D1559809

Also in Plains Histories

America's 100th Meridian: A Plains Journey, by Monte Hartman

American Outback: The Oklahoma Panhandle in the Twentieth Century, by Richard Lowitt

As a Farm Woman Thinks: Life and Land on the Texas High Plains, 1890–1960, by Nellie Witt Spikes; edited by Geoff Cunfer

Children of the Dust: An Okie Family Story, by Betty Grant Henshaw; edited by Sandra Scofield

The Death of Raymond Yellow Thunder: And Other True Stories from the Nebraska–Pine Ridge Border Towns, by Stew Magnuson

Food, Control, and Resistance: Rationing of Indigenous Peoples in the United States and South Australia, by Tamara Levi

Free Radical: Ernest Chambers, Black Power, and the Politics of Race, by Tekla Agbala Ali Johnson

From Syria to Seminole: Memoir of a High Plains Merchant, by Ed Aryain; edited by J'Nell Pate

"I Do Not Apologize for the Length of This Letter": The Mari Sandoz Letters on Native American Rights, 1940–1965, edited by Kimberli A. Lee

Indigenous Albuquerque, by Myla Vicenti Carpio

Law at Little Big Horn: Due Process Denied, by Charles E. Wright

Nikkei Farmer on the Nebraska Plains: A Memoir, by The Reverend Hisanori Kano; edited by Tai Kreidler

The Notorious Dr. Flippin: Abortion and Consequence in the Early Twentieth Century, by Jamie Q. Tallman

Oysters, Macaroni, and Beer: Thurber, Texas, and the Company Store, by Gene Rhea Tucker

Railwayman's Son: A Plains Family Memoir, by Hugh Hawkins

Rights in the Balance: Free Press, Fair Trial, and Nebraska Press Association v. Stuart, by Mark R. Scherer

Route 66: A Road to America's Landscape, History, and Culture, by Markku Henriksson

Ruling Pine Ridge: Oglala Lakota Politics from the IRA to Wounded Knee, by Akim D. Reinhardt

Trail Sisters: Freedwomen in Indian Territory, 1850–1890, by Linda Williams Reese

Urban Villages and Local Identities: Germans from Russia, Omaha Indians, and Vietnamese in Lincoln, Nebraska, by Kurt E. Kinbacher

Where the West Begins: Debating Texas Identity, by Glen Sample Ely

Women on the North American Plains, edited by Renee M. Laegreid and Sandra K. Mathews

A WITNESS TO HISTORY

George H. Mahon, West Texas Congressman

Janet M. Neugebauer | Plainsword by Kent Hance

Texas Tech University Press

This book is typeset in Minion Pro. The paper used in this book meets the minimum requirements of ANSI/NISO Z39.48-1992 (R1997). ∞

Designed by Kasey McBeath
Cover photographs courtesy of Southwest Collection, George Herman Mahon Box 285 and courtesy of US Army, George Herman Mahon, Box 582.

Library of Congress Cataloging-in-Publication Data
Names: Neugebauer, Janet M., 1935- author.
Title: A witness to history : George H. Mahon, West Texas congressman / Janet M. Neugebauer ; foreword by Kent Hance.
Description: Lubbock, Texas : Texas Tech University Press, 2016. | Series: Plains histories | Includes bibliographical references and index.
Identifiers: LCCN 2016048474 (print) | LCCN 2016051765 (ebook) | ISBN 9780896729889 (hardcover : alk. paper) | ISBN 9780896729896 (ebook)
Subjects: LCSH: Mahon, George Herman, 1900-1985. | Legislators—United States—Biography. | United States. Congress. House—Biography. | United States—Politics and government—1945-1989. | United States—Politics and government—1933-1945. | Lubbock (Tex.)—Biography.
Classification: LCC E748.M225 N48 2016 (print) | LCC E748.M225 (ebook) | DDC 328.73/092 [B] —dc23
LC record available at https://lccn.loc.gov/2016048474

17 18 19 20 21 22 23 24 25 / 9 8 7 6 5 4 3 2 1

Texas Tech University Press
Box 41037 | Lubbock, Texas 79409-1037 USA
800.832.4042 | ttup@ttu.edu | www.ttupress.org

For Nelda Thompson and Dr. Lawrence Graves

Contents

Illustrations   *xi*
Plainsword   *xv*
Preface   *xiv*

Chapter 1
The Early Years, 1900–1934   3

Chapter 2
The Plebe, 1935–1938   46

Chapter 3
The World on Fire, 1939–1945   98

Chapter 4
A Battered World Rebuilds, 1946–1952   161

Chapter 5
Security with Solvency, 1953–1960   216

Chapter 6
High Expectations, 1961–1963   290

Chapter 7
The Limits of Power, 1964–1968   334

Chapter 8
The Abuse of Power, 1969–1973   395

Chapter 9
Transitions, 1974–1978   447

Epilogue   477

Notes   *481*
Bibliography   *533*
Index   *553*

Illustrations

Following page **160**

Photo of Mahon used in his first campaign, 1934.

Mahon, General Marshall, and Subcommittee Chairman Snyder prior to War Department appropriations hearings, 1944.

Standing at the mouth of the Malinta tunnel where General Jonathan M. Wainwright surrendered to the Japanese, 1945.

Talking with Texas servicemen in Chunqking, China, 1945.

Subcommittee meeting with General Dwight Eisenhower in Frankfurt, Germany, 1945.

Inspection trip to Panama Canal Zone, 1946.

Meeting with James Forrestal, first secretary of defense, 1949.

Air Force appropriations panel of Defense Subcommittee, 1950.

Floydada, Texas, onions being presented to Speaker Sam Rayburn, 1951.

Ezra Taft Benson, secretary of agriculture, being invited to address the American Cotton Congress, 1953.

Mahon conferring with General Curtis LeMay, commander of Strategic Air Command, 1954.

George and Helen Mahon at the White House, circa 1955.

Talking with Charles E. Wilson, secretary of defense, 1956.

Mahon by the room where hearings of the Subcommittee on Defense Appropriations were held, 1956.

Mahon playing golf with President Dwight Eisenhower, 1957.

Mahon with the director of guided missiles and General Bernard Schriever after an inspection of missiles, 1957.

Mahon, General Lauris Norstad, and Representative Gerald R. Ford conferring in the House Appropriations room, 1959.

Admiral Hyman Rickover in Lubbock to speak at Texas Tech University, 1959.

President Kennedy and Mahon at the White House, 1962.

Mahon receiving an honorary doctor of laws from Texas Tech University, 1962.

A boa constrictor and Mahon in Panama, 1962.

General Douglas MacArthur talking with Mahon, 1962.

Mahon, President Harry Truman, and Jerry Hall of Mahon's staff, 1964.

Robert McNamara, General Maxwell Taylor, and Mahon prior to hearings on the 1965 defense budget, 1964.

A luncheon given for Madame Chiang Kai-shek, 1965.

Vice President Hubert Humphrey and Mahon walking through a hall of Congress, 1965.

Mahon going over his notes before addressing a national meeting of the Farm Bureau, 1966.

President Johnson giving one of the pens used to sign a supplemental appropriations bill to Mahon, 1966.

Mahon, in Washington, DC, speaking on the phone to Mayor Rogers in Lubbock, Texas, 1967.

A White House reception for General Westmoreland, who had returned from Vietnam to address Congress, 1968.

A White House meeting with President Johnson to discuss the Vietnam War, 1968.

George and Helen Mahon with Secretary of Transportation and Mrs. Alan Boyd, circa 1968.

Mahon aboard Air Force One en route to Fayetteville for the Arkansas–University of Texas championship football game, 1969.

NASA officials presenting an Apollo-Saturn V engineering scale model
to Chairman Mahon, 1969.

Secretary of Defense Melvin R. Laird prior to his appearance before
the Defense Subcommittee, 1970.

One of the "Googol Rags" sent to Mahon to use for wiping out the
national debt, 1971.

Mahon at North American Rockwell on an inspection tour concerning the
B-1 bomber, 1972.

At the White House on the night that President Nixon selected Gerald Ford to be
his nominee for vice president, 1973.

Meeting in the hall outside the door of the Appropriations Room after President
Ford addressed a night session of Congress, 1974.

George and Helen Mahon at the unveiling of Mahon's portrait, 1974.

President Ford and Mahon in the Oval Office, 1975.

A meeting with President Ford, 1975.

Mahon in his office with Deputy Secretary of Defense William Clements
and Prince Turki of Saudi Arabia, 1975.

Vice President Rockefeller and Mahon exchanging greetings at a dinner, 1976.

President-elect Jimmy Carter shaking hands with Mahon after a luncheon, 1976.

Mahon swearing in Speaker Tip O'Neill as speaker of the House, 1977.

CIA Director George H. W. Bush and Mahon conferring at CIA
headquarters, 1977.

Mahon receiving the Forrestal Award and medal from J. K. Kessler, 1977.

President Carter trying to convince Mahon and Jack Edwards not to fund
a new aircraft carrier, 1978.

Mahon and unidentified subcommittee members at one of the last
markup sessions he attended, 1978.

The first time I met George Mahon, I was a senior at Texas Tech University in 1964–65. Mr. Mahon had invited Sargent Shriver, a member of the Kennedy family, to Lubbock to make a speech about the Peace Corps. Mr. Mahon, as we called him, was a gentleman. Of all the people I've met in my lifetime, he best fits the definition of a gentleman. He spent a few minutes with me, but in that short amount of time, he made me feel like I was the only person in the world he was listening to, that he wanted my opinion, and that he was truly working for me and everyone else who was in attendance at the arena.

George Mahon came from humble beginnings and saw the world change during his lifetime to something he could not have foreseen as a young child. He grew up in a near state of poverty—but with plenty of love and compassion from his entire family. He was able to graduate from college, and he always remembered the people who helped him along the way. Judge Walter R. Ely in Abilene was one of his mentors. The judge helped him stay in college by providing him with money during his undergraduate years at Hardin-Simmons University. George Mahon never forgot Judge Ely. When George Mahon was sworn in as a member of Congress, the first letter he wrote was to Judge Ely, thanking him for all he had done for him and his career. Mahon was loyal to his friends and accommodating to his foes. He always tried to use a persuasive manner to get people on his side.

In his first campaign for Congress in 1934, there was very little difference on the issues between the candidates running for the Nineteenth Congressional District. Because of the Depression, they all supported many federal programs. In contrast, all the candidates running for Congress for the same seat in 2016 were against almost every federal program. However, the one issue on which all campaigns could agree—no matter the century—was the need for a good, solid farm program. Agriculture was the mainstay of the economy both then and now.

In that first race, the political pundits gave him no chance of winning. Mahon was born in Loraine, Texas and was serving as the district attorney in Colorado City. The large population center was Lubbock, where his opponent was a district judge. This placed Mahon at a significant disadvantage. However, Mahon's friends from high school, college, and Colorado City all volunteered to work the entire 19th Congressional District for him, and Mahon somehow managed to beat his Lubbock opponent. His hard work, personality, and loyal hardworking friends carried him to victory.

From his first day until his last day in Congress—a span of forty-four years—George Mahon was very accommodating to his fellow members of Congress. He was respected and admired by all, and I never knew of an enemy that he might have acquired along the way. He always tried to build political capital among his colleagues—an essential ingredient in getting things done. No doubt George Mahon would be appalled at the lack of civility in national politics in this day and time, and would attribute this lack of congeniality to the logjam that now prevails in Washington.

As a new member of Congress, he willingly served on some of the less desirable committees. For example, he served on the District of Columbia Committee. That is one appointment no member wants, but he agreed as a favor to the fabled leader of the Texas delegation, Sam Rayburn. George Mahon served with Sam Rayburn, who took him under his wing and became Mahon's mentor. This close relationship paid dividends when Rayburn became Speaker of the House in 1940.

Speaker Rayburn was of the opinion that one should "go along to get along," and that's exactly what Mahon did. He built up his seniority and was able to get on the Appropriations Committee in his third term. At that time, the military budget was not huge, but Speaker Rayburn advised him to take the position on the Military Appropriations Subcommittee because if the country went to war, it would be the biggest budget the country would ever see.

Once again, Mahon followed Rayburn's advice, and during the war became one of only five members of Congress who knew about U.S. plans to build the atomic bomb. This small group oversaw the spending for the super-secret Manhattan Project. He was one of only a handful of people who was trusted to engage fully in a project that would change the world. George Mahon was a man of trust, as well as being a gentleman.

After the war, Mahon, along with Richard Nixon and other select member of the House and Senate, was appointed to a special Congressional Commission to assess U.S. military capability around the globe. As a result, he spent a month traveling to many countries and his eyes opened to the problems of the postwar world. He was able to meet foreign leaders, such as General Chiang Kai-shek, the president of the Republic of China, and the shah of Iran, with whom he would have cordial relations for years to come. This special knowledge allowed Mahon to mold American foreign policy from his seat in Congress. Can you imagine if a congressman took a monthlong trip in this day and time, what would happen? The member would be attacked for taking a so-called junket.

With this experience, Mahon later became chairman of the Defense Subcommittee, and then served as chairman of the full Appropriations Committee from 1964 to 1978. Chairman Mahon was always careful to report his travels and make sure people knew why he was going someplace. For example, when he spoke about his trip to Japan and the Philippines, he mentioned their importance to US power and prestige, but also as a means to search for new markets for cotton. He understood his constituents and who he worked for. There were times that he received a lot of correspondence against certain things that he supported, but he was always careful to answer each and every letter in a thoughtful and measured way.

As Congress began to change in the middle of the twentieth century, Mahon stayed with the leadership. It proved difficult for him in the 1960s and 1970s. Most members of Congress are fortunate if they are ever close to one president, but Chairman Mahon was close to many presidents, especially President Lyndon B. Johnson and President Richard M. Nixon. In this book you will learn about Nixon calling him in the middle of the night after he announced he would be resigning as president of the United States. You can see that LBJ called George Mahon on a regular basis during the Vietnam era and asked him to support additional military appropriations. Chairman Mahon supported LBJ's war efforts and was the crucial member of Congress who could successfully ensure the passage of military spending during the controversial Vietnam War.

There are many congressmen who abuse their power by trying to get special deals for their friends, constituents, or their district. George Mahon didn't do any of that. Some have suggested that if Mahon had been as ruthless as LBJ, NASA would have been in Lubbock instead of Houston. George Mahon would not have been able to live with himself if he did something to take undue advantage of his fellow members—or the country—or supported something just to improve his personal standing in his home district. On rare occasions, George Mahon used his influence to help pass much-needed public construction projects, such as getting Interstate 27 extended from Amarillo to Lubbock and blocking unreasonable OSHA regulations that would be harmful to the cotton industry and his constituents.

George Mahon had a great sense of humor and could find humor in almost any situation. It was not unusual to receive handwritten notes from George Mahon. His wit would often find its way into clever notes.

Chairman Mahon also enjoyed taking the time to show the nation's capital to constituents when they visited Washington. He began doing this when very few people could make the trip from West Texas to visit him personally at the US Capitol. But, as he told me in the 1970s, he had done it for everyone's parents and their grandparents, and he would not stop now. He always made sure his constituents were treated like royalty. He knew that he worked for them and went above and beyond to pay proper respect to each and every constituent who visited Washington.

The book tells us about Helen, his wife and the love of his life. They made a great team, and the nineteenth Congressional District is a better place because of George and Helen Mahon. This book is both very informative and a must read for anyone who has any government dealings. You will realize the type of statesmen we had. Our present congressmen would do well to emulate this man and forgo the chaos that is so prevalent today. I hope you enjoy the book.

Kent Hance

This is the story of a man who went to Congress in 1935, when the House Committee on Appropriations still allocated a small amount of money to buy military horses. Forty-four years later, when George Mahon retired as chairman of that same committee, it was debating funds for a 2,000-mile-an-hour bomber. Spanning nearly a half century that took in almost the entire Cold War, Mahon's career grew from that of a country lawyer to one of the most powerful men in Congress. This book focuses on his signature work—service on the House Committee on Appropriations.

Mahon always kept a watchful eye on agricultural legislation, but he did not serve on that committee; therefore his impact was somewhat limited. However, his efforts on behalf of agriculture were recognized in 1964 when he was awarded the Knapp-Porter Award from the Texas Agricultural Extension Service because he had been "a vital force behind the growth of both Texas and U.S. agriculture."[1] I have provided examples of his service to agriculture to give the reader a feel for his work in that area.

He also served on other committees in Congress, but it is through his service on the House Appropriations Committee and the Subcommittee on Defense Appropriations that Mahon had the greatest national impact. I leave to others the pleasure of writing about his other congressional activities. I hope this overview of George Mahon's life will shed light on material in the Southwest Collection at Texas Tech University that is available for researchers to use.

During his time in Congress, Mahon had a front-row seat for some of the most important events of the twentieth century. He experienced the fear that Americans felt when Pearl Harbor was bombed, and he was determined to do his part in making US defenses so strong that something like that would never happen again. He was among a small group of congressmen who toured the atomic bomb lab at Oak Ridge, Tennessee, just prior to the nation's dropping of the bomb on Japan. After World War II he traveled to Europe with a select committee to survey the war-torn nations and to make recommendations to President Truman about the type of aid that was needed to rebuild these nations. This became known as the Marshall Plan.

He knew the trauma of a presidential assassination, having been in the fifth car in that fatal presidential motorcade in Dallas. He also knew the disappointment of a presidential resignation. He worked comfortably with the giants of government, enjoying the friendship and confidence of seven of the eight presidents with whom he served. He worked just as easily with his constituents in the Nineteenth Congressional District of Texas. Although their primary needs related to agriculture, when national defense became a priority for Mahon their interests turned in that direction as well.

Mahon had an uncanny knack for getting close to people. He communicated easily with constituents and convinced them of his concern for their problems. He did not promise to provide miraculous solutions, only to do what was possible. He grew up on a cotton farm and invested most of his discretionary income in two West Texas cotton farms, so he understood their problems. His constituents swelled with pride to see one of their own in a position of national leadership, and they were sure that he would be heard when speaking on behalf of their agricultural interests. Each year when Congress adjourned, Mahon spent time touring his district to strengthen the bond he had developed with his constituents and to hear their concerns. In this way he replenished his energy and renewed his spirit. He loved it, and so did the voters.

Mahon never aspired to any office other than representative of the Nineteenth Congressional District of Texas, and support from his constituents was rock solid for forty-four years. In Congress his ultimate goal was to become chairman of the full House Committee on Appropriations, and he reached that goal according to the mores of congressional politics, waiting his turn through seniority. Because his aspiration was always clear and unwavering, he was not susceptible to promises, flattery, or threats. Some of his colleagues and many political pundits considered him to be "unreachable." That may have been true, but he was accessible—always ready to help within the bounds of propriety, and his strong voice was always respected.

Although the Mahons were entertained by kings and queens, presidents and prime ministers, spending time at home gave them the most pleasure. They liked to play gin rummy or care for the plants on their balcony, where usually a few stalks of cotton could be found growing among the pots of geraniums and periwinkles. They also enjoyed listening to music. They accepted many invitations as part of Mahon's job, and when they returned the courtesies they did so at home with dinner prepared by Helen. Afterward they often played bridge with their guests. Although they grew to be worldly people of dignity and sophistication, they never forgot their small-town ways or the people who elected Mahon. The journey of a country lawyer from the dusty roads of rural West Texas to the marbled halls of the nation's capital seemed to be a natural one for them. As a team, they handled the many ups and downs with ease and confidence.

Mahon was a frugal man, who drove his cars for many years and resoled his shoes as long as possible. He came from a family of very modest means and learned at a young age to buy only what he could pay for. It was an irony that the defense bills he authored became one of the nation's largest expenditures. When he became chairman of the Subcommittee on Defense in 1949, the defense appropriation was $13 billion. When he retired it was over $116 billion!

Two threads hold this story together. The strongest thread is Mahon's ethos of accomplishment as demonstrated in public service. As a young man Mahon would often say that he wanted to be somebody, his way of saying he wanted to achieve and to have his work respected. Serving on the congressional committee that allocated funds for national defense during the Cold War provided a rich opportunity for accomplishment. New technologies, coupled with military officers who aggressively defended their budgetary requests for new weapons systems, provided a challenging situation. Mahon was up to the challenge. During his years of debating in college, he had learned how to win an argument through reasoning and persuasion. He rarely resorted to confrontation. He was a gentleman and expected others to behave likewise. Although he controlled the purse strings for the nation, he seldom talked about this. Everyone understood it. In the end he and his committee paid for what they believed would keep the nation safe.

Mahon had learned from a strict father that high moral standards, frugality, and a willingness to work hard were important traits. He had also learned from working at odd jobs after graduating from high school that a common laborer could work long and hard without ever getting ahead. That's when he realized that he must find a way to attend college, deciding that a law career would provide the opportunities he sought. It was his law degree that paved the way toward becoming county attorney and then district attorney, work that greatly increased his circle of friends and placed him in an excellent position in 1935 to win the seat for a newly created congressional district in Texas.

He was serving on the US House of Representatives Committee on Appropriations and the subcommittee that appropriated money for the military when the world drifted into the Cold War. Because of the massive amounts of money spent on defense over the next four decades, Mahon's decisions commanded national attention. Throughout his years on the Subcommittee for Defense Appropriations, and ultimately as chairman of the entire House Committee on Appropriations, he championed a strong national defense program; by retirement he had authored defense appropriations totaling in excess of $1.5 trillion.[2] During some of his years, defense appropriations consumed more than 50 percent of the total federal budget. In many ways George Mahon was defined by the Cold War, without which he would very likely have been just another West Texas congressman.

A second thread running through this story is the personal power that flowed from Mahon's ability to work collegially with others. "Unlike most of his fellow Texans here, Mahon has avoided local political hassles within the delegation or in state politics."[3] He often bragged that under his leadership the Subcommittee on Defense Appropriations was the most nonpartisan committee in Congress. The work was long and hard but taken seriously, and each person's opinion was respected. Because most of the work was done behind closed doors and often off the record, there was little opportunity to be in the limelight. That suited Mahon, who early on had decided not to talk about the way he intended to vote until after he had done so. In this way he could easily change his mind if new facts surfaced. So too with the subcommittee. Because much of their work was done away from the public eye, needed changes could be made without an unending barrage of questions from reporters. Mahon led both the full committee and the subcommittee with a strong, but gentle hand, which earned him the respect of all who worked with him. More than a politician, he became a statesman.

I have relied heavily on the George H. Mahon Papers housed in the Southwest Collection at Texas Tech University. Mahon was something of a pack rat, even saving magazine and news articles that he thought might be helpful when preparing speeches. He often dictated notes for his files in order to better remember what had happened and who had said what. Some of the most useful items for me were letters sent to his family. In these he often expressed his true feelings about others in Congress and the administration, political situations, and the world in general. From these letters, a unique source, one learns to know Mahon the husband, the father, the friend, and the colleague. Mahon spent a lot of time talking with others, especially constituents, but the conversation was about them, not him, and his inner person was always hidden. Incoming personal letters, even those that were flattering, were taken at face value if the writer's actions toward Mahon had been in keeping with the tone of the letters. While I have placed Mahon's work in context, this story is about the man, not the many venues in which he worked. The venues are explained only to help the reader understand the significance of his work.

Another important source of information for documenting Mahon's work has been the Government Documents Department of the Texas Tech University Library, which has a strong connection with Mahon. One of his first actions in Congress was to have the library designated a government documents depository. Having such items as the *Congressional Record* and House Reports close at hand was invaluable.

Time to work on this project was funded by a generous grant from the CH Foundation in Lubbock, Texas. The foundation's former director, Nelda Thompson, told me she had been offered an opportunity to work in Mahon's office in Washington, DC. She had declined because she was on the faculty of Texas Tech University and enjoyed teaching. She wondered aloud about what her life might have been like if she had accepted. I believe that experience would have been life-changing for her and I am deeply indebted to Nelda and the CH Foundation for the difference this project has made in my life. I am also indebted to Dr. Lawrence Graves for passing the project along to me. He worked on it for a number of years before his health failed. He contributed to this biography in an important way that I could not because many of the people he had interviewed were dead by the time I started working on it. His interviews were insightful and very helpful to understanding how colleagues viewed Mahon.

I am appreciative of the help provided by Tom Rohig, Julia Iturrino, Marilyn Garrett, and Susan Hildago of the Texas Tech University Library. They always went the extra mile in helping me with materials housed in the library.

Thanks also go to Dr. Tai Kreidler, Dr. Risita Moore, and Pam Brink for reading parts of the manuscript and calling my attention to problems. Any remaining mistakes are mine.

I am grateful to the staff of the Southwest Collection, especially Randy Vance, who filled in for me while I took time off for research and who has always been helpful in the Holden Reading Room. He has never complained about my clutter from the number of boxes I left on the tables. Catlin Leonard's help was also invaluable. I was somewhat careless with copies of material I used in the footnotes, and her ability to organize has been a lifesaver.

Finally, my warmest thanks go to my children, Gayle Carr and Joel Neugebauer, for always encouraging me with my research projects. And now, I hope you enjoy George Mahon's journey through life.

A WITNESS TO HISTORY

Chapter 1

The Early Years, 1900–1934

The long awaited day has now arrived. I will take the oath of office at noon today together with the other members of the House. . . . There are many things that I would like to write you but of course being very busy on an occasion like this I do not have the time. I get some satisfaction however, out of writing the first letter on the day of my taking the oath of office to one who has meant as much to me as you.

Sincerely your friend,
George H. Mahon[1]

The letter was written on the morning of January 3, 1935, to Judge W. R. Ely of Abilene, Texas. The bond between these two men dated back to 1920, when Mahon was a twenty-one-year-old struggling student at Simmons College in Abilene. It seemed that he would have had to end his schooling because of financial difficulties when the president of the college sent him to Judge Ely to ask for a loan.

In earlier conversations the judge had asked President Sandefer to keep his eyes open for some young man who showed promise but needed assistance to stay in school. Ely wanted to help. The stern, sometimes abrupt, older man answered Mahon's request, "Sure, son, how much do you need?" George told him he would like to have two hundred dollars to start with but would need more later on. They worked out a system whereby George would inform the judge when he needed money and would sign a note for 3 percent interest. A series of loans followed until George was finally practicing law in 1926 and could repay the money. Although the funds were fully repaid, the debt was never formally liquidated, and over the years the relationship grew to resemble that of a proud father watching his son grow in stature as he reached ever more challenging goals.

A deep sense of accomplishment filled the hearts of both men, and on January 10, 1935, Judge Ely answered the newly elected congressman:

> You do not know how grateful I am to have the first letter you wrote the day you became a Congressman, and how happy I am that you have attained this success. I have, for a long time, had great hopes for your future. The salary is not great, but the opportunity for service is large and the American Congress is the greatest legislative body on earth. To have a part in shaping legislative matters that mean so much to the destiny of the American people is a rare and sacred privilege. I hope that your course in Congress will be devoted to an ideal and that you will never ask yourself "What effect will this have on the next election?"[2]

The first session of the Seventy-fourth Congress convened in the Capitol at noon on Thursday, January 3, 1935, in accordance with the Twentieth Amendment adopted in 1933, which provided that Congress would henceforth convene on January 3 of each year, instead of March 4. This New Deal measure had ended the traditional lame-duck session that had delayed important legislative business every alternate year since the beginning of the nation. In 1935 January 3 was a beautiful day, with the temperature reaching a balmy fifty-eight degrees.

The general atmosphere was considerably more upbeat than two years earlier, when the Seventy-third Congress had convened. In 1933 failing banks and failing relief efforts had sent panic through the nation. By 1935 the panic had been arrested, but the Great Depression was still a major concern. The Democrats were in especially good spirits because they had gained seats in Congress in the 1934 election, the first off-year election since President Franklin Roosevelt had taken office. In November 1934 the pervasive discontent across the nation had significant political consequences, and the election gave the Democrats a two-thirds majority in both chambers of Congress. Historically, the presidential party loses congressional seats during off-year elections; however, during this election, new Democratic voters registered to vote in commercial centers of the West and in industrial cities of the North. Importantly, this growth took place outside the South, the traditional stronghold for Democrats.

Historian David M. Kennedy credits President Roosevelt's fireside chat in August 1934 for many of the new constituents. At that time, the president had asked Americans to judge whether the recovery was working by deciding whether or not they were better off than a year before. Few people were really better off, but many were encouraged by seeing the Democratic president taking some sort of action, and they expressed their satisfaction at the poll. The party's sweep of the 1932 election marked the first time in eighty years that both the White House and Congress were controlled by Democrats.

Mahon was one of the new Democrats in Congress, but he was not part of the new liberal group. He was a southern conservative Democrat with strong rural values that included believing in states' rights, a balanced federal budget, and limited expansion of the federal government. With Texans such as Vice President John Nance Garner and Representative Sam Rayburn in powerful positions, this was an exciting time to be an ambitious, young Democrat in Congress. Because of seniority, southern conservative Democrats were able to maintain control of Congress, but liberal voices would grow louder in the coming years.

According to the *Washington Post*, "Capitol Hill was a buzz of activity. Members of the House greeted old friends and made new acquaintances. Flocks of visitors stepped out of taxis and waited for elevators to take them up to the main floor where things were about to happen."[3] During the first day of a new Congress, rules were relaxed as friends and family freely mingled on the floor with the members of Congress. As the representative of the Nineteenth District of Texas, Mahon was allowed one ticket for opening-day admission to the House Gallery, and his wife, Helen, was on hand for the swearing-in ceremony.

Washingtonians viewed opening day in the Senate Chamber as very tame compared to the roll calls, elections, hand-clapping, and hand-shaking on the House side of the Capitol. In fact, the opening session of the House was generally considered the best show in town, so the largest number of visitors and reporters were there. First Lady Eleanor Roosevelt and a friend were among the visitors. After seeming to wander aimlessly among the crowds, they asked directions to the President's Gallery where a *Washington Post* photographer captured them listening closely to developments on the floor. Reporters also kept a close eye on the Speaker's Gallery, which was filled with the Byrns family. Joseph W. Byrns of Tennessee was elected speaker of the House that day. He had been majority leader and was the choice of the Democratic members when they caucused just prior to opening day. The *Post* reported that "Mrs. Byrns, one of the most charming of the long list of Speaker's wives, was attired in a black broadcloth suit trimmed in Persian lamb. Orchids on her left shoulder, white kid gloves and a quill-trimmed black hat pulled low over her silver hair completed her costume."[4]

Newspapers of the day devoted considerable space to such gossipy details that in later years could be seen on television. No record remains of what Helen Mahon wore on opening day, but Mahon wore a gray wool suit presented to him the previous September at the Panhandle-Plains Fair in Lubbock, Texas, the heart of the new district he was representing. The suit's wool came from sheep grown and sheared at the Textile Research Center on the Texas Technological College campus in Lubbock. Wearing this suit was in keeping with a tradition established by President George Washington who, at his first inauguration, chose a new American-made broadcloth suit as a symbol of his pride in the new nation. While there is no record of how often President Washington wore the broadcloth suit, Mahon wore his West Texas wool suit often, and as late as 1946, his father, J. K. Mahon, was still wearing the trousers at home in Loraine, Texas.

The clerk of the House of Representatives gaveled the House to order and presided over its deliberations until a new speaker was elected to take the place of Speaker Henry Rainey of Illinois, who had died of a heart attack in August 1934. As house clerk of the outgoing Congress, the clerk was authorized to prepare an official roll of the House members for the incoming Congress. Reverend James Shea Montgomery, D.D., chaplain of the House, offered the opening prayer, and in brief remarks Clerk South Trimble recognized the break with tradition represented by Congress's assembling in January. A roll call revealed that a quorum was present. In fact, 434 of 435 members had duly authenticated their credentials in accordance with the law of their respective states and the United States. One vacancy had been created by the death of Frederick Landis, who had been elected from Indiana's Second Congressional District.

The chairman of the Democratic Party, Representative Edward T. Taylor of Colorado, nominated Representative Joseph W. Byrns of Tennessee for speaker. The Republicans nominated Representative Bertrand H. Snell of New York. Representative George J. Schneider of Wisconsin was also nominated. Byrns was elected by a voice vote that strictly followed party affiliation. He received 317 votes, Snell received 95, Schneider received 9, and William P. Lambertson received 2. During the roll call, three members simply answered "present," thereby avoiding a vote for any of the nominees. This roll call became George

Mahon's first vote in Congress. Each candidate made a graceful speech of friendship and appreciation of the other nominees, after which Representative A. J. Sabath of Illinois, known as the dean of the House because he had the longest continuous service of any member, administered the oath of office to Speaker Byrns. William B. Bankhead of Alabama was elected majority leader; however, he remained ill during most of the Seventy-fourth Congress, and Edward Taylor of Colorado took over the leadership. A new whip organization,[5] led by Pat Boland of Pennsylvania, developed an uncanny ability to forecast the vote on any bill. Political scientist E. Herrington observed that "350 of the 561[sic] Members in Congress owed their seats to their pledge to back the New Deal. The leadership of the majority party was in the hands of staunch Southern Democrats whose first loyalty was to the will of the President."[6]

Members of the House of Representatives were sworn in en masse. After officers of the House had been elected, a message was sent to the Senate and the president signifying that a quorum was present and the House was ready to conduct its legislative business. The Senate did the same.

Mahon's second vote on his first day in office was "yea" on the resolution to require 218 signatures to get a bill discharged from a committee so that it could be debated on the floor and a vote taken. Since 1925 the rule had been that 218 signatures were necessary to get a bill discharged in the House. However, in 1931 the rule was changed to require only 145 signatures to force a vote. At that time Republicans were in control of the House, and Democrats liked the favorable odds for forcing a vote. Now the Democrats wanted more protection from such discharges, and because they controlled the House, the vote was 242-167 to return to the 218-signature requirement. As the *Washington Post* explained, "The celebrated 'discharge rule' had plagued the Administration all through the last session, routing a score of anti-Roosevelt petitions over the Speaker's desk."[7]

More than 2,400 bills were placed in the hopper on opening day.[8] Many members hoped to dispose of controversial legislation during the first session in order to have a briefer session the following year, an election year. After the business of organizing the Seventy-fourth Congress had taken place, the House of Representatives recessed at 4:32 p.m. It was scheduled to convene again at 12:00 p.m. on January 4, 1935.

The record of the preceding Congress had been long and productive in response to the despair created by the Great Depression. Although the Depression was far from over, an air of optimism prevailed throughout the country about Roosevelt's New Deal. The accomplishments of the Seventy-third Congress (January 1933–December 1934) were primarily related to relief and recovery. Among its accomplishments were the Agricultural Adjustment Act, the National Industrial Recovery Act, the Emergency Banking Act, and the establishment of the Tennessee Valley Authority. As historian James Patterson has noted, the Seventy-third Congress was "unprecedentedly generous in its grants of power to the President and executive agencies."[9] The next phase of President Roosevelt's program would focus on reform legislation that would change many aspects of American life—changes that would prove to be both exciting and disturbing.

George Herman Mahon was born on his paternal grandmother's farm in Claiborne Parish[10] in far northwest Louisiana on September 22, 1900. His grandmother had assumed ownership of the land when her husband died in 1870, and until 1903 George's father and his family lived with her. The farm was located near a post office called Mahon, apparently because young George's father operated a store in the vicinity. It was about seven miles northwest of the Claiborne Parish seat of Homer and approximately the same distance southeast of Haynesville, Louisiana. The fourth-class post office[11] was staffed at one time by George's aunt, Laura, and lasted only from 1888 to 1906, when insufficient business forced its closure. Claiborne Parish was largely rural farming country where cotton was the main crop. Its largest incorporated village, Homer, had a population of 1,157 in 1900 and 1,855 ten years later. The whole parish had only 23,029 inhabitants in 1900 and is still thinly populated.[12]

Although little is known of the Mahon family prior to the mid-1800s, for most of his adult life George was interested in his family's lineage. He even engaged the services of a genealogy firm in Washington, DC, to help with his search. However, they could learn only that the Mahons had been known in medieval Ireland, but when they came to America around 1800, the family scattered. George did discover that both sides of his family had migrated west from Virginia.[13] George's grandfather was George Thomas Mahon, born in Virginia in 1828 and raised as an orphan in Tennessee by an uncle, Charles White. George's grandmother on his father's side was Pollyann Kirkpatrick. She met George Thomas Mahon in Franklin County, Tennessee, and they were married there on February 16, 1848. In 1852 they followed Pollyann's family to the Homer area in Claiborne Parish, Louisiana. George Thomas died in 1870, leaving four small children. John Kirkpatrick (J. K.) Mahon, George's father, was born October 15, 1860, near Homer. He was the youngest, having been born only a few months before his father's death.[14]

On his maternal side George could trace the family back to his great-great-grandparents, Major Joshua Willis, who married Barbara Overton Winston. They moved to Louisiana in 1848. Their daughter, Barbara, also known as Patsy Ann, married James Madison Thomason, and that couple's daughter, Barbara Narcissa Thomason, married Thomas Marion Brown (George's grandparents). George's mother, Lola Willis Brown, was born September 29, 1870, in Claiborne Parish. She married J. K. Mahon in 1892 when he was thirty-two and she ten years younger. The couple had eight children.[15] George Herman was their fifth child and third son.

George's father became the head of the household when his older brother died in 1883. He realized that, as the senior man in the household, he needed more education, and so he attended a school at Mount Zion in Claiborne Parish conducted by a man named John Nelson. The session lasted just three months. He also went to school at Haynesville for one session. However, his efforts to make a living on the farm ended any further chance for an education.[16]

J. K. Mahon farmed for most of his life. From his marriage until 1903, he continued to live on the farm that had belonged to his mother. Only then could he afford to buy 160 acres about two miles from Haynesville. At the age of six, George was enrolled in the public school at Haynesville, walking to and from school with his brothers and sisters.[17] The family lived at the farm until they moved to Texas in 1908. Until he went away to college at age nineteen, George had lived most of his years in a family that included his grandmother Mahon, whom George described as having "a constitution of iron,"[18] and her unmarried daughter, Laura. "The conditions under which we lived were not ideal. Two families should not live under the same roof, particularly the mother or relative of the husband."[19]

George remembered that he and his siblings stood in awe of their father. In a short reminiscence written in about 1955 and entitled "My Father," the son wrote,

There is nothing lovey-dovey about my father. He is a stern, uncompromising sort. My mother must have longed for more affection than she ever got. My father was plainspoken at all times, but he was short on praise or flattery, fearing he might spoil us, or give us "the big head," a word that doesn't seem to be used anymore. My father is the most honorable man I have ever met and he is so conscientious he can tolerate nothing of a questionable nature. I have never heard him say "damn" or "hell," but if he were sufficiently provoked he would say "plague take it."[20]

He went on: "Papa was very frugal. He could hardly bear to spend or see anyone else spend an unnecessary nickel. With no worldly fortune and eight children and a wife, plus a mother and sister to provide for, it is understandable."[21]

George remembered that although his father's grammar was not especially good, he was a whiz at mathematics and had an uncanny memory, the best with dates he had ever encountered. He commented on his father's strong voice, which could be heard for miles when shouting at the livestock or calling a member of the household. He thought that was the source of his own strong voice, which was very helpful during his first political campaign for Congress, when he had to speak out on the campaign trail without a loudspeaker.[22]

The elder Mahon did take a few drinks and smoked an occasional cigar in his youth. At ninety-four years of age, his father still chewed tobacco. George did not drink alcoholic beverages but admitted to taking a "few chews and puffing a few cigars."[23] After reaching adulthood he did not smoke because he looked upon it "as a messy habit which does no one any good and does some people a lot of harm."[24]

Like his father, George always said grace at the table. Although his father insisted on stern decorum (perhaps defending himself against so many rambunctious children), George wrote, "I myself, having been repressed in my youth, have always insisted upon singing hilariously not only in the bathtub, but at the table during meals."[25]

George was somewhat sad that his father showed so little affection for his children, although he thought his father loved them. On one occasion he had told George, with appropriate reserve, that he was "a pretty creditable son." George was never whipped as a child and his siblings only on very rare occasions. "Actually, I know he is most proud of his children."[26] Somewhat wryly he said that the last time his father had kissed him he was eighteen and had been in Cisco, Texas, working on a construction project when he suffered a head injury that required several stitches. He reminisced that, "a child would have to be a very strong specimen indeed to grow up as the progeny of J. K. Mahon and not be profoundly influenced by his parent."[27] In public George referred to his father as "J. K. Mahon" but otherwise called him "Papa" until adulthood, when he changed his address to "Dad."

In 1925, as George was finishing law school at the University of Texas and preparing to start a career, his father wrote, expressing his pride in him: "Herman My dear boy (the family always called him Herman). When your life's career is ended. If this world is not made better, My prayers will have been in vain. Your father one who loves you, J. K. Mahon."[28] J.K. strongly encouraged his children to become community leaders. He believed the lack of formal education disqualified him from the opportunity.

After he had been in Congress for several years, George wrote his father to express his deepest feelings: "I am writing you to congratulate you on your seventy-ninth birthday. If I had it to do over again, I would still select you as my parent! Your counsel and example has been of immeasurable advantage to me throughout my life. I have always been proud of you, and as I have grown older, I have appreciated you even more. That is about all a son can say, isn't it? If I knew how to say more to let you know of my appreciation for what you have meant to me, I would say it." He signed it, "Your devoted son, George Herman Mahon."[29]

George's mother, Lola Brown Mahon, was far different in temperament from her husband. She was a sensitive woman, an artist, and interested in literature, especially poetry. After high school she attended a school at Daleville in Lauderdale County near Meridian, Mississippi, called Daleville Normal Institute, as George remembered it.[30] She painted many pictures, one of which hung in George's apartment in Washington for many years. She supported her children in their creative endeavors and tried to nourish the gentle side of their natures. She died on July 22, 1931, still a relatively young woman at age sixty-one.

J.K. Mahon was a tall man at 6'1", thin and energetic. George said he often complained of poor health, although it seemed he would live forever, and he almost did, dying at age ninety-seven. Each winter he suffered from bouts of influenza, commonly called the grippe in those days, and a doctor in Louisiana told him he would die if he didn't move to a dryer climate. (George suspected that some of the deaths in his father's family were caused by tuberculosis, but he could not prove that.) His father began to think of a drier climate and a place that would offer better prospects for a farmer. He also wanted to get away from the typhoid that was common in Louisiana. J.K. listened very carefully to glowing reports drifting back to Louisiana about land in West Texas opening up to farmers. He, no doubt, read the notices of cheap land that he saw in the post office or courthouse. He made two or three trips to West Texas and returned with stories about the wide-open spaces he found there but left no written record of these ventures.

Throughout Texas, railroads and land companies owned millions of acres along their tracks that they hoped to sell. Settlers were needed to make the railroad companies profitable, so they distributed one-page advertisements to attract prospective buyers and organized tours to carry trainloads of potential customers to various parts of the state. The Santa Fe Railroad, the Southern Pacific Railway Company, the Texas and Pacific Railroad Company, and others blanketed the state with their ads and made sure they reached surrounding states. These ads urged people to write the railroad's travel agents for more information. The *Dallas Semi-Weekly Farm News*, the *Fort Worth Star Telegram*, and other newspapers also carried stories about the fertile and cheap lands opening up in Texas and asked their readers to subscribe to the paper for more information. The Texas and Pacific Railroad Company also put ads in the *Texas Almanac* of 1904, listing twenty-nine counties of West Texas through which its trains ran. Mitchell County was one of the counties the railroad touted as the "Cream of Texas." The almanac carried a detailed description of each county in the state, as well as pages of ads about cheap land, farm implements, building materials, and other necessities for settlers.[31]

Settlement of West Texas had become possible in the 1870s, after the buffalo had been hunted to extinction and the Comanche and Kiowa Indians had been forced onto reservations in 1875. By then, there were enough white settlers, primarily cattlemen settling on the free range, that in 1876 the Texas legislature created fifty-five counties out of the enormous Bexar district that was created when Texas separated from Mexico. In January 1881 the legislature formally organized Mitchell County, and Colorado City[32] became the county seat on May 14, 1881.[33] The county was named for brothers Asa and Eli Mitchell, who came to Texas with Stephen F. Austin's original colonists, known as the Old Three Hundred.

In the 1904 edition of the *Texas Almanac*, Mitchell County was described as having "undulating prairies, traversed by numerous streams, with fertile and beautiful valleys with a scattering growth of mesquite, hackberry, and wild China."[34] Agriculture was the leading industry and source of wealth. The soil was a rich and fertile chocolate with sandy loam. There was plenty of water to produce large crops of almost every variety, including cotton, milo maize, kaffir corn, sorghum, Indian corn, oats, and others. The *Almanac* entry especially praised cotton, which it claimed averaged five hundred pounds to the acre, with boll weevils and caterpillars unknown. By 1900 cotton production had surpassed cattle ranching in West Texas, and before World War I thousands of farmers began immigrating to the region. Loraine was platted in 1906 to facilitate land purchases by settlers who were arriving daily. The town lay some 220 miles west of Fort Worth and 70 miles west of Abilene. Through the decades Loraine, Colorado City, and Westbrook were the only towns in the county. The terrain was nearly flat, with only Lone Wolf Mountain rising a few hundred feet above the plain. The Colorado River, one of the largest in the state, flowed through the county. The hot, dry climate was plagued with periodic droughts.[35]

Finally, after much thought and deliberation, J. K. Mahon made up his mind. The family would go to West Texas where the dry climate would be better for his health, and the fertile, newly broken land would provide better opportunities for a cotton farmer. In November 1908 he chartered a railroad car, known as an immigrant car, and shipped the household goods, farm tools, and livestock to Loraine. The family, including J.K.'s mother and sister, traveled on a passenger train going from Homer to Shreveport on the Shreveport and Northwestern Line and then westward to Loraine on the Texas & Pacific through Fort Worth and Dallas. This was the first train trip for George and his siblings and also their first glimpse of large towns.

The Mahon family stepped down from the train at Loraine, the first stop in Mitchell County. J.K. very likely chose this place based on the availability of land around the new settlement. He could have elected to live in nearby Colorado City, the county seat. However, as a religious man, perhaps the past reputation of Colorado City gave him pause about settling there. In earlier days, when cattle ranching dominated the whole area, Colorado City had been a wild town with a red-light district and more than a dozen saloons where cowboys caroused and whooped it up. This had all changed by the turn of the century, but for the present J.K. preferred to establish his home in a quieter environment.[36] Members of the Mahon family resided in Mitchell County for most of the remainder of the century, and descendants still live there.

When the Mahon family reached Loraine, they rented a house in town for a few weeks until J.K. could find a larger home for his brood of twelve.

He soon rented farm land near the small community of Valley View, seven miles north of Loraine, and began raising cotton. The name "Valley View" came from the beautiful view of the valley that sloped down from Lone Wolf Mountain.[37]

The Mahon children went to Valley View School from 1909 until 1911. The school had been built in 1905 with contributions from nearby farmers. Originally, the little school had one room and one teacher for the twenty-two students enrolled; by 1909 it had two rooms and two teachers. Subjects taught included basic studies in English and spelling, arithmetic, American history, and geography. The school also served as a community recreation center and a church.

Recreation came from within the community. Until a church was built just east of the school, Saturday night singing parties were held in the school. Several people played instruments such as the piano, fiddle, guitar, or mandolin. During the summer there was swimming in a hole at a neighbor's, or sometimes a group would venture south to Seven Wells at the mouth of Champion Creek where it joined the Colorado River. Because the chores of each day required most of people's time, there was little left over for recreation.

After three years J.K. sold his 160-acre farm in Louisiana and used the money to buy 60 acres two miles north of Loraine. As he accumulated more money, he bought additional acreage until finally he had a farm of 300 acres, which he owned for the rest of his life.[38] After moving to their own farm near Loraine, the children began to attend school there.

In 1908 Loraine was still a frontier town. Its growth was facilitated by the breakup of the great free-range ranches of West Texas and the coming of the railroad that brought settlers in and took their produce to market. Cotton quickly became the main cash crop, with about three-fourths of the farms in the county worked by tenant farmers.[39] By 1914 the population of Loraine was slightly less than eight hundred, but it supported more than forty retail and service businesses, among them a bank, an electric utility company, and a weekly newspaper, the *Mitchell County Times*. It also had a grade school, a high school, and a municipal water system.[40]

Although the elder Mahon owned his own farm, the needs of his family stretched his resources to the limit. He kept several cows and chickens and planted some fruit trees and a vegetable garden. In this way he produced enough for the family to get along, although there never was much cash to purchase anything but necessities.

Early-twentieth-century West Texas farm life was hard. There was no indoor plumbing or electricity for household appliances or farm tools and machinery. Able family members were expected to work from sunup to sundown all year. Each Mahon child was assigned chores. George was detailed to milk the cows; however, he was excused from greasing the windmill rotor because of his fear of heights. As he did the milking in the early hours before dawn, he made speeches to the cows from bits of paper posted on the wall. During his first campaign for Congress, George told about dragging a long sack down the row as he picked cotton bolls and feeling the sting of maize chafe on his neck when he helped with the harvest in the fall. He also remembered crying bitterly as a boy because he did not have a nickel to buy a little red top like the other kids had. His family simply did not have money to buy toys.

Travel was difficult and sometimes nearly impossible. Dirt roads were rutted, and during rainy weather they were almost impassable for horses, buggies, and the occasional automobile. Little national or international news percolated down to farm people in Mitchell County except that from the *Fort Worth Star Telegram*, read by those who could afford a subscription or were lucky enough to receive a used copy.

Businessmen actively promoted Loraine, causing it to receive much attention within Mitchell County. For example, one of the merchants periodically tied a five-dollar bill to a chicken's leg and threw it off the top of his building as a gimmick to attract people to Loraine. The lucky person who caught the chicken kept it and the money. There were picnics, barbecues, rodeos, and horse races. Medicine shows also attracted people, as did baseball games. The weekly dates of teenagers usually consisted of attending a party or church services.[41]

On occasion George Mahon spoke of his career and what lay behind it. In an interview after his retirement, he commented, "Well, you see, the whole background, the total explanation of what little success I may have achieved is predicated that I had ambition, that I had motivation, that I had encouragement, that I had friends, that I worked hard, and that I devoted my entire energy to trying to get some place in life."[42] "I wanted to be somebody," he said, then concluded, "So this was the whole, whether this was selfish or not, this was the motivation that kept me going."[43] In one of his notebooks he wrote about this a little differently, "Ever since I was a small boy and rode a mile to the mailbox to get the semi-weekly farm news [the *Dallas Semi-Weekly Farm News*] I have been interested in important world events. I longed for an opportunity to know more—to have a little part in the affairs of the world."[44] Years later, Mahon remembered that he was interested in politics by the time he was ten years old. He greatly enjoyed reading biographies of people who served in government and reading political articles in newspapers.

When he started school in Loraine, George was in the sixth grade and had already begun developing his lifelong ambition to "be somebody." He remembered that while he was still attending Valley View School, someone had said, "That boy might go to Congress sometime." This gave him something of a boost—but not enough to overcome the feelings of inferiority he harbored.[45] He believed people looked down on farmers and thought them inferior to those who lived in cities. One thing that bothered George, as a teenager, was driving into town in the family buggy. When they went to church, his father would often crack the whip and yell at the horse just as they were passing the house where George's girlfriend lived.[46] His father did not get an automobile until 1919, after George had left home.

George Mahon was curious about life, and for almost as far back as he could remember, he wanted to learn more, to expand his horizons as much as possible. This desire lasted throughout his life and became an important part of his success. He read constantly and paid close attention to what was happening around him. Ultimately, he was considered one of the most knowledgeable men in Congress on national defense issues.

George entered high school with much determination, and school was good to him except for one class he claimed to have passed only through the good graces of his teacher. He first learned about Shakespeare through Loraine Superintendent of Schools T. Stone Rives, who taught *Julius Caesar* and *Macbeth*. George went beyond his class work and read as much of Shakespeare as possible. He always loved poetry and read it often, memorizing parts he liked.[47]

One of the first books George remembered reading was about the lives of US military heroes, after which he thought he might like to be a military hero. He remembered staying home one Fourth of July and plowing while the family went off to visit relatives so he could earn enough to buy a book on the lives of the presidents. He had read that some people had used stenography as a stepping-stone in their courses. In later years he cited the career of James F. Byrnes of South Carolina, who started as a court reporter, went on to be a senator, and became a member of the Supreme Court.[48]

Mahon's fascination with history and politics caused him to think that he might like a civil service job. With that in mind he wrote to a company in Chicago in answer to an advertisement in the *Munsey Magazine* offering to rent a typewriter for $2.50 a month. When the typewriter arrived, George was surprised to learn the freight fee was $4.27, a sum he did not have. His father got the bill before George did and lectured him quite strongly about wasting money. Two things from this experience stayed with him the remainder of his life: how to type and to buy only what he could pay for.[49]

During high school George developed an interest in public speaking, "elocution" as it was called, and he enrolled in a class taught by one of the local teachers. He enjoyed the class although he was not a very good speaker and, in fact, did poorly in every oratorical contest he entered in high school. Reflecting on this problem later in life, George opined that he always lost these contests because he was "too awkward and backwoods-like to win, but [he] never lost hope."[50]

A tall, skinny kid, George towered over most of his classmates, which was embarrassing but made it possible for him to excel in sports. Already over six feet tall, he played center on the Loraine basketball team, which won the district championship in 1916.[51] He was also good at track and won five first places at one county track meet, the 50- and 100-yard dashes, the relay, broad jump, and high jump. Loraine High School won first place. George also fancied himself a baseball pitcher until he was "ingloriously knocked out of the box."[52]

In 1917 George passed the examination and received a certificate to teach second grade in Texas schools. He was a senior in high school at the time and had completed all of his required courses, so the principal allowed him to drop out of school for two months to teach in a small, two-teacher school at Brownlee, about six miles east of Loraine. Part of the time he stayed with a family near the town, and at other times he made the fourteen-mile round-trip from his farm home on a bicycle. By April 1918 he was back in Loraine High School, ready to graduate with his class.

After graduation George was eager to leave home and become independent. Believing that stenography could be a stepping-stone to a successful career, he enrolled in Tyler Commercial College in Tyler, Texas, advertised as the largest business training school in America. His coursework lasted about three months after which he worked briefly in Fort Worth. In October 1918 he moved to Nashville, Tennessee, to apply for a job at the DuPont Powder Plant, about sixteen miles outside of town. The job advertised was compressing powder at $4.50 per day. He arrived at the powder plant by train on a cold, rainy day, and when he inquired about a group of coffins on a rail siding, he was told that sixty employees of the plant had died the past week from influenza. George filled out the application and had his picture taken, but he did not take the job. On the train back to Nashville he realized he had a fever. Dousing himself with turpentine, Vaporub, and peroxide before taking a hot bath, he spent several days in bed, trying to ward off the influenza that was raging throughout the world and which ultimately took more than 20 million lives. While recovering he wrote to his sister Mary Agnes, telling her that no one would ever know how he wished for his "dear old West Texas home and mama."[53] However, his outlook improved after he recuperated, and he was able to secure a job in the Cumberland Valley National Bank keeping books for the discount teller. He had difficulty learning how to do the work required of him, though, and his supervisor recommended that he go back to the powder factory.

George then found a job in the office of the US district attorney, where he was able to use the shorthand and typing skills he had learned at Tyler Commercial College, although the job was to last only until the grand jury finished its work in December. While there, George discovered that he was learning something about law and liked this type of work. He typed nearly a hundred indictments, as well as warrants, subpoenas, and materials for the US commissioner. The assistant US attorney helped George find a room in the YMCA that he liked better than the one he had in the local hotel in downtown Nashville. The room had a little table on which he could write, and he could leave his clothes and books and everything else scattered around as he pleased. He was making seventy dollars a month and paying thirty dollars for room and board.

George wrote to his parents that one evening while he was working late, the assistant attorney opened the vault and showed him about twenty thousand dollars' worth of bootleg whiskey that had been confiscated. "These Tennessee bootleggers are a sight they catch them every day," he wrote. "They bring it [the moonshine whiskey] in here [Nashville] and sell it for $48 a gallon."[54] Although Tennessee was dry, Kentucky was wet and only about sixty miles away, so the situation was a lucrative proposition for the bootleggers. That year officials confiscated twenty-two Cadillacs full of moonshine whiskey. George promised to regale the family with more stories when he returned home.

In an earlier letter to Mary Agnes, George wrote, "I confess to you that I have had some dreadful experiences since I left Ft. Worth. I never knew before what home meant but I certainly know now. And, by the way, it's paradise. I also thought I knew the ways of the city but it all proved to be a bitter mistake."[55] By the end of December 1918, the job had ended, and George was back on the family farm near Loraine working for his father.

In March 1919 he followed his brother Marion to Cisco, Texas, approximately one hundred miles east of Loraine, an area in the midst of an oil boom. He found work with a construction crew building an ice plant. He carried mortar in a wheelbarrow for the bricklayers and earned three dollars for an eight-hour day. The work wasn't very hard, but a brick fell on his head, requiring several stitches. He and Marion shared a room at the local hotel for six dollars a week, and by doing their own cooking, they could live on sixty-five cents a day, thus clearing ten dollars for the week. George used part of the money he earned to repay two hundred dollars he had borrowed from Mary Agnes and to repay the Loraine Bank forty-five dollars. This money had been borrowed to finance his odyssey. He also invested five dollars in a Liberty Bond. George liked the bosses on the job, but he thought the workers were low-down and didn't enjoy being around them. By this time his view of common labor was well ingrained. In an unsigned and undated letter written to his sister Mary Agnes, he wrote, "If a man worked every day and lived to be an hundred years old he wouldn't make much out of common labor."[56] Although finding the money to go to college seemed like an impossible task, he knew he must find some way to get an education.

After several weeks George left Cisco and went home to work on the farm again. He helped with the milking and picked cotton. On Saturdays he helped his mother around the house. The cotton crop was better than it had been in many years, and J. K. Mahon was able to spare a few hundred dollars to help George get started in college. Together with the small amount he had been able to save from his own wages, George had enough for at least one semester. Initially, he considered the University of Texas in Austin, but he was concerned that it was too large and he was apprehensive about being adequately prepared to handle the courses. He visited Trinity University at Waxahachie, Texas, but was not impressed with what he saw. Returning by way of Abilene, he decided to enroll in Simmons College for the fall semester.

George spent very little money on himself and for months went without even seeing a movie. He was embarrassed because he had no extra money and seemingly little hope of getting any. As he wrote his sister, he had suspended relations with his high-school sweetheart although he still loved her. Frugality and a conservative outlook came naturally to him. These characteristics became part of his personality for the rest of his life. Through these months he showed a quiet but constant sense of humor. One letter he signed, "Hon G. H. Mahon." On another he wrote "The Wild Man." Always, he showed his love and concern for his family, especially Mary Agnes, whom he believed deprived herself of everything but necessities in order to help her brother and her family. He never forgot this.

In a letter to his daughter, Daphne, and her husband, written in the fall of 1969, after he had been in Congress nearly thirty-five years, George quoted the philosophy that he had held from his youth:

> The heights of great men reached and kept
> Were not attained by sudden flight:
> But they, while their companions slept,
> Were toiling upward in the night.

He went on to admit that "to be overly ambitious, to be always tense, to be always churning inside like George Mahon, is not for everybody." He remembered that his friends and his father had spoken of him in his late teens as a man destined for greatness. These expectations, he said, put him under great stress and strain and in a sense turned "the sweet milk of youth into clabber." He opined, "No young person should be put on the spot too severely by his admirers and loved ones and contemporaries. He must not be so tense that the joy of life is taken away. After all, just to live and be happy and to be pleasing to mankind is more important than their achieving greatness and distinction by the world's standards." He finished his letter to Daphne: "Had it not been for my elders pushing me so hard, and my own inner urge chastising me for every moment wasted, I would not have diverticulitis and today I would be sitting on the front porch on the farm rocking happily as Washington reels in dismay."[57]

In the fall of 1919, George Mahon rode the Texas and Pacific train to Abilene, where he found a city of nearly ten thousand poised to benefit from the post–World War I boom. Simmons College lay about eight miles north of the heart of the city on a barren sixteen acres surrounded by a barbed-wire fence that prevented cars from driving randomly across the land. Mahon rode a slow, chugging streetcar that traveled north out of the city through wheat fields, pastures, and patches of trees to Simmons Street on the southern boundary of the college.

Simmons College was founded in 1890 by the Sweetwater Baptist Association, which extended westward to El Paso. The first students enrolled in 1892, and for several years the college included high-school students among its approximately one hundred enrollees. One small red-brick building housed the entire college, with faculty on the first floor, classes on the second, and the girls' dormitory on the third. Boys lived in a crude dormitory nearby. As its largest donor, James B. Simmons, a Baptist minister in New York, lent his name to the college. By 1919 the school had grown to include an administration building, a men's residence hall and a women's residence hall, a gymnasium, and a science building. The college had lost its high-school students. Enrollment was 982, and the school was a standard, small liberal-arts college, with thirty-five faculty and staff members, including five with doctorates.[58]

When George entered Simmons College the student population had begun to pick up after the austere years of World War I, when enrollment had declined with the departure of some three hundred men for military service. Also, during the war years many activities had been curtailed and sports were discontinued. George reached the campus just as the new academic year was about to begin. A feeling of optimism was noticeable as the flapper era began to change the spirit of the campus and oratory societies started their activities for the fall semester. Opening-day chapel exercises on September 17, 1919, were especially exciting, with speeches from a bevy of visiting ministers, the return of old faculty members, and the appearance of several new ones, including the new football coach.

Friends, patrons, and students gathered to celebrate the twenty-ninth opening. President Thomas Jefferson Sandefer began the ceremony with the singing of "The Star-Spangled Banner." Divine guidance was invoked during the invocation, and the first chapter of Corinthians, on which Simmons College was founded, was read. Abilene Mayor Scarborough welcomed the students, promising that the residents of Abilene would do everything possible to make their stay a pleasant one. He went on to say that an important reason for men and women to attend college was the opportunities that were open to those who did so. Religion had a central role at Simmons College, which fit well with Mahon's beliefs and upbringing. The daily chapel services were conducted by the president, and faculty and visitors, especially visiting ministers, addressed the student body often.

After enrolling at Simmons, Mahon found a room at the Smith Boarding House near campus. Hazing was prevalent in the dorms, and he was concerned that it would interfere with his studying. Money was going to be a big enough problem; he didn't need another one. He secured a part-time job during the afternoons at Minter's Dry Goods Store and prayed that his father's cotton crop would be good enough to allow him to send more money. J.K. Mahon was able to send him $50 before Christmas, and George bought a dark gray suit that cost $47.50. He admitted that it was expensive, but he liked the suit and needed to be properly dressed for debates.[59] Willingly investing the time and money he had available in his career became a lifelong practice.

Simmons proved to be the right college for Mahon. He tried to make as many friends as possible, and within a year he had become one of the best-known and most popular men on campus. He genuinely liked people, and this affection was returned when he was elected freshman-class president and secretary of the Mitchell County Club, an organization of students from his home county.[60]

Initially, he was somewhat shy in class, and when his solid geometry teacher called on him using his first name from the enrollment list, he was too timid to tell the professor that his family called him Herman. From that day on he was George, and eventually only his family and a few of his oldest friends even knew his middle name or ever used it. It was only after he had gone into politics and left his home community that he started to pronounce his last name with a long "a," as in "day," instead of Muh-hon with the accent on the second syllable. People in the Loraine area still use this second pronunciation.[61]

He was a straight A student his first year. He took modern European history, freshman English, solid geometry, followed by trigonometry, principles of economics (which he especially enjoyed), education, and religion. At the end of his first semester, he had done so well that he was exempted from all examinations.[62] He had even developed some self-confidence. As he was leaving to return home for the Christmas holidays, he wrote in his journal, "I must say that work in Simmons College is very easy. A man that cannot make his grades here is very dull." Later, as he was finishing law school at the University of Texas, he added a note to this entry. "I studied well enough but had finally dissipated the pre-college days of fear of failing. I penned these lines rather extravagantly."[63]

During his years at Simmons College, Mahon tried to support himself in a variety of ways, including "batching"[64] for a time, which he said was bad for his health, managing a boarding house, and working part-time in the afternoons at a dry-goods store. His father couldn't offer much help because Mitchell County was experiencing a drought, and that meant poor crops. At the end of the fall term in 1920, his father wrote, "Conditions are such that we just can't afford to help you get through school, so you better come home at Christmas time." After a successful freshman year Mahon had no intention of giving up. That is when he went to President Sandefer with his appeal and received support from Judge Ely. Father Mahon also helped whenever possible, and the young Mahon sent his laundry home to his mother. Thus, he never had to leave school during his college days.

At Simmons Mahon continued his interest in debate, despite his lackluster experience in high school. A memorable event from his days in college occurred when he teamed up with a classmate to defeat the sophomores in the annual freshman-sophomore debate, which took place just before Christmas. He worried about one of his opponents, who had a reputation for being the best in the college, so he practiced until his presentation was memorized. Leading off with a twelve-minute speech for the affirmative on the question of whether Congress should provide for compulsory arbitration of industrial disputes, he pointed out that currently there was no way to settle such disputes and that the public had a right to have them solved. Ninety percent of workers were not members of unions, and, he argued, a minority of 10 percent should not be able to inflict loss on the other 90 percent or on the public at large. Government had been established to provide for the welfare of the people, and compulsory arbitration was necessary. The freshman team won 3-0.

Savoring this win, he wrote to his sister Mary Agnes about the victory, saying it was the first oratorical victory he had ever won and he was very proud of it. In his exuberance he ended his letter with quotes from faculty members about his ability: "I did not know you were in this institution. You have the making of an orator," Dean Julius Olsen said. "Mahon is the best speaker we have had in Simmons College since I have been here," said Lucian Campbell, head of the English department. "Mahon will rank with the best speakers in any college," according to Evan Barker, assistant English professor. He had reason to be proud but ended his letter with instructions to his sister to tear up the letter because somebody might accuse him of being boastful.[65] Mary Agnes was equally proud of her brother's accomplishment and preserved the letter.

Mahon also entered an oratorical contest sponsored by the Kiwanis Club and won with a speech entitled "Our Industrial Problem." His prize, given by the Abilene Kiwanis Club, was a gold Hamilton watch.[66]

When he had worked in the federal district attorney's office in Nashville, Tennessee, he had spent much of his spare time during evenings and weekends reading in the Carnegie Library. He took voluminous notes that were transferred to a journal he had bought in December 1918. He always referred to the journal as his Brown Journal, because of the color of the cover. When he read Shakespeare's *Macbeth* he wrote a critique and detailed synopsis of it. Soon poems and notes from books and periodicals that he read were added. Other additions included several essays he wrote, such as comments about plans he should make, comments about visits to the Tennessee state capitol, and remarks on the state penitentiary. Writings in his journal show that he read widely, both current publications as well as the Bible and philosophical writings. The comments also indicate a very active and reflective mind. This journal was an important resource when he composed material for his debates in college and for later speeches and writings.

The college paper and the yearbook show that oratory and debating played an important part in college life at Simmons, along with football, baseball, and track. Mahon became an official member of the Philos (Philomathion) debating society. In his sophomore year he and a teammate defeated Baylor, and in the fall of 1921 he served as president of the Philos Society. He also served on the Oratorical and Debating Council.[67] Each society had its picture in the annual *Bronco*, so Mahon was pictured along with officers of other college societies. Years later, in a short biographical sketch, he wrote that "George's college days were happy and extremely successful. Everything he did seemed to work out fine. While he was unable to win oratorical contests in high school he seemed to win easily many of the contests he entered in college."[68]

On April Fools' Day of 1921, students conducted chapel and spoofed the faculty in a stunt they had started the previous year. They did take-offs on various faculty members by dressing like the faculty members and imitating their words and actions. This was done without any rehearsal. Mahon impersonated President Sandefer, filling out his suit and vest with a pillow and combing his hair to resemble the president. Women members of the faculty filed in and took their places on the stage, followed by students impersonating faculty men. Mahon came in last and conducted the services. As the student newspaper reported, "George Mahon, as President Sandefer, was one of the stars of the occasion. From the tip of his wavy hair to the soles of his shoes he was as good an imitation of the dignified president of Simmons College as could be found anywhere." Mahon ended the exercises by announcing there would be no classes the rest of the day. The paper didn't report whether there were or not.[69]

Student government was established in 1920 and became one of the activities with which Mahon was identified. After World War I students generally demanded more control over their affairs. In November 1919 the student council sent a resolution to the faculty, seeking more social privileges. In September 1920 a committee of students and faculty worked out a constitution. There was a legislative assembly that established rules and a judicial council to apply the rules, subject to faculty approval. Rupert Richardson, professor of history and later president of Hardin-Simmons, called these changes "a noble experiment, perhaps the most important step in the history of student life in the institution."[70] Although at first the judicial council seemed a success, it soon deteriorated and was unable to control student activities. Clashes between classes couldn't be stopped. A freshman-sophomore contest usually ended in a row. On one occasion, somebody turned off the lights in the school gym and a riot ensued.[71] Mahon didn't approve of or take part in this rowdyism. Instead, he won election to the judicial council and worked to bring order out of the chaos on campus. He also helped redraft the student government constitution.

Mahon's letters to his family don't reveal much about his social life at Simmons, probably because there was little time for socializing. He went to church and Sunday school regularly and built a circle of friends from these activities, as well as from his part-time work and his boarding-house days. He did write home that he had met a pleasant young lady, a fellow student, at a junior theatre party. They had gone together to the South Side Baptist Church in Abilene, and he enjoyed going with her to the junior theatre party, and afterward to a café, where they had sandwiches and hot chocolate.[72]

As he said, these years at Simmons were happy ones that gave him a sense of accomplishment. Not only was he active in college activities and organizations, four of his poems appeared in the fall 1920 issue of the *Corral*, a campus magazine published by students. Three he had written before coming to Simmons: "Would You Like to Be," "'Tis Sweet to Hear," and "Gone" were written while he was in Nashville. The fourth, "The Exiled Lover," he wrote in the spring of 1920 at Simmons.

Would You Like to Be

Would you like to be a traveler on the wild and pathless sea
When the waves were beating high and the sprays were wetting thee;
When the captain's stern command could be heard above the roar
"To the pumps!" "To the pumps!" if you wish to reach the shore.
Would you like to climb the mountains, high, rugged—very steep,
'Mid the raging winds of winter, and the ice—the snow—the sleet,
And at last stand the victor on the sharpest, highest peak
With the rushing, dashing ocean lying at your very feet?
Would you like to be a king with a palace rich and grand
And have laid before your feet the choicest jewels of the land?
And all people would cease their struggles, cast away their arms, and stand
At a whimsical wish of yours or a beckon of your hand?
Or would you rather live in a plain and common land
And be pronounced by all that knew you as a just and righteous man,
And earn your modest living by earnest, honest sweat:
My friend, the God has created no nobler man as yet.

Geo. Mahon

The closing lines of "Would You Like to Be" seem to reveal that at the time he had not yet convinced himself he could become more than a high school teacher, although ambitions were developing within him. More importantly, the poem seems to provide an insight into his acceptance of people just as they were and his respect for work done well. Above all, Mahon's easy acceptance of others helps explain people's affection and esteem for him throughout his congressional district during his years in Congress.

By the end of his junior year, Mahon had completed the required courses for his bachelor's degree, leaving only electives to be taken. He remained undecided about his career but thought he might like to teach in college. For that he would need at least a master's degree, and he entered the University of Texas in Austin. He took religious subjects along with American history and some law courses and was able to transfer enough credits to Simmons to receive his bachelor of arts degree in absentia on June 5, 1924.[73]

As he began his first semester at the University of Texas, he worried about whether he could compete on the university level. He soon discovered the competition wasn't as hard as he had thought it would be. He was older and more serious about his course work than many of the other students. He did well in his classes and decided to study law.

As he had at Simmons, Mahon tried out for and became a member of the debating team. In the spring of 1923, he and a teammate debated teams from the universities of Oklahoma and Mississippi. The topic remained the same in each case: "Resolved, that the United States should cancel her war loans to her associates in the World War." In both debates Bell and Mahon took the affirmative, losing to Oklahoma and defeating Mississippi. In that year Mahon shared with two others the Boon prize for best extemporaneous speaker. The University of Texas had begun publication of a law review journal in 1922; two years later Mahon was listed as a member of the board of student editors.[74]

By the fall of 1923, Mahon began to think about his high-school sweetheart, Helen Stevenson. Although they had gone in different directions, they had never completely lost contact, staying in touch through letters while he was in Tyler and Nashville. Each had dated other people but made no real commitment. Now Mahon decided he was serious about Helen, and he renewed their relationship.

Helen Stevenson's family had moved to Loraine in 1915. They came from Sherwood, Texas, where her father, O. E. Stevenson, was the county judge of Irion County. According to family history, the Stevenson family migrated to Texas from Arkansas in the nineteenth century. Early in 1915 Judge Stevenson was contacted by a friend who was president of the bank in Loraine, asking him to come to Loraine to buy cotton for resale to textile mills. Mitchell County farmers had a bumper cotton crop in the fields, and there was no one locally who would buy the cotton.

Helen was fifteen years old when they arrived,[75] and she graduated from Loraine High School the same year as George Mahon. Although they had been classmates, they were each seeing other people until their senior picnic in 1917, when he asked if he might pick her up for the senior banquet that night. She accepted, and they began dating. After graduation Helen went to the College of Industrial Arts in Denton, Texas, a women's college, where she studied for one year before transferring to Southwest Texas State Normal

School for another semester. She then took the state teacher's examination and received certification to teach in Texas. For the next five years, she taught the fourth grade in several rural schools, ending up in Tahoka, Texas, in 1923. During the years that Mahon was in Fort Worth and Nashville, Helen wrote to him regularly to offer encouragement as he went through a series of changes. At one point he decided they should not correspond any longer because he could not afford a girlfriend and thought it not fair to "string her along." Helen did not agree, obviously, and they started seeing each other again, although there is no record of their relationship during his years at Simmons College.[76] After he enrolled in the University of Texas they would meet occasionally on weekends, and their relationship grew.

Initially they planned to be married in Austin on December 22, 1923, during the Christmas break. When the dean of the University of Texas law school died suddenly, school was dismissed, and Mahon wired Helen to come to Fort Worth so they could be married a day earlier. She arrived in Fort Worth on the morning of December 21, and they were married in the chapel of the First Methodist Church. As with many young couples, their finances were in a state of disrepair. Mahon had written Judge Ely for one of his two-hundred-dollar loans, but it was late in coming, so he married in his two-year-old suit. He later remembered that, in the afternoon, they attended the Majestic Theatre and spent their wedding night in the Texas Hotel. There was no money for a longer honeymoon, so on the evening of December 22, they left on the night train for Loraine, sharing an upper berth.[77] After spending Christmas with family, Helen returned to teaching in Tahoka, and Mahon went back to school in Austin. They did not see each other again until Helen resigned her teaching position in June of 1924 to join her husband in Austin.

By the end of the spring semester in 1924, George had satisfied most of the requirements for his law degree. The newly married couple needed money more than he needed additional courses, so Mahon accepted a position as superintendent/teacher of the school at Liberty Hill, Texas, a small town north of Austin. In later years he said he wasn't exactly sure why he had been hired at Liberty Hill but thought it was possibly because he had told them his wife had taught school for five years and could help him. At any rate, he got the job and later was offered a second year at an increase in salary from $1,600 to $2,500. Helen remembered that she was not able to secure a teaching position in the school because the previous superintendent's wife had whipped one of the students; however, she was allowed to substitute and ended up teaching nearly three-fourths of the year. They lived across the street from the school, and often George would run home to ask her advice. George was not accustomed to being a superintendent, but he learned quickly and enjoyed his year at the school. He made friends and practiced his oratory with speeches and poetry at chapel exercises. He also discovered that he had enough free time to do many things he liked to do.[78]

One of the chapel addresses he especially remembered was given on January 1, 1925, when he used as his title and theme, "Whatsoever a man soweth that shall he reap"(Galatians 6:7). In the eleven or so minutes it took him to give his message, he said in part, "If one sows a good disposition, and generous acts, and good thoughts he will reap a pure mind and a noble heart. If one is studious and desirous of advancement he will advance as surely as the night follows day." He went on to stress ambition and the rewards it would bring, ending with "so my New Year's message to you is, be ambitious, desire to lead your class, to be respected, to be honored. And as a guard against improper ambition there is none better than a Christian conscience."[79] That address reflected many of his lifelong beliefs and practices.

By the end of the school session in 1925, the Mahons had saved enough money to allow George to enroll for a summer term at the University of Minnesota Law School in Minneapolis where he was able to get the remaining courses that he needed. These courses were not offered in the summer at the University of Texas. Mahon carried lingering fears of the suspicion that Northerners were somehow smarter than Southerners, but as with his feelings of inferiority in the past, his fears were unfounded. He took three courses, scoring two *As* and a *B*.[80]

In Minneapolis Helen worked as a sales clerk in Dayton's department store while Mahon worked on the campus, pulling weeds out of a special kind of bent grass with which the grounds superintendent was experimenting. They lived in a one-room apartment. Feeling rather humiliated about having to dig out weeds, Mahon comforted himself as he sat on the ground by thinking about much of the philosophy of jurisprudence in one of his law courses.[81]

The Mahons would have liked to stay at the University of Minnesota to take more courses, but a little sound thinking and a shortage of money convinced them it was time to return to Texas. That fall they were back in Austin. The Minnesota courses were transferred to the University of Texas, and Mahon received his law degree in 1925.

Mahon lost no time in opening a law office in Colorado City, Texas, with his old high-school classmate, Charles Thompson, who was also serving as county judge. By the mid-twenties Colorado City boasted a population approaching four thousand. The streets were paved, a new sewage system was in operation, a city hall had been built, and the Col-Tex oil refinery was in operation. When Mahon and Helen arrived they rented a very small apartment until they were able to build a small house containing two rooms and a closet, but no indoor bathroom. It was just a few blocks from downtown and Mahon's law office.

The law degree that Mahon earned from the University of Texas admitted him automatically to the Texas bar. His first case was defending a black man charged with forgery. Initially, the defendant assured Mahon that he was innocent but confessed his guilt during the trial. At that point the best Mahon could do was plead for a suspended sentence. As he later remembered it, the judge admonished the jury not to listen to the "young Lochinvar."[82] The jurors issued a suspended sentence, which Mahon attributed to their desire to give the new attorney a break.[83]

Practicing law in a small West Texas town was not exactly a path to wealth. To earn additional income, the new partners decided to run for county office, Thompson for reelection as county judge and Mahon for county attorney. Both ran unopposed. Mahon's opportunity came when the county attorney for Mitchell County decided to return to private practice. As in other counties the county attorney assisted the district attorney in handling legal affairs for the county. Mahon's salary was $300 a year in contrast to Thompson's $2,600. For an additional $25 a month his duties included business coming before the County Commissioners Court and the Courts of Justices of the Peace, defending lawsuits involving the county, and serving as legal advisor to the county and precinct officials. In theory the position of county attorney might seem of some importance, but in a rural West Texas county with only three small towns, it more closely resembled civic work.

On May 9, 1927, the Mahons' only child, Daphne, was born in their small house on Chestnut Street. When they could afford to do so, they added on another room and a bath. Finally, they added a room across the back of the house. They lived in that house until moving to Washington, DC. In 1936, at the end of Mahon's first term in Congress, Helen returned to Colorado City after Congress had adjourned while George went to Philadelphia to attend the Democratic Convention. When she arrived home a neighbor who was a real estate agent suggested they buy a larger house that was on the market because of foreclosure. Helen protested that they could not afford the house, as did Mahon when he got home. However, the real estate agent was persistent and said the mortgage company was willing to take $5,000 for it. The Mahons bought the house and made the second floor into an apartment, which they used when in Colorado City. The lower floor was rented out. That was the only home they owned during his years in Congress. Mahon believed he was only in Washington, DC, to take care of business for the district; his home was in Colorado City, Texas.

In October 1927 the district attorney of the Thirty-second Judicial District resigned. The district included five counties, one of which was Mitchell County. Mahon knew the governor would appoint someone to fill the unexpired term, after which an election would be held to fill the position. Clyde Thomas, one of Mahon's friends, wanted the position and was widely endorsed by the bar at Big Spring, Texas, one of the cities in the district. Mahon also wanted the office and talked with Simmons College President Sandefer, with friends in Big Spring, and with his mentor, Judge W. R. Ely, who had by this time become a member of the newly formed Texas State Highway Commission. They all encouraged him and offered to help in any way possible.

On their advice Mahon went to Austin to talk with Governor Dan Moody, driving all night to get there. The governor did not seem to be impressed by a young lawyer who had tried only eight or ten cases and remarked that he thought Mahon was too young for the post. Mahon asked him how old he had been when he entered politics, whereupon the governor replied that he had been thirty-one. It later developed that about fifteen telegrams reached the governor's office in support of Mahon. The matter dragged on for some time, and Mahon called Ely to say that he had better withdraw his name in order not to embarrass any of his friends. Ely told him to "just sit steady in the boat. You're going to be appointed in the morning."[84] Mahon thought this was the biggest political break of his life and correctly attributed it to the work of his friends, especially Judge Ely. He served for seven years, being reelected every two years without an opponent.

Years later, Mahon recalled that this was the best possible political experience. As a criminal district attorney, he had to try a great variety of cases and contend with some of the best lawyers in the state. "You have to be able to stand on your feet and take the blows as they come. And you can develop self-confidence. You get experience, so this was very valuable to me," he explained.[85] He learned about people, as well as the law, as he tried cases that ranged from murder to theft of property, assault, bootlegging, and most other crimes capable of being committed. His debating experiences at Simmons College and the University of Texas proved valuable, and he gained even greater public-speaking skills as he stood before jurors to argue cases for the prosecution.

By the time Mahon was appointed district attorney, he and Helen were comfortably settled into the small-town life of Colorado City. They had developed a fondness for playing bridge with friends. Mahon became a Mason and was raised at the lodge in Colorado City on December 15, 1936. He also became a member of the Lions Club and supported other civic organizations. The Mahon family was Methodist and became lifelong members of the First Methodist Church in Colorado City, just down the street from their home. In 1928 George started playing golf at the Colorado Country Club on its nine-hole course with sand greens. He played the rest of his life and became a better-than-average golfer. In later years the game would provide him with badly needed respite from his congressional work. It also became socially and politically valuable in Washington, DC.

After the federal census of 1930 had been completed, three new congressional districts were awarded to Texas. Census data revealed that the Texas population had grown by nearly 25 percent in the previous ten years, making the state the fifth most populous in the nation. A notable feature of the new data was the increase in the Texas urban population. Forty-one percent of Texans were urban, residing in incorporated towns and cities of twenty-five hundred people or more. News of the three new congressional seats was welcome, but the state legislature argued for months over which areas of the state should have the new districts. Finally in May 1933, the governor signed the bill that created a new district in Bexar County, which included the San Antonio area; one in central West Texas, which included the San Angelo area; and a third in north West Texas, which included the Panhandle and South Plains area.

Although the number of Texans who actually lived on farms was less than one-half the total population, the growth in the western part of the state, where two of the three new districts had been formed, was primarily rural. Between 1920 and 1930 the number of farms in West Texas increased by nearly 70 percent. Most of this increase was the result of immigration from neighboring regions. Both cotton and cattle prices had fallen drastically after World

War I, but cotton began to recover by 1925. Ranchers, taking advantage of rising cotton prices, sold land instead of cattle. The Dallas and Fort Worth newspapers, widely read throughout Texas and Oklahoma, fueled a land boom by publishing long articles describing the fertile soil of West Texas. The land had to be broken, but the yields were far better than those from older land that was depleted after years of raising cotton. Additionally, the boll weevil, the scourge of cotton farmers in East and Central Texas, had difficulty surviving the cold winters in West Texas and was less of a threat. Even the sparse rainfall could be advantageous—West Texas farmers had less need for costly weed control. In the decade following World War I, the cotton belt quietly shifted from the Southeast to the Southwest, and enough people moved to West Texas to justify the allocation of two of the new congressional districts. With no incumbents these new districts were rich political prizes for the candidate who could win each district's initial election.

At thirty-two years of age, George Mahon was serving his fourth term as district attorney of the Thirty-second Judicial District and had gained statewide name recognition through his prosecution of a man who had drowned his wife in a lake near Sweetwater, Texas. His closing argument to the jury was considered a masterpiece, and many spectators came to hear it.

When 1933 began Mahon and his partner, Charles Thompson, looked forward to expanding their private law practice and becoming civic leaders in Mitchell County. Both were active in the Chamber of Commerce and their church. Their wives were leading members of the study clubs in Colorado City and belonged to the Texas Federation of Women's Clubs. However, when Mahon and Thompson learned that they were living in the newly created Nineteenth Congressional District, both men admitted they were interested in filling the seat, but they agreed not to run against each other. When asked in later years how the decision had been reached, all Mahon said was that they concluded that Thompson was needed more on his ranch than his partner was in the office. Moreover, most Texans were more interested in local than national politics. They believed that what happened at the county courthouse and in the state legislature had a greater impact on their daily lives than what happened in Washington. Thompson, who went on to have a distinguished career of his own, always said he thought Mahon had been a better congressman than he would have been.

Almost as soon as Governor Ferguson signed the bill in May 1933, District Judge Clark Mullican of Lubbock announced his intention to run. Since 1923 he had been judge of the Ninety-ninth Judicial District and had been judge of the Seventy-second Judicial District before that. The next day, May 17, while Mahon was in court in Big Spring, Texas, he told a reporter from the *Colorado Record* that he too intended to enter the race; however, he did not formally announce at that time. "There is no occasion to be hasty in the matter," he said. "My announcement will come at the proper time, and I am pleased to know that I do not anticipate opposition in either Mitchell, Howard or Scurry counties, the three largest counties of my judicial district."[86] Three others soon announced their candidacy: State Senator Arthur Duggan of Littlefield, Fred Haile of Spur, and District Judge Homer L. Pharr of Lubbock. They were joined later by Taylor White, a high-school agriculture teacher of Tahoka; J. A. (Swede) Johnson of Lamesa; and Joe H. Thompson, a retired lawyer from Plainview. None of these last three campaigned much and very likely paid the twenty-five-dollar filing fee more for name recognition than anything else or because they hoped a long shot might win if a split vote caused a runoff. All of these candidates ran in the Democratic primary. This election took place at a time when one-party politics dominated Texas elections; the Republican Party did not put up a candidate to represent the new district.

The Nineteenth Congressional District took its shape partly by being split off from the Eighteenth Congressional District. Prior to 1933 the Eighteenth Congressional District had been represented by Congressman Marvin Jones from Amarillo, and it included fifty-three counties south from the Oklahoma border and east from the New Mexico state line to west of Wichita Falls, Texas. The new district got twenty-one counties from the Eighteenth District, and the remaining four counties were split off from the Sixteenth Congressional District, represented by Congressman Ewing Thomason of El Paso.[87] The new Nineteenth District stretched from the New Mexico border to Haskell County on the east and from Hale County on the north to Mitchell on the South, taking in twenty-five counties. The size of these districts indicated the scarcity of people in rural West Texas, where ranching and stock farming were the predominant livelihoods. Mahon was well-known in the southern part of the new district, but he was almost unknown in the northern part, and he expected to find his strongest competition there. Initially, he was a little hesitant about entering the race and decided to seek the advice of two men whose opinions he greatly valued. A. R. Mauzey, judge of the Thirty-second Judicial District, urged him to run, as did his old friend and mentor from Abilene, W. R. Ely, who was chairman of the State Highway Commission. Ely told him that a candidate could never know whether or not people would vote for him, and the only thing to do was get out there and see. Despite his misgivings about being young and less experienced than Mullican and Duggan, he entered the race.

Mahon knew the size of the district meant that to win the election a candidate would have to contact and appeal to the 254,567 people scattered over 23,924 square miles. In fact, the new district was larger than the combined areas of Connecticut, Vermont, and New Hampshire. Approximately 143,720 people lived on farms and would be especially difficult to contact to ask for their votes; however, all of the candidates faced the same challenge. In sixteen counties of the twenty-five, there was no town with 2,500 people, and in the whole district only 26 percent lived in towns of 2,500 or more. Only a handful of voters would live in any one community. Mahon also knew that the population was almost completely native-born white, probably as much so as any congressional district in the entire country. The census of 1930 listed 8,124 Mexican Americans (who were at that time not classed as Caucasians), 6,214 Negroes, and 1,028 foreign-born whites.

Mahon did not begin campaigning immediately because the election was more than a year away and he still had a job to do as district attorney. The summer months were spent preparing for the September term of the Thirty-second District Court, which was one of the busiest in history, with nearly two hundred cases on the docket. The Thirty-second District, serving 72,000 people, was the largest in West Texas. Although the boundaries of the district were also redrawn in 1933, the number of cases remaining on the docket was quite large.

Traditionally, Mitchell County candidates for any upcoming election launched their campaigns with the first edition of their local paper in January of the election year. In 1934 the *Colorado Record* published announcements for several candidates who were running for various offices, including Mahon. He established his campaign headquarters in the bank building in Colorado City, with his wife as office manager.

When he announced his candidacy, George Mahon made a statement that actually expressed the sentiments of each of the other candidates. He was in favor of the general idea of the New Deal for all people, the policy that was moving the center of power from Wall Street back to Washington. He believed there should be equitable representation and an equitable share of the benefits of government for the people of West Texas. He agreed to work in harmony with the people, the party, and the president. Mahon advocated an agricultural policy that emphasized the expansion of foreign markets because Texas exported many commodities. He wanted to discontinue the policy of issuing tax-exempt bonds, and he wanted the immediate payment of a soldier's bonus.[88] He wanted to take the profit out of war by drafting industry as well as manpower. He would cooperate with the national administration to expand home ownership both in the country and in towns. He was in favor of an old-age pension and equal representation for every county and citizen in the Nineteenth District. As district attorney he had compiled an impressive record for law enforcement and justice. He was known to be levelheaded and fair-minded, which encouraged many to believe he was just what was needed in Congress. When he retired more than four decades later, people were still saying the same thing.

Soon after formal announcements were published, a group of enthusiastic Democrats met in a Colorado City hotel to organize the "George Mahon for Congress Club of Mitchell County." Law partner Charles Thompson was elected as the club's president, and Lloyd Croslin was the secretary. The vice president and treasurer positions were filled by officers from City National Bank. Thompson led the tributes by saying, "I know George Mahon probably more intimately than any man in this meeting tonight and I cannot speak too highly of his sterling qualities, his ability, and his integrity." These characteristics would be praised over and over in the years to come. Others also paid tribute to the man whom they believed had the strongest qualifications to fill this new congressional position. The rally ended with a staunch resolve to launch an aggressive campaign in support of "our man." George Mahon for Congress clubs were organized throughout West Texas for the purpose of networking, raising campaign funds, and getting out the vote.[89]

Mahon was an easy sell, especially in the southern part of the new district, where people were familiar with his strong work ethic and personal integrity. For the previous seven years they had watched him at work as the county attorney, then as the district attorney. They admired his achievements despite a lifetime of very limited financial resources. They were confident that he would also be successful as their representative and would work diligently on behalf of their interests. Now Mahon's task was convincing the whole district of his strengths.

He began by putting together a team to work with him. As county judge of Mitchell County and Mahon's law partner, Charles Thompson was the natural choice for campaign manager. The two men had been close friends since high school. Thompson proved to be a strong ally, who was outgoing and ready to organize supporters throughout the district. Years later Mahon recalled that campaigns were not long and expensive in 1934.

On the first day of June, Thompson orchestrated a rally in Colorado City of Mahon supporters from all over the area, complete with speeches and a special concert by the "George Mahon for Congress" band from Loraine. Caravans of two or three cars went out regularly into the district where six or eight men would spend the day holding political meetings and urging support for Mahon. Thompson often went with them and frequently accompanied Mahon or went by himself to speak for him.

Lloyd Croslin, a high school teacher in Colorado City, agreed to become Mahon's advance man. School was not in session during June and July, when the campaign was in full swing. There is no record of his receiving a salary for this work; however, this was not new for him. During the Great Depression, the State of Texas issued scrip (a form of credit) to state employees instead of pay because money was not available. During the previous year Croslin, a native of Lubbock, had demonstrated his interest in working for the Democratic Party. He had been active in the Lubbock Young Democrats and represented West Texas as a delegate at the initial national convention of Young Democrats held in Kansas City in 1932. In late 1933 he had been a delegate to the party's state convention, held in Fort Worth. In December 1932 he had organized a Young Democrats Club in Colorado City to build among young people a greater understanding of Democratic Party principles. Because most Texans believed that true political power rested with local officeholders, these clubs were a strong voice of concern about state and national issues.[90] The clubs also became a strong pool of workers for any candidate on the Democratic ticket. Because Mahon inspired confidence in him, Croslin decided to support him instead of any other candidate. Additionally, if Mahon won, there just might be employment with a steady paycheck instead of scrip.[91] Croslin's organizational skills were his biggest asset. In each town he arranged for a time and place for Mahon to speak, a pickup truck for him to stand on when he spoke, and somebody to introduce him and work for him afterward. Many times Mahon had to speak without a microphone; fortunately, his voice was strong enough to be effective without one. In some small towns he could be heard by everyone, even if they weren't attending the gathering.

Thompson and Croslin helped Mahon put together a campaign that caused Clark Mullican to remark in a speech at the end of the first Democratic primary, "That bunch from Mitchell County is the best-organized I've ever seen. They have resident organizers in every county and community. They have a man here."[92] The other candidates could not match Mahon's organization, and they seldom even ventured out of their own area to campaign. Haile, for example, did not begin his campaign until sixty days before the first Democratic primary. He and the others had committees of supporters who worked mainly within their own communities. A month before the primary, Mullican toured the northern part of the district, and when he returned to Lubbock, he was startled to find that Lubbock County's votes might have to be shared with three new men in the race: Taylor White, J. A. Johnson, and Joe Thompson. He warned that unless Lubbock County came alive to the fact that a congressional race was going on, they were approaching the last roundup as far as electing a congressman. He feared Lubbockites hadn't yet awakened to the fact that the district extended beyond the boundaries of the county.[93]

Shortly after Mahon had entered the race, his brother Durward offered a bit of advice that George followed faithfully, then and for years to come. Durward told him to subscribe to newspapers all over the district and try to get the editors on his side because their help would be very valuable. Additionally, he would get information about what was going on in that particular locality. He concluded his advice with, "I feel that the most effective campaign would be by personal contact with each individual possible over the District, not the long-drawn out bull session, but meet all of them personally that you can possibly do briefly."[94]

Radio was of limited use because most farm homes were without electricity to power a radio, even if they could afford one. Battery-powered radios were expensive, and television had not yet climbed above the horizon. County newspaper editors showed little interest in national campaigns and were unwilling to print news about those candidates unless they were paid twenty-five or thirty cents a column inch. The important races were for mayor, sheriff, school board, and others at the local level.

Texans were fiercely proud of their rugged individualism and ability to take care of their own, but during the Great Depression they joined the rest of the country in looking to the federal government for help to get them through the hard times. West Texas was hit especially hard. It was part of the Dust Bowl where severe droughts raged throughout most of the 1930s. When cotton prices fell to a nickel a pound, there was no money to pay farm mortgages. Farmers had always operated without much ready cash, but now barter became commonplace. Chickens, milk, and butter were traded for clothing, shoes, and other manufactured necessities. Magazine salesmen offering subscriptions to farm and ranch journals would take goods in trade and drove from farm to farm with chicken cages in their cars and pieces of traded iron strapped on the roof. Political candidates were as strapped for money as everyone else. In an effort to economize, they drove to many towns together and occupied the same platform for their speeches. In addition to saving money, this practice allowed the audience to better compare one to the other. However, Mahon remembered years later that there were no debates among the candidates; each one spoke separately.

In their search for votes, political candidates focused on current conditions and tried to tailor their speeches and written statements to address them. It was no surprise that they all believed the biggest challenge lay in how to help farmers. All eight of the congressional candidates said that if elected they would work to reduce taxes in one way or another, especially for those with low incomes. Also, payment of a soldier's bonus ranked high on their list of legislation to support.

A federal law was passed in 1924 to provide adjusted compensation for veterans of World War I. They were to be paid $1.00 for each day of active duty served inside the United States and $1.25 for each day served on active duty overseas. The intent of the law was to make the veterans' pay during the war comparable to civilian workers, whose wartime wages reached an all-time high. Veterans had been issued certificates that would mature and be paid with interest in 1945. As the Great Depression worsened, Congress passed a bill in February 1931, allowing veterans to borrow up to one-half of their money, but President Hoover vetoed the bill. In the summer of 1932, approximately twelve thousand jobless veterans marched to Washington, DC, in an attempt to get Congress to make the appropriation. Failing to understand the urgency of their situation, Hoover ordered them driven from the city with teargas and bayonets. News of their disheveled retreat stuck in the hearts and minds of most Americans. There was widespread agreement on the need to pay the bonus money immediately when these veterans needed it most, not in 1945 when many would already be dead. President Roosevelt also opposed payment immediately because when he entered office he was trying to carry out his promise to cut government expenses.

The memory of World War I was still fresh for many West Texans, causing an antiwar sentiment to grow. Newspapers carried wire service stories about Japanese aggressions in the Pacific and their goal of dominating that part of the world. When Hitler came to power, the national press kept a watchful eye on his maneuverings and shifting of power within his government. The *Sweetwater Reporter* noted that treaties and alliances were being negotiated, armaments were being increased, and military preparations were under way. The result would be war, perhaps not in the next few years but eventually, and it would be more disastrous than World War I.[95] Although they feared war and wanted to stay out of another, most people believed that one was coming. Mahon and the other candidates stressed the need for an adequate national defense, although they did not spell out exactly what they meant.

As the campaign moved into 1934, Mahon seemed buried in the pack, somewhere behind Mullican and Duggan. To the charge that he was too young to be a congressman, thirty-three-year-old Mahon quoted from a list of other Texans who had also entered politics at a young age: he mentioned Congressman Marvin Jones, who was thirty-one years old at the time of his election and had formerly represented most of the counties in the new Nineteenth District; Vice President John Nance Garner, who was thirty-five when elected to the US House of Representatives; and Texas Senator Tom Connally, who was forty when first elected to Congress. Just for good measure, Mahon threw in Thomas Jefferson, who was twenty-six years old when elected to the Virginia House of Burgesses.[96] At times his youth seemed to be in his favor. He had an abundance of energy and a quick memory. He could recall instantly the name and some interesting fact about a person when he met him—or her—a second time. Mahon had a friendly smile and a firm handshake to go along with his dark hair and tall stature. He genuinely liked people and never really met a stranger.

The rural nature of the Nineteenth Congressional District was a good match for Mahon. His game plan was to come to a community and search out places where he could meet people: a post office, barber shop, soda fountain, or café. He would introduce himself, shake hands, talk about local conditions and events, then hand people his card and ask for their vote. Not every town had a newspaper, but forty-two of them did, and he carried a list of each one, along with the name of the editor and publisher. He never missed stopping at a newspaper office to visit with the editor and ask for his or her support. Country editors wasted little time on publishing handouts that politicians provided, hoping they would be printed without charge. Mahon avoided that trap by attaching a check with whatever notice he wanted published, together with a personal note to the editor. A number of editors responded with brief comments about him, although not really official endorsements for his election.

Driving from town to town, Mahon often saw farmers working in their fields. He would stop and wait until the man plowed to the end of the row. He then would get out of his car and visit with him about crops, weather, and local conditions. He could do this as one who had dragged a tow sack down a cotton row and who had felt maize chafe on his neck. He would hand out a copy of his campaign literature, shake hands, ask for their vote, wave, and drive on.

In 1934 the candidates in the congressional race seldom mentioned the shortcomings, real or imagined, of their opponents. They tended to congregate on holidays like the Fourth of July and Labor Day. Six of the congressional candidates made their way to Plainview on July 4 to talk about their platforms. Several hundred people gathered late in the afternoon to listen to them for two hours. The *Plainview Evening Herald* reported that this proved that the interest in politics was strong and the speeches only showed that there were no real differences in the issues stressed by each candidate, but it made no comment about the cash drawing that had brought about two thousand ticket holders to the bandstand.[97]

"Trades days"[98] provided the candidates with great opportunities to proclaim their virtues through speeches to those who cared to listen. Some of the larger towns in the new district claimed crowds of five or six thousand who attended trades days. Mahon was especially good at mingling with the people, eating countless cookies and slices of apple pie as he made his way through the crowds and shaking hands all around. This kind of campaigning became the core of Mahon's campaign strategy for the next forty-four years. He always believed it was important to meet one-to-one with his constituents and let them make up their minds after talking with him.

As often as possible, the candidates for the Nineteenth Congressional District spoke at special occasions and at meetings of civic clubs and local political organizations, and at schools and churches. Mahon proved to be especially good at this. He spoke at commencement exercises at McMurry and Hardin-Simmons colleges in Abilene and at high-school graduations. He attended the Methodist church in Sweetwater regularly, and several times spoke before Sunday school classes. Mahon combed the district tirelessly. Judge

Mauzey virtually shut down his Thirty-second District Court for the summer, which gave Mahon the opportunity to travel the district three or four days a week. He made sure he covered the larger towns, especially Lubbock, Lamesa, and Plainview in the northern part of the district. His opponents could be expected to win a fair share of the votes there, and he needed the exposure. He did not neglect smaller communities, however. In fact, during the last ten days before the election, he made eighteen speeches, starting in the towns in the western part of the district.[99] Of the eighteen towns in which he spoke, only six had a population of more than a thousand residents, six were unincorporated, and three didn't even have a bank.

At the end of his first campaign for the Democratic primary, Mahon went home to Colorado City to await the results. The last month on the campaign trail had completely exhausted him. He had driven up and down countless dirt roads, speaking to audiences several times a day without a microphone, standing in the open or under whatever cover he could find from the relentless sun, and sleeping in sweatbox hotels. All he could do was hope that he had campaigned in such a way that people would vote for him, as his friend and mentor Judge Ely had advised.

The Democratic primary was held on Saturday, July 28, 1934. Mahon polled 19,524 votes to Mullican's 10,881 and Duggan's 9,781. With several counties slow in reporting their vote tallies, Mullican and Duggan waited for nearly a week before Mullican was declared to be the runner-up and, therefore, Mahon's opponent in the Democratic primary runoff. Mahon had won in sixteen counties while Mullican and Duggan had each won in three counties. Haile trailed behind with a victory in two counties. Pharr had carried one. After the primary results had been finalized, most of the candidates wrote brief statements for the district newspapers, thanking voters for their support. Mahon said that he was under everlasting obligation to the people of the congressional district for their votes and their wonderful consideration of his candidacy. Mullican said he approached the runoff with confidence and that with the help of his many friends he would win.

Two things stand out about these leaders. First, Mullican had been right when he said that there were no differences among the candidates on the issues. Second, the absence of complaints and bitterness showed the nature of the campaign and the political temper of the times. For Mahon and Mullican there was no underlying dissatisfaction with the outcome.

The campaign for the runoff lasted for another month, with the two men conducting it pretty much as they had the first time around. Once again, Mahon feared that his youth might be against him, and Charles Guy, editor of the *Lubbock Morning Avalanche*, tried to whip that horse one more time when he wrote, "We can send a boy to do a man's job—or we can send a man to fill the bill."[100]

Although he did not know it at the time, Mahon had really charmed one woman he met, Grace Guy, wife of the editor. According to Freda McVey, Guy's biographer, "Grace met the personable and handsome young Mahon in Guy's office one day on one of her rare visits to the newspaper. Later, as they drove home, Grace said, 'Charlie, I'm going to vote for him.' 'The hell you are,' Guy exploded. 'The paper is supporting his opponent, who's from Lubbock. Mahon is from Colorado City.' 'I think he's really honest,' Grace responded. Exasperated, Guy thundered, 'You vote for him, and I'll never again buy you a poll tax.'"[101] Grace knew it was time to be quiet and kept her secret for years. Finally, she confessed that she had voted for "that honest young man, George Mahon." By then Guy, who had become an avid supporter, roared with laughter and couldn't wait to tell Mahon.[102]

Both candidates toured the district, making as many speeches as possible, and their support organizations worked much as they had done earlier. Mahon's were stronger than Mullican's because of the friends he had already made on the campaign trail. Also, Mullican lagged behind because a support organization was not formed in Lubbock until the second round had begun.

Mahon's youth was a help rather than a hindrance as he traveled the remote areas of the district. He cultivated the image of being just like his constituents. He said he hadn't run for office for the people but with them. Once when Mullican said he was going to get down among the people to run, Mahon gleefully replied that he didn't have to do that because he was already there. He never mentioned his opponents by name and urged his workers not to. With his stress on benefits for all the people rather than special privileges for some, he created a populist image that proved to be a winner.[103]

During this first campaign Mahon tested many of the techniques and habits that stayed with him throughout his career. He developed a strong cadre of friends and supporters whom he never overlooked or forgot. He constantly worked at sharpening his memory for names, faces, and personal details. He began compiling a list of people he had met and put them in what he called his "little black book," a six-by-nine-inch loose-leaf notebook. He included the names of mayors, city officials, businessmen, and other people he had met and knew. When he went home to the district, the black book went with him to be consulted as he went from town to town. In Washington, as he wrote an increasing stream of letters, he was able to use a person's first name. He never let his enthusiasm for interacting with his constituents wane.

The month's campaigning did not really change the results. Mahon emerged with 35,054 votes and Mullican with 19,122. Mahon won all but three counties of the district (Lubbock, King, and Yoakum) and carried the larger counties except for Lubbock. His majority was especially strong in the southern counties. Mullican had gained only 4 percentage points over the first primary, and Mahon had carried both Lamb and Dickens counties, the home counties of Duggan and Haile.[104]

In 1932 the Texas Democratic Party had resolved at its state convention that all white citizens of the state who were qualified to vote under the constitution and laws of the state were eligible for membership in the state Democratic Party. In effect, this limited party membership to whites, and since the Democratic primary in 1934 was a party function to determine candidates for office, Negroes were excluded from voting. The Texas Court of Civil Appeals at San Antonio had upheld the action of the state convention when it was challenged in 1934.

Under state law candidates were required to report their campaign expenses. This report was to include all money spent by the candidate and others on his behalf. Mahon's files do not contain a copy of the final report; however, a list of checks written to cover expenses indicates that he wrote $1,793.30 in checks to cover expenses for the primary and runoff campaigns.[105] There is no record revealing the source of this money, although it is logical to assume that supporters contributed part of the money in addition to the time they volunteered to work on his behalf.

When the second primary had finished and the combatants had retired from the field, it was time to think about what had happened. Mahon told a reporter from the Lubbock *Avalanche-Journal* that he felt under an everlasting obligation to the people of the district for the votes given him on the previous Saturday and asked for their goodwill and support as he filled the great task before him. He declared that he was incapable of truly expressing his deep appreciation for their votes and confidence.[106] Mullican's statement was a little longer. He extended his sincerest congratulations and his warm personal friendship to the winner, the voice of democracy had spoken, and everybody should stand behind him as he moved on. One thing emerged: None of the candidates had known really what kind of a job he would be getting into. Along with the rest of the country, Texas was struggling with the misery of the Great Depression and with the most severe drought in its history. The new congressman-elect would have to begin defining his responsibilities within the main issues of the national campaign in addition to deciding how best to serve the people of the Nineteenth District.

After the dust had settled from the runoff election, a reporter asked Mahon to what did he attribute his victory. He said he didn't know; then, after thinking for a few minutes, he said, "I wasn't running for Congress. WE were running. I took the people into partnership."[107]

Chapter 2

The Plebe: 1935–1938

One-party politics operated virtually undisturbed in Texas from the turn of the century into the 1940s, with political life in the state being controlled by the Democratic Party. "On the surface, the party often gave the appearance of at least some internal competition among its rival leaders, and this competition appeared to give voters some voice in party affairs."[1] In fact, candidates seldom differed from each other on policy, but rather "based their campaigns on personality differences, on moral issues like Prohibition, or on symbolic appeals to religious, family, or agrarian values."[2] Voters in the Nineteenth District were mostly rural, belonged to Protestant denominations, were members of families that had several children, and stressed the importance of family life. George Mahon appealed to these voters because he possessed the characteristics they considered important.

He was frugal, hard-working, and honest. Winning the second Democratic primary in August assured his election to the Nineteenth Congressional seat in November because the Republican Party did not offer a candidate for the office in 1934. When their candidates ran for offices in the general election, 5 to 10 percent of the vote was all they could expect to garner. In fact, the Republican Party existed chiefly to dispense federal patronage when a Republican was president.

The primary campaign and the runoff campaign had been so strenuous that many years later Mahon could still remember how exhausted he felt. For several months he had traveled around the district making hundreds of speeches, and although he felt drained, the next three months demanded even more from him. Before leaving for Washington, he still had to wind up his affairs as district attorney, which included prosecuting cases already scheduled for trial. He finished the last of these just before the general election on November 6, 1934, and telegraphed his resignation to Governor Miriam Ferguson.

As time permitted, he and Helen continued to enjoy their usual social activities, which consisted of evenings playing bridge or forty-two[3] with friends, attending church and Sunday school, and visiting with their families in and around Loraine. Mahon had been a member of the Lions Club in Colorado City for several years, and he continued to attend its meetings. His election to Congress added to his prestige as a speaker, and he spoke to civic clubs when possible.

As he continued to wind up his affairs at home, he became increasingly preoccupied with thoughts of living in Washington, DC. Years later, in a short manuscript he wrote entitled "Early Days in Congress," he remembered that he had seen no more than three or four live congressmen by the time of his election, and now he would be working with more than four hundred of them in the House of Representatives. He approached his new job with awe.[4]

Mahon knew a fair amount about Texas state politics, but he was just beginning to learn the intricacies of national politics. For advice he turned to Marvin Jones in Amarillo, a veteran of Congress since 1916 and the representative of the entire area before the Nineteenth District was carved out from the Eighteenth District. When Mahon won the Democratic primary runoff, Congressman Jones wrote to offer congratulations and encouraged him to ask for any help that Jones might be able to provide. His letter crossed with one from Mahon asking whether he might talk with Jones in Amarillo. Jones replied that he would be glad to meet as soon as he returned from a trip.[5] This was the beginning of a long and cordial relationship between the two men.

Congressman Jones had been a member of the House Committee on Agriculture since 1921 and its chairman since 1930. In addition to being considered a key committee of the House of Representatives, it was an important one for rural West Texas, where most constituents earned their living farming and the remainder earned their living from services to the agricultural community. The committee was created in 1830 to ensure that agricultural interests had equal legislative power with manufacturing and commercial interests. New Deal agricultural programs were becoming as important as the weather for West Texas farmers.

One hallmark of American public life in the 1920s and 1930s was patronage politics, especially during the Great Depression years when jobs were very hard to find. Postmasters were appointed in Washington upon a recommendation from the House member of the district. In December 1934 Jones began to send Mahon his recommendations and to invite comments from him.

Jones would still have to propose the appointments to the postmaster general, but he allowed Mahon to take credit for several nominations that were made in this way. Mahon usually concurred with Jones's suggestions for nominees.[6] In this small way Mahon began to build his political base in the new district with people who owed their job to their congressman. In addition to becoming political supporters, postmasters were able to provide valuable grassroots information concerning local problems and local reactions to legislation. Jones became one of Mahon's mentors, although he was careful not to impose on him unnecessarily because of the many commitments that Jones had as chairman of the House Committee on Agriculture. The friendship these two men formed in the months before George left for Washington, DC, was very helpful to the new congressman.

On August 19, 1934, Henry Rainey, speaker of the House of Representatives died of a heart attack, requiring the election of a new speaker before the House could return to open session. After the upcoming general election in November, the majority party would caucus to choose the new speaker. The Democrats were heavily favored and in all probability would retain the speaker's chair. Ten candidates announced their interest in the open position and began canvassing friends for support. Among the Democratic candidates, Sam Rayburn was a leading contender. He had the most seniority in the Texas delegation, having been elected in 1912, and he was considered to be the dean of the delegation. Rayburn believed that nearly twenty-two years in the House qualified him for the post and that he was not being presumptuous in seeking the position of speaker of the House. At the end of September, he wrote Mahon asking for his support.[7]

Mahon feared that he was caught in a predicament even before being officially elected. There was a good chance that Marvin Jones would also run for speaker. As Mahon's neighbor and mentor, if he did decide to run he would ask for and expect Mahon's support. If Jones ran and lost, the winner would not regard Jones's supporters as friends. If Mahon backed Rayburn and Jones won, he would be at a disadvantage if he needed Jones's support for some later purpose. If he backed Jones and Rayburn won, he would have lost the opportunity to make a friend of the House speaker. However, House Majority Leader Joseph Byrns of Tennessee had the edge since the House traditionally elevated the holder of that position to the speakership. He had written Mahon early in August saying, "If you are elected and I earnestly hope you will be, and you feel that I merit this advancement by precedent, service rendered, and my past progressive record, I will deeply appreciate your support."[8] Mahon was flattered to be asked for help by one of the House leaders before he had even been formally elected.

A letter from Representative Hatton Sumners, chairman of the House Judiciary Committee, asking Mahon to support Sam Rayburn complicated the matter. Trying to avoid making enemies before he even got to Washington, Mahon wrote to Jones, enclosing a copy of the letter from Sumners. He wrote that because Jones was a neighbor and could certainly be considered a candidate for the speakership, Mahon did not want to agree to support Rayburn until he knew Jones's plans. However, if Jones was not interested Mahon asked to be told of this so he would know how to proceed. He was relieved when he received Jones's reply releasing him from his promise of support: "I have just announced that I am not a candidate. I want you to know of my deepest appreciation of your very generous attitude, and I am writing you so that you may feel free to take any course which to you may seem proper."[9] Mahon then wrote Rayburn, "It is a mere formality for me to say so but nevertheless I want to assure that I am for you in your race for Speakership one hundred percent."[10] By return mail Rayburn expressed his thanks.[11] Learning to move cautiously and keep one's eyes wide open while searching for a solution was important in politics, where friendships could make or break a career. This was a skill that Mahon would hone for many years to come.

Rayburn lost the race for the speaker of the House, but Mahon won a friend. The battle over the speakership became quite bitter, and many newly elected Democrats backed Byrns. Mahon's loyalty to his fellow Texan could possibly have cost him later, but with the unexpected death of Byrns in 1936, Rayburn's power grew. George Mahon had made a good decision.

Mahon looked forward to being a part of the Texas delegation, and after the late August runoff election congratulatory letters began to pour in. Hatton Sumners, an important member of the Texas delegation, sent congratulations on his election. Across the bottom of the letter he wrote in longhand, "Any time any way I can be useful command me."[12]

Tom Blanton, an eighteen-year veteran congressman from Abilene, also wrote to offer his congratulations and advice. Blanton was one of the most contentious members of the Texas delegation. On one occasion he had nearly come to blows with Rayburn on the House floor. Now he confined himself to offering advice to a newcomer. He urged Mahon to appoint a newspaperman as his chief clerk, who would look out for the newspaper publicity in his district. He cautioned him to avoid anybody from Lubbock because the town was a pivotal part of his district, and this would mean that, sooner or later, his appointee would want his job and give him trouble, just as so many secretaries had done to congressmen who had befriended them.[13] During the 1930s only men were considered qualified to be secretaries to congressmen, and some did run for the office after they had learned the ropes. The advice came too late as Mahon had already appointed Lloyd Croslin, his advance man during the campaign, to be his secretary. Mahon was impressed with Croslin's organizational skills, and there is no evidence that he considered anyone else.

However, Blanton offered other advice that proved to be worth having. He said he would send a copy of the rules manual of the House of Representatives, which was as important as a hammer and saw to a carpenter. Without this, Blanton wrote, and without an intimate knowledge of the rules and precedents, a member was absolutely helpless. "You will be surprised when I tell you that there are not over fifteen members of the House who really know the rules and precedents. I know of members who have been in Congress twenty years and who don't know how or when to file a motion to re-commit, and who, without help, are absolutely unable to get the floor when they want it."[14] There is no evidence of how Mahon responded to the letter, but he did take the advice seriously and learned everything he could about how the House of Representatives operated.

Long before he left Colorado City for Washington, Mahon discovered that fellow Democrats had learned of his election and were offering their help and friendship. In addition, Sam Rayburn wrote on August 27 to congratulate him on his "smashing victory last Saturday" and to offer his assistance in any way he could before Congress convened. John J. O'Connor, who aspired to party leadership, wrote from New York's Sixteenth District to congratulate him and offer his services. A. J. Sabath wrote from Chicago, as the longest-serving member of the House, to send congratulations and an offer of assistance at any time. After the election Jim Farley, national Democratic campaign chairman, thanked Mahon for his share of the party's great national victory.[15]

Initially, Mahon was flattered to receive these letters, but he later learned how superficial they were when, early in his career, he failed to get consideration on a matter and went to see Marvin Jones about it. "Your colleagues will pat you on the back, but they will be looking after themselves and their constituents, and they will rarely find time to pave the way for you. The only way to make progress in Congress is to stand on your own two feet and make your own way," Jones told him.[16]

During the months before going to Washington, Mahon traveled through the new district, talking with friends he had met during the campaign and making new ones as he went along. This was the beginning of a forty-four-year routine. Throughout his political career George Mahon was energized by traveling through the district and interacting with constituents on a one-to-one basis.

On Saturday morning, December 15, 1934, Mahon, Helen, and seven-year-old Daphne boarded a Texas and Pacific train at the railroad stop just a few blocks down the street from their home in Colorado City. After transferring in Dallas, they reached Washington, DC, on Tuesday, December 18.

For their first night they stayed at the New Willard Hotel on Pennsylvania Avenue, about a block from the White House. The next day they looked for an apartment and found a small one with housekeeping facilities in the Roosevelt Hotel on Sixteenth Street. About thirty congressmen, along with two senators, also lived there while in Washington, as this was much less expensive than living in a house. Among them were Ewing Thomason and his wife, Abbie, who lived just across the hall from Mahon and Helen. Thomason was the representative from the Sixteenth Congressional District, headquartered in El Paso. Prior to the redistricting, Colorado City was in Thomason's district, so he and Mahon already knew each other.

The day after arriving in Washington, Thomason took Mahon to Vice President Garner's office, where the vice president greeted Mahon with "Come in, plebe." He offered the two a prelunch nip of bourbon, which they declined. Garner told Mahon that, as a young man, he ought to go places in Congress. Mahon noted in his journal that he thought the vice president was a pretty smooth man with lots of energy and practical sense. After a short visit with Garner, they joined Texas senators Morris Sheppard and Tom Connally for lunch in the Senate dining room, and in the following days Mahon met other members of the Texas delegation.[17]

Soon after his arrival in Washington, Mahon bought a journal and began filling it with an account of his new experiences, just as he had done when he moved to Nashville. It appears that initially he intended to write daily, but demands on his time caused daily entries to become weekly entries until, finally, entries were made only randomly, often months apart. This journal, which he simply called his Green Journal because of the color of the cover, was similar to a diary: understanding the full meaning of many entries depends on a prior knowledge of the story, and only the writer has such knowledge. In that respect he intended himself to be the only reader; however, at other times he included so much detail that he possibly anticipated other readers at some future date. The first entry was made on December 28, 1934, and contained what he remembered from his arrival in Washington ten days earlier. He wrote that Texas senator Morris Sheppard had told him that he was fearful of the future. When Mahon questioned him about this fear, Sheppard would only say that he was anchored to the president. In parenthesis Mahon wrote, "I think he is a good man but not a great man."[18] It is not clear whether he was referring to Senator Sheppard or the president.

Office space would not be available until Congress convened in January, but Marvin Jones loaned Mahon a small amount of space that had been allocated to his Committee on Agriculture. It was located in the Old House Office Building, currently the Cannon House Office Building, and for the first time, on December 28, 1934, Mahon went to the office, where he soon began to receive welcoming visits from members of the Texas delegation. Fritz Lanham of Fort Worth, a veteran of fourteen years in Congress, who became one of his good friends, came by to welcome him to Washington, DC. According to a journal entry, Lanham seemed to Mahon to be anxious to give advice that might be useful, so he listened to the older congressman's tips. First, Lanham advised, never reveal your thoughts about a piece of legislation in advance of discussion on the floor. He said he had often changed his mind on a bill after he heard it discussed thoroughly.[19] Another sound piece of advice that Lanham gave was not to speak very much on the floor of the House. He said that he had known many good men who hurt themselves by speaking too much. He offered three guidelines: Speak only if the bill particularly affects your district, if you are a member of the committee sponsoring the bill, or if you have special knowledge about the bill. Lanham also had advice on how to campaign: Do it in off years, and then try to speak on noncontroversial matters; mail should be answered promptly; and it is wise to do little things for constituents and other congressmen whenever possible.

The day turned out to be an interesting one for Mahon. He had lunch with newspapermen, had his picture taken for newspapers in front of the Old House Office Building with the Capitol in the background, and in the afternoon paid forty-five dollars for the first tuxedo he had ever owned.[20] Mahon, the "plebe," was beginning to get his feet on the ground and to find his way around. One piece of Lanham advice he had no trouble following was calling him by his first name; it was quite the thing to address a colleague by his first name, Mahon learned.

The Mahons' first social engagement in Washington came on the evening of December 26, 1934. Congressman Martin Dies from Orange, Texas, who later became chairman of the House Un-American Activities Committee, hosted a dinner for Texas Congressmen Luther Johnson, R. E. Thomason, George Mahon, and their wives. Three newspapermen were also included. Mahon noted in his journal that after dinner they went to the Gayety Theatre, "which is a rather wild downtown show."[21] No doubt the show did seem wild to the Mahons, who were accustomed to church activities and bridge games for entertainment. According to an advertisement in the *Washington Post*, the burlesque show at the Gayety Theatre featured Hinda Wausau, a buxom blonde, in a very low-cut gown, who had come directly from the Casino de Paree in New York. Mahon and Helen were rapidly learning that there was much more variety in the nightlife of the nation's capital than in Colorado City, Texas.

When the Mahons went to Washington, they left a small-town life with small groups of friends. They entered a world of sophisticated social events where guests might be diplomats, high-ranking military men, or prominent members of the administration and where liquor flowed freely. The Mahons attended many social functions; however, they never became "socially minded." Being on the list of society's hostesses was not one of Helen Mahon's goals. Neither of them had been reared in homes where alcohol was served, and they now showed little interest in that kind of socializing. They did acquire a number of close friends with whom they played bridge or whom they entertained at home with Helen's cooking.

As with any club or association, the members of Congress were judged and evaluated by their colleagues. One soon learned what to do and what not to do. Mahon was determined to find his place by observing the written rules and those not written—or even spoken. He intended to advance as far as he could.

The Depression had pushed cotton to five cents a pound and destroyed the likelihood of promising employment for many college graduates in Texas. The ten-thousand-dollar annual salary that Mahon was to earn in Congress was far greater than the income earned by West Texas farmers and greater than his earnings as county attorney, which had often amounted to slips of paper from the state, promising to pay at a later date.[22]

During their first days in Washington, the Mahon family marveled at the broad boulevards and majestic classical architecture. It seemed like the most beautiful city in the world. Wanting to see as much as possible, they took many little tours around town. They saw every part of the capital and were especially impressed by the Bureau of Printing and Engraving and the $7 billion they saw in the vault. They were even allowed to hold $1.2 billion in hundred-thousand-dollar bills in their hands. From the Capitol they could look down across the lawn to the grand statue of General Grant, and then on along the mall past the Washington Monument to the Lincoln Memorial and the White House beyond that. On the mall, by contrast, stood the row of wooden buildings left over from World War I that were then used as government offices.

The House of Representatives convened the Second Session of the Seventy-fourth Congress at noon on Friday, January 4, 1935. The previous day the session had opened with the swearing-in of members of Congress, and on this day excitement ran high as President Roosevelt arrived in the House chamber to deliver his State of the Union address. Mrs. Franklin Roosevelt; Mrs. James Roosevelt, the president's mother; Mrs. Anna Roosevelt Dall, the president's daughter; her two children; and other family members were among the guests in the Executive Gallery. Again, Helen had a seat in the gallery, and Mahon held Daphne on his lap for the address. Senators, cabinet members, and the Supreme Court justices were already seated when the president entered on the arm of his son James at 12:24 p.m. A lone incident marred the excitement of the president's arrival at the Capitol, when police seized a man who rushed out of the crowd yelling, "We want our bonus."[23] Veterans were pushing for immediate payment of the adjusted compensation certificates issued in 1924 but not scheduled to mature until 1945. President Roosevelt opposed early payment because the federal treasury could not afford the expense; however, many congressmen disagreed with him, and the veterans' bonus became a controversial issue in 1935.

Roosevelt was given a wild ovation as he entered the House Chamber. From the dais below the speaker's chair, he announced that change was the order of the day throughout the world. A new order was rising from the disintegration of the old. This new order, in the United States, was in the spirit and intent of the Constitution. Throughout the speech he stressed that the time had come to replace recovery with reform—not just cure the symptoms but remove the cause. Roosevelt wanted the federal government to provide three types of security: (1) security of a livelihood through better use of the land (2) security against the major hazards and vicissitudes of life and (3) security of decent homes.

To address the security of livelihood, he announced that he was ready to submit to Congress a plan that would replace federal relief with public-works jobs for 3.5 million people. He made a distinction between those who were employable but not able to find jobs and those who were unemployable because of age, illness, or handicap. Work for the employable would not compete with private industry but would consist of the type of jobs that private industry could never undertake, such as clearing slums, improving rural housing and existing roads, rural electrification, reforesting of the watersheds of the nation, preventing soil erosion and reclaiming blighted areas, and constructing a national highway system to handle modern traffic.[24]

Roosevelt did not specify a price tag, but in the budget he later sent to Congress, it was revealed that $4 billion, in addition to the $880,000 allocated from previous appropriations, would be needed to fund the work-relief bill. President Roosevelt called the Emergency Relief Appropriation Bill the "Big Bill." He did so with good reason; it authorized more spending than the sum of all federal revenues in 1934. In the Senate, Huey Long from Louisiana raged, "This isn't a relief bill, it's a boodle bill."[25] When it passed in April, Mahon wrote in his journal, "We have now enacted into law the $4,880,000,000 work relief bill. Could it be true that a great peace time expenditure like this might be a noble and worth[while] thing? After all we are not spending the money of the poor and hungry, because this class has no money to spend. Therefore, when the government spends this huge sum perhaps those who have the money will contribute to the welfare of the poor and needy."[26]

The Emergency Relief Appropriation Act became law on April 8, 1935. It funded a number of "alphabet agencies" such as the PWA (Public Works Administration), WPA (Works Project Administration), REA (Rural Electrification Administration), and CCC (Civilian Conservation Corps). According to historian Conrad Black, "These New Deal relief programs were invaluable. They salvaged the lives of tens of millions from utter misery and hopelessness, endowed the country with a vast infrastructure, and vitalized much of the environment at bargain cost."[27] These programs did, indeed, prove to be helpful to the Nineteenth Congressional District. According to a press release in 1938, Mahon announced that his district had received more PWA grants than any other congressional district in the United States.[28]

Mahon's first official act as a US congressman came on January 7, 1935, when he requested that the library at Texas Technological College in Lubbock (renamed Texas Tech University in 1969) be designated a federal documents depository. This meant that Texas Tech would receive copies of publications from most federal agencies, including the publications of many agencies created before the college library attained depository status. Included in the depository would be records of earlier census returns, a complete set of the *Congressional Record*, the first journals of Congress, and others. These documents are important to support the research required in graduate-degree programs. President Bradford Knapp and librarian Elizabeth Howard West had earlier requested that Mahon do this. Mahon checked with Elmer A. Lewis in the House documents section to confirm that, as a congressman, he had the authority to assign depository status to a university library in his district and learned that he was correct. Thus began the first of many actions that Mahon would take on behalf of Texas Tech University. He wanted it to become one of the nation's outstanding schools.[29]

On January 31, 1935, as a new Democratic member of the House, Mahon and Helen attended a reception at the White House. This was an annual event to which members of Congress and their spouses were invited. Mahon was impressed with the president's pleasing and impressive personality and remembered that FDR appeared to be in excellent health.[30]

As the Mahon family took up life in the nation's capital, they had no idea how busy their days would become. Although they were not especially interested in Washington's social whirl, they did attend a number of social events that required the attendance of congressmen, and they also began to receive an unending stream of visitors from home. There was a belief that one couldn't attend to official duties and also spend time on the affairs of one's constituents. George Mahon proved just how mistaken this belief was. He and Helen not only liked people, they really enjoyed having them visit. Years later Mahon recalled that he always thought of himself as the hired hand and friend of the voters of the Nineteenth Congressional District. He described serving the needs of his constituents as thrilling.[31] During his years in Congress, Mahon could almost always find time to spend with people from the district who were in the city. Even in later years, when he chaired the Appropriations Committee and its Subcommittee on Defense Appropriations, he could usually find time to see visitors and would never allow his office staff, on their own authority, to turn people away. In handling the affairs of their constituents, the Mahons worked as a team. Helen was a gracious hostess for visitors. She came to the office at least two days a week and, without pay, helped with office work or showed visitors around the Capitol and other parts of the city.

Although conditions had improved since 1933, the country had yet to fully recover. In fact, the original momentum of the New Deal was showing signs of waning, and the Depression was far from over. According to historian Alan Brinkley, "National income remained more than forty percent lower than six years earlier. Farm prices continued to languish far beneath their 1929 levels, which at that time had been uncomfortably low. Ten million people, twenty percent of the workforce, remained unemployed."[32] New Deal programs seemed to be faltering, and by 1934 opposition from both the right and the left was building. During that summer, conservatives organized the American Liberty League, claiming that New Deal programs were moving the nation toward socialism. According to historians Joseph Siracusa and David Coleman, "The true explanation of conservative discontent, of course, went deeper than this. The Depression had toppled the high priests of finance and industry from their exalted position, and stunned by their loss of prestige, embittered businessmen sought a scapegoat and vented their spleen on the essentially conservative Roosevelt."[33] Opposition also came from the left, escalating into a number of popular protest movements that many feared might alter the face of American politics.[34] The loudest voices among the protesters belonged to Louisiana senator Huey P. Long, known as the "Kingfish,"[35] and to Father Charles E. Coughlin, a Catholic priest from Detroit. They were not friends or allies, but their constituencies often overlapped, and their movements represented part of the same kind of political discontent.[36]

There were also other dissident movements. One that caused great concern for Mahon, as well as for President Roosevelt, was led by Frances E. Townsend, a sixty-year-old unemployed physician in California. He proposed a plan that would pay all citizens over sixty years of age two hundred dollars a month, provided they agreed to forgo all gainful employment and spend all of the money in the United States within thirty days of receipt. In addition to caring for the elderly, Townsend believed his plan would end the Depression when these monthly checks stimulated the economy and created new jobs. Many constituents in the Nineteenth District favored the Townsend Plan. In fact, people in the district were mustering support for a candidate in the upcoming 1936 election who pledged to vote for the Townsend Plan if elected to Congress.

Townsend proposed to pay for his plan with a 2 percent transaction tax that would be levied each time a product changed hands along its journey from raw material to final sale. He believed a tax of this nature was more equitable than a retail sales tax, because a sales tax falls heaviest on those least able to pay it.[37]

In January Representative John S. McGroarty introduced a bill in the House to make the Old Age Revolving Pension, commonly known as the Townsend Plan, a national program. A Democrat from California, McGroarty owed his 1934 election to support from Townsend clubs.

Mahon opposed the bill in spite of numerous petitions from the district, most containing more than one hundred signatures, in favor of the Townsend Plan. He always opposed it because it would require approximately $24 million per year of federal money to support it. In his Green Journal he wrote, "One of the major things wrong with this country is that too many people are wanting something for nothing. . . . The Townsend Old Age Pension Plan of $200 per month for each person over 60 is a sample of the popularity of such an idea."[38] However, Mahon did recognize the need for some type of old-age assistance and preferred the president's Social Security plan. Among the many letters he received urging him to vote for an old-age pension bill, the following one indicates how desperately some kind of old-age assistance was needed in the Nineteenth District as well as in other parts of the nation.

February the 28 1935

> Dear sir en regrd to the old age pintion we was advised to rite you our condition just us 2 we Bouth us worked hard all our lives my husband are 70 past I am 62 past and we haven't got any way making a living we Bouth are in Bad helth we Bouth try to live a Christian life we are mostly on well fair we owen our little home we use our oil stove and oil lamp we can Buy even medicine or clothes and if we could just get aBout 30 dollars a month we would Be OK We can't make 10 dollars a month Regular so We haven't eny in come at all We done all We could to help you all out and We Would feel afful thankful if you all Will help us en our old Worn out lives yours truly."[39]

In response Mahon thanked the writer, saying,[40] "I assure you that I am heartily in favor of a solution of this problem during this Session of Congress."

Designed to benefit approximately 30 million people, the Social Security bill was signed into law on August 14, 1935. This bill was intended to provide a broad program of unemployment insurance and old-age pensions. Launched by an appropriation of $95 million and beginning in 1949, it was to be supported by a 6 percent payroll tax to be paid by employers and a 3 percent salary tax.

This act had a long history. Early in 1933 a bill was introduced to provide federal unemployment insurance; however, because committee agreement on the bill had not been reached by 1934, President Roosevelt appointed a Cabinet Committee on Economic Security headed by Secretary of Labor Frances Perkins, the first woman cabinet member. Secretary of Agriculture Henry Wallace; Secretary of the Treasury Henry Morgenthau, Jr.; Attorney General Homer Cummings; and presidential aide Harry Hopkins were also on the committee, which was really "an advisory body of technical experts who would hammer out the precise terms of social security legislation."[41] According to Secretary Perkins, it was expected that the committee's recommendations were to be based on a practical knowledge of the needs of the country, the prejudices of the people, and the nation's legislative habits.[42] They were expected to remember that this was the United States in 1934–1935, not another nation at some other time.

Even before his inauguration, Roosevelt realized the necessity of unemployment and old-age insurance. The growing strength of those advocating the Townsend Plan was worrisome. In some districts it became the chief political issue, and its supporters were being elected to Congress.[43] There were fears that public pressure for the adoption of this plan, or something similar to Huey Long's Share-Our-Wealth proposal, would become irresistible. Those fears caused many congressmen to look favorably on the administration's plan for Social Security. The Depression had left millions destitute and exposed the fact that traditional methods of meeting large-scale needs through state, local, and private charity were inadequate in a modern industrial society. A genuine need for some sort of economic-security program became obvious with the widespread popularity of proposals such as the Townsend Plan, which sent a strong message that the public was willing to accept action by the federal government.

The bill that was enacted into law contained programs designed to provide unemployment insurance, old-age pensions, aid to dependent children, relief for the indigent elderly, and aid to the blind. In order to secure sufficient backing from both Republican and Democratic congressmen, the Roosevelt administration conducted an eighteen-month public-relations campaign to educate the public. On August 17, 1935, Congress voted overwhelmingly in favor of the Social Security Act. Also in August 1935 a large majority of Texans in a statewide referendum voted in favor of old-age assistance. The vote was necessary for the state to be able to provide matching funds for the fifteen dollars of federal funds allotted per eligible person.

The pension system was based on insurance principles. It consisted of a payroll tax levied on both employees and employers in industrial and white-collar jobs that began at 1 percent for each for the first three thousand dollars of annual earnings. The money was put into a trust fund earmarked for the payment of pensions to employees who contributed. The amount of the pension was to vary according to the amount of an individual's earnings prior to retirement, thus the benefits were a matter of right and not dependent on need.

Based on actuarial principles, the first monthly benefits from this program could not be paid until 1942, and this fact emphasized the need for old-age assistance for the elderly who could not wait until 1942, or who were not eligible. The old-age assistance program authorized matching grants to states that adopted a program to assist the indigent aged. The federal government would reimburse the state for half of any amount up to thirty dollars per month paid to an indigent person sixty-five years of age or older. Money was dispensed based on need, not as a right. This program was intended to be a backup system to provide for the elderly until the old-age insurance program matured. After that, it would remain to help only those needy persons who were not eligible for the insurance program.

The third and fourth programs were also based on charity. One program provided money to blind adults who needed assistance, while the Aid to Dependent Children program operated through federal grants to help states support needy children deprived of normal parental support when a parent died, was incapacitated, or was absent from the home. Under this program, reimbursement amounted to approximately one-third of the money spent on each child.

Like all freshmen congressmen, Mahon hoped to be assigned to key committees, especially those that dealt with bills having an impact on national policy. He was particularly interested in agriculture, for that was where he could best represent the interests of his constituents, but he knew that getting a seat on that committee was unlikely. West Texas already had Marvin Jones at the helm as chairman of the House Committee on Agriculture. Before Congress had even convened, George visited with Hatton Sumners, chair of the House Judiciary Committee, who encouraged him to write the House Ways and Means Committee, asking for a seat. Since the reorganization of Congress in 1911, each party in the House of Representatives had a Committee-on-Committees to distribute committee assignments. In the Democratic party, this committee consisted of the members of the House Ways and Means Committee, the speaker, and the majority floor leader (or the minority floor leader when the party was in the minority). Such a method was designed to eliminate arbitrary choices by the speaker, who, in the past, had used committee assignments as rewards or punishments to control legislators.[44]

Mahon soon learned that he would have to channel his request through Sam Rayburn, the dean of the Texas delegation. He also learned that there was no possibility that he would receive a seat on the House Judiciary Committee or any other key committee. Like other freshmen, he would have to wait until the more senior members had been assigned, despite the fact that there were open seats on some of the most powerful committees in Congress. Six seats were open on the House Ways and Means Committee and five on the House Appropriations Committee; however, an assignment to a key committee would come only after several years, when he had acquired some seniority. For the time being, his service would be closely scrutinized by party leaders to see how he fulfilled his responsibilities and how well he worked with other committee members. The tradition of seniority in Congress permitted members with the longest continuous service to be assigned a seat on the most prestigious committees, and seniority on a committee determined who would become the chair. Mahon was assigned to two standing committees, the Committee on the Census and the Committee on Civil Service. He was also assigned to the Committee on Insular Affairs, not a standing committee. Only the standing committees met with regularity; others met at the call of the chair, and that did not happen often.

The Census Committee was one of the oldest standing committees of the House, but members did not consider it to be very prestigious, despite the fact that the appointment of representatives based on population had a far-reaching effect on the state of the nation. The Civil Service Committee investigated and reported all bills pertaining to the civil service of the federal government and considered legislation pertaining to the retirement system for federal employees. The work of this committee was becoming more important at this time because of the growing number of federal employees during the New Deal. Also, throughout the country there was a movement in favor of a merit system for selecting federal employees instead of the spoils system of political appointments.

It was, however, a seat on the Insular Affairs Committee that proved to be a lucky break for Mahon, who was determined to meet as many other congressmen as possible and to learn the ropes quickly. The Committee on Insular Affairs, established in 1899, wrote legislation concerning civil governments for each of the island possessions of the United States. The committee also reported legislation concerning the clarification of the citizenship status of inhabitants of the islands; ratification and confirmation of actions of the Philippine and Puerto Rican legislatures; and matters relating to public works, harbor improvements, wharves, roads, railways, telephone and telegraph cables, electricity, trade and tariff laws, prohibition, education, taxes, bond issues, and relief from hurricanes and the Depression. Additionally, it issued reports on the social, economic, and political conditions in the island possessions. In 1946, when the Philippines gained independence, the committee was abolished, and its reduced legislative responsibilities were transferred to the House Committee on Public Lands.[45]

At the end of March, Mahon wrote in his Green Journal that during the previous week he had attended some very interesting meetings of the Committee on Insular Affairs.[46] No doubt one of the more interesting items discussed during committee meetings was an invitation to attend the inauguration of the new government of the Philippine Islands in November, with the new government paying all expenses for committee members who could attend.

Also, in March 1935 he attended a banquet honoring Frank Murphy, former governor of Michigan, who had been appointed governor general of the Philippines. He wrote to his father and Aunt Laura that "it was quite an affair for a country boy."[47] The Insular Affairs Committees of both the House and Senate had been invited, and Mahon sat with three other congressmen and three senators. He did not name the congressmen, but the senators at his table included Ernest V. Gibson (R-VT), Peter G. Gerry (D-RI), and William Gibbs McAdoo (D-CA). McAdoo monopolized the conservation and was most interesting, although Mahon wrote that he didn't admire him personally. He also wrote that he didn't know that people could serve with such elegance, reporting that "many distinguished senators, the Attorney General of the

United States, and other men of note were present."⁴⁸ One of the things that impressed him most was that they began eating at 8:30 p.m. and concluded the meal at 11:00 p.m. He also wrote that he was proud of his membership on the House Insular Affairs Committee.⁴⁹

The Texas delegation in the House, made up of all the representatives from the state, consisted of twenty-one men in 1935. The group met every two weeks to discuss bills before Congress that were of particular interest to Texans. Congressmen from other states followed a similar pattern. Texans in the House of Representatives met at the beginning of each new term to select a chairman of the delegation, a vice chairman, and a secretary-treasurer. At the January 1935 meeting, Mahon was chosen secretary-treasurer and Fritz Lanham of Fort Worth was elected chairman.⁵⁰ Members were allowed to bring guests to the biweekly meetings, and in March when Mahon's longtime friend and mentor from Abilene, Judge W. R. Ely, was in town, he attended as Mahon's guest.

Mahon made his maiden speech in the House on March 13, 1935. He urged the immediate passage of a bill that would make emergency crop loans available to farmers. Several weeks earlier a bill providing $60 million to cover emergency loans for 1935 crop production had passed the House and the Senate, but the passage of an appropriation bill was needed to provide the money for these loans. Mahon stressed the importance of making the money available immediately because planting time was imminent. The deficiency appropriation bill that was under consideration in the House at that time contained the crop loan item, and with very little opposition it was speedily passed and sent to the Senate for consideration.⁵¹

On April 1 Mahon introduced his first bill (H.R. 7171) to amend Section 108 of the Judicial Code to create a new federal judicial district for the state of Texas. The new district would be made up of counties that had been in the Amarillo, Lubbock, San Angelo, and Abilene divisions of the Northern District of Texas. Mahon argued that it was unfair for the people of West Texas to be compelled to travel three hundred miles or more to appear before a federal judge, as was the case at that time. Two of the judges in the Northern District lived in Dallas, and one lived in Fort Worth. Mahon believed that a new district was justified on the basis of the service it would render to the growing population of West Texas. Additionally, according to the 1934 Annual Report of the Attorney General of the United States, the Northern District was six to twelve weeks behind in hearing cases. He testified before a subcommittee of the House Judiciary Committee that the population in West Texas had increased 92 percent since the creation of the district and that 43 percent of the population of the Northern District lived in the San Angelo, Abilene, Lubbock, and Amarillo divisions. Representative Hatton Sumners, chairman of the Judiciary Committee, was from Dallas, and he was not in favor of the bill; thus, it did not get out of the committee. The previous year, Congressman Marvin Jones had introduced a similar bill to create the Northwestern District of Texas, and it also did not get favorable consideration from the House Judiciary Committee. Perhaps this was one of the reasons he had cautioned Mahon about members making friendly overtures of help but not really working for each other.

Mahon then introduced a bill (H.R. 8311) that would amend the Judicial Code to establish a new division within the Northern District. That bill did not get out of the Judiciary Committee. Two of the judges in the Northern District were serving in an emergency rather than permanent capacity, and a bill did pass the House and Senate to make these positions permanent. When Mahon learned that one of the three judges planned to retire in December 1935, he wrote to President Roosevelt asking him to appoint a judge who resided in the western portion of the district. Once again he made the argument that traveling more than three hundred miles to appear before a federal judge worked a hardship on more than a million people who lived west of Fort Worth.[52] His pleas were in vain. When one of the temporary district judges retired, the spoils system prevailed, and Roosevelt appointed a man who had done several political favors for him. The new judge lived in Dallas. West Texans were very disappointed, but Mahon had to let the matter rest. He could not afford to get into a quarrel over this. The appointment of federal judges was presidential and senatorial patronage, which was beyond his prerogative. He had put forth his best effort, but West Texas would have to wait.

An interesting aspect to Mahon's first legislative effort is the correspondence to and from Judge Clark Mullican, now district judge in Lubbock. In one letter Mullican thanked Mahon for a copy of H.R. 6021, a bill relating to home mortgage relief. Then he wrote, "From time-to-time these new and strange laws leading forward to desired betterment of conditions must have the rough edges knocked off. Study them deeply, with the future welfare of the country and of humanity in mind, vote your convictions and damn the consequences. . . . I long ago realized the court bill was doomed. Western Texas cannot yet hope to cross swords with the other more powerful sections of the

State, but our day will come. The form letter you sent me relating to the new court should satisfy our people that you did all that could be done under the circumstances."[53] Just a year before Mullican and Mahon had been opponents for the congressional seat, and now the two were working together on the court bill. Their mutual respect for each other was obvious in their correspondence. During the campaign each man spoke only of his own ability and desire to serve the people of the district. There was no mudslinging, so when the campaign was over, the path was clear for these two strong men to work cooperatively for the good of West Texas.

In April 1935 Mahon also met with Secretary of the Interior Harold Ickes to request one hundred thousand dollars of Public Works Administration money to survey the underground water resources of West Texas. The money would permit the completion of work started by the Geological Survey, which had provided a preliminary report in 1934, raising questions about the presence of sufficient underground water for extensive irrigation in the area. A newspaper in the Nineteenth District, the *Sudan Beacon*, reported, "Mahon also conferred with Dr. Mead[54] of the Bureau of Reclamation in an effort to assure funds for making irrigation loans to individual farmers. Mr. Mahon has already secured an interpretation from Federal Housing Administration officials which would allow that agency to insure loans made by local banks for this purpose. Dr. Mead is of the opinion that direct loans may be made possible through an allocation of funds from the Public Works appropriation. However, nothing definite may be determined at this time because the President has not announced his plans for administering the new appropriation."[55]

Mahon offered an amendment in the House appropriations bill for the Interior Department for fifty thousand dollars to conduct a survey of West Texas underground water resources, but the amendment was defeated by six votes. He had hoped to lobby Senators Tom Connally and Morris Sheppard in an attempt to get the amendment approved in the Senate, but that did not happen.[56]

Mahon remembered that, during his campaign for office, "he was repeatedly exposed to the concept that a vast river from the Rocky Mountains underlay the entire Texas High Plains, and the area's groundwater supply was inexhaustible."[57] He decided that the idea of an inexhaustible water supply probably came from the early pioneers who could find water wherever they drilled. The water they pumped was for household use, livestock, small vegetable gardens, and a few trees. This amount was very small compared to the large-capacity irrigation wells that were being dug to water crops. Shortly after being sworn in, Mahon sought the counsel of hydrologists from the US Geological Survey. He hoped to prove, or dispel, the theory of unlimited water from underground streams. "These studies, completed in the late 1930s and the early 1940s consisted only of inventories of wells and springs—they did not contain an analysis of these data, and therefore, did not summarize the magnitude of the area's groundwater supplies. For this reason these studies, to be dubbed the WPA reports because they were funded by the Federal Public Works Administration, were not widely used or appreciated by the general public."[58] Although the reports lacked analysis, time proved that the WPA studies were essential to scientists in the 1970s, who relied on them to determine the effect of large-scale irrigation on the groundwater reservoir.

Besides working for his district, Mahon remained active in national matters and was an FDR loyalist in the clash between the Roosevelt administration and Wall Street over regulating public-utility holding companies. In a letter to Helen's father, Judge O. E. Stevenson, Mahon wrote, "I stayed with the President on this and in view of the recent developments, you can well imagine I have no cause for regret. I do not think the Members of Congress are corrupt but in view of some of the things that have been done and said, I am glad that I cannot be in any way linked to those who opposed the President on this issue."[59] He was referring to the Public Utility Holding Companies Act. A Federal Trade Commission study revealed that in a holding company several companies were pyramided on top of each other primarily for the purpose of allowing the top company to milk the assets from those on the bottom and force rate increases on consumers. Sam Rayburn introduced the bill opposing this practice in the House and led the floor fight. However, he could not protect what was known as the "death sentence" provision in the bill. That would have given the federal government the "power to compel the dissolution of every holding company which could not establish an economic reason for its existence—whose continuation, in other words, was not necessary to the operation of a geographically and economically integrated system."[60] This proved to be one of the bitterest contests in Rayburn's legislative career because of the enormous influence of lobbyists. The defeat of the death sentence caused near chaos in the House and marked FDR's first major defeat in that chamber.[61] In all, twenty-nine Democrats abandoned the administration on the death sentence amendment, and having done it once made it easier for them to do so again.[62] Considering Rayburn's difficult struggle to get this bill through the House, voting against any part of it would have been political suicide for a newly elected Democratic congressman.

In July Mahon also received a letter from his brother Durward, who was practicing law with a firm in Dallas, Texas. Durward wrote, "Though I am not in favor of too much Government ownership and control, I do believe that the good derived from utility holding companies does not in any manner equal the harm caused by their existence. . . . My point is that the harm created by this strong and powerful association of utilities will eventually make itself more felt, and it does not look as though the Government should allow private organizations to become more powerful than the Government itself."[63]

On August 11, 1935, near the end of his first session of Congress, Mahon wrote in his journal,

> It has been almost eight months since I left Colorado, Texas for Washington. I doubt that I have greatly improved during these eight months in mind, body, experience, or spirit. The trouble is, I have been utterly absorbed in doing small detailed things. I guess this is true of every new Congressman. Congressman South of Texas remarked yesterday that he had depreciated more, lost more in confidence, during the last eight months than during any similar period in his life. Maybe when the "tumult and the shouting dies" and we return home after the session of Congress there will be a golden residue of profit that we cannot now comprehend.[64]

After having been at the center of the action during his days as district attorney, Mahon felt somewhat disillusioned by the mundane tasks that took up most of his time. In Washington the veteran congressmen were at the center of action, and the newcomers had to watch what was going on but were seldom consulted about any of the decisions being made.

During his first year in Congress, Mahon learned that the national legislative body did not have all the glamour he had imagined. He told his journal, "For that if there are any great looking men in the House and Senate I have yet to see them. I do not mean that they are not fine, good men—honest and sincere. But great? I must say no. As a child and even as a young man I was a hero worshipper. I suppose that the closer we get to the so-called great men, the more real and ordinary they become."[65]

Many people considered the Seventy-fourth Congress to be one of the stormiest in peacetime history. Mahon seemed to agree when he told a reporter, after returning to Colorado City, "It was a strenuous session. Some of these who have been in Washington for years say it can be compared only with the war Congress."[66]

Returning to West Texas gave Mahon's spirits a much-needed boost. The recent rains that had increased prospects for good crops and Agricultural Adjustment Act payments to farmers convinced him that the Nineteenth District was making a comeback from the Depression and drought. During an interview with a reporter for the *Sweetwater Reporter*, he expressed his admiration of President Roosevelt, though he made it clear that the man who led the country out of the depths of depression was no miracle maker, as some apparently thought he was. The spotlight that had shone so brilliantly on the success of the president during his first months in office had actually made him a target for criticism as time wore on. This happened when the Supreme Court declared that some New Deal legislation was unconstitutional. While not attempting to defend or praise every move the president made, Mahon stressed his belief that the humanity and rights of the people were paramount in the president's mind. According to Mahon, the outstanding accomplishment of the session was the passage of the Social Security bill. It would take some time to perfect the plan and would be costly to pay for; however, he told the reporter, "The greatest clamor from my district was for old age pensions. Hundreds of letters from persons in every walk of life urged me to approve such a plan."[67] The reporter asked Mahon what he considered the most dramatic moment of the session, and he said it was the president's personal appearance in Congress when he returned his veto of the bonus bill.[68] "That was a most delicate subject, and it took nerve and tack; but the President returned the vetoed measure with a powerful appeal, as dramatic an occasion as [one] might imagine."[69]

Mahon predicted the reelection of Roosevelt in 1936, and he could have also predicted his own reelection. Although the first session of the Seventy-fourth Congress was arduous, the Social Security bill, an important plank in Mahon's platform, had become the law of the land.

During the six weeks he planned to be in West Texas, Mahon was determined to contact as many constituents as possible in the district to talk about his work in Washington and answer their questions. In early August he received his formal invitation to attend the inauguration of the new government of the Philippine Islands in November 1935. The boat was scheduled to leave Seattle on October 16 and return on December 14. Japan and Shanghai were ports of call on the trip. Mahon was apprehensive about being gone for two months because he believed he should be visiting with constituents, so he wrote to Judge Ely for advice. Ely replied, "By all means, go. . . . We have practically lost all foreign markets, but our chief competitor in cotton fabrics is Japan, and you might get a lot of good ideas by going over there. Another thing, it will help you with your people as you will be with the Vice-President and that will not hurt your standing with him."[70] He accepted the invitation for Helen, Daphne, and himself. During his interview with a reporter from the Sweetwater newspaper, he made sure constituents knew that the trip was not a junket. He wanted them to know that the Philippine government was paying for their ship passage and all the expenses while they were there. Any other expenses would be covered by Mahon. Additionally, President Roosevelt had requested that he make the trip as a member of the Committee on Insular Affairs. Mahon claimed that Republican Senator Borah's (R-ID) charge that the trip was "the greatest junket of the generation" was just a slap at the administration.[71]

After the inauguration the group was scheduled to stop in Japan, which, as Judge Ely pointed out, would be valuable to Mahon in representing the people of West Texas because that nation was one of the world's largest consumers of cotton. In articles published in newspapers throughout the district, Mahon stressed the fact that this trip would provide an opportunity to learn more about conditions in the cotton and textile industries and their relationship to trade between the United States and the countries of the Far East. Expanding trade and foreign markets had been a plank in his campaign platform in 1934. He believed the future of the cotton industry and the economic welfare of West Texas depended to a large extent upon world trade and foreign markets that would be impacted by developments in the Far East. Last, but not least, the trip was also touted as an opportunity to become more closely acquainted with congressional leaders such as Vice President Garner, Speaker of the House Joseph R. Byrns, and Senator Tom Connally of Texas. Sensing that leaders in the Democratic Party approved of him, he believed these contacts would be valuable in the days ahead. Many newsmen were also scheduled to make the trip, and if his congressional career proved to be a long one, these contacts could be useful. To let constituents know that his focus was still on West Texans, news articles circulated throughout the district to tell people that his Washington office would be kept open by his secretary, Lloyd Croslin, who stood ready to help constituents in any way possible.

Mahon had made a wise choice. Although intellectually curious, both he and Helen were somewhat provincial. They had traveled very little outside of Texas and had never been to another country. Not only did they enjoy the trip thoroughly, they gained important knowledge about the nations and people of the Far East. Because he had more free time than during his days in Washington, he wrote often in his journal. These fresh, firsthand impressions show an ambitious young couple learning from their experiences and growing in sophistication. Making the trip was not financially easy, as they spent nearly one thousand dollars of their own money, but they hoped the friendships they made would be beneficial to his career. In addition to investing in his career, Mahon was also shaping it to represent national interests, rather than just regional ones. In some ways deciding to make this trip was similar to the new suit he had bought with the fifty dollars his father sent to him when in college. Both were a good investment, although they took a big bite out of his available resources at the time.

At 8:05 p.m. the evening of October 10, 1935, the family departed Colorado City on the Texas and Pacific train. The next morning they were met in El Paso by Congressman Ewing Thomason and his wife, Abbie. The day was spent touring the city and Juarez, Mexico, after which they took the night train to Los Angeles, arriving the next morning in time to spend that day sightseeing. That night they boarded the train with Senator Tom Connally and his son Ben for San Francisco. Another day was spent sightseeing, and they spent the night in San Francisco before traveling on to Seattle the next morning, where they spent a day sightseeing. On the morning of October 16 they boarded the SS *President Grant*.

After ceremonies at which the governor of Washington and the mayor of Seattle spoke, the ship departed for Victoria, British Columbia. At each port of call during the trip, host couples were assigned to each congressman and his family, which allowed them to see and learn far more than most tourists. The usual banquets, luncheons, and other glamorous types of entertainment were also part of every stop.

Ports of call along the trip included cities in Japan, China, and the Hawaiian Islands. Mahon filled more than one hundred journal pages with his reactions to the cities he visited, the people he met, and how they earned a livelihood, and his thoughts about the impact these people would have on the world. These impressions would prove valuable in the years ahead. He also took along reading material from the Department of Agriculture and the State Department relating to the US cotton industry.

The stops in Japan, both going and returning, were especially important to Mahon. He was determined to gather as much information as possible about that nation's use of cotton. According to his journal, in 1934 the United States sold approximately $133 million worth of raw cotton to Japan. This amount was equal to the entire Texas production that year. In return the United States bought textiles and raw silk.[72] On the return trip, while anchored in Kobe, he inspected one of the largest textile mills in Japan, Kanegafuchi Spinning Company, where he saw American and Egyptian cotton being spun together. The company, headquartered in Tokyo, also had other plants. That mill had a payroll of twenty thousand employees who earned less than fifty cents a day in US money, and Mahon quickly understood that there was no way that American labor could compete with Japanese labor.[73] Impressed with the industriousness of the Japanese people, he wrote, "I have some prejudice against the Japanese but I cannot deny that the laborer is worthy of his hire. The Japanese really deserve some measure of success because they are working to earn it. Our people have grown soft and more accustomed to luxury."[74]

China was another port of call that interested Mahon because, according to his journal, in 1934 the United States sold $18 million worth of raw cotton to China and bought $10 million in furs. He was shocked by the misery of the "boat people," and in Shanghai he mentioned this to the US ambassador to China. The ambassador replied that the Chinese people were actually happy. They had been poverty stricken for generations and were used to it. Comparing their happy faces to the worried faces of Americans, the ambassador decided the Chinese were really happier than Americans. Mahon had a hard time accepting this explanation, especially after sitting next to the wife of one of the diplomats at a banquet and noticing that "she had on a diamond as big as a lima bean."[75] The extremes of wealth and poverty were glaring, and he wrote, "One cannot fully realize the depressing feeling that 'China' gives him without actually seeing and smelling for himself."[76] Despite his disappointment with China, he believed Shanghai was the most interesting and colorful city in the Orient. He also noted, "In China the people generally are interested in their families but not in the nation. They are not willing to fight for China. They are not patriotic and nationalist in spirit like the Japanese or Americans or English or French."[77]

Finally, on November 10 the SS *President Grant* arrived in the Philippine Islands. In Baguio the congressional group was given a special tour of the largest gold mine on the island. According to Mahon's journal entry, refined gold from the mine, about five hundred thousand dollars' worth per month, was sent to the United States. Later, they had lunch with Governor Frank Murphy, one of the honorees at the dinner party Mahon had attended the previous January. After the luncheon the group rode a train to Manila, about 160 miles from Baguio. On the way they passed a river where several people were bathing, and Mahon wrote, "The modest [modesty] of a woman bather was striking. She sat down in the water and turned her back as simply as she could. However, she kept on bathing her arms and limbs."[78] Another interesting habit of the Filipino women that he noticed was the cigars they smoked. They were about two inches longer than American cigars.[79] He also noticed that the men wore very thin shirts that were not tucked in. On November 12 Mahon attended a joint session of the Philippine House and Senate to hear speeches by Speaker Byrns of the US House of Representatives and Vice President Garner.

Mahon described November 13 as the most interesting day on the Islands. Two carloads of congressmen were taken on a 125-mile trip across the island. They inspected a coconut mill that processed about sixty thousand coconuts per day. The meat of the coconut was ground or shredded, then dried and packed for shipping. The poorer coconuts were dried and sold as copra. The copra was pressed for its oil and the residue fed to cattle. The United States bought the dried coconut and oil from the copra. The oil was a main ingredient in soap and was also used in margarine. The residue from Philippine copra was an advantage to Southern farmers in the United States because it did not compete with the cottonseed meal they produced, which was also used for cattle feed. Coconuts were by far the biggest business of the islands.

In a conversation with Mahon, Senator Nye of North Dakota remarked that if the independence of the Filipinos was successful in the face of British opposition, it would be a real accomplishment. The British wanted to keep a firm hold on their possessions in the Far East and believed that if the Americans withdrew from the Philippine Islands, that would be the beginning of the end of the white man in the Far East. Mahon wrote, "I have always been pro-British but I am more pro-British now than ever."[80] Within the next two years, with the world hovering on the brink of war, Mahon would turn his concerns from trade to security and change his mind about the Philippines.

On November 15 Manuel Quezon was inaugurated with much pomp and ceremony. Approximately twenty-five thousand people attended. The crowds were so large that they blocked the streets and disrupted the inauguration parade. Mahon wrote, "On the evening of Nov 15 we went to the Inaugural ball which was the most strikingly artistic feature of the Inauguration."[81]

In the days remaining, Mahon joined other congressmen for an inspection tour of Corregidor, which he described as "perhaps the strongest fortress in the world."[82] With another group he inspected US submarines in the harbor. The group was allowed to remain on board for a dive that lasted an hour while the crew went through numerous drills.

On the afternoon of November 20 the SS *President Jefferson* left Manila Bay to begin the journey home. Mahon wrote, "The sea was very calm in Manila bay. The water was smooth and peaceful and shone like a mirror. I predict that the future of the Philippines will not be so smooth and peaceful as was the bay on this 20th of November. The Filipinos do not realize how good America has been to them. If they secure the independence they seek it will be the most unfortunate thing that has ever come their way."[83]

On the return trip he read a book about the Philippine economy and wrote, "In 1933 they were our 9th best customers—I think they now rank thirteenth—we are by far their best customers buying more than 80% of all goods which they export. One fourth of our foreign trade is with the Far East and it is hoped that we can continue to have a large share in the commerce of the Far East."[84]

After leaving Yokohama, Japan, on the return trip, Mahon wrote, "Really the Japanese people are a great people. The Filipino people will probably never be a great people because of the climate in which they live. The Japanese are favored with a good climate and seem to be full of energy and ambition. Climate is one of the most primary factors in a life of a nation. It is not so much race and color as it is climate that counts. Of course, race is a very important factor, and I do not mean to discount it."[85]

On the ship from Japan to Honolulu, there was much discussion about Japan, and Mahon recorded, "Speaker Byrns expressed a view that seems sensible—Japan does not want war with us any more than we want war with Japan. If Japan should be at war with us she would have to devote all her resources in an effort to win. Russia and China would seize this opportunity to wipe Japan off the face of the earth. Japan is a great threat to the maritime nation of Britain and would for several reasons side with the US."[86]

An article in the *Washington Post* indicated that when the ship stopped at Yokohama, Vice President Garner was scheduled to meet with Japanese officials in an attempt to improve relations, which had chilled between that country and the United States.[87] Speaker Byrns believed the vice president's mission had been successful.

In Hawaii they toured the Oahu Sugar Plantation. According to journal entries the plantation produced eighty thousand tons of sugar per year.[88] During their two-day stay in Honolulu, the Mahon family swam at Waikiki beach and then joined the group for a tour of Pearl Harbor and Schofield Barracks, where military men paraded in review.

During the trip from Honolulu to Seattle, Mahon recorded several pages of his thoughts about cotton production in the United States. He was convinced that the federal policy of reducing acres to force the price up would ultimately be destructive to producers. He believed that the AAA program and the Bankhead Bill had provided relief, but only temporarily.[89] Because the United States produced only about 40 percent of the world's cotton, if production continued to decline, other countries would simply increase production and fill the world's demand. Furthermore, when foreign textile mills changed their machinery to handle the type of cotton that was grown in other nations, they would not change back, should the United States decide to increase production again, because of the large expense involved in such a change. If the United States could not sell its cotton abroad, producers would be limited to the approximately 6.5 million bales that could be consumed in the domestic market. "My position is that our plight is bad enough with a foreign market, and that without a foreign [market] we are utterly ruined. Texas exports about 90% of her cotton. Where would she be without a foreign market at all— ruined!"[90]

Just prior to their arrival in Seattle, the sea began to roll so badly that many passengers complained of having trouble staying in bed at night. The rolling was gentle and did not make people sick; however, Mahon wrote, "Senator Connally's chair tipped over and he fell to the floor while we were engaged in a game of bridge."[91]

When the ship docked in Victoria, British Columbia, on December 15, customs officers and baggage porters boarded the ship. The souvenirs that Mahon and Helen had bought amounted to less than the three hundred dollars allowed in duty-free items. He checked their luggage with a porter who was to take it to the Northern Pacific Railroad station, and then they went to lunch, where Helen was surprised with a birthday cake. Members of the congressional group gathered around her table to sing "Happy Birthday" on her thirty-fifth birthday. The Mahons boarded the night train for home, and

Mahon wrote, "Billings, Montana, Kansas City, Dallas and home—with a capital 'H.'"[92]

The family arrived in Colorado City, Texas, the night of December 19, just in time to celebrate Christmas before they had to make the trip back to Washington for the second session of the Seventy-fourth Congress, which convened on January 3, 1936. Spending Christmas in Texas and making the long trip back to Washington in time for the opening of Congress became an annual ritual repeated for nearly half a century.

The memories of their two-month trip lasted a lifetime, refreshed again and again by reading the entries Mahon had made in his Green Journal. In years to come, Mahon would make many trips abroad, and the entries he made in his Green Journal would be a benchmark for measuring how much his outlook on life had matured.

When interviewed before leaving for the Philippine Islands, he told a reporter from the *Sweetwater Reporter* that he expected the second session, which was scheduled to begin on January 3, to be more serene because the "recovery-reform" legislation was out of the way. He anticipated that Congress would concentrate on balancing the budget, a step that needed to be taken.[93]

On January 3, 1936, the "more serene" Congress that Mahon had predicted the previous September convened at noon. The House got off to a lively start with some sharp criticism about the State of the Union address being given at 9:00 p.m. instead of the time-honored tradition of noon. This change would allow as many people as possible to hear the president on the radio, a medium that had proven to be a very effective tool of communication for people like Father Coughlin. Coughlin had used the radio as a great centralizing force to spread his philosophy into even the remotest rural community. Now President Roosevelt intended to do the same.[94]

Not all members of Congress agreed with the change, and Republican Minority Leader Bertrand H. Snell quipped, "Is there going to be anything in that message which will not stand the usual light of the midday sun?"[95] Snell voiced the Republican sentiment when he complained about Roosevelt using the time that had been set aside by Congress for the dignified reception of a message from the president to open his political campaign for reelection.[96] Other Republicans threatened to object, but none did; thus, House Majority Leader William Bankhead determined that, since there were no formal objections, the new time was accepted. Among the usual deluge of bills dropped in the hopper for consideration that session was the Vinson-McCormack bill for the payment of a soldier's bonus and a neutrality bill that would give the president wide powers to prohibit shipments to belligerent countries and make other restrictions designed to keep the United States out of war. At 1:15 p.m., the House recessed until 8:45 p.m.

On the night of January 3, the House chamber was filled to capacity to hear President Roosevelt as he attacked power-seeking minorities, both at home and abroad. The first half of the address focused on the war clouds gathering in Europe and Asia. He stressed the need for neutrality that included an embargo against selling arms, ammunition, or implements of war to the nations in conflict. He also advocated a strong defense to prevent an attack that would cause the United States to become embroiled in war, should it break out. The last half of his address was an attack on critics of the New Deal, those financial and industrial groups that fought the return of control of the federal government to Washington. His defense became a litany of New Deal legislation. He challenged his opponents to come forward and propose that Congress repeal these measures. He finished by declaring this the beginning of a new era, a humanitarian era. Two days later, the *Washington Post* carried a photograph of robed and hooded members of Ku Klux Klan No. 6 at Ballston, Virginia, participating in funeral services for a Klan member.[97] Obviously, this new era of government, focused on humanitarianism, needed to grow considerably to reach all people.

Roosevelt's challenge that critics of his New Deal programs come forward and ask Congress to reverse this legislation was answered by the Supreme Court. On January 6, by a majority of six to three, the judges ruled against the entire Agricultural Adjustment Act, invalidating AAA processing taxes, benefit payments, and all farm production controls. The court ruled that the Agricultural Adjustment Act was unconstitutional because it taxed one group for the benefit of another, and more importantly, it interfered with states' rights to legislate agriculture, which was intrastate, not interstate, commerce.

The comprehensiveness of the ruling stunned the administration and those members of Congress who supported farm legislation. The president called a meeting at the White House that lasted more than two hours to try to salvage some part of the legislation. Agriculture Secretary Wallace; Attorney General Cummings; AAA Administrator Chester C. Davis; Senator Bankhead (D-AL), member of the Senate Agriculture Committee; and Marvin Jones (D-TX), chair of the House Committee on Agriculture, attended. When the meeting had ended, Wallace, Bankhead, Davis, and Jones went to the Department of Agriculture to continue the discussion. Marvin Jones offered the only statement made concerning the ruling, when he said he believed that Congress had a moral obligation to pass an appropriation to pay the farmers who had already signed crop-reduction contracts. Meanwhile, all payments stopped, as did the collection of all processing taxes. Many members of Congress believed something should be done, but most were undecided about what course to take. Some even talked of a constitutional amendment curtailing the power of the Supreme Court.

Mahon was very concerned. Within days after the announcement of the Supreme Court decision, he attended a meeting of 150 farmers called by Agriculture Secretary Wallace. After the meeting he announced in a press release to district newspapers that the far-reaching effects of the decision should not be underestimated. A practical farm program must be worked out. He tried to reassure farmers that Congress would have to honor the contracts already signed by farmers. He went on to say that he believed some features of the former program were not well suited to the rapidly growing Nineteenth District, and he would watch any new plan closely to assure fair recognition for West Texas farmers. He pledged to devote his best efforts to placing the farm industry on a stable foundation and closed with "the fight for equality of agriculture has only begun."[98]

Once again, letters from the district began to pour into Mahon's office pleading with him to encourage Congress to find a substitute program that would allow farmers' payments to continue. A Mitchell County study of the benefits received during the three years of the AAA's life revealed that it had put over a million dollars in the pockets of farmers and cattlemen in that county alone.[99] One constituent wrote:

Hon. Geo. H. Mahon:

Dear George I suppose you are getting quite a lot of mail these days but nevertheless I feel that should I not say a few words you might forget the boys at the forks of the creek. Realizing that A.A.A. is a dead issue according to the decision of the robed owls on the mahony [mahogany] roost [he was poking fun at the Supreme Court Justices who had recently moved into a new building that was lavishly adorned with mahogany] and agriculture is just where the present administration found it helpless hopeless and penniless so to speak. Now George you are a man of unquestionable intelligence integrity ability and the nerve to do things and believe me the people are expecting it of you. You realize the plight of the farmers as well as I and the people are not going to submit tamely to threadbare alibis from their Representatives always. I know that you are up against a tough bunch but we are in a tough spot ourselves here. I know your ability as an attorney, so first tear into those bullies and give them <u>Hell</u>.

I want you to know that people will not sit idly by and see their homes taken from them put out into the road like an unwanted cat or dog and make no protest, so do your stuff George we are betting on you. With kindest regards and best wishes.[100]

To which Mahon replied,

Dear Friend:

I thank you for your letter regarding a new farm program. The Senate passed a new farm bill Saturday and the House will probably take the matter up during this week. We have already appropriated money for feed-seed loans and for payment of outstanding contract obligations.

Because of my desire to contribute all I can in the formation of new policies, I am glad to have every expression of interest from our West Texas Farmers.[101]

Many who criticized the Supreme Court's rulings against New Deal measures argued that the court was thwarting the will of the people. This argument did not hold up against the results of a poll, conducted by Dr. George Gallup of the American Institute of Public Opinion, that was released by the *Washington Post* on January 5, 1936.[102] It revealed that 59 percent of Americans opposed the Agricultural Adjustment Act and 41 percent favored it. As might be expected, 92 percent of Republicans were opposed and 70 percent of Democrats favored the act. The South was the only section of the nation that was in favor. That section was also heavily Democrat, and planters there had received more than $140 million up to October 1935 for restricting cotton, tobacco, and other crops. A surprising fact revealed in the poll was the opposition of states like North Dakota, South Dakota, Nebraska, Minnesota, Wisconsin, Missouri, and Ohio. The number of rural families in each state, the amount received by each rural family, and the proportion of Democrats to Republicans had a telling impact on the way each state voted. For example, farm families in Iowa comprised one-third of the state's population and received approximately $216 per farm family during 1935. Iowa voted in favor of AAA. In contrast, farm families in Ohio made up one-sixth of the population and received approximately $53 per farm family; this accounted for Ohio's vote against the act. It seemed that a large number of Americans were happy that AAA would again just refer to the American Automobile Association. President Roosevelt did not agree with that.[103]

While the administration was stunned by the comprehensiveness of the Supreme Court's ruling, it had a substitute program waiting in the wings. The Soil Conservation Act of 1935 was amended and became the Soil Conservation and Domestic Allotment Act, which was signed into law on February 29, 1936. "It was worded to circumvent the Supreme Court by making its main purpose soil conservation, which promotes the general welfare. Farmers were sent invitations, instead of contracts, to reduce their acreage of designated crops. Reduced acres were to be planted in soil-building crops for which they would be paid out of the general treasury. It was clearly stated that no taxes would be levied to cover this expense."[104] The act also transferred the responsibility to states for making the payments that would be underwritten by federal grants. Marvin Jones, chairman of the House Committee on Agriculture, characterized the act as justice for the farm family; as his biographer, Irwin M. May, observed, "He consistently mixed concern for family welfare, frontier humanitarianism, and Christianity in his considerations."[105]

Soil conservation was on the minds of all West Texans as gigantic dust storms raged across the land during the drought of the 1930s. With slightly more than two inches of rain since the previous fall, the topsoil was dry enough to take to the air with the slightest breeze, and breezes had not been slight during the spring of 1935 in West Texas. Through the months of March and April, high winds blew forty-seven days out of sixty-one. During most dust storms, visibility was limited to one mile or sometimes as little as five hundred feet. Topsoil from Texas farms was carried as far as Washington, DC, where it caused a light rain to become muddy before reaching the ground. This "yellow rain" was a common occurrence on the Great Plains. Trying to protect their land, most farmers left sorghum stubble and cotton stalks standing until planting time, but the severity of the drought outstripped their efforts. Chambers of commerce did everything possible to avoid having their town considered a part of the Dust Bowl. They feared such a designation would cause a mass exodus, leaving only ghost towns. On March 11, 1936,

Mahon bitterly criticized Pathe News Service from the House floor for producing a newsreel that portrayed his district as the heart of the Dust Bowl,
where neither man nor cattle can live. He had seen the newsreel the evening
before while attending a movie in the capital city and became quite angry
with what he considered an unjust portrayal of West Texas. From the floor
he pointed out that the development of West Texas had been remarkable and
most of the counties in his district paid a record number of poll taxes for the
year.[106] In refuting the Dust Bowl portrayal, Mahon sounded like the president of a chamber of commerce in West Texas and for the same reason—fear
of stigmatism that would ultimately cause depopulation.

As the 1936 presidential election began to appear on the horizon, the Democratic Party's speakers bureau asked Mahon to make campaign speeches
around the country, including two in Virginia. In Danville, he was introduced
as "just an ordinary cowpuncher who got elected to congress but who proved
to be born a silver-spurred orator, who is a master of arts in public speaking."[107]
Mahon reviewed the record of New Deal legislation and, while admitting that
not all of it was perfect, told the audience crowded into the courtroom of the
municipal building that they had only to look at the business index to see
what the Democrats had accomplished. As to the mounting debt, he said it
was less than one-tenth of the national wealth, and any business whose debts
were only one-tenth of the assets would be considered extremely solvent. He
said businessmen who were criticizing the president were not using the same
facts they gave their stockholders in the last annual reports. The next month,
when he spoke again in Mansfield, Virginia, he stressed that humanitarianism
had become the paramount consideration of the Roosevelt administration.
He challenged listeners to compare the status of the farmer, the homeowner,
and the average citizen during the Hoover administration with their status
under President Roosevelt. In closing he admonished, "That's a comparison
the Democrats mustn't permit the country to forget."[108] Those championship
debating skills, first developed in college and then honed so well during his
district attorney days, gave George Mahon an impressive platform presence.
He quickly attracted the attention of party leaders.

In January 1936 a bill for early payment of the soldiers' bonus passed both chambers of Congress, then overrode a presidential veto. It was known as the Vinson-Patman-McCormack Bill and differed from the Patman Bill of the previous year in that bonds were to be issued to the veterans instead of printing new currency, which would have happened under the Patman Bill. In June bonus bonds were mailed to three million veterans of World War I.

At the end of World War I, returning veterans received a severance bonus of sixty dollars. While on active duty they had been paid $1 per day, which compared unfavorably with those who had been exempted from service and earned from $8 to $20 a day in shipyards or munitions factories. Congressional advocates pushed for more equitable compensation, and in 1924 legislation was passed authorizing adjusted service certificates of $1.00 per day for domestic service and $1.25 per day for overseas duty plus interest that would accrue from 1925 to 1945. This meant that each veteran would receive approximately one thousand dollars, but not until 1945. When Wright Patman (D-TX) entered Congress he pushed for immediate payment of the certificates, and the arguments he put forth in 1929 became a seven-year crusade that was ultimately successful in 1936.[109] Roosevelt vetoed the bill because he argued that what people called the "bonus" was really 3.5 million endowment policies, taken out in 1925, that would mature twenty years later, or upon the death of the veteran to whom the money was due. To compensate for the delay in payment, Congress agreed to add 25 percent to the allowance for each veteran, plus 4 percent interest for twenty years.[110]

More than eleven hundred veterans in Lubbock County were eligible to receive bonds. An editorial in the local newspaper indicated that "a check of Lubbock veterans indicates the men will buy homes, buy needed clothing, furniture, cars, etc., will pay out on insurance, on their business and a hundred and one other items of daily life."[111] Merchants were expecting business to increase from this inflow of cash, which was estimated to be approximately $4 million throughout the district. Because of its larger population Lubbock County expected to receive between $350,000 and $400,000, but not all of the bonus money was spent wisely. One man filed charges with the Lubbock justice of the peace against his wife, who had persuaded the veteran to allow her to place his $500 in the bottom of her shoes for safekeeping until they got home. She then said that she wanted to go "up the street" to buy some wearing apparel and would return shortly. That was the last he saw of his wife and his bonus money.[112]

About the middle of May, Congress increased the speed of its work in order to adjourn in time for the political conventions. The unusual amount of stress that resulted from this push was thought to be part of the cause of Speaker Joseph Byrns's death. Late in the afternoon of June 3, 1936, he became ill and was taken from the House to his suite in the Mayflower Hotel. The Capitol physician, Dr. George Calver, was summoned, and the illness was diagnosed as a heart attack. At 11:00 p.m. that night Byrns suffered a cerebral hemorrhage and died at 12:14 a.m. His death shocked officials throughout the capital. Although the strain of the previous few weeks had been taxing, Byrns had appeared to be in excellent health. Now the rush on Capitol Hill had to cease to allow for funeral preparations, and the expected date of adjournment was pushed off until mid-June. The House was required to elect at least a speaker pro-tem who could sign bills that were passed from that time until the end of Congress. At 11:00 a.m. on June 4 the House was called to order to handle its sorrowful business. Representative William B. Bankhead (D-AL) was unanimously elected "in an atmosphere of awed solemnity."[113] Bankhead, the House majority leader, was the son of a former senator and the father of Tallulah of theatrical fame. In 1935 he had unsuccessfully sought the speakership and because of his own fragile health had not been able to attend a single day during the first session. He must have wondered about this office that had seen three of the last four speakers die while holding it.

When Congress adjourned on June 20, Mahon attended the Democratic National Convention in Philadelphia. Because he and Sam Rayburn were the only two congressional delegates representing Texas, he believed it was more important to attend the convention than to return to Colorado City to begin his campaign for reelection. Also, an attorney in Big Spring had written to say, "In my opinion, the Townsend group is not nearly as strong as they were two years ago in this section of the country, however, they still have a following who try to make up in noise for their lack in size. I do not think that they will hurt you materially."[114] Despite passage of the Social Security Act, there were still people who believed it was worthwhile to pressure their congressman to advocate for the Townsend Plan. The impetus behind this movement was the thought of receiving two hundred dollars a month immediately instead of thirty dollars per month in the future from Social Security.

At the convention he was joined by his longtime friend and former law partner, Charles Thompson. Thompson represented the Nineteenth Congressional District as a member of the National Executive Democratic Committee. Meanwhile, Helen and Daphne returned home to Colorado City.

Mahon hurried home after the Democratic Convention ended to begin campaigning by the first of July. E. B. Speck, a retired Baptist minister, was his opponent. Speck, a kind, well-meaning, elderly gentlemen, was a Townsend-ite. Although Mahon's files were filled with letters and petitions containing numerous names of constituents asking him to support the Townsend Plan, he had avoided talking about it in public. Now he would have to speak out.

Because only about three weeks remained before July 25, the date of the first primary, Mahon used district newspapers to tell constituents why he would not be able to shake everyone's hand and personally ask for their vote as he had done before. He also used these news articles to let people know that he was away from the district because of the increasingly important tasks the party was asking him to perform. He ran an ad in the *Lubbock Morning Avalanche*, explaining that he supported farm legislation, the payment of the soldiers' bonus, old-age pension legislation, and other measures important to West Texas. He also claimed to have cooperated fully with each individual and with the people in each county and town in the performance of personal services in Washington.[115] He told voters that he would only support Social Security, which paid no more than thirty dollars per month to those who qualified, instead of the Townsend Plan, which was to guarantee two hundred dollars a month to every individual sixty years of age and older.

Mahon tried to show people how their tax burden would become unbear-able when the ordinary taxpayer had to make up the $20 billion difference. All taxes were then producing only approximately $4 billion per year. He believed the federal government could not afford the difference between what the sales tax would raise and the approximately $24 million required annually to fund the plan.

This was a harsh message for many older people who had been left almost desperate by the Depression. However, there were many voters in the district who agreed with Mahon. One of these was Charles Guy, editor of the Lubbock newspaper, who predicted that Speck could go into the election with every Townsend vote and still be a long way from Washington.[116] Mahon welcomed this about-face from Guy, who, with his 1934 editorials supporting Clark Mullican, had cautioned voters against sending a boy to Washington to do a man's job. After Mahon won the 1936 primary, Guy wrote in an editorial, "The fact that the Democratic National Campaign committee has called Mahon to stump the East for the Roosevelt-Garner ticket is not alone a compliment to the personable young man from Colorado City. It also is a compliment to the people of the entire Nineteenth District who, twice hand running, have voted to send Mr. Mahon to the lower house in Washington."[117] He went on to say that if Mahon kept on in the way he was going in Washington and with his contacts, he would be in Washington a long time. Everyone loves a winner! Guy often laughed about getting on the bandwagon only after Mahon had proven himself, but Mahon never commented on it. He understood the importance of support from the editor of the largest newspaper in his district and always remembered his father's admonition about getting "the big head." In addition to the endorsement of newspaper editors, Mahon had developed a network of support among postmasters in the district because he had appointed many of them. His files are filled with letters from these postmasters, keeping him abreast of the attitudes and problems in their hometowns.

Despite Mahon's whirlwind canvass of the district, he won the primary by a three-to-one majority, which in the one-party politics of Texas meant he had won the election. Most voters believed Mahon had made a fine start in Congress. They liked the way he had quietly learned the ropes by studying the problems involved in legislative matters as well as looking after the interests of his constituents. The list of economic benefits to the district was impressive. More than $5 million had been received in seed/feed and crop production loans; AAA payments amounted to nearly $22 million; Federal Land Bank loans to farmers amounted to over $22 million; and over $3 million had gone to fourteen hundred urban homes refinanced by the Home Owners' Loan Cooperation.[118] Mahon emphasized these facts in his campaign, leading people to express approval of his honesty, industriousness, and the intelligent way he performed his duties. They predicted that, given time, this West Texan would be influential in shaping the legislation of the nation. After all, they believed he had been influential in bringing much-needed economic benefit to their district.

After the primary he and Helen traveled to Dallas to join in the festivities scheduled for "Garner Day" at the Texas Centennial celebration. On August 5 Vice President and Mrs. Garner arrived from Austin with Governor Allred, who had been their host in the governor's mansion the night before. Their motorcade from Austin was escorted by state highway patrolmen. Mahon joined other members of the Texas delegation and many longtime Garner supporters for a luncheon in the grand ballroom of the Hotel Adolphus, while Helen attended a luncheon for Mrs. Garner in the main dining room of the same hotel. That evening they were among the one thousand invited guests for a dinner at the Baker Hotel, where seventy-five people were seated at the speaker's table. This was followed by a Texas-sized gathering in the Cotton

Bowl, where fifteen thousand people gathered to hear the vice president praise Texans for looking to the future while celebrating the accomplishments of the past. He said that people who attended from throughout the nation would leave with a better idea about the potential of Texas. He ended by saying, "I am awfully glad and proud to be a Texan."[119] Before his arrival the newspaper had forecast a celebration of "Texanic" proportions. Indeed, it was. When the celebration was over, the Mahons returned to Colorado City, where George hoped to spend the remainder of the year visiting with constituents and accepting invitations to speak at events throughout the district.

That did not happen. Sam Rayburn, who headed the Democratic Party's national speakers' bureau for the presidential campaign, remembered Mahon's success in Virginia earlier that year. Rayburn also had the task of furnishing speakers for Democratic candidates in upcoming House and Senate races. By the middle of October, he had scheduled Mahon for a week of speaking engagements in New Mexico. Mahon eventually went on to Chicago to confer with Marvin Jones of the House Committee on Agriculture. Jones was managing Roosevelt's campaign in the farm states of the Midwest. After this, Mahon went to the Democratic National Committee headquarters in New York to confer with Rayburn and other party leaders, then on to Connecticut, New Jersey, and Pennsylvania for Democratic rallies. He did not get back to Colorado City until nearly time for the general election on November 3. As usual, Lloyd Croslin kept his office open and helped constituents. However much constituents might have been disappointed because they were not able to talk with Mahon, they were very proud to see one of their own winning the respect of party leaders so quickly. This tall, handsome, and serious young congressman had not only captured the admiration of his constituents, he was rapidly capturing the admiration and respect of party leaders also.

In late September, before leaving for New York, Mahon wrote to several members of the House to encourage them to vote for Rayburn as majority leader when the party caucused the next January. In a letter to Mahon, Rayburn expressed his reticence in asking colleagues for their vote because he believed they might think he was using his position as chairman of the speakers' bureau to promote himself. Mahon was happy to do this for his fellow Texan, and favorable replies were received from nearly every person he asked to vote for Rayburn. Only a few wanted to wait until January before making a definite commitment. In a letter to Rayburn, Mahon wrote, "Of course, I am for you 100% and would like to render whatever little assistance that may be within my power."[120]

After the 1936 presidential election, when Roosevelt was reelected and the Democrats won control of the House, Rayburn wrote from Washington, DC, to thank Mahon for sending a clipping from the Dallas newspaper. In his big, bold hand he penned a postscript: "When are you coming here—you could help me a lot in my battle for the leadership."[121] The campaign for majority leader was very important to him because if he won he would be next in line to become speaker of the House, a position Rayburn dearly wanted.

It was the end of December when the Mahons were able to return to Washington. Before leaving the district, Mahon told a Lubbock newspaper reporter, "No matter how much wheat we make; no matter how much cotton; no matter how many unemployed go back on payrolls, it will make little difference to us if we go to war. Our keeping out of war is not only important. It is essential. We must steer clear of conflict if it is humanly possible—come what may. The biggest problem we'll have in Washington during the term of Congress starting Jan 5 is that of American neutrality."[122]

The Mahon family was back in Washington in time for the opening of the Seventy-fifth Congress on January 5, 1937. Before leaving Colorado City, Mahon predicted a long and important session. This Congress was filled with an unprecedented Democratic majority. The day before Congress convened, the Democrats caucused in the House chamber and elected Sam Rayburn majority leader. He triumphed over John J. O'Connor of New York by a vote of 184-127 after a tense afternoon when eight New York Democrats bolted from O'Connor to Rayburn.[123] With Garner presiding over the Senate, Rayburn's elevation placed two Texans in very powerful positions.

O'Connor, fighting for victory to the bitter end, berated the New York representatives because they had agreed to vote for the Texan instead of him. Realizing, however, that the die was cast, his motion made the vote for Rayburn unanimous. O'Conner remained chairman of the powerful Rules Committee, and agreed to do everything in his power to carry out the administration's program. Later Rayburn told reporters, "Of course, I feel mighty good about it. All I can say is that when the Administration's program is fixed, after consultations between Congressional leaders and the President, that program will be my program 100 per cent."[124] He further said that he anticipated no difficulty shepherding his majority of 332 Democrats to go along with the program. This statement would come back to haunt him before Congress adjourned.

After determining that a quorum was present, Speaker of the House William B. Bankhead (D-AL) was returned to the speakership by a routine vote. He waxed eloquent after taking the oath of office and promised to "at all times endeavor to be just and fair and equitable . . . to try to measure up to the illustrious traditions that have been handed down to me by those great predecessors whose portraits hang in the outer corridor."[125] Earlier, Democrats had elected Senator Joseph T. Robinson (D-AR) as majority leader of the Senate. He was unopposed.

Six women were among the lawmakers of the Seventy-fifth Congress. One of them, Mary T. Norton of New Jersey, was chair of the District of Columbia Committee, and in that capacity she frequently clashed with Thomas Blanton of the Seventeenth District in Texas. Blanton, who was on the House Appropriations Committee, also served on the District of Columbia Subcommittee, which was responsible for appropriating the money with which the District of Columbia operated. In her clashes with Blanton, it had been reported that Norton gave him a "few legislative lickings that made history on the Hill."[126] Blanton was not returned to Congress in the 1936 elections. In future years Mahon chaired the District of Columbia Subcommittee and the House Appropriations Committee.

On January 6 the House and Senate met in joint session to open the electoral certificates and count the votes of the electors for the president and vice president. President of the Senate James Garner presided. Four tellers, two from each house of Congress, certified that each certificate was in proper form and counted the votes. Tellers ascertained that Roosevelt and Garner had each received 523 votes, while the opponents, Alf Landon and Frank Knox, had received 8 each. Their report was delivered to the vice president, who then dissolved the joint session.[127]

At 2:00 p.m. the House and Senate returned to hear President Roosevelt's message on the state of the union. Roosevelt, speaking to a crowded gallery, said he believed that "the President should in every fourth year, insofar as seems reasonable, review the existing state of our national affairs and outline broad future problems, leaving specific recommendations for future legislation to be made by the President about to be inaugurated."[128] He asked Congress to consider three measures immediately: extending the life and powers of authorizations that would expire that month, prohibit arms shipments to Spain, and pass a deficiency appropriation bill to take care of relief requirements. Also, he stated that plans for reorganization of the executive branch would be presented to Congress shortly. He went on to stress that current problems made it mandatory for this government to perform, not just theorize, in order to prove that democracy was superior to more extreme forms of government for getting action when it was needed. His administration had met that challenge, although it required unprecedented activities of federal leadership. Rejecting the idea of a constitutional amendment, Roosevelt declared, "Means must be found to adapt our legal forms and our judicial interpretation to the actual present national needs of the largest progressive democracy in the modern world."[129] He challenged the judicial branch to do its part in making democracy successful by allowing implied powers to be effective instruments for the common good.[130] While the president was suggesting that the Supreme Court and the federal judiciary had become an obstacle to the full functioning of American democracy, just across the Capitol Plaza members of that high tribunal were having lunch in the private dining room of their new building. They gave no indication of being the least bit aware of the president's words.[131] The stage was now set for the biggest clash of Roosevelt's second administration.

"In the 1930s the flood of New Deal legislation made a titanic duel with the judiciary all but inevitable," wrote historian David M. Kennedy.[132] By the end of 1936 the Supreme Court had declared nine major New Deal bills unconstitutional, and President Roosevelt feared that ultimately all of them would suffer the same fate. Additionally, he was concerned that returning prosperity would blunt the need for his progressive reforms. "As his second term began, Roosevelt was, therefore, determined to strike boldly. In the waning moment before prosperity had fully returned, he must protect the New Deal and prepare the way for further reform. He struck on three fronts: at the judiciary; at Congress; and eventually at elements within his own party, particularly its entrenched southern wing."[133]

On the morning of February 5, the president called Democratic congressional leaders to the White House to reveal his plan for judiciary reform that was to be sent to the Senate that afternoon in a special message. Attorney General Homer S. Cummings briefly explained the proposal to Vice President Garner, House Judiciary Chairman Hatton Sumners, Senator Alben W. Barkley, Speaker Bankhead, House Majority Leader Rayburn, Senate Majority Leader Robinson, and Senate Judiciary Chairman Henry F. Ashurst. Cummings proposed to add one new Supreme Court justice for each sitting justice who refused to retire at seventy years of age. Ostensibly, this was for efficiency as the backlog was claimed to be quite large. In truth, it was designed to provide enough justices in favor of New Deal legislation to assure the survival of what was still considered constitutional. Silence followed Cummings's explanation, then Vice President Garner said, "Mr. Attorney General, before that law comes back up here for the Boss's signature, many, many moons will pass."[134] He was correct. The bill was introduced in the Senate, and after much arm-twisting, many promises, and even a few threats from the president, it failed to pass. It did, however, monopolize most of the energy in Congress that year.

Reform of the judicial branch of government was not new. It dated back to John Adams, when Congress reduced the original six justices to five, and it had happened intermittently until the New Deal. "Thus, in the context of our history adding and subtracting justices for essentially political reasons was a well-established practice, and although each change in the number of justices had aroused the fears of defenders of the Constitution, the outcry had been short-lived, and the effects on the Court over the long run were negligible."[135] When FDR suggested reform of the judicial system, he was accused of "court packing," which damaged his credibility with the American people and helped split the already fragile unity of the Democratic Party. Southern conservative Democratic congressmen feared that an attack on the Supreme Court would jeopardize the institution of white supremacy. Despite their conviction that the court had overstepped its boundaries with recent legislation, many joined a coalition with Republicans to battle liberal legislation in the future. Opponents of the court-packing plan in Congress passed the Retirement Act on March 1, 1937, which provided a generous retirement package for the justices. It was designed to encourage older justices to retire and thereby weaken the argument for adding extra justices. President Roosevelt, however, refusing to be appeased or to compromise, tried to use support for the court fight as an excuse to purge the party of conservatives who only halfheartedly supported his New Deal programs.

Mahon's stand on this legislation reflected the feelings of many Americans. He voted against the bill to reorganize the Supreme Court and to allow judges to retire with full pay. Many legislators still paid homage to President Roosevelt, but they had lost some of their zeal for reform in the face of so many challenges to long-standing political and legal traditions. More often than not, their constituents reacted sympathetically to their feelings of doubt.[136]

In a letter to Fred C. Haile, one of his opponents in the 1934 race, Mahon wrote, "Now, I did not deserve any congratulation for voting against the Sumners Bill which provided for retirement of Federal Judges after reaching the age of 70 years upon an annuity of $20,000 per year, with so many of the people represented by me lacking the bare necessities of life. . . . I am rather liberal in my views, and I am hopeful that some compromise can be worked out that will be somewhat agreeable to the President, the Congress, and the Country."[137]

News clippings in his scrapbook indicate that editors in his district were pleased with his vote because it was protective of their financial interests.[138] Another letter to a former dorm mate and fellow debater at Simmons College revealed deeper feelings. He wrote, "Of course, being an average American, I have always, more or less, had a subconscious tendency to worship the Supreme Court like the pagans worshiped the Sacred Cow."[139] Since the controversy had started Mahon researched the backgrounds of the justices and concluded that they "are no better than my constituents—no better than the rest of us." He believed they were subject to politics and prejudices just like other people, especially if they had been involved in battles with members of an opposing party. Mahon continued, "Chief Justice Hughes stepped off the Bench in 1916 to carry the standard of the Republican Party and undertake to drive Woodrow Wilson out of the White House. The California vote had not come in, but Hughes, thinking he was elected, posed for [the] photographer as the President-elect. Mr. Hughes and his eight associates are not any more akin to God than the farmers and school teachers and business men of my Congressional District."[140] On the other hand, Mahon did not think the president had been straightforward in his first message about the Supreme Court, but in his speech on March 9, he made more sense. Although Mahon was not in complete agreement with Roosevelt, he did believe some new blood was needed on the court. "During the last four years we have had new blood in the Presidency and in the Congress, and I think it would be a fortunate thing if some of our Supreme Court Justices would resign."[141] He was not in favor of a constitutional amendment, nor did he believe additional judges would change our form of government. He closed, "Please treat this letter in confidence as I am still blundering around in my own mind in search of the light."[142] Mahon's belief that additional judges would not change our form of government, and his continued attempts to support the party, was in line with Sam Rayburn's view of matters; however, he differed with Rayburn by voting against the bill.

In June, during a hearing on appropriations, Mahon spoke in the House in favor of granting complete independence to the Philippine Islands in 1938 or 1939, instead of waiting until 1946, as Congress had previously agreed to do. At that time a bill for $140,000 for administering the US government in the

Islands was being debated. As a member of the House Committee on Insular Affairs, Mahon took the opportunity to remind the House that from the date of occupation until that time, the United States had spent approximately $900 million, in addition to the cost of military support, to govern the Islands. He believed the money could be better spent in the development of own institutions of the United States. Also, this would be legislating for neutrality because as long as the United States maintained sovereignty in the Philippines, it was liable to be drawn into a conflict in the Orient. "This is most unfortunate, and this untenable position should be terminated at the earliest possible moment. It is one of the major threats to peace for the United States." He went on to say, "I do not want my remarks to indicate any lack of consideration for our 'little brown brothers' across the sea."[143] His attitude toward people of color was definitely paternalistic; however, his idea about granting independence early contained much foresight when one considers the number of American lives that were lost defending the Islands during World War II.

When Mahon returned to the district after Congress adjourned, he told a reporter for the *Abilene Reporter News* that his belief in President Roosevelt had not weakened. Mahon said, "He has lost some ground, of course, but he could not be expected to maintain the highest peak of popularity. It is well to remember that no president has ever been extremely popular throughout eight years in the White House."[144] Mahon also did not believe the party split was serious but was fearful that if it did become serious, the split would hurt farm legislation because prior to this, strong presidential leadership had been able to get nonagricultural representatives and senators to vote for farm programs almost as enthusiastically as representatives from farm areas. Mahon indicated that this had led to the charge of a "rubber stamp" Congress, but a Congress broken into factions can accomplish little worthwhile legislation. Stressing how friendly Congress had been to farmers, he pointed out that $500 million had been appropriated to continue AAA payments, a 3.5 percent interest rate was being continued on Federal Land Bank loans, the soil conservation program had expanded, CCC camps were being continued, and the vocational educational program had been liberally expanded. All of this was an indication that President Roosevelt believed an appropriate farm program was essential to the national well-being.[145] He voiced optimism about the accomplishments of the special session.

Later that month Mahon praised a joint meeting of service clubs in Big Spring, Texas, for their strong interest in governmental affairs, emphasizing that was the best way to curb any threat of a dictatorship that they feared Roosevelt might try to establish. The new type of government implemented by Roosevelt was designed to correct a system of exploitation that had flourished in years past. "Social legislation," he said, "was not exploitation, but conservation of our natural and human resources."[146] Defending his loyalty to the Democratic Party and the president, he challenged the audience to name an administration that had done more for West Texas. He also reminded his listeners that he was keenly aware that a representative who does not vote to the benefit of his people will not long endure. He thanked them for not expecting the impossible of him, for understanding the limitations of public officials.

In November the Mahons returned to Washington in time for George to attend a special session of the Seventy-fifth Congress that convened on November 15, 1937. He had spent the previous two months traveling throughout the district, talking with farmers and attending meetings to learn their views about new farm legislation that was to be the first business of the session. After listening to many different views, he concluded that the majority of farmers in the district favored a program with compulsory controls of cotton acreage; a uniform basis of allotment of acreage for each farm in a county; a moderate acreage reduction program; and adjusted payments that were equivalent to parity, which would amount to sixteen cents a pound for seven million bales of domestically consumed cotton. Most West Texas farmers wanted legislation that would encourage the operation of farms by tenants or owners and discourage large corporations that operated with hired labor. Producers also objected to any discrimination against farmers whose land had not been in cultivation over a five- or ten-year period. Mahon told a reporter for the *Abilene Reporter News* that "any bill passed will have to apply to the entire nation, and since the problem is quite different in each locality, the bill which is finally passed will, of necessity, be a compromise between the various groups."[147]

The special session of the Seventy-fourth Congress, which lasted from November 15, 1937, until December 21, 1937, was disappointing to all concerned, especially President Roosevelt. He failed to get final action on an executive reorganization bill, on wages-and-hours standards, on a new farm bill, or on a bill that would create "Seven Little TVAs." The discouraged and dispirited president was not the same man who had calmed the nation's fears and ringmastered the special session of the Hundred Days in 1933. Furthermore, the strain of the previous four years was so severe that many believed they could see it etched in his face.[148] When the session ended, the split over

President Roosevelt's attempted "purge" that had earlier caused concern for Democrats was now deeper. Becoming bipartisan, the opposition issued a "Conservative Manifesto" that was the clear expression of an antigovernment political philosophy. It was the beginning of a powerful conservative counterattack against the expansion of federal authority and federal institutions. "The crystallization of this new conservative ideology, as much as the New Deal that precipitated its articulation, was among the enduring legacies of the 1930s."[149]

The Seventy-fifth Congress, which had convened on January 5, 1937, at the height of the recovery movement, ended in the depths of a depression within a depression. The Third Session, which convened on January 3, 1938, and adjourned on June 16, 1938, was given over to the president's battle for reorganization of the executive branch. Unfortunately, the bitterness and suspicion aroused in the attempt to reorganize the Supreme Court clouded the picture. The Seventy-fifth Congress was a balky and nonproductive one.

As Congress debated, Mahon became disappointed and wrote to one of his constituents, "I feel that the agricultural bill will likely be disappointing to the farmers of our section, but I hope that it will be helpful in many ways. It seems the best that could be worked out in view of the strong conflicts in interests between the various sections of our county."[150] He did, however, secure the passage of an amendment that would prohibit a person from increasing his government payments by dismissing tenants from his lands.

In Texas more than 57 percent of the farmers were tenants. That number exceeded the national average of 42 percent.[151] Tenancy occurred predominately on cotton farms, 70 percent of which were operated by tenants. By 1935 relief roles in rural areas were higher than ever.

The general farm aid bill that passed was the Agricultural Adjustment Act of 1938. According to agricultural historian Murray Benedict, "The 1938 act left the main features of the Soil Conservation and Domestic Allotment Act of 1936 substantially unchanged but spelled out more fully the procedures to be used. It stressed particularly the use of price-support loans and purchases, and authorized the imposition of marketing quotas to regulate the flow of agricultural commodities onto the market."[152]

The secretary of agriculture was authorized to enter into crop production contracts with farmers that determined allotments of soil-depleting crops. The act also authorized parity payments to cotton growers but limited individual payments to ten thousand dollars.

Disappointment with the progress of the agricultural bill just added to an undercurrent of disappointment that Mahon had been experiencing for the past two years. Years later, in an autobiographical sketch, he wrote, "During my second term, my unhappiness and frustration became much more acute. It became apparent that a Representative who was not a member of a major committee, such as Agriculture, Ways and Means, Appropriations, or Judiciary, had very little chance to distinguish himself in important fields. Many Texans had key positions in the House at that time, and there was little chance for a newcomer from Texas. I sought to get in position to become a member on Ways and Means or Appropriations. I made no major effort toward membership on any other committee."[153]

He was also experiencing a letdown from his days as district attorney when he was at the center of the action and was challenged by some of the best attorneys in Texas. The "waiting time" that every new congressman must endure was weighing heavily on him. He continued, "I felt that I was in the big league, but I was not on the team. The sedentary life on the bench did not appeal to me."[154] He turned to colleagues who had mentored him before, such as Sam Rayburn, Marvin Jones, and Ewing Thomason. They encouraged patience and assured him that the time would come when a seat on a major committee would be open to him.

Despite being somewhat depressed, the years of waiting were not without rewards. Staying on the floor regularly, he had a chance to closely watch everything that went on. That would not be an option in later years, when committee meetings were in session both mornings and afternoons. Also, he tried to learn as many of the rules as possible and took pride in being able to call any member of the House by name. He was conscientious in answering letters from constituents, and he regularly read all the district newspapers. Although many miles away, he stayed abreast of the accomplishments and problems of the people he represented.

As soon as Congress adjourned, the Mahons returned to Colorado City, where George reopened his office. Lloyd Croslin and George Witten, Croslin's assistant, were in charge of the office while it was open. Upon arriving, Mahon told a reporter from the *Colorado Record*, "I'm elated over finding this country soaked by recent rains. I'm anxious to get out in the country and get my feet wet."[155] It was already the end of June, and there were many voters to talk to before the July primary.

Mahon's campaign in 1938 was easier than the previous two. He had no opponent. Constituents were well pleased with his acceptance by the national party leadership and his unflagging attention to their needs. A cursory examination of his papers reveals the importance he attached to agricultural legislation. Although he served on the Insular Affairs, Civil Service, and Census and Elections committees, there is very little material in his files to document his work on these committees. In contrast, he saved voluminous and detailed information about every piece of agricultural legislation. Additionally, most of his comments and addresses in the House dealt with farm bills. The Nineteenth District was predominately agricultural, and constituents were grateful for his attention to these matters. He was also helped in the election by a comment to a *Lubbock Morning Avalanche* reporter by Amarillo congressman Marvin Jones, chair of the House Committee on Agriculture. Jones, who was in town to visit relatives, told the reporter that George Mahon "is one of the finest, cleanest and ablest young men in the congress."[156] Additionally, Speaker Bankhead wrote the following letter, and Mahon sent a copy to the editors of most district newspapers. There is no evidence that Mahon requested the letter from Bankhead; however, supporting party members at election time was common practice for party leaders.

My dear Mahon:

Now that the strenuous labors of the last session of the Seventy-fifth Congress have been ended and our records made, I cannot resist an impulse to write you an expression of my deep appreciation of your cordial cooperation with me in carrying forward our program of legislation.

It has been a very genuine personal satisfaction for me to have served with you in the House and no one is in a better position than I to have observed the fidelity, diligence and ability with which you have performed the duties of your office as Representative of your District, and I congratulate you upon the high character of public service you have rendered.

Wishing you a happy and beneficial vacation and with the assurance of my personal esteem and good wishes I am,

Sincerely your friend,
Wm. B. Bankhead, Speaker.[157]

Voters in the Nineteenth Congressional District saw no need to change their representative. However, some other congressmen from Texas did not fare so well. Morgan Sanders from Canton, an eighteen-year veteran in the House, failed to be reelected. He was on the House Ways and Means Committee and was near the chairmanship because of his seniority. His defeat meant a seat on this important committee would likely be open to another member of the Texas delegation, and the Democratic Committee-on-Committees would decide who to endorse for the committee assignment. "In one of the more notable features of the reorganization of Congress in 1911, each party created a committee-on-committees to distribute committee assignments, on the theory, still asserted, that a party committee offers at least an opportunity for all party members to receive suitable assignments."[158] In 1938 the Democratic Committee-on-Committees was composed of the Democratic members of the Ways and Means Committee, the speaker, and the majority floor leader. At this time Sam Rayburn was the majority floor leader and the senior member of the Texas delegation; thus, his endorsement was crucial.

In addition to sponsoring tax legislation, the House Ways and Means Committee also appointed a committee-on-committees that elected members to other House committees. Mahon discreetly expressed his interest in filling the seat to some of his colleagues, such as House Majority Leader Sam Rayburn, Bob Poage of Waco, and Ewing Thomason of El Paso. All agreed to support him, especially Ewing Thomason. Wright Patman, who also wanted the seat, made his wishes public and began writing to members of the delegation for support. Patman had just been reelected for his sixth term in the House and was the twelfth-ranking member of the Banking and Currency Committee. Milton West from Brownsville, who had just won reelection for his fourth term, also threw his hat in the ring.

During the summer of 1938, Rayburn came to Colorado City, Texas, to confer with Mahon in his home. He was concerned that there might be a struggle within the Texas delegation for the seat on the Ways and Means Committee. Rayburn reminded Mahon that the road would not be smooth. After the meeting Rayburn wrote, "I am now as I have been for you for anything you want and can get. I think it will be an easy matter for you to get this place unless we get caught up in the seniority swirl which will be made by Wright Patman in order to get the endorsement of the Texas Delegation to Ways and Means Committee."[159] On August 23 Mahon wrote to Ewing Thomason, "Sam has been very friendly toward me, but I realize that he could not afford to insist upon my election to the Ways and Means Committee in view of developments."[160]

Mahon knew only too well what this meant. Two years before he had asked for a place on the Appropriations Committee but had withdrawn his request rather than get into a struggle with W. D. McFarlane of Graham, Texas, who represented the Thirteenth District and had also wanted the seat. McFarlane had seniority over Mahon. Now McFarlane had been forced into a runoff election for his congressional seat, and it looked as if he would lose. Once again, rather than cause a rift within the Texas delegation, Mahon decided to seek a seat on the Appropriations Committee if McFarlane was not reelected. This would not be a disappointment to him as his long-term goal had been a seat on one of the two committees. "We had an agreement in the Texas delegation that when an opening came up that might be assigned to Texas, the senior man was supported, generally speaking. There were some that tried to break that rule, from time to time, and it had been broken successfully a time or two but not too often. So I bided my time and things broke for me and I got to be a member of the Appropriations Committee."[161] McFarlane did not win reelection, and Mahon had the support of the Democratic Committee-on-Committees and the Texas delegation for the assignment that he wanted. Instinctively, he knew that playing by the rules instead of trying to beat the system was the best approach for the long haul, and he wanted to remain in Congress for many more years.

Although Mahon was personally concerned about the final outcome of the congressional elections in Texas, many others in the nation were concerned about presidential interference in the elections of Southern conservative Democrats who were not supportive of President Roosevelt's New Deal programs. The president tried to purge them from Congress. "No American President since Andrew Johnson had taken a more active part in congressional elections."[162] The triumph of the conservative Democrats over the candidates that FDR supported hurt the New Deal cause. The failure to purge these men "revealed that Roosevelt, though personally popular, could not transfer his popularity to those he supported."[163] Furthermore, his attempted purge further intensified the liberal-conservative split within the Democratic Party. This encouraged conservatives to stand their ground more strongly and damaged Roosevelt's prestige. "The most important change was the huge Republican gain in the House."[164] In the new Congress, when the conservative Democrats joined forces with the Republicans, the coalition could stop bills that were considered too liberal. In the years to come, Mahon often voted in tandem with the conservative coalition. However, he was careful to vote with the Democrats when the fate of a bill was being decided strictly along party lines. As a representative from a one-party state, he understood that completely ignoring the needs of the Democratic Party would be fatal to his career.

Chapter 3

The World on Fire: 1939–1945

T he opening of the Seventy-sixth Congress on January 3, 1939, marked the beginning of a new direction in Mahon's career. During the annual Democratic caucus before the opening of Congress, there had been a heated debate about the two vacancies on the House Committee on Appropriations. Some members strongly believed that Texas already had more than its share of seats on important committees and the openings should go to other states. However, not everyone agreed with that, and two Texans fought hard to see that one of the seats would be offered to George Mahon. House Majority Leader Sam Rayburn and Milton West of the Texas Fifteenth Congressional District, the same district that former vice president John Nance Garner had represented, were very active on his behalf. Democrats seeking appointment to a particular committee had to have the blessings of Sam Rayburn and the support of members of the Ways and Means Committee. West was a member of the Ways and Means Committee, and Rayburn had promised to support Mahon in 1936 and again after the mid-term elections in 1938 if Mahon would abide by the rule of seniority, which meant waiting his turn. In the caucus Rayburn and West successfully encouraged party leaders to closely examine Mahon's performance in Congress—his willingness to work long hours and to assume responsibility. His record was found to be in good standing, and while his votes were not just a rubber stamp for every bill the administration tried to get through the House, his dissenting votes did not cast any shadow of doubt on his loyalty to the Democratic Party. Indeed, in 1939 only six of the twenty-three Texans in Congress voted with the administration on all bills.[1] Mahon and Nat Patton (D-TX), representative of the Seventh Congressional District, were the only two who voted against the administration on only a single occasion. Mahon's drive, party loyalty, and the strong support from Sam Rayburn won him the recommendation of the caucus for a seat on the Appropriations Committee. His official appointment came from the Ways and Means Committee, with strong support from Milton West.

The House Committee on Appropriations had been created on March 2, 1865, just before the end of the Civil War. At that time some of the duties of the Ways and Means Committee were given to two new standing committees, Appropriations and Banking and Currency. "The rationale for the creation of an Appropriations Committee was the growing inability of the Ways and Means Committee to perform its two traditional tasks of raising revenue and allocating appropriations."[2] The workload had increased greatly as a result of expenditures during the Civil War. In addition to redistributing the workload, Congress was trying to hold appropriations down as much as possible, especially because strenuous demands for money were increasing. It was believed that the closer scrutiny of appropriations, guided by a more single-minded group performing this operation, would produce a more efficient government.[3]

The jurisdiction of the Committee on Appropriations is fixed by clause 3 of Rule XI of the House of Representatives. It provides that all proposed legislation on matters relating "to the appropriation of the revenue for the support of the Government" shall be referred to this committee. Other rules exist to govern "riders" that are attached to appropriation bills to ensure that they retrench expenditures or place genuine limitations on the expenditure of money in a general appropriation bill.[4] Each January the president sends a proposed federal budget to Congress, and the first body to act on it is the House Committee on Appropriations. Appropriation bills "originate in the House by virtue of tradition rather than by constitutional prerogative. But tradition has legitimized that and fixed a sequence for appropriation bills that is equally inflexible."[5]

Over the years since its creation, the political power of the Appropriations Committee has waxed and waned. Taking seriously its mandate to restrain extravagant and illegal appropriations, the original committee reduced the national debt but became unpopular within a few years. Jealousy over the power to disburse money grew in the House and among executive departments until disgruntled members finally reduced the responsibilities of the Appropriations Committee. By 1880 appropriations for agriculture and rivers and harbors was handled through the legislative committees,[6] and on December 18, 1885, responsibility for six more appropriation bills was given to legislative committees. This left only six of the original fourteen bills with the Appropriations Committee, which led to "extravagance and confusion . . . There was little, if any, coordinated consideration of the overall needs and condition of the finances."[7]

By 1920 the drawbacks of this system were obvious to the whole country. Waste and extravagance were the result of legislative committees simply going their own way instead of working in tandem to allocate the nation's money efficiently. On June 1, 1920, there was a reconsolidation of jurisdiction over all appropriations in the Committee on Appropriations. The following year the Budget and Accounting Act was passed, establishing the national executive budget system and creating the General Accounting Office. These were "unquestionably, the most fundamental and consequential national fiscal reforms since 1885."[8] Incredible as it might have been, roughly 120 years after the government was organized, the United States was the only major nation of the world that had not yet established a national budget system. When Mahon took his seat on the House Appropriations Committee, its jurisdiction had not changed since the reconsolidation of 1920.

The committee is expected to help the House attain its monetary goals. This involves a two-step process: passing a bill in Congress to authorize a program or activity, and then passing a bill to allocate money to fund that program or activity. As Richard Fenno explains, "The Committee is not expected to appropriate every last nickel requested. But it is not expected to vote so little money that the program, as conceived by the House, cannot survive."[9] Appropriating an insufficient amount of money to allow the program to survive would be, in effect, legislating, and the committee is not authorized to do this. However, there is great room for differences of opinion about what constitutes "sufficient" and "survival." Conflict can, and often does, arise over a program or activity that might have to be reduced in size due to a smaller appropriation than was originally requested. This happens because the committee is aware that although its duty is to appropriate money to fund a program that already has the support of Congress, it is expected to fund the program as economically as possible. In order to fund a program economically, the committee is given discretion to stretch the limits, and in stretching these limits it acquires considerable influence; however, this influence should not reduce a program or activity to the point of prohibiting the enactment of legislation already passed.

When Mahon became a member of the House Committee on Appropriations, the painstakingly detailed work of the committee was done by ten subcommittees.[10] Requests for money to be appropriated by each subcommittee arrived in bill form with detailed information about the history of previous appropriations, estimates of anticipated expenditures, and explanatory schedules. The pertinent House legislative committees also submitted supplemental data to justify the expenditures, which amounted to a fiscal and factual explanation of the necessity and purpose of each proposed appropriation. In addition, each appropriations subcommittee conducted hearings at which representatives of the relative department, or agency, were questioned to secure additional information that subcommittee members believed was necessary to develop policies and purposes for the appropriated money. A stenographer recorded and transcribed the hearings, which were published in a separate volume. The work of a subcommittee often took six weeks or longer, and the printed hearings frequently exceeded several thousand printed pages. When their work was finished, the subcommittee chairman presented a report of the bill to the full committee along with a printed report and a printed copy of the hearings. The full committee then considered the bill, adopted such amendments as it deemed necessary, and reported the bill to the House. An appropriation bill was given early consideration when it was put on the House calendar, the scheduling system for moving bills to the House floor for debate and a vote. The procedure remains basically the same to this day.

Members then were—and continue to be—selected for the Appropriations Committee based on several characteristics designed to ensure the overall stability of the committee. A potential member must be a responsible legislator who will conform to the basic House norms, both formal and informal; be a person who will seek consensus and be responsive to the legislation passed by the House; must understand that the committee is dependent upon the House and be willing to share information with other House members; be a person who is willing to work hard at legislative tasks without expecting public recognition (hard work becomes their badge of identity); be a member from a "safe district,"[11] so reelection concerns will not overshadow House concerns; be a person whose working style is based on cooperation, mutual respect, and the ability to compromise; be a person who works well with party leaders; and someone who represents a geographical distribution of party strength.[12]

Traditionally, there has been a great esprit de corps in the committee. Working together, day after day, creates a tightly knit group whose members are willing to do favors for each other, including voting together. Fenno explains: "The sense of Committee unity, of in-group solidarity fostered by the style of hard work brings immense satisfaction to individual Committee members. They will behave, therefore, in ways calculated to preserve it."[13]

Because the committee controls the purse strings it wields considerable power, but if its actions anger the House, the jurisdiction of the committee can be severely curtailed. Although the committee exists to serve, that service commands great respect because, as Fenno observes, "A desire for economy in government may well be among the most durable strands of American public opinion."[14]

In 1789 the first appropriations bill was a single bill that covered thirteen lines in the statutes and allocated $639,000 for the expense of running the nation. By 1939, when Mahon was appointed to the committee, the federal budget had risen to $9,492,329,000,[15] and history has proven that the end was nowhere in sight.

Mahon hoped to be assigned to one of the major subcommittees, perhaps the Subcommittee on Agricultural Appropriations. Once again, he had to serve an internship, and committee chairman Edward T. Taylor (D-CO) assigned him to two lesser subcommittees: the District of Columbia and the Treasury and Post Office.[16] The Subcommittee on Appropriations for the District of Columbia, along with the House Committee on the District of Columbia, was one of the least desirable of the lot because Washingtonians couldn't vote so there was no electorate, nor were there dams, highways, or federal projects with which to reward the constituents and gain votes for good service. Also, while Mahon was taking care of the District of Columbia it would be difficult to take care of his own Nineteenth District. Since 1801 Washington had been governed directly by Congress, and not until 1878 did Congress set up a system whereby the president, as part of his patronage, appointed three commissioners to be responsible for running the city. Presidents seldom paid much attention to these appointments, with the result that through the years political operatives came to dominate, showing a consistent disregard for city affairs, except to give their friends appointments to city departments.[17] This continued until 1967, when the appointed commissioners were supplanted by an elected mayor and city council.

Mahon expressed his disappointment to Chairman Taylor, who replied, "Be a good soldier and when an opportunity comes for you, I will give you a break."[18] Despite his impatience, appointment to the District of Columbia subcommittee provided exactly the experience he needed. When the subcommittee chairman, Ross Collins, resigned later in 1939, Chairman Taylor asked

Mahon to take over and he accepted. Although Representative Casey, a Democrat from Massachusetts, had seniority in Congress, the seniority rule was not binding in the appointment of a subcommittee chairman. Both Mahon and Casey were freshmen on the Appropriations Committee.[19]

Historically, the responsibilities of the chair had not been considered very demanding. Mahon was expected to take care of subcommittee business, chair the meetings, and report on the annual budget. Generally, the group worked on the annual bill for several weeks and near the end of the cycle of appropriation bills took it to the floor for debate and passage. As a rule, few amendments were offered during the debate, which took only a few hours and attracted few members. Unless Mahon committed some blunder, or failed to do his homework, he could expect few problems. This was an excellent opportunity to gain experience as a subcommittee chairman, and he served in this position until December 1943.

The District of Columbia subcommittee faced problems for which there were no good solutions. In 1939 Congress passed a law fixing the federal government's contribution to the city at $6 million per year. The remainder of the $55 million city budget had to come from city business and other local taxes. This was a problem in light of the influx of tens of thousands of war workers each year, which created a demand for more schools, roads, sewer lines, and all the other needs of a growing city. Before World War II Washington had been a southern country town of approximately sixty-five thousand that members of Congress left before the inevitable heat and humidity of summer. The "cave dwellers," wealthy old-time residents on Massachusetts Avenue, also fled to their country homes in Maryland and Virginia.[20] By the later stages of World War II, the population had grown to over a million, but Congress provided little help. One member of the House, a persistent critic, thought they should cut out the $6 million grant and leave the city to its own devices. Another wanted to substitute a tax on all federal property in the District. Still another wanted to charge tuition for all children from Virginia and Maryland who were taught in the District schools.

Under Mahon's leadership the subcommittee took its responsibilities seriously and worked diligently to deal with the problems. Members actually toured the schools, hospitals, police, and fire departments to learn how they operated. Trying to find enough money to solve District problems proved to be a valuable experience for Mahon. When taking the proposed budget to the House floor, he pointed out that the annual grant had been fixed by law, thus ending the debate. He shot down a proposal to tax federal property in the District by reminding the House that states and cities would drool at the thought of being able to tax federal customs houses, hospitals, and other federal properties. He pointed out, calmly, that this would cost hundreds of millions of dollars annually, thus squashing that proposal. He lost the tuition battle, however. Congress might overlook the other aspects of city government, but children of members living outside the District came to the city's schools, and they didn't want the expense of tuition.[21]

Mahon believed that Washington was the capital of the greatest nation on earth and that it should be maintained as the most beautiful one. Unfortunately, that was difficult to do with a Congress that thought only of cutting expenses and using the savings to strengthen defense in light of a European war that was gaining in intensity. The editor of the *Washington Post* was grateful for Mahon's interest, and after he had been on the job for two years, the editor wrote, "It is the District's good fortune that Mr. Mahon has had some experience dealing with municipal problems of the Nation's Capital and that he is a straight-forward, fair-minded young man who wants to give the District a 'square deal.' . . . Those who know Mr. Mahon have no doubt that he will work conscientiously in the position to which he has been assigned."[22]

Residents of Washington were not prepared for the problems caused by the huge influx of people in the years leading up to World War II. As David Brinkley observes in his book, *Washington Goes to War*, "Their placid, comfortable town was becoming a noisy, crowded, expensive city—a place that newcomers liked to joke combined the charm of the North with the efficiency of the South."[23] New construction helped alleviate the problem of new arrivals, but sometimes not even streets or sewers existed. In one section of the city, a new school had been built but was overcrowded as soon as it opened. In another, funds had been allocated but starting construction was not a priority. Additional police stations were needed, but even if they could be funded, suitable men were not available to recruit as policemen. Several thousand families were on welfare, but there never was enough money for them all, and for those who did receive help, the money was well below the average for other cities. At committee meetings, the room was filled with people who came to complain about these problems and others. In addition there were the undesirable "alley dwellings," where many African Americans settled as they fled from the South to take the menial jobs they needed and were allowed to have. Whole families crowded into windowless rooms only big enough for one person and without lights or plumbing. Dirt streets became quagmires in wet weather. Open-air privies served as toilets, several thousand of them made from barrels sunk into the ground.[24] Still the people came, sometimes as many as seventy thousand in a year, often with families in tow. Mahon's committee faced a continuing stream of city officials and representatives of civic organizations who complained of increasing problems caused by the never-ending influx of people. Members of the House liked to complain on the floor that their constituents had been treated poorly, especially by government, when they came to the city. With that they pretended to have satisfied their responsibility without offering solutions for the chaos that seemed to be bearing down on the District.

Despite the problems in some parts of the city, life in high society continued pretty much as usual, and Mahon received a lot of ink in the press because of his reaction to it. Late in 1942, dollar-a-year man Bernard Baruch gave a lavish dinner party at the Carlton Hotel.[25] The *New York Journal American* reported it on December 21, 1942, with pictures and glowing details. Leading government officials attended, including Office of Price Administration head Leon Henderson, as well as War Production chief Donald M. Nelson, and economic director James F. Byrnes. Harry Hopkins, one of President Roosevelt's closest advisors, and his new wife, were honored guests at the dinner. When Mahon read about the party and letters began to pour into his office complaining about it, he promptly wrote Henderson, requesting that he include rules that would prohibit such elaborate dinners in the food-rationing program he was soon to announce. The dinner had included caviar, baked oysters, and cold tongue among other delicacies. Rare French champagne was served, as well as expensive French wine. Because the average citizen was often not able to buy even the staple cuts of beef and other ordinary foods, Mahon wrote that he could not agree with anyone serving such grand dinners. "Apparently foods of the choicest varieties have been served with lavish splendor and prodigality reminiscent of prewar days. . . . I think the average American citizen is abundantly willing to economize on foods and even to go hungry occasionally if this will help win the war. But fair play is not only right, it helps morale and promotes national unity which is so essential at this time."[26] Just for good measure he sent a copy to Agriculture Secretary Claude R. Wickard. His letter reached the newspapers and was copied around the nation, along with accounts of the dinner. In a letter to Lubbock newspaper editor Charles Guy, Mahon expressed some concern that his reaction might be seen as the work of a publicity hound, but he believed his response to the forty-dollar-a-plate dinner and the headlines it stirred up were amply justified, especially since many grocery shelves in Washington were empty.[27] Party leaders recognized that seeking publicity had not been one of Mahon's priorities when they appointed him to the House Appropriations Committee; however, they also knew, since he had spoken on the House floor about his irritation with the manner in which the Pathe News Service portrayed West Texas as a dust bowl in 1935, that Mahon would speak out when he thought the public needed to be better informed about a situation.

In September 1939 Mahon moved his district office from Colorado City to Lubbock because it was more centrally located and the fastest-growing city in the Nineteenth District. In an interview with a *Lubbock Morning Avalanche* reporter that month, Mahon said he thought the American people held a deep-seated belief that American soldiers should not be sent to fight in any foreign country. He stated that he believed Europe had been embroiled in controversies for hundreds of years, and the United States should stay out of them. They had plenty of men, and what they really needed was supplies. "I think we ought to trade with all alike, and thus stay out of trouble. Let them come here and get it at the water's edge, and let the responsibility be theirs from there on."[28] He went on to say how personally satisfied he was that Congress had appropriated a billion and a half dollars to build up the US military forces. He believed US troops could defend and preserve the integrity and security of America. However, President Roosevelt more realistically alluded to the part the United States would have to play in world affairs when he said in his 1940 State of the Union address, "I can also understand the wishfulness of those who oversimplify the whole situation by repeating that all we have to do is to mind our own business and keep the nation out of war. But there is a vast difference between keeping out of war and pretending that this war is none of our business."[29]

Until the late 1940s there was a strong current of isolationism in American thought. From the days of George Washington, the nation had put its faith in isolation, believing the oceans would be adequate protection from the type of aggression that had caused problems in Europe for centuries. Emphasis was put on a navy that could keep potential enemies away from the country's shores. When danger did seem imminent, citizens were drafted, and after the fighting was over, they returned to civilian life, leaving only a very small military force intact. World War I was a good example. After peace had been declared, the armed forces were allowed to lapse into obscurity. In the National Defense Act of 1920, Congress had authorized an army of 280,000 along with a reserve program, but during the 1920s and 1930s Congress failed to appropriate enough money to fund that many personnel. Army personnel usually hovered somewhere between 130,000 and 190,000. In fact, total appropriations never reached $500 million for the army and navy together.

During the 1920s and 1930s the idealism of President Wilson, as well as the idea of participating in any international peacekeeping organization, created a certain amount of fear in the minds of many Americans. Memories of World War I were still troublesome to many, and they were determined not to become involved in another global conflict. They believed neutrality and a weak military would keep the nation out of future wars. Many writers and lecturers argued that our involvement in World War I was a mistake, brought on by the propaganda of international bankers and arms dealers who wanted to line their pockets with excessive war profits. Americans were encouraged to look inward, letting the rest of the world go its own way, which was easy to do, because their attention was focused on problems at home, especially the Great Depression that caused widespread suffering for nearly a decade.

Beginning in 1934 Senator Gerald P. Nye of North Dakota held extensive hearings that produced volumes of evidence accusing bankers and arms dealers of leading the nation into war simply to gain profits. Although the reliability of the evidence was questionable, the isolationists in Congress heard exactly what they wanted to hear, and the accusations of profiteering caused such apprehension that armaments manufacturers were reluctant to accept government contracts. The anxiety caused by these hearings, coupled with the invasion of Ethiopia by Mussolini, brought on the first Neutrality Act in 1935. The act prohibited the sale of arms materials to belligerent nations and warned US citizens not to expect protection if they traveled on ships belonging to any party involved in war. It was hoped this legislation would isolate the United States from European problems. A year later the second Neutrality Act extended the first one and also prohibited loans to belligerent nations. In 1937 another act tightened the previous ones by making it unlawful to travel on ships registered in belligerent countries and authorizing the president to restrict sales of all items to cash-and-carry on ships belonging to the purchasing nation. Munitions were not to be sold under any circumstances.

After Hitler invaded Austria in 1938, President Roosevelt, though continuing to profess neutrality, believed that ultimately the United States would have to halt the dictator's march. He also believed it was wise to begin rearming by using funds formerly spent on emergency relief measures.[30] This would help bring the country completely out of the Depression, and he hoped to persuade the American people to accept this shift of funds by arguing that it would protect US borders. The shift could also provide aid to combatants who were sympathetic with American policies. Hopefully, Southern and Western congressmen could be persuaded to accept rearmament in lieu of public works projects, if this shift were accompanied by expressions of determination to stay out of war. In 1939, as Hitler's aggressions continued and the crisis deepened, Congress repealed the embargo on arms shipments and authorized the export of munitions to belligerents on a cash-and-carry basis only. Buyer nations would pay cash for nonmilitary commodities that would be transported on their ships. "There was never a sharp turning point when Roosevelt's absorption with domestic matters left off and his concern for foreign affairs began. Despite the President's later talk about shifting roles from 'Dr. New Deal' to 'Dr. Win the War,' the fitful rush of events would allow no simple shift. While Roosevelt was struggling with recession in March 1938, the Nazis overran Austria. While he was still trying to purge conservative Democrats later that year, Hitler charged into the Sudetenland. While the President was jousting with a rebellious Congress in 1939, Hitler swallowed the rest of Czechoslovakia and turned his eyes in new directions."[31] President Roosevelt believed he clearly understood Prime Minister Churchill's warning that if the United States failed to help England, it would soon be overrun by Hitler and the Americans would be left to fight the Nazis alone. If that happened, neither the Atlantic nor the Pacific Ocean would be the protective barriers they had been in times past.

From his earliest years in Congress, Mahon supported neutrality legislation. Although he did not join in debating the issues as each piece of legislation came before the House, he voted in favor of each act. As late as 1939 he was sure the United States could, and should, stay out of any conflict between other nations.

A steady stream of mail poured into Mahon's congressional office concerning the issue of neutrality. Mahon was in favor of the cash-and-carry plan that allowed any nation to buy nonmilitary products if it paid cash and transported the products in its own ships. This plan was intended to avoid the type of event that historian David M. Kennedy believes "had led to war in 1917, when German U-boat attacks on American ships, and the alleged desire to protect American loans, had apparently made war inevitable."[32] One constituent wrote:

For your information will state that from my contacts with people in all walks of life in West Texas and all over the state for that matter I find that about 95% or more are in favor of the so called cash and carry plan which the President had advocated.

Many people think the Isolationist group in the Senate is playing Politics, or most of them, the others fighting it because the President is for it. As the writer sees it we are an ally of Hitler under the present neutrality law and the great majority of our people hope that Hitler will not run a bluff over our United States Congress as he has done over the small Countries of Europe.

It would be a great consolation to Germany if the new neutrality bill should be defeated. Hitler is watching the United States Congress closer than he is watching the western front.[33]

Mahon replied, "I am firmly convinced that you are correct in assuming that practically everybody in our section of Texas is favorable toward the recommendation of the President as to neutrality. I voted with him on this subject when it came up at the last session, and I shall vote with him again at this session. I think the House will take the measure up for consideration and probably finish it before the end of the week."[34] Another constituent wrote:

Geo. I notice from the press that you are in favor of changing the neutrality law as the Pres. wants and in my humble opinion that is the entering wedge into the war.

Geo. This is one time that Cash and Carry is the same as declaring open hostility on Germany for we know they do not have the money and we know that they do not have the ships to come for the goods.

What did France or England ever do for us that we should mess up in their wars and fight for them? I served 13 months trying to save Democracy and now they want it did again. I am ready to enlist in the service to day to defend this country against any people on earth but I am not in favor of fighting their fight.

Geo. There is only one way to be neutral, and that is to be absolutely neutral, Cash and carry is the entering wedge and looks to me that it is planned that way by the munitions and arms Mfgs.[35]

Mahon answered, "It is impossible to know just what turn the legislative situation will take here, but I am certainly hoping that in the end a reasonably satisfactory neutrality law may be worked out. I cannot express too strongly my opposition to involvement in the European war. I think we are crazy if we permit ourselves to be dragged into this European controversy which has been raging in one form or another for scores of years. Frankly, I do not believe we are going to get into it. I find on every hand here among officials a determination to stay out of the European trouble."[36]

In the 1940 election Republicans played on the antiwar and anti–New Deal sentiment as much as possible. They had been gaining seats in each election since 1936, and by the fall of 1940, they needed only forty-eight more to capture control of the House. Democratic incumbents had little time to campaign because the Seventy-sixth Congress remained in session for 366 days, the longest in history. Also, their war chests were rapidly dwindling. Members from single-party states, such as Mahon, remained in Washington through September and October to keep Congress in session and be ready to respond if international developments required congressional action.

Adding to the troubles of Democrats, a power struggle was growing within the Democratic Party between the faction that supported President Roosevelt and the faction that supported Vice President Garner. The Roosevelt faction was committed to having Negroes vote everywhere. They were part of the group described as the ill-used one-third, and that one-third was an important power base for the New Deal. Large Negro colonies existed mainly in the North, but the Roosevelt faction hoped to end the various devices used in the South to restrict black votes. The Garner faction feared this idea. Control of local elections and states' rights had always been basic political tenets for Southern Democrats. An additional concern was the fact that the 1936 convention in Philadelphia had abolished the two-thirds rule for selecting a presidential candidate. In the past, Southern Democrats, with almost one-third of the delegates, had veto power. After the change, a candidate only needed a bare majority and was not as dependent on the blessings of the Southern coalition. Although Roosevelt and Garner tried to prevent the situation from becoming an open power struggle, New Deal and traditional Democrats were not simply separate wings of the same party; they held contradictory concepts of government and society.[37]

Mahon was sympathetic to the Garner faction; however, he voted with the administration when he could do so with what he called "a clean conscience,"

which meant when his vote was compatible with the majority of his constituents. As stated earlier, in 1939 he had voted against the administration on
only one bill. He tried to be loyal to President Roosevelt; however, he believed
his first and strongest loyalty was to the American system of government and
his second to his constituents, most of whom were opposed to civil rights for
blacks.

In an interview conducted in 1980, after his retirement, Mahon remembered,
"The war clouds in Europe were becoming more and more ominous. One day
Edward Taylor, the aging Chairman of the Appropriations Committee, said to
me, 'Young man, I want to put you on the War Department Subcommittee on
Appropriations. There is controversy over buying a number of planes. Whether they should try to prepare for 5,000 . . . and I would like for you to serve
on this committee.'"[38] Mahon replied that he knew nothing about the mili-
tary and had no military service because he had been too young to serve in
World War I, but Taylor told him that didn't make any difference. Mahon then
asked for time to consider the offer. Immediately, he found Sam Rayburn and
Ewing Thomason and asked their opinion about accepting this assignment
with no military background. Both told him to take it and take it quickly.[39]
They emphasized that the world situation was such that the War Department
Subcommittee could become a very important subcommittee. Being veterans
of Congress, they also understood that Mahon was being appointed to the
subcommittee because it was likely that Taylor believed he could encourage
him to vote the way the chairman wished. They also knew Mahon's ultimate
success on the committee would not depend as much on his knowledge of
military affairs or economics as it would on the approval of the chairman,
along with seniority. Mahon was from a "safe district," one that had a single party, and as long as national Democratic leaders were satisfied with his
performance, they would continue to support him publicly in his district as
well as in Congress, thus assuring him an opportunity to gain more seniority.
In light of these factors, Rayburn and Thomason could see this would be an
assignment with great potential for success. This was, in fact, the break that
Chairman Taylor had promised at the time of appointing him to the District
of Columbia subcommittee.

Mahon reported back to Chairman Taylor that he would be pleased to
receive the appointment, which became effective June 1, 1940. Forty years

later he was still telling people, "This had a very important impact on my Congressional career."[40] According to an article in *Fortune* magazine in 1958, Mahon had been hoping and waiting for a seat on the Agricultural Appropriations subcommittee because he believed he could help his constituents most from that position. However, "A deadlock developed in the six-man subcommittee on the Army [which included the Army Air Corps at that time] over whether to appropriate for 3,000 or 5,000 planes. Chairman Taylor favored the higher figure. When he learned that Mahon felt the same way, he enlarged the subcommittee to seven members and appointed Mahon to the vacancy."[41] Though Mahon was somewhat confused over being assigned to a subcommittee about whose work he knew nothing, there was logic to this action. In keeping with the broad budget-cutting goal of the Committee on Appropriations, the chairman and ranking minority members deliberately appointed individuals to subcommittees where little, or no, clientele interest existed. Members who lacked a major stake in the appropriations of an agency would be more likely to cut where it is needed.[42] As Fenno explains, "Putting men on subcommittees where they have a vested interest in the subject matter should be avoided wherever possible. However, it is hardly possible to find anyone whose constituency interest is completely disassociated from all activities for which appropriations are made. The factor of objectivity is one of the considerations in making selections."[43]

In 1939 a $293,985,547 appropriation bill for the War Department came out of Senate and House conference and was sent to the president for his signature. It provided for the purchase of fifty-five hundred planes for the Army Air Corps. Among other provisions, the bill provided for five new major air bases to be located in Panama, Alaska, and Puerto Rico, and two in the United States.[44] President Roosevelt believed that aerial warfare would cost less money and fewer lives and be more likely to succeed than traditional land and sea strategies. "Pursuant to that aim, Roosevelt asked Congress in January 1939 for a special appropriation of $300 million for aircraft construction. That request marked the decidedly modest origins of a rearmament program that would in time pour forth an avalanche of weaponry,"[45] writes David M. Kennedy. The nation was beginning to understand the danger it faced from the European war, and Congress was debating whether to put more money into military preparations.

On June 18, 1940, a second supplemental bill to cover emergency items that were needed before the end of the fiscal year was reported to the House.

The bill was for nearly $58 million and when combined with appropriations already approved would bring federal expenses to $15.3 billion, nearly $2.2 billion below that initially requested in the budget for the year. After Representative Taber presented the bill, Mahon asked for the floor, and instead of addressing the bill, he used his time to affirm his support of the House Un-American Activities Committee, chaired by Martin Dies from the Second Congressional District of Texas. Mahon stated that he was pleased with the growing spirit of patriotism in the country and said, "The new spirit of loyalty to our own country goes hand in hand with the determination among all true Americans that the enemy aliens, the followers of false and foreign isms, the so-called 'fifth columnists,' shall be uprooted and banished from the land. . . . Our citizens will not tolerate the existence of a 'fifth column' in this country."[46] He went on to say that the so-called Dies Committee had caught the imagination of the American people, and "it would be impossible to exaggerate the wholesome influences which have been generated by the committee."[47]

Many people disagreed that the influence of the Dies Committee was wholesome. It was accused of spending time going after New Dealers in President Roosevelt's administration and liberal thinkers in the artistic community rather than those suspected of being enemy aliens. There were many complaints that Dies would not investigate the Ku Klux Klan because of his ties with the Texas Klan. In answering a constituent complaint about his support of the committee, Mahon wrote that "the overwhelming majority of the people in West Texas favor a continuation of the Dies Committee."[48] Martin Dies was born in Colorado City, Texas, and was a protégé of both Sam Rayburn and John Nance Garner, just as Mahon was. This may explain some of Mahon's fascination with Dies. In addition to believing that voting against funding the House Un-American Activities Committee would be contrary to the wishes of the majority of his constituents, Mahon also held many of the beliefs that were prevalent throughout rural West Texas, beliefs that contained a great fear of anything foreign or different. West Texans, like many in the Midwest farming belt, had little or no interaction with foreign trade, foreign citizens, or foreign ideas, in contrast to people living in port cities along coastal areas. Mahon's trip to the Philippines in 1935 was enlightening, but it was not long enough to dispel some of his long-held convictions.

In August 1940 Mahon was asked to accompany three other members of the

War Department subcommittee to Alaska to inspect two bases for which $100 million had been designated to strengthen US defenses there. Alaska was within four or five hours' flying time of cities such as Vancouver, Seattle, Portland, and Tacoma. Initially Mahon thought "the trip was not worthwhile and not justifiable."[49] However, subcommittee chairman J. Buell Snyder insisted that he go because the group was scheduled to inspect army posts and equipment all the way across the West and the Southwest on the return trip. Also, they hoped to inspect aircraft factories in Seattle. Snyder believed the information gathered would be very useful because Mahon knew so little about military matters and the War Department subcommittee was responsible for decisions involving billions of dollars for defense installations. Mahon had never flown in a plane before and was concerned that he might suffer from air sickness because he had had trouble climbing the windmill back home to grease it.[50] Dreading the thought of flying, he tried to back out but, ultimately, agreed because subcommittee chairman Buell Snyder assured him that he could leave the group if flying became a problem. On the morning of departure from Bolling Field,[51] he was asked to sign a paper absolving the government of any blame in case of an accident or death. He did this apprehensively and then was required to practice putting on a parachute.[52] After the army transport plane was airborne, he quickly discovered that "flying was not like climbing up a windmill tower."[53] It was, in fact, the thrill of a lifetime—being able to see the beauty of Washington, DC, from the air. His anxiety seemed to subside as he recorded several entries in his journal about the beauty of the land from the air.

The army had constructed airfields at Anchorage, Fairbanks, and Annette Island, but the number of armed forces and the extent to which the United States intended to use the bases for offensive measures were military secrets. Tokyo was within easy range of modern-day bombers. If an aggressor nation gained possession of Alaska, the main body of the United States would be less than 750 miles away, and airplanes made this distance seem even smaller. In fact, Alaska was closer to Tokyo than Tokyo was to Honolulu. Since 1938, the army, navy, and territorial agencies had been working to make Alaska as nearly impregnable as possible.[54] Mahon's group inspected defense installations for which money had been appropriated to determine whether additional money should be appropriated in the next fiscal year.

Mahon was anxious to have the *Congressional Record* indicate that when he failed to vote on bills in the House it was because he was away on an official leave of absence. Ewing Thomason (D-TX) agreed to put in the leave of absence for him, and Mahon advised his secretary, Lloyd Croslin, not to say much about his absence in answering letters. He asked Croslin to just say he was out of town on business for the War Department Appropriations subcommittee. He was concerned that constituents would believe Alaska was outlandishly far away for a trip while Congress was in session.

When Mahon got back to Seattle, he found a long letter from Croslin bringing him up to date on everything that had happened in the office and in the House while he was away. In closing Croslin reported an earlier conversation with Thomason. "He said to tell you that he talked to Frank at Hyde Park the other night and Frank said it would be all right for you to stay away another week if you wanted to . . . that he would try to manage until you'all got back, etc., etc. But he did say that he would like to know if you were coming back by Fort Bliss [located near El Paso, Texas, in Thomason's district] so that he [Thomason] could wire some of the folks there to be on hand. And he also said that if you had a good opportunity that you might make some appropriate remark to the press about their able Congressman and to the effect that Fort Bliss ought to be doubled in size."[55] Obviously his colleague and his office staff were having a good laugh at Mahon's expense about his reluctance to fly and also to be away while Congress was in session. Mahon, however, was thankful just to have his feet back on US soil, and he recorded in his journal, "I stole away [from the group] to the Presbyterian church to thank the Lord for so wonderful a trip."[56]

While Mahon was making this trip, Helen and Daphne visited with family and friends in Colorado City. They returned to Washington in time to welcome him home. One wonders whether, as he shared his experiences with them, they realized this was just the first of many such trips that in the coming years Mahon would make to gather firsthand information about defense appropriations that were being spent at various locations. In addition to providing necessary information, each trip expanded his horizons and political perspective, broadening his focus to include national needs, rather than primarily regional ones.

Although Mahon had a lot to learn about defense, he already knew the importance of looking after the welfare of his district. In May he wrote to Major General Brees, commanding officer of the Eighth Corps Area at Fort Sam Houston, asking that he consider Lubbock or Big Spring for the location of air corps facilities that were part of the military expansion then taking place.

After pointing out the advantages of each city, such as favorable weather for flying, adequate transportation, and cooperation with the Civil Aeronautics Authority Student Pilot Training Program at Texas Technological College, he wrote:

> It is my sincere conviction that the area offers unusual advantages for a location of air corps activity, such as pilot training facilities, a mechanic's training center, and air corps depot for re-fueling, supplies, shops, and so forth. I do not know, of course, what problems you will have to work out in the contemplated expansion of the air corps, but I believe that the advantages offered by this area merit consideration for a part of the programs.
>
> I want to assure you that all local authorities as well as myself will stand ready at all times to cooperate fully with you and your staff in the formulation of any plans which might involve these cities.[57]

Although he was not successful, this was the first of many attempts to encourage the location of military facilities in his district.

Speaker William B. Bankhead died on September 15, 1940, and for the third time in eight years, a new speaker had to be selected. This time, when Mahon voted for Sam Rayburn he didn't have to wonder whether it was the wise thing to do. Having been majority leader for many years, Rayburn was the natural choice, and he went on to hold the position of speaker for twenty-one years, longer than anyone else. In November 1940 President Roosevelt was elected to a third term. He was faced with a build-up to war and domestic conflicts endemic to the New Deal and its critics.

Throughout 1941, defense industries were plagued with strikes. During early October thirty-one strikes and one lockout, involving more than 21,630 employees, held up work on defense projects.[58] Many Americans were confused and angry about the reluctance of the president to ask Congress for legislation supporting government seizure of companies where strikers were hindering defense production. Constituent mail was heavy from West Texans, who were angry that their sons were serving in the military for twenty-one dollars per month, while defense workers, who were exempt from military service and were making more money, decided to strike in favor of even higher wages.

Mahon agreed. On April 3, 1941, he spoke on the House floor against the strikes saying:

> Mr. Speaker, this conference report provides for more than $4,000,000,000 additional for national defense. I think the appropriation is in the public interest and I am for it, and I am for such taxes as may be necessary to raise all or part of that sum. However, I share the view of the overwhelming majority of the Members of this Congress when I say that I want this money spent right and without waste or graft, and spent promptly for the defense of this country.
>
> I believe the American people are tired of having their pleas for action in regard to the slow-up of the national defense answered with the statement that the situation is being investigated. The patience of the people is about exhausted. What the people of this Nation want is action—and action now. [Applause.]
>
> I say that this hold-up of our national defense is nothing short of an outrage against the public welfare of our Nation. I hope the Mediation Board will act, and I hope the President will act and act with increasing firmness and promptitude. As for myself, I am ready for the Congress to supplement investigation with action—and action now—for the defense of our country.[59]

Mahon's opposition to the strikes partly reflected the anti-union sentiment prevalent in Texas. Although unions were not attempting to organize agricultural workers, even the idea that this might happen was threatening to West Texas farmers. Most farms in the Nineteenth District were family farms, and work consisted primarily of the labor of family members. It was difficult enough to find money to pay migrant laborers to help at the time of harvest, and the thought of having to pay union wages for nonfamily workers caused much concern. The following letter from a constituent and Mahon's answer to a letter from the district judge in Lamesa, Texas, illustrate how emotional the subject of unions and strikes had become in West Texas.

> As a wife of a World War veteran and the mother of a nineteen year old boy that another war is "staring in the face" I am writing to you.
>
> We are so tired of strikes holding up defense industries. Seems there could be something done to stop it. Let our boys go to work in the factories. Most of them would be glad to work, and put these strikers in camps someplace and teach them some patriotism on a dollar per day (or less), just what

the boys get in camps.

My husband says tell you to take our present secretary of labor [Frances Perkins] out in the middle of the Pacific and leave her in a canoe.[60]

On April 29, 1941, Mahon wrote the following answer to District Judge Louis B. Reed:

The people have been greatly incensed over the hold-up in the national defense program. Strikes in key national defense industries have played havoc with several aspects of the program. It has been the disposition of the President to minimize the seriousness of strikes, and Mrs. Roosevelt has, herself, rather ridiculed the idea that strikes were of great consequence. I have been an admirer and supporter of the President for a long time and I speak of him as a friend and not as a critic. I am compelled to say that I think he has been entirely too lax in dealing with the strike situation. I do not know whether he is afraid that he will do more harm than good, or whether he has so many ties with certain groups in labor that he does not feel at liberty to cross them too violently. I prefer to think that he feels that the situation will work out better by the method which he is employing.

Personally, I feel that Mrs. Perkins has been a stumbling block as the Secretary of Labor.[61]

Encouraged by the prospect of warborne prosperity in 1941, leaders of the Congress of Industrial Organizations (CIO) were determined to complete the task of organizing unskilled workers as rapidly as possible. These workers were found mainly in the steel and automotive industries. Historian David M. Kennedy writes, "Labor had two great fears in wartime: that prices would rise while workers' ability to negotiate wage increases would be curtailed and that the great industrial unions born in the 1930s would decompose under the triple burden of management pressure, public hostility, and worker indifference. The isolationism of many union leaders, including conspicuously John L. Lewis, was due, in large part, to their memories of labor's setbacks in the World War I era, when inflation more than ate up all of workers' wages and the mood of hyperpatriotism helped management to crush the AFL's [American Federation of Labor] great membership drives, notably in steel."[62] Moreover, it was unlikely that new workers hired during the war would have the degree of commitment to unionism that union members had. Despite the strikes, most defense workers regularly put in six- or seven-day weeks. In

1944, in a letter to one of the postmasters in his district, Mahon wrote, "John L. Lewis and the CIO have raised a slush fund to defeat all Members of Congress who have opposed strikes and who have voted accordingly. I am on the John L. Lewis 'black list.'"[63]

Strikes continued off and on throughout the war, and Mahon continued his opposition to unions. In 1943 he wrote to his family back in Texas: "Saw Frank Roosevelt April 13 when he dedicated the Jefferson Memorial in Washington. He looked pretty good. I imagine he is pretty worried tonight about the coal strike situation. I have been in favor of showing John L. Lewis for several years that this country did not belong to him and his racketeering gang, but I have been in the minority. I blame the President for not putting Lewis in his place long ago. I wish Lewis might have lost his life today as a substitute for some good American boy who died today in North Africa. If the American people are not mad they ought to be."[64]

On a cold and gloomy Monday President Roosevelt addressed a joint session of Congress, declaring, "Yesterday, December 7, 1941—a date which will live in infamy—the United States of America was suddenly and deliberately attacked by naval and air forces of the Empire of Japan."[65] At the end of his address, Congress declared war against the Imperial Government of Japan.

The Mahon family learned about the attack on Pearl Harbor while returning home from the Naval Academy at Annapolis, Maryland. Sunday afternoon excursions to nearby towns had become a favorite pastime for the family, and trips to the Naval Academy had the added attraction of visiting with the two midshipmen that Mahon, as a representative, was allowed to appoint. About 3:30 p.m. news of the attack flashed over the car radio. "I knew that the President would ask for a declaration of war on the following day, and I knew my vote would be an emphatic 'aye,'" he wrote to his father.[66] For months he had anticipated war, despite his support of neutrality and his claims that the United States could avoid being caught up in the conflict. He dreaded having to vote in favor of becoming entangled in the problems of other nations, but this attack on American soil made the task easier for him to accept, just as it did for many other Americans.

Daphne missed school and went with her parents to the House of Representatives to hear President Roosevelt deliver his message on December 8 and to witness the vote on the war resolution. "It is hard to realize that we have been so close to big events. We will follow events in the Pacific area with even greater interest on account of our 1935 trip to that part of the world,"[67] Mahon wrote. He remembered the pageantry in Manila which the army, under General MacArthur, staged for the congressional delegation attending the inauguration of Philippine president Manuel. In the same letter to his father, Mahon described General MacArthur as "probably the greatest genious [sic] in our Army, certainly an attractive personality."[68]

Four days after the Japanese attack, Americans found themselves in the thick of World War II, when Germany and Italy declared war on the United States. Congress approved an extension of the draft for all men between twenty and forty-four years of age. All men between eighteen and sixty-four had to register, but only those twenty years or older would be called. There was some objection to men under twenty-one actually seeing service, although England had a national conscription bill that required compulsory service by women and men from eighteen and a half to fifty years of age.[69]

As Washington, DC, moved to a wartime footing, many changes became apparent. There was fear of air raids, although there seemed little chance of that happening so far from enemy bases. Mahon wrote to his father on December 14, 1941, that air raid precautions were being taken in the apartment house where he and eight hundred other people lived. "We are to assemble in certain portions of the basement in case of an alarm. I would be in charge of morale in the so-called air raid shelter. Imagine me in such a position! Helen also has a job on our floor. People are assigned to watch the roof for incendiary bombs."[70] He noted that Washington, DC, was then a war capital for the fourth time in the life of his father, who was born in 1860.[71] Mahon was concerned about the Japanese in the newly declared war, but he feared Germany more. He ended the letter by telling his father that the rent money from the farm he had bought in 1928 had been put in defense bonds. "This year we will be sad for many reasons, yet happy for many others. We will be thinking of you frequently during the Christmas season. Our love and best wishes to all."[72]

Once again Americans would experience the upheaval of war. All metals were diverted to war materials. The manufacture of automobiles and household appliances, such as radios and vacuum cleaners, was halted to free up metals and manpower for planes, guns, or tanks. Three shifts, with 168-hour working weeks, became the norm. Producers who could not obtain war orders were faced with curtailing production because raw materials were restricted for total war production. *United States News* on December 19 announced, "The automobile industry, with a huge backlog of war work, now is ordered to curtail passenger car output 75 per cent below the previous year by next January. Manufacturers of slot machines and pin ball games are ordered out of business by February, and output of other automatic devices is to be slashed 75 per cent at the same time."[73] This would conserve both labor and materials. The manufacture of juke boxes required skilled labor and ingenious engineers, both of which could be used more advantageously in defense work.[74] Rubber could only be used on orders carrying an A-3 or higher priority. Industrial and civilian rationing was near at hand. Endangered sea lanes threatened the supply of rubber, tin, tungsten, chromium, burlap, and silk. All this meant a reduced standard of living for civilians. Price controls were also instituted. However, record production levels in 1940 meant that durable supplies in warehouses, or in homes, would carry the country for at least two years. Clothing the military meant fewer apparel goods for civilians. The output of war materials was expected to triple because at least 50 percent of production would be needed to equip the military. It was anticipated that production of consumer items would drop to the Depression levels of 1933–1934.

Before a short recess for Christmas, Congress passed a supplemental appropriation for $10 billion to purchase more guns, planes, and munitions and to support a two-million-man army. The president was also granted the same extensive war powers that President Woodrow Wilson had during World War I. He was given the authority to reorganize government functions for defense and to censor outgoing communications to foreign countries. He was also given extensive control over the property and transactions of aliens. A 150,000-ton expansion of the naval fleet was also authorized.

The Mahon family remained in Washington for the Christmas season. During December the House had been meeting every three days although there was not much business to conduct. Many members believed they should be close by in the event something developed on the international scene that needed their response. Work at the office was more hectic than usual as correspondence flooded in, but he and Helen stole a few moments to celebrate their eighteenth wedding anniversary. Mahon described those as "18 happy years."[75] Daphne's Christmas recess began on December 23, and on Christmas Eve the office staff came for dinner. In a Christmas letter to the Charles Thompson family in Colorado City, he bragged that Daphne had made seven As and one C-plus on her last report card. He also confessed that "the longer I stay away from West Texas the more I realize that I love it very, very much."[76]

A New Year's Day editorial in the *Washington Post* called 1942 the "Year of Preparation." The writer noted that the old year was actually rung out a month before. "Lulled by a sense of false security because of our oceanic ramparts," the United States crossed the Rubicon on December 7, 1941.[77] Failure to adequately prepare sooner meant that an offense could not be mounted before 1943. "And so grievous has been our past neglect that every minute of the national time in 1942 must be made to yield 60 seconds worth of distance run."[78] Now it could no longer be business as usual, of talking instead of doing. An all-out effort was mandatory.

In President Roosevelt's State of the Union address he vowed to carry the war to the enemy, and he told Congress it would end only with the end of militarism in Germany, Italy, and Japan. "We are fighting today for security and for peace, not only for ourselves, but for all men, not only for one generation, but for all generations. We are fighting to cleanse the world of ancient evils, ancient ills."[79] In order to do this, the United States had to be capable of putting weapons in the hands of those who needed them, and production of war materials had to be increased. The president instructed the appropriate departments to increase production of planes to 60,000 in 1942 and to 125,000 in 1943. The increased production of tanks would reach 45,000 in 1942 and 75,000 in 1943; production of anti-aircraft guns was increased to 20,000 in 1942 and 35,000 in 1943; production of merchant ships was increased to 8 million deadweight tons in 1942 and 10 million in 1943.[80] In January 1942 Roosevelt stated "War costs money. So far, we have hardly even begun to pay for it. We have devoted only 15 percent of our national income to national defense. As will appear in my budget message tomorrow our war program for the coming fiscal year will cost 56 billion dollars or, in other words, more than one-half of the estimated annual national income. This means taxes and bonds and bonds and taxes. It means cutting luxuries and other nonessentials. In a word, it means an 'all-out' war by individual effort and family effort in a united country."[81] A United Press reporter estimated the per capita cost would amount to $427.80 for every man, woman, and child in the nation.[82]

On Sunday, January 25, 1942, George wrote to his father, "We passed the biggest appropriation bill this week in the history of this or any other government. I made a speech on the bill. Among other things we are providing for the purchase of 33,000 airplanes. The Lord willing, the day is coming when we are going to smash Japan off the map."[83]

In a speech that Mahon made in the House on January 23, 1942, concerning the $12.5 million bill for defense appropriations, he stressed his belief that citizens wanted Congress to appropriate every dollar necessary to purchase the equipment, planes, ammunition, and guns necessary to win the war. However, he was equally convinced that it was the moral duty of each member of the House to ensure that every dollar appropriated went into national defense, not war profiteering. He pointed out that national defense should not become "a cloak for covering up inefficiency, bad judgment, and waste." Wise spending would provide more materiel that would reduce the loss of human life. In subcommittee hearings it was revealed that labor costs, including large amounts of overtime, cost of material, overhead, and improved airplane design with better equipment had resulted in a net increase of 20 to 25 percent in production costs during the last year and a half to two years. Mahon voted for the appropriation bill but wanted the *Congressional Record* to show that he believed excessive war profits existed and he wanted these taken out of war.[84] The House debate revealed that the bill would provide only thirty-three thousand planes, of which twenty-three thousand were bombers and ten thousand were training planes. More money would be needed to reach the sixty-thousand-plane goal the president had laid out in his State of the Union address.

The war effort strained electric power facilities, and daylight saving time was instituted. The uniform, one-hour advancement was expected to reduce demand 2 to 3 percent in the late afternoon and early evening, thus saving several billion kilowatt-hours of electricity.[85]

In June 1941 Mahon sent a telegram to Lubbock city officials, announcing that the War Department had decided to locate an advanced pilot training base there. The initial allocation of $4.6 million was for construction of buildings, with prospects for more in the future.[86] By December personnel began arriving at the Lubbock Army Air Force (LAAF) training base from Brooks Field in San Antonio. Early in 1942, cadets began to arrive for the intensive training program that would provide a commission as second lieutenant upon graduation. Pilots who received their wings at LAAF Base flew bombers such as the Flying Fortresses, Liberators, and B-26 and P-47 fighters. They also flew transport and cargo planes in the European and Pacific theaters. The second-oldest training base in the Army Air Force Central Flying command, Lubbock Army Air Force Base trained more than seven thousand bomber, fighter, and transport pilots from 1942 to 1945. Early in 1944 emphasis was shifted to training instrument pilots.[87] Nearly two thousand flyers received their instrument training in Lubbock before the base closed on December 31, 1945.

In April 1942 a second flying school was located north of the city. More than $5 million was allocated for the project. The Lubbock Chamber of Commerce and the city commissioners did significant promotional work to secure the bases. Mahon's seat on the War Department Appropriations Subcommittee of the House Committee on Appropriations was also helpful because he was able to arrange appointments in Washington for city officials that might otherwise have been rejected. As military people testified before the subcommittee to support requests for new facilities, Mahon repeatedly asked military officials about the possibility of locating some of these installations in the Nineteenth District. Initially, he was told that the altitude was too high for engines used in the training planes. However, his persistence, coupled with new technological developments, soon caused those requesting money for new installations to realize that Lubbock would be an acceptable location after all. The city fathers, and those who were lucky enough to land construction contracts, were overjoyed with the decision made by the War Department and Mahon's support throughout. The money was most welcome on the heels of the Great Depression.

During the war the Roosevelt administration had two powerful groups with which to deal: business and labor on one side and agriculture on the other. Labor was in a strategically sound position to win wage and organizational concessions from industry. Early on, President Roosevelt decided to prevent wages from rising too high through price controls. He believed that if wages rose, prices would follow. Producers of grain, milk, meat, and other foodstuffs would also be forced to raise prices to meet increasing production costs. To keep producer costs as stable as possible, the administration paid farmers and middlemen as the need arose.

The president's concerns were supported by protests that Mahon received throughout 1943 from across the state. The question of paying subsidies of various sorts vexed Congress throughout World War II. Inflation hovered over the country and kept increasing as prices and wages rose. Since taxes were not raised enough to keep pace with rising income, and the situation was helped along by a growing scarcity of nonwar goods, something had to be done to prevent runaway inflation. This was especially true because the administration borrowed money through the issuance of bonds, rather than taxing away surplus.

Subsidies were one answer, along with price- and wage-control laws. There was a fairly general consensus that farmers should be encouraged to produce more food and fiber for consumption by the allies and the civilian population. The administration proposed to pay consumer subsidies, which were amounts paid to processors and distributors to take care of their increased costs, thus holding the prices of many foods at a reasonable level. These payments met with general approval from the public and the press, and by the end of the war were being made for eighteen food groups and agricultural products, including beef, butter, sugar, canned and frozen vegetables, flour, and peanut butter.[88] The subsidies were called "consumer subsidies" because they had the effect of putting money in the pockets of consumers through lower food prices in relation to rising wages. Labor groups and those on fixed incomes were especially appreciative, while the farm bloc and its supporters spoke out strongly against what they called the socialization of American agriculture.

Mahon was against consumer subsidies. He spoke only once during the debate in the House, and then only briefly, but he made his stand clear. He was for price controls and favored continuing the Commodity Credit Corporation, but as he saw it, the Commodity Credit Corporation that was being debated was concerned mainly with consumer subsidies rather than those for producers. He was against subsidizing consumers by helping to pay for their meat, butter, milk, and bread bills from the federal treasury. Production had to be stimulated, but it didn't seem quite ethical to him "for the Government to be paying a part of the grocery bill of all people at the greatest period of prosperity and widespread employment in the Nation's history."[89] He didn't understand why people whose incomes were good should demand an increase in their wages just because bread went up a penny a loaf, milk a penny a quart, and meat and butter a few cents a pound.[90] He admitted there were a few people who weren't well off, although the total income of the country was about $150 million, but that didn't justify helping to pay the grocery bills of both rich and poor. He was in favor of price control and against uncontrolled inflation, as were the people he represented. He thought most people could afford to pay a little more for their bread, milk, and meat. Everybody should be willing to sacrifice a little for those fighting on the battlefronts of the world. "Let us be Americans who are worthy of our country in this great and tragic hour—Americans willing to make the necessary sacrifices."[91] Mahon believed money spent on consumer subsidies would reduce the amount available for defense. This was the beginning of a strong stance in favor of defense spending rather than nondefense, or public welfare spending, a position that he would support for many years to come.

After several days of debate, Wright Patman (D-TX) introduced an amendment to remove section 3, thus permitting consumer subsidies. Mahon joined in defeating the amendment, although votes were not recorded, and then in passing the bill to continue the Commodity Credit Corporation. The Senate concurred, and the bill made its way to the president, who promptly vetoed it. Congress went a second round early in 1944, and again FDR sent back his veto. On February 24, 1944, the Senate concurred with the House in a joint resolution to continue the Commodity Credit Corporation to June 30, 1945, with no mention of consumer subsidies, which were, therefore, to continue in effect.

The appropriation bill for the Treasury and Post Office drew another comment from Mahon, this time against an amendment that would bar executive and administrative offices from sending millions of pieces of mail free of postage. Although he wasn't on the Appropriation subcommittee responsible for this bill, he opposed such a restriction. It would hamper the war effort by requiring more manpower to process government mail, and he thought it was a bad thing to do when farmers were crying for help, as were the army and navy. "It is time to rise above petty politics and differences as between one side of the aisle and the other and come down here and carry on our functions as representatives of the people in such a way that we may merit the confidence of the people."[92] This time Mahon was on the losing side, at least temporarily. Francis Case (R-SD) introduced an amendment to the Keefe Amendment to bar the legislative branch as well from free mail. The House preserved free mail for itself by disposing of this amendment in short order, after which they approved Keefe's by a vote of 204-201 and sent the bill to the Senate without a recorded vote. Mahon was on the conference committee for the bill and had the satisfaction of seeing the Keefe Amendment thrown out and the question of free use of the mail sent to the Joint Committee on Reduction of Nonessential Federal Expenditures.

During the fall of 1943, the American Institute of Public Opinion, under the direction of Dr. George Gallup, conducted a poll that revealed that many Texans were critical of Roosevelt, and many of the state's congressmen were becoming cool toward New Deal programs. Texas would be a rich prize for the Republican Party if it could be wooed away from the Democrats, and it seemed that might be possible. In fact, the state went Republican in the Hoover-Smith campaign of 1928, when Democratic candidate, Alfred E. Smith, polled only 48 percent of the vote and Herbert Hoover received 52 percent. Its twenty electoral votes were coveted by the Republicans. A statewide survey conducted in 1943 by the institute revealed that in the previous three presidential elections a smaller number of voters favored the Democrats than at any time. In 1932, 89 percent favored the Democrats and 11 percent the Republicans. In 1936 the number favoring Democrats fell to 88 percent and to 81 percent in 1940. By 1943, only 78 percent favored the Democratic Party and 22 percent favored the Republican. Voters were interviewed from thirty different communities, both urban and rural, including Lubbock and Big Spring, within the Nineteenth District. Although Texans were trending slightly toward the Republican Party, it would have taken a major and unforeseen event to put Texas in the Republican column. The majority of the voters were still willing to stay with the Democratic Party and, certainly, West Texans with George Mahon.[93]

Life in the nation was shaped by the war effort. Like many other families, the Mahon family had a victory garden in Washington. Victory gardens were a positive way for all Americans to feel they were contributing to the war. By eating their home-grown vegetables, they reduced the demand for mass-produced vegetables, allowing the War Department to purchase them more cheaply. While people were willing to sacrifice, there was a negative aspect to doing without. In contrast, the vegetables that were enjoyed by so many families were a type of reward. "In 1943, these gardens provided more than a third of all the vegetables grown in the country."[94]

Located a few blocks from their apartment, the Mahon victory garden was on a hillside that had been plowed up to accommodate sixty gardens. Space throughout the city was being turned into victory gardens. A playground behind their apartment house had been plowed up, but the only garden they were able to get was a little farther away. A whole garden was about sixty feet by twenty-six feet, but they could only acquire one-fourth of a garden, which was approximately fifteen feet by twenty-six feet. They planted radishes, tomatoes, onions, and three rows of black-eyed peas. According to letters that

Mahon wrote to his family, they truly enjoyed taking care of it.[95] Although they lived in the midst of a city, the Mahons never lost their love for growing things. The four window boxes in their third-floor apartment brimmed with color from the petunias and geraniums. George painted the boxes green. In letters that he wrote home Mahon often mentioned how pretty the flowers were and how much he enjoyed them.

Mahon also wrote his family that he was not too concerned about shoe rationing. Although he had not bought a pair in two years, he believed what he had would last at least two more years with help from the neatsfoot oil he put on them. However, he believed that Helen and Daphne would use their allotment. In a letter Mahon told his father, "We laughed about buying a new package of gum and chewing a whole piece instead of just a half. I think people who never chewed gum or ate candy before are doing so now because it is scarce. Diamonds are precious because they are scarce, you know."[96]

In February 1943 Mahon's assistant, George Whitten, left for the army, causing Mahon to work many nights in order to do Whitten's work in addition to his own. By the end of the month, however, he and Helen found time to have dinner in the home of Dr. Splawn, who had been the president of the University of Texas at the time George attended. Now, he was on the Interstate Commerce Commission. Speaker Rayburn, two other congressmen, and their wives were there also.

Mahon often met interesting people as part of his duties as congressman. In a letter to his father he shared the following:

I have met two interesting personalities recently. Mr. Eddie Rickenbacker, whose picture was on the front leaf of your Life Magazine came to the Capitol and had lunch with the Texas Members of Congress (in a private dining room) and gave us an off the record talk about the experiences which he had had and his outlook on the war situation. It was interesting to be with him, but I must say that I was disappointed in him as a man. He did not measure up to my expectations. He is not a big man in my opinion. On the front leaf of the Time Magazine a few weeks ago was a picture of Major General A. A. Vandergrift of the Solomons. He was the man in command of the Marines who landed in the Solomon Islands last August and licked the Japs on Guadalcanal Island. Well, he appeared before the 43 members of the Appropriations committee and gave us a marvelous story of the whole campaign. He saw what happened in the land and air fighting and saw most of the dramatic sea battles. It was a thrilling thing to hear him tell about these things. . . . I think General Marshall is going to invite us over to the War Department soon and give us a report on the trip to North Africa with the President. These high lights compensate us for much of the rather uninteresting work which we must do on our appropriations committee.[97]

The war in the Pacific was a growing concern in 1943, and in February Madame Chiang Kai-shek, first lady of the Republic of China, addressed Congress, speaking in the Senate first and then in the House. Madame Chiang was in the United States for personal medical care and also to request more arms to fight the Japanese, who had invaded China in 1937. She referred to Japan as "a waiting sword of Damocles, ready to descend at a moment's notice. Let us not forget that Japan in her occupied areas today has greater resources at her command than Germany."[98] She warned Congress that the longer Japan was left in control of these resources, the stronger that country would become. She also pleaded with Congress to understand that the threat from Japan was just as serious as that from Hitler. The *Washington Post* reported that the members of the House "interrupted her speech in the middle and jumped to their feet, cheering and giving the rebel yell. In the packed galleries, although it was against the rules, the spectators did likewise."[99] While in Washington Madame Chiang Kai-shek stayed in the White House as the guest of President Roosevelt.

After Pearl Harbor many Americans strongly sympathized with China's brave struggle against the Japanese invaders. The enthusiastic reception given to Madame Chiang Kai-shek by the press, especially the *Washington Post*, also encouraged a favorable reaction to her visit. Mahon's favorable impression of her can also be traced to closer feelings for the Chinese people after touring parts of their country in 1935 when his ship to the Philippines put into Chinese ports to take on needed supplies. Added to this was the fact that he, like many other Americans, had for years given his nickels and dimes in Sunday school to help Methodist missionaries in China.

On Friday, February 26, Mahon and Helen attended a tea for Madame Chiang Kai-shek that was held in the ballroom of the Shoreham Hotel with more than twenty-five hundred guests in attendance. Hosted by the Chinese ambassador and Madame Wei, it was the only official function honoring Madame Chiang, who remained seated throughout because of her health. All of Congress, the Cabinet, high-ranking officers of the army and navy, officials in governmental agencies, and army, navy, and military attaches of the embassies and legations were invited. At the tea a buffet table reaching from one end of the room to the other offered food that was apparently as lavish as the menu for the dinner party given for Harry Hopkins and his new wife in December 1942 that had caused Mahon to complain so bitterly to government officials. However, this time Mahon and Helen seemed to enjoy the event.

During 1942 the administration had grown concerned about spiraling inflation caused by too much personal discretionary money from the abundance of war-industry jobs and too few consumer goods available for purchase. Certain commodities were rationed, and a limit on wage and price increases was imposed; however, it was easier for the administration to enforce savings or to tax away excess personal income. The Revenue Act of 1942 lowered the personal exemption, causing an additional thirteen million people to pay income tax. This increased the tax on incomes by $7 billion, and by the end of the war "in the aggregate individuals for the first time now paid more in income tax than did corporations, a pattern that held and even deepened in the postwar years."[100] Withholding tax from paychecks at the time of earning was initiated in 1943. There was much concern that when withholding first went into effect taxpayers would experience a double tax bite because they would be paying two years' tax in one year. Previously tax was reported and paid the year after income was earned; however, in 1943, taxpayers would be liable for 1942 income taxes and would also have taxes on 1943 income withheld. This double bite was alleviated by a one-time forgiveness of any 1942 income tax under fifty dollars and a forgiveness of 75 percent of any tax over that. Mahon voted against the tax bill because it canceled most of the revenue from the 1942 income tax. He was in favor of raising taxes as much as possible to cover the cost of the war.

In a letter to his father, Mahon wrote, "We have up a new tax bill this month. I am undecided how to vote. I think we ought to have a withholding tax but I think every body ought to pay their full 1942 taxes too. I cannot understand people who are unwilling to give dollars when others are giving up everything including their lives. . . . The American people have probably never been so aware as they are now of the importance of the farms of the Country. I hope the good Lord will give us good seasons and that the crops will be bountiful. Had a little visit recently with Chester Davis, the new Food Administrator. I think he is a pretty good man. Of course, the real answer is largely up to the people on the farms."[101]

On May 11, 1943, British prime minister Winston Churchill and his high-level military advisors arrived in the United States for talks with President Roosevelt and United States military advisors. Only days before, the Axis powers (Germany, Italy, and Japan) had lost their foothold in Africa with the fall of Tunisia. Now these two Allied leaders and their military advisors were meeting to speed up plans for defeating the Axis powers. This was the fourth of such conferences between the two heads of state. Churchill had been in the United States shortly after the bombing of Pearl Harbor and had addressed Congress on December 24, 1941, to show his nation's support. On this visit to the United States, he again addressed a joint session of Congress on May 19, renewing the pledge that Britain would remain in the war until both Germany and Japan were defeated. He also stressed the necessity of providing immediate aid to China and taking more of the burden of the war in Europe off Russia's shoulders. There was some speculation that Britain might consider pulling out after Hitler was defeated because that nation had been under attack from Germany since 1939. His pledge to remain in the war was reassuring to Congress and the nation. Famous for his oratorical skills, Churchill held the attention of a packed House for fifty-two minutes. Later he met in executive sessions with the foreign relations committees of both houses. According to the editor of the *Washington Post*, "It reflected the hunger of Congressmen for news and background information about the war. This was the first opportunity the great majority of Senators and Representatives had had to get a firsthand report on the Tunisian campaign or the war in general in recent months."[102] Pointing to a lack of cooperation between the White House and Congress, the editor wrote that legislators were expected to approve vast sums of money for the war without being kept informed by the commander-in-chief about how the battle was going. He admonished both the administration and Congress to bridge this dangerous gap.

The Mahons were present at Churchill's address to the House, and George wrote to his family of his impressions: "The Churchill visit is over. I had heard him in December, 1941, but I really enjoyed hearing him again. Helen was in the Gallery when he spoke. We were a little embarrassed that Wally and the former King Edward got almost as big a hand as Churchill. There is a lot of speculation here as to what will happen next. Nobody thinks that Victory is just around the corner. How I know everybody must wish that it were, and that is especially true in the case of fathers and mothers of sons in the Service."[103]

In December 1943 Mahon resigned as chairman of the District Appropriations subcommittee because his work on the War Department Appropriations subcommittee required more and more of his time. Although he was glad to be rid of what was considered a thankless job, officials of the District of Columbia thanked him profusely for his unselfish devotion to duty and his keen grasp of local problems. Letters in his files contain remarks such as, "a profound regard for your caliber of leadership . . . Your untiring devotion and the high intelligence which you have displayed in your work as Chairman . . . No one could have served the District better than you; Your thorough, impartial and fair consideration of our problems has been an inspiration to me."[104] Despite the fact that they were losing a respected leader, the people from the District of Columbia with whom he had worked for four years expressed their satisfaction about still having a friend in Congress, but for Mahon his war department work was a top priority and grave responsibility.

Revenues were an issue at every turn, and although new revenue was necessary to support the war, every effort to raise money produced a sharp confrontation between the executive and legislative branches. The treasury department requested $12 billion in 1943, but President Roosevelt insisted that the request be pared down to $10.5 billion. However, with the election of 1944 looming, Congress was unwilling to raise taxes and passed a bill providing only $2 billion, a bill that also made substantial tax concessions to business interests. Furious at the limited revenue the bill provided and at its inequities, the president sent an angry veto message to Capitol Hill in February 1944. The measure, he said, was "wholly ineffective" for meeting national needs. With its "undefensible privileges for special groups," he went on, "it is not a tax bill but a tax relief bill providing relief not for the needy, but for the greedy."[105] In a letter to his father Mahon wrote, "You have heard a lot of discussion about the tax question and the veto of the President. This bill was not especially good, but it was better than nothing at all, providing for additional Federal taxes in the sum of over two billion dollars and bringing the total Federal taxes to about 42 billion dollars annually. Taxes are high on both the rich and the poor. For the duration of the war, however, I should like to see them higher in order that we could do a better job in defraying the expenses of the war and sharing in a small measure the burdens of the men who fight and die."[106]

Senate Democratic Majority Leader Alben Barkley, a longtime supporter of President Roosevelt, voiced his personal irritation at the president and resigned, calling the veto message "a calculated and deliberate assault upon the legislative integrity of every member of Congress." He called on his colleagues to override the veto. They did, by overwhelming margins, and Senate Democrats reelected Barkley leader as well.

On two counts Roosevelt had met a stinging defeat at the hands of an intransigent Congress. "First, the measure was inadequate for its intended purposes. Second, it was the first revenue act ever passed over a presidential veto. It was but one more indication of the conservative coalition in national affairs."[107] The conservative coalition was formed of southern conservative Democrats and northern Republicans. Because of the conservative nature of these two groups, it was natural that they would vote the same way on legislation they considered too liberal.

Mahon had an opponent for the 1944 primary, C. L. Harris, the same person who had run against him in 1940. Although Harris had not polled a very large number of votes in 1940, there was concern that voter dissatisfaction with President Roosevelt and the New Deal would generate a movement to "clean house" of all officeholders. Mahon announced for office in all of the district papers, but he did not intend to actively engage in campaigning until early summer, about a month or so before the primary to be held at the end of July. He did, however, begin an active correspondence with people in the district, especially the postmasters. He had appointed many of them and could count on their support. Early in the year he also corresponded with Charles L. South, former representative from Coleman, Texas. South wrote: "Now that I am removed from the scene of action, I can look back and see that you are peculiarly well fitted for this service; you have a good mind, you are clean, honest, and while not courageous to the extent that you will take unnecessary risks, you have plenty of courage."[108] Mahon handily won his election in the district, and President Roosevelt also won an unprecedented fourth term.

As 1945 began, Democrats in Washington felt renewed optimism, with the party firmly in control of Congress. The Allies were drawing a tight ring around Hitler in Europe, and in Asia US forces were moving toward a show-down with Japan. There was, however, one dark cloud on the horizon. President Roosevelt could no longer hide his failing health after he did not deliver his State of the Union message to Congress in person.[109] In his message, which was read by Mr. Miller, one of the president's secretaries, President Roosevelt predicted that "1945 [would] be the greatest year of achievement in human history."[110] He predicted the end of the Nazi-Fascist reign in Europe, "the clos-ing in of the forces of retribution about the center of the malignant power of imperialistic Japan," and the beginning of an organization of world peace.[111]

Historian David McCullough has written, "In deference to the tragedy of war and the President's limited strength, the inauguration at noon, Janu-ary 20, 1945, was a somber affair lasting less than fifteen minutes. It was the first wartime inauguration since Lincoln and the first ever held at the White House. The ceremony was conducted on the South Portico before a crowd that included a number of disabled soldiers. A thin crust of snow covered the lawn. The day was grim. There were no parades. The red jackets of the Marine Band were the one note of cheer in the whole chill, muted scene."[112]

Two days later President Roosevelt, in strict secrecy, boarded his private train for Norfolk, Virginia. There he boarded a navy cruiser for the island of Malta in the Mediterranean Sea where he met Winston Churchill. From Malta the two men flew on the *Sacred Cow* to Yalta, a Black Sea resort in Soviet Crimea, where they met Joseph Stalin. Items on the agenda for the meeting included the rebuilding of Eastern Europe, especially Poland, after the war ended; the fate of Germany after defeat; Soviet participation in the war against Japan; and membership rules and voting procedures in the newly formed United Nations.[113] Although the leaders hoped to resolve problems, different interpretations of the discussions and agreements actually set the stage for future complications.

President Roosevelt, whose health was even more fragile than the Yalta agreements, left for his summer home in Warm Springs, Georgia, soon af-ter returning to Washington. He died there on April 12, 1945. About 1:00

p.m., while sitting in front of his fireplace as an artist drew his portrait, he complained of a terrific pain in the back of his head and collapsed. He had suffered a cerebral hemorrhage, and by 3:30 p.m. he was dead. At 7:00 p.m. Chief Justice Harlan Stone administered the oath of office to the thirty-second president of the United States, Harry S. Truman.

President Roosevelt's funeral service was held in the White House on April 14 at 4:00 p.m. After the service his body was placed aboard his train for a journey through the night to Hyde Park. The next day he was buried near the main house in a garden where he had played as a child.

The following week Mahon wrote to his daughter, Daphne: "No, we did not get to go to the White House to pay tribute to the President, but we did see the funeral procession. Roosevelt was a very great American, and I am mighty sorry we have lost him. We will have to vindicate our faith in democracy by showing that we can take in our stride the loss of our greatest leader and still go forward to better things and better days. Now for the first time we feel that we personally know, rather that the President and his family personally know us."[114]

Mahon and President Truman had both been elected to Congress in 1934 and became acquainted during their visits to Sam Rayburn's "Board of Education." This was a hideout that Rayburn had in the Capitol, a small room below the House of Representatives, where he would invite colleagues for drinks after Congress recessed for the day. Although Mahon did not drink alcoholic beverages he was often invited, and he enjoyed the lively political talk that included discussions about strategies and events on Capitol Hill. The gatherings gave Speaker Rayburn a chance to work more closely with the Democrats in Congress—to maintain control over the party and encourage cohesion in voting for party programs.[115] In fact, Truman was attending a "Board of Education" meeting when he was summoned to the White House to learn of President Roosevelt's death.

In a letter to his nephews who were on active duty, Mahon wrote, "Shook hands with Harry Truman this week. Speaker Rayburn said, 'You remember George Mahon!' President Truman said, 'Sure, I visited his town last year.'[116] He doesn't seem like a president, but he is your new Commander-in-Chief and we are wishing him luck."[117] In June, he wrote to his father, "Had a little visit yesterday with President Truman at the White House. He was in his shirt sleeves and apparently feeling good."[118]

Mahon's first business encounter with Truman as the president was at a meeting at the White House on June 15, 1945, during which he asked President Truman to help get the public announcement made about a new veterans' hospital to be located in Big Spring, Texas. Mahon had worked hard to get this hospital located in West Texas, and the Veterans Administration had delayed far too long in announcing its decision. Constituents feared some sort of shenanigans might cause the decision to be changed, and the endless excuses Mahon was forced to make were becoming embarrassing. He explained this to the president, who agreed and picked up the phone to talk to someone in the Budget Office. After the conversation the president told Mahon, "You just forget it. This is taken care of." And it was. Mahon was so pleased that he misspoke and said, "Harry, this has really been great." Embarrassed, he then said, "Pardon me, I should have said Mr. President." President Truman replied that Harry was the way Mahon should address him; however, Mahon was careful never to make that mistake again. Although he had known Truman for many years and knew Lyndon Johnson and Gerald Ford even longer, he always addressed them as Mr. President out of his respect for the office.[119]

In the letter to his nephews, he also wrote, "Did I tell you about the seed corn that Henry Wallace, former Secretary of Commerce,[120] gave me for Easter! I have sent it to Dad to plant for me. He will have to hood the tassels so that it will not lose its identity."[121] Secretary Wallace knew of Mahon's interest in agriculture and thought he would enjoy planting the Hybrid Golden Bantam seed corn to see how well it would grow in Mitchell County. He sent most of the seed corn to his father. His brother-in-law Ernest Meadows also received some. Correspondence files do not contain information about how the corn grew.

In early 1939 a group of foreign-born scientists who had left their homelands to escape the tyranny of fascism had become increasingly concerned about the military application of atomic energy. This group included Enrico Fermi from Italy; Leo Szilard, Eugene Wigner, and Edward Teller from Hungary; and Victor Weisskopf from Austria. Despite all the talk in the United States about letting European governments settle their own disputes, these men knew the Nazi government was supporting nuclear research at the Kaiser Wilhelm Institute in Berlin, and they were convinced that the military consequences of a breakthrough in that research would enable Hitler to dominate the world.[122] In August they persuaded Albert Einstein to write a letter to President Roosevelt, encouraging a liaison between the government and the scientists because it was difficult to fund the necessary research on limited university budgets. Alexander Sachs, an informal advisor of the president who was familiar with the subject of atomic energy, presented the letter to Roosevelt in October 1939 and, according to historian Vincent Jones, "persuaded by Alexander Sachs' urgent arguments, President Roosevelt agreed to investigate the desirability of providing some preliminary support for independent and private research."[123] He established the President's Advisory Committee on Uranium and charged the members with making recommendations based on the ideas presented by Sachs and the scientists. Despite some skepticism within the group, they recommended funding for research.

Throughout 1940 news from the war front in Europe became increasingly depressing, despite the claims of many congressmen, including George Mahon, that Americans would not be sent to fight these battles. However, news from the research laboratories was promising, and additional funds were made available. Despite the obvious potential for military use, government officials left the actual research in the hands of civilians but charged the army with production because the bomb would be delivered in Army Air Force planes. It was believed that an atomic bomb could be developed within three or four years. When American involvement in the war became a stronger possibility, large expenditures of money were seen as necessities, not as extravagances.[124] On December 6, 1941, details of a new organization were announced to those persons who would be responsible for exerting the maximum effort to develop the new bomb that could be the decisive weapon in defeating Nazi Germany. The next day Pearl Harbor was attacked, and the United States declared war on Japan.

In June 1942 President Roosevelt decided that the Army Corps of Engineers should have the responsibility for building and maintaining the production plants and power sources needed to build the atomic bomb. In the Corps of Engineers, the basic unit for supervising construction was an engineer district, with the district engineer being responsible to a division engineer of one of the eleven geological divisions in the United States. Engineer districts usually took the name of the city where they were located, but the new district had no definite location so it was called the Manhattan Engineer District because one of the offices was located in Manhattan. Titling it the Manhattan Engineer District, or the Manhattan Project, provided an additional element of security since the first location was actually at Knoxville, Tennessee. Brigadier General Leslie R. Groves became district engineer.

As early as 1943, George Mahon and other members of the War Department Subcommittee of the House Committee on Appropriations became suspicious about some unusually large expenditures listed under the general heading of "Expediting Production." In their watchdog role over federal spending, they probed for more information. Later when Undersecretary of War Robert Patterson and Colonel C. F. Hofstetter appeared before the committee, requesting permission to transfer funds from other War Department appropriations to build new plants that would develop a new explosive more powerful than anything available in the past, details were extremely vague, which aroused even more suspicion.

We now know that one of the reasons for the vague information was the fact that President Roosevelt and General Groves believed that compartmentalization of information about the project would provide an added element of security; therefore, those appearing before the Appropriations Committee really did not have all the information to reveal, even if they had wanted to do so. Concealing information about the Manhattan Project meant funding for it had to be concealed as well; thus, the unusually large expenditures for "Expediting Production." Several people involved in the project knew part of what was going on, and all of them understood it could be the lynchpin in winning the war, but only a few had complete knowledge of the project.

Initially, subcommittee members went along, partly because the money had already been allocated to the War Department and was now simply being used in a different manner from the one specified at the time of the original request for appropriations. They wanted to cooperate in every way possible to win the war, but they were concerned about unspecified funds because of the potential for waste and excessive war profiteering. In his history of the project, General Leslie Groves explains, "During the war period, military appropriations were often made with little public debate, although the discovery of the Manhattan Project by the Appropriations Committee testifies to the alertness of the committee members."[125]

General Groves described the unorthodox manner of securing funds. "Before July 1, 1945, the majority of our money came from two sources—Engineer Service, Army; and Expediting Production; the latter being under direct supervision of the Under Secretary of War. In justifying our requests for these funds, we were handicapped not only by the very size of the project and its many uncertainties, which made it impossible to budget in advance, but by the overriding need for secrecy, in the spending as well as in the getting."[126]

George Mahon remembered an especially tense moment in 1943 when

Congressman Albert J. Engel (R-MI) told Undersecretary of War Patterson that he knew about the construction at Oak Ridge and he intended to visit the site in the near future. Also, he requested further details about the expenditure of funds. Engel was the most likely member of the subcommittee to question how the army was using money that had been appropriated to it. In private life he worked as an accountant and undoubtedly understood the art of moving money around better than other members of the subcommittee. Also, he was the ranking minority member of the subcommittee, and his intense questioning, which bordered on insurrection, would not be seen as disloyalty to the Democratic administration. Members of the subcommittee worked in close harmony, and there is no evidence that others disagreed in any way with Engel's concerns. He was told that the nature of the project was highly secret; therefore, he could not have the information he sought. Finally, he was persuaded to forget about visiting the site.

While Mahon and the other members understood that extreme secrecy was necessary for the war effort, they were all becoming concerned that they might be part of a $2 billion boondoggle that could easily destroy their political careers. They supported Engel's determination to get straight answers from those in charge of the Manhattan Project. Project officials realized they could not evade the congressmen forever and decided to brief the leaders of the House and Senate. Thus, on February 18, 1944, Secretary of War Stimson, General George C. Marshall, and Dr. Vannevar Bush, who was director of the Office of Scientific Research and Development, visited Speaker Rayburn in his office. In a secret session that also included Majority Leader John W. McCormack and Minority Leader Joseph W. Martin, information about the Manhattan Project was revealed. They were told that if the project was successful, it would produce an atomic bomb that could end the war. They were also told that many scientists in the United States believed that Germany was working on a similar project, making it necessary to act swiftly. The congressional leaders assured Secretary Stimson that the House would cooperate completely and only a partial explanation to a few members of the Appropriations Committee would be necessary. On June 10 Secretary Stimson and Dr. Bush briefed the Senate leadership and received the same guarantee of secrecy and cooperation.[127] According to notes in Mahon's files, none of the Democratic congressional leaders conferred with his subcommittee, so questions about the army's secret use of money were certain to resurface.

And the next problem did surface in February 1945, when a request came forward to transfer additional War Department funds to "Expediting Production." This time Congressman Engel objected vigorously, demanding a detailed explanation. He also threatened a full congressional investigation if the information was not forthcoming. Secretary Stimson interceded and showed Engel information about the cost of real estate, housing, roads, and other costs but did not reveal full details of the project. However, project administrators realized that it was now time to share the secret with members of the appropriations committees in the House and Senate. The administrators intended to get President Roosevelt's permission to do this; however, he died before they could meet with him. Later President Truman agreed that five members of each committee should visit Oak Ridge. In May 1945 Congressmen Clarence Cannon (D-MO),[128] J. Buell Snyder (D-PA), George Mahon (D-TX), John Taber (R-NY), and Albert Engel (R-MI) were selected from the House Committee on Appropriations to make the trip. The congressmen were very favorably impressed with what they saw. After returning to the airport in Washington, Congressman Taber said, "General, will you come over here a minute—I want to ask you a question."[129] General Groves's first thought was, "Well, here it comes." He was astounded when Taber said, "There is only one thing that worries me, General. Are you sure that you are spending enough money at Oak Ridge?"[130] General Groves replied that he thought enough money was being spent; however, in an undertaking as new as this one, it was hard to know. Secretary Stimson was pleasantly amazed when Groves reported the conversation to him. According to Groves, "During the entire period, we were allocated approximately $2,300,000,000 of which $2,191,000,000 were expended through December 31, 1946."[131]

After returning home Mahon recorded his memories before any part could fade. Understanding the extreme importance of secrecy, his handwritten account was put under lock and key until after the atomic bomb was dropped. The omissions in his account were considered so highly secretive that he did not record them, which explains the dashes in the account that follows:

A Fantastic Interlude

John Pugh, Clerk of the Appropriations Committee, called me on the telephone Thursday, May 17, 1945, and asked me to be in the Capitol at 12 o'clock noon in the office of Chairman Clarence Cannon for a highly important meeting.

Riding up the elevator to the second floor to the Chairman's office I did not notice that Secretary of War Henry Stimson was on the elevator with me, but as we stepped off the elevator into the Chairman's office I noticed that the man near me was Stimson. In the room was Major General [Leslie] Groves of the Pentagon Building and a congressional group of four men. Stimson said that he wanted us to go down and inspect the secret project at Knoxville, Tennessee, for which we had appropriated $1,800,000,000. He said the explosive being made at this project was apparently going to be a success; that the chances for success were better than 99%. The greatest secrecy was urged upon us. The time is rapidly approaching when this new weapon will be used and it must be a surprise, explained the Secretary.

It was agreed that we would leave by plane from Washington on Wednesday, May 23, for the Knoxville Airport, leaving at 7 a.m. General Groves called for me at the apartment at 6:30, and we had a nice visit on the way to the National Airport. . . . We took off promptly at 7 o'clock. Major Henry Dayton Orr, who is from Lubbock, was pilot. He went with TWA as a pilot in 1934. He was friendly—A. B. Davis of Lubbock is his friend.

In about 3 hours we were at Knoxville. I was put in a car with Capt. King as driver and Brig. Gen. [Thomas F.] Farrell as special guide. We drove about 20 or 30 miles west of Knoxville to the project. The name of the town at the project is Oak Ridge—70,000 people. About 79,000 people work on this project. . . . After lunch we went to the pilot plant for the project at Hanford, Washington. . . .

At this plant we wore badges which would register any radio-activity to which we might be subjected by the plant. We saw silver covered or aluminum, I believe, covered cylinders of uranium about 1 inch in diameter and 4 inches long which are put into a vault sort of thing by the hundreds where they create an intense heat and are transformed in 3 months into a different element called plutonium. Then by a chemical process the plutonium is separated and this is the explosive element. This is the Hanford, Washington project [process].

The place where this new product is made into explosive bombs is near Santa Fe, New Mexico. There are three processes in use at the Clinton Engineer Works—the official name of the Knoxville project. The pilot plant works on a small scale. You have to stay far away from the working uranium. The rays can be kept away by about 15 feet of concrete or 20 feet of water. The finished cylinders are handled in water and by intricate devices. (A few of these cylinders do not set up much radioactivity. It takes several hundred of them arranged in perfect order in carbon block containers.)

We then went to a huge plant built in a "u" shape where the uranium is processed by being blown through many pipes in cylinders which have to be air tight. It is a very huge plant which must have cost many many millions. We were given the exact cost.

That night after supper we discussed the project at further length. The next morning we went to the Y12 project which extricates the precious element in more pure form than the other projects. The material is brought from the piping process plant to this plant for further refinement. Dr. E. O. Lawrence perfected this process. (We went to the great power plant the day before—great power is used in the plant, especially in Y12.)

The atomic weight of uranium is 238 but some of the atoms are 235. The whole idea of $1,800,000,000 plant is to separate the relatively small number of 235 from the 238. This is done in the Y12 plant by firing the atoms in a circular vacuum through a highly charged electrically magnetized field. $400,000,000 of government silver is used in creating the magnetism. The racing atoms go in a circular direction and the 235s have a tendency to follow a little shorter pattern and are thereby caught in the process. The process is repeated in a smaller machine.

Finally we were carried to the building where the 235 is washed up and becomes the finished product. It is green in appearance, it looks like coarse crystal, like metal filing. It is dry looking, looks brittle. It is put in a gold cup a little bigger than a tea cup and is taken by an officer to the New Mexico plant to be made into bombs. The bombs may weigh 5,000 pounds but the weight of the product in the Washington [state] bombs will be — pounds; in the Clinton-Lawrence product plant the weight of the product will be — pounds.

A small quantity of the product will not explode; it might flash a little fire. It takes a certain amount to generate the explosive energy.—— pounds of this stuff is as powerful as 20,000 tons of TNT???

The first bomb will be dropped on the Japanese from an airplane. The bomb will have a proximity fuse adjusted in such a way that the bomb will explode while quite a way from the earth. It will absolutely wipe out every thing within a distance of two miles. The intense heat will melt everything. A great ball of fire will be generated which will rise to an altitude of 30,000 feet. It is not out of the question to assume that a few of these bombs will end the war with Japan.

The source of supply which we are using is in Canada and the Belgium Congo in Africa. We are trying to corner the supply. The Germans were working on the process but we destroyed their plant. The British know of the project and are partners with us in a way. The Russians may not know much about it. A scientist from Italy is one of the key men in the project. Many of the European scientists are in on the deal. There are a few scientists at the Clinton plant but the largest aggregation is in New Mexico where the actual finishing touches are being put on the bombs. General Groves said he was trying to hold all these men but some of them might leave for Europe. He bemoaned the fact that he lacked the authority to shoot one of the men who knows too much.

We came home by plane on Thursday afternoon, arriving at about 2:30 P.M.[132]

In 1970 Mahon contacted an official of the Atomic Energy Commission to confirm the accuracy of his notes. The official added some further explanatory material and said the notes were remarkably accurate. This final draft was intended for Daphne and included a short prologue, providing background for the visit. In the prologue Mahon wrote,

> We did not want to be part of a $2 billion boondoggle, but we were convinced that the gamble on the secret weapon was probably worth taking. Congressman Albert Engel was the most skeptical of our group, but as we were provided with tidbits of information Albert Engel would go along.
>
> The later-to-become famous George Marshall, Chief of Staff of the Army, and Under Secretary Bob Patterson were very stubborn about giving information, but they gave enough to prevent a rebellion in the committee.
>
> When we were at last notified that we were going to have an opportunity to inspect the facilities which we had been financing we were admonished that we could tell no one in our family or otherwise where we were going.
>
> Before leaving on the trip I told my wife and daughter, Daphne, I could tell them nothing as to where I was going or later as to where I had been.[133]

The first atomic bomb, nicknamed "Little Boy," was dropped on Hiroshima on August 6, 1945. In this bomb, a wedge of uranium was fired at a uranium target producing as much energy as twenty kilotons of TNT. On August 9 a second bomb, nicknamed "Fat Man," was dropped on Nagasaki. Using a more advanced nuclear principal, the second bomb exploded by crushing a hollow sphere of plutonium into a core of highly fissile material. Using two different methods of explosion, these bombs "brought death and destruction on a horrifying scale,"[134] as General Groves explains.

The afternoon of August 6 Mahon was working in his Lubbock office when a *Lubbock Morning Avalanche* reporter called to ask if he knew anything about the bomb that had been dropped on Japan. Mahon had been expecting this because earlier in the day he had received a phone call from Major General George Richards, budget officer for the War Department, saying the story had "broken." The congressmen who were in on the atomic bomb secret had known for weeks that it could be dropped at any time. After expressing concern about the horrific potential of the atomic bomb going forward, Mahon told the reporter that the potential for destruction made it mandatory that international peace be achieved.[135] Thirty-five years later, in a 1980 interview, Mahon reminisced that he believed dropping the atomic bomb changed the history of mankind because prior to its development many lives could be lost in a war but civilization would not be destroyed. However, after the bomb the destruction of civilization had become a very real possibility. "It is a frightful thing," he said. "I don't know; maybe mankind would be better off if the bomb had never succeeded."[136] Judging it in the light of what he knew at the time, however, he continued, "In the short run it was a wonderful thing for America, ending the war and saving thousands of American lives."[137] He always believed it would have cost an unacceptable number of American lives to storm Japan. When the story filled the newspapers, eighteen-year-old Daphne told her mother, "Now we know where Daddy went on that trip!"[138]

The fire-bombing that took place during the summer of 1945 had already weakened the resistance of Japan, and finally the devastation of the atomic bombs convinced the Japanese leaders that the "prompt and utter destruction" promised in the Potsdam Declaration was actually happening. On August 14 the Japanese emperor announced an end to the war by accepting the Allies' terms of surrender.

On August 16, 1945, Mahon joined a group of seven legislators led by J. Buell Snyder, chairman of the House Military Appropriations subcommittee, and Major General George J. Richards, budget officer of the War Department, on an inspection trip of US military installations around the world. The purpose of the trip for the congressmen was to get out in the field to learn firsthand how the more than $214 billion appropriated to fight World War II had been spent and how expenditures could be reduced now that the war had ended. The alternative was to rely completely on information from the War Department, which provided only a one-sided interpretation, regardless of how correct that interpretation might be. The thirty-nine-day trip that ensued indicates the extent of US involvement in the war effort and the country's power and influence at the war's end.

Included in the group were J. Buell Snyder (D-PA), chairman of the House Appropriations Subcommittee for Military Appropriations; George H. Mahon (D-TX); W. F. Norrell (D-AK); Joe Hendricks (D-FL); Albert J. Engel (Ranking Republican-MI); Francis Case (R-SD); Harve Tibbott (R-PA); Robert E. Lambert, committee clerk, who was responsible for compiling the subcommittee report; Maj. General George J. Richards, War Department budget officer; Brig. General L. W. Miller, Army Air Force fiscal officer; Brig. General Joseph F. Battley, deputy chief of staff, ASF; Brig. General William L. Mitchell, deputy chief of staff, AGF; and Colonel Robert J. Wood, OPD, WDGS. The trip was made in a C-54 army plane. The group visited the major headquarters in each of the theaters, where they attended an extensive orientation conference. Their task was to inquire at length about the number and type of installations, expenditures for the installations, supplies and equipment on hand, and personnel problems. A questionnaire was left at each theater headquarters to be completed and returned to the subcommittee. After the conferences they met with the commanding officer and his staff before inspecting the installations and facilities such as airfields, ports, hospitals, roads, supplies, equipment, and personnel centers. Upon returning home, a report was to be compiled for the Appropriations Committee based on information gathered during the inspections and the completed questionnaires.[139] Chairman Snyder also inserted the report in the *Congressional Record*.

On his return Mahon made several attempts to write a narrative of the trip from the notes he had taken. Information about installations in Europe was very scant and general, so the narrative was probably never really completed. He very likely ran out of time to finish and polish it; in letters to family members, he often lamented that he lacked the time to record his memories of events that he considered important. His narrative, an official diary of the trip, a letter to his family written on the flight to Washington, DC, and reports in the *Congressional Record* provide information for the following summary.

Leaving Hamilton Field, California, the first stop was Hickam Field, Oahu, Hawaii. From there they went on to other installations in the Pacific, Far East, Middle East, Europe, and finally home. For thirty-nine days they held conferences in the headquarters of each US military installation. These conferences were designed to collect facts that could be used in shaping future plans for military appropriations. The 1946 fiscal year budget allocated $128 million for the Pacific area alone, and Mahon anticipated that roughly 50 percent could be turned back because of the termination of the war.[140] Similar situations existed in other regions. At each stop along the way, arrangements were made to allow time to visit with enlisted personnel. Many of them were resentful of War Department policies, and they wanted Congress to know the truth as they saw it. The troops were very anxious to return home. One of the soldiers in the Red Cross canteen on Kwajalein Island described it best: "We are not homesick anymore; we are nervous and high strung—tired and weary from the monotony."[141] Monotony was prevalent among men who were compelled to live for long periods on small Pacific islands.

On the island of Tarawa, scene of one of the Marines' bloodiest battles, they saw remnants of Japanese pill boxes and concrete dugouts. They commented among themselves that it was obvious the United States attack was a surprise because the pill boxes faced away from the area where the landings were made.[142]

Moving next to the island of Canton, the inspection party was fed food that was poor, and they suspected that the troops were not being fed properly. Morale was low, and many of the men seemed quite disgruntled. The inspection group requested an extensive briefing about this. They learned that one of the reasons for the delay in redeployment was the necessity to leave troops to guard US military equipment. Also, good water was a problem on most of the Pacific islands.

In American Samoa native soldiers wore uniforms that consisted "of a sort of wrapped skirt affair of navy blue with red border plus a shirt and headdress." Mahon also noted that some in the party were impressed with the beauty and symmetry of the native women.[143] In the Fiji Islands the inspection party slept in grass huts with concrete floors. They were also feted by a native chief, who prepared a drink called cava-cava. "It was made of juice from a certain tara root, cocoanut [sic] juice, rice, leaves, etc., the making of which involved several Fijians washing their hands in it and mixing a bunch of nondescript vegetables. Happily, those who drank it lived."[144] Representatives Snyder and Engel were given the honor of drinking the sacred potage. After all, they were the ranking members of the subcommittee.

After leaving Fiji, the group visited New Caledonia before going on to Australia, then to Guadalcanal and Guam. On Guam they inspected B-29s that were loading food and supplies to be dropped to United States prisoners of war in Japanese prison camps. They also inspected internment camps where captured Okinawans were kept.[145]

The plane circled Iwo Jima but did not land. The congressmen got a good look at Mount Surabachi where the Marines had raised the American flag and noted that the island was barren with no trees or vegetation after the battle.

On August 30, the day that General MacArthur left Manila for the occupation of Japan, the group inspected installations near Naha, Okinawa, the main army port. Destruction was everywhere. The Japanese had defended the island by using tunnels that honeycombed the rocky hills. An interesting feature was the large concrete tombs built by the natives.[146]

Next stop was Manila, where a conference was held at General MacArthur's headquarters. After the conference they toured Manila and the surrounding country to see the intense destruction before sailing to Corregidor on a small boat. In 1935, when Mahon had attended the inauguration of Philippine president Immanuel Quezon, he toured the military installation on Corregidor and described it as "perhaps the strongest fortress in the world."[147] However, under intense pounding from the Japanese aerial and naval forces, coupled with an extreme shortage of food and drinking water, the fortress had surrendered, bringing about the fall of the Philippines to the Japanese. "Had a good look at Bataan," Mahon wrote in his narrative, "and from the boat saw the road where the 'March of Death' began. Manilla [sic] Bay was dotted with sunken Jap ships. The Navy officer in charge stated that he had moved some 400 ships of all kinds and was using many of them to extend the breakwater."[148]

After leaving Manila the group traveled on to China. The first town they saw was Pei-shiyi, where Mahon was struck by the primitive working conditions. "Chinese were breaking rocks and spreading the smaller rocks out by hand on the runway. A large roller, which was pulled by hand by scores of Chinese, was in operation. The Chinese chanted as they pulled the roller along. In carrying dirt and rocks, they had a stick across their shoulders with a bucket-looking affair swinging from each end. This type of construction was a far cry from the gigantic dirt-moving enterprise which we saw on Okinawa in which the largest and most powerful machinery was used to do the job of airfield construction."[149] They proceeded on the thirty miles to Chungking, where they were met by the colorful US ambassador, Patrick J. Hurley. Lt. General Albert Wedemeyer, commanding general of the Chinese theatre of operations, was also on hand to welcome the dignitaries. Hurley took Mahon and part of the group to town in his Cadillac, which was famous for having been flown over the "Hump" in 1938.[150] Others rode in Wedemeyer's jeep. Mahon also stayed at the ambassador's home. The group attended a dinner given by Generalissimo Chiang Kai-shek on September 3 at his country home several miles out of town. Mahon was seated next to Dr. Wong, head of the Chinese War Production Board.

The next day most of the party had lunch with the Chinese minister of war, General Chenchang; however, Mahon joined subcommittee chairman Buell Snyder and Albert Engel for lunch in the home of Ambassador Hurley, where they met Mao Tze-Tung, leader of the Chinese Communists, and Chou En-Lai. In all, about twenty people were present. Ambassador Hurley had flown north to escort the Chinese Communist leaders to Chungking for conferences with Chiang Kai-shek and representatives of the central Chinese government. Hurley was working for unification of the dissident political groups in China, and the luncheon had no particular relation to the congressional group that just happened to be in town at the time. However, the presence of the Chinese Communist leaders provided a good opportunity to introduce the two groups to each other, and this was done by hosting a luncheon in honor of Mao Tze-Tung, who made it plain that he wanted to be addressed as "Mr.," not "General." Chou En-Lai, who wanted to be addressed as "General," was very friendly and spoke intelligible English, in contrast to Mao, whose lack of English made him somewhat difficult to visit with. The congressmen teasingly called Chou "General Joe." As mementos of the occasion, Mahon asked for, and received, the place cards of Mao and Chou, in addition to that of Dr. Shao Litze, general secretary of the People's Political Council. Mahon noticed that the Communists were dressed in very ordinary uniforms made of blue denim without any decorations, in contrast to the more elaborate dress of the Chinese officials.

Later that afternoon the congressional group went into town to do some shopping but discovered that the long war with Japan had caused consumer goods to be very scarce. The streets were crowded with people celebrating the final victory over Japan, which had taken place just days before. Later, the delegation attended a victory tea at Chiang Kai-shek's headquarters before returning to army headquarters, where arrangements had been made for them to meet several groups of enlisted men from the States. Here Mahon met Sergeant George Whitten, who was stationed there with the 14th Air Force. He was very surprised because he thought Whitten, who had been Mahon's secretary in Washington for many years before enlisting, was stationed in India. They had a good visit, catching up on what had happened since they had last seen each other.

The last evening in China was spent at a dinner in the home of Lt. General Wedemeyer. It ended with one of Ambassador Hurley's famous Oklahoma-territory, ear-splitting war hoops. While in China, the congressional group was briefed on the situation there by Brig. General Caraway, son of former senator Caraway, and General Wedemeyer. Mahon described the briefing as excellent.

A criticism made by General Wedemeyer of Japanese tactics was that the Japs proceeded in all their major efforts in a piece-meal fashion. When they committed themselves to a program, they did not put everything they had into it and were always vulnerable. . . . Vice President Wallace visited China at the request of the President, and when he returned he reported to President Roosevelt that the Chinese would collapse within two months after his visit. . . . We had a lot of trouble with the Chinese because they wanted such an excessive number of divisions. They had 246 divisions, entirely too many, in view of the fact that only a relatively small number could be sustained by the Chinese economy. . . . Forty-seven percent of the Chinese soldiers were suffering from malnutrition. . . . The Generalissimo wants us to have a military mission here to help train the Chinese. He also wants our help in a road construction program. . . . General Chiang seems to think that the French and British want to move in and exploit the victory that has been won. . . . We have about 60,000 men in China, 30,000 of whom are in the Air Forces, 5,000 in the training program, 7,000 with combat troop, 14,000 with services of supply. . . . One hundred and nine-two [sic] million dollars is the sum which we expect to furnish in supplies to China within a six month period. . . . India got about one million dollars in lend-lease. Total to China was about 809 million dollars. At the end of the war, the title of unused lend-lease property reverts to the United States. China has got under lend-lease 302,000 rifles, 13,000 light machine guns, 3,000 heavy machine guns, and large quantities of grenades and ammunition. The Chinese have furnished us the equivalent of 208 million dollars, but we have had no real lend-lease agreement with China by reason of the fact that the Chinese monetary system is in such a hectic state. . . . The Chinese will inherit considerable industry in Formosa and Manchuria. The talk is that the Chinese may employ the Japs to run this industry. Perhaps we should have an American industrial mission to China.[151]

Mahon believed the central Chinese government would fall because of widespread corruption. In addition to corruption in the government, thieves' markets, where stolen American supplies and equipment were sold, were everywhere. When the military police could prove theft, local authorities would do nothing about it because they were receiving a kickback. Additionally, Mahon saw two distinct classes of people—masters and coolies, or slaves, who worked for a cup of rice and a cup of tea each day. It was to the advantage of the warlords to keep the coolies in slavery, causing them to believe their only hope was Mao Tze-Tung, who promised them a piece of land on which they could raise enough food to live, not just exist. Family loyalty to the warlords was strong, something that Mahon had noticed when he was there in 1935. In his 1935 journal account of the trip to the Philippines, he wrote that the Chinese would only fight for their family, not for their country. At that time he believed national unity was a major problem.

On the morning of September 5, the group left for Kunming, China, and arrived at the landing field used for so many of the planes that had flown over the "Hump" from India. They learned that, despite the heavy air traffic, there was never a mid-air collision because of the precise timing of the flights; however, six-hundred planes did crash trying to fly over the Hump. This location was also the end of the Stilwell Road, along which a four-inch-wide pipeline had been laid that brought oil and gas into China. About 65 percent of the petroleum that came in was gasoline. The group inspected a tank farm and learned that 50 percent of the personnel were Texans. At Kunming Mahon also visited with a group of American prisoners, who had recently arrived from Mukden.

The congressmen found a very dusty city filled with characteristic Chinese odors, but the atmosphere at six thousand feet was fine. "At Kunming we stayed at the Red Cross Hotel. It was a very-well constructed building, but we were cautious however not to drink any water in Kunming that had not been boiled or treated and not to let bath water in the hotel get into our eyes. Fortunately, the night we spent in Kunming was Wednesday night—not Saturday night—and there were some of us who didn't feel called upon to take a bath!"[152]

Next they flew the Hump at sixteen thousand feet, one of its lower points.

Oxygen had to be used for part of the trip. They landed at Chabua airport in Issam, India, where a series of military installations, warehouses, and airports were the focal point for traffic over the Hump. Air traffic was slow the day they arrived because the war with Japan had ended several days before. Only 1,460 tons were flown over the Hump that day.

From Issam the group traveled on to Calcutta. From the air they could see the Brahmaputra River as well as the Ganges. On the trip to the hotel, "We got our first close-up view of the great and filthy city of Calcutta. Indians and sacred cows were on every hand."[153] The group inspected port installations and an engine repair depot, where five hundred engines were overhauled each month for the 4,035 planes in the China-Burma-India theatre. Over two thousand natives, who were paid about forty cents a day, were employed at the depot. "One of the interesting operations which we saw in the port area was the large installation where American trucks were being unpacked and assembled. General Motors has a large installation here for the purpose of helping the Government in this work."[154]

From Calcutta the group traveled on to Agra, India, to inspect an airport and depot. "After lunch with the Colonel and his staff, we drove out to the Taj Mahal and saw what most of us thought was the most beautiful shrine we had ever beheld. . . . We weren't too happy about pulling off our shoes, particularly since a rain had just fallen and we had to walk through shallow water which covered spots here and there on the marble pavement surrounding the Taj."[155]

The next stop was Delhi. On Sunday they attended an extended conference in the war room at headquarters before attending religious services in the army chapel. Following that, they attended a conference with enlisted men from several states before having lunch with them. The next day Mahon attended a luncheon conference with approximately fifty officers from Texas. That evening they were honored at a reception in the palace of the English viceroy Waivell. "We went through the elaborate palace and saw the beautiful furnishings. The British go to great length to put on style and impress the subject people. . . . It was quite evident that the Indians do not now love the British very much. Our Indian driver at Calcutta said that the people of India wanted to be free and independent like the people of America. I told him that there were so many factions in India that the country would probably destroy itself if it should be granted independence. He assured me that the Indians could get along and that the information which I had was British propaganda!"[156]

In Karachi they inspected the installations there and observed long lines of soldiers who were being processed for shipment home. They had lunch at the officers' mess.

As we left the dining room, we were encountered by a number of young officers of the Air Transport Command who engaged us in conversation and bitterly protested the policies of the Air Transport Command and the Army, generally, in that part of the world. We had a long conference with fifty or sixty officers in the reception room at the club and took note of the many complaints which they registered. We cancelled our previous arrangement to leave Karachi immediately after lunch and proceeded from the Officer's Club to the Red Cross headquarters where we had a meeting with a large group of enlisted men. There were numerous complaints, particularly with reference to a lot of material that had been hauled by Air Transport from the Peacock Project in Africa to India, some of which was destroyed after having been flown to India, according to the complaints. There were also complaints about "The Hump" operation. We took due note of all complaints and had a very frank discussion about the whole situation with the Commanding Officer, Colonel Holterman.[157]

Representative Albert Engel's account of the stop in Karachi is slightly different. His report, inserted in the *Congressional Record*, states plainly that General Richards, the army budget officer accompanying the group, tried in vain to hurry the group along in order to avoid having the congressmen confer with the unhappy officers. When he threatened that the plane would have to leave without them, Engel told him to go ahead and also to leave the conference area because he wanted to hear what the officers had to say without any interference from Richards. Angrily, Richards told the officers they were to report anything they said to Engel to their commanding officer. The young officers then told their stories about the flying in of personal items and many items that were quickly destroyed. This shouldn't have been a surprise as Engel had recently ridden in Ambassador Hurley's Cadillac, which had been flown over the Hump for his personal use. As before (when problems were encountered getting information about funding the atomic bomb), Engel was the one who spoke out for the group, demanding the truth.

They left Karachi late that afternoon for Abadan, Iran, landing after dark. "We were told how hot the weather got in Abadan, but the weather was pleasant on the night and early morning of our visit. We were told that on the ordinary day, the temperature was 117 [degrees] in the shade, 170 [degrees] in the sun. We saw very little of our installations in the Abadan area, but we were told about the situation. . . . We observed the large refinery there."[158] Early the next morning they took off for Teheran. Mahon recorded that

The British-Iranian oil refineries were very much in evidence. The oil comes from the oil fields about 125 miles northeast of Abadan. The River which is formed by the confluence of the Tigres and Euphrates is called the Shett-al-Arab. We saw the town of Khorramshahr just a few miles north of Abadan. Here are our main depots, and they were obvious from the air as we flew over. We were told of the surplus supplies which we have at Khorramshahr. It is quite a port. We flew almost directly north over the desert-like country toward Teheran. Here and there we would see the automobile and truck roads which were used in delivering trucks and supplies through the Iranian corridor to the Russians. We also saw the railroad upon which we had spent a lot of money and which we had used in delivering the vast quantities of supplies into Russia.[159]

Upon arrival the congressmen went to headquarters and got the best report they had received from any stop on the trip. The mission of the military installation in Iran was to serve as a conduit for aid to Russia. There were six thousand troops there at the time of Mahon's inspection; however, Mahon expected that number to be reduced to twenty-six hundred in approximately six weeks. He recorded

We have a $35,000,000 equity in the highway [from Abadan to Kazbin, west of Teheran]. . . . The British part is $7,000,000. The British were to do the maintenance, but they failed to do so, and that is why we have such a large American investment in the road. 140,000 measurement tons of supplies have been declared surplus. We are dismantling many railroad cars. There are 3,663 cars here; also, 4,000 trucks. UNRRA [United Nations Relief and Rehabilitation Administration] has taken some of the stuff from this area for Greece and Serbia. Most of the trucks have a remaining life of about 55%. The railroad cars are worth about $2,000 each. Apart from the road, etc., our installations in Iran cost us about $32,000,000. Personnel peak was 29,500 plus 6,000 ATC [Air Transport Corps] troops.[160]

Takeoff time was to be 3:00 p.m. However, the American ambassador had made an appointment for the group to see the shah of Persia at 4:00 p.m., and he informed the group that it would be poor diplomacy to skip the visit. "We changed our plans and went to see the Shah, and we were very glad we did."[161]

While waiting for the appointed time, Mahon and some others went sight-seeing about the city. They went to the Russian Embassy and persuaded a guard to let them in. "Inside the Embassy we saw a plaque upon which in gold lettering reference was made to the historic meeting of 'The Big Three' in that particular room."[162] Mahon was impressed by the clear water that had been brought from a nearby mountain through underground tunnels and flowed down a gutter on each side of several streets. At the proper time they walked up to the White Palace, the home of the shah. "The guards about the grounds were surly and well-armed. They didn't seem too happy about our being there. But the warmth of the greeting of the Shah made up for all this. Mahon described the visit in detail:

Promptly at 4:30 we were admitted to the palace, much more elaborate and beautiful than our own White House, and standing on priceless Persian rugs, we shook hands with the handsome 26-year-old Shah of Persia. He had on an ordinary brown business suit, talked good English, and made quite a hit with our party. He expressed concern over Russian and British imperialism but complete faith in the integrity and intentions of the United States in Iran.

In the course of the conversation, I asked him if he had any doubt about the attitude and good faith of our American troops in Iran. He smiled and said, "To use an American expression, 'gosh no!'"

There was talk about justice and democracy, imperialism, visas for Persian girls who had married American boys. Some member of the party, perhaps Mr. Norrell, brought up the subject of irrigation, and we had quite a talk on that subject. Francis Case, of course, presented the subject of horses, after I had asked the Shah about his recreation and if he liked to ride horses. The Shah said that the closer the people lived to nature and the soil, the better they are. . . .

Chairman Snyder was in fine form as he sat on the settee with the Shah and rested his feet on an elegant Persian rug. We had been warned that the audience with the Shah would last only 15 minutes, but the Shah kept us for one hour and ten minutes. We had coffee before leaving. Finally the Shah rose, shook hands with us which meant we were free to leave the palace.

As we were sauntering down the front steps, we saw him get into his

Packard and drive up a tree-covered land, chasing away some dogs from the palace garden.[163]

Years later Mahon penciled in a note to his narrative that in 1972 the same shah still presided in Iran and he had visited with him several times in the United States. In 1978 the eldest son of the shah, who was deposed in 1979, lived in Lubbock, Texas, while receiving pilot training at Reese Air Force Base; however, there is no evidence that Mahon had any bearing on the decision of Reza Pahlavi to receive his training at a base in the Nineteenth District.

The next morning the group left for Jerusalem. On the way they passed over the city of Baghdad and speculated about the ruins of ancient Babylon. "Prior to our arrival over Bagdad [sic], I asked Major Hayes, our pilot, if he wouldn't circle the city at a low altitude and let us take a good look. He replied with a wisecrack, 'Well, you know, we cannot afford to circle too low over Bagdad [sic] on account of flying carpets!'"[164] Mahon noted in his narrative that Baghdad was ruled by a twelve-year-old regent who would become king when he was of age and that the British dominated Iraq. He also noted that just a few days before, former president Herbert Hoover had recommended that $150 million be spent reviving the irrigation system of Iraq, which had been destroyed by goat-raising nomads, so several million more people could live there. This would provide an outlet for the Arabs so the Jewish people could make a national home of Palestine.

From the plane the group tried to locate as many biblical landmarks as possible before landing in Lydda. They were met by representatives of the United States foreign service and taken in army cars the thirty miles to Jerusalem. Along the way they saw many cactus hedges, lemon and olive trees, a few camels, and overloaded donkeys. "Women seemed to carry the burdens while the men often rode the donkeys. One particular sight was most impressive and inspiring. A man was riding a donkey while his wife walked along beside him with a bundle balanced on her head, while holding an umbrella over the man's head!"[165]

Most of the time in Jerusalem was spent sightseeing. After making an extensive tour of the temple area, they gathered in an upper room where their hosts served coffee, chocolate candy, and water. "We were all afraid to partake, but Chairman Snyder could hardly refuse to accept the courtesies which were offered us. The penalty which he suffered was most of the following day in bed at the hotel in Cairo!"[166] They also visited King Solomon's quarry, which had been used as a bomb shelter during the war. Following supper they boarded the plane for a one-hour flight to Cairo.

In Cairo the group stayed at the Shepherd Hotel, where they had wonderful accommodations, compared to local conditions. Mahon recorded, "In the long ago when Napoleon occupied Europe, he used the Shepherd Hotel as his headquarters, the hotel having been remodeled on several occasions since that date."[167] Following a two-hour report on the Middle East command, they had lunch at the Red Cross center with the servicemen at the center. Then they departed for an eight-mile trip to the pyramids, which impressed Mahon so much that he wrote, "This Great Pyramid has kept an eternal vigil over this portion of the Valley of the Nile for five thousand years, and it is not likely that even an atomic bomb would ever move it from its present location."[168] Later the group toured the Egyptian museum, where Mahon was also impressed with the King Tut collection and wrote, "The gold casement of King Tut's tomb and the various things contained therein were most astounding."[169] The day ended with dinner at the Mena House near the Pyramids of Giza, and Mahon recalled that "it was here that Churchill, Roosevelt, and Generalissimo Chiang Kai-shek met for a conference."[170] The Big Three met there in 1943 to plan Overlord, the invasion of Europe.

Before 10:00 the next morning, they were airborne on the way to Greece. The pilot gave the island of Crete a wide berth because planes had recently been shot at in that area. They landed at an airport approximately eighteen miles out of Athens, which was being used by American military forces. After the usual briefing the group traveled by car to the city for lunch and then went to the Acropolis. They left at 4:00 p.m. for Naples. The next day they received a briefing, which included an outline of the Italian campaign, in the Caserta Palace, which was being used as the headquarters. In Naples they inspected port facilities and an ordnance depot, and Mahon reported, "At the port, personnel were observed loading out for return to the US. There were many sunken ships in the harbor—some were being used as piers."[171]

The next stop was Rome and an audience with Pope Pius XII. Mahon wrote, "The Pope was very gracious and read a short speech in English to our party which later was published in the Papal newspaper."[172] After the papal audience the group toured the city to see historic sites, including Mussolini's balcony, from which the dictator had delivered many of his public speeches.

The following day the group traveled on to Frankfurt, Germany, flying through the Brenner Pass, where there was much evidence of the bombing that had taken place there. They flew over Innsbruck and circled Hitler's chalet at Berchtesgaden before landing in Frankfurt. After lunch there was an orientation and briefing in the War Room at headquarters, and "after the conference, the group toured the city and noted the destruction therein which was very complete. On return to the Guest House, the group was met by General Eisenhower who talked to the members of the party for nearly an hour."[173] Redeployment and occupational duties were the main subjects discussed in Frankfurt.

The following morning they landed at Templehof Air Dome, Berlin. After lunch they conferred with Lt. General Lucius D. Clay at the headquarters of the US Group Control Council in the former Luftwaffe headquarters building, which had not been damaged during the war. General Clay's office was in former Field Marshal Goering's office. The group was then taken on a tour of the city, where they saw the Reich Chancellery, Hitler's dugout, the Reichstag building, and the Brandenburg Gate. Mahon recorded, "The drive through the city indicated that the destruction in Berlin was many times greater than that in London—some estimated the damage was 10 times as great. In general, the main streets have been cleared by piling up rubble on the sidewalks or within the buildings. Many German women were working at this. Very few men of military age were observed in town. The male population apparently consists of old men and boys not more than 12–13 years of age."[174]

They left Berlin the next day for Paris, where they were briefed at the headquarters of the Theater Service Forces. Later, they were entertained at the King George V Hotel and attended the Folies Bergère for the evening's entertainment. The following morning they inspected the ordnance depot on the base, which was the largest ordnance depot on the continent. Here a tire rebuilding plant was operated by German POWs under the supervision of a small American detachment. At 1:00 p.m. they took off for Bovington Airport, thirty miles south of London. That afternoon they toured the city, seeing many historic sites and inspecting the bomb damage, most of which had been cleaned up. Later, they were briefed at the headquarters of the United Kingdom Base Section headquarters before departing for the Azores. Representative Joe Hendricks, Democrat from Florida, had to remain in London because of illness. This was September 22, which was Mahon's birthday, and the group honored him with a "sing-song," which included "Happy Birthday." He reported, "In the Azores we were held up for two or three hours with a little engine trouble. I visited the soldiers for a long time. Met several Texans—one of the boys was from Big Spring. They were glad to talk to us and wanted us to help them get home. The boys at many places have practically nothing to do and they get unhappy, if not definitely bitter about the situation."[175]

Mahon concluded his letter home, written on the final leg of the trip: "We have nearly two million troops in Europe, and I had a chance to see but a few of them. We have eight million tons of Army supplies in Europe. . . . America is on trial all over the world, and I hope we will be big and decent enough to set a high standard. Our boys have made a lot of friends for us all over the world."[176]

The group arrived at National Airport in Washington at 4:30 p.m. on September 23, after having been gone for thirty-nine days on the inspection trip. The following day they had a committee meeting with General George Marshall. The congressional group reported their findings to President Truman at the White House on September 24, 1945, and on October 4, 1945, subcommittee Chair J. Buell Snyder reported the group's conclusions to the House.

The congressmen recommended that the United States retain possession of the captured islands in the Pacific in order to prevent ever having to sacrifice American lives to take them again. They suggested further study be conducted to determine the most economical way to operate the bases on the islands. Surplus war stocks, including lend-lease items the borrower did not want to pay for, should be sold as soon as possible to avoid further theft and depreciation of equipment, and to expedite demobilization. It was suggested that private airlines should be encouraged to operate the worldwide system of airways, landing fields, weather, and traffic control facilities that had been established during the war. After the thirty-nine-day air trip it was obvious to the congressmen that air travel was the way of the future and these expensive facilities should be maintained in order to prevent having to rebuild them at a later date. They urged that the demobilization process be expedited because a lag in the discharge program was causing the War Department to lose prestige among troops caught in the lag. The group stated that "G.I. Joe has not only been a good soldier but a good ambassador for the United States. He deserves definite, straight-forward statements from the War Department on what to expect and when."[177]

The congressmen recommended that current appropriations for the War Department be reduced by at least $27.5 billion. However, they stressed the importance of ensuring the continuation of research and development in jet propulsion, radar, rocket projectiles, and atomic power because "this war has destroyed old concepts of frontiers and perimeter defense."[178] They also stated that because China was "the largest and most fruitful single field in the world for United States foreign trade,"[179] it would welcome military and economic assistance from the United States.

They also recommended the creation of a commission of the scientists who had worked on the atomic bomb project, the Joint Chiefs of Staff, the State Department, and Congress to study all phases of atomic power. Pending the findings of the commission, the congressmen recommended that atomic secrets not be released.

Finally, the group recommended that the United States inform "every country asking aid that here as there, wealth is produced only by work and if supplies or credits are furnished, repayment must be assured."[180] The United States was not to be considered a country of unlimited wealth.

President Truman and Congress followed most of the recommendations of the subcommittee; however, many US dollars were sent around the world to help nations rebuild—with no repayment. Also, attempts were made to aid China militarily and economically, but the political climate of that nation negated any attempts to help. Information gathered on the trip made it possible to recover more than $27.5 billion from funds that had been allocated but were no longer necessary because hostilities had ended.[181] When the recovered funds were added to the reduction in appropriations because the war was over, the subcommittee believed it had saved the taxpayers over $52 billion.

The year ended with a solemn but beautiful sight for Washingtonians. The national Christmas tree was set aglow with red and green lights. It was the first time the tree had been lighted since President Roosevelt and Prime Minister Churchill turned on the lights in December 1941. In those sad days Wake Island had just fallen to the Japanese and Torbruk was about to fall. During the next four years the tree remained dark to prevent interference with nighttime blackouts of the city. The war was over, but the horror of it was still vivid throughout a weary world. After turning the lights on, President Truman encouraged the crowd gathered there to "remember that the spirit of Christmas is the spirit of peace, of love, of charity to all men . . . We must strive without ceasing to make real the prophecy of Isaiah: 'they shall beat their swords into plowshares and their spears into pruning-hooks; nation shall not lift up sword against nation, neither shall they learn war any more.'"[182] The editor of the *Washington Post* praised the president. Additionally, he admonished readers to remember that "there is also prophecy in the Book of Revelations[*sic*]—the prophecy of a dreadful Armageddon."[183] He speculated that the atomic bomb could become the symbol of our lost innocence, causing the story of mankind to become a story that had already been told because the bomb had the power to destroy mankind, thus ending the possibility of any future chapters to the story. His concern foreshadowed the fears of world leaders for the next four decades. Mahon's seat on the War Department Subcommittee of the House Appropriations Committee placed him in a position to become one of the world leaders who daily worried about the atomic bomb's power to destroy civilization and the skyrocketing cost of protection from this catastrophe.

Photo of Mahon used in his first campaign, 1934. (Courtesy of Southwest Collection, George Herman Mahon, Box 584)

General George Marshall, Subcommittee Chairman J. Buell Snyder, and Mahon just prior to hearings for War Department appropriations, 1944. (Courtesy of Southwest Collection, George Herman Mahon, Box 582)

Standing on the very spot at the mouth of the Malinta tunnel where General Jonathan M. Wainwright surrendered to the Japanese. On September 2, 1945, the day after this photo was taken, General Wainwright joined General MacArthur on the USS *Missouri* to receive the full surrender of Japan, 1945. Left to right: Rep. Albert J. Engel, Rep. Frances H. Case, Rep. George H. Mahon, William F. Norrell, Rep. J. Buell Snyder, General George Richards, Rep. Harve Tibbott, Robert L. Lambert, Joseph E. Hendricks. (Courtesy of US Army, George Herman Mahon, Box 584)

Talking with Texas servicemen in Chungking, China, 1945. (Courtesy of US Army, George Herman Mahon, Box 584)

Subcommittee meeting with General Dwight Eisenhower in Frankfurt, Germany, 1945. (Courtesy of US Army, George Herman Mahon, Box 584)

Inspection trip to Panama Canal Zone. Left to right: Albert J. Engel; General Ray E. Porter, Deputy Commander, Panama Canal Department; General Willis D. Crittenberger, Commanding General, Caribbean Defense Command and Panama Canal Department; Harve Tibbott, 1946. (Courtesy of US Army, George Herman Mahon, Box 584)

Meeting with James Forrestal, first secretary of defense. Left to right seated: Rep. Clarence Cannon, Chairman of House Committee on Appropriations; Rep. George H. Mahon, Chairman of Defense Subcommittee; Secretary Forrestal; Rep. Albert J. Engel. Standing: Robert E. Lambert, executive secretary; Rep. Robert L. Sikes; Rep. Harry R. Sheppard; and Rep. Charles A. Plumley, 1949. (Courtesy of US Army, George Herman Mahon, Box 582)

Air Force appropriations panel of Defense Subcommittee. Left to right: Rep. Dean, Rep. Jamie Whitten, Rep. George Mahon, Rep. Errett Scrivner, Rep. Glen Davis, and Sam Crosby, appropriations staff, circa 1950. (Courtesy of Southwest Collection, George Herman Mahon, Box 602)

Floydada, Texas, onions being presented to Speaker Sam Rayburn, 1951. (Courtesy of Southwest Collection, George Herman Mahon, Box 582)

Inviting Ezra Taft Benson, secretary of agriculture, to address the annual meeting of the American Cotton Congress held in Lubbock, Texas. Left to right: Rep. W. R. Poage, Rep. George H. Mahon, Senator Lyndon B. Johnson, Secretary Benson, and Senator Price Daniel, 1953. (Courtesy of Southwest Collection, George Herman Mahon Box 582)

Conferring with General Curtis LeMay, commander of Strategic Air Command, after inspecting Offutt Air Force Base near Omaha, Nebraska, 1954. (Courtesy of Southwest Collection, George Herman Mahon, Box 582)

George and Helen Mahon at the White House, circa 1955. (Courtesy of Southwest Collection, George Herman Mahon, Box 584)

To George Mahon — with kindest regards
C. E. Wilson — 2-16-56

Talking with Charles E. Wilson, secretary of defense, 1956. (Courtesy of Southwest Collection, George Herman Mahon, Box 582)

Mahon at entrance to the room where hearings of the Subcommittee on Defense Appropriations were held, 1956. (Courtesy of Southwest Collection, George Herman Mahon, Box 285)

Golf game with President Dwight Eisenhower. Left to right: President Eisenhower, Prime Minister Kishi of Japan, George Mahon, and Senator Prescott Bush, 1957. (Courtesy of Southwest Collection, George Herman Mahon, Box 582)

After inspection of missiles in California. Left to right: William Holiday, director of guided missiles, George Mahon, and General Bernard Schriever, Western Development Division under the Air Research Development Command, 1957. (Courtesy of Southwest Collection, George Herman Mahon, Box 582)

George Mahon, General Lauris Norstad, and Rep. Gerald R. Ford confer in House Appropriations committee room, 1959. (Courtesy of Southwest Collection, George Herman Mahon, Box 582)

Admiral Hyman Rickover in Lubbock to speak at Texas Tech University. He presented a bottle of water taken from under the North Pole to Mahon. Left to right: Bill Pfluger, president of Texas Tech University student body, Admiral Rickover, Mahon, and Robert Goodwin, president of Texas Tech University, 1959. (Courtesy of Southwest Collection, George Herman Mahon, Box 582)

Mahon with President Kennedy at the White House, 1962. (Courtesy of Southwest Collection, George Herman Mahon, SWCPC #394, E-2)

Mahon received an honorary doctor of laws from Texas Tech University. Left to right: Fred Moore, president of Mobil Oil, Mahon, and Robert Goodwin, president of Texas Technological College, 1962. (Courtesy of Southwest Collection, George Herman Mahon, Box 584)

Mahon posing with a boa constrictor during an inspection tour of the jungle training school in Panama, 1962. (Courtesy of Southwest Collection, George Herman Mahon, Box 78)

Mahon talking with General Douglas MacArthur after a luncheon in the Speaker's Dining Room. Congress had passed a resolution giving MacArthur the thanks of the nation for his public service, 1962. (Courtesy of Southwest Collection, George Herman Mahon, Box 581)

Kindest regards to
Hon. George Mahon from
Harry Truman
12-11-64

Mahon, President Harry Truman, and Jerry Hall of Mahon's staff, 1964. (Courtesy of Southwest Collection, George Herman Mahon, Southwest Collection Photo Collection #394, E2)

Robert McNamara, secretary of defense, and General Maxwell Taylor, Army Chief of Staff, confer with Mahon just prior to hearings on the 1965 defense budget, 1964. (Courtesy of Southwest Collection, George Herman Mahon, Box 586)

The head table at a luncheon given by Rep. Otto Passman, chairman of subcommittee for Foreign Relations, to honor Madame Chiang Kai-shek, who was in the United States, 1965. Left to right: Rep. Garner E. Shriver, Mahon, Madame Chiang Kai-shek, Rep. Otto Passman. (Courtesy of Southwest Collection, George Herman Mahon, Box 581)

P

Mahon and Vice President Hubert Humphrey walking through a hall of Congress, 1965. (Courtesy of Dev O'Neill, George Herman Mahon, Box 582)

Behind the stage going over his notes for the hundredth time before addressing a national meeting of the Farm Bureau, 1966. (Courtesy of Southwest Collection, George Herman Mahon, Box 584)

After signing a Supplemental Appropriations bill, President Johnson gives one of the pens to Mahon. Rep. McFall in the background, 1966. (Courtesy of Southwest Collection, George Herman Mahon, Box 586)

r

Mahon in Washington, DC, talking with Mayor Rogers in Lubbock, Texas, 1967. (Courtesy of Southwest Collection, George Herman Mahon, Box 584)

At a White House reception for General Westmoreland, who had returned from Vietnam to address Congress, 1968. (Courtesy of Southwest Collection, George Herman Mahon, Box 586)

At the White House for a meeting with President Johnson to discuss the Vietnam War, 1968. Immediately in front of the fireplace is Richard Helms, director of the CIA. Left to right: General Maxwell Taylor, Senator Young, Secretary of State Dean Rusk, Chairman Carl Hayden of the Senate Appropriations Committee, Senator Margaret Chase Smith, President Johnson, Chairman L. Mendel Rivers of the House Armed Services Committee, Frank Bow, the top Republican on the House Subcommittee for Defense Appropriations, Clark Clifford, advisor to the president, Rep. Bill Bates, Chairman George Mahon of the House Committee on Appropriations, Senator Stennis, Secretary of Defense Robert McNamara, and three unidentified people on the far left. (Courtesy of Southwest Collection, George Herman Mahon, Box 586)

George and Helen Mahon with Secretary of Transportation and Mrs. Alan Boyd, circa 1968. (Courtesy of Southwest Collection, George Herman Mahon, Box 582)

Aboard Air Force One en route to Fayetteville for Arkansas–University of Texas Southwest Conference championship football game. Left to right: Rep. Hammerschmidt, President Nixon, Rep. Pickle, Sen. Fulbright, Rep. Jim Wright, Sen. John McClellan, unidentified, Rep. Bob Price, Rep. George Mahon, and Rep. George H. W. Bush, 1969. (Courtesy of Southwest Collection, George Herman Mahon, Box 586)

NASA officials presenting an Apollo-Saturn V engineering scale model to Chairman George H. Mahon, 1969. Left to right: Dr. Thomas O. Paine, NASA administrator, Chairman Mahon, Dr. Wernher von Braun, director, Marshall Space Flight Center, NASA, Dr. George E. Mueller, associate administrator for manned space flight, NASA. (Courtesy of Southwest Collection, George Herman Mahon, Box 581)

To my good friend and James Chairman — George Mahon — with warm regards —
[signature]

Secretary of Defense Melvin R. Laird just prior to his appearance before the Defense Subcommittee. For eight years Laird served on this committee. Left to right: Mahon, Rep. William E. Minshall, Laird, and Rep. Robert L. Sikes, 1970. (Courtesy of Southwest Collection, George Herman Mahon, Box 585)

One of the "Googol Rags" sent to Mahon to use in wiping out the national debt, 1971. (Courtesy of Southwest Collection, George Herman Mahon, Box 607)

DON'T LET DEBT GO TO A GOOGOL
$1,000,000,000,000,000
000,000,000,000,000,000
000,000,000,000,000,000
000,000,000,000,000,000
000,000,000,000,000,000
000,000,000,000,0
GEORGE MAHON

Mahon at North American Rockwell on an inspection tour concerning the B-1 bomber, 1972. (Courtesy of Southwest Collection, George Herman Mahon, Box 584)

At the White House on the night that President Nixon selected Gerald Ford to be his nominee for vice president following the resignation of Spiro Agnew. Man on extreme left is Rep. Kuykendall, 1973. (Courtesy of Southwest Collection, George Herman Mahon, Box 586)

Meeting in the hall outside the main door of the Appropriations Room after President Ford addressed a night session of Congress, 1974. (Courtesy of Southwest Collection, George Herman Mahon, Box 586)

George and Helen Mahon at the unveiling of his portrait in the Rayburn Room of the US Capitol, 1974. (Courtesy of Southwest Collection, George Herman Mahon, Box 602)

George Mahon and President Ford in the Oval Office at the White House. Mahon was urging the President to veto the energy bill. December 16, 1975.

Mahon and President Ford in the Oval Office. Mahon was urging the president to veto the energy bill, 1975. (Courtesy of Southwest Collection, George Herman Mahon, Box 602)

A meeting with President Ford to discuss the suspension of American grain sales
to the Soviet Union. Left to right: Wilmer Smith, Agriculture Council of America
representative from New Home, Texas, Mahon, President Ford, Senator Carl Curtis of
Nebraska, and Ray Davis, ACA representative from Potter, Nebraska, 1975. (Courtesy
of Southwest Collection, George Herman Mahon, Box 602)

Mahon in his office in the Rayburn Building with Deputy Secretary of Defense William Clements and Prince Turki of Saudi Arabia, 1975. (Courtesy of Southwest Collection, George Herman Mahon, Box 602)

Mahon and Vice President Nelson Rockefeller exchange greetings at a dinner honoring Rockefeller at Chevy Chase Country Club, 1976. (Courtesy of Southwest Collection, George Herman Mahon, Box 602)

President-elect Jimmy Carter shaking hands with Mahon after a luncheon in the Speaker's Dining Room for House committee chairmen, 1976. (Courtesy of Southwest Collection, George Herman Mahon, Box 602)

Mahon swearing in Speaker Tip O'Neill as Speaker of the House. Traditionally the most senior member of the House of Representatives swears in the Speaker at the beginning of a new Congress. O'Neill and Mahon both have their right hand raised, 1977. (Courtesy of Southwest Collection, George Herman Mahon, Box 602)

Mahon and CIA Director George H. W. Bush confer at CIA headquarters, 1977.
(Courtesy of Southwest Collection, George Herman Mahon, Box 602)

Mahon receiving the Forrestal Award and medal from J. K. Kessler, 1977. (Courtesy of Southwest Collection, George Herman Mahon, Box 602)

President Carter trying to convince Mahon and Jack Edwards, the top Republican on the Subcommittee for Defense Appropriations, not to fund a new aircraft carrier, 1978. Left to right at the table: Frank Moore, White House staff, Jack Edwards, George Mahon, President Carter, Secretary of Defense Harold Brown, unidentified staff. (Courtesy of Southwest Collection, George Herman Mahon, Box 602)

Mahon and unidentified subcommittee members at one of the last mark up sessions he attended, 1978. (Courtesy of Southwest Collection, George Herman Mahon, Box 602)

Chapter 4

A Battered World Rebuilds: 1946–1952

As the guns of World War II fell silent, the conflict shifted to ideological differences between the United States and the USSR. The result was a power struggle over how to reconstruct the war-torn governments that lay in shambles. Although the roots of this struggle dated back to World War I, the new superpowers did not openly clash until their differences emerged about the future of Europe and Asia. Drawing from a deep reservoir of distrust and sharing almost no common ideology, it was not surprising that ultimately a strong rivalry replaced the American-Soviet alliance that existed during the war.[1]

At the end of the war, Soviet premier Joseph Stalin expected spoils to compensate for the heavy price his nation had paid with a ravaged economy and casualties that numbered more than twenty million, compared to approximately three hundred thousand American deaths. Stalin also wanted a ring of communist buffer nations on his borders to prevent a fourth invasion of Russia within the twentieth century, so he kept the massive Red Army mobilized and maintained control over as much territory as possible in Eastern Europe. He was troubled that the United States did not withdraw to North America, as he believed Roosevelt had agreed to do at Teheran. He knew the power vacuum created by the war would make it easier for the Soviet Union to control all of Europe if the United States would return to its prewar isolationism.

President Truman also clearly understood that the war had created a power vacuum and that the United States would have to remain in Europe if there was to be a counterbalance to the USSR. He believed an American presence provided the only hope of rebuilding Europe with self-determined governments and multilateral economic cooperation among the nations. As attempts to cooperate with the Soviet government failed, the Truman administration began to see Stalin as just another Hitler who was forcing his own authoritarian form of government on the war-torn nations. In this environment of fear and distrust, an impasse known as the Cold War developed. Although direct conflict between the two superpowers did not occur, a massive arms race and proxy wars kept the world on tenterhooks for more than forty years. The Cold War became the impetus for unprecedented US involvement in world affairs. It also became the impetus for an arms race that meant unprecedented defense spending in both the United States and the Soviet Union. Unbeknownst to Mahon in 1946, his position on the Subcommittee for War Department Appropriations would soon put him in the midst of this whirlpool of events.

In the aftermath of World War II, many returning veterans found a different country from the one they expected. Victory did not mean a total peace that would allow everyone to return to the calm, good old days, as had been the case after World War I. Instead, the United States emerged as the strongest noncommunist nation in the world and moved into a position of international leadership. The average person on the street did not seek or want this new role because the problems that came with it seemed to defy solution. Nevertheless, policy makers in Washington believed the nation's destiny—its freedom and democratic institutions—had become dependent upon counterbalancing an aggressive Soviet Union. The war that leveled old Europe had spurred the development of aircraft that could easily reach North America; thus the oceans no longer provided the security they had in the past. As Americans realized that peace meant a heavy, increasingly expensive burden for the United States to bear, their frustrations often turned to anger. They did not want to make any more sacrifices. They wanted a respite from world problems, time to make their lives more comfortable and to rebuild the families that had been fractured during the war. This was not to be.

Many historians point to 1946 as a turning point when events unfolded that ultimately hardened the positions of East and West. The first was a speech by Stalin in early February in which "he blamed 'monopoly capitalism,' not Hitler, for the onset of World War II and implied that it must be replaced by communism if future wars were to be avoided."[2] Americans were alarmed. In fact, Supreme Court Justice William O. Douglas considered it the declaration of World War III.[3] Following this event, George Kennan, US chargé d'affaires in Moscow, sent an eight-thousand-word telegram from the Soviet Union to the secretary of state on February 22. Kennan characterized the Soviets as being bent on destroying the American way of life. He believed their goal was world conquest, but because the Soviets thought that inevitably capitalism would fall, they were in no hurry and had no timetable.[4] Avoiding unnecessary risks, they were prepared to drift into problem areas, wherever they surfaced. Kennan recommended "long-term, patient but firm and vigilant containment of Russian expansive tendencies."[5] His "Long Telegram" ultimately provided the rationale for a policy of containment designed to halt the spread of communism.

Then on March 5, 1946, former British prime minister Winston Churchill delivered his "Iron Curtain" speech at Westminster College in Missouri, declaring that "from Stettin in the Baltic to Trieste in the Adriatic, an iron curtain has descended across the continent. . . . From what I have seen of our Russian friends and allies during the war, I am convinced that there is nothing they admire so much as strength, and there is nothing for which they have less respect than weakness, especially military weakness."[6] This became one of the most famous speeches of the entire Cold War era. "Iron Curtain" was a term Churchill used to describe the boundary between the totalitarian communist countries of Eastern Europe and the democratic countries of Western Europe. He wanted to convince Americans that the Soviets were becoming a threatening menace in Europe, and he proposed that English-speaking nations join together to check any westward advance of the Iron Curtain. He believed the atomic bomb was the most likely tool to make this happen. He also wanted to stiffen President Truman's attitude against the Soviets. The tone of Churchill's speech increased the Soviet Union's fears that the United States wanted to dominate the world and caused an intense effort to eliminate all Western influences from the Soviet Union.[7]

As Churchill had hoped, these events did have an impact on Truman, encouraging him to toughen his policy toward the Soviet Union; however, American military forces, the instrument for enforcing a strong foreign policy, were demobilizing. After the war a tired nation and a cautious Congress tried to return to normality, which meant rapid demobilization, increased domestic programs, a balanced budget, and lower taxes. With finite financial resources available, when any one area of government expands, others must contract. At this time national defense was the area of government that contracted. Focusing on domestic needs was a legitimate goal, but it was not compatible with national security goals at a time when the United States was assuming greater commitments in the world.

Among those pressing for rapid demobilization and a return to normality were Mahon and his constituents in the Nineteenth District. In a letter to a constituent, he wrote, "Ever since V-E Day, I have been doing everything in my power to have the demobilization program speeded up."[8] He remembered the homesick men he had talked with during his inspection trip around the world, and he encouraged military officials with whom he had any contact to do something—anything—to bring the men home faster.[9] Like many congressmen, Mahon did not clearly understand that the international situation was really not peaceful, despite the recently won victory. Tyrants had tumbled, but now another seemed to loom on the horizon; therefore, military strength was just as important as ever.

Postwar foreign-policy objectives and responsibilities were very different from prewar days, but that was not the predominant thinking of most Americans, which made the years from 1946 to 1950 a time of conflicting priorities in the United States. Most people expected the years to be peaceful and taxes to be lower than wartime levels. They just wanted the world to go about its business and leave them alone. Running counter to this was the restlessness of the USSR. Being one of the only two superpowers left after the war, the Soviets were using this opportunity to take control of weaker countries on their border. Their aggressive behavior alarmed noncommunist nations, causing many to fear that their ultimate goal was control of the entire world. That would make another war a real possibility. Despite this situation, President Truman was determined to have a balanced budget, and reducing military expenditures would go a long way toward making this happen. Sharp cuts were made in all military expenditures during 1945 and 1946, and soon troop strength of more than twelve million during the war had been reduced to slightly more than one million. Those who mustered out of the services as well as those who advocated more domestic programs were pleased with his approach. However, many military officers, as well as people in the State Department, believed that vastly increased foreign commitments required strong military forces. America's tradition of citizen armies drafted to respond to conflict, then demobilized during peacetime, could no longer provide the necessary security against planes that could easily cross the oceans to deliver an instant fatal blow. Military leaders advocated maintaining battle-ready forces because there would be no time to mobilize. These forces-in-being, as well as the weapons to counter a possible attack, required defense budgets that were as high as during wartime. This expense was confusing for many, but so was the idea that America was really not at peace, that a Cold War was developing.

President Truman has been described as a "hard money man," determined not to spend more than was collected in taxes. Because a balanced budget and lower taxes were priorities, reducing military expenditures became an important goal of his administration. During World War II he had served as chair of the Senate Special Committee to Investigate the National Defense Program, a bipartisan committee formed to investigate waste and war profiteering in military contracts. The committee was credited with saving over $10 billion, which convinced Truman that huge sums were being wasted in defense. From his experience on this committee, he developed a basic distrust of generals and admirals when it came to spending money.[10] Additionally, the Republican Congress was determined to reduce taxes; thus, revenues were down. After expenditures for interest on the national debt, foreign aid, and domestic programs were subtracted from revenues, the remaining amount was allocated to defense. This became known as the "remainder method" and caused endless debates and power struggles that lasted for the next fifteen years about what constituted adequate military expenditures when the United States was not actively involved in a shooting war. Defense budgets following World War II, which were as much as twelve times higher than those prior to the war, had to compete against strong public pressure for domestic programs and lower taxes.[11] The result was defense budgets that were based on monetary restrictions, not budgets that were based on the best advice of military leaders. According to Warner R. Schilling, "Defense preparations have no meaning except in their relationship to the foreign policy purposes of the nation, but this relationship is not always easy to establish."[12] Because only a handful of congressmen understood the link between military strength and foreign policy, a serious gap began to develop between the two.

Appropriation requests for the War Department (army and air force) and for the navy (navy and marines) were submitted separately at that time, which allowed each department to act as though national defense was its sole responsibility with no need to coordinate plans with the other. This caused an expensive duplication of weapons. Members of the War Department and Department of Navy subcommittees of the House Committee on Appropriations examined the items in each budget, focused on eliminating waste in the purchase of particular items, and then approved funds without attempting to get military leaders to coordinate their responsibilities for national security. Critics accused them of often not even requiring an explanation of what foreign threats were looming and how the budget being considered would provide adequate security against those threats.[13] Moreover, in hearings, sub-committee members heard primarily from military officers whose task it was to secure as much money as possible for their individual service.

In 1946 Mahon agreed with other members of the War Department sub-committee that the president was responsible for deciding the strength of the army and navy, despite the fact that the Constitution charges Congress with the responsibility of providing for the common defense. After World War II the executive branch of the government had the best scientific, technical, and military expertise to properly determine which military requirements could best respond to enemy threats.[14] Also, because defense expenditures had to compete for available revenue with nondefense expenditures, the task should fall to the president and his advisors to consider security threats, nondefense requirements, and public sentiment when allocating funds through the annual budget. At other times, however, Mahon strongly defended the right of Congress to provide for the military. Until the Korean War it was common for the administration, Congress, and the public to vacillate on how much national security should cost the nation.

Although defense budgets from 1946 through the 1950s were marked by inter-service fighting over a smaller and smaller piece of the budget pie, there were other factors that made military leaders very aggressive about securing money for their services. Military technology was undergoing a rapid change that impacted ships, aircraft, weapons systems, electronics, and other fields, causing service arsenals to become quickly obsolete. Not only was the cost of this new technology skyrocketing, its complexity required a long lead time—that is, a longer interval between placing an order and its actual delivery. This was problematic because weapons with a long lead time might need to be ordered even before money was appropriated. Some lead times could extend to ten years, and service leaders had no way of really knowing what the world would be like when orders arrived.[15]

The House, especially the Committee on Appropriations, accepted the presidential request for reduced defense expenditures for fiscal year 1947 and, after holding hearings on annual budgetary requests, sent to the Senate a War Department appropriations bill for $7.1 billion, $117 million below administration requests. The army received the most generous portion of the total funds only because troops and supplies were needed in occupied areas. During hearings, army witnesses testified that they believed any future attack would be a surprise, and battle-ready ground forces would be vital. Army Air

Corps spokesmen countered this by arguing that for the first time in history, Soviet airpower made the United States vulnerable to attack from any point on the globe. They reasoned that this fact made American planes carrying atomic bombs the most effective and efficient deterrent; thus, the security of the nation depended on Army Air Corps weapons. To support this strategy they requested a seventy-group air force.[16] Actually, future events proved that a foreign policy of containment would still require ground forces, but people in general and Congress in particular were greatly impressed by the technology of airpower. The arc of World War II, from the bombing of Pearl Harbor to the dropping of the atomic bomb from an airplane, was vividly etched in American memory; thus, it is easy to understand why the House Subcommittee on War Department Appropriations was so impressed with airpower. Technology and a smaller defense budget proved to be a hard combination for the army to beat.

Considering itself the national guardian of the purse, the House Committee on Appropriations worked diligently to fund all bills as economically as possible, which usually resulted in greater budget cuts than the Senate Committee on Appropriations demanded. For example, in 1946 the Senate passed a $7.6 billion bill for fiscal year 1947 War Department appropriations that restored all of the House cuts. Even after differences were resolved in conference, final appropriations were greater than the House had initially recommended. Almost from its inception the Senate Committee on Appropriations has served as an appeal body to consider government agency requests that have been reduced, or even eliminated, by the House Committee on Appropriations. The Senate believes it is protecting national interests by providing adequate funding for an agency to function effectively when the House has exercised too much restraint in its reductions.[17] Because the Conference Committee[18] often splits the difference in order to get agreement between the two chambers, it is not uncommon for the final bill sent to the president to be larger than the House has recommended.

Congress adjourned on August 2, 1946, ending the shortest session since America entered World War II. Congressmen welcomed the early ending in order to campaign and, perhaps, get a well-deserved rest. Mahon learned that he would have an opponent in the upcoming election. A former member of the Texas state legislature from the Nineteenth District had announced his candidacy during the first week in May. Mahon had announced previously. Marcus "Hop" Halsey was a veteran who had received an honorable discharge after nine months of service to finish his term in the state legislature. When the term ended he then enlisted in the Marine Corps and served in the South Pacific. The thirty-one-year-old Lubbock native came from a well-known family in the drugstore business and had money, which could make a difference in a campaign. He also had a radio show, featuring a hillbilly band, which reminded listeners of how successfully Governor W. Lee "Pass the Biscuits, Pappy" O'Daniel had used this gimmick in his campaigns.

Halsey was rapidly gathering a following throughout the district. His platform promised (1) twenty dollars a month for everyone over sixty-five, whether the state matched it or not; (2) a 20 percent pay increase for teachers; (3) the elimination of the national debt; (4) a firm stand against communism in the United States; (5) an exemption from income tax for people earning thirty-five dollars a week or less; (6) the weeding out of dishonest people from the labor unions; and (7) in order to keep the peace, a promise by Halsey to encourage Congress to tell other nations that they would not have support from the United States if they were wrong. He singled out Great Britain as needing to be shown the error of its ways.

Halsey's candidacy appeared to be a worrisome challenge for Mahon. After reading in the *Lubbock Morning Avalanche* Halsey's announcement that he would be running, one concerned constituent wrote:

> I am afraid that you have the most serious race before you that you have had since your first election to Congress. There is a great deal of unrest in the country and dissatisfaction with existing conditions. A lot of it is natural unrest which always exists in the time of uncertainty after war when there is a great surplus of purchasing power and a shortage of goods, but . . . this government of labor unions, by labor unions, for labor unions has made many good men wonder if the Democratic Party hasn't sold its birth right for a mess of pottage. Lots of people are well fed up with the way the labor unions are running the country, and Mr. Truman's announcement on the ill-advice of a half shot economist in the Commerce Department last fall that the wages of union laborers working for big companies could be raised thirty per cent without any raise in prices did not increase his popularity nor that of the Democratic party in your Congressional District.[19]

Letters from other constituents flowed in, expressing similar concerns. Mahon was also apprehensive about his constituents' reaction to the fact that Halsey had served during World War II, while he remained in Congress. Although he believed he could ultimately win the race, Mahon knew his work was cut out for him. His two biggest challenges would be reminding voters throughout the district of his voting record in Congress (he had voted in 99 percent of the roll calls) and reminding them that his eleven years of seniority would permit him to serve on committees that could be of greater benefit to the district than those of a newcomer.

Running on his record seemed to be the strongest defense. To do this he persuaded friends, who were also his campaign workers, to print a newssheet that would explain, in detail, his work in Congress for the past eleven years and his service to the district. In June he wrote to the editor of the *Colorado City Record* to let him know he would soon be contacted to do the printing. The newssheet would look like the *Record*, but have only four pages, filled with Mahon stories and photographs to let his constituents know how well he had performed his congressional duties. It was called "The George Mahon Journal" and could be easily passed out by volunteers. It was distributed to all residences of the Nineteenth District, both rural and in towns.

His record in Congress was impressive for a farm boy who had come up the hard way, and he claimed the hard way gave him a better insight to the problems of the common man. As the "Journal" pointed out, he had not been able to spend much time in the district lately because Congress had been in session for all or part of every month, except four, since January 1940. However, during those six years Mahon's congressional career grew in importance because decisions made by the War Department Subcommittee of the House Committee on Appropriations had an international impact. Although money appropriated to win the war had left a large national debt, the atomic bomb had hastened peace and gave the United States a military advantage following the war. Mahon's cooperation in funding the development of the bomb was emphasized, with reprinted comments from former secretary of war Henry Stimson, Manhattan Project coordinator General Leslie Groves, and current secretary of war Robert Patterson, praising the subcommittee for its work during World War II. Although Mahon had grown comfortable working with national leaders, he never forgot that most of his constituents were farmers, and he stayed abreast of matters affecting agriculture. A photograph of Mahon with Secretary of Agriculture Claude Wickard had a caption stating, "He has fought the battle of the REA during his entire Congressional service, and one-third of the rural homes in his District are now provided with electricity by REA."[20]

Another article reminded readers that Mahon had worked diligently to dispose of cotton surpluses overseas. During his trip around the world in 1945, he had talked with General Lucius Clay about reviving the German textile industry with US cotton instead of rayon and synthetic fibers. Upon returning home he had conferred with President Truman and Secretary of State Byrns about requiring new German and Japanese textile mills to use American cotton instead of synthetics, especially while they were receiving American aid. The "Journal" noted that his efforts had been instrumental in reducing surplus cotton stocks, a large part being West Texas cotton, from six million bales to a few hundred thousand.[21] This was the kind of help that West Texas farmers wanted from their congressman, and a newcomer could not possibly have the important connections that Mahon had because of his seniority.

In 1946 Mahon was serving on three subcommittees of the House Committee on Appropriations. He was chair of the Government Corporations subcommittee and the ranking majority member on both the Independent Offices subcommittee and the War Department subcommittee. The newly organized Government Corporation subcommittee handled appropriations for forty government corporations. Among others, it appropriated money for the Commodity Credit Corporation, Reconstruction Finance Corporation, and Federal Farm Mortgage Corporation, important to farmers because of the loans they provided for people involved in agriculture. He was the number-two man on the Independent Offices subcommittee, which appropriated funds for twenty independent offices of the government, including the Veterans Administration and the Public Roads Administration. This was important to rural West Texans, who had a vested interest in any bill providing money for paved roads. After the death of J. Buell Snyder (D-PA) in February 1946, Mahon had become interim chair of the War Department subcommittee, the largest and most powerful of all the subcommittees in the Committee on Appropriations. It handled more money than any other committee in Congress or any legislative body in the world. This committee was charged with providing funds that would impact the policy of the postwar military establishment.[22]

Readers were reminded, again and again, that committee assignments were extremely important to congressmen because Congress was run by com-mittees. Assignments were based on seniority, and a new member would not have a chance to receive any of the committee assignments that Mahon held because of his years of service and hard work. In 1946 he was the seventh man from Texas who had been a member of the Appropriations Committee since the Civil War and the second man from Texas since the Civil War who had been a member of the War Department subcommittee.[23] Because money is power, Mahon's position on the House Committee on Appropriations was a coveted one. All these factors were amplified in "The George Mahon Journal."

Although his strong and well-documented record strengthened the confi-dence of his supporters, the Lubbock chapter of the Texas Negro Voters League endorsed Halsey in the *Lubbock Morning Avalanche*. No reason was given, but the chapter president did say that no candidates had made overtures toward the league, and the endorsement was an experiment to see whether the black community would vote for candidates endorsed by the league. Particular can-didates for other statewide offices were also endorsed.[24] This was the first time that African Americans had been permitted to vote in Texas primaries, and there is no evidence that league endorsement helped any of the candidates.

Of the 44,420 votes cast, 25,676 were for Mahon. He won by a margin of 17,744 votes, and in Lubbock County he won by a margin of two to one. As soon as the votes had been counted, Mahon issued a statement in district newspapers, thanking voters for their confidence in him and promising to work even harder during the coming term. Then he hurried back to Washing-ton to continue appropriations work on the War Department subcommittee. Later that summer, after Congress had adjourned, he spent time covering the district to personally thank voters and listen to their concerns.[25] In the general election that November, Democrats did not fare as well nationwide as Mahon did in his district, and Republicans gained control of Congress.

On New Year's Day, the twenty-one representatives from Texas met to elect new officers for 1947–1948, and Mahon was elected chair of the Texas con-gressional delegation. The delegation met each week in the Speaker's Dining Room to discuss pending legislation. Mahon considered the group important because many of them were ranking members on important committees, and they had become his allies. During the meetings they also discussed members' bills pending before Congress, and they supported each others' bills when possible. By tradition, the member who was ranking in seniority and had not previously served as chairman was elected for a two-year term. Mahon's twelve years in Congress gave him the seniority needed to follow Milton West from Brownsville. The following day the Democrats caucused to take care of their usual business of recommending members for open seats on committees before the second session of the Eightieth Congress convened on January 3. Under the Legislative Reorganization Act of 1946, which became law with the opening of this session, House and Senate committees underwent a drastic reorganization. Both parties had to reassign all of their members to newly established committees, and in the House the number of standing committees was reduced from forty-eight to nineteen. This meant that those caught in a merger of committees could suffer loss of some seniority: a member might be the number-three person in terms of seniority on his old committee, but after the merger there would be others with more seniority. Mahon was not affected by this, and because subcommittees assumed even more importance as part of the larger committees, his power actually increased. On the other hand, the Legislative Reference Bureau was enlarged, allowing standing committees to receive a greater amount of information about the bills they were considering. The Reorganization Act also increased the salary of congressmen from $10,000 to $12,500 and provided for retirement income and additional office help for members.

Although the power of subcommittees increased with the reorganization of committees, Mahon actually lost some power when he had to turn his interim chairmanship of the Subcommittee on War Appropriations over to Albert Engle (R-MI). This was the first time since 1929 that Republicans had assumed control of both chambers. In his State of the Union address, President Truman stressed the need for both parties to work together. Only then could he hope to get any of his desired legislation passed. However, except for foreign policy, he had little success getting what he requested, mainly because Republicans were opposed to the cost of his domestic welfare programs.

On January 2, in a letter to Eldon Mahon, who was to take the oath of office as Mitchell County attorney on that day, Mahon advised his nephew that the quality of his service would be far more important than the number of convictions to his credit and that fairness with all would create an invaluable foundation of trust. Subconsciously describing himself, Mahon wrote, "The office of County Attorney is a good starting place for a lawyer. He can make it a stepping stone, or he can make it an avenue to laziness and procrastination. I know you will grow as fast as you can in your profession, and I wish you all the luck in the world."[26] Mahon himself had, indeed, made the office of county attorney a stepping-stone to greater opportunities.

With traditionally conservative Republicans in control of Congress, there was pressure at every turn to cut government expenses and reduce taxes. The most obvious place to make cuts was in appropriations to the War and Navy departments because this represented the largest slice of the budget, and most Americans believed a return to normality meant less money for military expenditures. Additionally, President Truman was committed to an $11 billion ceiling for the War Department (Army and Army Air Force) budget for fiscal year 1948. Army witnesses testifying before the War Department Subcommittee for Appropriations cautioned against a cutback of the ready forces-in-being that would be needed to counter a surprise attack, but most congressmen did not seem to understand that conflict during the Cold War would not necessarily be just a replay of World War II on a larger scale. A foreign policy of containment could well involve the United States in limited wars instead of a general war. Mahon was one of those who believed the Army Air Force should be built to seventy groups, but he expressed no concern about reducing ground troops. When subcommittee chairman Albert Engel (R-MI) led the move to reduce Army Air Force funds, Mahon objected. Knowing he would be overridden in committee, he waited until the bill reached the House floor, where his amendment to keep Army Air Force appropriations at their original level got the needed support from L. Mendel Rivers (D-SC), who was serving on the House Armed Services Committee. In the end, conventional troops were reduced in both the army and navy. Research funds for the development of a ballistic missile were also reduced. As early as 1947 it was becoming obvious that congressional support of airpower was growing at the expense of ground troops.[27]

In late February a British diplomat informed the State Department that Great Britain would no longer be able to provide troops and military aid to Greece and Turkey. Since the end of the war, British aid to the anticommunist government in Greece had been the crucial factor that allowed the government to survive attacks from communist guerillas. Without aid, Greece would likely move into the Soviet orbit, which would undermine Turkish independence and possibly bring the Iron Curtain down around the eastern Mediterranean.[28]

President Truman and his foreign-policy advisors believed it was important to meet and contain the communist challenge wherever it appeared; however, in 1947 the American public was not keen about making the sacrifices necessary to maintain armed forces strong enough to meet this challenge. Most preferred to rely on the United Nations to solve international problems or threaten the use of the atomic bomb when all else failed. America had just witnessed "the most rapid demobilization in the history of the world."[29] Increasing the strength of the armed forces to support this new foreign policy as it was developing required military expenditures that would undermine the drive for a balanced budget that was so important to President Truman and to the Republican Congress. However, in this particular situation the president was convinced that it was necessary to prevent the communists from moving into the Mediterranean area when the British pulled out, so he undertook the task of convincing Congress to provide economic and military aid.

President Truman first gained the support of congressional leaders, such as Senator Arthur Vandenberg (R-MI), chair of the Senate Foreign Relations Committee, who advised him to paint a very dark picture for Congress and the American people, in fact to "scare hell out of them." He believed it would take this to overcome old isolationist beliefs and convince Americans that Soviet encroachment in the Mediterranean was a serious problem for the United States as well as England. On March 12, 1947, when the president addressed a joint session of Congress, he emphatically stressed the danger that awaited and ended his address by asking Congress to support "free peoples who are resisting attempted subjugation by armed minorities or outside pressures."[30] That one sentence represented a sharp break with the past and defined American policy for the next generation and beyond.[31] Known as the Truman Doctrine, it started the United States on the path to helping victims of aggression throughout the world during times of peace as well as war. In May Congress granted $400 million for economic and military aid to Greece and Turkey. Despite critics on the right who objected to the cost and those on the left who objected to supporting a monarchy in Greece and a dictatorship in Turkey, Truman managed to gain the support of the majority of Americans, in addition to Congress. Just as importantly, politicians learned that using the fear of communism to scare hell out of the American people was an effective tool that could be used to increase foreign aid and defense expenditures for the next forty years.

Mahon received a letter from Marshall McNeill, of the Scripps-Howard Newspaper Alliance, asking for a statement of his views on the Truman Doctrine. McNeill wrote, "It has been called the gravest decision ever to face a peace-time Congress."[32] Mahon replied:

> Marshall, I don't see how at this stage of the game a Member of Congress could oppose the proposed loans to Greece and Turkey. It is more or less our announced policy; our Nation has stuck its neck out and we cannot vacillate on such an important issue. We will just have to go ahead and cooperate with Greece and Turkey with the view of helping them stabilize their Government and economy.
>
> I hate Communism, as all right-thinking Americans must hate it, but I don't view this thing as an effort to repel Communism so much. I think of it as an effort on our part to help maintain the independence and freedom of Greece and Turkey. It is the view of our military people that if Greece and Turkey should capitulate to Russia, the whole of the Mediterranean world would fall under the domination of Russia. While I am no military man, I believe that the capitulation of Greece and Turkey to Russia would seriously threaten the peace of the world and imperil the security of the United States in the years to come.
>
> I don't think for a moment that we can feed the entire world or install our democratic system in every nation in the world. As great and powerful as our Nation is, we have some very definite limitations, and I don't want us to undertake to overstep ourselves. When the President announced his policy with regard to Greece and Turkey, I was very much depressed over this further burden which our Nation is being called upon to bear, but I believe the failure to follow through on the program would shoulder upon us an even greater burden.[33]

The Truman Doctrine was the cause of a flood of letters into Mahon's office. He often jotted down thoughts about the contents of letters as he read them. Scrawled across the top of one page are the words, "There are about as many different ideas on the situation as there are people. Truman has posed a very grave question." At the time of reading his mail, he usually made notes that would help later when he dictated an answer. In one he wrote, "I hate Communism wherever it may be and I do not believe in appeasement, but I deplore all this loose talk about Russia. I think we ought to tread softly and carry a big stick[34] and find a way to live at peace with Russia. It must be done. . . . Aid to Greece and Turkey poses many grave questions. I do not know all the answers. Occasionally questions arise here when it is impossible to know with complete certainty just what to do about things. . . . I shall give the matter my earnest attention and hope and pray that I may have the wisdom to do the right thing when Congress takes action."[35]

Another constituent, a professor at Texas Technological College in Lubbock, wrote:

I wonder what Americans would think if Stalin should ask his Supreme Soviet (if that is the name of his top parliament) for a huge loan for Venezuela and Costa Rico to stop the spread of American capitalistic penetration in those countries—and ask further for soldiers and munitions to see that it is properly administered! We might then realize how Russians must have thought of our own recent proposal—made right in the midst of an effort at peaceful agreement in settling problems of the Big Four. If we wish to help feed starving Greeks without demanding the right to choose their form of government, that might be a neighborly deed. But if we are picking up where England failed, it will lead us to the same end. So much that is being said about Russia today sounds like children blustering at each other. There are signs, I am glad to note, that some members of the Congress wish to temper the terms first suggested by the President.[36]

To which Mahon answered:

On Monday or Tuesday the House will appropriate $300,000 to prevent starvation in Japan and Germany. It looks like it ought to be sufficient for us to defeat our enemies, but in view of the fact that we occupy these areas we are required to prevent starvation. It is a most distasteful and unhappy situation from my viewpoint, but General MacArthur says "send me food or send me more Divisions."

The loans to Greece and Turkey disturb me even more than the matter of assistance to occupied areas. I think 80% of the children in Greece have tuberculosis, and I have the utmost sympathy for them, but they are so far away our people do not realize their plight and in spite of the Gallup poll to the contrary I do not think the American people are wholeheartedly in favor of sending either food or military and political assistance to Greece. Of course, I think most people would like to prevent actual starvation, but the facts are hazy and the implications of the whole thing are such that all thinking people are worried, or ought to be.

As you know, our foreign policy provides that we must keep Russia from dominating the Mediterranean and we must keep the British Empire as a buffer between us and Russia—but that is too big a subject for this letter. I am completely out of patience with these people in and out of Congress who declare war on Russia every day and apparently do everything in their power to stir up bad relations between this country and Russia. I think if we will keep our mouths shut, "tread softly and carry a big stick" we would lessen the likelihood of war and have an opportunity of good feeling between this country and Russia.[37]

Constituents from the Nineteenth District seemed to be more concerned about the cost of supplying aid to Greece and Turkey than they were about helping a monarchy rather than a democracy. Some people did notice that these were not governments of free people, but most just wanted a balanced budget and reduced taxes. Mahon's response to constituent mail reflected the views of many Americans. Although the Soviets were becoming increasingly difficult to deal with, many people remembered sympathetically the aid of the Soviet Union during World War II. Moreover, they were reluctant to become deeply involved in the affairs of other nations.

Historian John Lewis Gaddis writes that when President Truman implemented the Truman Doctrine, he understood "that we [the United States] have to have something positive and attractive to offer, not just anticommunism."[38] It would be more effective to provide hope than to instill fear. In that same vein, in 1947 George Kennan, author of the "Long Telegram," was serving in the State Department in Washington, DC. At the direction of Secretary of State George Marshall, he gave form to the European Recovery Program. The concept was made public by Secretary Marshall in a June 1947 commencement address at Harvard University. Ultimately it became known as the Marshall Plan and committed the United States to the rebuilding of Europe. As Gaddis explains, "Several premises shaped the Marshall Plan: that the gravest threat to western interests in Europe was not the prospect of Soviet military intervention, but rather the risk that hunger, poverty, and despair might cause Europeans to vote their own communists into office, who would then obediently serve Moscow's wishes; that American economic assistance would produce immediate psychological benefits and later material ones that would reverse this trend; that the Soviet Union would not itself accept such aid or allow its satellites, thereby straining its relationship with them; and that the United States could then seize both the geopolitical and the moral initiative in the emerging Cold War."[39]

The Soviets were invited to participate in the Marshall Plan, but State Department officials expected them to decline because of American insistence on free trade and shared financial disclosure. Although the financial burden on the United States would be great, the results were expected to be beneficial as well because the nations receiving aid would buy American goods that could be delivered in US ships. Additionally, raw materials could be imported from Europe, providing new investment opportunities for American capitalists. American leaders believed they must find foreign markets if another depression was to be diverted, and war-torn Europe offered little hope before the Marshall Plan.

The House of Representatives adopted H.R. 296 on July 22, 1947, which created the Select Committee on Foreign Aid.[40] Representative Charles A. Eaton (R-NJ), chair of the House Foreign Affairs Committee, was appointed chair of the new committee, which was divided into two subcommittees, one to study European and one to study Far Eastern conditions. Eaton was also chair of the subcommittee to study Far Eastern conditions. Representative Christian A. Herter (R-MA) was appointed chair of the group to study European conditions; that subcommittee became commonly known as the Herter Committee. Eighteen additional House members whose committee assignments dealt with foreign aid were appointed by Speaker Joe Martin. In an article in the *New York Times*, Washington bureau chief Arthur Krock wrote, "Chairman Eaton and Vice Chairman Herter were pleased [with Speaker Martin's choice]. Their colleagues come from the ranks of the hard and serious workers of the House."[41] Because of his strong work ethic and position on the Appropriations Committee, Mahon was appointed to the Herter Committee. Another member was Representative Richard M. Nixon (R-CA). The committee was charged with making an on-the-spot survey of economic conditions in Europe and reporting back to the House on the potential of the United States to meet these needs.

After World War II a major worldwide problem was the economic rehabilitation of the war-torn nations, and the United States—the only solvent nation—assumed a position of leadership. Under the Constitution, money bills must originate in the House—hence, the need for someone on the House Appropriations Committee to be part of a firsthand inspection and evaluation. Krock wrote, "When the executive foreign policy of the United States turned from the first application of the Truman Doctrine—piecemeal assistance to 'governments threatened by outside pressures of armed minorities'—to the Marshall Plan—material aid in the general economic rehabilitation of the world, beginning with Europe—the House of Representatives assumed importance in that policy equal to that of the Senate."[42] The report of the Herter Committee greatly impacted the funding of the Marshall Plan because the testimony of the nineteen representatives, leading members of their committees, convinced a very isolationist House of Representatives of the dire need for this aid.

Before his trip to Europe with the Herter Committee, Mahon sent a newsletter to the district, explaining why he would not be making his usual rounds during the congressional recess. He began by saying, "The question of feeding and financing Europe with American taxpayers' dollars has become of increasing concern to Congress and the American people. There must be an end to it some time. It cannot go on forever unless we are to dangerously deplete our own country. There must be a new approach to the question. The Secretary of State has suggested the so-called Marshall Plan."[43] Direct aid from the United States, such as aid to Greece and Turkey, had been going to European countries, and Mahon hoped the Marshall Plan would establish boundaries for the amount and duration of the aid. This position was welcomed by conservative West Texans.

Mahon was diligent about keeping constituents informed through district newspapers about his congressional work and travels. He let them know that he would be out of the country for approximately six weeks and that he would still have time to visit each of the twenty-five counties in the district when he returned. Although his work was not directly related to agriculture, his constant flow of communication made his constituents feel that he was in touch and concerned about each of them. Being drawn into his work, whatever it was, gave them a feeling of pride that their representative had been chosen for select committees such as the Herter Committee. This was apparent when the editor of the *Lubbock Morning Avalanche* wrote that the people of the Nineteenth Congressional District would be following the trip with special interest because their representative was the only Texan "accorded the distinction"[44] of being chosen for the committee. He went on to write that the committeemen were "recognized in Washington as the real work-horses of Congress."[45]

The committee's first meeting was held in New York on August 26, 1947. According to Mahon's notes of the meeting, Charles E. Bohlen, a Soviet expert who held the third-highest position in the State Department, reported on the situation in Europe. Bohlen said, "The U.S. would be inclined to give 'Friendly aid' if European countries would help themselves. We do not want these countries just to make out a list of merchandise which they would like to have. . . . We are interested in what is really needed in Europe not so much as to what the Europeans <u>say they need</u>."[46] Near the bottom of the page of notes, Mahon wrote, "I am not interested in 'Foreign' aid unless this so-called Foreign aid is to the best interest of the U.S.," and at the very bottom of the page he wrote, "You cannot have one-world until Russia is shown that countries can get along without Russia. Russia is playing for our failure—not for their success. My parting question to Bohlen at the first meeting was what if we withdraw from Europe. His answer was in effect that all Europe would swing into the Russian orbit. It would be the Rest of the world dominated by Russia VS the Western Hemisphere (I feel more like an enthusiastic internationalist than ever before)."[47]

On August 27 the Herter Committee boarded the RMS *Queen Mary* and set sail for Southampton, England. London was headquarters for the inspection trip. During their time at sea, day-long meetings were held with economists and staff members who prepared committee members to better evaluate the economic and political situation in the countries they were to visit and recommend possible programs for aid.

In a news release from England to papers back in the district, Mahon wrote that the country was in the midst of a severe drought that was causing a marked reduction in the food supply. The war had been over for two years, but food, gasoline, and clothing were still rationed. Although these items were produced locally they were exported, "the idea being to acquire more dollars to be used for the purchase abroad of raw materials and food."[48] He continued that the British were a sturdy lot. "They are unwilling to admit defeat; they are determined to prevent the collapse of their country. This is the impression which I got in conferences which we held with officials of the British Government."[49] In London they conferred with Foreign Minister Ernest Bevin and Minister of the Board of Trade Sir Stafford Cripps.

The whole committee traveled on to Germany to inspect the Ruhr, the center of Germany's coal, iron, and steel production, before dividing into smaller groups for an intense study of five different areas—Great Britain; Austria and Germany; Italy, Greece, and Trieste; France and the Low Countries; and the state of agriculture throughout Europe. Mahon was assigned to the group charged with inspecting Italy, Greece, and Trieste. It was chaired by Thomas A. Jenkins (R-OH) and nicknamed itself the "Jenkins Raiders." Newly elected representative Richard Nixon (R-CA) was also in this group. During their time in these countries, political, labor, business, and peasant leaders were interviewed, in addition to government officials. Committee members talked with workers and farmers in their homes; made trips through shops, market places, and factories; and were offered many opportunities for unrestricted observation of postwar conditions.[50]

Italy, the first stop, was primarily dependent upon the United States for coal and grain. Even before the war the country had not been self-sufficient in food, but the war and a severe drought had worsened the situation, and the cost of transportation for both grain and coal was very high. Russia had also been sending a small amount of wheat, but through various manipulations, it was getting a lot of ink in the press that made it appear that most of the aid to Italy was coming from the Soviets. In one of his personal notes, Mahon wrote, "We ought to use our wheat in a most decisive and strategic way."[51] In the same note he wrote that the American flag and the letters *USA* should be prominently displayed on any containers of foodstuffs from the United States. The Italian government was not considered stable, and the group concluded that a stable government in addition to an increase in commercial activity, including especially US food aid, would greatly diminish the threat from communism in Italy.[52]

The next stop was Trieste, the second-largest seaport on the Mediterranean. At the end of World War I, Trieste was made a part of Italy, and following World War II it had been placed under a military government until a peace treaty with Italy was finalized. The Allied powers occupied the western section, and Yugoslavia occupied the eastern. The Italian peace treaty, signed on September 15, 1947, established the Trieste Free Territory with a civil governor to be appointed by the United Nations Security Council. On the night the treaty was ratified, the subcommittee arrived in Trieste. During that night two thousand Yugoslav troops, with horse-drawn artillery, twice tried to force their way into the city. American military authorities resisted both attempts, and the Yugoslavs withdrew.[53] Mahon wrote in his notes "Sept 16, 1947—Trieste (we arrived in Trieste evening of Sept. 15, Monday. 1 dead and 57 in Hosp. from last night)."[54] He described it as one of the danger spots of the world and noticed that an air of uneasiness prevailed throughout the city.[55] Chairman Jenkins's report concluded that Trieste could prosper from its shipping business, but communist harassment was definitely a hindrance.[56]

The group's last stop was Greece. Reports that Mahon sent to newspapers in the district are a good source of his observations there. In one report he declared that Greece was in worse shape than any other European country. Because of the $300 million in aid already sent to that country, people were not starving, but devastation from the war was heavy. More than two years after hostilities had ceased, most highways, railroads, and ports were still not operative. Guerilla warfare carried on by the communists and bandits caused an estimated 250,000 people to flee farms and villages for cities, where they lived in the worst of conditions. This left many acres of wheat land idle, though a worldwide grain crisis loomed in the near future. Terrorists raided the countryside from neighboring Bulgaria and Yugoslavia, communist nations that kept unusually large military forces near the border. Communists also filled government offices there and in Italy and Trieste. Demanding high wages and constantly threatening strikes, they hoped to destroy the economy with inflation and then establish a police state. The local people did not want communism, but the congressmen feared that desperation would force these countries into the communist bloc.

In the committee report submitted when the group returned, the most pressing needs of Western Europe were defined in three categories:

- **Foodstuffs, fuel, and fertilizers**
  These items ranked first, both in urgency and cost of acquisition. Without adequate food there was no hope of expanding production in these war-torn countries; an increased amount of coal was necessary to turn the wheels of industry; and without increased amounts of fertilizer the exhausted soil would only yield smaller and smaller crops.

- **Commodities to be processed and certain types of specialized equipment**
  Commodities to be processed, such as wool, cotton, and lumber, were needed if industry was to grow. Also, agricultural and mining equipment was needed.

It was recommended that the Export-Import Bank,[57] already established by Congress, be used to oversee the purchase and delivery of items in this category. It was believed the Export-Import Bank would be the best bridge to return these financial activities to private channels.

- **Capital goods and equipment**
  These items were needed for long-range reconstruction and recovery. It was recommended that the International Monetary Fund, in cooperation with the International Bank for Reconstruction and Development, be used for these items, with the hope of attracting private capital for long-range construction programs.

To finance food, fuel, and fertilizers, the committee recommended that the Emergency Foreign Relief Authority be established as a corporation under federal charter. The corporation would enter into an agreement for these urgent items and would determine the best form of repayment according to the recipient country's ability to pay. The corporation would also be charged with providing "incentive goods," such as shoes, clothing, tobacco, and cigarettes, and other American consumer goods that would encourage laborers to work harder and reduce absenteeism. Congressional control was to be established through a semi-annual report from the corporation to Congress. All other materials were to be self-liquidating commercial transactions.

It was a hard sell to get a Republican Congress to agree that European aid was necessary because old isolationist feelings surfaced again after the war. Those who believed European aid was vital to prevent the spread of communism worked hard to convince others who focused primarily on trying to cut federal spending.[58] On December 16 Mahon spoke in the House in support of the $509 million appropriation bill that would provide interim aid for Austria, France, and Italy. He called the foreign-aid bill a national defense program and reminded fellow members that he had always stood ready to take calculated risks, such as appropriating money for the atomic bomb, to defend the nation. "If there is anything fundamental in my political philosophy it is this question of a strong national defense."[59] He went on to state that if Moscow pushed the Iron Curtain to the Atlantic Ocean, the necessary increase in US military capabilities would cost billions. Any money spent now to halt communism would save the American taxpayer money in the long run. "We have learned from two world wars that you cannot ignore Europe and the rest of the world and, at the same time, look after the best interest of the United

States."[60] He admitted frankly that he also supported European aid because it served the military and financial interests of the United States, not just the humanitarian needs of the war-torn nations. He believed that a rebuilt, democratic Europe could provide a strong market for American agricultural products and manufactured goods. It was vital to the American economy to find new markets overseas to replace the demand for products created by the war. He understood that failure to do so had the potential for returning the United States to the prewar depression. The extensive debate lasted through the winter of 1947–1948.

Answering those who complained that US citizens were still suffering from a shortage of both consumer and petroleum products, Mahon reminded them that the shortage would continue to exist whether or not products were exported to Europe. He concluded his remarks in the House: "I think we would all like to be isolationists if we could safely afford to be, but we cannot afford the luxury. . . . [W]e must assume our position as the dominant power on earth in promoting peace, security, and stability. It is not so much a question of helping people in faraway lands, rather it is a question of helping Tom, Dick, and Harry, and their families, and all our people in our own country."[61] In later years Mahon declared that he could learn more from an on-site inspection than he could from reading reams of printed material. Apparently, this happened during his trip to Europe with the Herter Committee because his isolationist views began to wane after the trip.

Funding for the European Recovery Plan, known as the Marshall Plan, was debated for twelve days in the Senate and seven days in the House before being passed in the spring of 1948. A year after his Harvard speech, Secretary of State George Marshall, working tirelessly, had overcome the major opposition to the Marshall Plan.[62] Through the Marshall Plan, $13.34 billion in aid was to be provided to European nations between 1948 and 1952. While hastening recovery, it promoted political stability and demonstrated the commitment of the United States to Europe.[63] Truman wrote privately a few days after final passage of the program, "Our neighbors are not afraid of us. Their borders have no forts, no soldiers, no tanks, no big guns lined up."[64]

The Marshall Plan also became a strong tool for implementing containment, which had become the primary focus of the nation's foreign policy. By providing economic aid to the struggling democracies of Europe, the Marshall Plan worked in tandem with the Truman Doctrine, which provided military aid. In fact, President Truman called them "halves of the same walnut."

By 1948 two important trends were becoming entrenched in American politics. The first, containing the expansion of communism, meant increasing military and foreign-aid budgets. The second, "scaring hell out of Americans," allowed fearmongering to become an effective way to get public support for additional defense expenditures. Another two decades would pass before the American public seriously questioned these concepts.

Daphne graduated from Duke University on June 7, 1948, with a major in English. Later that month she married Duncan Holt of Greensboro, North Carolina. They had been dating for two years and were married in a suburban Methodist church that the Mahon family regularly attended. She was at home the first weekend in May to make plans for the wedding, which was a modest one. Friends of hers and Duncan's from Duke were attendants.[65] Her cousin Bryan, son of John Mahon from Loraine, sang at the wedding.

Friends of George and Helen offered their home and spacious garden for the wedding reception. The Carters also attended the same church as the Mahons. Mahon described it as "a lovely affair."[66] Although he was somewhat sad to see her marry and leave home, he wrote to his brother John, "We like Duncan very much, and we are hoping that he and Daphne will be very happy together. Of course, they are on their own having severed the apron strings."[67] However, despite his rather stern comment about severed apron strings, the Mahons gave the newlyweds a new Chevrolet for a wedding gift. The couple went to Virginia Beach, Virginia, for their honeymoon and a week later returned to Washington, where they stayed in the Alban Towers apartment while Mahon and Helen returned to Texas. Duncan kept Mahon's Washington office open during July and August before returning to Duke in September for his last year in law school.

After the wedding, cousin Bryan spent an additional week with his aunt and uncle. George Mahon wrote to his father about an interesting event as they walked by the White House. "To our amazement and delight, the President's secretary insisted that we tarry a moment and shake hands with the President. The President was in fine fettle. . . . No doubt the approaching election was somewhat responsible for the cordiality of our reception at the White House! It is terrible the way people suspect the motives of politicians!"[68]

Congressional night sessions lasting until nearly midnight were often necessary in order to adjourn by mid-June. Generally, Mahon's days were quite full.
At about 10:00 each morning he left his congressional office in the Longworth
House Office Building for the Appropriations Committee office in the House
of Representatives to work on marking up[69] a bill or to attend hearings. At
noon each day Congress convened, and Mahon had to be either in the chamber or close enough to answer the bell for a roll call. About 6:00 p.m. he returned to his congressional office to sign letters before going home. On most
days he took material home to read that evening in preparation for the next
day. Often he lamented that he was so busy he really had no leisure time to
enjoy friends or family.[70] In August 1948 he and Helen spent nearly two weeks
making the trip back to Texas, taking time to vacation and rest along the way.
He did not have an opponent, and they had voted by absentee ballot in the
July primary, so this quiet time was especially enjoyable. They always looked
forward to returning to Texas, and being rested made their time with constituents more rewarding. However, on the national scene Democratic politics
were anything but peaceful.

The Democratic National Convention opened in Philadelphia on July 12.
Mahon decided not to attend, begging off because of work. Truman and Barkley were chosen for the ticket, but many leading Democrats openly opposed
Truman. According to historian James Patterson, "Rarely in the modern history of American politics had so many leading party figures rebelled openly
against an incumbent President seeking re-nomination."[71] The political party
that had led the nation for so long was experiencing deep ideological tensions,
and Truman was caught in the crosshairs. Conservative Southern Democrats
bolted the Democratic ticket because of disagreements about the civil-rights
plank in the platform. They united under the States' Rights Democratic Party,
known popularly as the Dixiecrat Party, and J. Strom Thurmond (D-SC) ran
against Truman. Fielding L. Wright, governor of Mississippi, was nominated
for vice president. Truman's "whistle-stop" campaign drew huge crowds as
his train crisscrossed the nation. Sam Rayburn was with him in Texas to lend
support there. On election day President Truman "won against the greatest
odds in the annals of presidential politics,"[72] writes his biographer, David Mc-
Cullough. He was reelected with 304 of 521 electoral votes. Dewey received
189, Thurmond 38. In popular votes Truman received approximately 24.1
million, Dewey approximately 21.9 million, and Thurmond fewer than 1 million. Just as important, the Democrats recaptured the majority in the House

and Senate.[73] After the election there was a lot of soul-searching in an effort to explain what many people had considered impossible.

Although Mahon did not have an opponent, he believed he needed to spend time in the district, listening to constituent concerns and strengthening his contact with supporters. Early in March 1948 he had received a troublesome letter from Lloyd Croslin, his former secretary in Washington and the manager of his first campaign in 1934. Croslin, living in Lubbock at the time, reported hearing rumors that Houston oil millionaire Hugh Roy Cullen was offering five thousand dollars to anyone who would run against incumbent officeholders in Texas. Cullen was one of the strongest Republicans in the state, and the Republican Party was growing in strength in West Texas. The rumor of an opponent proved false; nonetheless, Mahon decided to spend time in the district instead of attending the Democratic National Convention. He could not really be effective in the 1948 presidential election because he had consistently voted against federal civil-rights bills, FEPC,[74] anti–poll tax bills, and anti-lynching bills. He and the majority of constituents in the Nineteenth District believed these matters should be settled at the state level; therefore, he had difficulty supporting the Democratic national platform. Moreover, he wanted no part of the party squabble because he had no intention of siding with the Dixiecrats. The 1948 Democratic National Convention was crucial to the party but not to Mahon. He was able to remain above the fray of party politics because he was from a safe district, and he wanted only one other position in all of Congress. He hoped to become chairman of the full House Committee on Appropriations when Chairman Clarence Cannon resigned. As long as he continued to be elected and continued to be "Cannon's protégée in good standing," unfinished work would be an acceptable excuse to avoid situations where party conflicts might cause problems for him.

Voters in the Nineteenth District were pleased with their representative, which was obvious from an editorial in the *Big Spring Herald* entitled, "Mahon Deserves Unopposed Campaign." The editor went on to write, "Because he is quiet and unassuming, a type of man whose name may seldom be found quoted at length upon this and that issue, his record is the one thing which has earned him the support of his district."[75] He praised Mahon for, among other accomplishments, being selected to serve on the Herter Committee, whose members were known for their conscientiousness and ability to work hard. The editorial was carried verbatim in many other newspapers throughout the district. Mahon was indeed safe in his district, and he intended to spend time among his constituents to ensure that that situation did not change. Mahon publicly supported the Democratic ticket in the general election, and when the results were final, he dutifully gathered Democrats in the district for a fund-raising dinner. Approximately twenty-five hundred dollars were sent to national party headquarters to help defray the cost of the campaign.

In 1947 the National Security Act merged the Navy Department and the War Department into the National Military Establishment under the direction of a secretary of defense. It also created a separate Department of the Air Force from the old Army Air Force. The Senate confirmed James V. Forrestal as the first secretary of defense on September 17, 1947, and the provisions of the act took effect on September 18, 1947. The act was intended to bring cohesion and direction to the military establishment through unified planning, programming, and budgeting. Hopefully this would reduce wasteful spending and inter-service conflicts. It was also hoped that the act would create a closer relationship between the required level of defense preparations and foreign policy.[76] Nothing of the sort happened.

The National Security Council was created under the same act to advise the president on security matters. According to plans the three services would be guided by two planning documents: the Basic National Security Policy (BNSP) and the Joint Strategic Objectives Plan (JSOP). These documents were intended to provide guidance that would help the Joint Chiefs develop budgets to support the nation's strategic policy. In reality, they became practically useless because they could be interpreted in many ways, and each service interpreted them to suit its own goals. Each service saw the major part of national security as its own charge, which resulted in much duplication. This caused budgets that ran as much as 15 percent over the ceiling established by the administration. Consequently, the Office of the Secretary of Defense had to make cuts, and often these were percentage cuts across the board, without regard to priorities. Developing a defense budget in this manner was not really satisfactory to any branch of the service. There was no planning for integration, there was too much duplication, many areas of national security were not well covered, each service was busy protecting its own territory within the budget, and there were no criteria for choosing between competing programs. Competition among the three services for as large a piece of the pie as possible became intense. Padding expected expenditures to offset possible cuts became common practice in addition to spending time concocting arguments in favor of more money in the next year's budget. With the creation of the Department of Defense, the process of developing each annual budget began approximately a year before it was to be submitted to Congress. To control expenditures the Truman administration established a ceiling for the budget.

Democrats gained control of Congress in the 1948 election, and when the Eighty-first Congress convened in January 1949, Mahon became chair of the Military Establishment Subcommittee of the House Committee on Appropriations. This marked the first time in history that one subcommittee handled appropriations for the entire military budget. Clarence Cannon, chair of the House Committee on Appropriations, tapped Mahon for this position. Mahon's longtime aide, Ralph Preston, remembered that his appointment had been something of an alphabetical accident. When two people were appointed to a committee in the same year, alphabetical order was used to determine which one had the most seniority.[77] Both George Mahon and Harry Sheppard (D-CA) were appointed to the Appropriations Committee in 1939, so Mahon was considered to have more seniority than Sheppard. Additionally, Mahon's ability to work harmoniously with Cannon and the fact that the two shared a similar conservative fiscal philosophy were a big plus for him. On June 13, 1946, Chairman Cannon praised Mahon from the floor of the House of Representatives, saying, "I think that in all my service here in the House I have never seen a Member rise more rapidly, and more deservedly, than . . . the distinguished gentleman from Texas, Mr. Mahon. His capacity for leadership, his sound judgment, and his interest in the maintenance of essential Federal activities at a minimum of expenditure have placed him on committees holding the purse strings over some of the most important departments of the Government."[78] Mahon's ethos of hard work, willingness to accept responsibility, and respect for others were marking him as someone who could get the job done without alienating those with whom he worked.

This latest appointment placed him in one of the most responsible positions in Congress because the subcommittee for all defense appropriations would approve the largest expenditures of any subcommittee. After the president sent his budget to Congress in January, each administrative agency sent its justifications to the appropriations subcommittee responsible for preparing the bill that provided operating funds for the agency. These justification documents supported the agency's requests and compared the current budget to earlier ones. The subcommittee summarized the documents it received and used the information during the hearings that followed. The hearings allowed agency leaders and other interested parties to defend the agency's budgetary requests and also to answer questions from subcommittee members. When the hearings were concluded, the subcommittee met to mark up the bill. This consisted of deciding what dollar amount to recommend for each item that was presented. The final bill, together with an explanatory report, was then prepared and presented to the full House Committee on Appropriations for approval. Rarely were changes made. The next step was sending the bill to the House for debate and a vote. Mahon, as chair of the subcommittee, was responsible for scheduling and presiding over the hearings, presiding over the markup sessions, writing the bill and the subcommittee report, presenting the report to the full committee, and managing the floor debate when the bill was considered in the House. The defense appropriations bill passed by the Senate was almost always different from the House bill, and Mahon then led the House conferees in conference deliberations.

For fiscal year 1950 (July 1, 1949–June 30, 1950), President Truman requested $15 billion for defense, more than one-third of the entire federal budget of $41.9 billion. In April 1949 Mahon presented the subcommittee's bill to the full House, where it passed. This was the first bill ever written for the entire Department of Defense, and he received broad nonpartisan praise from many in the House. Representative C. A. Plumley (R-VT) said that he "wanted to take a moment to pay tribute to the chairman of the subcommittee, the gentleman—and I use the term in full appreciation of its meaning. . . . He has had an unprecedented burden involving the enactment of appropriations for all branches of the armed services under the National Security Act in one bill. . . . He has been fair. . . . He is well informed. He has our complete confidence because of his outstanding ability and his demonstrated qualification for the leadership he has exemplified."[79] Mahon's files, currently housed at Texas Tech University, contain many letters from constituents and a scrapbook full of news articles from local and Texas-wide editors, praising him for his work on this bill. One rather short letter sums it all up. A constituent from Lubbock wrote, "Congratulations. You make all of us whom you represent proud of you. Keep up the grand job you are doing."[80]

Mahon was one of many in Congress who had led the fight for a fifty-eight-group[81] air force instead of the forty-eight-group one requested by President Truman, and he stressed the importance of stockpiling strategic materials such as tin, magnesium, cobalt, and rubber. He hoped to ultimately see a seventy-group air force. He justified his position by saying that the taxpayer must find consolation in the fact that the huge sums were being spent for national security and for the peace and happiness of Americans—in short, to prevent World War III. He said on the floor of the House:

> If war comes soon, we are appropriating too little. If we have miscalculated the dangers, if the threat of war is just a deceptive mirage on the horizon, we are appropriating too much. The likelihood of the outbreak of war in the near future was a pertinent subject of inquiry by our committee. Among those with whom we discussed this subject were Secretary of Defense Louis Johnson and former Secretary James Forrestal,[82] Secretaries Royall, Sullivan, and Symington, General Omar Bradley, Admiral Denfeld, General Vandenberg, General Wedemeyer, and General of the Armies Dwight D. Eisenhower. These men did not predict an early outbreak of war, but they agreed that some unpredictable development might throw us suddenly into conflict. This, however, was not anticipated.[83]

He went on: "I would have no part in deceiving the people of this country. The bill before us does not prepare this country for the immediate outbreak of war. A minimum of $50 billion would be required for that purpose."[84] That would have been more money than the government could collect that year through taxes. According to the *Congressional Record*, Mahon argued, "No military man before us recommended complete preparation for war. Nothing would please a potential enemy better than to have us bankrupt our country and destroy our economy by maintaining over a period of years complete readiness for armed conflict. Such a course would not only destroy our economy, but it would also probably destroy our democracy, destroy the essential natural resources of the country, and perhaps lead to a military dictatorship. Our country proceeds on the theory that our best interests are promoted by taking certain calculated risks. That is what the military people say, and I think we are compelled to agree with them in that statement."[85]

Later, critics argued that Mahon's committee did not, during the hearings, request information about the criteria used to determine the size and kind of military forces requested. The committee also failed to inquire about exactly what kind of protection the nation could expect from the amount allocated to each of the services.[86] Often Mahon claimed to be reluctant to ask military witnesses for too many specifics because he believed that too much information was already being made public and available to the Soviets. Despite his concern, it is very likely that Soviet spies had already had more information about US military forces than most members of Congress.

The accusation that the subcommittee was more comfortable in a watchdog role than in examining the strategic planning behind defense spending became a recurring theme of historians writing about congressional examination of defense budgets during the Cold War. Congressional committees lacked the time and research staff available to the military and executive departments; however, more challenging questions from Mahon's subcommittee about how the military budget was prepared and how it would support foreign policy, especially containment, might have encouraged more congressional debate and input about the best balance between defense and domestic expenditures.[87] Additionally, during the markup phase of budget deliberations, each line item was examined to ferret out waste and mismanagement before settling on a final dollar figure. This very process caused the subcommittee to believe it had done its job of funding the defense program as economically as possible and diverted its attention from learning if the defense budget it had approved was really the best one to support the nation's foreign policy. In fact, the increased amount of funding that Mahon supported for the air force, without questioning how the money would be used, would not be used for more strategic aircraft, such as heavy bombers, but would be used to purchase planes to transport troops. All the services competed for strategic missions—such as carrying atomic bombs or using atomic weapons that would become a strong line of defense—and gave short shrift to supporting conventional warfare. In the near future a hard lesson would be learned about the importance of conventional warfare—of having adequate ground forces and the ability to transport them from location to location.

From the floor of the House, Mahon declared, "In cash appropriations the bill exceeds the President's budget by $53,497,100. In contract authorizations the bill exceeds the President's budget by $577,755,000. Many reductions were made in the budget, but there is an over-all increase of the budget in the bill which is brought about by the action of the committee in providing for additional aircraft and expansion of the Air Force."[88] The increase was brought about to ultimately reach the seventy-group program. Mahon went on to say that he believed there would have been no Pearl Harbor in 1941 if the United States had been prepared to strike a quick and deadly blow to Japan—and the only force that could strike that devastating blow was the air force. It was considered the first line of defense because it could immediately carry the battle to the interior of the enemy's homeland. Thus, Mahon thought the air force must be in state-of-the-art condition and always ready to strike. However, in this case added money for the air force would not have provided any more striking power. Although the Army and Navy were important, the subcommittee believed the idea of trying to split the national defense appropriations into three equal portions was nonsense that could not adequately meet national-defense requirements, and Mahon expressed this belief on the House floor.[89] However, one member of the subcommittee, Representative Taber (R-NY), managed to insert a clause in the appropriation bill, authorizing President Truman to spend the additional money "only after he had made a finding as to its 'necessity.'"[90] This meant the money would not be spent because it was contrary to the president's position on the amount of money that should be spent on defense. He was shaping the defense budget by overall budget restrictions, rather than by recommendations from military people and from Congress. The *Washington Post* reported that the important question was whether President Truman or Louis Johnson, secretary of defense, would permit the air force to spend the extra money.[91] This question was raised during the debates in both chambers, and floor leaders stressed the fact that the bill only permitted the money to be spent; it did not demand that it be spent. This meant there was a high probability that the money would be impounded.

Texas congressmen voted in favor of the bill. "I'm for as great an Air Force as might be needed to defend the United States and prevent war," Sam Rayburn said. "My people in Texas want this nation to keep strong, and I think a powerful air force is the best way to do it."[92] From 1946 to 1952, Texas had twenty-seven active air force bases, which also helped keep the state's economy strong, so support from Texas congressmen for a powerful Air Force was politically wise. Mahon voted in favor of the increase although his subcommittee voted for only a fifty-five-group air force. Just for good measure, proponents pointed out that Army General Dwight Eisenhower agreed that a seventy-group Air force was necessary. The bill that was ultimately sent to the president contained funds to support a fifty-eight-group air force. When the Conference Committee report was being debated in the House, it was pointed out that the president would simply impound the money, thus circumventing the will of Congress to increase the size of the air force. Mahon responded, "I do not think it would be proper for the will of Congress to be circumvented. I would not object, as I know other Members would not object, to any reasonable economies in Government. But economy is one thing, and the abandonment of a policy and program of the Congress another thing."[93] However, it would be another two decades—and many debates in Congress—before impoundment of appropriated funds by the executive branch would be curtailed.

In answer to concerns that Congress was making the same mistake in reducing defense spending that had been made after World War I, Mahon made the point that the 1950 defense budget was more than 3,000 percent above the amount spent on defense four years after World War I.[94] As of June 30, 1950, Congress had provided $49.33 billion for the Department of Defense since 1946.[95]

Despite the long hours of hard work that were required, one of the rewards of Mahon's position was interacting with leaders who had left their mark on the nation and the world. On March 21 Mahon wrote to his sister-in-law, "My subcommittee goes into the 9th or 10th week of hearings this morning at 10 o'clock. We always meet at 10 in the morning and adjourn about 4:30 or 5:00 in the afternoon. General Ike Eisenhower, one of the heroes of the war, will be our star witness this morning. Our hearings are always behind closed doors with no spectators and newspaper people permitted. In other words, we do not get any glory for all the work we do but we have many interesting experiences."[96]

In April 1949, communist forces, one million strong, crossed the Yangtze River and moved south to take control of the last provinces still loyal to Chiang Kai-shek. The fall of China to communism was complete by October 1, 1949, when the People's Republic of China was officially inaugurated. With more than five hundred million people, this became the largest communist nation in the world.[97] In September of that same year, above-normal radioactivity over the North Pacific and later over the British Isles indicated that Russia had detonated an atomic bomb. On September 23 Truman announced that an atomic explosion had taken place in the USSR. Although the United States had known that other nations would eventually have the bomb, this event had occurred several years earlier than expected. The international situation had changed drastically. Stephen Ambrose and David Brinkley observed that "the Soviets now had two trumps, the bomb and the Red Army, to the West's one."[98] By the end of 1949, the whole world was polarized into two distinct spheres—one dominated by the USSR and the other dominated by the United States. Mutual fear and distrust drove these spheres further and further apart. The United States believed the communists were just lying in wait for the economic and political instability of war-torn nations to force them to accept communism, and the USSR believed that unfriendly democratic nations had encircled the Soviet Union, thus making its borders vulnerable to the type of invasions that had been a plague throughout its history. Leaders of each group poured all their energies into defending their side of the argument.

The loss of China, the Soviet's explosion of an atomic bomb, and increased hostility toward the West in public speeches by Soviet leaders became a wake-up call to the State Department. Policy planning staff members were convinced that budget limitations were responsible for a military strategy that hindered the implementation of the nation's foreign policy of containment. In January 1950 President Truman ordered the departments of state and defense to conduct a general strategic reassessment. The result was NSC-68,[99] the first comprehensive defense strategy oriented to the needs of the Cold War.[100] The document recommended that the United States assume, unilaterally, the defense of the noncommunist world.[101] This meant "an immediate and large-scale build-up in our military strength and that of our allies with the intention of righting the power balance and in the hope that through means other than all-out war we could induce a change in the nature of the Soviet system."[102] The document argued that the West "lacked conventional forces and was critically weak in Europe."[103] The Soviet Union, on the other hand, possessed an overwhelming superiority in ground troops and an expanding economy. "By 1954, it was estimated, the Soviet Union would have the nuclear capability to launch a devastating attack upon the United States."[104] The document rejected both withdrawing to the Western Hemisphere and doing nothing or launching a preventive war. Unlike previous assessments that envisioned an expanded conventional conflict, NSC-68 urged preparation for a cold war that would require constant preparedness for immediate retaliation. There would be no time to mobilize and train forces. The recommended preparation stressed

strengthening ties with our allies and increasing military strength in preparation for either a limited or a general war. This meant increasing the number
of ground troops as well as increasing the number of pilots and planes. Preparing for any type of war during peacetime proved to be a hard sell to the
American people, who believed that democracies armed only in response to
actual aggression. Arming to deter war made no sense to most of them, but
that would change before the year was over.

Back in the district, constituents reacted to Mahon's new appointment on the
Military Establishment subcommittee with pride and hoped that he would
be able to help the district even more than before. They speculated that his
position as chair of the subcommittee that approved military expenditures
would enhance the district's chances of getting Lubbock Army Air Force Base
reactivated. Politics play a major role in the decision to locate government
installations, whether for armed services or other agencies. When all things
appear equal—or nearly equal—installations are often put in locations most
beneficial to congressmen. Why not reactivate a base in the district of the
congressman who so strongly supported the air force?

In April Mahon arrived in Lubbock with two planeloads of air force officials on an inspection tour to determine what problems would be involved
with reactivation. The group, which included Undersecretary of the Air Force
Eugene M. Zuckert, inspected the physical properties and met with city officials to secure the assurance of help with such things as housing needs for personnel. Three days later, the Lubbock newspaper carried headlines announcing that the base was to be reopened as soon as possible.[105] In November 1949
the name of the base was changed to Reese Air Force Base in honor of 1st Lt.
Augustus F. Reese, Jr., a native of nearby Shallowater, Texas, who was killed
in World War II. It was to become a permanent advanced training school
for twin-engine planes, and with it came an annual payroll of approximately
$6 million for twenty-seven hundred military personnel and 650 civilians.
Purchases of supplies, such as food and gasoline, were expected to add nearly
another $6 million annually to the local economy.

In December, while the Mahons were in Lubbock for the Christmas holidays,
George made a trip to the farm near Spade, Texas, that he owned with his

brother Durward. Mahon wrote to Daphne that they hoped to make 350 bales of cotton from the farm. He ended the letter: "I am very relaxed and happy over this exciting and wonderful world."[106]

When the president's fiscal-year-1951 military budget was examined after it reached the House Subcommittee on Military Establishment Appropriations, members were concerned that it was inadequate in terms of the international situation. Domestic economic considerations, rather than funding requests submitted by the services, were primarily responsible for a $13 billion ceiling. At subcommittee hearings Mahon expressed his concern about reduced Army forces, with increased tensions abroad after the communists had taken control of China and the Soviets had exploded an atomic bomb. Director of the Budget Frank Pace and Defense Secretary Louis Johnson were called in to discuss the reasoning and strategic policies upon which the budget was based. Pace said that the budget belonged to the president, and Johnson argued that the smaller budget actually increased military efficiency. This rationale apparently satisfied the subcommittee members, who agreed that it was up to the president to determine what the military budget should be. This was contrary to Mahon's reasoning of the previous year that it was up to Congress to determine the size and composition of the military budget, and thus the increase in air force funding. In presenting the subcommittee's bill to the full House in April 1950, Mahon argued that America's industrial potential, which permitted the nation to fight until victory was achieved—not forces-in-being—was the basis of the deterrent strength of the United States. Events later in the year would challenge the soundness of his argument against adequately prepared forces-in-being. Moreover, he had long advocated a stronger air force to deliver atomic weapons that could produce victory in a matter of minutes, making a nation's industrial potential almost a moot point. This illustrates the difficulty that congressional appropriations committees experienced in formulating the right questions and securing the necessary information to determine whether the defense budgets they approved would provide the right mix of forces to protect the interests of the United States in the world. This confusion would continue for the next fifteen years because, according to Samuel Huntington, "both established political ideas and military doctrine hampered change."[107]

On June 25, 1950, North Korean forces crossed the Thirty-eighth Parallel, launching a surprise attack on South Korea. "Within a few hours of receiving the news, Truman requested a meeting of the U.N. Security Council, and later that afternoon the United Nations adopted a US-sponsored resolution declaring the North Korean action a 'breach of peace,' demanding that the aggressor withdraw beyond the 38th parallel, and calling upon all members of the United Nations to assist in the enforcing of the resolution."[108] Almost instantly the type of concerns expressed in NSC-68 became cold, hard realities. The stronger ground forces of the communist bloc were invading an independent nation. The pressure had been ratcheted up a notch from the internal political pressures exerted in war-torn European nations.

Since 1940 Korea had been part of Japan, but after World War II the northern half was occupied by troops of the Soviet Union and the southern half by the United States. The Thirty-eighth Parallel was to serve as a line of demarcation until a single Korean government could be organized; however, during 1948–1949 both superpowers withdrew their troops despite the lack of a united government. A UN–sanctioned election placed Syngman Rhee in power in the American-supported Republic of Korea, and Kim Il-Sung took control of the Soviet-supported Democratic Republic of Korea. There was no election in the North. Although a civil war began to develop over which faction would govern the entire country, neither side could invade the other without the support of its superpower, and that support was not forthcoming until January 1950. According to historian John Lewis Gaddis, Stalin concluded the time was right to seize territory in Asia after Secretary of State Dean Acheson publicly identified America's "defense perimeter" in the western Pacific and it did not include Korea. Any seizure would have to be done by proxy to prevent open conflict with the United States; thus, Kim Il-Sung received the approval he had long sought to take control of South Korea. He assured Stalin that it would take no more than a few days.[109]

A swift reaction by the United States and the United Nations surprised both Kim Il-Sung and Stalin. At the time the Soviets were boycotting the UN Security Council because the People's Republic of China had not been given the seat occupied by the Republic of China, commonly referred to as Nationalist China; thus, representatives were not present to veto the UN resolution calling on countries of the world to join a police action that would drive the invader from the Republic of Korea, with the United States to direct the military operations in Korea. As Gaddis points out, "What Stalin had not anticipated was the effect it would have on the Americans: this unexpected attack was almost as great a shock as the one on Pearl Harbor nine years earlier, and its consequences for Washington's strategy were at least as profound."[110] And because President Truman believed it was just this sort of action in the 1930s that had led to World War II, it took only hours for his administration to decide to come to the aid of the Republic of Korea. The stage was now set for a three-year war, not the three-day war originally predicted by Kim Il-Sung.

Active-duty military personnel had been so drastically reduced that only a skeleton force of the Eighth Army, on occupation duty in Japan, was readily available to send to Korea.

David McCullough, Truman's biographer, writes that "years of slashing defense expenditures, as a means to balance the budget, had taken a heavy toll. And while the policy of 'cutting the fat' at the Pentagon had been pushed by Republicans and Democrats alike—with wide popular approval—and lately made a noisy crusade by Louis Johnson, it was the President who was ultimately responsible. It was Truman's policy—and along with the 'fat,' it was now painfully apparent, a great deal of bone and muscle had been cut. For all its vaunted nuclear supremacy, the nation was quite unprepared for war, just as such critics of the policy as James Forrestal had been saying."[111] In previous years Secretary of Defense Forrestal had not been the only one saying the nation was not prepared for war. Army officers were also concerned that cutting the budget for troops was an unwise decision that would return to haunt the nation. This happened when thousands of ill-prepared and outnumbered Americans were killed in Korea while the US Army was becoming fully battle ready.

Constituents sent letters to Mahon, demanding to know why ill-trained and ill-equipped troops were sent into Korea to be slaughtered. Those asking the hardest questions were women. One letter is typical: "Our boys can't expect to win over tank equipped units with just guns. Why didn't we get equipment there before we put the men in? Why didn't we know the thing was going to start? There are always so many whys."[112] Mahon answered that there was equipment in Japan, but it was not adequate and could not be gotten to Korea in time. He wrote that men and weapons were being poured into Korea at that time, but of course he said nothing about his speeches on the House floor favoring increased funding for the air force at the expense of the army—nothing about his conviction that air force planes and the atomic bomb were the best means for stopping enemy aggression. This was a clear example of the surprise attack that army witnesses before the subcommittee had predicted for several years, and now all the air force bombers on earth were not stopping the North Koreans. Furthermore, the atomic bomb was basically useless because of the fear that dropping one would cause a nuclear war with the Soviets.

The North Korean attack compelled the Truman administration to change its concept of the Soviet threat. Previously most believed it consisted primarily of internal political subversion in economically vulnerable nations. Now they understood that it could easily include armed aggression, and this meant the nation would have to rearm to "increase the size and readiness of our Armed Forces should action become necessary in other parts of the world."[113] The attack became the catalyst for implementing NSC-68.

The appropriations committees of both houses had been in almost continuous session since the outbreak of the conflict, and supplemental bills totaling more than $30 billion for defense appropriations were sent to Congress before the end of fiscal year 1951, bringing total military appropriations to $48.26 billion, almost a 400 percent increase over defense appropriations for fiscal year 1950. These supplemental requests were based on military estimates of requirements, rather than budgetary ceilings. Congress became more concerned with appropriating an amount sufficient to take care of the situation in Korea than with cutting appropriations in its usual watchdog capacity.[114] Because American lives were involved, most members of Congress quickly closed ranks behind the administration until the crisis was over. "The FY 1951 supplements that were presented to Congress may be viewed as part of a broader program for the orderly expansion of land, sea, and air forces above the estimated Korean requirements in order to bring America's military power, at least momentarily, into line with its widened perception of its political commitments abroad."[115] The army gained the most. With American lives involved it was easier to secure funding for a general buildup immediately rather than later when the shooting stopped.

Initially, news from the Korean battlefront was very bleak. In fact, administration officials were concerned that retreat would soon become rout; however, by the first week in August, the retreat was halted at Pusan, on the southeastern coast of Korea, and under the command of General Walton Walker, the Eighth Army broke out of the Pusan perimeter to begin marching northward. On September 15 General MacArthur successfully landed on the western coast of Korea at Incheon, which allowed him to recapture Seoul thirty miles to the east. When the North Korean Army became caught in a pincer movement, the war changed completely. MacArthur then organized all of the troops for a northward march. President Truman granted him permission to cross the Thirty-eighth Parallel and continue his northward drive only if Chinese troops did not enter the conflict. Initially Kim Il-Sung had invaded South Korea in the hopes of unifying the whole peninsula under his control; now Truman hoped to unify it under US control. Everything was going so well that MacArthur announced that the troops would be home by Christmas. Then the war changed again, this time within sight of the Yalu River boundary between North Korea and China. The Chinese, thirty-three divisions strong, entered the conflict as they had threatened to do if UN forces crossed the Thirty-eighth Parallel. Endless waves of Chinese troops, well armed and well trained, sent UN forces into an epic retreat during the bitter cold winter. By early December 1950, it became clear that the United Nations forces in northern Korea were facing defeat. Chinese communist forces had split the United Nations forces into two groups. Forces on the west coast retreated southward, abandoning Pyongyang, the North Korean capital. Forces in northeastern Korea were cut off from retreat by land and had to be evacuated by sea. MacArthur insisted that he be granted permission to expand the war into China, even using nuclear weapons if necessary. President Truman and the Joint Chiefs vetoed this move, fearing an all-out nuclear war that would mean annihilation for all.

By April 1951 general dissatisfaction had surfaced about the United Nations police action in Korea. Additionally, problems existed with General MacArthur over President Truman's strategy to keep the war limited to the Korean peninsula and to conventional weapons. MacArthur repeatedly disobeyed presidential orders by commenting publicly about his strategy for conducting the war and sabotaging Truman's attempt to negotiate a settlement of the conflict by offering to work out a settlement of his own with China. MacArthur even threatened invasion of China if the conflict was not resolved. His outspoken opposition amounted to insubordination. The final straw was a letter to Representative Joseph Martin, Republican speaker of the House of Representatives, which Martin read on the House floor. This letter supported Martin's views that a second front should be opened in Asia and Chinese Nationalist forces should be used in the fighting. In a radio broadcast that same day, Truman explained to the nation that if MacArthur's course of action was followed, the United Nations would be in grave danger of expanding the conflict in Korea into a general war, which was precisely what the United States was trying to prevent. He also said that the United States stood ready to negotiate an agreement that would restore peace to the area, but it was not ready to appease the aggressors. Because of MacArthur's insubordinate behavior, President Truman relieved him of his command in Asia on April 11, 1951.

Although the cost of the Korean conflict and the national deficit were growing at an astronomical rate, what stood out in the mind of most Americans was the firestorm that swept the nation when MacArthur was relieved of his command. President Truman, General Omar Bradley, chairman of the Joint Chiefs of Staff; and the chiefs of the army, navy, and air force believed MacArthur's strategy would widen the war to include the Soviets. Truman and his generals advocated for a limited war because they believed a wider war could very easily escalate into World War III. After relieving MacArthur, the president failed to take his case to the public, where he could have easily defended the constitutionality of civilian control over the military. MacArthur had been insubordinate to the commander-in-chief of the United States military, and this could not be tolerated. Many Americans figured out the logic of Truman's action, but an even larger number rose up to defend MacArthur. Their defense also reflected the frustrations that most Americans were feeling about the Korean War and the difficulty that United Nations forces were having pushing the aggressors back to the Thirty-eighth Parallel.

Mahon told a reporter from the *Lubbock Morning Avalanche* that "General MacArthur has had a distinguished military career and I regret that he found it impossible to cooperate with our military leadership in this country."[116] Trying to remain calm and above the fray, he refused to comment on the wisdom of MacArthur's removal because it would not have been politically smart to disagree publicly with the president, who was a Democrat. Trying to sidestep the main question, he said he believed the United States should continue to rapidly build its military strength and "seek to prevent a general war, but that in the event of a general war we [the United States] should get in a position to win it."[117] However, the editor of the Lubbock newspaper felt no deference for a Democratic president. He moved his editorial to the front page and strongly questioned President Truman's decision to remove MacArthur, writing that the communists throughout the world had been handed a victory. "[W]e frankly fear that the President's action will prove one of the costliest in the history of the nation."[118]

Letters pouring into Mahon's office from constituents were ten to one in favor of MacArthur and against the president. These angry people failed to realize that the main problem was not about the soundness of the nation's foreign policy or a commanding general's idea about conducting war. The problem was insubordination, and the Constitution is clear that the president is commander-in-chief of United States military forces. Generally, those favoring the president's action were attorneys and university professors, who regretted that matters had reached the breaking point, but they understood that the military is subject to civilian control. One attorney from Plainview, Texas, sent a three-word telegram that said, "Don't say anything." A letter from an irate constituent began, "Dear Sponger, Parasite, and Business Failure." The writer not only chewed the president into small pieces, he also took a swipe at Mahon when he wrote, "I wrote you five years ago about the mess that we are now in with Russia. You came back with a soft soaping letter,—saying,—that you did not know what was the best thing to do. Well, I have never known of any one getting one of you politicians over the barrel yet. You tell me of one good thing that you have done up there,—AND, I will tell you a hundred things that you haven't done, that you ought to do." He closed with, "And by the way, there are too damn many people that are on the pay roll up there, doing NOTHING."[119] Mahon answered that he saw a great deal of impatience and exasperation in the letter, which he believed the writer felt about the situation generally, but not about Mahon personally. He went on to explain that he was also frustrated and felt that the administration could have handled the situation better.

In the midst of the frustration that Mahon felt about believing it unwise to express his honest opinion in public, he managed to weave a bit of dry humor into the diplomacy of his answers to emotionally charged letters that demanded the impeachment of President Truman and spilled over to insist that two terms was long enough for any politician. An angry constituent wrote, "There must be a side line that makes a man want to hang on in Washington, or he can not promote a paying business back home. If the latter is the case then he certainly should not be running our government."[120] Mahon answered that he believed a restriction on term limits was good for the president because that position was so powerful; however, because his term was only two years in duration the voters could remove him anytime they wished. The general tone of the answer was that it was appropriate to "throw the rascals out" as long as he was not considered one of the rascals.

In answers to constituent letters, Mahon did not allow his anger to show when he criticized President Truman for not settling the problem diplomatically. In his heart he favored General MacArthur because he liked him better than President Truman, although in his mind he knew that the president was right. He expressed shock over the way MacArthur was removed and believed much of the trouble "has been brought about by inexcusable bungling by the Executive Branch of the government."[121] He believed President Truman should have been able to head off a public break with MacArthur just as General Eisenhower had managed to work with difficult subordinates, such as General Patton, during World War II. In his answers to letters he also stated his strong support of the House Un-American Activities Committee and his belief that the president should have removed Secretary of State Dean Acheson. There is no record about exactly why he was against Acheson; however, he said often that he was opposed to communism in any form, and during the Alger Hiss trials Acheson had refused to deny his friendship with Hiss, who was accused of being a communist. This put him in the position of being considered "soft on communism." This attitude was not unique to Mahon since many Americans opposed Acheson's strong support of British opposition to widening the war in Asia, and there were many calls for his resignation.

When General MacArthur returned to the United States, he addressed a joint session of Congress to defend his position. Many times applause interrupted his speech, which finally ended with the now famous line that "old soldiers never die, they just fade away." Mahon supported his address to Congress and was among those who applauded loudly. MacArthur also testified before joint Senate committees on the armed services and on foreign relations. After the secretary of state, the chairman of the Joint Chiefs, and the chiefs of staff testified, it became obvious that his views did not have the support he claimed. They all supported the administration's objective to limit the conflict to Korea. General Bradley is remembered for saying it best: "This would involve us in the wrong war, at the wrong place, at the wrong time and with the wrong enemy." Truman's biographer, David McCullough, wrote that "the principle of civilian control over the military, challenged as never before in the nation's history, had survived and was stronger than ever."[122]

In a family letter Mahon confided,

Believe me, it is time for me to think of a little something harmonious and beautiful because I have been going through a terrific strain here. . . . But worse than the work has been the pressure generated by the return of General MacArthur. It is perfectly obvious that old soldiers never die and they don't even fade away. I have never seen people in such a frenzy over any-body. I have tried to be very down-to-earth and restrained about the whole MacArthur proposition. . . . One Congressman got a message from a couple of old ladies, 'Impeach Truman, but if you can't impeach him, kill him!' . . . The pressure of this thing is about to kill all of us. I think Truman could have handled the matter in a much better way and, of course, the Adminis-tration has done so many foolish and indefensible things, like failing to fire the fur-coated stenographer at the White House, etc., that one cannot blame the people for being angry.[123] In addition to other factors, the Republicans are whipping it up for the political campaign of next year. . . . As for me, I am trying to put the country first and let the chips fall where they may.[124]

In most answers to letters, Mahon stated clearly that he considered the welfare of the country more important than the welfare of the Democratic Party; however, he was careful not to openly oppose the party.

President Truman's proposed military budget for fiscal year 1952 reached the House on April 30. It requested expenditures of $60.7 billion, four times the absolute limit for fiscal year 1950. Most of the funds were to be used for mil-itary equipment and supplies, with some being reserved for construction of bases and other facilities. Over $34 billion ($34.7 billion) was for the purchase of the most up-to-date kinds of heavy equipment, such as planes, tanks, ships, electronics, artillery, and ammunition. This was intended to make substan-tial progress toward modernizing the combat equipment of the armed forces. Funds requested for research and development were approximately 20 per-cent more than requested in fiscal year 1951 and two and one-half times that requested in fiscal year 1950. The budget was based primarily on military re-quests set down by the Joint Chiefs of Staff. Civilian leaders from the executive branch deferred to military leaders, and budget ceilings were not enforced.[125] Because each service got what it requested, inter-service rivalries were re-duced to a minimum. "Subcommittee Chairman George Mahon frankly told the House that the defense of the nation was a 'long-haul proposition.'"[126] The "long-haul" concept meant maintaining forces-in-being indefinitely to meet any unexpected emergency.

The president's fiscal year 1953 defense budget was cut by $4.5 billion in the full House Committee on Appropriations. The bill that passed provided

$46,680,270,000 for the Department of Defense. Foreign aid, as well as military spending, was subjected to severe scrutiny. In fact, when Mahon presented the bill to the House, the debate was almost hostile. Members expected a much smaller bill because truce negotiations had begun in Korea and the public was clamoring for economy. People seemed to have forgotten the death and destruction that the first troops had suffered in Korea because budget cuts weakened the army after World War II. Mahon told them that "the truth is that the world situation is still highly explosive and dangerous. We have by no means achieved our goal of adequate military strength."[127] He reminded them that the country had not been in a program of all-out mobilization and it made no sense to back down on the military program at home when the United States was trying to be strong at the negotiating table. He had no patience with the idea of weakening the military just because the shooting war was winding down. He told the members that he believed allowing the military to become weak would be sowing the seeds of World War III, and he would not be a party to that.

House members questioned him aggressively about waste and the money that the services already had in their accounts. The defense department had received $174.7 billion since the start of the Korean conflict; however, not all of this money had been spent because of the time lag between ordering weapons, such as planes and carriers, and the settling of accounts upon delivery. This was the money that House members thought should be used for expenses instead of appropriating more. Mahon explained that because it was obligated it could not be touched until the weapons on order arrived. He also reminded them that canceling procurement orders was the biggest waste of all.

Mahon reported to the full committee that the Korean conflict was costing $5 billion per year or approximately 10 percent of the overall military expenditure. He said the Department of Defense had furnished him with estimates that the cost in 1951 was $5 billion for ammunition, movement of troops, and combat, and the same was expected for the fiscal year ending June 30, 1952. The remaining 90 percent of military expenditures was for the overall buildup and maintenance.

The largest cuts were in procurement funds for army weapons and equipment and in shipbuilding for the navy. Construction of the navy's second "super" aircraft carrier was dropped, and money for plane production was reduced. Money for aides of top-ranking inactive officers, including General

MacArthur, was eliminated, and a limit was placed on the number of officers in the upper grades. Rather than demoting officers, a freeze on promotions would be enforced.

Global preparedness met more opposition in Congress than at any time during the previous two years, but this was an election year, and congressmen were talking loudly about cutting expenses. They did this in the House to the tune of five hundred thousand dollars, and the cuts amounted to good news that they could take home to constituents during the Easter recess.

On April 10 Mahon wrote to his family, saying,

> For the first time in three months I am sort of down to earth and relaxed. Since Congress met I have had hanging over my head the responsibility of handling the hearings and the Floor debate on the 50 billion dollar military appropriation bill. After 12 weeks of hearings, we finally wrote the bill, presented it to the House and we passed it yesterday afternoon. I got kicked about in the House debate more this year than ever before, but I did my share of the kicking and came from the battlefield with some degree of personal satisfaction! When amendments were offered, I made very logical speeches against them, but the House steam roller ran over me time and again and flattened me out. It was very interesting though.
>
> In the Appropriations Committee we had cut the military budget by 4 and a quarter billion dollars. On the Floor further cuts were made over my protest in the sum of one-half billion dollars. The military people have made so many mistakes and have been guilty of so much unnecessary wastefulness everybody wanted to kick them in the teeth, including me. My only concern was not to go so far as to actually hurt our defense program.[128]

In the same letter he continued, "I notice in the morning paper that Ike is coming home for sure. A friend from Lubbock took me to the $100 per plate Jefferson-Jackson Day Dinner in Washington sometime ago—the one when President Truman said he would not be a candidate again. Before going to the dinner, I shuddered to think of what some of my West Texas friends would think of me for going to a dinner which was to be addressed by Truman. But the burden of my heart rolled away when Harry announced that he would not run again! I felt that this announcement ought to dissipate a lot of bitterness. Nobody seems to be excited about any of the candidates."[129]

Although Mahon's attitude about President Truman was very favorable when he became president in 1945, it had changed by 1952. Truman's stand on civil rights was a hot-button issue with the Southern conservatives and also with Mahon's constituents. Mahon voted with the Southern conservative bloc in Congress more often than not, and segregation was one of the binding forces of this group. Additionally, Mahon and many of his constituents still harbored some ill will toward Truman after the MacArthur controversy.

On Easter Sunday, April 10, Mahon wrote to his family in Texas that he and Helen were expecting their grandson, George Mahon Holt, to visit for the first time since he had been born on March 11, 1952. "His parents are going out for a drive. I am a little suspicious; I am afraid that this may be just the beginning of this sort of thing! For Easter we gave the proud parents a flash light camera. George and I will probably have our pictures taken today. Then tonight we have turkey dinner together."[130] Actually, this was just the beginning of the sort of thing that provided Mahon and Helen some of the happiest moments of their life. Although he enjoyed spending time with his family more than with anyone else, he was not much for helping with household chores. In the midst of one of his Sunday family letters, he wrote, "Helen has now completed the washing of the dishes from last night's party and I can now suspend this letter for a while and resume my dictation later!"[131] Their company the night before included Daphne and Duncan. After dinner, they all played bridge. Other favorite pastimes were listening to the radio and playing Scrabble.

In July, when Congress recessed, Mahon joined General Omar Bradley and four other officers on a trip to Thule, Greenland, for an unpublicized inspection of the northernmost US base. Greenland belonged to Denmark, but that country allowed a US Air Force base to be located there. Greenland was covered by a block of ice that was ten thousand feet thick in places, and it had a population of twenty thousand people. An Eskimo village, seventy-eight miles north of Thule, was the northernmost permanent human settlement on earth.

Thule Air Force Base was important because it was the point of departure for the shortest arctic route from an American base to Moscow. It was 2,762 statute miles from Moscow and only 500 miles from the western edge of Soviet territory, which made it ideally suited for medium-range bombers, or

B-36 bombers, carrying atomic bombs. Although the United States had bases in Saudi Arabia and Libya that were closer to Moscow, Mahon wrote in his notes of the trip that "Thule would be easier to defend and supply."[132] Thule Air Force Base could also be used as a fueling stop for planes taking off from the United States and could be a haven for crippled planes returning from any future conflict, just as Iwo Jima had been during World War II. Because it would be the takeoff point for attacks on the Soviet Union in the event of World War III, the base was considered quite vulnerable; it would likely be the first place bombed by the Soviets in a war. In his notes Mahon also wrote, "There is a limitless danger to civilization in the arms race between this country and Russia."[133]

Mahon had personally handled appropriation bills that provided $239 million for the construction of the base, which was funded under the code name BLUEJAY to protect its secrecy, and he wanted to see how the money had been used. Construction costs were unusually high because engineers had to use six feet of gravel as a base for runways and five feet for buildings so that heat from the buildings and plane engines would not thaw the earth, causing the buildings and pavements to settle unevenly. Walls of buildings were four inches thick and heavily padded with insulation. Windows had three panes to prevent the transmission of heat and cold. Service personnel appeared to be happy, and the place was a beehive of activity. In order to make their tour of duty even more attractive, it was limited to one year.[134]

In a letter to his father, George wrote, "I got back to Washington in time to listen to some of the Democratic Convention in Chicago. I do not know very much about Governor Stevenson.[135] (I think Helen is going to claim kinship to him). . . . I stayed up until 3:30 . . . in order to hear his acceptance speech before the convention. I thought it was the finest speech that I have heard in many months. . . . I rather imagine that he will conduct the political campaign on a very high plane."[136]

The convention chose Senator John J. Sparkman (D-AL) as the vice presidential candidate. The Mahons knew the Sparkman family because for years they had all attended the same church in Washington. Mahon had also become friends with General Eisenhower through many subcommittee hearings and other occasions. "There is no doubt that he is a fine American," Mahon wrote to his father, "though I think he knows very little about the non-military and non-foreign policy aspects of our government. His running mate Senator Nixon and I spent six weeks together on a trip to Europe with the so-called Herter Committee in 1947. He is a nice fellow. It would appear that whoever wins, we will have a pretty good President, but the sad truth is that neither Adlai or Ike can wave the magic wand and brush away the sins and ills of this sick and troubled world." [137]

Undoubtedly, he knew that two delegations from Texas were planning to attend the Democratic National Convention, and this would cause a power struggle over which one was seated. Governor Allan Shivers led one group of conservative and middle-of-the-road Democrats known as the "Shivercrats." This group was opposed to the Truman administration, the New Deal, and Truman's Fair Deal program. The second group, led by former congressman Maury Maverick, was known as the "Loyalists." The Loyalists supported the liberal wing of the national Democratic Party. The Shivercrats were determined to send unpledged delegates to the national convention, and the "Loyalists" believed the national committee should refuse to seat any delegates who were not pledged to support the party nominee. Although Mahon's conservative political philosophy was compatible with the Shivercrats and the Democratic delegates from Lubbock were pledged to back Governor Shivers at the national convention, with a storm of this nature brewing, it was a good time to be out of the country on business. Taking sides in a party squabble could prove detrimental to his career if the side he opposed won the struggle. As mentioned before, Mahon's ultimate goal of becoming chair of the House Committee on Appropriations when Clarence Cannon retired was based on continuing to be elected and staying in Chairman Cannon's good graces. What he wanted most would not come from the convention; thus, it was better to be in icy Greenland inspecting military facilities than caught in the heat of a party fight.

When Mahon returned to the district in September 1952, he told *Lubbock Morning Avalanche* reporters that "America is much stronger today than at the outbreak of the Korean war, but it will be two years before the nation's military might will be at the 'safety point' for an all-out war. . . . I am optimistic over the progress we have made in our military buildup. . . . It has been a mixture of butter and guns, an effort toward business as usual plus larger defense production."[138] He added that he had been one of those who wanted the military buildup to go even faster than it had; however, if an all-out war could be prevented, he would have advocated the wrong approach. On the other hand, if war did come in the next two years, America would not be adequately prepared, and the reductions would be a tragic mistake. He also predicted that because defense spending was to be reduced, taxes could be reduced substantially.

Before leaving Washington, Mahon said he had conferred with the military and intelligence officials and saw no relief from world tension and danger. "In my judgment, our mounting military strength here and abroad is a more significant factor in our campaign for peace and world stability than day-to-day developments in Korea."[139] He predicted that if America was forced into an all-out war, it would not be fought in Korea.

He tried to console his constituents about waste in military spending by saying, "Much of it was caused by the 'so called crash programs' immediately after the outbreak of the Korean war because no one knew when that war might produce an all-out explosion. . . . There is bound to be some waste in a program involving billions of dollars, but I think the military has been made cost conscious through congressional and other investigations."[140]

He let it be known that his Lubbock office would be open, but he would not spend much time there. He got enough of staying in the office when he was in Washington, so he wanted to get out and talk with the people. As he traveled around through the Nineteenth District, Mahon learned that Texas was sizzling under a drought that had already bankrupted an estimated two thousand farmers and ranchers and threatened at least seven thousand more. Approximately 80 percent of the cotton crop was lost and about 12 percent of the grain crops. Over all, it was estimated that $100 million had already been lost because of the drought.[141]

In September Mahon announced that he would be supporting the national Democratic Party in the November elections. Having won the primary in July without opposition, this would be his tenth two-year term, and so far none of his opponents had proven to be a serious challenge. This was not only a compliment to his record but an economic godsend because campaigns were expensive. He told a reporter for the *Lubbock Morning Avalanche* that his "support of the Stevenson-Sparkman ticket does not, however, represent his complete personal or political agreement with the national nominees, with President Truman and many other national Democratic leaders. . . . 'I long have been in disagreement, on certain issues, with many of the party leaders. I still am and I expect to be. I am in violent disagreement on the questions of Texas tidelands, compulsory FEPC and repeal of the Taft-Hartley law. I still decry, as I consistently have decried, waste and corruption in government.'"[142]

As he said, Mahon did not agree with national leaders of the Democratic

Party on the Texas tidelands issue. In Texas the controversy became a major issue in the 1952 presidential election. This controversy between Texas and the United States involved title to more than two million acres of submerged land in the Gulf of Mexico. When Texas was annexed to the United States in 1845, it was required to retain all debts and was allowed to keep all unoccupied land that could be sold to liquidate those debts. There was no problem for one hundred years; however, the discovery of oil within the three-league boundary of submerged land set the stage for legal disputes over ownership. Texas leases cost oil companies more than federal leases, but this money was an important addition to the state's public-school fund. A controversy arose after the 1948 presidential election when President Truman directed the attorney general to file suit against Texas to acquire title to the tidelands. Truman had twice vetoed congressional legislation allowing Texas to retain ownership of the land. During the 1952 presidential campaign General Eisenhower declared in favor of ownership of the tidelands by Texas and said that, if elected, he would sign legislation guaranteeing such. Democratic candidate Adlai Stevenson said he would veto such legislation.

Dwight Eisenhower and Richard Nixon were swept into office with nearly ten million more votes than the Democratic candidates. Eisenhower was a moderate Republican and a war hero who promised to end the war in Korea and clean up the "mess in Washington." He pledged to go to Korea to break the stalemated peace talks, to battle corruption in Washington, and to fight communism at home. President Truman, angry about the implication that he had not done all he could to end the war and of being accused of creating a "mess in Washington," charged Eisenhower with demagoguery. Unfortunately, by election day these two men had become bitter enemies, after years of working together. Truman had offered to support Eisenhower for the presidency in 1948, and in 1949 Eisenhower had served as chairman of the Joint Chiefs of Staff under Truman. Now, any respect they once had for each other was replaced with bitterness, and the next two and a half months became one of the most hostile transitions in the twentieth century.[143]

The election proved to be a bloodless coup in Texas that gave further impetus to a two-party system. This started with the States Rights Party in 1948, then settled down somewhat until General Eisenhower promised to sign a quitclaim bill returning the tidelands to Texas. After the election many people decided that voting Republican was not a crime after all. However, the pundits did not expect this trend to continue with any great momentum because the mid-term election in 1954 would not likely have a Republican candidate with the warm personality of Ike. Predictions were that the Democrats in Texas would pick up many votes at that time.

At the end of November 1952, three members of the House Committee on Appropriations were sent to Europe to check on money being spent on the construction of US bases. Glen Davis (R-WI) and John Riley (D-SC) accompanied Mahon. Because voters were complaining about the amount of money being spent abroad, the next Congress was expected to closely examine the whole picture of foreign aid, including military bases, and committee members wanted to have firsthand knowledge of the situation if budget cuts were sent to the Subcommittee on Defense Appropriations. During their month-long inspection trip, the group inspected bases in England, Germany, Italy, and North Africa. They also conferred with NATO commander General Ridgway in Paris. The trip had been arranged before Eisenhower was elected.

Upon returning, Mahon issued a press release in which he announced, "Economic aid has been expensive, but it has saved Western Europe from chaos and Communism. Economic recovery has been accomplished in most areas."[144] He went on to say that he believed the aid could be practically eliminated during the next year, but commitments for military assistance should be fulfilled because those were the bases from which the United States would wage war should it break out. He acknowledged that haste and poor planning by the army engineers and the air force had caused the waste of several million dollars, but that had been brought under control, and waste at the end of 1952 did not exceed 5 percent of total expenditures. That meant, unfortunately, that construction of the bases was costing 5 percent more than it should have. The committee was disappointed with the progress in France because there was disagreement with the United States on procedures. However, the United States and the countries of Western Europe were vastly better prepared to fight a war than they had been eighteen months earlier. Mahon believed this preparedness was the greatest deterrent to war. He said, "I can confirm the reports of others who have visited Europe this year that there is absolutely no evidence of war hysteria."[145] He also stated that he believed the reason the military program was moving so slowly was the fact that the nations of Western Europe did not feel the situation was urgent any longer. When the Korean conflict broke out they were more concerned, and it was easier to find agreement on the military program. Despite difficulties, the United States could not afford to withdraw but must stand firm and strong.

Mahon also believed that American civilian personnel should be removed as soon as the countries involved could provide their own personnel for the installations. "When Congress meets we will take decisive action to drastically reduce the number of Americans in Europe who are undertaking to administer our various programs. Not one person overseas with whom I talked doubted that we have too many American civilian employees abroad. They are in each other's way and they are creating ill will in many areas. We are suffering from over-administration."[146] He said he would recommend to General Eisenhower that a high-level policy committee of representatives from the executive and legislative branches be appointed to reexamine the entire overseas spending program before any further appropriations were made. He was critical of the waste and lack of planning under the Truman administration. Mahon concluded the press release: "Our objectives in many areas are not too well defined. We ought to decide what we are trying to do, whether or not we can afford to do it, and proceed on a specific basis, not haphazardly as is not too often the case."[147] With that task behind him, he and Helen welcomed Christmas.

On December 23 Helen met Mahon in New York, and they returned to their apartment in Washington to spend their first Christmas alone in many years. Daphne, Duncan, and nine-month-old George Holt were visiting with Duncan's parents in Greensboro, North Carolina. Mahon had been away for five weeks, and there was a lot of catching up to do, in addition to just being thankful to be at home safe and sound. His ship had been delayed for twenty hours in Southampton, England, because of strong winds, and he had experienced a pretty rough crossing to New York.[148]

Helen must have believed there was still a Santa Claus when she opened the many gifts that Mahon brought home. He had bought a service for eight of Royal Worcester china and a revolving silver tureen in London, a jewel case in Heidelberg, gloves in Naples and Madrid, three Hummel figurines from Germany, and an assortment of scarves from Italy. He had also brought home cashmere sweaters for Daphne. Helen gave him a wool robe and a pewter pitcher for his extra cup of hot chocolate in the mornings.[149]

When Truman became president he led a nation that was anxious to return to its traditional foreign policy of noninvolvement that required only a small military. When he left the White House, his legacy was an American presence on every continent and a greatly expanded armament industry.[150] An arms race was rapidly gaining momentum, and public acceptance of it was based on more than fear of Soviet aggression. Military leaders insisted that they must have the newest and best weapons to protect the nation; defense-industry workers and owners of weapons industries were dependent on the jobs the arms race created; and politicians involved in defense were enjoying their ever-increasing importance. Many aspects of American life were impacted. Fear, combined with economic opportunities and the acquisition of power, fueled an arms race that would dominate the American psyche until nearly the end of the century.

Chairmanship of the Subcommittee on Defense Appropriations (formerly the Appropriations Subcommittees for the Army, Army Air Force, and Navy) had grown ten-fold in importance since the interim between World War I and World War II. Likewise, George Mahon's power in Congress had grown at least ten-fold since the day he had experienced anxiety about accepting a position on the Subcommittee for War Department Appropriations.

Chapter 5

Security with Solvency: 1953–1960

The predominance of the Democratic Party in Washington was shattered in 1952 when the Republicans captured the presidency and both houses of Congress. Because the majority party in each chamber chooses the committee chairs, Mahon lost his position as chair of the Subcommittee on Defense Appropriations to Representative Richard B. Wigglesworth (R-MA), and Representative Clarence Cannon (D-MO) lost his position as chair of the House Committee on Appropriations to Representative John Taber (R-NY). Mahon then became the ranking member of his subcommittee. Mahon could look forward to becoming chair again when the Democrats regained control of the House of Representatives. During the Eisenhower administration, both Mahon's reputation and his workload grew.

Several factors contributed to the Republican victory. Foremost was the enormous personal popularity of Dwight Eisenhower, followed by his promise to go to Korea and end the fighting, of which Americans had grown so weary. Allegations of corruption in the Truman administration and the declaration that there were no communists in the Grand Old Party also had an impact. "The Republican pledge to do something about Communist enslavement—and it was never very clear exactly what—brought millions of former Democratic voters into the Republican fold, especially those of East European descent."[1] Eisenhower promised to "clean up the mess in Washington." Finally, there was widespread concern with the rising deficit, which historian James K. Patterson believes had spurred Eisenhower to enter the race.[2] He campaigned on a promise to balance the budget while maintaining a strong national defense without raising taxes. He would reconcile security and economic solvency.

Inauguration Day was chilly but sunny, with an unusually large, festive crowd on hand to celebrate with Ike, their hero from World War II. Responding to their mood, "his grim, determined expression gave way to that famous grin, and he shot his hands over head in the old V-for-Victory sign."[3] In his inaugural speech Eisenhower spent no time denouncing the programs of past administrations; instead, he summoned Americans to another crusade—a crusade for peace. "The world and we have passed the midway point of a century of continuing challenge. We sense with all our faculties that forces of good and evil are massed and armed and opposed as rarely before in history."[4] According to historian Robert J. Donovan, this tension defined and influenced most of what President Eisenhower did in his eight years as president.[5] It hardly sounded like a victory speech for the first Republican to occupy the White House in two decades, but Americans of every persuasion seemed pleased.

"The Inauguration of last week was terrific," Mahon reported to his family. "There was only one sour note. Some people were a little disappointed that the Vice-President's dog, Checkers,[6] was not in the parade!"[7] About seventy-five constituents from the district were in town for the festivities, including the Hockley County Sheriff's Posse, which came to ride in the inaugural parade. "I was very proud of our District, and the Hockley County boys and girls. The head guy of the Posse was Lindsey Dycus, a boy who used to go to school [with] me in Liberty Hill,"[8] Mahon wrote. By 1953 Dycus had become a prosperous farmer in Hockley County.[9] The posse waited in line several hours before taking its place in the parade, which was so large that many groups did not get to pass the White House until after dark. It was nearly 7:00 p.m. before the president and Mamie entered the White House, their new home, to dress for the inaugural balls they were attending.[10] Mahon wrote to his sister:

The Inaugural Committee gave Helen and me a couple of choice seats near the White House so that we could review the parade along with Ike and Mamie and other notables. Other Members of Congress, of course, were given similar seats. Well, we were serving ham sandwiches, hot coffee and tea, and other first-aid items in our office, and we did not undertake to proceed one mile from the Capitol to the White House for reviewing the parade. We, of course, saw it from the Capitol area. We gave our choice parade tickets to a good farmer-friend and his wife from Lockney. You can imagine how thrilled they were, and how pleased we were to extend this little courtesy to a couple who had come so far to see our new President inaugurated.[11]

Helen enjoyed being in the office to entertain visitors, who were mainly constituents. She served refreshments to about sixty people who stopped in during the day. The office looked pretty bad after the festivities were over, with potato chips scattered on the floor, spots of grease, and crumbs of bread. But Mahon considered the solution pretty simple: "We just got busy and 'cleaned up the mess in Washington.'"[12]

Helen was not the only one on hand to greet constituents when they came to town. Mahon had five young women and an errand boy working in his congressional office. His 350,000 constituents kept everyone busy, running errands and securing information for them, which caused him to remark in a letter, "I am not so sure that we are doing very good in the congressional capacity, but in the field of errand running, we are strictly on our toes!"[13] Mahon actually enjoyed serving the needs of his constituents. He believed that they really did not want their representative in Washington to be some big shot who might be indifferent to their needs. They wanted someone they could like and trust, someone who cared about them. If their representative happened to be important nationally they were proud, but if they didn't like him, his political days were numbered.[14]

With the inauguration behind him, President Eisenhower considered one of his most pressing problems to be the reduction of the Truman adminis-tration's budget for fiscal year 1954. Submitted to Congress before the Dem-ocrats left office, the budget requested total expenditures of $78.6 billion. Of this amount, $41.2 billion was for defense.

Because the new president was a lifelong fiscal conservative, reducing ex-penditures was a top priority, and the most likely place to trim expenses was in the Department of Defense. As Lawrence Korb[15] points out, "Unlike other federal agencies, the Pentagon receives no long-term commitments from the Congress. This is different from most other federal agencies where the budget process consists mainly of costing out approved and continuing programs."[16] With more than 50 percent of the controllable expenditures in the federal budget allocated for defense, those appropriations were the easiest to manip-ulate.

Efforts to reduce defense spending generated many conflicts and compro-mises over the next decade, and his position on the House Subcommittee for Defense Appropriations placed George Mahon in the middle of the action. Because there was not one "right" defense budget, military leaders, Congress, and administration officials were annually immersed in a great intellectual and political struggle as they hammered out a defense budget they hoped would protect the nation. The defense budget was—and still is—a political document where compromises are made from many options, and power wins out.

NSC-68 identified 1954–1955 as a "target date" by which time Soviet air-atomic power would be much closer to that of the United States, and coupled with their superior ground forces, the USSR would be in a favorable position to attack the United States; thus, American military strength needed to be increased to meet the threat that was expected to peak at that time. President Eisenhower argued that the Soviet threat was constantly shifting in scope and direction; therefore, military strength should be maintained at a steady level that could meet any threat over the "long haul." He did not believe that World War III was imminent. When taking office he argued that the Soviet threat was as strong as it would be for the foreseeable future, and he relied on his military experience to support his interpretation of the world situation. A gradual increase and steady maintenance of forces over the long haul was considered adequate for national security, rather than arming for a particular date by which Soviet danger was predicted to peak.[17] If necessary, the president was prepared to threaten the use of America's powerful nuclear arsenal to deter aggression—a less costly strategy than maintaining conventional troops.

The impact of military expenses on the domestic economy was a primary factor in the "long-haul" approach, and this created tension between those who placed defense first and those who placed the economy first. Some historians argue that Eisenhower's cuts in the defense budget were made on economic grounds, not military, with deficit spending, one of the economic pitfalls of the Cold War, being uppermost in his mind.[18] The concept of an economic-military balance and the long haul had been part of General Eisenhower's campaign rhetoric; therefore, it was not surprising that they became important initiatives in the new administration. In the first half of 1953, the fiscal year 1954 budget was revised to reflect a $5 billion reduction in defense.[19]

Added to the $6.5 billion reduction already recommended by the Truman administration with the cessation of hostilities in Korea, reductions in the defense budget resulted in $11.6 billion less for fiscal year 1954 defense appropriations. Both the air force and the navy received major cuts; however, the army actually received a slight increase that was to last only until hostilities actually ceased in Korea. The president presented the revised budget to Congress as an interim measure until Charles E. Wilson, the incoming secretary of defense, could take a new look at the entire defense policy.[20] Actual changes in specific military programs were to begin taking place in the fall of 1953, and the reformulated policy became known as the "New Look."

President Eisenhower's concept of governmental budgets was shaped by traditional beliefs that dated to the Jeffersonian era. Iwan Morgan states these beliefs were that "balanced budgets symbolized commitment to limit the size and functions of the federal government, to protect states' rights, and to safeguard free enterprise."[21] The president's new cabinet, with the exception of Secretary of State John Foster Dulles, was made up of corporate executives, fiscal conservatives who believed that deficit spending was basically immoral. Determined to balance the budget and cut taxes, they strongly supported cutting the defense budget in order to reduce government expenditures. Stephen Ambrose, Eisenhower's biographer, writes, "Defense expenditures were to be reduced by approximately twenty percent and greater efficiency was to take the place of greater size. . . . A middle course between military demands and economic stability was the goal. As part of this, Eisenhower was determined to force the Europeans to spend more on defense and to achieve political and military unity."[22]

The Joint Chiefs, carryovers from the Truman administration, could not accept the New Look military program, and President Eisenhower replaced them with new chiefs in August 1953. The replacements also believed the threat to American security was no less than during the previous administration, and they could see no justification for retrenchment. They stood firm "against pressures for economy, following instead the logic of external threat and existing national commitments, including the new commitment to a greater effort in the continental defense field."[23] Differences of opinion continued about the force levels necessary for national security. Many congressmen rallied to the side of the chiefs. President Eisenhower was persistent, however, in his effort to convince one and all that large-scale land wars were a thing of the past, and thus conventional ground forces could be reduced. By threatening the use of America's nuclear arsenal, he intended to deter wars and rely on smaller, stronger, and battle-ready forces-in-being should deterrence fail. In so doing he changed the focus of national security from containment to deterrence, a less costly approach.

On March 5, 1953, Joseph Stalin died in Moscow, and his successor, Georgy M. Malenkov, "declared in a speech that there was no issue between Moscow and Washington that could not be resolved by peaceful means."[24] By the end of July, an armistice was signed in Panmunjom to end the hostilities in

Korea. At that time many Americans believed the armistice was the result of the nation's atomic arsenal and Eisenhower's military reputation.[25] Historian John Lewis Gaddis, however, believes Stalin's death actually had a greater impact on the armistice than Eisenhower's veiled threat to use atomic weapons. He argues that one of the biggest problems with using atomic weapons was determining a target. "The atomic bomb had been developed for use against cities, industrial complexes, military bases, and transportation networks. Few of these existed on the Korean peninsula, where United Nations forces were confronting an army that advanced mostly on foot, carrying its own supplies, along primitive roads and even improvised mountain paths."[26] Guerilla warfare was far more effective under these conditions. Few congressmen or administration officials gave this point serious consideration, and possession of the world's largest arsenal of atomic weapons became a determining factor in shaping foreign policy and defense budgets. Reliance on nuclear weapons to the detriment of land forces also became a point of disagreement for critics during the next decade.

Early in his administration President Eisenhower, a native Texan, made a big hit with Texas congressmen who, at different times, were invited to the White House for lunch. He was trying to strengthen his ties with these Southern conservatives, who often voted with Republicans against liberal legislation. This was also part of the president's patient but persistent efforts to bring congressmen around to his way of thinking. The previous November he had had a strong showing at the ballot boxes throughout Texas, and now he intended to capitalize on that windfall. The day Mahon attended breast of guinea hen and wild rice were served. He remarked to a reporter, "It was a good idea. . . . We had a wonderful time. Of course, I won't comment on it further. I've always liked Eisenhower personally very much."[27]

Later that week Mahon and several other congressmen attended a ninety-minute meeting in the president's office that was all business. No humorous stories were exchanged. They were briefed about the national debt, the tax burden, and the Korean War and were provided a general overview of the international situation. Allen Dulles, chief of the Central Intelligence Agency; General Omar Bradley, chairman of the Joint Chiefs of Staff; and Joseph M. Dodge, director of the Bureau of the Budget, took part in the presentations. When it was over, reporters wanted information, but no one would reveal any of the details. Mahon commented in a press release to district newspapers, "I believe in freedom of the press, but I think some Americans in recent years, by unnecessary loose talk, have given the enemies of our country entirely too much information which is of no value to the American public, but of very great value to our enemies."[28] In the same press release he acknowledged that the job of being president was a superhuman one, but Eisenhower looked exceptionally fit. Mahon stated his belief that the president was entitled to as much assistance as possible from Congress and the American people. He went on to say that all should work together in finding answers to the problems facing the nation—that it was in everyone's best interest to put the welfare of the country above party affiliations.[29]

In February Mahon took advantage of an opportunity to do something that would be important to his constituents when he accompanied Senator Lyndon Johnson (D-TX), Senator Price Daniel (D-TX), and Representative W. R. Poage (D-TX), a member of the House Agricultural Committee, to the office of Ezra Taft Benson, the new secretary of agriculture. The group extended an invitation to Secretary Benson to address the American Cotton Congress during its annual meeting to be held in Lubbock on June 27. They also talked with him about overall agricultural problems such as declining prices, acreage controls, and farm labor difficulties, as well as the effect of a devastating drought in West Texas. Mahon reported that Benson was easy to talk with and was well informed about agricultural problems. This effort on Mahon's part counterbalanced the amount of time and energy he devoted to defense budgets that did not directly serve the needs of his district, and it is also a typical example of how he tried to help his constituents. Outside of committee work, his chief contacts were with officials in the Department of Agriculture, and a week seldom passed that he did not confer with members of the House Committee on Agriculture.[30] West Texas was one of the newest cotton-producing regions in the country, and it was also one of the largest, often producing 10 percent of the nation's crop. The Nineteenth District alone accounted for one-seventh of the US annual production; thus agricultural legislation was vitally important.

Before long, however, Mahon began to realize that Benson's concept of handling agriculture was to get the government out of it, completely. The elimination of price supports would be difficult for West Texas farmers, because market prices were rapidly declining as the conflict in Korea ended, but the cost of tractors and other modern equipment was constantly rising. Additionally, their problems were intensified by a severe drought. In a newsletter to the district, Mahon praised Benson, but he revealed his disillusionment in a letter to family members. "Of course, I have to be careful what I write. In the first column I spoke kindly of the new Secretary of Agriculture, but since I wrote the column Benson has kicked up a storm of protest over his lukewarm attitude toward support prices for farm products. I have been taking some kidding from my colleagues, but I do not mind it. In fact, I have said, and will repeat publicly from time to time that while I did not support our new president in the campaign, I feel that the welfare of the country comes first and I shall help him and his Administration in any way I can."[31] Mahon's attitude was admirable; however, the balanced budget that the president believed was best for the welfare of the country and the vested interests of his constituents were at odds where agricultural policy was concerned. Despite the frugal and conservative nature of the Nineteenth District, West Texans favored a generous agricultural policy, and Mahon supported the same.

The Korean conflict had offered farmers a brief respite from low prices; however, by early 1953 average farm prices were 10 percent lower than in early 1951, and cattle prices were down 30 percent.[32] Secretary Benson agreed with President Eisenhower that fixed price supports were not economically sound. He intended to move away from 90 percent of parity as quickly as possible because it encouraged production of huge quantities of unneeded commodities.[33] He believed that returns to farmers should be based on market prices, and price supports should be only an insurance against disaster. This fit well with Eisenhower's philosophy of reduced expenses and getting government out of the business of agriculture. Benson wanted to remove government controls, a break with policies of the New Deal and the Fair Deal, just when prices were declining and farmers were suffering from a harsh cost-price squeeze.[34] Farmers became increasingly angry as prices slipped downward.

Mahon was on hand to greet Secretary Benson at the Lubbock airport when he arrived to attend the cotton conference in June. At Mahon's request, Benson agreed to reserve time before the conference started to observe firsthand the impact of the drought on the Southwest—a drought that was then in its fourth year. In addition to touring the area surrounding Lubbock, Benson met with delegations from New Mexico, Colorado, Oklahoma, and across West Texas. After seeing how severe the situation was, he promised help from the administration to prevent further loss to farmers and ranchers. On June 29 he announced that $8 million in disaster funds would be available for 152 drought-stricken counties in Texas and 40 in Oklahoma. The aid was designed to meet the three biggest needs: an extension of credit, provision of feed for livestock, and a relaxation of freight rates for feed going into the drought-stricken areas and for cattle being shipped out.[35]

Secretary Benson delivered the closing address for the three-day cotton conference in the gymnasium on the campus of Texas Technological College. Approximately seventeen hundred persons were present to hear him say that the administration would take steps immediately to check the disastrous losses from the drought, which was considered to be as severe as the one that had created the Dust Bowl in the 1930s. Benson, a descendant of Mormon pioneer farmers in Utah, impressed the audience with his sincerity. The *Lubbock Avalanche-Journal* reported that Benson said the United States had become "the world's residual supplier of cotton because other cotton-producing nations are selling for less than our 90 per cent support price. Federal restrictions on exports, imposed when the Korean situation developed, caused other nations to increase production until world production now exceeds world consumption."[36] He went on to say, "The buying power of farm operators' net income for the past four years has averaged about 10 per cent lower than any year from 1942 to 1948. . . . Last year it was 22 per cent lower than in 1947. The farmer is being squeezed between low farm prices and high, rigid farm costs."[37] The secretary pledged to carry President Eisenhower's campaign promises to the American farmer, including the pledge for price supports. Benson said he had no intention of giving up any of the farm programs until he had something better to replace them.

At a luncheon earlier that day Benson had praised the spirit of West Texas farmers who, he claimed, didn't want anything they couldn't pay for. He also admired their sense of humor, as he had heard many jokes about the drought. Mahon told a Lubbock reporter, "I think the interest shown by the Secretary is very wholesome. It will have a good effect, but it will take time and energy to implement and improve the new program."[38] Mahon missed a vote taken that day in the House Appropriations Committee on funds for the military establishment, but he believed it was important to stay in Lubbock for the final day of the meeting. Important as his appropriations work was, it did not benefit his district as much as matters relating to agriculture; therefore, Mahon was careful to make the most of an opportunity such as this.

Finally, on July 24 the House passed the Hope drought bill which provided $150 million for emergency drought relief. This bill made it easier for farmers to borrow money from the federal government. Prior to the passage of the bill, no emergency loans were made for less than $2,500, but this bill allowed smaller loans for farmers who couldn't get credit elsewhere.

"I had a terrific week in Washington," Mahon wrote to his brother-in-law in July. He went on to record that the main business of the House during the week was the $34 billion Military Appropriations bill and that "the Republicans were in charge of the legislation, but I was in charge of the Democratic side of the debate, and we had some very interesting and spirited controversies over the question of what to do about our national defense program." According to Mahon,

> The Republicans apparently had searched the Congressional Record and had read many of my previous speeches with the thought of quoting them back to me and somewhat embarrassing me. I will send you the Congressional Records which contain most of the debate. I think you will enjoy reading parts of it. Maybe I was too self-confident, but I was not taken aback by the old speeches which I made earlier this year or in 1950, and which the Republicans quoted back to me. I told them that I thought my old speeches were pretty good! I was seeking to raise the bill for the Army, Navy, and Air Force to the over-all total, which President Eisenhower had requested. The Republicans had cut his request by over $1,000,000,000. My point was that we should restore most of the cut and assign the increase to the Air Force in order that the Air Force could more rapidly achieve its goal of 143 wings, which have been determined by the Joint Chiefs of Staff as the minimum requirement for this country in the event of a big war.[39]

Earlier Mahon had told a reporter for the *Houston Post*, "I do not believe President Eisenhower had anything to do with where the cuts were made. It was Secretary of Defense Charles Wilson, Deputy Secretary Roger Keyes, and Assistant Secretary William McNeil who pinpointed the defense 'economy' in the Air Force."[40] This was very likely just a way of avoiding the president's wrath, as it was always risky for a congressman to take a public stand against any incumbent president's power and prestige.[41]

In his July letter Mahon was referring to a heated debate that had taken place on July 1, 1953, in the House, about slashing approximately $6 billion from the amount previously requested by President Truman. This cut was challenged by top military brass. Mahon led the fight to increase the air force budget by over a billion dollars, but his amendment was rejected by a voice vote. Had the amendment passed, the bill would have been sent back to the Appropriations Committee with instructions to add the funds. His motion to recommit forced a roll call in which the amendment failed by a vote of 230-161. He declared that the military budget had been made up by Secretary of Defense Wilson, whom he considered inexperienced in military matters, and it ignored the recommendations of the Joint Chiefs of Staff. Mahon pleaded with House members not to weaken the country's defense by cutting funds that were needed to allow the air force to build the 143-wing force that had been recommended by General Hoyt S. Vandenberg, former air force chief of staff. Later he told a reporter that "even the President cannot foretell the future. . . . Eisenhower joined the rest of us in 1950 in believing a $16.5 billion defense budget was ample. That was just a few weeks before the Korean war started." He ended his speech in the House with, "I warn you—today is the day of decision in our country's history. Many of you will go out of here and make July 4 speeches about keeping our nation strong. The decision is yours to make here today."[42]

Mahon believed the administration was gambling on the absence of war with the Soviets. He hoped this gamble would prove to be right; however, he knew that in the past the USSR's aggressive moves had often been timed to coincide with America's retreat in military preparedness. Just after the last great reductions in the defense budget, war had broken out in Korea, and before that the Soviets overran Eastern Europe shortly after the US postwar demobilization and defense cutbacks. He had also been uneasy since Stalin's death. He believed Stalin's age was a deterrent to war, but he was not sure of the incoming leaders. No one really knew how aggressive they would be.

Mahon and Senator Stuart Symington led the fight in their respective chambers to restore the reduced money to the air force budget for fiscal year 1954, but neither was successful. President Eisenhower intervened with a letter to Representative Errett Scrivner (R-KS), a member of the House Subcommittee on Defense Appropriations, who managed the Republican side of the debate in the House. In the letter the president declared that he was completely conversant with the budget, that it represented his views and had his personal endorsement. He went on to say that the armed services had traditionally requested more than they needed and that the Air Force already had some $25 billion of unspent appropriations from previous years. He used his military prestige to prevent increases in appropriations.[43] The committee reports on the defense bills from both chambers did not provide any details about the military-political issues of the defense cutbacks.[44]

The Soviets' possession of the atomic and hydrogen bombs convinced Mahon that the United States had become just as vulnerable to attack as the USSR had been when the United States alone possessed the atom bomb. Guided missiles were being developed to defend the country, and it was hoped they would provide a defense superior to interceptor planes or anti-aircraft fire, but they were costly. Now that the shooting had stopped in Korea, Mahon believed the military budget could be trimmed somewhat but not drastically reduced. He advocated saving money by keeping a lid on nonmilitary, or domestic, programs. He supported a pay-as-you-go approach that would be financed with increased taxes. However, tax increases were anathema to Republicans.

In a press release to district newspapers, Mahon reported that in meetings of the Appropriations Committee, he sat in an old chair "which was used in Constitution Hall in 1921 at the ill-fated international Conference on the Limitation of Armament called by Charles Evans Hughes, then Secretary of State."[45] Although new leather chairs had been recently ordered for the committee, he and Chairman John Taber of New York asked to keep their old ones because they were more comfortable. Despite the ribbing they got from their colleagues, they continued to use the squeaky old chairs during meetings.[46] Apparently, the Appropriations Committee did not wield the economy ax quite so heavily on its own requests as on the budget in general. The committee allowed twenty-nine thousand dollars to purchase 225 new leather swivel chairs for House members, yet Mahon believed he could get along fine with the chair he already had. This story of frugality helped to maintain the image of a representative who was careful about spending the taxpayers' money.

When Mahon returned to the district, he described the Eighty-third Congress as "cooperative," despite members voting with a greater degree of independence from party leadership than in past years. He told a reporter with the *Lubbock Avalanche-Journal,* "This does not mean that there was a tendency on the part of Congress to be a rubber stamp for the President. Far from it. There was considerable crossing of party lines on major votes, a healthy sign in my judgment. The higher duty is not to vote for or against the administration in power on the issues that arise, but rather to vote for the best interests of this country. Likewise, I am not critical of the first session of the 83rd Congress. I think it did about all that could have been expected of it under the circumstances."[47]

He emphasized that no miracles had been performed and predicted that the second session would provide a better test of Republican leadership. He went on to say,

> We are thankful that an agreement has been reached to stop the shooting, but there is every indication that there is no good way to deal with the Communists and that the Korean peace will prove to be as frustrating as the Korean War. . . . The fiscal picture is clouded by the necessity for continued high level spending. . . . We can't get off this peak spending all at once. . . . But we must keep up our guard on the domestic and foreign fronts and work our way through this difficult situation. We must not lose our faith in each other nor should we lose faith in our Commander-In-Chief, the President. We must not permit our frustrations to lead us to defeatism. This country is essentially sound to the core and tremendously powerful. I hope we will not sell ourselves short at the international conference tables or in matters involving our domestic economy.[48]

Mahon did one of the most important things expected of him by his constituents. As *Congressional Quarterly,* a special service reporting, congressional activities to newspapers throughout the country, reported George Mahon was present for 97 percent of the roll calls, and he voted "on the record" each time he voted. He did not pair his vote with that of a colleague to conceal whether he voted "yea" or "nay." Mahon's record was not surpassed by any other member of the twenty-one-man Texas delegation; only Representative Jack Brooks from Beaumont and Representative Brady Gentry of Tyler equaled it. This record was especially meaningful in light of the heavy committee work that occupied many of his waking hours.[49] Mahon believed that being present to vote was only one part of it. Voting wisely was the second—and more important—part. Wise voting meant being in tune with his constituents' wishes, and he tried to do that by being a careful listener. Mahon's voting record in the first session of the Eighty-third Congress indicates that, despite his public admiration of Eisenhower, he really did not rubber-stamp the administration's bills. He voted with Eisenhower's requests on two key bills—the bill that would return the tidelands to the states (the House passed this bill) and the bill to reduce foreign aid by $212 billion (the House defeated this bill). He voted against Eisenhower's key requests to grant statehood to Hawaii (this passed the House); to authorize thirty-five thousand new public-housing starts (rejected by the House); to reduce soil conservation payments from $195 million to $140 million (the House rejected the reduction); to block expansion of the Tariff Commission to seven members, which would allow Republicans to remain in control; and to reorganize the Department of Agriculture. He also voted to authorize private utility development on the Niagara River and Falls, to increase the national debt limit, and to discontinue a tax on the movie business. He spoke in favor of this last bill and was one of its most active proponents. It passed both chambers by a large majority. By comparison, on key votes Senator Lyndon Johnson voted with the administration four times and against twice; Senator Price Daniel supported Eisenhower three times, voted against him twice, and did not vote one time.

After Congress adjourned, Mahon spent four months in the district warning farmers that, "because of the drought in recent years and because of the new cotton lands in New Mexico, Arizona, and California the new cotton program is going to be a terrific shock to the people of the cotton states."[50] He reminded them that although Texas was experiencing a drought, predictions were for a surplus in 1954, hence the need for allotments to control production. The new program allowed a national allotment of nearly eighteen million acres, which was 16 percent below the acreage that farmers were allowed in 1950, the last year when acreage controls were in operation. A shift in cotton production to western states meant that older cotton-producing counties would experience a drastic reduction in acres as the national allotment was apportioned to many more farmers. In some cases farmers would be allowed to plant only 44 percent of their 1950 allotment.

There was speculation that farmers participating in the program might be required to plant their remaining acres in crops that would not be harvested in order to control overproduction. Because of the surplus of grain sorghum, that crop would not be an option. While the cotton program would provide

90 percent of parity in price, Mahon said there would not be 90 percent of parity as far as income was concerned. He believed the national acreage allotment was too low and hoped that Congress would raise the figure to about twenty-two million acres. Farmers would have to vote in their counties to accept the program or be forced to sell their cotton on a glutted market. Mahon worked continuously with county officials and officials in Washington to secure the best possible control program because thousands of acres of cotton land and the economic survival of thousands of West Texas farmers were at stake.

The year ended on an especially joyful note for the Mahon and Holt families. Christmas together had been a happy time for them, and three days later a granddaughter was born. On December 28, 1953, Betsy Helen Holt joined the family.

Eisenhower's New Look military program was formally presented to the American people in his 1954 State of the Union address. He announced that the nation's great and growing arsenal of nuclear weapons would be used, as needed, to keep the peace. He stressed that these weapons had changed the relationship between men and material and would permit a reduction in the use of troops; thus, the airpower of the air force and the navy would receive the greatest emphasis in the new budget. Technology was causing ground troops to become obsolete, and their expense would undermine the nation's economy. The troops that were maintained would constitute a professional corps that could be put into action quickly in either partial or all-out mobilization. Finally, military and nonmilitary measures for continental defense would be strengthened.[51]

The defense budget submitted to Congress reflected the president's new concept. The administration intended to build the air force to 137 wings by the end of fiscal year 1957, in line with the plan to include nuclear weapons as part of the military's arsenal; ground forces were to be reduced. Indigenous forces would be used to withstand any initial attack against allies until the United States could bolster these forces with sea- and airpower. Weapons possessing state-of-the-art technology, instead of conventional fighting power, were to be the primary response from the United States. The core of the nation's fighting ability was rapidly shifting from troops to weapons. Greater emphasis was also to be put on continental defense. Before 1954 there had been very little support for defense of the American continent; however, the

Soviet explosion of a thermonuclear device in 1953 increased the fear of an outside attack. To guard against the possibility of a long war, reserve forces were to be strengthened through training in the use of all modern weapons and techniques. It was reasoned that reserve forces were cheaper to maintain than regular forces and, with modernization, could be quickly mobilized for defense. Historian Edward A. Kolodziej writes:

> The New Look touched all the important political bases: small and big wars would be deterred; the military establishment would be streamlined and modernized and the blessings of science and technology incorporated into its weapons arsenals; America's allies would be reassured of American military support; the communists everywhere would be put on clear notice that they would pay dearly through massive retaliatory attacks against their homelands if they should commit aggression against the United States or its friends; the government's budget would be balanced, defense spending cut, and taxes lowered; and Americans would be spared most of the grating personal inconveniences and sacrifices of the cold war.[52]

Most Americans responded favorably. They were tired of high taxes and military service. The fact that the president was a retired army general gave increased credibility to the New Look.

Initially, Congress had little difficulty accepting the doctrine. A majority believed it was a logical solution to the technological revolution in military weapons, to the growing communist military threat, and to the diminishing willingness of Americans to bear the financial and human burdens of worldwide commitments. The president's assurance that the nation was actually secure strengthened their support of the new priorities. The critics who called for even greater military spending were outnumbered by those who wanted a balanced budget, a reduction of the national debt, and reduced taxes. Kolodziej writes, "It was not an accident, therefore, that a reconstituted tax system which was to leave an additional $7 billion in private hands was closely linked to the President's New Look budget message."[53] The military establishment was left with little choice other than shaping their budget requests to fit the new fiscal policy.

Near the end of January 1954, the House Subcommittee for Defense Appropriations began hearing testimony from military officials. Mahon confided in his family:

Secretary of Defense Charles Wilson was rather cold toward Congress when he began his work last year, but he has learned that he needs the understanding of Congress if he is to carry out his program. Last Monday he had our Committee over to the Pentagon to lunch, admitting that he was trying to soften us up. He is a pretty able and clever old codger. He is rich and could be basking in the sun in Florida, but he has chosen the harder part. One of his predecessors cracked up and jumped off a building.[54] I told Secretary Wilson last year that he should try to do his work without worrying himself to death. Wilson said, "I won't do that. A successful business executive is one who wears a worried look on the face of his assistant!" His best crack this year in connection with the heat and pressure of his job was, "I try to make decisions and then not worry about them." As President Truman said, "If you can't stand the heat, stay out of the kitchen and let someone else do the cooking.[55]

In March a group of Puerto Rican nationalists opened fire from the gallery in the House of Representatives. At the time, Mahon and other members were standing for a vote on a bill that would permit recruiting agricultural workers from Mexico. Just as Speaker Joseph Martin finished counting the vote, the shooting started. Mahon thought it was some prankster with firecrackers until he saw other House members diving for cover. Immediately, he stepped through a doorway that shielded him from the gunmen. Shortly after the incident, a reporter from the *Lubbock Morning Avalanche* contacted Mahon by telephone and learned that he was unharmed. None of the bullets came within fifteen feet of him. Mahon said he didn't believe the shooting had anything to do with the bill regarding Mexican labor, although one of the gunmen appeared to be aiming for Majority Leader Charles Halleck (R-IN), who had just finished speaking in favor of the bill. Representative Alvin M. Bentley (R-MI) was critically wounded. Mahon said that although this was the first time in the history of the House that such a thing had happened, he was in favor of stricter policing of the visitors allowed into the galleries of the House and Senate.[56]

In April House debate began on the $28.7 billion military appropriation bill for fiscal year 1955. The House reduced the amount that President Eisenhower had requested by $1.2 billion. Mahon told the House that although progress was being made in the use of guided missiles, the United States was "vulnerable to atomic attack but he said the US retaliatory strength is such that 'only the most foolhardy enemy' would risk starting a war."[57] He believed that atomic and hydrogen bombs might become completely neutral because no nation would dare use them, just as neither side would use poison gas during World War II. Representative Errett Scrivner (R-KS) pointed out that the United States currently had twenty-one thousand air force planes, plus ten thousand for the navy and Marine Corps. The Soviet Union had approximately twenty thousand, which gave the United States an edge of three to two.

After the military bill had cleared the House, Mahon wrote to Daphne and Duncan that "I did not have a prepared speech and did not participate very much in the proceedings. I did have one violent colloquy with Mr. Gavin because he inferred that I had suppressed Air Force appropriations in the past, but it was taken completely out of the record."[58] What Mahon actually said on the House floor on April 29, 1954, was that he was disappointed "when the gentlemen from Pennsylvania took time out gratuitously to make a baldfaced misstatement about me . . . Unless the gentleman's memory has forsaken him, he well knows that in previous years as a Member of the House, regardless of the wishes of the administration, I have been a champion of strong national defense. . . . I rise merely to correct the gratuitous slap by the gentleman from Pennsylvania."[59] The quiet and unassuming George Mahon had been pushed to the limit of his patience! There are two editions of the *Congressional Record*. One is printed daily, and the permanent, bound one is printed after a session is over. Members of both chambers are allowed to edit their remarks before publication in the permanent *Record*.

In May Mahon made news in the *Lubbock Avalanche-Journal* by stating, "The nation has developed no adequate air defense against atomic attack, but that the U.S. Air Force is superbly prepared to launch a devastating unstoppable counterattack . . . within seconds after hostilities begin."[60] He went on to say that he believed an attack by the Soviet Union was unlikely because that nation was even more vulnerable to an air attack and leaders in the Kremlin were well aware of this situation.[61] His comments indicated that he would publicly support President Eisenhower's New Look, which focused on retaliatory airpower rather than large ground forces, despite some problems that he and Representative Sikes had uncovered during the hearings.

Apparently, Mahon was beginning to recognize a major shortcoming of the New Look military strategy. Because the Soviet Union and the United States had both accumulated sizeable nuclear arsenals, neither side could risk the massive retaliation that would result from a Pearl Harbor–type attack against the other side. Representative Robert L. F. Sikes (D-FL) also spoke on the House floor about this issue. Unfortunately, both congressmen fell short of offering an amendment that would address the problem. Neither man tried to increase appropriations for ground forces that could be used where, in effect, atomic weapons were neutralized. Although the New Look was economical, it was not balanced, and before the year was out this became obvious.

The communist bloc took advantage of this weakness by supporting a proxy war in Indochina, where nuclear weapons could not be used because of the threat of proliferation into a full-blown nuclear war. President Eisenhower toyed with the idea of entering the conflict with air strikes to help the French, if he could get multilateral support. When that was not forthcoming, the National Security Council drafted a paper exploring the possibility of using small atomic bombs at Dien Bien Phu, but the president responded, "We can't use those awful things against Asians for the second time in less than ten years."[62] Nor would public opinion or Congress support the use of ground forces, in part because the army and marines had been reduced to the point that there simply were not enough troops to send. The situation was similar to Korea; however, in this case, troops of a dangerously low level were not sent in to be slaughtered. This exposed a major weakness of relying on air-atomic weapons to solve all global conflicts. Dien Bien Phu fell to the Viet Minh in July 1954, and at the Geneva Conference the French government agreed to partition the country at the Seventeenth Parallel.

During the debate GOP opposition was voiced against an amendment by Frederic R. Couderat, Jr. (R-NY), that would bar President Eisenhower from sending troops to fight in Indochina without specific congressional consent. According to the amendment, congressional approval would be required to send troops into conflict, or the United States would have to be attacked to send troops without Congressional approval.[63] Mahon and Lyndon Johnson, who were later in Lubbock for the presentation of a Medal of Honor to the widow of an air force pilot who had lost his life in the Korean War, stated publicly that they were opposed to sending American troops into action in Indochina.[64] These statements are worth remembering.

Despite President Eisenhower's emphasis on smaller government, federal spending actually increased to such a level that Congress was forced to raise the national debt limit. The federal deficit rose by $4 billion for the year ending June 30, 1954. This was 25 percent more than the deficit for the previous year. A 3 percent reduction became the goal for the next fiscal year.

When the House recessed for Easter, Mahon went shopping. He had not bought a new pair of shoes in two years, and the tires on his old Chevrolet were three years old. The remainder of the time was used to catch up on his correspondence. To his family he wrote, "Our military appropriations bill of twenty-eight billion dollars will be before the House for debate April 26. My work will not be so heavy thereafter. Since I do not have the leadership in handling the bill I have tried to take it a bit easier this year."[65]

Spring can be pleasant in Texas, and Helen was enjoying a visit with Daphne and her family in May when "lonesome George" wrote to her, "Everything about the apartment reminds me of you; the gin rummy score pad, my dirty shirts on the floor. The dresser drawers all open, the dirty dishes in the sink, and more appropriately than anything else—the candy in the pretty candy jar!"[66] However, he managed to lift his spirits with a golf game with President Eisenhower at Burning Tree Country Club in Maryland. Representative Les Arends (R-IL) and Representative Scrivner (R-KS) completed the foursome. When the game was over, the president gave Mahon one of the golf balls he had used, saying, "Give this to your grandson."[67] The manufacturer of Titleist golf balls furnished the president with golf balls on which was inscribed "The President."[68] Earlier that year Mahon had sent Daphne a place card autographed by Admiral Arthur Radford, chairman of the Joint Chiefs of Staff. He had sat next to Radford at a luncheon and knew that the autograph, like the golf ball, would be a nice memento that would help give Daphne's children a sense of their grandfather's place in history.

Helen recalled during a 1985 interview that when President Eisenhower wanted to play golf, an aide from the Oval Office would call Mahon and say, "Mr. Green has died. What time can you get away for the funeral?"[69] At the agreed-upon time, Mahon would go to the White House and ride from there with the president to the golf course. Mahon often spent weekends playing golf with congressmen, military leaders, and presidents. He and Helen also played bridge and accepted social invitations from these people. Early on he had made a decision to use persuasion, rather than a forceful personality, to impact legislation. The friendships he formed helped him get his ducks in a row before committee hearings were conducted or legislation came to the House floor. This approach created a type of power that was difficult to challenge.[70] No doubt his golfing buddies also used the game as an opportunity to influence Mahon to be more receptive to their viewpoints.

The Mahons enjoyed listening to the radio, especially the Arthur Godfrey program, and watching baseball on television. Mahon was also an avid reader. Weekends were often spent driving to various small towns near the city, and by the time they retired from Washington, they were familiar with most of the countryside. Movies provided another enjoyable type of entertainment. Mahon claimed not to like television; however, he watched it more than he wanted to admit. He and Helen enjoyed watching Norman Vincent Peale on Sunday morning. In late summer of that year, they also attended a backyard dinner given by the Connallys, and he wrote to his sister, "So many people seem to have charcoal broilers which can really cook a tasty steak. I haven't inquired lately, but I imagine that thick juicy steaks are still expensive!"[71]

In late July 1954 Daphne's husband, Duncan, received notice that he had passed the Texas bar exam, and Mahon wrote, "I think Mama Mahon and I are perhaps as thrilled and delighted as you and Daphne are. I do think that is a great compliment to you, a very great compliment, that you should pass the bar on the first try. The fact that you are a 'foreigner'[72] I thought would militate against you, at least for one try. That you passed and made good grades, is really very wonderful."[73]

"We went by the French Embassy a few afternoons ago and I got to shake the soft little hand of the famous nurse from Deinbienphu [sic]," Mahon wrote to his sister. "She seemed to be a very grand person. Another courageous personage visited us this past week and spoke to a Joint Session of Congress, President Rhee of South Korea."[74]

Lieutenant Genevieve de Galard-Terraube, known as the "Angel of Dien Bien Phu," was in the United States to receive the Medal of Freedom from President Eisenhower. It was awarded for her outstanding contribution to peace and can be given only for service outside the boundaries of this country. Lieutenant de Galard had been a flight nurse for the French Air Force in Indochina, where her bravery during the siege of Dien Bien Phu captured the admiration of the world. After assisting with many evacuations of casualties, she was stranded at the battle scene when the plane she was on overshot the runway and was completely destroyed by the Viet Minh. For the next two months she cared for the wounded at a field hospital. Although the French capitulated, the Viet Minh allowed her to continue her work. Finally, she was evacuated to French-held Hanoi. Representative Edith Nourse Rogers (R-MA), chair of the House Veterans Affairs Committee, sponsored a congressional invitation for Galard to visit the United States. It was hoped that her visit would help recruit nurses for military duty. Several hundred guests attended the reception at the French Embassy to show their admiration for Lieutenant de Galard's heroism.[75]

At the same time, Republic of Korea president and Mrs. Syngman Rhee were in the United States for an official state visit. In addition to attending many social functions, President Rhee addressed a joint session of Congress. Before and after his address, he was loudly applauded by a packed chamber; however, a wall of silence rose when he called for a preventive war against the People's Republic of China. He asked the United States for navy and air force support, with South Korea and Nationalist China furnishing ground troops. He stressed that the communist bloc intended to lull the United States into talking peace until their nuclear capability was large enough to destroy the US. He added that such a war against China would likely cause the Soviet Union to enter the conflict, which would provide an excellent opportunity for the United States to destroy the Soviet centers of productivity. The reaction was one of shock and dismay. The editor of the *Washington Post* wrote, "Congressmen could scarcely believe that any high official of any country would deliberately advocate a course of action calculated to start an atomic war."[76]

After returning to the district in September, Mahon told a staff writer for the *Lubbock Morning Avalanche* that the world picture was not bright because "the Communists continue to make gains at our expense. The free world did not win in Korea, and it lost in Indochina. The Geneva Conference was a sharp setback for us.[77] . . . In Europe, the Communists have been successful thus far in defeating the EDC [European Defense Community] program for Western Europe which we have sponsored."[78]

He went on to say that he believed the United States was stronger militarily than at any period in peacetime history, but the Soviets were even stronger. Military appropriations had been reduced because the shooting in Korea stopped. Employment was high and business was enjoying large profits, but the farmer's income was sharply down. Some decrease in farm income was inevitable after the war, but the administration was largely responsible for the reductions. "The Republicans appear to feel that the new flexible support farm program is their greatest accomplishment in two years. In my opinion, it is their greatest mistake to date, and I vigorously opposed it, feeling that the 90 per cent program was in the interest of both the farmer and the people generally. . . . The farmer will be badly hurt, and there will be no corresponding benefit to the consumer and taxpayer and no solution to the problem of crop surpluses. Crop controls in 1955 will probably be more rigid than at any time in the last 20 years."[79]

The 1954 mid-term election posed no problem for Mahon because he did not have an opponent. In contrast, Republicans did not fare well nationally in the election. Democrats campaigned vigorously and won control of both chambers of Congress. Shortly after the election Mahon undertook an inspection tour. He described his trip as "operations getting the feel of the field . . . Bull sessions with military in the field ought to help more than endless tramps about military bases, but I will do some of that too."[80]

Stopping first at Briggs Air Force Base near El Paso, Texas, to inspect the guided-missile program, he learned that the commanding general was "hampered in his training operations by reason of the failure of Congress to give him the green light on the acquiring of additional land for guided missile firings."[81] Mahon promised to bring this situation to the attention of the appropriate people in Washington. Now, with the Democrats in control of the House, he would be responsible for such matters when he, once again, assumed the chairmanship of the Subcommittee on Defense Department Appropriations. From El Paso he went to San Francisco to meet with the National Guard officers and Reserve officers of the Sixth Army. In his report of the trip, he wrote, "I was convinced that the Reserve Program lacks effectiveness by reason of the fact that there is no way to compel attendance at meetings of Reserve Officers, etc."[82]

After inspecting other military installations in the San Francisco area, including the MATS (Military Air Transport System) program at Travis Air Force Base, he traveled by train to Nebraska, where he spent a day at Offutt Air Force Base, ten miles south of Omaha. General Curtis LeMay, commander of the Strategic Air Command, was his host. In his report after returning, Mahon wrote, "By all odds, the most interesting thing I did on the trip was to spend a day with General LeMay. He is the most impressive man, and the briefing which I got—it lasted seven hours—was the best I have ever had. I wish our entire Subcommittee might go to LeMay's headquarters on some appropriate occasion and have the briefing which is given there."[83] Mahon believed the air force was the branch of service most likely to deter war with the Soviet Union because its planes were capable of delivering fatal blows in response to an attack. He obviously admired LeMay's ability to develop the Strategic Air Command into an effective shield. Generally, Mahon respected people who could get the job done, even if their forceful, brusque, and sometimes crude behavior was very different from his own. It is also likely that LeMay let Mahon see only the best of his personality in order to keep the dollars flowing in from Congress.

While he was away Helen visited Daphne in Houston, and George's letters to her were truly love letters: "I want you to be rested and feeling wonderful when I see you. Don't lift George and Betsy unnecessarily and don't be in a dither all the time. Just enjoy them. I will be glad to see them too."[84] It was signed: "Much love from your adoring husband—Geo. Herman."[85] A week later he wrote that he was relaxed and feeling wonderful. He planned to meet Helen in Colorado City, where they were to spend a few days wishing relatives and friends "Merry Christmas" before driving to Houston. "I know you have enjoyed Daph and Dunc and the children. I am looking forward to Xmas with them. Say, I hope we won't have a lot of society during our stay in Houston. . . . This would give us a chance to be with each other at home and we could go out at night too by arranging for baby sitters. . . . Officially we just would not be in town—we could just explain to people that we wanted to make Xmas a time for family association and rest. Love and Kisses—George."[86]

The Mahon and Holt families had a joyful Christmas together in Houston. In addition to a good, long visit with Daphne and Duncan, Mahon ate a lot of his favorite foods, slept later than usual, and romped with the grandchildren. Shortly after Christmas he and Helen set out for Washington by automobile. When they got to Eunice, Louisiana, their car was the fourth in a pileup. Mahon, who was asleep in the backseat, got a cut on his forehead when he was thrown against the backseat, and Helen bruised her elbow and ribs against the steering wheel. Mahon's cousin, who had a Ford dealership in nearby Baton Rouge, took the car in for repairs, and a few days later they were on their away again. They arrived back in Washington on the first of January, in time to attend a traditional New Year's Day party, where everyone ate a big helping of black-eyed peas for good luck during 1955.

Mahon was busy when he got back to Washington. After nearly two months away, correspondence was piled up, waiting for him. With the Democrats in control, he returned to his position as chair of the Subcommittee for Defense Appropriations. Representative Clarence Cannon (D-MO), who also returned to his former position as chair of the full House Committee on Appropriations, conducted the greatest reorganization since 1921. He raised the number of subcommittees from eleven to thirteen and regrouped the membership of each. He returned jurisdiction over military construction to Mahon's subcommittee. Despite Cannon's reputation for being cantankerous, Mahon respected the older man and found ways to get along with him. Cannon learned that Mahon could be trusted to get the job done, and as each year passed he grew to depend on his protégé more and more.

The first month of the new session was unusually busy, with most of the attention focused on passing a resolution regarding the defense of Formosa. On January 29 President Eisenhower signed into law H.J. Res. 159-PL 4, which gave him the authority to use force in defending Formosa and the nearby Pescadores Islands against the People's Republic of China. Keeping the western Pacific islands in the hands of "friendly" governments was considered vital to the interests of the United States. Controversy surrounding this resolution centered on the omission of the specific area that the United States would defend with force. In supporting passage, many congressmen believed that failure to pass the resolution would have put the nation in an even more dangerous position.

In January 1955 Lloyd Croslin, a Lubbock attorney who had been Mahon's personal secretary in 1935 when he first came to Washington, asked for a ruling from the Internal Revenue Commission to determine if the "other natural deposits" section of Section 611 of the new Internal Revenue Code would cover water drawn from the Ogallala Aquifer. Section 611 provided that a tax deduction was allowable for the annual depletion of "mines, oil and gas wells, other natural deposits, and timber." Representing the High Plains Underground Water Conservation District #1 in Lubbock, Croslin asked for a depletion allowance for Marvin and Mildred Shurbet of Petersburg, Texas. Croslin argued that the annual inflow, or recharge, to the aquifer in West Texas was approximately two to ten feet less than the drainage from irrigation wells used in growing cotton, grain sorghum, and wheat. Because the water was used faster than it was being replenished, the value of the land was being driven down; thus landowners were entitled to tax relief just as oil well owners were entitled to tax deductions as their wells were depleted through mining the resource below. In 1893 the Texas Supreme Court had ruled that groundwater is a natural resource, like the soil, and as such it belongs to the landowner.

When Croslin appeared before the commission, Mahon was with him. In March he wrote to Croslin, "Lloyd, I had a letter from Tom McFarland about the tax case. He seemed to be encouraged. Some time ago I talked to Colin Stam about the case, but I did not get anything helpful from him. I have hesitated to get in touch with the boys down at the Bureau of Internal Revenue. However, the time for their decision is approaching and if you think I should do anything, I had better do it pretty soon."[87] Croslin and Ray Lawrence, a Lubbock accountant, were spearheading this movement. The IRS refused to grant the allowance, and it took nearly a decade to resolve the case through the state and federal courts. In 1963 the US District Court for the Northern District of Texas ruled that groundwater in the Southern High Plains of Texas is a depletable natural resource and eligible for a federal income tax deduction. During the long struggle Mahon supported the group through phone calls to people in Washington and by arranging hearings before federal agencies. West Texans hailed this as one of Mahon's most important accomplishments for the district because of the importance of water in earning a livelihood in this semi-arid area. Unfortunately, Lloyd Croslin did not live to see the final ruling handed down.

During the Christmas holidays the Mahons had decided to give up their apartment in the Alban Towers and gave the landlord thirty days' notice after returning to Washington. They wanted to be closer to the victory garden they enjoyed so much. After searching briefly, they found an apartment that was closer, but unfortunately it had only two rooms, which they considered a drawback. Their landlord at Alban Towers wouldn't hear of their leaving and offered to remodel their apartment with a completely new kitchen and new paint throughout. Mahon insisted on an air conditioner, and the landlord agreed to do the wiring if Mahon would buy the air conditioner and pay an additional twenty-five dollars per year for electricity. That was too good to refuse and they agreed to stay, moving into an adjoining apartment while the work was done. A lot of other remodeling was also done in the building, and its name was changed to Alban Towers Hotel. The new air conditioner was installed in May, and Mahon loved it. In fact, this old West Texas farm boy had grown quite dependent on air conditioners, and as Helen wrote to Daphne while they were in Lubbock that summer, "I must tell you about Daddy, there is an air conditioner in the apartment[88] and when he came in at lunch today I hadn't turned it on so he almost had a fit, he wanted it on right at once. I came to the office so I could write to you all and he told me not to turn the conditioner off while we were gone."[89]

He even saw to it that his father also received an air conditioner in Weatherford, Texas, but he had trouble getting the old man to keep it turned on. At one point he wrote to a friend, who worked for the local utility company, asking that his father be billed for no more than seven dollars a month, and Mahon be billed for the remainder of the charges. However, this had to be a closely guarded secret, because he knew his father would not tolerate a son paying part of his electric bill.[90] Even the inexpensive rate didn't seem to convince the old gentleman that he should enjoy the comfort of cool air during the summer. So Mahon tried again. On July 2 he wrote to his father, "Hope you all are feeling fine and be sure and keep that air conditioner going because I know how nice it is to keep cool. Another thing, they told me that the cost is more to run one if you turn it on and off, than just turning it on in the morning and leaving it on all day."[91] Mahon loved his father very much and enjoyed doing nice things for him.

When they returned to their newly remodeled apartment they decided it was just right for company, and the Mahons hosted a dinner party for the office staff. Actually, Mahon had agreed to prepare the dinner by himself. In a letter to his family, he wrote,

> I took to the Appropriations Committee Room with me, the cookbook entitled "Joy of Cooking" and when I was not busy interrogating a witness, I read portions from the cookbook. Prior to this date [February 14, when the party was held] 12 luscious steaks had been procured and were in the freezing tray. Helen had bought the baking potatoes for me. I went to a hardware store and got some baking nails, meaning twenty penny finishing nails. I stuck one into each potato in order to insure a little more even baking. Texas Highway Commissioner, Marshall Formby, of Plainview was one of my guests. He said that he had never been to a dinner before where he had been served nails. I explained that people in Washington were so nervous and

frustrated they went away unhappy if you didn't serve them nails! I got four kinds of greens for the tossed salad. I had some especially fine French olive oil, some garlic vinegar and vitamin salt. The salad was really crisp and nice but it was not sufficiently tasty. I could do a better job next time. It was fun to put all of these ingredients into a large salad bowl and mix them up with my hands. My fingernails have never been so clean! Massaging the potatoes with bacon grease before baking them was fun too. One of my troubles was that nearly everything had to be done at once. Some people wanted their steak rare, others medium, etc. About that time the broccoli was ready to take off the stove, and I wanted to make the salad at the last minute so the greens would be good and crisp. Of course, it wasn't very much trouble to take out the baked potatoes. Helen and I went out to Bethesda, Maryland, some five miles away and bought some very cleverly made and decorated ice cream. It was a George Washington Birthday Special. When the meal was over and I had had my Postum[92] and others had their coffee, it was agreed by all, with tongue in cheek that I had done a pretty good job. At any rate I had not had so much fun since about 1919 when I cooked for a farming crew on a farm near Dallas for a couple of weeks. Life can be beautiful and cooking can be fun, but it is an awfully messy art and quite expensive![93]

In March Helen returned to Colorado City to attend the funeral of a long-time friend, Ewell Thompson, who had died of lung cancer. She was the wife of Charles Thompson, the high-school classmate of both Mahon and Helen, and Mahon's law partner when he decided to run for Congress in 1934. After the funeral Helen went on to Houston to visit with Daphne and family. Duncan was then a lawyer with Sinclair Oil Company.

In a family letter Mahon wrote,

"We had quite a battle in the House last week over the tax bill. In a two-party country such as we have—and the two-party system in my judgment is a pretty good system despite its weaknesses—one has to occasionally vote with the Party leadership as a gesture of Party Loyalty. Of course, you will know that I was not very enthusiastic about the tax cut. I think we ought to balance the budget before we cut taxes but in view of the fact that President Eisenhower had intimated that he was going to cut taxes next year, some of the Democrats felt that the Democratic Congress should pass a reduction effective January 1, 1956. There seems to be little likelihood that the reduction will actually become the law."[94]

Subcommittee hearings on President Eisenhower's defense budget began in January, and by May the bill was ready to present to the full House. The second New Look budget experienced greater resistance than the previous one. There was a growing sense among House members that the budget would not provide the right mix of forces needed to fulfill growing US commitments around the world. The emphasis on air-atomic weapons appeared to create a weakness that had become obvious during the Indochina crisis of 1954 and again during the Formosa crisis, when the administration admitted that using ground troops in Formosa was not an option because of the small number available. That left only atomic weapons, and in addition to being reluctant to use atomic weapons against Asians a second time in little more than a decade, President Eisenhower also acknowledged that using atomic weapons for massive retaliation would cause problems with European nations. Despite these facts, air force appropriations were increased at the expense of army and navy appropriations, which meant a further reduction in the size of the land force on active duty. Two members of the Subcommittee on Defense Appropriations, Representative Daniel Flood (D-PA) and Representative George Andrews (D-AL), argued that these cuts were actually designed to balance the budget and it would never be balanced, even with unwise military cuts. They offered amendments that would have restored army and navy funds to their levels of the year before, but their amendments were defeated by a voice vote.

Mahon was one of those who led the fight against the restoration of funds, claiming the cuts reflected "bookkeeping changes rather than real savings."[95] By leading the fight against increased funds for the navy and army, Mahon was subtly supporting increased funds for the air force without having to take a clear stand against the other services. In future years Mahon would use this technique to influence the defense budget. Keeping the total appropriation at or below the amount requested by the president, Mahon would decrease some line item expenditures and increase others, thereby supporting one branch of the service over another. Mahon's subcommittee could not actually write defense policy, but he did rearrange line item amounts in ways that came pretty close to creating policy. President Eisenhower did not always agree and would often refuse to spend any additional funds allotted. Appropriations chairman Clarence Cannon stated his belief that only weapons of massive retaliation would be useful in the next war. He believed the reserve army forces that Eisenhower advocated would only be used to keep martial law after an attack. In the end, the opportunity to cut expenses so tantalized most congressmen that they seemed to have forgotten the recent losses to the communist bloc in Korea and Indochina, where massive retaliation was not a practical option. They appeared to be willing to follow the recommendations of a great military leader without questioning the logic behind his reduced land forces. The defense budget for fiscal year 1956 was $31.5 billion. The president's second New Look military budget survived, but the seeds of opposition had been sown.

The House Appropriations Committee announced it would conduct a gloves off investigation of defense buying that was causing the taxpayer to lose his shirt. Mahon said, "The profits of industry engaged in defense production business have been soaring as though they were jet propelled, at supersonic speeds. The taxpayer is being taken for a ride."[96] One aircraft producer, doing most of its business with the government, was enjoying a 242 percent increase in net profits since 1950.

Mahon said the full House Appropriations Committee had hired experts to examine contracts where profits seemed excessive and make recommendations that could be used by the committee in establishing new buying procedures. He also charged that Defense Secretary Charles Wilson, who was appointed for his business ability, had done nothing to bring expenses down. He said, "The Secretary . . . is a genius in the field of business and management, but if he has knocked any heads together in industry in an effort to get defense costs down to reasonable levels . . . I have not heard about it."[97] The editor of the *Lubbock Morning Avalanche* agreed with Mahon's concern, recommending that "Mr. Mahon's Subcommittee should knock a few heads together, if necessary, and jar some sense into the way our tax dollars are spent."[98]

During July 1955 the Soviet Union staged an impressive air show just outside of Moscow that Western powers called "perturbing" and an "unprecedented shock." A number of heavy bombers, a turbo-prop intercontinental bomber, a supersonic single-jet pursuit aircraft, a twin-jet all-weather fighter, and a twin-rotor helicopter were displayed. The number and variety of new planes in the show challenged a theory held by some American defense officials that the Soviets could produce only a few handmade intercontinental bombers compared to the large-scale production of US planes. It appeared that the Soviets were geared up for the latest assembly-line methods. Additionally, US officials were surprised that the Soviets had produced what could turn out to be the first all-jet passenger plane for civilian use. These were paraded for the benefit of foreign observers and just in time to make a big impression before the Big Four conference scheduled in Geneva. Senator Stuart Symington (D-MO), fearing that the United States did not have the degree of superiority it had enjoyed in the past, told reporters, "It is the duty of the administration to give us the facts on what was seen at Moscow so that we can do whatever is necessary to maintain our air superiority."[99] Mahon told the same reporter that he thought the United States was moving too slowly in building up the air force. He said, "I think we are a little naïve to be surprised by these developments and I have so told Defense Secretary Wilson and Air Force Secretary Talbott."[100] Mahon would make no prediction about the full implication of the air show, but he believed the Soviets were making the most of an attempt to deal from a position of strength at the 1955 Geneva conference. While the Pentagon denied that Soviet planes were equal to those of the United States, they admitted that Russian jet engines were larger than previously and must be more powerful.[101] Newspapers throughout the district carried the story before it was later proven that the large number of aircraft was actually waves of planes that circled around and flew over the crowd again and again. Soviet leaders hoped this would impress American observers. It certainly did, and it also fueled the arms race.[102]

When Congress adjourned, Mahon traveled to Europe to attend a meeting of the Interdisciplinary Union in Helsinki, Finland, on August 24. Founded in 1889, this was a meeting of representatives from the parliaments and congresses of twenty-nine nations, including the USSR. The purpose of the union was to promote personal contacts between members of all parliaments in an effort to promote international peace and understanding. Its mission states: "By providing its members with the opportunity for unrestricted and frank discussion, it can powerfully contribute to developing the spirit of mutual comprehension between nations, which is the only solid foundation for a stable international order." It also prepared the way for action to be taken by official international organizations and acted as a clearinghouse for public opinion concerning decisions that would affect the whole world. The number of votes was determined by the size of the population, and the United States had twenty-one votes. The Soviet Union had twenty-two, India had nineteen, and the United Kingdom had fourteen.

Mahon was one of twenty-five delegates from the United States, and he served on the Committee on World Disarmament. Helen accompanied him, but he was careful to see that all of her expenses were covered with their personal money. In Stockholm, where they joined other US delegates on their way to Helsinki, the group attended a reception hosted by the American ambassador, John Cabot. They found Ambassador Cabot quite friendly, despite the jokes about the Lodges speaking only to the Cabots and the Cabots speaking only to God. In the land of the midnight sun, Mahon wrote that one morning he awakened at 3:30 a.m. and found it was light as day. Scandinavia also had no flies, so there were no screens on the windows. Most Swedes spoke English, but few in Finland did. Mahon marveled that in Swedish hotels linen sheets were used, but when they stayed more than one night, the sheets were not changed. He also commented that double beds were unknown in Sweden.[103]

A problem arose in recognizing the delegation from China when the meeting began. The Republic of China, with headquarters in Formosa, claimed to be the legitimate delegation. The People's Republic, with headquarters in Peking, had not yet been recognized by many nations, including the United States, nor had it been recognized by the United Nations. The US delegation voted to leave the conference if a delegation from the People's Republic of China was seated, and for a while it appeared this would happen. Because the question was so difficult to resolve, neither group was admitted.

Items on the agenda included the conditions of a true and peaceful co-existence between the nations, the strengthening of the inter-parliamentary union, immigration and emigration (especially refugee problems), the powers of the chair in legislative assemblies, and changes in the by-laws. Earphones provided effective translations in English, French, and Russian. In 1955, 80 percent of the debate was conducted in English, compared to ten years before, when 80 percent was conducted in French. At least one member of the US delegation spoke to every item on the agenda, and by the end of the meeting the American point of view on every issue was well known.

Mahon rated the conference as better than expected. Sessions began promptly at 10:00 each morning and continued until about 1:15. After lunch they reconvened from 3:00 to 6:00. The Soviet delegation and their interpreters were seated in a long row in front of the US delegation. Mahon wrote to family members, "If you make the slightest gesture of friendship toward the Russians they almost eat you up with kindly gestures. All for a subtle purpose, in my opinion."[104]

Evenings were filled with dinners and entertainment such as concerts; a performance by the Finnish Ballet, one of the greatest in the world; and a boat trip along the Finnish coast line. Mahon wrote home that he brought along a shirt made of Dacron for dress wear. He just washed it after each wearing, and it dried in a couple of hours. Though it made his laundry problem much simpler, he felt a little guilty about not wearing cotton.[105]

Before the conference began and after it was over, he inspected military construction programs on the continent. This had become his responsibility when Cannon returned control over money for military public works to the Subcommittee on Defense Appropriations. When the bill for the continuation of construction of US military bases overseas came before his subcommittee, Mahon insisted that several million dollars for additional new bases in Spain, England, and France be stricken from the bill. He said, "I think our overseas bases have been a great deterrent to war, but I am getting more and more skeptical of this program, particularly from a long-range view-point, and I have grave doubts that it should be expanded. The whole program of our having American bases and troops in Sovereign countries abroad rests upon a rather shaky foundation. I plan to visit a number of bases and confer with our own people and citizens and officials of other countries."[106]

Along with the inspection tour, he and Helen took time for a vacation in Switzerland and Italy. They flew from Sweden to the continent and back again, but most of their European travel was on trains, which Mahon decided were much nicer than trains in the United States. They had a compartment for six on the train in England and enjoyed visiting with English people in the same compartment. The trains had large windows, so they had a great opportunity to see the countryside. He also wrote that upon further observation, accommodations for second- and third-class passengers were quite inferior to first class. Mahon noted that at mealtime they had to pay fifteen cents extra for a bottle of water.[107] Although they both felt the trip was a bit expensive, they considered it the opportunity of their lifetime.

He also wrote home that the people were always more interesting than the countryside, but Americans were generally unpopular all over Europe. They lived in little clans and looked down upon Europeans. They made no attempt to learn the European languages or appreciate the customs. In fact, Europeans thought most Americans were arrogant, inconsiderate, and overbearing. "It is a shame, I am told, that Americans do not capitalize on our marvelous opportunity. [I] ask on every side when I have a good opportunity, 'How long will it be before the Europeans begin to feel somewhat secure and tell us to pick up our marbles and go home?' Of course, we cannot pick up the billion dollars plus that which we have invested in air fields and military installations. I was responsible for slowing down the program a bit in the last Congress and I am trying to make up my mind what we really ought to do about this awkward and difficult situation."[108]

The fly in the ointment for Mahon was the publicity in newspapers about congressional junkets. According to these articles, over two hundred legislators had traveled abroad after Congress recessed in 1955. Most of these trips were financed with congressional funds and counterpart money furnished to traveling congressmen by foreign nations that received US aid. Many congressmen were impressed with how lavishly these funds were dished out. For personal expenses some nations provided as much as three hundred dollars per day. Transportation was often in military planes. Wives and children also traveled with the congressmen; in fact, there was one incident where a mother-in-law went along with the family. Mahon was mentioned as one of the Texas congressmen who went to Europe that year; however, he had always been careful to let others know that he paid Helen's expenses out of his own pocket. Some of these news articles made their way into district newspapers. One of them estimated these trips cost at least five thousand dollars of taxpayers' money and probably an equal amount was supplied by the foreign nations being visited. It went on to say, "Our own Congressman George Mahon, not given to goofing up his constituents' tax money, has succumbed to the congressional urge to travel in far lands. George might well employ his time in his district to find out how voters feel about an 84th Congress whose record is far from distinguished. He might be getting opinions of people to guide him in the government's obvious determination to socialize everything and everybody—all in the name of democracy. . . . Wings of high-flying Congressmen should be clipped, and they should be grounded in the U.S. where they can (even if they seldom do) render outstanding service to their constituents."[109]

There is no record of Mahon's reaction to the article; however, a postscript in one of his letters from Europe reads, "Well, we are now safely landed in Rome. About all of Congress seems to be here."[110] Although he visited military installations the better part of each day that he was on a government expense account, it appears that some of his constituents believed he had developed a case of the same "junket fever" that held many other congressmen in its grip.

Christmas was spent with Daphne and her family in Houston. This time they rode the train back to Washington, leaving Houston on December 27 and arriving in Washington on December 29. That provided just enough time to eat their traditional large helping of black-eyed peas on New Year's Day and to rest up a bit before the opening session of the Eighty-fourth Congress on January 3. Helen was one of the "regulars" in the gallery. She had not missed an opening day in the twenty-one years since Mahon had come to Congress in 1935. That evening they attended the annual dinner for congressmen and their spouses given by the Women's National Press Club. After listening to the president's State of the Union address the next day, the festive atmosphere of renewing old friendships and catching up on all that had happened during the recess gave way to serious work and spirited debates.

President Eisenhower's fiscal year 1957 military budget was characterized by repetition. There were no major changes in the level of spending or the size of military forces.[111] The only change was an increase in funds for guided missiles. Airpower continued to be emphasized, and the role of conventional weapons was further diminished. The army's budget was cut to $7.8 billion.[112] The administration could not muster up the same kind of support for its recommendations that had been achieved previously from the public and Congress. "The publication of General Matthew Ridgway's attack on the New Look in his *Memoirs* and an article in the *Saturday Evening Post* sharpened the dissonant effect of army complaints."[113] A noticeable development was the manner in which the army organized its criticisms into a well-defined strategy. Previously, these criticisms had consisted of isolated jabs at parts of the administration's military policy. During the hearings for the 1957 military budget, General Maxwell Taylor, the army chief of staff who had replaced General Matthew Ridgway, succinctly presented the army's position when he said,

I am aware of the fact that many students of the world military situation regard only one type of war—the general nuclear onslaught—as being sufficiently important to cause much concern. I believe that as parity is approximated in numbers and types of atomic weapons between East and West, every effort will be made on both sides to avoid the general atomic war. But, at the same time, I cannot believe that the Communist bloc will give up aggression as an instrument of policy. It appears probably by pressure on the soft spots about the Soviet periphery through subversion, guerrilla actions and *coups d'etat*; by small-scale wars; and the ever present threat of their large armies the Communists will continue to seek extension of their boundaries at the expense of the west. Failure to respond quickly and effectively to these types of warfare will permit piecemeal loss of important areas belonging to friends and allies. Such failure would create situations which might expand into the general war that all parties seek to avoid.[114]

General Taylor went on to say that the world's trouble spots all had one characteristic in common: any military action there would require ground forces, with a very limited role for weapons of mass destruction. He acknowledged the need for deterring a general war but also stressed the necessity of suppressing a small war as quickly as possible. To carry out this mission, he asked that active forces be increased to 1.5 million; that conventional weapons be modernized and a large stockpile maintained; that the development of anti-aircraft and antimissile guided missiles be stepped up; and that air and sea transport services be increased. To do this the army would require a larger share of the military budget, or the overall budget would have to be increased. The army received a sympathetic hearing from Congress, but nothing more.

This was an election year, and members of the Defense Appropriations subcommittee attempted to ask more questions than before. Part of this questioning was led by Mahon, whose questions directed to Secretary Wilson challenged the wisdom of Secretary of State Dulles's policy of brinkmanship.[115] He wanted to know what the Department of Defense was doing in regard to being battle-ready should Dulles's statesmanship go over the brink.[116] Although Wilson's answer was not really adequate, Mahon failed to probe deeper to learn precisely how Wilson intended to handle a conflict that might require ground troops instead of nuclear weapons.

Despite the threats of Congress to exercise more control over raising and supporting military forces, the subcommittee appeared reluctant to demand straight answers from the Department of Defense about how their budget requests actually supported foreign policy. Mahon was one of the few committee members who even spoke up at all, but he failed to probe as deeply as he could have. Perhaps he feared that had he done so, he would have incurred the wrath of the president, who, as a retired general, assumed that he knew far more than any congressman about the kind of military protection the nation needed. However, many historians believe that it was President Eisenhower's dogged determination to reduce federal spending that was a major factor in his reluctance to allow more money for defense—not knowledge gained from his military experience.

By the end of the hearings, it was obvious that the subcommittee members recognized the lack of limited war capabilities and slow progress in missile development, but they did not get answers from Defense Department officials about how they intended to solve the problems. Some action was taken, however, through allocations for aircraft procurement to build toward 137 wings. In May, after sixty-five hundred pages of hearings, Mahon authored a $33 billion military appropriations bill that was passed by the House. From the House floor he said, "By reason of the fast-growing long-range Russian heavy jet bomber fleet and other factors, this country is subject to the greatest peril that it has ever been subjected to in its history."[117] He believed that there was a fifty-fifty chance that the Soviet Union was already ahead of the United States in producing the first intercontinental ballistic missile (ICBM), but it would probably take at least five years before it could produce those missiles in any number. A large part of his concern was based on the false impression created by the Soviet air show in July 1955. The bill that passed the House contained $500 million more than the president requested for procurement of the B-52 bomber. Again Mahon paid only lip service to the army's pleas for greater funding for conventional weapons, and his committee manipulated the allocations in the budget to favor the air force. The Senate joined the House in increasing air force funds, but that was not the end of the debate. On Armed Forces Day the row between the army and the air force "leaked" to the public, much to the chagrin of the administration. This caused Senator Stuart Symington, former air force chief of staff, to advocate a Senate investigation that would more clearly establish the role of each service in the nuclear age.

Mahon, however, turned his attention to the cost of military procurements. During the hearings Air Force Secretary Donald Quarles told the subcommittee that the United States had the knowledge and skill to produce an ICBM, and success was only a matter of time. The biggest discussion in the annual defense appropriations bill surrounded the B-52 program. Mahon argued that Boeing Aircraft Company, which made the planes, had a backlog of $2 billion in orders, and he did not favor additional funds for Boeing over those already in the bill.

Congress adjourned in late July 1956, giving Mahon a couple of weeks to wind up his business in the Washington office before going to the Democratic National Convention, which began on August 13. He was a delegate, but he did not vote for Stevenson or Kefauver. After the convention he realized those two might have been the best vote-getters the Democrats had. In answer to the question about his running for the Senate seat vacated by Price Daniel when he became governor of Texas, Mahon said, "I like the work I am doing."[118] He made it clear that he was not, and would not be, a candidate.

In November, after Congress had adjourned, Mahon, Representative Errett P. Scrivner (R-KS), and Representative Harold C. Ostertag (R-NY) toured the Boeing facilities in Seattle. All three were on the Defense Appropriations Subcommittee of the House Appropriations Committee and aware of the huge backlog at Boeing. They were joined by Representative Don Magnuson (D-WA) of Seattle, who was also on the Appropriations Committee, but not the same subcommittee. The group was looking for firsthand information relating to the major military items that would appear in the next year's budget, and they believed such information would be worth more than many hours of testimony. They inspected Boeing's flight test center, the Renton transport division, the final assembly area in Seattle Plant No. 2, and the company's new supersonic wind tunnel that was nearing completion. Next they were briefed in the company boardroom and later inspected the Boeing pilotless interceptor facilities. The press was not allowed to accompany the congressmen on the tour, and there is no official report of their findings. Before leaving they inspected the navy's Pier 91 in Seattle, the Puget Sound Naval Shipyard at Bremerton, the Keyport Torpedo Station, and the Bangor Naval Ammunition Depot.

Twelve of the twenty-one Texas members of Congress ran unopposed in 1956. Mahon was one of the unopposed, despite rumors of an opponent. At the eleventh hour, forms were requested through an intermediary for the rumored opponent, but they were not returned. In June, announcing his candidacy from Washington because Congress was still in session, he promised that he would continue to view the needs of his district as his principal responsibility; however, he also believed that serving his district meant serving the nation as well.

Upon returning to Lubbock for his annual tour of the district, Mahon was interviewed by a local reporter. He emphasized that the Soviet Union was rapidly gaining strength in military striking power, especially in the fields of intercontinental bombers and missiles. He believed this had happened within the past year. With nearly two decades of service on the House Subcommittee on Defense Appropriations, and currently being the chair, Mahon basked in the glow of media reports calling him one of the best-informed civilians in the nation on the comparative strength of the United States and the Soviet Union. He said, "We are still ahead, but Russia is gaining. Russia is now capable of launching an intercontinental attack upon us. She has more jet fighters than we have, although I think ours are better. She has 400 submarines to attack our Navy and shipping lanes. That is several times the number Germany had at the start of World War II."[119] The Soviet Union was then undergoing an industrial revolution similar to the one that had taken place in the United States during World War II, and it was speculated that within the next decade the USSR would produce more steel than the United States. Both nations had enough military strength to destroy each other, and Mahon believed it was wise to develop some sort of inspection program that would limit the arms race. However, until that could be worked out, he believed the only alternative was to stay ahead in the arms race. This would require that the national defense budget remain at approximately $37 billion.

When asked whether there were any areas where defense spending could be cut, he replied, "I had thought that Mr. Wilson's [Secretary of Defense] high-priced industrial team might get things running on a more economical basis. He has affected some economies to be sure, but nothing of any real noteworthiness. In this era of general prosperity, I see no reason why we shouldn't be able to pay as we go and still maintain an effective defense program."[120] "Pay as you go" meant higher taxes, and Republicans were opposed to that. It was good publicity for Mahon to tell reporters that "pay as you go" with higher taxes was a good idea; however, there is no evidence that his constituents agreed and no possibility the Republicans would let that happen.

Mahon let it be known that he stood ready to help the Democratic ticket in any way that he could to prevent Republicans from repeating their 1952 victory in Texas. He offered to help any Democratic candidate from constable to president and insisted that he thought Stevenson had a real chance to win in November. On October 29 he was the keynote speaker at a Democratic rally that raised $4,250 from four hundred persons who came to support the party. At the Caprock Hotel in Lubbock, he "traced the blame for that military threat to the 1953 decision by the GOP to whack a $5 billion Air Force

Build-up program off the Air Force budget."[121] He was referring to Secretary of Defense Charles Wilson's budget cut that Eisenhower approved. Mahon labeled Wilson as "one of the most inept members of the cabinet" because he believed this had given the Soviets supremacy in the production of the intercontinental jet bomber and of jet fighters.[122] It is not known whether or not Mahon did this intentionally, but it was this type of fearmongering that supported the Cold War and boosted the arms race.

During his thirty-minute speech, Mahon also defended Adlai Stevenson's suggestion that H-bomb testing end and criticized the GOP tight-money policy that was hurting American farmers. He said, "No Democrat shouted politics when Eisenhower went to Geneva and when Stassen departed for the disarmament conference, but when Adlai Stevenson suggests that if elected President he would take the initiative in trying to abolish H-Bomb tests, the Republicans cry politics as if to say 'Don't get on our territory, we have a patent on peace and disarmament proposals; and any ideas on this vital world subject from a Democrat candidate are political and unacceptable.'"[123] Mahon said he would be opposed to curtailing H-bomb tests if it would cause the United States to lose its lead in nuclear weapons, but he did not believe it impacted the nation's position relative to the Soviet Union.

He called attention to the fact that the Eisenhower administration had spent $45 billion more in four years than the last four years of the Truman administration, which included the Korean War. He made it plain that he was not against spending for defense, but he labeled as false the administration's claim that the prosperity was based on peace. He claimed that the prosperity was based on the highest defense spending, together with the highest rate of nondefense government spending in the history of the nation—an interesting insight.[124]

Mahon also labeled the cuts in agricultural support the unkindest of all and said broken promises had been the order of the day. Because it took more grain or cotton to buy homes, appliances, etc., the businessmen were hurt just as much as the farmers since they made fewer sales. He feared American agriculture was moving toward a depression. As he called upon the audience to consider party responsibility, he reminded them that four more years of Ezra Taft Benson were more than the farmer and businessman could take. He encouraged them to vote for the team, that voting for the man (Eisenhower) was like voting for a half-truth.[125] The ballroom was crowded with loyal Democrats who interrupted him many times with applause that was soon drowned out by a landslide victory for Eisenhower a week later, even in Texas. However, this time Eisenhower was not able to carry others on his coattails, and the Democrats retained control of Congress. This meant Mahon would continue to chair the Subcommittee on Defense Appropriations.

December was a sad month for the Mahons, as Helen's brother died on December 9 from a heart attack. He lived in Fort Stockton, Texas. Before returning to Washington after the funeral, the Mahons were fêted with an old-time "sing-song" in Loraine. Relatives and longtime friends gathered to wish them well for another term in Congress. After a visit with J. K. Mahon in Weatherford and with the Duncan Holts in Houston, they returned to take up work once again.

In January 1957 President Eisenhower requested $35.5 billion for the Department of Defense in fiscal year 1958.[126] During hearings Treasury Secretary Humphrey told Mahon there were places where the defense budget could be cut, but when pressed about where, he could not provide solid recommendations. The Subcommittee on Defense Appropriations was reluctant to question administration officials too aggressively in light of the president's overwhelming victory the previous November. They believed that the voters wanted him to continue pushing economic measures and that any cuts in the defense budget would be pleasing to most people. Thus, Mahon did not push for greater military preparedness as he had done the year before but rather claimed that an adequate defense program could be secured for $2.6 billion less than the president requested. The bill that came out of the Conference Committee cut defense by $2.3 billion, with the army bearing the brunt of the cuts once again, despite the fact that its requests had been the least of the services.

In the heat of their search for ways to cut the budget, Congress seemed to lose sight of the fact that the defense budget was to "allocate limited money resources to maximize the security and foreign policy interests of the nation."[127] Just reducing the budget became more important. Despite the experience in Korea, appropriations subcommittees in both chambers failed to evaluate defense requests in terms of meeting political objectives. They were primarily concerned with a lower overall defense budget. Congress and the administration sought the cheapest way to provide security and military programs under a predetermined ceiling. An alternative method would have involved choosing the most effective programs, then determining the amount necessary to fund them. The consequences of the approach taken would be disturbingly obvious just four months after the 1958 budget went into operation.

According to historian Edward A. Kolodziej, there were many similarities between the defense budgets of fiscal years 1958 and 1951. In each case, the Soviet threat was considered to be reduced. Also, the military services were openly opposed to the secretary of defense and the president, who wanted to reduce defense expenditures. On one of the pages in his "Appropriations" file, Mahon scrawled across the page "Shades of Pre Korea."[128] The pressure for economy and reduced spending overpowered everything else when each budget was prepared and ceilings were imposed. In each instance Congress was as determined as the executive branch to save dollars, and both times major adjustments had to be made in the next session.[129]

On *The American Forum of the Air*, an NBC Sunday program, in August 1957, Mahon urged President Eisenhower to "knock a lot of heads together to end the squabbling between the military services."[130] The year before Mahon had defended the rivalry as a healthy thing, but now he believed it had gotten so far out of hand that it was a danger to the nation. Mahon's appropriations files contain notes that he collected for use in preparing the speech that he would make on the House floor when he introduced the bill for defense appropriations. These notes provide a deeper insight into his thinking. "I might very well point out that probably we could save over a period of years many billions of dollars if we had better unification," he wrote. "Last year I said the jealousies were to some extent helpful, but my consideration is now that these jealousies and rivalries among the services have gone so far that the cause of national defense is being seriously impaired and the cost to the tax payer is extremely high."[131]

His opponent on the program, Representative Hugh Scott (R-PA), challenged Mahon for allowing his subcommittee to reduce Eisenhower's requested defense budget by nearly $3 billion, arguing that it would deprive the United States of needed missiles, ships, and planes. Mahon answered that "there was 'an Iron Curtain' between the services which is 'terribly expensive.'"[132] He argued that a defense budget of $35 billion to $38 billion was adequate if a dollar of value was received for each dollar spent. Scott thought Congress should do something about unifying the services, but Mahon contended that Eisenhower had to take the leadership and ask Congress to help with the problem.

Inter-service rivalry dated back to the Truman administration, when the services were reorganized under the Department of Defense. However, it intensified during the Eisenhower administration because the president and the secretary of defense failed to establish a well-defined mission and role for each service. When this situation was combined with the lack of strong civilian control of the Defense Department and shrinking defense budgets, the rivalry became bitter. Each service believed that funds were inadequate for its needs, and each tried to curtail the programs of the other services in order to obtain a larger portion of the funds available within the ceiling established for the whole defense budget. Lacking an overall plan, each service made decisions independently of the others, causing conflicting doctrines, duplication of expensive weapons systems, and a tendency to ignore less-glamorous roles, such as transporting troops. Finding a place in the scheme of massive retaliation for air-atomic weapons became the top priority for each of the services. During these years, service chiefs also sought outside allies and often went over the head of the Department of Defense to gain the support of congressmen. Historian Samuel P. Huntington writes that inter-service rivalry was tolerated for a number of reasons, one of which was that it allowed the Joint Chiefs to attack the amount of the military budget allocated to the other services without attacking the overall budget. It was also advantageous to the president and Congress to have the services direct their criticism toward each other, rather than at Congress or the executive branch for the amount of money allocated to national security. Additionally, if the services accepted a restricted budget, they had greater freedom to do things their own way. Although they had fewer dollars than they wanted, each could spend them as they pleased. Huntington observed: "Inter-service rivalry not only strengthened civilian agencies but also furnished them with a whipping boy upon whom to blame deficiencies in the military establishment for which possibly they could be held responsible."[133] The inter-service rivalry also caused a dramatic shift in all the services toward high-tech weapons, which resulted in a proliferation of these expensive weapons.[134]

The pleasures of domestic life provided a necessary balance for Mahon as he grappled with the many challenges of appropriating enough money for an adequate defense. "We have a new car ordered!" Helen wrote to the family in June:

> We have ordered an air conditioned Pontiac station wagon. It is to be Chevron blue, trimmed in Sheffield gray. One of the Members of Congress is a Pontiac dealer and we are getting the car at cost plus $50. . . .

We have gone home on the train for the past two years but this year we decided that we would take a little trip on our way home and so get the station wagon and then use it while we're in the district. It will take, as we understand, until about the 1st of August for it to arrive. Don't misunderstand me, the 1948 Chevy and the 1950 Chrysler are still running perfectly and we can't stand to think about giving up either one of them for a new car. . . . George was quite thrilled when the White House called and asked him to play golf with the President and the Kishi from Japan last week. . . . It was the first time newspaper people or photographers have been allowed out at Burning Tree, and of course he was quite taken back when he found all of the people there taking pictures. None of the pictures that were carried in the papers mentioned George because there were two foursomes of them playing and they only mentioned names of the first foursome but he was in all the pictures that were in the newspapers and on Television. . . . This really has been a very big year for George and of course he deserves every bit of it. I sometimes hate to see him work so hard, but after all his work has brought him a great deal of satisfaction and distinction.[135]

When Mahon returned to Lubbock after Congress adjourned, he told a reporter for the *Lubbock Morning Avalanche* that the last session revolved primarily around the budget because Congress sensed that the people wanted a retrenchment of government. Mahon's attention, however, was focused on defense cuts, civil rights, and agricultural legislation. He was disturbed by the sharp budget cutbacks by the Defense Department but not alarmed. He claimed that it was not the fault of Congress for not appropriating enough money for defense, although it did reduce the budget by $2.3 billion. This was done to force more economy and efficiency in the military program. "The reduction by Congress of the defense budget is not responsible for the slowdowns and cutbacks in the defense program," he stated.[136] He pointed out that, although the United States was working on forty-five missiles, each for a different purpose, we were in a "nip and tuck" race with the Soviets on ballistic missiles. He said the United States was ahead in some respects, and the Soviet Union was ahead in others, and it would be ten years before either side could launch a full-scale attack or be ready to defend itself adequately in a war. He believed that defense spending must remain high, and he had no confidence in disarmament talk. There had been no real change in the international scene. It was still East against West, and both sides were becoming stronger, which meant that both sides were more vulnerable to a destructive attack. Because of this there was no expectation of a tax cut in the foreseeable future.

"I opposed all civil rights legislation," Mahon told the reporter, "feeling it was unnecessary and not in the best interest. The issue was being used as a political football by segments of both parties. I feel that all citizens should not only have the right to vote, but should exercise it. Lyndon Johnson and Speaker Rayburn did an unbelievably good job in working out a compromise on civil rights legislation. They got the northern Democrats and the Republicans to agree on a bill that was far less harsh than originally anticipated."[137] Although he was opposed to civil-rights legislation, Mahon did not sign the Southern Manifesto in March 1956. This document condemned the 1954 Supreme Court ruling of *Brown v. Board of Education*, which abolished segregation in public places. Neither Sam Rayburn nor Lyndon Johnson signed the document.[138]

While Mahon was making his rounds through the district, news broke that the USSR had attained a major breakthrough in modern science. On October 4 the Soviets successfully launched into orbit a 184-pound satellite named Sputnik, meaning "traveling companion" in Russian. It circled the earth at eighteen thousand miles per hour and was claimed by many to be as significant as the splitting of the atom. When a second satellite was launched a month later that carried both scientific instruments for studying space and a dog, Laika, with medical instruments strapped to its body, it seemed obvious that the Soviets were working to put a man in space.[139] These two events were considered a victory in the race for space, which had military significance since the control of outer space was considered a vital factor in future wars.[140] If nuclear weapons could be mounted on such rockets, then traditional armies, navies, and air forces would become obsolete. Americans panicked because they considered the satellites as evidence that US space exploration lagged behind the Soviets, constituting a threat to national security. This was also a psychological blow that shattered the complacency of the 1950s. Stephen Ambrose and David Brinkley captured the mood of the nation when they wrote: "Americans were frustrated, angry, ashamed, and afraid all at once."[141]

Despite the fact that the Soviets had beaten the United States three times, first in testing an ICBM, and then in launching two satellites, President Eisenhower refused to show alarm. Ambrose again writes:

The American B-52 fleet of 1957 was incomparably the best delivery system in the world of that time, far superior to the Russian bomber fleet, and enjoying the additional advantage of access to airfields around the Soviet Union. Sputnik, however, coupled with Soviet boasting about their progress in ICBMs, suddenly made Americans feel naked and vulnerable, stripped of a retaliatory capacity. American weapons, Khrushchev declared, including the B-52, belonged in museums. Eisenhower knew how ridiculous such an assertion was, but like so many of his countrymen he nevertheless was fearful that the Russians had stolen a march on the United States, that Sputnik proved the enemy had better rockets and missiles than the Americans possessed.[142]

The president calmly sought advice from scientists, military officials, and cabinet members about how to deal with the psychological blow of Sputnik, but spending more money seemed to be the primary remedy presented by each group. He was concerned that if he increased spending, as they recommended, the balanced budget of the previous two years would be gone. National sentiment was otherwise. Groups and individuals across the board wanted more money spent on national security. Many people believed national security was more important than a balanced budget. Eisenhower claimed to be concerned that if the United States spent so much money on weapons that it became a garrison state, our way of life would be lost. If the United States lost its way of life, there would not be much left to defend.[143]

In November, while in Lubbock, Mahon warned the nation that the United States must spend more money for ballistic missiles and earth satellites; however, such a move could not become a spending spree.[144] That month the Gaither Report was delivered to the National Security Council. Named after Committee Chair H. Roland Gaither, this report was the result of a charge by President Eisenhower to the Security Resources Panel of the President's Science and Advisory Committee to review the nation's defense readiness. The report was classified, but through "leaks" the press secured and printed the contents. It stressed that a "missile gap" existed between the United States and the Soviet Union and recommended that approximately $44 billion be added to the defense budget during the next five years. It also recommended that missiles be perfected and used to back up the bombers of the Strategic Air Command. Finally, it recommended that fallout shelters should be built for each family. President Eisenhower ignored most of the recommendations, but he did increase funding for intercontinental missile development and for civil-defense programs. However, Democrats did not ignore the report. They smelled a campaign issue and began attacking the president for allowing a "missile lag" to develop that would leave the United States vulnerable to Soviet attack.

Mahon spent the final months of 1957 visiting missile bases and plants in order to acquire firsthand knowledge of the situation before returning to Washington to handle defense appropriations for fiscal year 1959. On January 7, 1958, the second session of the Eighty-fifth Congress opened with the usual backslapping, hand-shaking, and chorus of greetings that disguised the tension most congressmen felt about the so-called missile lag. Sputnik had launched deep concerns that the superiority of Soviet rocket technology made the United States vulnerable to attack, and President Eisenhower's "chins-up" messages did not really ease the nation's worries about falling behind in the arms race.

On January 9 the president's State of the Union address stressed the need to build a genuine peace instead of simply relying on military strength as a deterrent to war. He said, "But what makes the Soviet threat unique in history is its all-inclusiveness. Every human activity is pressed into service as a weapon of expansion. Trade, economic development, military power, arts, science education, the whole world of ideas—all are harnessed to this same chariot of expansion. The Soviets are, in short, waging total cold war. The only answer to a regime that wages total cold war is to wage total peace."[145]

Eisenhower stressed that since the Korean armistice, the United States had spent $335 billion in building and maintaining a strong military shield. Using the best intelligence available to him, he predicted that this nation would have the required missiles to sustain this shield. Because of the necessity for utmost secrecy, President Eisenhower could not share with the American people his proof that there really was not a "missile gap" or a "bomber gap," as many feared. In 1956 the CIA had inaugurated a series of high-altitude flights over the Soviet Union in planes called the U-2. Images from a camera developed by Drs. Edwin H. Land and Harold Edgerton indicated that the Soviets were not building launching sites for ICBMs, meaning the United States still had a substantial lead in strategic weapons. President Eisenhower believed he could not share this top-secret information with the public, but he personally was convinced that the psychological impact of the Soviet announcements was greater than any physical threat. A larger threat was the possible loss of the confidence of the American public should it learn that their president had broken international law by flying over the Soviet Union. Eisenhower feared a loss of respect from Americans more than he feared a military threat from the Soviets.

In his State of the Union address, President Eisenhower also announced that Americans wanted the harmful rivalries within the military branches to stop. Hoping to reduce inter-service rivalries, he proposed a reorganization of the Defense Department that would give the secretary more control over his department. After much debate in Congress, this latest reorganization placed the line of authority from the president to the secretary and to the unified field commanders. The Joint Chiefs of Staff were bypassed in the line of authority and would henceforth only advise the secretary and president. This would greatly curtail their lobbying activities in Congress for weapons and money on behalf of their separate services. Military officers were still allowed to express their views to Congress; however, the secretary of defense had to be informed before they did so. Congress would continue to appropriate money to each service, but budgetary requests had to come from the secretary to the president. This allowed the secretary to consider overall policy in formulating a final request for the president, and it was hoped that this would reduce inter-service rivalries. President Eisenhower got his reorganization but not without a vigorous debate in Congress. Initially, chairs of the Armed Services Committees in both chambers feared the loss of power in determining what was needed to provide for the common defense, but ultimately a compromise was reached and the bill for reorganization passed.

Because two powerful Democrats, Representative Carl Vinson and Senator Richard Russell, both Georgians, led the protest against reorganization in Congress, Mahon did not express his views publicly until the dust had settled. When things calmed down he told Liz Carpenter of the *Houston Post* that "knocking heads together" would not end the inter-service rivalry. After more than fifteen years of working with military appropriations, he advocated a "no nonsense" approach and greater unification. He believed the Pentagon should be reorganized along functional lines, not around air, land, and sea forces, as in days past. For example, all people working on missiles should be one group; all pilots should be in another. He advocated putting all the service people in one uniform, making it easy to transfer from one service or group to another, and making the Joint Chiefs objective advisors instead of lobbyists for their services. He was bothered by the fact that the Joint Chiefs did not hammer out overall policy together but, instead, were tied up in an inefficient power struggle to see which chief could get the most for his service. Mahon stressed that the Soviet Union was becoming truly powerful because of the industrial revolution then under-way, and the US defense budget was increasing annually in order to stay abreast. He believed the inefficiency and duplication caused by living in the past were far too costly.[146]

In his address President Eisenhower announced that he would ask for a $1.3 billion supplemental defense appropriation for fiscal year 1958 and would increase, by approximately $4 billion, budget requests in fiscal year 1959 for missiles, nuclear ships, atomic energy, and research and development. He proposed to finance this increase from revenues and stressed the need for efficiency and careful management. He asked the American people to understand the situation and to be ready to make intelligent sacrifices. He said that talking in general terms about reducing federal spending and then fighting the reduction of a federal grant that touched one's own interests was counterproductive.

Stress was greater than usual during the early part of 1958 as Congress tried to deal with the crisis caused by Sputnik and the alleged "missile gap." Apparently, Mahon was preoccupied to the point of forgetfulness, and he wrote his sister, "Helen is doing fine, but I am continuing to slip a little. Recently, I parked down at the Capitol and not only left my keys in the car, I forgot and left the engine running. The policeman told me about it the next day. He had finally spotted the car and cut off the engine. He didn't know whose it was, but I found my keys in it at the close of the day. Sort of wish somebody would steal it because it's not running very well!"[147]

Despite President Eisenhower's slow and calm response to Sputnik, a chain reaction was set off in Congress that caused many to examine more closely how their committees affected national security. This ultimately resulted in lobbying for greater defense spending. Leaders of both chambers were involved. Senator Lyndon Johnson, chair of the Senate Preparedness Subcommittee; House Speaker Sam Rayburn; and Representative Clarence Cannon, chair of the House Appropriations Committee all disagreed with the president's budget ceilings, and they pressured the administration for more defense spending. They were joined by others in Congress and in the military who believed that something had to be done to counter the Soviet threat. If the president was going to abdicate leadership, they threatened to take the lead.

Appropriations committees in both chambers of Congress reexamined their basic charge to fund programs as economically as possible. They were not to reduce funds to the point that programs suffered, and in the wake of Sputnik, Congress was somewhat chagrined by the strong emphasis on economizing the year before. The New Look program was seen as undercutting defense programs that were important to national security. In examining the defense budget for fiscal year 1959, the emphasis was on programs more than reducing dollars. This was obvious in Mahon's presentation of the fiscal year 1959 defense appropriation bill in the House, which revealed a shift of emphasis from reducing dollars to funding crucial programs. Recognizing that sufficient funds had not been provided in the appropriations bill for fiscal year 1958 to support a number of crucial programs, he said, "Last year, just prior to this time, we passed the annual defense appropriations bill. There was talk of economy, efficiency and how to cope with service rivalries. Money aspects of defense loomed large on the horizon. We said the defense budget was too fat, that it was unnecessarily big to finance the specific programs which had been submitted to Congress for funding in the President's budget. . . . In hindsight it is obvious that the budget submitted to us last year should have made more provision for rocketry and space age weapons."[148]

In preparing these remarks Mahon's mind must have reflected back to 1951, when he tried to account for defense appropriations that proved inadequate to cover the unforeseen conflict in Korea. Now a similar scenario had unfolded. In his remarks he tried to absolve the Democrat-controlled Congress from any responsibility in the alleged defense lag. He claimed that the lag happened because the Department of Defense and the president did not adequately support the programs that were needed. He argued that the requests for supplemental money submitted by the administration in 1958 were to fund new programs, not to rush old programs to completion. He also argued that the $2.5 billion cut in the 1958 defense bill did not affect Defense Department operations. The department had sufficient carryover funds to take care of any authorized programs and simply did not take advantage of all the authority it had. Republicans pushed back on this argument, and ultimately appropriations committees in both chambers shared the blame for not ferreting out operational gaps in the bill.[149] Both parties were in agreement, however, that defense spending should be increased; and Mahon questioned the new secretary of defense, Neil McElroy, strongly about why his fiscal year 1959 budget requests were increased only marginally from the past year.

Charles Wilson had retired in 1957. Some members of the House Appropriations Committee, such as Mahon, had served longer in their position than Defense Department officials in the administration. Over the years Mahon had listened to the arguments of many career military officers as well as the ever-changing retinue of officials from the Department of Defense, and this experience began to instill in him enough confidence to question the administration about how the funds requested would provide national security. As many in Congress and the public saw it, national security was fragile in light of the Soviet space accomplishments of the previous fall, and Mahon wanted to know why more was not being done to strengthen the military. He was critical of reductions in military manpower, and the House passed a bill that added $99 million to keep the army's strength at nine hundred thousand. When the appropriations bill reached the Senate, that chamber added $1.6 billion for additional bombers, two assault ships for the Marines, and more airlift for the army. After leaving the Conference Committee, the appropriations bill that was accepted by both chambers provided $39.6 billion for defense—$826 million more than the president had requested.

Budget debates had to be put aside during the first week of April when Mahon received word that his father had died in Weatherford, Texas. The ninety-seven-year-old patriarch of the family had enjoyed good health until a few weeks before his death, when an attack of flu began to sap his strength. Just as recovery seemed imminent, he fell and had to be hospitalized. Less than a week later he died. Services were held in the First Methodist Church in Loraine, and he was laid to rest in the cemetery where his first wife, Nola, was buried. Mahon's mother had died in 1931, and several years later J.K. had married a woman from Weatherford, Texas. In a letter to his sister Mary Agnes, Mahon wrote, "Of course I have thought a lot about Dad. I do not seem to have many regrets. Dad lived such a remarkably fine life and left such a profound impact upon his family and many others, it would be hard to have many regrets over his passing in view of the fact that there was no real hope that he would ever be well and active, mentally and physically, again. In response to sympathy letters, I usually include this line, 'My father had lived such a full and wonderful life we have found reasons to rejoice even in our sadness.'"[150] However, there was one regret that he mentioned in the letter to Mary Agnes. Neither the newspaper nor the minister had mentioned that John Mahon had been a good Christian and an inspiration to his family. Those qualities were very important to the Mahon family. In the same letter Mahon wrote that since returning from the funeral, "life has dealt pretty strenuously with me here. I have so much more to do than I can get done I often get pretty weary and frustrated."[151] He closed with an admonition to his sister to divide some money that was left with their sister Cary. He wrote that he didn't mean to be crotchety, but he definitely wanted his sisters to have the money.

Before long, happy thoughts replaced grief. When Mahon arrived at his office on the morning of May 5, he learned that Helen had called from Houston. He was on his way to the office when she tried to reach him at their apartment. Helen had been in Houston for several days awaiting the birth of Daphne's third child. He returned the call and learned that Laurel Ann was now part of the family. In a note to Helen that day, he wrote, "I think that is a wonderfully sweet name."[152]

On the weekend of May 25, Mahon and Helen went to Groton, Connecticut, where Helen christened the USS *Skipjack*, the navy's newest atomic submarine built by the Electric Boat Division of General Dynamics Corporation. It was the first of a new class of nuclear-powered attack submarines designed to achieve unprecedented underwater speed and maneuverability. Frank Pace, Jr., was president of General Dynamics, the nation's second-largest defense contractor, which did 85 percent of its business with the US government. Prior to this, Pace had served as director of the Budget Bureau and secretary of the army under President Truman. He and Mahon had known each other since his days of testifying before the Defense Department subcommittee in the 1940s. After leaving government service, Pace developed quite a reputation in the business world and appeared on the cover of *Time* magazine on January 20, 1958.

For the big event Helen was attractively dressed in a red-and-gray silk dress with a full-length red coat to match. Her black hat had a large red rose on the back that matched the coat. To complete her ensemble she wore black patent-leather shoes and carried a black patent-leather handbag. According to tradition, after the countdown the sponsor must break a bottle of champagne across the bow for good luck just as the ship slides into the water. If the bottle does not break, one of the officers on board will break a bottle of champagne to ward off bad luck. This time the bottle broke easily. Helen was given a jeweled watch inscribed, "*U.S.S. Skipjack*, May 25, 1958, New London, Conn.," and a case with the broken champagne bottle.

During the festivities that weekend, Helen was pleased to learn that the wife of the *Skipjack* captain had graduated from Duke University and remembered Daphne. The weekend provided many happy memories for Helen, but no one enjoyed all of it more than granddaughter Betsy, who is reputed to have told all who would listen that her that "grandmommy" hit a boat with a bottle of shampoo. Champagne was not a familiar word for most toddlers, especially in a family that did not drink alcoholic beverages.

Charles Guy, editor and publisher of the *Lubbock Morning Avalanche*, accompanied the Mahons. Years later, reminiscing about the trip he wrote in one of his editorials, "Cong. George Mahon and I flew with Admiral Russell from Washington to Groton, Conn., a couple of years ago to see the commissioning of one of the new, big atomic-powered submarines. I was impressed by Russell's comments and attitudes on what this country's policies and defense strategies should be. After we left Admiral Russell, Congressman Mahon remarked: 'It always makes me feel better to talk to a military man of the stature of Jim Russell. It gives me confidence that, come what may, our country will come through.' Admiral Russell had made me feel the same sense of confidence."[153]

When Congress adjourned, Mahon did not spend as much time as usual in his district. On October 16 he flew to Brussels on the preinaugural Pan American jet passenger service across the Atlantic. After attending the World's Fair, he and Scott Crosby, a staff member of the Appropriations Committee, proceeded on to the Middle East to get a firsthand look at what had become the number-one trouble spot in the world. The two made the trip at the request of Representative Clarence Cannon, chair of the House Committee on Appropriations. Their task was to check as deeply as possible into the operations of the Central Intelligence Agency overseas in preparation for a hearing with Allen Dulles when the agency's budget proposal was submitted for fiscal year 1959.

Since 1957 the CIA had been training native undercover agents in the Middle East to suppress opposition to the monarchies that supported the monopolization of oil by foreign companies, including the United States.[154] Western dependence on Middle Eastern oil made it crucial to keep these monarchies on the throne to stem the rising tide of nationalism in the region. Gamal Abdel Nasser of Egypt urged the nationalization of the oil fields. Early in 1958 he announced the formation of the United Arab Republic (UAR). Fearing a greater alliance between Nasser and the Soviet Union, the Eisenhower administration spread a lot of loose talk about Nasser's friendliness toward communism. Officials "had no evidence to support such a charge and solid evidence against it, beginning with the fact that the Communist Party was outlawed in Egypt."[155] At this time an active arms race had developed in the Middle East, with the United States supplying arms to Saudi Arabia, Iraq, Jordan, and Lebanon; the Soviet Union supplying Syria and Egypt; and France selling arms to Israel.

After touring the region for a month, Mahon concluded that war could easily break out because of the arms race between Israel and the Arab countries. He believed that sending US troops to Lebanon had a stabilizing influence but did not really settle any of the problems. Nasser's popularity was based on Arab nationalism rather than outside political forces, and in opposing him the United States appeared to be opposing freedom. Mahon did not believe that war would break out by design; rather he believed that "the greatest threat of war seems to lie in chain reaction possibilities which might spring from the boiling and bitter controversies of the Middle East and Far East."[156]

Reporting to Chairman Cannon, Mahon wrote: "I talked with the personnel and studied the records. I looked at various installations. I studied the report of auditors, talked with the auditors, conferred with the Ambassadors in regard to their estimation of the CIA, etc. . . . There are a lot of things we did not learn but I do think we made some progress toward a better understanding of the Central Intelligence Agency and I believe we can have a pretty down to earth hearing with Allen Dulles when he submits his budget next year. I did not do anything spectacular and I must confess I am not wise enough to know how and to what extent the CIA program ought to be modified."[157]

On a more positive note, during his travels through Belgium, Germany, Austria, Italy, and France, Mahon was impressed with the prosperity and confidence in these countries. He also spent some time with General Lauris Norstad, the NATO commander, and learned that tension had been reduced because the threat of war between the NATO counties and the USSR was not perceived to be as great as in times past. Berlin was still a worry, but General Norstad agreed that the greatest threat was escalation from tension in the Middle East or Asia. Mahon was also pleased that he did not see any of the "Yankee, go home" attitude that had existed previously.[158] He was favorably impressed with the public relations efforts of the US ambassadors in Europe.

He believed that the withdrawal of military forces would seriously endanger Europe, but he also recognized that NATO countries must be required to assume a greater role in financing weapons and providing economic assistance. He wrote, "We just do not have enough American dollars to sop up all the troubles of the rest of the world."[159] However, he did not see how the defense program could be further reduced; therefore, a defense budget of $42 billion would be required for 1959. "We are in a period of long-range competition for world power and world peace. A sustained defense program of real quality pitched toward minimum manpower levels and maximum modernization and efficiency goals is what we must continue to strive for."[160] He and Scott Crosby sailed home on the *Queen Elizabeth*.

When the first session of the Eighty-sixth Congress convened on January 7, Democrats held almost two-thirds of the seats in both chambers, making President Eisenhower the first US president to serve with three sessions of Congress controlled by the opposition party.[161] Sam Rayburn was reelected speaker of the House for the ninth time since first assuming that position in 1940. In 1951 he had surpassed Henry Clay's record for serving the most days and terms as speaker. On March 4, Rayburn began his forty-seventh consecutive year in Congress, also setting a new longevity record by surpassing the record of Speaker Joseph G. Cannon (R-IL), who had served for forty-six years.

Representative Joseph W. Martin, Jr. (R-MA), lost his position as minority leader to Charles A. Halleck (R-IN). Publicly, it was argued that Halleck, being younger, could provide more vigorous leadership. Privately, it was known that many Republicans were unhappy with Martin's close cooperation with Rayburn in the past. They complained that he did not show enough partisanship to be an effective leader. "Martin attributed his defeat in part to GOP election reverses, saying a 'fall guy' was needed."[162] In addition to continuing to serve as the chair of the Defense Department Subcommittee of the House Committee on Appropriations, Mahon was appointed to the Reduction of Nonessential Federal Expenditures Committee, a committee to study and recommend reductions in federal spending.

Having run what was historically the largest peacetime deficit the previous year, the administration was determined to have a balanced budget in fiscal year 1960. The $40 billion defense budget sent waves of disagreement through Congress and the services. If this amount had been proposed before Sputnik, the president would have been praised, but now there was concern over the adequacy of the nation's preparedness. Although the Joint Chiefs signed a statement declaring the fiscal year 1960 defense budget "adequate" with "no serious gaps," when pressed for information during testimony before the appropriations committees, they quickly admitted that they had initially requested a lot more money.

Hearings were barely under way when Mahon typed a quick note to a former employee in his congressional office. It contained some interesting thoughts about his work (typos have been corrected to reduce distractions).

The month of January passed very rapidly. We have been in defense hearings two weeks. The other committees get the headlines because our hearings are not public. It is fantastic the way Lyndon Johnson gets headlines, but he deserves them because of his uncanny ability to lead the Senate around by the nose. Symington gets into the defense picture from time to time. He is unstable, and I would be frightened if he should ever take over the reins of government. I think he would get us into war. He just has no balance. The caddies out at Burning Tree know that Symington is not to be trusted. Unfortunately he is not well known by enough people. On the surface he is attractive and quite a fellow. Carl Vinson pulled quite a stunt to get rid of Overton Brooks as number two man on Armed Services. He did not want Brooks to succeed him so he maneuvered the creation of the Space Committee and got Brooks appointed chairman. Now Kilday is the number-two man on Armed Services. I have some fine young Republicans on my subcommittee as replacements for Wigglesworth, Scrivner, and a couple of others. We have drawn up a set of committee rules this year, and my work is not so nerve wracking. I have unlimited time but no member can question a witness more than 30 minutes and a minor witness no more than 15 minutes. This helps handle Flood.[163] Of course, by unanimous consent a member can get more time, but this doesn't happen often. We do not permit any questioning of a witness until he completes his main statement. I am doing a better job controlling the Committee and I am getting better cooperation. Jerry Ford is the top Republican and I work well with him. Scriv and Wig[164] were erratic. . . .

Admiral Momsen (Retired) is going to give me two hours in the morning for the purpose of giving me ideas on the Navy. We are to have breakfast at the Carlton. I am going to try to knock the big carrier out of the budget, and I think he can help me. He is a submarine man, in view of Naval Headquarters. There I guess you see a lot of Naval people.[165]

On a more personal note, he continued, "I got two new suits at Lewis and

Thomas Saltz last month. They are handsome but they really made us poor. Helen's apartment is now outstanding. She has a new American Oriental rug, as you know, and three rugs I brought her from Turkey. She has two big brass trays and a lot of other brass and copper I brought her from Cairo. The place has never been like this before. Wish you could see it."[166]

The fiscal year 1960 budget included substantial funds for developing intercontinental ballistic missiles, such as the nearly operational liquid-fuel Atlas,[167] the Titan,[168] and the ultimate solid-fuel Minuteman,[169] all air force projects, as well as funds to continue development of two competing air-defense systems, the air force's Bomarc[170] and the army's Nike-Hercules.[171] The latter two were intended for protection against enemy bombers rather than ICBMs. There were no funds requested in the budget for the Army's Nike-Zeus,[172] the only missile in production designed to cope with ICBMs. When questioned by the appropriation subcommittees in both chambers, Secretary of Defense McElroy admitted that his department had not developed a clear plan about which air-defense systems to support and would welcome congressional direction. Weapons proliferation of this type is typical of each service's determination to acquire more and more high-tech weapons, thus garnering a larger share of the budget.

Although Congress had grown accustomed to refereeing the annual money quarrel between services, congressmen reacted so strongly to this situation that the Defense Department was required to draw up a new plan for continental air defense, which was submitted to the Senate Armed Services Committee on June 12. This plan, which was not made public, cut back both the Nike-Hercules and Bomarc while increasing funds for the Nike-Zeus program. This situation underscored the weakness of President Eisenhower's policy of using budget ceilings rather than well-defined missions to exercise central control over the services. "The weakness of central control during this period is reflected by the fact that not only were the services duplicating weapons systems but that any resolution of service disputes by the Secretary of Defense was quickly evaded by the supposedly subordinate services."[173] Dealing with the conflicting requests of the individual services and the administration in regard to the nation's defenses was extremely frustrating and provided an added incentive for Congress to take the lead in defense matters. More importantly, the Democrats in Congress sensed an issue that could be used in the upcoming presidential election, and they organized into a loyal opposition to fight the administration.

The armed services continued to emphasize their differences over strategic doctrine in their never-ending competition for money. Army General Maxwell Taylor and Navy Admiral Arleigh Burke argued that the nation's atomic retaliatory power was already excessive and that the air force did not need a budget almost as large as the other two services combined. Both stressed the importance of building capabilities for fighting limited wars. In response, Air Force General White emphasized the continued threat of total war and the need for the capability to destroy a major part of the Soviet nuclear delivery forces. In the end, Congress appropriated some additional funds for modernizing army equipment (most of which had been designed during World War II) but nothing approaching the $3 billion a year sought by General Taylor.[174]

The House and Senate held different views about the president's request for $39.24 billion to run the Defense Department in 1960. In the House Subcommittee for Defense Department Appropriations, $1.2 billion was cut from some programs and $800 million added to others, generating a net reduction of $400 million. The bill that was presented to the full House on June 3 cut all of the $260 million requested for a conventionally powered aircraft carrier and $500 million in air force programs, including the Bomarc missile. However, the subcommittee did add $200 million for army procurement, $255 million for antisubmarine warfare programs, and $172 million for the Atlas and Minuteman ballistic missiles. When the bill was presented to the full House, it passed without change.

The Senate Appropriations Committee added $746 million to the bill, which included $380 million for a second navy nuclear-powered carrier (rather than the conventionally powered carrier requested by the Defense Department). The bill also restored one-half the cut for the Bomarc that was in the House bill. After the Senate approved the bill, it was sent to conference.[175]

In conference a bill for $39.22 billion was approved for the Defense Department for fiscal year 1960. This amount was $20 million less than the president had submitted in his budget request. In conference Mahon argued strongly against the nuclear-powered aircraft carrier, calling attention to the fact that cost estimates had risen nearly $55 million since the navy first requested the ship. Instead, $35 million was approved for advance planning and procurement for such a carrier. The House adopted the conference report by a voice vote, and the Senate adopted it by a roll call vote of 85-0. On August 4 it was sent to the president for his signature.[176]

On August 8 Mahon told his family that the final defense bill had cleared the House the previous week and the president was very pleased about a few things the House had done at his request. The Tuesday before the conference bill cleared the House on Thursday, President Eisenhower asked Mahon to come to the White House for a late afternoon visit before going home. "I tried to get away in 15 minutes realizing he is a busy man, but he was in a talkative mood and I stayed for 45 minutes. He tried out part of his television speech on the labor bill on me."[177] No doubt President Eisenhower also let him know how pleased he was with Mahon's efforts to cut both the conventional and the nuclear-powered aircraft carriers from the defense bill, although the nuclear carrier did receive partial funding for advanced planning.

The week after Father's Day Mahon was enjoying a particularly lazy Saturday and decided to start his weekly family letter:

> I had almost said earlier that I had wasted part of the wonderful day out at Burning Tree. I played like a champ. One over par on the front side and 3 over on the back side. Eisenhower and George Allen, thin and fat respectively, were there riding in baby blue electric carts with fringes on top. Ike was in Canada with the Queen yesterday, as you know. Poor Ike, I felt sorry for him on the Admiral Strauss contest and I felt sorry for Strauss, too. Fortunately, I have not had but one letter from the District about the action of the Senate. Our Senators are involved, and I would not want to judge their actions. It was all a sad affair. The Admiral seemed to have contempt for the Senate. He must be a bit arrogant. I thought before the vote that he would be confirmed. I know that some of the Senators were deeply troubled over what to do.[178]

Mahon was referring to the failure of Lewis L. Strauss to be confirmed as secretary of commerce. He had been appointed interim secretary on November 13, 1957, after serving as chairman of the Atomic Energy Commission for five years. Democrats accused him of not answering questions thoroughly during his confirmation hearing, having withheld vital information from the Joint Atomic Energy Committee, and distorting his role in the Dixon-Yates affair.[179] They argued that his conduct was "lacking in the degree of integrity and competence essential to proper performance of his duties as Secretary of Commerce."[180] Majority Leader Lyndon Johnson led the fight against confirmation in the Senate, which resulted in the first rejection of a cabinet nominee in twenty-five years. Also, it was the first rejection of a major Eisenhower appointee in six years. On June 30 Strauss resigned and Under Secretary Frederick H. Mueller was confirmed as secretary of commerce.

At the end of August, Helen and a young man from Sterling City, Texas, who worked for another congressman, drove to Colorado City. Mahon planned to follow after Congress adjourned, which he hoped would happen within the next two weeks. When he wrote his last family letter for that session, he included a few tips for bachelors. "Don't forget that the leavings of an egg on a plate form the most obstinate glue known to man; if all the other dishes are dirty, don't try to fry a steak in a thin pie pan. It burns too quickly; don't put a crooked piece of bread in the toaster. It won't pop up and the toast is burned; don't think that a beefsteak is ruined because it gets dark after being in the refrigerator a few days."[181] Mahon was always a little lost when Helen was away, and at those times it was quite obvious that he functioned much better on the floor of Congress than on the kitchen floor.

On September 10 Mahon voted to override President Eisenhower's veto on the public works bill. He agreed with Eisenhower and did not want to vote against him, but the matter was being decided strictly along party lines. He could not afford to vote against the Democratic leadership on this matter.[182] Mahon voted with the conservative coalition on all eleven key roll calls.[183] "For their part, one of the gains for the southerners from the informal alliance with Eisenhower was a tepid approach to civil rights questions by the White House."[184] Bills were proposed in the House and the Senate that authorized antibombing penalties in civil rights confrontations and empowering the Justice Department to subpoena offenders of voting rights. Both bills were pigeonholed in committee, and leaders from both houses vowed to carry the fight into the next session. "At the end of 1959 key provisions of the 1957 act were being tested in the courts. The Civil Rights Commission and the Justice Department's Civil Rights Division, both created by the 1957 statute, were seriously hamstrung in the efforts to carry out the act."[185]

After Mahon returned to the district, a reporter from the *Lubbock Morning Avalanche* customarily interviewed him and ran a rather lengthy article that provided an overview of the work of Congress for the previous session. This was informative and helpful to the constituents who would be talking with him in the coming months. In October 1959 a reporter also interviewed Helen, the "silent partner" who worked very hard on behalf of the Nineteenth District. For twenty-five years she had faithfully handled what she referred to as "the chore of the day." In addition to managing a home, this included acting as hostess for visitors from the district, an office assistant, a chauffeur, an "errand girl," and even getting the car serviced. When in Washington she was the "unofficial mother" for the office staff. They were entertained in the Mahon home often for dinner and song fests. Helen told the reporter that she considered acting as chauffeur when they were in the district to be one of her greatest and most interesting contributions. As she drove to the widely separated towns, her husband had time to work on his speeches or take care of clerical duties such as drafting answers to correspondence. This added greatly to the time in his schedule and gave them uninterrupted time together, a rare commodity for a public servant. Helen truly enjoyed touring the district with him as she made new friends and renewed old friendships in each town they visited.[186] The "first lady" of the Nineteenth Congressional District was more than just a wife; she was always a working partner on the George Mahon team.

In October Mahon spoke to the Texas Tech Tax Institute. In his address, entitled "Federal Fiscal Affairs," he bemoaned the fact that the federal government was not living within its income. The federal debt, which had been raised six times during Eisenhower's administration, totaled $295 billion, a whopping increase from the $1.9 billion in 1917, at the beginning of World War I. Interest alone was approximately $1.4 billion in 1959. Mahon advocated raising taxes to cover expenditures, especially costs for defense. He blamed "back door" spending[187] for much of the deficit; however, the writer of a letter to the editor of the Lubbock Morning Avalanche pointed out that when President Eisenhower vetoed a bill relating to back-door spending, Mahon voted to override the veto: "Mr. Mahon's vote in this instance connotes just how interested he is in cutting spending. I think that what will ultimately destroy our economic system is this constant bickering between the various sections of the nation to obtain more of the government's cash outlay."[188] At times Mahon's appeal for frugality appeared to be political.

Christmas that year was spent in Houston with the Holts. A good time was had by all, especially the grandchildren who enjoyed having Granddad make a fire in the backyard so they could toast marshmallows. There was a little excitement, however, when Betsy's hair was set on fire from some fireworks. It was just sparklers, and everything was brought under control quickly with no serious burns. On the way back to Washington, Mahon and Helen stopped to visit with Duncan's parents in Greensboro, North Carolina. When they arrived home, there was lots of mail to answer and colds to recover from. They had traveled over twelve thousand miles since returning to the district in September, so it was good to be in their apartment again.

By 1960, Americans were generally confused about the true state of the nation's security. Military experts declared there was a "missile gap," and the president declared that was not correct, that his military experience allowed him to evaluate the situation better than his critics. Mahon entered the debate by declaring there was no "deterrent gap." Early in the year he had supported the president's claims that the United States was capable of deterring a Soviet attack. He maintained that the nation's deterrent force was the whole of our military forces and different from the single missile component—that the United States was clearly the superpower that was best prepared for all-out war, if necessary. The president welcomed support from a well-known Democrat; however, this was an election year, and many more voices would be heard before the year ended.

A summit meeting between President Eisenhower, Prime Minister Harold Macmillan, Premier Nikita Khrushchev, and President Charles de Gaulle was scheduled to open in Paris on May 16, 1960. On May 5 Premier Khrushchev announced that an American spy plane had been shot down over the Soviet Union four days earlier. Initially, the United States stated that the plane was a missing U-2 plane on a high-altitude weather mission from a base in Turkey and that there had been no deliberate intention to violate Soviet airspace. However, on May 7 Khrushchev announced that the pilot, Francis Gary Powers, had confessed that he was employed by the CIA and that he had been on a four-thousand-mile photo spy mission from Pakistan to Norway. The State Department tried to deny that there had been any authorization from Washington for the flight, but finally on May 11 President Eisenhower took full responsibility.

Eisenhower believed that the information Khrushchev shared with him at

Camp David in 1959 had been the truth about Soviet missile capability be-cause information gathered from U-2 flights confirmed what he had said. For this reason, and in light of the upcoming summit meeting, Eisenhower want-ed the U-2 flights stopped. According to notes taken by the president's aide at a meeting with the CIA and other leaders in the intelligence community, "The President said that he has one tremendous asset in a summit meeting, as re-gards effect in the free world. That is his reputation for honesty. If one of these aircraft were lost when we are engaged in apparently sincere deliberations, it could be put on display in Moscow and ruin the President's effectiveness."[189]

To protect his "reputation for honesty" Eisenhower developed a fetish about keeping the U-2 flights a secret. Also, admitting that he was involved in questionable activities would be personally embarrassing since he would be revealing to the world that his reputation for honesty was greater than his actual honesty. Eisenhower's biographer writes, "The odd thing about this fe-tish was that the U-2 was no secret to the Soviets, and had not been since the very first flight, back in 1956. Indeed, all the governments involved—British, French, Turkish, Norwegian, Formosan, and others—knew about the U-2. The people who did not know were the Americans and their elected repre-sentatives."[190]

When Khrushchev arrived in Paris he announced that the summit could continue only on the condition that the United States declare that it would not violate Soviet airspace again. He wanted a six- to eight-month postponement of the meeting, and he canceled the invitation that had been extended to Ei-senhower to visit the Soviet Union in June. Eisenhower said he would not ac-cept that ultimatum, although the U-2 flights had already been cancelled. The Senate Foreign Relations Committee conducted a closed-door inquiry into the flight and concluded that there were no compelling reasons for the May 1 mission and that it should not have been conducted. They also concluded that strong direction from the top had led to the conflicting statements of May 5, 7, and 9.

With the breakup of the summit, the best chance of slowing the arms race during the sixties, seventies, and eighties was lost. Both Eisenhower and Khrushchev had been on the verge of making major concessions in the direc-tion of mutual trust, with Eisenhower agreeing to an unsupervised test ban on nuclear weapons and Khrushchev to allowing inspection teams in the Soviet Union.[191] These good intentions ended with the collapse of the meeting.

Mahon was disappointed with the handling of the U-2 incident. He ex-pressed his disappointment in a family letter:

I do think that the faith of the country in the Republican leadership has been badly shaken by the U-2 airplane incident. People apparently are glad we have a U-2 and they do not want to put a halo over Mr. K's head but many of them will find it difficult to understand why we blundered so badly when we got caught. I have never been so shocked over the handling of a big national crisis. Secretary of State Chris Herter told the Senate Foreign Relations Committee last Friday that he had never heard of the U-2 until we got caught. I like Ike but we just do not have the careful coordination and planning at the top that this great nation needs. I have known this for a long time. If the people ever find it out for sure, and they probably won't, they are going to be very unhappy.

About the U-2, as you will suspect, all the money for the Central Intelligence Agency, including the U-2 and a multitude of other things, is hidden in the Defense Appropriation bill which I handle. The CIA money is handled on a super-secret basis by five members of the Subcommittee. Chairman Cannon of the full Appropriations Committee presides when we discuss CIA appropriations. We have Director Allen Dulles before our 16-member Subcommittee each year for a discussion of what supposedly goes on inside Russia, the magnitude of the threat to our security, etc. At these meetings Mr. Dulles tells us what he knows and surmises but he does not tell us how he finds out what he knows. That is done before the 5-member group. I have known of the U-2 for the duration of the project, about 4 years.

My work is very arduous but the U-2 aircraft incident is indicative of the tremendously interesting facets of some of it. My trip to Europe in 1958 had principally to do with our secret operations overseas. I have never talked about the details of these things but in view of public statements recently made, a brief reference from me does not seem to be inappropriate. I feel strongly that the officials of our government should keep their mouths shut with respect to our spy operations.

I do not see the President very often. He wrote me a letter of thanks not long ago. I went out to the plane when he returned from his humiliating trip to Paris. He had a very friendly "Hello, George" for me. He had earnestly hoped to make a great contribution during his latter days of service as President to the cause of peace. In view of Khrushchev's objectives and attitudes, it is hard to know just what the President could have achieved but I think his hopes are shattered now and that he is in many ways a very sad man. The President has not been physically strong enough to run his Administration with an iron hand the way it should be run, but his desires and intentions have been of the highest.[192]

From every corner critics charged Eisenhower with neglecting the nation's security. He was enraged over these charges and responded that, based on his previous military experience, he knew more than others about what was needed to protect the nation. Information gathered from U-2 flights convinced him there was no "missile gap," but his argument was losing credibility because he would not tell the public about the flights. Instead, he wanted everyone to "trust Ike." This did not happen, and many continued to question him harshly, especially Democrats with an eye on the fall elections.

Initially, it was hoped that Congress would adjourn for the year before the conventions got under way; however, in an unusual move party leaders decided to reconvene after the conventions. Lyndon Johnson requested the postconvention session, claiming there was not enough time to finish all the work that had to be done. After the Democratic convention nominees John F. Kennedy and Lyndon Johnson met at Hyannis Port, Massachusetts, where they announced that they intended to devote their full time and energy in the postconvention session to five key issues: a farm bill, medical care for the aged, aid to education, minimum wage, and common-site picketing and housing. However, none of these bills was cleared for the president before the session ended.

Organized labor had hoped that dividends would flow from the Democratically weighted Eighty-sixth Congress that had taken office in 1959, but the failure of Congress to pass a new minimum-wage law was a major defeat. The bill that Mahon voted against in the House was modified after its introduction to reduce the proposed minimum wage from $1.25 to $1.15 per hour. He had also voted against the increase in 1955, when the wage was raised from $0.75 to $1.00.[193] Mahon was inclined in 1960 to vote to raise the wage but not to broaden the coverage.[194] Letters from constituents were heavily opposed to the bill and included petitions containing long lists of voters. Some farmers mentioned a concern that farm laborers would be included, thus reducing their profits greatly. Many believed increased wages would add to an already inflated economy. Others feared that small businessmen would be bankrupt or would have to reduce the number of employees. Most letters came from businessmen, not laborers. However, one letter from a waitress asked Mahon to vote in favor of the bill because the expense of a special uniform required for her work actually reduced the wages she was earning. Mahon replied that he believed a federal minimum-wage law infringed on states' rights: "I personally feel that the federal government should not completely dominate the lives of all our people. I doubt that it is practical at this time to pass a minimum wage law which would cover everybody who works. In fact, I feel that a federal minimum wage law to be applied universally to all workers is not in the best interests of the country."[195]

However, the Civil Rights Act of 1960, an outgrowth of the 1957 act, authorized federal judges to inspect local voter registration records and impose criminal penalties on anyone who obstructed another person's attempt to register or vote. Although this act was designed to help blacks register and vote, only an additional 3 percent voted in the 1960 election.

Mahon voted against the Civil Rights Act of 1960 (H.R. 8601). In a letter to Daphne, he wrote, "Of course, you have been reading in the papers about the Civil Rights controversy in the House and Senate. It is a bit ridiculous that this kind of circus should be going on at a time when so much important legislation needs to be considered. The Senate is not taking action upon the appropriation bill which we have sent over in recent weeks and we are going to have quite a log jam. We had hoped to adjourn for the Democratic Convention July 1 but I'm afraid that this may not be possible."[196]

Civil rights legislation was a strong point of contention between Northern and Southern Democrats during 1960. Mahon had the temperament of a Southern conservative, and he argued that individual states should determine who was eligible to vote. In view of that, he did not believe it was prudent for the Senate to spend time debating a voting rights bill while delaying action on defense appropriations, a matter that was clearly within congressional jurisdiction. On May 6 President Eisenhower signed a civil rights bill that became Pub. L. No. 86-449.

The split between Democratic liberals and Southern conservatives, who voted with Republicans, watered down much of the Democratic Party's cherished legislation. The coalition was as effective at stopping legislation as a presidential veto. The Democratic presidential and vice presidential nominees, Kennedy and Johnson, were committed to a liberal platform, and they found that the coalition blocked their bills for medical care for the aged, school aid, and minimum wage. A pay raise for federal employees was enacted, but only over the president's veto.[197] In 1960 Mahon voted on 96 percent of the roll calls. He voted in agreement with the majority of Southern Democrats slightly over 50 percent of the time and against the remainder. He also voted with his party 76 percent of the time on party unity roll calls.[198]

Democrats were convinced that the president's defense budget of $41 billion was not adequate. One committee member after another questioned Secretary of Defense Thomas S. Gates, Jr.—who had replaced Neil McElroy on December 1, 1959—and his subordinates in an effort to find reasons to increase the appropriation for defense. They insisted that soon the Soviets would have a three-to-one lead over the United States in ocean-spanning missiles. Because Atlas missiles were just beginning to come on line in the Strategic Air Command and an antimissile defense system did not yet exist, they were convinced that America was vulnerable. "After protracted and critical hearings on the nation's defense effort, Democrats agreed that it was inadequate and added more than $600 million to the administration's $41 billion military budget. But they couldn't force the president to spend the extra money, most of which was frozen by the Budget Bureau."[199] This rankled many congressmen, who believed his refusal to spend the appropriated money was an erosion of their power to raise and arm military forces.

In addition to the frustration of inter-service rivalry, Congress was annoyed when it learned that each service planned its own budget independent of the others. The importance of cross-service programs such as the Navy's request for another carrier, the size of the army's ground forces, or the size of the manned bomber program for the air force were never discussed among the Joint Chiefs. Clearly, a coherent strategic plan was lacking. Duplication in some areas—such as expensive weapons programs—and gaps in others—such as airlift support for ground troops—were common. Members of the House Subcommittee for Defense Department Appropriations were frustrated with the Joint Chiefs, whom they criticized for not exercising leadership.[200] Their attack on the chiefs, drawn heavily from General Taylor's testimony, implicitly took issue with the president and the secretary of defense for their inability to control the services and to produce a cohesive defense policy for the nation to which the military branches could repair. The chiefs were criticized for not exercising leadership in setting up guidance for the various branches. "The Joint Chiefs of Staff should look at what is available and for what purposes and attempt to match it with needs."[201]

For example, it was thought that the combined forces of the Marine Corps and the army should be considered to comprise the total ground forces, and the combined airpower of the navy and the air force should be considered the airpower capability of the United States. Considering each separately caused each service to argue for a larger share of available resources when in fact the combination would have met a large part of the overall need.

In June Mahon wrote in his Green Journal, "Developed a constant fairly sharp pain very low in abdomen. Had Xray of lower intestines. Was told by Navy Hospital doctors that I had a few diverticuli in lower intestine but not more than would be expected. Had another attack in summer with slight fever. Had sharp attack in October and Dr. J. C. Douglas of Lubbock, without Xray pronounced my trouble diverticulitis. It took about 10 days to get back in fair shape."[202]

With hearings on the defense budget behind him, Mahon prepared to attend the Texas state Democratic convention to be held in Austin on June 13–14. He was a delegate. During the convention he had a good, long visit with Lloyd Croslin, who had been a close friend and colleague since 1934, when Croslin spearheaded a movement of young Democrats for Mahon during his first congressional campaign, then accompanied him to Washington as his first secretary. On June 22, 1960, the fifty-year-old Lubbock attorney died suddenly of a heart attack. With his death a strong and reliable "pipeline" of information from the district was broken. In a letter to Daphne, Mahon wrote, "We are so sad about Lloyd's death. It hardly seems possible that this could have happened."[203]

Mahon was also a delegate to the Democratic National Convention in Los Angeles. Johnson wanted his colleagues from Texas to be there, believing they would be helpful to his bid for the nomination. Before leaving for Los Angeles Mahon assumed the race would be between Johnson, Kennedy, and Symington. While on the West Coast he also spent an extra week inspecting military installations. After returning to Washington, the defense bill was finalized and sent to the White House for the president's signature. At that time Mahon summarized the actions of the Eighty-sixth Congress in national defense for the *Congressional Record*. This included calendar years 1959 and 1960 and fiscal years 1960 and 1961. He praised the lack of partisanship in the work that had been done. He understood that defense spending would become a central theme in the campaign, and lavishing credit on both parties allowed both to share any blame in the upcoming months.

According to Mahon's summary Congress, rather than the executive branch, often "carried the ball, provided the drive and determination, provided the initiatives that have sparked our most spectacular gains in defense."[204] He believed the most important actions of Congress were the reduction of funds for marginal projects, such as the Bomarc, thus downgrading their priority and raising the priority of other projects by increasing their funds. Congress was entitled to a large share of credit for the rapid development of the Polaris missile weapon system that Mahon said, "has captured the imagination of the world."[205] It had captured Mahon's imagination because a Polaris submarine could fire missiles twelve hundred miles while submerged. After firing it could move away, thus denying the enemy knowledge of its location. He expressed disappointment that the president had frozen the additional funds for six months, causing a delay that could not be made up. However, in 1960 Congress again aggressively supported the program by allocating more money for fiscal year 1961 than the president had requested, thus bringing the total to five fully funded Polaris submarines and components for seven more. Finally, the president released all but a small amount of the money to the Navy.

Mahon also cited money provided, but not included in the president's budget request, to maintain an airborne alert that would allow a portion of the B-52 bomber force to be in the air at all times and ready for instant action in the event of a surprise attack. More importantly, an around-the-clock alert would prevent complete destruction of the force on the ground from Soviet missiles. Congress refused to accept a cutback for the B-70 bomber—a follow-on bomber for the B-52. Funds were provided to move this program beyond the prototype stage into production. Testimony in Appropriation Committee hearings revealed that the program was cut back because of "the fear that expenditure ceilings would be exceeded."[206] Congress also took the position that the budget requests for the intercontinental ballistic missile program were inadequate. The sum of $12 million above the amount requested was allocated for the Atlas program, the only operational ICBM. Additional funds were provided to accelerate the Minuteman program.

In each session of the Eighty-sixth Congress, funds were provided to modernize the army in preparation for limited war, but the executive branch froze most of the money. These funds included money to procure high-speed, long-range aircraft for troop movement and to accelerate the Nike-Zeus program that theoretically could destroy enemy ICBMs. In the end Congress did not increase the dollar amount of the overall defense budget but shifted funds from low-priority programs to high-priority programs. In addition to reducing funds for the Bomarc air-defense missile, Congress emphasized the need to eliminate duplications in the services, reduced funds for civilian employees, and insisted that the services use more efficient contracting methods.

Mahon predicted that defense spending would become a central theme in the campaign, and it did. The Democratic candidates charged President Eisenhower with allowing a "missile gap" and a "rocket gap" to develop, thereby forcing America into retreat around the globe.[207] As campaign rhetoric heated up, the big question became whether or not national defense was adequate for the country. In the 1952 campaign Republicans had gained a lot of ground by accusing Democrats of being soft on communism. Now, in the 1960 campaign, the tables were turned, and Democrats retrieved the lost ground by hammering away at Republicans about the "missile gap." Mahon ordered ten thousand copies of his extended remarks from the *Congressional Record* printed at his expense. The remarks summarizing congressional defense initiatives designed to strengthen national security were sent to all Democratic members of Congress, major newspapers, radio and TV stations throughout the nation, correspondents of major rank listed in the *Congressional Directory*, and all Democratic campaign workers in the Nineteenth District. Those working for the Kennedy-Johnson ticket had ammunition ready to use. Among the many letters in Mahon's files acknowledging receipt of these remarks is a letter from Kennedy's campaign headquarters and one from Kennedy himself.

Although President Eisenhower was adamant about budget ceilings for defense spending in the name of economy, there was much waste in the proliferation of weapons systems by competing branches of the services. Historically, the United States did not maintain large military forces in time of peace, and this inhibited the growth of a large munitions industry. During times of conflict the civilian industries, those generally adaptable to both the mass production of consumer items and weapons, quickly converted to weapons production. However, technological advances since World War II had produced highly complex weapons systems that required scientific engineering skills not found in most industrial firms. The result was the growth of a munitions industry dependent on defense contracts, which meant increased pressure on the military services and congressmen to buy new weapons systems. Under President Eisenhower budget ceilings allowed each service to spend its allocated funds as it saw fit. Thus, the competition for a greater share of the budget pie developed through the procurement of cutting-edge weapons systems. Too many competing projects managed to secure congressional funding primarily because the secretary of defense did not exercise firm control over the budgets coming from each service branch. Additionally, the Joint Chiefs of Staff did not meet together to discuss which systems were likely to be most effective and most efficient. This approach paved the way for duplication and waste through the large sums of money lost to munitions industries because initial concepts for weapons did not prove viable.[208]

The final year of President Eisenhower's eight-year administration was the least successful. Congress approved only 30.6 percent of his proposed legislation.[209] Democrats held nearly two-thirds of the seats in both chambers of Congress and had held a majority since the 1955 session. The president's crusade for peace, launched in his inaugural address, did not end the Cold War. When he left office in 1961 he could only claim to have avoided war. The collapse of the Paris summit was largely the result of his poor judgment. Republicans had promoted President Eisenhower as a kindly grandfather; now however, many people saw him as an old man at the head of an old party, surrounded by old advisors who dealt with old problems. He could not anticipate new problems or adjust to the winds of change.[210] The second session of the Eighty-sixth Congress left behind "a record of indifferent accomplishment and spirited partisanship."[211] The presidential campaign left a trail of glowing embers from the heated debates about the adequacy of national defense.

In contrast, Mahon's power and prestige had grown. During the previous fifteen years of service on the House Appropriations Committee Subcommittee for Defense Appropriations, he had gained valuable knowledge about what it takes to provide security for the nation and why the costly new weapons systems required so much of the federal budget each year. In fact, he believed his years of experience provided a knowledge base that was greater than that of any of the secretaries of defense who had served during the same years. Turnover was a problem for the secretaries, coupled with the fact that there was no single solution for providing national security. Each service had its own concept of what would best protect national interests. As Mahon and his colleagues on the subcommittee refereed the inter-service squabbles year after year, they developed an expertise that helped them identify some of the strengths and weaknesses in the various concepts. In contrast, each new secretary who came on board was faced with getting up to speed. Having no knowledge base about military weapons, he had to rely on the World War II heroes who were the chiefs to decide what was needed. This situation allowed the military rather than the civilian secretary to actually control the Department of Defense.

During the campaign Mahon made speeches on behalf of the Democratic nominees, referring often to the leadership of Congress in providing the nation's defense. In September he wrote to Helen, "Made a big speech at El Paso airport along with others as we waited for Kennedy plane (I really did). Heard Kennedy twice in El Paso Monday morn. And we then flew to Lubbock. Got here 20 minutes late. I was Master of Ceremonies and introduced LBJ & JFK. I was on the ball OK. Kennedy did fine. LBJ had an off day and got off poorly. Crowd good etc. . . . Heard Kennedy address the preachers at Houston. He was magnificent. . . . After seeing Kennedy address the preachers and talk without notes in El Paso and Lubbock I have decided he may overshadow Nixon. Could be wrong. Have about decided Kennedy will be next President. He has it and I doubt that Nixon has."[212]

Historian James T. Patterson writes that Kennedy made a very important decision to address the issue of his Catholicism head-on when he spoke to a group of Protestant clergy in Houston, Texas. Houston was known as a stronghold of Protestant strength, and Kennedy managed to soften the religious rhetoric of the campaign by emphasizing how strongly he felt about the separation of church and state. According to Patterson, if Kennedy had tried to evade the issue, he very likely would have alienated Protestant voters, thus ensuring his defeat.[213] It is likely that his address was also a relief for Mahon, who was a staunch Methodist. However, many voters in the district were not relieved, as the final votes revealed. Late in August Mahon wrote in a letter:

The House sessions were brief during the past week and I stole out to Burning Tree a couple of times. On one occasion I took as my guest a Jewish doctor who formerly lived in an adjoining apartment and who is one of our medical Father Confessors. People of Jewish descent are not encouraged to visit the Club but I made up my mind to speak my mind if anyone should complain, what with the big Civil Rights planks in both platforms. Ike was there, of course, both days. My friend got a big kick out of Ike when his party overtook us on the 9th hole. Ike and his son and grandson and another person made up the foursome. David[214] had about a fifteen foot putt. David missed but he rimmed the cup and ran his ball against the President's purse which the President had placed just beyond the hole. The press is barred from Burning Tree else you might have read this in the paper. We had no business in the House last week but we have a full schedule for the next couple of days. The Senate passed the minimum wage bill. I voted against it some time ago when the House passed it.[215]

Before the letter was mailed to Daphne, Helen penned a footnote, saying she was pleased to learn that Daphne would be attending a Democratic tea at the Shamrock Hotel in Houston. She reminded Daphne to speak to Lady Bird Johnson and let her know who she was.

The Friday before Election Day, Mahon was in Fort Worth, where he and three other congressmen spoke at a rally for Lyndon Johnson. In a note to Daphne and Duncan he wrote, "LBJ made the best speech I ever heard him make but only 2 min. of it was on the TV. Apparently Tricky Dick is getting a huge reception in Texas. But our boy Kennedy is going great guns and he will win unless he is blocked by the religious issue. Mother and I will be glad when it is all over. . . . I do not have another speech scheduled but I will be busy up to the wire. Wasn't that fantastic that oil man Hunt came out for the Demos. That might tend to make some of the big shots have a second thought. I cannot think of anything more stupid than for Texas to go Republican. They will cripple the prestige of their state in Washington and make it harder for Texans to get what they want in Washington, regardless of who wins the Presidency. If the religious issue is as strong as it appears to be I do not see how Kennedy can carry Texas or the nation. Well if Kennedy loses it will assure 4 years of misery for Nixon. Times will be rough whoever is President."[216]

A one-hundred-year political tradition was broken when both the Republican and Democratic platforms contained a strong civil-rights plank. Southern conservatives had been able to prevent this in the past, but now their strongest rallying point, segregation, was under attack, and Republicans hoped for a third straight victory in the Lone Star state. That did not happen, and Texans' votes helped provide a razor-thin margin for Kennedy and Johnson. This was one of the closest elections in history. Voters in Lubbock County turned out in record numbers to vote for the Nixon-Lodge ticket, but

Democrats were elected to all other offices. Lyndon Johnson was favored over John Tower for US senator, and Mahon did not have an opponent.

Mahon and Helen left the district early in December and spent time with the Holts in Houston. They seemed to enjoy the grandchildren more than usual. "More than ever before it was just plain fun to be with them."[217] They spent a pleasant five days driving back to Washington, arriving there on December 19. Christmas was quiet. Their gift to each other was new chairs for the apartment. Although there was just the two of them, they hung their stockings and opened their "gifts from far and near with much enthusiasm."[218]

With the election behind them, the days were less stressful. "Everyone says I'm looking better now," he wrote to his family, "and I have gained three pounds since returning to Washington. The tired look is gone. . . . While walking home from church on Christmas Day a pretty girl in a midget sport car stopped at the intersection and waved, 'Hello Congressman.' This made me feel awfully young. Her children waved too!"[219]

During the leisurely days Mahon reflected on how he could cut corners and save time:

I found last year that if I always put hat checks and car storage checks in the same pocket every time, I cut down the fumble time by 90%. The pocket selected for these items is the upper, outer left breast pocket of the coat. Fortunately, I never go out without my coat! My glasses case is chained to my shirt and cannot get far away from my shirt pocket. This has saved me hours, perhaps days of time! The innovation for 1961 is this: Without fail and under all circumstances I put my car keys in my right-hand pants pocket. This is a little awkward when I have on an overcoat but I will save hours of fumble time, always finding my keys without thinking and as a matter of routine. I think I've got the car key problem licked because I will never be going to the car without my trousers on. Other time-saving projects are under study.[220]

Chapter 6

High Expectations: 1961–1963

The "New Frontier," a term coined by John F. Kennedy that became the theme of the Kennedy administration, ushered in an era of high expectations. The steady stream of intellectuals flocking to Washington was reminiscent of President Roosevelt's administration and the New Deal. David Halberstam described them as "the best and the brightest." Even Lyndon Johnson was impressed with their brilliance; however, after describing the new cabinet members to his mentor, Sam Rayburn replied prophetically, "Well, Lyndon, they may be just as intelligent as you say. But I'd feel a helluva lot better if just one of them had ever run for sheriff."[1] Despite their political naiveté, national leadership had passed from the old guard to the young and energetic New Frontiersmen, who believed they could get the country moving again. Mahon was also impressed with these bright, young minds, especially that of Robert S. McNamara, the new secretary of defense. Additionally, he was pleased that during a Democratic administration almost two-thirds of the seats in each chamber were held by Democrats. He hoped this would make it easier to get approval for the kind of defense bills that he thought were necessary to protect the nation.

Early in January, before inauguration fever seized the city, the Mahons attended a birthday dinner at the Mayflower Hotel, honoring Sam Rayburn, who had been elected to his tenth term as speaker of the House. This was also the beginning of his forty-ninth year in Congress, where he had served longer in the House of Representatives than any person. On January 31, 1951, he had set the record for the most days served as speaker when he surpassed Henry Clay's service record of 3,056 ½ days, and on June 12, 1961, he doubled Clay's record as speaker.[2] Mahon told his family in a letter, "Bobby Kennedy and wife came by for a little visit just prior to the dinner. . . . About mid-way in the dinner, John Fitzgerald Kennedy himself came in and sat at Rayburn's table for a few minutes and visited. Our table was nearest to the door and as he was leaving he stopped to shake hands and remarked that he had not seen us since the election. He was looking wonderful."[3]

Later that month Mahon took time from his work to go with Helen to the Pentagon to view the film that had been taken during his 1945 trip around the world. Much of it had been shot from a jeep on bumpy roads. Although it was difficult to see, they both enjoyed watching it and were impressed by its good condition after fifteen years. They also viewed some film taken when he appeared on *Face the Nation*. In telling his family about it, he wrote: "Had the man re-run some of the TV *Face the Nation* shows upon which I have appeared. CBS had given me films of the appearances, but I had never looked at one. Should have looked at them before. Saw lots of things I was doing wrong. Will send copy of this to Daphne. Have complained that she did not stand sufficiently erect. The round-the-world film demonstrated to me just how much I myself slump! Hadn't realized it."[4]

In a letter to his family back home, Mahon wrote: "Saw Ike at 8:00 church service last week at the Presbyterian Church. His minister always has a special communion for Members of Congress on the day that Congress convenes. Dick[5] was there and a number of other big shots. Dick presided at the Joint Session of Congress when the results of the Electoral College were announced. He made a little speech at the end of the proceedings and did quite well. Got a big hand."[6] This was the first time in a century that a defeated presidential candidate presided over the session of Congress that declared his opponent the winner.

Mahon also confided in a later letter that during the campaign Nixon was almost always present for church, even if he had to fly two thousand miles on a Saturday night, but that he had not attended services at the Methodist church Mahon attended since the election. "The pastor worked hard for Dick, saying the closing prayer at the Republican Convention, and he was unhappy over Dick's backsliding. Helen told him [the pastor] to cheer up, that he would just have to be satisfied with us plain Democrats! This is an interesting sidelight on human nature. The Nixons are O.K. and, of course, they are tired, emotionally exhausted and disappointed."[7]

The Mahons were up early on Inauguration Day and quickly packed the car with food for guests in the office, as was their custom. Eight inches of snow had fallen the night before, and several hundred army soldiers worked through the night trying to clear the streets in temperature that was ten degrees below freezing.

Mahon reported to his family:

We had to hit the street before eight o'clock, if we were to have the best chance to make the six miles through the grave yard of stalled and stranded cars which partly blocked the streets and parkways to the office. . . . We made it beautifully! Helen and the office staff were serving coffee and refreshments to friends in the office by 10 o'clock. A TV was available in the office so we could keep track of happenings. We had taken down all my extra sweaters, top coats, etc., and this was fortunate because two of our guests did not even have overcoats. The wind was blowing a gale and it was very cold. I almost froze and some of you can imagine how many clothes I had on! I sat with other Members of the House on a high platform reserved for us. I did not wear a top hat, but I did wear my best blue suit. As the Cardinal continued to pray or lecture the Lord, whichever it was, I sneaked my trapper's cap with ear flaps out of my pocket and put it on.[8] Some of us wanted to leave the stand before everything was over, but the way was blocked. For sure the New Frontier is the hard way![9]

Mahon was not able to see Kennedy's inauguration because so many people were standing in front of him, but he did hear the inaugural address and told his family: "The speech was magnificent. He may not make a popular President but I pray he will make a good one."[10]

Back in the office Helen and the office staff served food to about forty people, mostly constituents, who watched the parade from Mahon's office windows and on TV. They actually saw more of the activities than Mahon did. He and Helen were at home by 7:00 p.m. tired, but happy with the day's events. They decided not to attend any of the inaugural balls, which cost fifty dollars a couple, nor the one-hundred-dollar-per-seat gala the previous night, which they considered just a political affair intended to pay off the debts run up by the Democrats. The gala, a variety show at the Armory, included such celebrities as Jimmy Durante, Ethel Merman, Maurice Chevalier, and Leonard Bernstein, all of whom were staying at the apartment house–hotel where George and Helen lived, so they saw them without the expense. Later in the week, however, he and Helen had dinner on the presidential yacht *Sequoia* with an old Texas friend, John Connally, who was President Kennedy's new secretary of the navy.

"Full of vigor" was a good description of the inauguration of the youngest man ever to serve as president of the United States. Despite an exceptionally cold day, with the temperature in the low twenties, Washington was warmed by the sense of purpose in President Kennedy's "New Frontier," as Americans were admonished to ask not what their country could do for them, but what they could do for their country. Kennedy also committed the nation to "pay any price, bear any burden, meet any hardship, support any friend, oppose any foe, to assure the survival and success of liberty."[11] Few Americans understood the far-reaching entanglements this commitment would lead to in the coming decade.

One of the brightest of the New Frontiersmen was Robert S. McNamara, a Republican. He had become president of Ford Motor Company on November 9, 1960, just one day after John Kennedy's election and less than five weeks before he accepted an offer to serve as secretary of defense in the new cabinet. Although his knowledge of defense matters was meager, he immersed himself in the subject, and being a quick study he set out to become an aggressive leader. At forty-four, just a year older than the new president, McNamara seemed a good fit with the new generation of young, intelligent people who were champing at the bit to replace what they considered the old, tired Eisenhower administration. Under the 1958 Defense Reorganization Act the secretary was given greater authority over the military, and McNamara intended to use every bit of it. He extracted an agreement from President-elect Kennedy to be allowed to make his own choices about who would work under him. No political favors were to be repaid in his department. His biographer observed, "In the months that followed, McNamara undertook the largest overhaul of the department's budget and administration, the nuclear forces and the even larger non-nuclear, or 'conventional,' forces since the United States plunged into World War II."[12] This had a major impact on the dynamics between the Department of Defense and Congress, which was manifested in a decline of congressional initiatives designed to influence defense policies through appropriations. McNamara's changes, seen by many in Congress as an improvement over the indecisiveness of President Eisenhower's defense secretaries, were favorably received. "Enthusiasm over the forty-four-year-old supermanager came from both sides of the aisle in the spring of 1961: from Democrats who had called for a stronger and more centralized defense effort since Sputnik, and from Republicans who agreed that Eisenhower had let U.S. defenses slip,"[13] writes Deborah Shapley. McNamara would take care of that with the largest peacetime defense buildup in the history of the nation, causing the defense budget to grow from $41 billion in 1961 to $49 billion in 1964.

Understanding the importance of support from members serving on the House Subcommittee on Defense Appropriations, McNamara stopped by Mahon's office for a friendly visit early in January. He made a favorable impression. Through the years many administration officials had stopped by Mahon's office in order to have an open line of communication when questions arose concerning budgetary matters. "I have been in touch with a lot of the top outgoing people in the Eisenhower Administration," Mahon wrote to his family. "Many of them are good friends and many of those coming in on the Kennedy team are good friends of mine."[14]

In the same letter Mahon reported to his family, "We have already started some of our committee hearings. Our first witness was Mr. Allen Dulles, the head of Central Intelligence Agency. It is very interesting to hear him talk about our undercover activities in various parts of the world. Mr. Kennedy is certainly inheriting a difficult situation. It is fortunate that he has youth and vigor. I hope he may have the wisdom to follow the right course. Nobody knows in detail just what the right course is."[15] On a more personal level, he wrote, "I have been working almost day and night since my return to Washington. Helen has helped me a lot and the office staff is now back in Washington in full force and we are getting a lot done."[16] One of the things that he and Helen were able to get done was their income taxes. In a later letter to his daughter and son-in-law, he wrote: "We have the income tax in final form except for the final copy of the return for the tax collection. This is our biggest year for income tax. A lot of things we have been depreciating have been depreciated out and there was not as much to charge off. The tax man said he was amazed at our taxable farm income—that he thought I was the only man he had helped who wasn't taking a net loss on his farm! I guess a number of the Members have show place type farms like a lot of businessmen have in certain brackets."[17]

In February 1961 the Kennedy administration sent a bill to Congress that would provide $2.3 billion in federal aid to education for construction of elementary and secondary classrooms and for improvement of teachers' salaries. The president called it one of the most important pieces of domestic legislation of the session. Plagued with opposition from civil rights groups and religious groups, the bill passed the Senate in May; however, on August 30 the House voted by a 242-170 roll call vote not to even consider the bill. In June a group of women met in Lubbock to declare their opposition to any kind of federal aid to education and to draft a letter to Mahon stating their position. It was signed by 127 women who vowed to attempt to organize a statewide group in opposition to education aid. They wrote, "As God-fearing American citizens wishing to stand firmly against further encroachment upon our civil liberties; as mothers who wish freedom of choice to be preserved for our children; as constituents of the 19th Congressional District; we urge you not only to oppose the Federal Aid to Education Bill by casting your vote against it, but we also urge you to use the influence at your disposal and publicly work to defeat the bill."[18] One of the women wrote, "The government's money cannot buy excellence in learning." Another stated, "It is my feeling, who accepts the king's shilling, inevitably becomes his slave."[19] They need not have worried. Mahon voted against the aid-to-education bill, as he had always done in the past. He was one of the Southern Democrats who joined forces with Catholics and Republicans to defeat the legislation because he believed it would give the federal government too much control over the administration of local schools, which could possibly lead to their integration. The strength of special interests in American politics was obvious.

Early in February Defense Secretary McNamara held a background briefing for the press corps in which he outlined his management concept of a five-year plan and task-force studies. Reporters pressed him for an answer about the Soviet lead in missiles, and McNamara said that the intelligence reports that he was privy to indicated that the United States, not the Soviets, was ahead in missiles. This made headlines because some of Kennedy's strongest campaign rhetoric was about the "missile gap" that had been allowed to develop during the Eisenhower administration. After Sputnik was launched in 1957, many Americans became concerned that if the Soviets had rockets that could launch a satellite, they also likely had rockets that could deliver a nuclear warhead into the United States. President Eisenhower tried to calm this fear by assuring the public that US retaliation would be so devastating to the Soviet Union that nothing of that sort would happen. However, the Democrats picked up the idea of a missile gap and made it a campaign issue. During the campaign Kennedy declared the Soviets had more missile power than the United States, and "he used it even after classified briefings by General Earle

Wheeler, who told him that the United States was not behind any country in nuclear delivery capability."[20] It was after a few drinks that McNamara told reporters that any gap was in favor of the United States. His comment made headlines, and an angry president told the press that McNamara was incorrect because no studies had been made to indicate that the United States was ahead.

According to biographer Deborah Shapley, "The gaffe faded quickly—for congressional Democrats had ridden the missile-gap charge as hard as Kennedy had and were not eager to embarrass themselves or the President. . . ."[21] Classified intelligence through the Spring gave firmer evidence of lower numbers of operational Soviet missiles, so obviously the concept of a "missile gap" was subject to interpretation. Although the United States appeared to have fewer intercontinental ballistic missiles, there was no hard evidence about the number the Soviets really had, only estimates. Moreover, the air force had aircraft that could be refueled in route in order to deliver nuclear warheads to any location in the Soviet Union. The Soviets did not have this capability. While there might have been a gap in the number of missiles, Mahon was convinced there was no "deterrent gap." He considered this the most important point because US deterrent forces could survive a first attack and deliver a fatal blow in retaliation.

Determined to be a strong and activist secretary of defense, McNamara decided to gain control of his department through control of the budgeting process. He implemented a planning, programming, and budgeting system to analyze defense expenditures. Budgets were to be the outgrowth of programs that supported force requirements, and force requirements were to correspond to military missions that in turn were related to national security objectives.[22] Plans and cost analyses drawn up by the services were forwarded to the secretary, who made the final decisions in the budget that was submitted to the president. This was in sharp contrast to the budget ceilings used by previous administrations, under which each service received an amount of money that could be used pretty much as it pleased, causing a lack of integrated missions and much duplication of expensive weapons systems. The new process was to be a cost-reduction program that stressed the concept of buying what was needed when it was needed, rather than bearing large expenditures that resulted from each branch of the services trying to protect its own turf. The national importance of such an approach is more clearly understood when one considers that the Department of Defense had for a decade spent over half of every tax dollar.[23] Military leaders were not impressed, to say the least, but congressmen were. After Secretary McNamara appeared as a witness at hearings on the defense appropriations bill, Mahon wrote to his family, "My present estimate is that he is about the ablest cabinet member I have ever encountered. Hope he continues to measure up to such a high standard. I am afraid he might be breaking himself down. He works from 7 to 7 and the pressure upon him is terrific."[24] Mahon admired McNamara because of his determination to make service unity and efficiency high priorities. Inter-service rivalry, which allowed the duplication of weapons systems, had proven to be an expensive wastefulness that McNamara intended to end. Mahon himself maintained that that "civilian administration at the Pentagon is essential, claiming that top businessmen can run a more efficient, economical operation than military men."[25]

At the outset, President Kennedy and Secretary McNamara changed the nation's overall defense policy from one that relied on the threat of nuclear weapons and massive retaliation to deter a war to a more flexible policy that stressed conventional methods of warfare as well. "Administration planners did not believe that nuclear weapons were credible in a confrontation with the Soviet Union except in the most desperate situations."[26] McNamara continued to strengthen nuclear forces but also strengthened conventional forces in order to respond to a broader range of threats. He and President Kennedy believed that Soviet strength in long-range bombers and missiles was continually increasing, thus making the American policy of massive retaliation suicidal. If the United States ever decided to retaliate with nuclear weapons, the Soviets had the capability to strike back, setting off a conflagration that would become a mutual catastrophe. Moreover, the threat of massive retaliation had not really been effective in stopping Soviet aggression. Berlin, Korea, French Indochina, and Lebanon were clear examples of aggression that had not been stopped with nuclear weapons because the consequences of using them would have been too great. Kolodziej writes, "The threat to use military force was viewed as credible only if a potential aggressor believed that the United States would actually implement its threat if its interests were challenged."[27] McNamara, with President Kennedy's support, argued that the United States needed a broad range of defenses that could counter any threatening force, but nuclear weapons were to be used only in the most desperate situations.

After being in office only three months, President Kennedy asked Congress for an additional $650 million, of which $1.3 million was for the acceleration of the Polaris program; then on May 25 he addressed a joint session of Congress to request $2.65 billion to increase the capability for conventional warfare and to help governments threatened by wars of national liberation. He intended to reorganize the Army so it could fight smaller wars. That would require more armored personnel carriers, more helicopters, and more howitzers. He also wanted a national civil-defense program that included bomb shelters in public places such as subway stations or in mine shafts. His requests for supplemental defense appropriations continued through the year, and by October he told reporters that he had increased defense spending by more than 14 percent. This included "a 50 percent increase in Polaris submarine construction; a 100 percent increase in Minuteman missile production; a 50 percent increase in the number of strategic bombers on fifteen-minute alert; a 75 percent increase in troop airlift capacity; a 150 percent increase in anti-guerrilla forces."[28] This reflected the president's decision to strengthen nonnuclear forces in order to have a wider choice of options than humiliation or all-out nuclear war, which he believed was the case with a policy of massive destruction.[29]

In June Defense Secretary McNamara admitted at a news conference that there were horrendous examples of waste in the military establishment. But he said they were no worse than in big private companies. "It is a mistake to assume that government departments are less efficient than large aggregations of men and materials."[30]

The final report prepared by Chairman Mahon of the House Subcommittee for Defense Appropriations commended McNamara for the manner in which he had tackled these problems since taking over six months earlier. The committee also gave him a year to head off threatened "chaos" at top levels, but it served notice that it would move to order corrections if they were not made. In August 1961 the final version of the defense bill, as agreed upon in conference, passed the House and Senate. The $46 billion bill was the largest that Mahon had ever handled during peacetime. It had been increased from the previous year by $5.9 billion, to the highest level since the Korean War. Space funds were nearly doubled in an effort to beat the Soviets to the moon.

Mahon was greatly relieved after it had passed the House, and about six o'clock that evening he and Helen left his office to have supper at a nearby restaurant. Upon returning they learned that the president had been trying to reach Mahon. He returned the call and learned that President Kennedy had called to thank him for the way he had handled the civil-defense portion of the bill. The final version of the bill contained $207.6 million for the Department of Defense to begin civil-defense programs in accordance with Pub. L. No. 87-144. The day before Mahon had been at the White House to assure the president that everything would be okay; however, Kennedy was still somewhat concerned. Now everything was in order. International tensions caused the president to insist that shelters were needed to protect citizens from a possible nuclear attack, but funds to provide these had not been included in the budget requests in time to allow debate during hearings in the House.

A funding request was added by the Senate, and only during the conference to settle differences between the House and the Senate bill did members of the House Appropriations Committee have a chance to consider this addition. McNamara told the conferees about the addition ahead of time, and they strongly supported it before the conference version was returned to the full House for approval. On August 26 Mahon also received a letter from McNamara, expressing appreciation for his support on the civil-defense appropriation, although neither the subcommittee nor the full House Committee on Appropriations had been given adequate time to carefully investigate the budgetary request. McNamara wrote: "I, therefore, wish to reaffirm the commitments made to you, your Committee and the Senate Defense Subcommittee during the hearings in connection with the Third Amendment to the President's Budget for fiscal year 1962. I want to assure you that I have carefully re-examined the programs contained in the budget justification material which was presented to your committee in support of the budget estimate contained in the above referenced amendment. . . . I will be most happy to send you and your Committee a monthly progress report and am enclosing a report of our progress to date."[31] When Mahon received McNamara's timely reports, he believed his favorable opinion of the secretary was confirmed.

Despite having knowledge that the missile gap was in America's favor, President Kennedy dramatically increased military spending. This decision, combined with his boasting in the fall of 1961 about America's superiority over the Soviets in nuclear weaponry and declaring that a US first strike on Soviet territory was not out of the question, encouraged the Soviets to respond with a "long-term military buildup that brought them approximate parity with the United States in nuclear weapons by the early 1970s. Kennedy's defense policies thus served to escalate the arms race and, paradoxically, to reduce America's nuclear lead in the long run."[32]

Before 1961 no authorization was required prior to appropriation of military funds, except those for construction. However, in 1959 the Armed

Services Committees attached a rider (Section 412b) to the construction authorization (Pub. L. No. 86-149) that required legislative authorization prior to appropriating funds to procure aircraft, missiles, and ships, beginning in 1961. The legislative committees hoped thereby to recapture a large portion of the control over the defense program that was being exercised by the appropriations committees at that time.

In 1961 this proviso required enactment of two separate procurement authorizations (in addition to the regular construction authorization). One, totaling $12,571,000,000, was for the regular Department of Defense budget requests for aircraft, missiles, and ships. The second, totaling $958,570,000, was in response to President Kennedy's July 25 request for additional funds to build up military forces in response to the Berlin situation.

In July Mahon became acting chair of the full House Committee on Appropriations. He presided in the absence of eighty-two-year-old Chairman Clarence Cannon (D-MO), who had fallen in his bathtub at home, breaking three ribs and cutting a gash over his eye. Mahon was the second-ranking Democrat on the committee, and he presided over the full committee meeting when a vote was taken on the new money bill for military construction. A Texan had not chaired the House Committee on Appropriations since James P. Buchanan, who died in 1936.

The strong leadership exercised by Secretary McNamara in gaining control of the sprawling Department of Defense, coupled with firm presidential support, encouraged congressional confidence in the secretary's management ability. It also reduced end-runs to congressmen by the Joint Chiefs and helped bring inter-service rivalry under control. In conjunction with legislative approval of new weapons systems under Section 412b, the Subcommittee on Defense Appropriations was able to spend more time determining whether the defense budget would adequately support the administration's foreign policy and less time refereeing the budgetary power struggle between the services. Ultimately, this resulted in less congressional influence over defense policy. Congressional committees do not have the time, or resources, to study how defense appropriations fit into the larger scheme of total budget expenditures required to run the nation. That is a function of the executive branch of government.

When McNamara first took over the Department of Defense, he turned to the Joint Chiefs of Staff and their chairman, Lyman Lemnitzer, asking them what changes needed to be made in the budget Eisenhower had left them.

The chiefs' answer proved to be only a rehash of requests they had submitted to former Secretary of Defense Gates and President Eisenhower that had not been approved. Later McNamara said to Henry Glass, one of his assistants, "Do they think I'm a fool? Don't they have ideas?" Glass suggested that Mc-Namara ask to increase the number of Polaris submarines to be produced. "What number should we ask for?" asked McNamara. "Seven," said Glass. "Why seven?" McNamara asked. "That's the number Mahon wants," said Glass. The way the Pentagon had been run, Mahon's wishes were often the starting point for its requests. "That's a hell of a way to build a program," said McNamara. "It's not *logical*."[33]

This method was not logical according to the way the legislative process was intended to work. Requests for military expenditures should be compiled in the Department of Defense, forwarded to the president for any changes, and included in his annual budget. Upon reaching Congress, requests for military expenditures should be sent to the House Armed Services Committee for legislative approval before being forwarded to the House Appropriations Committee for funding. Basing weapons requests on what the House Subcommittee on Defense Appropriations would likely fund became the de facto routine because previous secretaries could not control the department enough to get a consensus of opinion about which weapons systems were needed for national defense. More importantly, it was not logical according to the new methods of cost analysis that McNamara intended to see used by the Department of Defense as a basis for determining the purchase of weapons. This would become a major difference during McNamara's tenure.

Prior to the 1958 Defense Reorganization Act, the Armed Services Committees in both chambers of Congress used great latitude when writing authorization legislation for the procurement of military hardware. These bills provided blanket permission to purchase aircraft, ships, and weapons systems. It also allowed each service to decide how much of its annual budget to spend on research and development. For example, the air force might be authorized to procure missiles or twenty thousand aircraft with no attention given to the fact that a similar authorization for the navy would cause expensive duplication. Moreover, the lack of integrated planning often meant that neither branch would be required to provide necessary support for other service branches. For example, both the navy and air force were so focused on strategic aircraft that carried nuclear weapons that neither assigned a very high priority to airlift for troops or cargo, despite the fact that this support was important. Each service secretary was free to determine what weapon systems were deemed necessary to support the mission of that particular service branch. While the blanket authorizations allowed the Armed Services Committees to preserve their legal and jurisdictional authority, this loose legislation was too broad to be a reliable tool for shaping defense policy. Any congressional impact had to come from the defense appropriations subcommittees of each chamber through the appropriation of money to procure specific weapons systems or support particular research and development. Thus most of the real battles between Congress and the Pentagon were fought in the hearings of George Mahon's subcommittee and its counterpart in the Senate, through the power to loosen or tighten the purse strings.[34] It has been pointed out that during President Eisenhower's administration members of Mahon's subcommittee often acted as referees, using funding allocations to actually determine which weapons systems were to be procured and which research was to be continued.

With more than twenty years' experience on the subcommittee that appropriated military funds, Mahon's judgment was respected by both the Pentagon and the administration. Ruling by persuasion rather than the arbitrary use of power, he had managed to accumulate a sizeable power base of his own, and it was widely believed in the Pentagon that if a program could pass the review of his subcommittee, it was likely to be a good program.[35] Although the previous method of building a defense budget may not have seemed logical to the new secretary, Mahon's preference for the Polaris submarine was logical. He knew that the lifespan of these submarines could easily stretch to thirteen years, and their solid-fuel missiles had an even longer lifespan. Moreover, these submarines and their missiles could not be destroyed easily because their location was very difficult to detect. This provided greater deterrence than fixed-based weapons that could be knocked out because their location was known to the Soviet Union.[36] Mahon apparently felt that he was more qualified to make decisions about defense budgets than were some of the early secretaries who had served for far fewer years than he and who couldn't even get control of their own department. He managed his subcommittee very smoothly and effectively persuaded committee members to move funds around to support the weapons systems that the committee believed were most important. A clear example of this was the additional funds appropriated to strengthen the air force during the Truman and Eisenhower administrations.

Prior to World War II, the main interest of Armed Services Committees, in both chambers, had been exercising control over military pay and the number of personnel because these items made up the largest expenditures for national defense. However, the technological advances in weaponry since World War II reduced the importance of troops and increased the importance of weapons systems, and when the Armed Services Committees failed to keep up with this change it meant that some very important decisions would be made elsewhere. During debate over the 1958 Defense Reorganization Act, several senators finally realized that by allowing the appropriations subcommittees to assume much of the decision-making responsibility for weapons, they were actually delegating part of their power to others. Arguing that they had been negligent of their duties, the senators started a movement to insist that the Armed Services Committee of each chamber conduct hearings before writing specific and detailed authorization bills for military expenditures each year. The requirements for this change were found in Section 412b of the Defense Reorganization Act and applied to any money spent after December 31, 1960.

Just prior to the inauguration of John Kennedy, President Eisenhower's farewell address sounded a warning to the nation, when he stated that "this conjunction of an immense military establishment and a large arms industry is new in the American experience. The total influence—economic, political, even spiritual—is felt in every city, every statehouse, every office of the federal government."[37] He admonished Americans to be cautious about allowing this military-industrial complex to become so powerful that it endangered the nation's liberties or democratic processes. Eisenhower's remarks were not really heeded until the Vietnam War years when antiwar activists referred to them to call national attention to the costs of national security.[38] Despite Eisenhower's warning, the power of the military-industrial complex grew so rapidly that it ultimately became the dominant feature of the US economy and the lifeblood of many communities. Correspondence in Mahon's defense-appropriations files illustrates how closely many congressmen and their constituents were involved with the defense industries. In April his old acquaintance Frank Pace, then chairman of the board of General Dynamics Corporation, wrote, asking Mahon to understand the wisdom of appropriating more money for B-58s, although the defense budget did not request funds for future procurement of this plane, nor did it request funds for the B-70. Pace was concerned because

General Dynamics and its partner Grumman Corporation had the contract for building the B-58s and was scheduled to build a portion of the wing of the B-70. He called Mahon's attention to the fact that their largest plant, located in Fort Worth, would be forced to lay off approximately seven thousand workers by October 1962 unless more orders were placed by the Department of Defense.

Mahon's answer offered no encouragement for Pace. He wrote that after exploring the situation with the Pentagon, he believed the B-58 program would not be revived, and the sharp differences of opinion made the B-70 program a very controversial matter for the Appropriations Committee that session.[39] In a letter to Mahon, Secretary McNamara explained that he would not request more funding for B-52s or B-58s because previous appropriations would provide an inventory of more than seven hundred of these planes by the end of fiscal year 1966, and he considered that an adequate amount. If a decision was made later to add more bombers, money could be appropriated in future years. He also pointed out that "restart costs" would be less than the cost of continued production of unnecessary planes.[40] Secretary McNamara was convinced that manned bombers, the backbone of the nation's retaliatory force, were very vulnerable to a surprise attack. With that in mind, he intended to speed up the production of missiles, especially the Polaris and the Minuteman. He also ordered the Strategic Air Command to keep a larger portion of the bombers in the air at all times, and the remainder were to be ready to take off on fifteen minutes' notice. His emphasis on missiles had the additional benefit of allaying the nation's concern about any missile gap.[41]

Mahon's files also contain correspondence from Representative Jim Wright of Fort Worth, who appeared before Mahon's subcommittee to testify about the seriousness of the situation. Wright stressed the fact that the proposed budget did not request money for a single manned bomber, thus procurement would be terminated by the middle of 1964 when the last of the B-52s and B-58s on order were built. Because the USSR was rapidly building bombers and missiles, he argued, the United States was creating a "bomber gap." Furthermore, ballistic missiles had never been fully tested and once launched could not exercise judgment if a change was necessary, as a pilot could in a bomber. He pleaded with the committee to include appropriations in the upcoming bill that would allow additional bombers to be purchased. Texas senator Ralph Yarborough also testified before the Senate Department of Defense Subcommittee, Committee on Appropriations in June, arguing in favor of continuing defense contracts with General Dynamics because the aeronautical industry had diversified the economy of the Southwest from an extractive one depending on mineral resources and agricultural products to an economy that included aerospace, electronics, and nucleonics. He stressed the contributions of General Dynamics to the community of Fort Worth by tapping unused manpower resources in the area. Even the nearby colleges and universities had benefited.[42] The impact of the growing defense industry was one of the most complex problems that the Defense Department and Congress had to deal with. The munitions business had become a major US industry, and the increased number of defense contracts inevitably had a marked influence on almost every aspect of American life. The unanswered question was whether the influence would ultimately be positive or negative.[43]

Despite Mahon's lack of encouragement for Frank Pace, the final defense appropriation passed by Congress did include $515 million for the production of either B-52s or B-58s. It also included funds to speed up the development of the B-70. The president had not requested these funds, and in October Secretary McNamara announced that they would not be spent. He declared that production of B-52s and B-58s would end in 1962 because the United States had a bomber force "sufficient to perform its mission through the late 1960s and early 1970s."[44] The committee did not flatly insist that the president reverse his decision to let B-52 and B-58 bomber production come to a halt the next year or his projected cut in funds for the two-thousand-mile-an-hour B-70 bomber. It did, however, express concern and put into the bill not only the $220 million sought for the curtailed B-70 program but also the $130 million that President Kennedy had cut from former president Eisenhower's bomber budget and another $100 million for good measure. The committee left it up to the president to determine on which bombers this $450 million should be spent. McNamara made it known that he would not recommend that the president spend extra funds on manned bombers because he wanted to concentrate on missiles.[45] Congressional discussion of the necessity of manned bombers would be continued the next year.

The first year of any new administration is spent largely on building a team that can work together to implement the new president's initiatives. During 1961, however, much of that time and energy was spent coping with international crises. President Kennedy had hardly settled into office before the Bay of Pigs fiasco monopolized everyone's attention, taking time that could have been spent fleshing out the president's defense program. An invasion of Cuba, at the Bay of Pigs, was initially conceived under the Eisenhower administration. Approximately fifteen hundred Cuban exiles were trained in Guatemala by the CIA to lead what was supposed to be a surprise popular uprising against Cuban prime minister Fidel Castro. Security leaks were rampant in both Cuba and the United States, but the plan went forward and on April 16, 1961, the exiles landed. Trying to mask US involvement, President Kennedy withheld any overt military support, and Castro's forces swiftly crushed the invasion, causing enough blame to provide a generous share for everyone in the administration.

Then in August Soviet premier Khrushchev ordered the construction of a wall separating East Germany from West Germany and also separating the two Berlins. A major factor in his decision was the outflow of East Germans to the West through West Berlin, which was rapidly draining the country of professionals and skilled laborers. The wall set off a clamor by Cold War hawks insisting that the president challenge the Soviets by halting the building of the wall. However, President Kennedy, understanding that the Soviets could seal off their own boundary if they wished, remained calm. Khrushchev's threat to sign a separate treaty recognizing the sovereignty of East Germany, struck fear in West Berliners located more than a hundred miles inside East Germany. If this happened their status as a free city would have to be negotiated with East Germany, and it was highly unlikely that this would be granted. Many in the United States also waited with bated breath, fearing that a confrontation there could set off a nuclear war.

In a family letter Mahon wrote:

In spite of adversity and embarrassment the President has remained calm and has shown no disposition to panic. . . . I have never seen the people so upset. I hope the President doesn't get upset and that he keeps a steady nerve. Not since 1945 have I been as worried about war. I think the chances are fairly good that we will avoid it. I have been to the White House this year more than any other year. A month or so ago the President had Senator Russell of Georgia, the Secretary of Defense, and myself come to his office for more than an hour of discussion on the Berlin crisis and what to do about it. This was of course flattering to the Senator and me. The President leaves his desk and sits in a little straight-up rocking chair and puts both feet on a coffee table. There are two couches facing each other about 5 feet apart and the coffee table is between them. His guests sit on the couches. This arrangement is probably designed to help the President make his back more comfortable. The President looks pretty good but the stress and strain are telling a little. Nothing could be much more back breaking than the Presidency. Visits such as the one just described don't get in the paper for obvious reasons. Those who call on the President off the record enter through a special gate and to the back and enter through the White House itself, not through the Presidential office set-up where the press is located. . . . I have voted against and worked against many domestic spending programs at this session as in previous years. I strongly favor a program of economy wherever possible.[46]

Mahon observed that in 1961 his mail from constituents showed a marked increase over former years. The mail reflected their concerns about a wide range of legislation, including calls for reduced spending. However, the majority of the letter writers expressed their satisfaction with the way Mahon had voted on various bills. "I think this growing interest is healthy," he told a reporter from the *Lubbock Avalanche-Journal.* "In the long run, people get the kind of government they want and for which they work."[47] Among the letters he received were many from members of the John Birch Society, asking him to help impeach Chief Justice Earl Warren. Mahon answered that he would be required to vote in the House if impeachment proceedings were carried through, but he would not take a stand on the matter until all of the evidence was in. He discerned that many people in the South equated support for civil rights with sympathy for communism, and because they were distressed with Justice Warren's stand for civil rights, they believed he was a communist.

On August 31 Speaker Sam Rayburn left Washington for an extended rest at his Bonham, Texas, home. He said he had been suffering from lumbago and was going to take a long vacation but could return on short notice if he was needed during the closing days of the session. Mahon wrote to his daughter and son-in-law that Rayburn looked very bad, and he feared he would never return.[48] Majority Leader McCormack was elected speaker pro tempore and continued in that post for the remaining twenty-seven days of the session.

On October 2 Rayburn entered Baylor Hospital in Dallas for medical tests, and three days later doctors reported that he had incurable cancer. He weakened rapidly, and at the end of October he was "taken home" to the Bonham hospital, where he died on November 16 of paralysis of the lungs, a complication from his illness. Rayburn had served 48 years, 258 days as a representative (continuous service) and 17 years, 62 days as speaker (twice interrupted). He was buried in Bonham, and among those attending the funeral were President Kennedy, Vice President Johnson, and former presidents Eisenhower and Truman.[49] After Rayburn's death Wright Patman was the senior Texas member, and Mahon was number two. Next in line were Albert Thomas and W. R. Poage, each with twenty-five years of service.

The Mahons attended the funeral, going first to the Rayburn home to express their sympathy to relatives. At the church seats were reserved for members of Congress; their wives sat in the back. Mahon was pleased with the service, which was conducted by a hard-shell Baptist preacher.[50] George and Helen went to the cemetery with Representative Carl Vinson (D-GA). When the graveside service was over they spoke with former president Truman but lamented that they did not have a chance to speak to former president Eisenhower. As Mahon and Vinson walked along talking, with their heads turned down, a voice called out "Hello, George," and when he looked up, Eisenhower was standing there with his hand out, having gotten out of his car to speak to them. He looked fine and was very friendly. Later Mahon wrote to him and "told him I thought it was wonderful for him to come to the funeral."[51] He did not tell Eisenhower, but he thought it was good that he and Truman had patched up some of their differences. He believed it was foolish for two ex-presidents to be angry with each other.[52]

In October at a Fort Worth rally approximately five hundred Democrats passed a resolution declaring that henceforth they would be Republicans. William A. Horan, acting as chairman of the Democrats, said the rally was a grassroots repudiation of the one-party system in Texas. In 1961 John Tower had won a seat in the Senate as a Republican, and the group agreed to begin working to elect a Republican governor in Texas.

That fall Mahon made his first hole-in-one at Burning Tree Country Club. "I made the hole-in-one on the 11th hole using a number 4 iron, 165 yards."[53] Another foursome was near the green where Air Force General Timberlake saw the ball roll into the cup. He called back to Mahon's group, which included Karneil Singh from Delhi; General L. L. Lemnitzer, chairman of the Joint Chiefs of Staff; and John McClure, a Washington lawyer. In keeping with tradition, the country club pro sent the golf ball to the manufacturer, who later returned it in a plaque to commemorate the event. He duplicated his score card, which he sent to family and friends.

Mahon believed that in 1961 he had worked harder than any other year in Congress. In fact, it was not unusual that he had to work seven days a week. He and Helen were eagerly counting the days until Congress adjourned so they could vacation for a few leisurely days. Helen planned to accompany him on a trip west to inspect military installations before returning to the district. As usual, Mahon was careful to see that he paid for her part of the trip. They traveled by train, going by way of Minneapolis for a few days of vacation before beginning the inspection tour. They visited the University of Minnesota, where Mahon had attended classes in the summer of 1925. They also stopped in at Dayton's, the department store where Helen had worked while Mahon was in school, and they ate at some of the nice restaurants they couldn't afford when they were there as students. Mahon wrote to Daphne that it was like a second honeymoon.[54] From Minneapolis they continued on by train to Great Falls, Montana, to inspect the Minuteman missile site at Malmstrom Air Force Base. In 1959 Malmstrom AFB was selected to be the first Minuteman ICBM base because it was close enough to the Soviet Union to put most strategic targets within the range of the Minuteman missile. This also made it possible to substitute the Minuteman for the Jupiter and Thor missiles in Turkey, which were removed when the Soviets removed their missiles from Cuba. Malmstrom AFB was part of the Strategic Air Command. The next stop was the Strategic Air Command Headquarters at Offutt, Nebraska, before the Mahons boarded the train for home by way of Chicago. Mahon was especially interested in visiting these sites because he believed there was a possibility that a Minuteman missile base might be put near Lubbock, and he wanted to learn more about the advantages and disadvantages of having it in his district.

After celebrating his 61st birthday he wrote to Daphne and Duncan, "Being 61 is no problem. It was last year when I became 60 that the real shock came.

That shock has been fully absorbed and I am quite contented and happy. I am very much excited about the .410 gauge shotgun which Helen gave me. The 12 gauge has been just a little too much bang for a man of my age."[55] The new gun would be nice for hunting dove and quail when he was in Colorado City.

In early October when Mahon returned to the district during the inter-session, he recapped his year for reporter Kenneth May of the *Lubbock Avalanche-Journal*. He admonished Americans to adopt an attitude of cautious optimism instead of negative pessimism concerning the relative strengths of the communists and the free world. He predicted that the United States would not back down on the Berlin crisis; however, he did not expect the situation to degenerate into a shooting war. He predicted that the Cold War would be just one crisis after another. He interpreted Russia's new series of atomic tests as a sign of weakness and further proof that the United States was far ahead in atomic capability.

Mahon also spoke about a trend toward fiscal conservatism becoming evident throughout the country, which pleased him. He believed the government should live within its means and that the balanced federal budget promised by President Kennedy the following year was sorely needed. He stated that Americans were showing more interest in government, and he believed that was a good sign.

Pointing out that in 1961 defense appropriations were boosted $5 billion over the previous year, he was convinced that the additional funds were necessary in order to give the United States more "deterrent" power and "a better bargaining position at the conference table."[56] While a lower level of defense spending had been sufficient in past years, he added, "No one knows what the right amount is. We are not widening the gap in our military superiority over Russia, but neither are we losing ground."[57] He believed that ultimate victory in the East-West conflict "will go to the side which is able to maintain its power and stability. There could be victory without war. War [is] not inevitable."[58] Mahon predicted that as the Soviet people became better educated, they would be increasingly restless under the communist regime. However, this would take many years, but patience was the key ingredient in dealing successfully in the contest with the communists. "Fear, self-pity and negative thinking will get us nowhere in this contest," he told the reporter.[59]

Mahon deplored the Soviets' resumption of atomic testing as a sign that

Soviet leaders were uncertain of their capabilities. He also stated that Roswell L. Gilpatric, deputy secretary of defense, had been correct in a recent news article when he warned against using atomic weapons and stated that the United States had enough power remaining to crush an aggressor after sustaining a first blow. Gilpatric's warning about using atomic weapons was not new, but Mahon believed it was timely. The United States always had the power to fight a very devastating war, and Mahon believed the increased defense budget provided more deterrent power, more power to strike back after sustaining heavier losses, than might have been estimated. Mahon also believed the United States would have to resume testing if the Soviets continued to do so or the nation's weapons would run the risk of becoming outdated.

Increased spending for conventional defense weapons and the activation of additional military units were needed because a war might not start as an atomic conflict, and "there is no need to swat the fly on a friend's forehead with an axe."[60] The Nineteenth District congressman was disappointed that domestic spending had not been reduced in an effort to balance the budget during the year. He had voted against three major administration bills: the aid-to-education measure, the housing act, and the aid-to-depressed-areas bill. Mahon reported that he had helped kill President Kennedy's request for a foreign-aid program on a five-year basis instead of one year at a time because he believed Congress should maintain a close watch over spending. However, this would not prevent the administration from planning ahead.

"Looking for a bright side, federal spending in 1949 was 15 per cent of the gross national product. In 1961, it was 15 per cent, also," Mahon noted. "However, in our period of greatest prosperity I think we should be operating on a balanced budget. That is something we have done only six times in the last 31 years." Mahon did not mention that the gross national product had grown considerably between 1945 and 1961, which meant that 15 percent was a much larger dollar figure.

That December there was a problem in Slaton, Texas, one of the cities in the district, regarding discrimination incidents at the public swimming pool. Allegedly a young Mexican American girl and a Slaton High School Mexican American boy had been denied admission during the summer months when the pool was open. The young girl's father, who was a member of the GI Forum, contacted Dr. Hector Garcia, state chairman of the GI Forum in Texas, and Dr. Garcia lodged a complaint with the Department of Labor. The Labor Department threatened to blacklist thirty-one area farmers who were using bracero labor[61] if the pool was not integrated within thirty days. Representatives from Slaton contacted Mahon, who was making his rounds in the district at the time. He immediately wired Secretary of Labor Arthur Goldberg in Washington, urging that the January deadline for integration be withdrawn and that city officials be given a chance to handle the problem themselves. The pool was closed during the winter months, and Mahon believed matters could be worked out before it opened again the following summer. A copy of the telegram was also sent to Representative Harold Colley (D-NC), chairman of the House Agriculture Committee, and to Representative Bob Poage (D-TX), the vice chairman. Slaton officials and Mahon strongly maintained that integration was not the problem. They believed the root of the problem was that the Department of Labor was very unsympathetic toward the bracero program that made it possible for farmers to use cheap Mexican laborers instead of union workers and that this problem was part of an attempt by the department to unionize farm workers. Union people had been in the Slaton area asking farmers whether they would employ union workers, and many people were upset about the attempts of unions to infiltrate farm workers. In the agreement between the United States and Mexico regarding the employment of braceros, discrimination was just grounds for canceling the contract, and in light of the international agreement it was imperative that Slaton officials get the problem solved quickly. Ultimately they were given until March 1, 1962, to integrate the pool. Senator John Tower, a Republican, joined Mahon and Slaton officials in expressing outrage over the matter, indicating that it was not a partisan incident.[62]

However, partisan politics did enter the picture on the local level. A Republican from Crosby County took this opportunity to write a letter to the editor of the *Lubbock Avalanche-Journal*, theorizing that the Democrats simply created a problem that Mahon could quickly solve, thus making him look good. The writer did not believe Mahon had the power to do anything about the problem and that he was actually being used as a tool by the ultraliberals in Congress. His support of the New Frontier administration along with his cooperation with Texas Senator Ralph Yarborough and Representative Bob Poage, both of whom the writer considered ultraliberals, was proof that the liberals wanted him to look good and get elected again.[63] A Democrat answered that the complaint was designed to make Mahon look bad and possibly hurt him at election time. The writer wrote, "I am strongly in favor of a two-party system in Texas, and I don't blame the Republicans for nurturing ambitions. But they must arm themselves with more than ambition and ruses if they hope to gain representation in the 19th Congressional District in the foreseeable future."[64]

~

The Mahons spent time with the Holts during Christmas. The grandchildren were still a great joy to them, but as they grew older some of the normal antics of adolescence were annoying. They also discovered that a home with three children was much livelier than their home with one child had been. In a family letter Mahon wrote, "I guess the thing that upsets me most is that the children don't replace the cap on the tooth paste. Replace it! You can't find it. I think they throw it away."[65] His frustration was short-lived, however, as he told his Green Journal, "I have a new set of Wilson Staff golf clubs which I bought for my Christmas present in Omaha, Neb., last October. I think I am going to play much better. I bought Helen a new portable TV for Christmas."[66] After a leisurely drive they arrived in Washington on New Year's Eve and attended church services that evening to give thanks for their safe trip. On New Year's Day they attended a black-eyed-pea party given by the National Press Club. In addition to ensuring good luck for the coming year, they wished many of their Texas colleagues a happy new year. Watching the Cotton Bowl game on TV was especially pleasant. The Longhorns from the University of Texas, Mahon's alma mater for law school, were rated number three in the nation and started the game as the underdog to the Rebels from the University of Mississippi, rated number five in the nation. The Longhorns won 12-7, making this the first victory by a Southwest Conference team in the Cotton Bowl in five years.

~

Mahon wrote home, "The opening of the House of Representatives will be more interesting this year than usual. It won't be routine in view of the absence from the scene of the late Speaker Sam Rayburn. John McCormack has been the Democratic leader, hence the number two man in the House for 16 years and he will no doubt be the new Speaker. He is not too well liked by liberals or conservatives, Democrats or Republicans. However, under seniority rules and practices and in the absence of a strong candidate in opposition, he is scheduled to take over as Speaker. This does not mean he will control the House insofar as votes on issues is concerned. I think Members in the next session will be rather cautious from the standpoint of new legislation and I certainly hope so."[67]

Before McCormack was elected speaker there were rumors that Mahon might be elected as a dark horse.[68] He was being encouraged by Representative Clarence Cannon, chair of the House Committee on Appropriations, to seek this position because Cannon did not believe the House would elect McCormack, but he thought Mahon had a chance. During a phone call on December 2, 1961, Cannon suggested that Mahon discreetly contact some of his friends to express an interest in being speaker. Mahon agreed to give the matter consideration and get back in touch with him. After the phone call Mahon dictated a memo about the conversation for his files. In it he stated that he intended to contact no one but at a later date would call Cannon to tell him he did not think it desirable to get into the race.[69] Mahon understood that being elected speaker was unlikely because McCormack had been speaker pro tem during Rayburn's absence. He had been majority leader of the House and was well qualified to take over the second-most-powerful post in the nation. Additionally, Mahon was one of those who had pledged support to McCormack early on.

Late in January Helen had surgery to remove two polyps from her colon and was hospitalized in Georgetown University Hospital. She was pleased with her surgeon and with the care she received. Fortunately, the preceding October Mahon had secured a hospital insurance policy that covered most of the expenses. He had expected to be the one who needed surgery for diverticulitis, having had two attacks in 1960, but he had been well since. After she recovered, Mahon wrote in his Green Journal that they might not have more than another decade of good health in which "to enjoy life robustly . . . It seems we should not work day and night but should take time out occasionally to try to get more out of life. We have no financial worries. We should spend more money for pleasure. Maybe we should go to Puerto Rico for Easter! I want to give this whole matter more thought. When and if we get to be 70 we might not be well and alert enough for full enjoyment of golf, travel, etc."[70]

On February 10 Mahon met with Clarence Cannon's subcommittee on the Central Intelligence Agency and listened for five hours to John McCone, who succeeded Allen Dulles as the head of the CIA. In his Green Journal Mahon wrote that he had learned more about the U-2 flights over Cuba and Red China, that US satellites were doing a good job of photographing parts of the

Soviet Union, and about the work of the agency in general. Detailed information is lacking because of the secretive nature of the activities. Mahon wrote that he thought McCone would be more interesting than Dulles.[71]

During the first week of March, Speaker McCormack asked Mahon to preside over the House during consideration of the quarter-of-a-billion dollar labor retraining bill. Mahon voted against the bill as well as against the Urban Affairs Department bill and the federal-aid-to-colleges bill. He did vote in favor of raising the debt ceiling to $300 billion. He understood that it was necessary to pay for government obligations and believed those members who voted against raising the debt ceiling after voting in favor of appropriations that made the increase necessary were just playing politics. He also wrote to the Holts, "Jno.[72] Glenn really took Washington by storm. Mother was down for the joint session of Congress. I have not been too excited about the celebrations but I really was thrilled by the success of the mission. Glenn has conducted himself wonderfully well. He has real talent. I cannot imagine anybody who could have done better or as well as he has done."[73] Since December 1961 the United States had been trying to match or surpass the flight of Soviet cosmonaut Yuri Gagarin, who successfully orbited the earth. After a number of failures, the flight of Colonel John Glenn was successful. When he orbited the earth three times on February 20, 1962, and landed safely in the Atlantic Ocean near Bermuda on the same day, fear of a missile gap began to subside.[74]

On May 28 Mahon was awarded an honorary doctor of laws degree from Texas Technological College in Lubbock. He was also in Lubbock on May 12 with the secretary of the air force to celebrate Armed Services Day.

Billy Sol Estes, a Texas wheeler-dealer, got a great deal of space in the press during May. He ultimately served two prison sentences for fraud involving false agricultural subsidy claims and using nonexistent anhydrous ammonia fertilizer tanks as collateral for bank loans. Rumors of help from friends in high places went as high as Secretary of Agriculture Orville Freeman and Vice President Lyndon Johnson. Mahon, wanting his family to completely understand his position on the matter, wrote home:

> Some businessmen had complained to me last fall that Billy Sol was building too many elevators and storing new grain for free for the first six months. This hurt his competitors. Last December from Houston I called the Department of Agriculture's top grain storage man, Mr. Moseley, of the Dallas

office, and told him about these complaints. I had talked to him and the U.S.D.A. people here on several occasions in recent years to the effect that a lot of people complained to me that the grain storage people were making too much money. I did this on a confidential basis because I did not want the elevator men to accuse me of trying to prevent their making a legitimate profit, and I did not know whether they were being paid too much or not. I cautioned officials, always pointing out that a scandal on undue profits might be brewing. My purpose was to make the U.S.D.A. men more alert. Officials did reduce rates a year or so ago. The legitimate grain storers came to Washington and raised a big protest. In cautioning against a scandal, I did not dream that a Billy Sol Estes type scandal was in the making. . . . I am very grateful that Billy Sol is from Pecos and not our District even though he had tremendous investments in our District. I did not know him too well, but I had seen him a few times, especially in January of this year when the Democratic fund-raising dinner was held. . . . Estes never did call on us for a favor and, insofar as we know, he has never written us a letter. . . . People will be smeared for answering his letters and for accepting small favors such as a lunch, but there is nothing wrong with things like that, especially during the time Estes was thought of as a saintly man with a Bible in one hand and a church contribution in the other. Taking money from him is a different story, of course. . . . Apparently the fullest investigation is being made and will be made by Congress, the FBI and the government generally. This is imperative. When the story broke weeks ago I talked to the right people in government, including Secretary Freeman (whom I consider an honest man), and urged the fullest investigation. The press has never interviewed me as to Estes, and I am glad to have my name out of the sorry mess; but in reply to people who have written, I have expressed my sentiments without reservation.[75]

In June 1962 the Supreme Court, in *Engel v. Vitale*, ruled against compulsive prayer and other religious observances in public schools. The ruling shocked many conservatives who feared that antiestablishment trends would encourage a permissiveness that could undermine the nation's values. The minister of Mahon's church spoke from the pulpit against the court's decision. When he finished the congregation gave him a loud "Amen." Mahon believed the court was wrong but hoped that those who were so upset about prayer being banned from school would remember that it had not been banned from the home and that those same people just might begin to spend more time exercising this important freedom at home. Prayer, Bible studies, and church attendance were regular activities in the Mahon family.

In July he wrote to his family: "I have made three trips to Texas this year. More than usual. On the last trip I left by Air Force plane last Friday noon and returned at midnight Saturday. Along with several congressmen from several states and the Secretary of the Interior Mr. Udall and other Interior Department officials I went to the ground breaking of the Canadian River Dam, about 30 miles north of Amarillo. This is a $102 million project which I helped get authorized by Congress in 1949 and 1950. More than half the money will be spent on a pipe line to channel the water from the lake to 11 cities, 8 of which are in the 19th Congressional District. The largest city to be served is Lubbock (and Amarillo) and the southern most town is Lamesa."[76]

At the end of July, Mahon and Helen were guests of Larry O'Brien, a presidential aide, and his wife. "He seeks to help the President with his problems with Congress. As you know, the President is having many problems in this area as you can well understand," Mahon later wrote to his family.[77] They also had dinner on the presidential yacht *Sequoia* as it travelled down the Potomac River. Other guests included Mike Mansfield, the leader of the Senate, and Wilbur Mills, chair of the House Committee on Ways and Means. Mahon was also the guest of Secretary of State Dean Rusk at a dinner honoring Prince Souvanna Phouma, prime minister of the Royal Government of Laos.[78]

Mahon had a Republican opponent in 1962, but the final vote was forty-nine thousand to twenty-three thousand in his favor. He described 1962 as the roughest year of his congressional service. Members of the John Birch Society[79] kept up a steady drumbeat of complaints about everything they could think of, and the Billy Sol Estes problem took a lot of time and energy that could have been used for other matters. Additionally, the crops were poor on Mahon's farm. "This was the year I went to the Naval hospital and got some expert advice and began taking some exercises for my sore back with excellent results."[80]

By the time that H.R. 9751, the Armed Services Committee authorization bill for fiscal year 1963, was debated in the House, a showdown between the administration and Congress had narrowly been avoided. Many committee members were still angry that extra funds provided in the fiscal year 1962 defense budget to be used on the B-70 bomber had been impounded. The new aircraft was to fly two thousand miles per hour, for approximately six thousand miles at eighty thousand feet. It was to be a follow-on bomber to the B-52 and B-58 and had been in development since 1955. President Eisenhower was not overly impressed with the plane and kept it in research and development status during his presidency. When McNamara came on board as secretary of defense, he was more impressed with the potential of missiles, believing they could do the same job as the bomber and at much less cost. The Chiefs of Staff agreed with McNamara, with the exception of General Curtis E. LeMay, chief of staff for the air force. LeMay had powerful friends in Congress, including Representative Carl Vinson (D-GA), who chaired the House Armed Services Committee, and LeMay went over the head of his boss, Secretary McNamara, to persuade Vinson that the nation should not rely solely on missiles but should continue to have a large inventory of manned bombers. He knew that Vinson was a powerful person in Congress and was not afraid to use his power whenever it suited him to do so. Vinson's committee had a reputation that dated back to fiscal year 1949 for favoring airpower, having authorized more money for airpower than President Truman would spend. President Eisenhower also refused to spend the extra money authorized for airpower, but even powerful congressmen, such as Vinson, were somewhat reluctant to publicly insist that they knew more about what was needed for defense than one of the nation's most celebrated military heroes from World War II. However, the situation changed when President Kennedy took office and appointed Robert McNamara as secretary of defense. Neither man had served as many years in the military as Vinson had served on the Armed Services Committee. Vinson also defended his position with the argument that the Constitution charged Congress with providing for and maintaining the armed forces; therefore, the president should not challenge directives from Congress despite the fact that as commander-in-chief he could use available weapons as he believed best. Vinson was convinced that his many years of authorizing the procurement of weapons systems provided him with the knowledge necessary to substitute his judgment for the judgment of the secretary of defense.

By the time of the fiscal year 1963 authorization bill for the armed services, the designation of the aircraft had been changed to RS-70, which meant that its function was expanded to include reconnaissance as well as bombing, in hopes of persuading Congress, as well as the secretary of defense, to speed up development of the plane. Most of the committee supported Vinson's determination to insist that the air force chief of staff spend the appropriated money despite the decision of the secretary of defense and the president to likely impound the money they had not requested. In an attempt to make the committee's (actually Carl Vinson's) judgment prevail, the bill was to be written "directing" the administration to spend the money instead of "authorizing" it to spend the funds.[81]

Red flags went up immediately. If the administration ignored a directive from Congress, then Congress would have to take action, which meant begin impeachment proceedings, or lose much of its power.[82] Beginning impeachment proceedings against a Democratic president would benefit only Republicans. And if the wording was allowed to remain, the House Appropriations Committee and the Subcommittee on Defense Appropriations would lose their prerogative to determine exactly how much money should be appropriated for the aircraft. The Armed Services Committee was responsible for determining which weapons systems could be procured and for establishing funding limits, but the House Subcommittee on Defense Appropriations was responsible for determining exactly what the dollar figure would be.

George Mahon well understood that Vinson was stepping across the line, and he decided to do something about it. He had the support of Democratic leaders such as Speaker McCormack and Majority Leader Carl Albert, neither of whom wanted an open quarrel with the administration just so that Vinson and LeMay could have their way. He also had the full support of the fifty-member House Committee on Appropriations, all of whom clearly understood the power they would lose in Congress if Vinson's wording prevailed.

Just days before the bill was to be debated on the House floor, an unannounced meeting was scheduled between President Kennedy and George Mahon.[83] When Mahon learned that the president had the same concern about the upcoming bill and planned to take the matter in hand in order to avoid a public quarrel with Congress, he returned to the House chamber to find Vinson. He told Vinson he would lead the fight against him, and that the Democratic leadership was on his side as were the fifty members of the appropriations committee. Vinson knew this meant losing some necessary votes, and he gladly accepted an invitation to the White House to work out a compromise with the president. Kennedy poured his charm on as thickly as he knew how and convinced Vinson to use "authorize" instead of "direct" in the wording of the forthcoming bill. Kennedy agreed to immediately send a letter to Vinson, promising to have McNamara restudy the RS-70 situation. McNamara also sent an immediate letter to the same effect. Both letters were read in the House during the debate on the following day and put into the *Congressional Record*.

The bill that ultimately passed authorized the Department of Defense to spend $491 million more on the RS-70 than it had initially requested. This would allow six aircraft to be built instead of the three requested by the Department of Defense. Vinson claimed victory because the bill forced the Department of Defense to realize that the committee meant what it said: "We are not going to stand idly by and see ourselves heading down the road that had nothing at the end but missiles."[84] When a reporter asked Mahon for his opinion, he just smiled and replied, "No comment."[85] The 1962 controversy over funds for development of the RS-70 resembled the controversy over funds for procurement of bombers in 1961. It also reflected the concern among air force officials and sympathetic congressmen that the administration was placing undue reliance on missiles as the core of the nation's strategic retaliatory forces during the middle and late 1960s. "'Bomber men' said that missiles were unreliable and lacked flexibility in use; 'missile men' said that bombers were expensive and vulnerable to advance anti-aircraft defenses."[86]

For fiscal year 1963 Congress appropriated $48 billion for the Department of Defense, exclusive of funds for civil defense, military construction, or foreign military assistance. This amounted to the largest defense appropriation since the Korean War. The current bill contained $1.6 billion more than fiscal year 1962 and almost $8 billion more than fiscal year 1961.[87] When the bill was initially introduced in the House, Mahon told members that this bill amounted to a levy of $258 on every man, woman, and child in the United States. He claimed it was necessary because of increased threats against the nation's security, especially in the area of intercontinental ballistic missiles. He went on to say that during the 1950s the United States was so preponderant in nuclear weapons that the defense budgets could safely be lower. However, Soviet developments in nuclear weaponry and intercontinental ballistic missiles made it necessary to raise the defense program to a higher level. He also pointed out that from end of the Korean War through the bill he was introducing (fiscal year 1963), defense spending had increased 9 percent and nondefense spending had increased 85 percent.[88]

For the first time the defense budget drawn up by Secretary McNamara was presented in terms of programs such as strategic retaliatory forces, general forces, continental air and missile defense forces, and airlift and sealift forces, which reflected the military missions they were designed to serve. This had been sorely lacking during the Truman and Eisenhower administrations, when arbitrary ceilings were imposed to keep defense budgets in line with the rest of the economy. In order to remain below these ceilings, costly ground troops were reduced and bombers were increased. Many congressmen, including Mahon, predicted that any future conflict would be a nuclear one, and aircraft carrying nuclear bombs were basically all that was needed for national defense. When the Korean War broke out, the fallacy of this argument became obvious as the small number of ground troops available were sent into battle and miserably slaughtered while troop levels were being built up again. Defense budgets during the past two decades were not truly designed around the missions they were expected to serve.

The House appropriated $47.8 billion, which included $52.9 million more for the RS-70 aircraft and $42 million more for the Dyna-Soar, a manned space glider, than was initially requested in the president's budget. A total of $223.9 million was earmarked for the RS-70, a much smaller amount than the $491 million that Representative Carl Vinson wanted to "direct" the Department of Defense to spend. However, when the bill reached the Senate, $491 million was appropriated by that chamber. The difference was split in conference, and the Department of Defense actually received $362.6 million for the aircraft. This was $191.6 million more than requested in the original budget. The Senate appropriated a total of $48.4 billion for defense, and the final amount worked out in conference was $48.1 billion. When the military did not get the money they wanted from the House Subcommittee on Defense it was common practice to take their case to the Senate, where increased funding was standard. By the end of 1962, no information had been released about the reevaluation of the RS-70, as promised by Secretary McNamara, and it became obvious that the extra money that had been appropriated would be impounded. In a similar vein former president Eisenhower, addressing a Republican fund-raiser in Washington, DC, said the fiscal year 1963 defense budget should be substantially reduced. He argued that it was the result of unjustified fears and that more spending would not necessarily lead to more strength.

The Cuban missile crisis of October 1962 caused Americans to fear that their worst nightmare might become real with a nuclear attack from Soviet missiles installed in Cuba. The events unfolded against a background of tension between President Kennedy and Soviet premier Khrushchev. Tension began to develop following the failed Bay of Pigs invasion in April 1961. It was further fueled that June when the two men met at the Vienna Summit. At that time Khrushchev threatened to negotiate a separate peace with East Germany that would endanger the Allied presence in West Berlin. Building the Berlin Wall in August actually relieved some of the pressure, but when it was learned that Cuban premier Fidel Castro had been given nuclear attack weapons to protect the island from a US invasion that he feared was imminent, the tension was ratcheted up another notch to crisis status. Although Castro and Khrushchev had little hope of winning a direct confrontation with the United States, nuclear missiles striking American cities could cause serious damage and the loss of lives. The close proximity to the United States precluded any warning time if the missiles were fired. After many days of high-level administration meetings and negotiations, President Kennedy addressed the nation on television on the night of October 22. He announced that any attack from Cuba would be treated as an attack from the Soviet Union and appropriate retaliation would follow. He also announced a quarantine on Cuba. It was called a quarantine rather than a military blockade because a blockade would have been considered an act of war. The quarantine was designed to prevent the arrival of any additional military weapons. People hunkered down, expecting the worst. Grocery store shelves were stripped of food and water as people stocked their fallout shelters in anticipation of an attack.

After the president's address, Mahon issued the following statement: "The President is our spokesman in foreign affairs and I shall support him to the limit. I am pleased with the decisive action which he has taken. It was made mandatory by the recent assessment of developments in Cuba. It is fraught with grave risks, but it is safer than a policy of weakness."[89] He praised President Kennedy for his patience in this situation and predicted overwhelming support from Congress and the American people. In the same folder of his defense files in which he placed a copy of his public statement are two typewritten pages entitled "Notes on Cuba, October 1962." These pages contain a brief sketch of the problems with Cuba from 1958, when the United States suspended arms shipments to dictator Batista because he was using them to suppress the revolution led by Fidel Castro through President Eisenhower's suspension of diplomatic relations with Cuba on January 3, 1961. By then Castro had publicly aligned his government with the Soviet Union and China. When President Kennedy took office, plans were already under way for the US-supported invasion of Cuba, at the Bay of Pigs, by Cuban exiles. Referring to President Kennedy, Mahon wrote, "He supported the April 1961 invasion, but did not order sufficient U.S. Military participation to insure success of the effort. This was a mistake. The U.S. could not escape responsibility for the invasion, therefore it should not have allowed the effort to fail. I am convinced that the U.S. cannot permit the construction by the USSR of a major military base in Cuba."[90] He voted for the congressional resolution authorizing the president to use any means necessary, including military forces, to deal with the Cuban situation. He also believed the problem was less complicated at the time of the Bay of Pigs invasion and should have been settled then. He noted that Congress had done all that it could short of a declaration of war. "I regret, as I believe all Americans do, our past errors in dealing with the Cuban situation. . . . I shall continue to do all I can toward a policy of strength and firmness. . . . Take sufficiently strong action."[91] In these notes he seems to be journaling as a way of dealing with his true feelings while maintaining a public posture of support and loyalty for the president.

At the eleventh hour both Nikita Khrushchev and President Kennedy agreed to avoid a nuclear confrontation that had the potential to destroy the world. The missiles were removed from Cuba, and the quarantine was lifted. Although not made public at the time, the two leaders also agreed that American missiles would be removed from Turkey.

After Congress had adjourned at the end of November, Mahon joined William E. Minshall (R-OH), a member of the defense and foreign aid subcommittees on appropriations, and two members of the defense subcommittee staff for a trip through Central America and the Caribbean to evaluate the effectiveness of foreign assistance programs there and to get a feel for the extent of communist influence in that area.[92] The group left from San Antonio, stopping first in Mexico City. At each stop along the itinerary, they visited with the US ambassador and CIA personnel. Mahon wrote home: "Almost without exception, the people we have seen in Central America are much disappointed that JFK did not figure out a way not only to dispose of the missiles but also to invade Cuba and liquidate the Castro communist regime. The communists with Cuba as a base are reportedly playing havoc with Central and South America."[93]

While in Mexico City, Mahon also met with the agricultural attaché for Mexico about the bracero farm labor program. Publicly the Mexican government was opposed to the program, but privately the attaché was much in favor of renewal. Mahon's Spanish was very limited, and although he could ask questions, he couldn't always understand the answers. In a letter he wrote back home, he said his goal was to get someone to teach him how to say, "Please don't talk so fast, dadgummit!"[94] The group then traveled to Guatemala, where a revolution had taken place just two days before and the airport had been bombed; however, the situation was under control by the time they arrived. Mahon wrote to Helen, "Insofar as I have been able to learn from the standpoint of American standards there is not an honest official in Central or South America. Graft in public office to feather one's nest is considered perfectly all right."[95]

From Guatemala they flew on to San Salvador and Managua, Nicaragua, where they stayed for two days and visited with the ambassador, Raymond Telles, the former mayor of El Paso. Then they went on to Panama City, where Navy Captain Bob Hailey, the head of naval intelligence, was their escort. In 1937 Mahon had appointed Hailey, a Big Spring, Texas, native, to the Naval Academy. They visited the military headquarters of the area and the US Army Jungle Warfare Training Center at Fort Sherman, where Mahon had a photograph taken with a boa constrictor draped around his neck. The United States had a military force of approximately eight thousand in Panama. From Panama they flew to Barranquilla, Colombia, on the northern tip of South America. After leaving there they traveled to Kingston, Jamaica, then to Guantanamo naval base in Cuba, where the United States had staged its unsuccessful invasion attempt the previous October. Mahon caught a navy flight from Cuba to Montego Bay, Jamaica, where he boarded a Pan American jet for Miami. Changing to a flight for Dallas, he finally arrived in Colorado City on December 9, where Helen was waiting for him.

Initially he had been reluctant to make the trip; however, after returning he used the information that was gathered for several years in considering foreign-aid appropriations.[96] A memo in his office files regarding the trip provides an insight into problems that the United States encounters when interfering with the governments of other countries. "Ambassador Tom Mann [ambassador to Mexico] and others in Central America pointed out that we often assist in kicking out one dictator without having a satisfactory replace-ment. That is what we did in Cuba. We contributed to the overthrow of Batista but we didn't have a good man to take over. This produced Castro. In too many countries the same situation exists. We tend to try to help eliminate the bad dictators but we often jump from the frying pan into the fire because we do not have a good replacement to sponsor."[97] Although Mahon had taken his golf clubs to play should he have an opportunity, the tales that he brought home were more interesting than his score card.

When President Kennedy's $51 billion defense budget was sent to Congress for fiscal year 1964, Mahon vowed to find a way to make meaningful reduc-tions without cutting into any of the "muscle" of national defense. Reflecting his concern about the predicted $11.9 billion deficit from an overall budget of $98.9 billion, he told a reporter, "We need to make up our minds whether we can and should live within our means. I, personally, believe we should live within our means."[98] He did, however, believe defense spending was largely justified. It was spending for social programs that he objected to most.

He anticipated that it would take many long hours of testimony in com-mittee hearings to settle the differences of opinion concerning the Skybolt and the Nike-Zeus missiles and the RS-70 supersonic bomber. McNamara planned to discontinue the Skybolt air-launched nuclear missile because "it would have had the lowest accuracy reliability and yield of any of our stra-tegic missiles—without the relative invulnerability and short time-to-target of a Minuteman or Polaris."[99] Additionally, it seemed that public cussing and discussing of the Cuban missile crisis would never end. The president was releasing very little information, which left the field wide open for various "experts" to tell everything they knew and shape the story the way they want-ed. Early in March 1963 Mahon asked for permission for one minute to ad-dress the House, and that was enough for him to blast away at all of those who had "loose tongues." Identifying a gap "in the intelligence of those who are daily revealing the secrets of the intelligence operations of the U.S. Gov-ernment,"[100] he leveled his criticism at Democrats and Republicans alike. He said those who wanted be in the headlines so badly that they were willing to jeopardize national security were demonstrating bad judgment. More im-portantly, their bad judgment would help adversaries identify the location of covert operatives. At best this would cause our sources of information to dry up, and at worst human lives could be lost. "Our immaturity and indiscretion in these constant disclosures is making us the laughingstock of the world," he went on.[101] He admonished people to understand that "our national survival to a great extent depends upon our knowledge of our enemies' activities. . . . It is difficult enough to obtain information from closed Communist societies. The American people, the press and the officials of the executive and legislative branches of the Government must stop making a most difficult task more difficult."[102] He ended by saying that there was plenty of room for criticism of the government without revealing sensitive intelligence information. Allen Dulles agreed with Mahon's speech. In his book *The Craft of Intelligence* Dulles pointed out that although the concept of a democratic government implies openness, not secrecy, many governmental actions go beyond the public's need to know. Mahon's remarks were widely covered by the press, and the editor of the *Baltimore Sun* called Mahon the voice of discretion.

Back in the district, Charles Guy, the editor of the *Lubbock Avalanche-Journal*, criticized him for not going far enough. Guy insisted that he should have made it clear that the reason the administration was being criticized was their bungling in Cuba. He did not agree with Mahon's belief that the problems of the administration should be kept under wraps. Guy's stand on this matter seemed to reflect the atmosphere of the sixties, a time of rebelling against traditional ways of life—a decade when exposure often counted for more than discretion.

The first week in September was a more relaxed time for Mahon, and he and Helen traveled to New York, where he received the American Political Science Award. In each odd-numbered year one Democrat and one Republican in each chamber was recognized for distinguished Congressional service. The purpose of the award was to call attention to effective legislative service that might not otherwise be noticed. It emphasized the importance of free elections in bringing individuals with high abilities and varied talents into public service. Members of the Washington press corps nominated, by secret ballot, a dozen or more whom they considered deserving of the honor. The American Political Science Association then investigated the nominees and narrowed the number to four recipients. Representative Thomas B. Curtis (R-MO), Senator Clinton P. Anderson (D-NM), and Senator Leverett Saltonstall (R-MA) were the other recipients in 1963. At the ceremony it was said of Mahon that he discharged one of the most difficult and important tasks in Congress with quiet distinction. "Under his guidance, one billion dollars a week flows from the Capitol to the Pentagon. His zealous concern for the national defense is tempered by concern for the nation's economy. His respect and friendship for the military establishment is tempered by a commitment to civilian control. Sympathetic to every proof that more money is needed for military security, his questions and relentless demands for facts are quieted only by proof. An acknowledged expert in his field, he commands the attention and respect of all his colleagues."[103] Mahon was the first Texan to receive this award.

Congratulatory letters from constituents reflected the pride felt through-out the district for his service. One, describing himself as an independent Republican Mahon supporter, wrote, "The merited honor in being chosen a recipient of this highly coveted award makes all of us West Texans stand taller with pride."[104] Another wrote, "I must admit that it makes me feel just a little proud to live in a district represented by such an able and sincere Congress-man. . . . It makes a constituent feel that he is well represented when folks in various parts of the country know the good job that George Mahon from Lubbock, Texas is doing for the entire nation."[105] And last, but not least, a con-stituent wrote, "Are they just now getting around to recognizing what a good many of us have known for a long time?"[106] In the same file is a carbon copy of a memo written to a member of his office staff, thanking her for an editorial from the *Fort Worth Star-Telegram*. He wrote that he may not have known about the editorial except for her but admonished her to be more conscious of the date of newspaper clippings. He was not fussing, just asking her to be more observant in the future. Not much escaped his eagle eye! The editor of the *Lubbock Avalanche-Journal* wrote that although he did not agree with all of Mahon's positions on public issues, he did agree with the American Polit-ical Science Association that Mahon exemplified the best traditions of legis-lative service in discharging one of the most difficult jobs in Congress with quiet distinction, yet maintaining the respect of all his colleagues.[107] This was a well-deserved honor for a man whose work was usually done behind closed doors during hearings, many of which were off the record. If he had wanted publicity, reporters would have been waiting for him at the end of each day, but that was not his style. He went to Washington to serve his district and the nation, not himself.

In November 1963 President Kennedy scheduled a trip to Texas to raise mon-ey for the 1964 election. At this time he also hoped to bring together the conservative and liberal factions of the Democratic Party in Texas. Lyndon Johnson, already in Texas to take care of last-minute arrangements, met the presidential party when it arrived in San Antonio on the afternoon of November 21. George Mahon was in the group, having departed in Air Force One from Andrews Air Force Base that morning with President Kennedy. After the San Antonio festivities he boarded Air Force Two with Vice President Johnson for the brief flight to Houston where Representative Albert Thomas (D-TX) was honored. Later that night he flew to Fort Worth with President Kennedy. He recorded: "I flew with the President last night from Houston, to Fort Worth, arriving at about 11:10 pm. We made the long ride to the Texas Hotel (where I stayed in Room 1310). I had an intimate visit with the President while en route to Fort Worth. He told me what he was going to say about Defense in his Fort Worth speech. He said he was deeply involved in the mil. Budget for the next year—that he wanted to level off def. spending. We talked about the great things which had been done in defense—airlift—conv. Weapons increase, etc. etc. I told him we didn't want to go up with def. spending but not down much either. I will always treasure this visit."[108]

The following morning the group proceeded by plane to Dallas. Mahon was in Air Force Two with Johnson. He wrote, "While flying from Fort Worth to Dallas I sat and talked with LBJ and Lady Bird. LBJ talked about Yarbrough's statements as reported in the press and pointed out he, LBJ, had said nothing. I congratulated LBJ for riding in the car to the plane in Fort Worth, etc. and Lady Bird said she always was kind and LBJ said that he always turned the other cheek. Something real clever was said on a related subject but I cannot recall it now. We had a real rough landing at Love Field and Lady Bird was very indignant. LBJ and I said it was a real bad landing. Larry O'Brien who was in the President's plane said they had a rough landing too. Larry had walked by our car as we were taking off to Dallas in the motorcade—from Love Field to Dallas."[109]

The group went by motorcade through the streets of Dallas to the Trade Mart, where President Kennedy was scheduled to speak at noon. Mahon, Congressman Walter Rogers (D-TX), and presidential aide Larry O'Brien were in the fifth car in the motorcade. Mahon recorded the events as follows:

> I heard the shots fired which killed the President of the United States. We had made a right turn at an intersection and were beginning to turn a curve to the left, near the end of our long tour of the city. There was a tall yellow

brick building on the right from whence the shots appear now to have been fired. . . . The first shot rang out more like a big firecracker, a backfire or a shotgun. There seemed to have been a brief pause and then two more shots. People began to fall and duck and sprawl on the grass in front of the yellow building. When the shooting started I held up my arm and raincoat to protect my head, as tho this would help. I don't know why I did not crouch down in the seat. At that stage I knew that something was wrong because the motorcade had sped up and people were running for cover. . . . There was confusion and then we sped up at a high rate of speed following the cars in front. We stopped momentarily and a press or photo man from the car in front climbed up on the back of our convertible where he was not too safely anchored. . . . We finally got to the mart where the luncheon was to be held and circled into a parking and circle area. We were told by an officer that the President's car was headed for the hospital and we dashed in that direction at a high rate of speed. We turned in to the hospital and stopped at the curb— not too many people were about. . . . Ray Roberts who was ahead of us was at the hospital and he said the President and Connally had been shot. He spoke of Connally being shot through and through and said the President's head had apparently been shot off. I walked up to the car and looked at the thick puddles of blood in the back seat. It was the President's Blue car with a D.C. license. I saw the priest go in to give Kennedy the last rites. My first reaction was when I knew that Kennedy was shot and probably dead that the name of Texas had been badly hurt. I was angry with Dallas and wanted to get government agencies out.[110]

Government agencies in Dallas brought in federal money, which helped the economy.

After the shooting Larry O'Brien seemed to be stunned. He did not respond to questions. If he said anything I do not recall it. I walked with him to the hospital door and returned to my car. Much later when I was inside the hospital I left momentarily to report to the group and the Secret Service had knocked an FBI man down at the door and pinned him to the floor. He tried to rush in the room where Kennedy was and did not show his card. He said "FBI" and pushed forward. . . . Yarbrough went into the hospital. Later Tiger [Olin Earl] Teague and I went into the hospital and talked with Ted Clifton as to the situation and what to do. This was after LBJ had left with some of the

fellows. Carter of LBJ's staff later left in a car with great haste without divulg-
ing where he was going. Soon Mrs. Kennedy, Larry O'Brien and others left
the hospital and Teague and I walked outside the hospital and joined other
Texas members including Sen. Yarbrough. . . . We decided to return to the
airplane and get back to Washington by one of the planes on the trip or commercial. We saw the President's plane roll from the parking apron in a short
while. At that time I did not know that the President's body, LBJ and a few
others were aboard. Secret Service men told us to stand by and probably the
No. 2 plane, the Vice President's plane, would take off for Washington soon.
Yarbrough and I walked to the plane and made arrangements to leave with
our party and several others, secret service men, etc, at once. We had been
told earlier at the hospital that LBJ had left the hospital for security reasons.
Not until we got to the airport did we know that Sarah Hughes had sworn
LBJ in as President of the United States in the aircraft.[111]

Mahon was able to get aboard Air Force Two and at approximately 3:30
p.m. took off for Washington. When airborne he began making notes in a
small brown notebook he had in his pocket. After writing for a few minutes
he noticed that the Secret Service man sitting across from him was crying bitterly. Upon returning to Washington Mahon wrote a narrative from his notes.
Referring to that day's events, he stated, "Initially, the presidential party was
scheduled to proceed to Austin on the evening of November 22 for the Texas
Welcome Dinner honoring President Kennedy, Vice-President Johnson, and
Texas Governor John Connally." According to Mahon's notes, the president
was to have said at the end of his speech, "Finally, I said in Lubbock in 1960,
as I said in every other speech in this state, that if Lyndon Johnson and I were
elected, we would get this country moving again."[112]

President Kennedy's trip to Texas "focused on enhancing the president's
image in Texas and opening up the checkbooks of wealthy contributors in
a pivotal electoral state."[113] It was also an opportunity to bring about a more
harmonious relationship among Texas Democratic leaders. In Texas the
Democratic Party was split. On one side, the conservatives, such as Governor
Connally and George Mahon, followed the old beliefs of their forefathers,
beliefs that emphasized states' rights and downplayed civil rights. Many of the
same beliefs were held by Mahon's constituents, which made it easy for him
to vote with the conservative coalition in Congress. Vice President Johnson,
more of a moderate Democrat, sided with the conservatives in Texas against

liberal Democrats, who were more in tune with northern liberal Democrats. Ralph Yarborough was a liberal Democrat, thus closely attuned to many of President Kennedy's programs. As the Democrats quarreled among themselves, Texas Republicans, who were growing in strength, were pleased because they believed enough liberal ideas would push the conservatives over into the Republican Party. That was exactly what President Kennedy hoped to prevent. He needed as much Democratic support as possible in order to win Texas's twenty-five electoral votes in 1964, especially in light of their razor-thin victory in 1960.

Helen and three of her friends were playing bridge that Friday when the phone rang. It was the maid of one of her friends, Mary Brooks. After talking on the phone for a minute Mary said, "Oh, was he killed?" Initially, Helen thought Mary was referring to her poodle that had gotten out of the house and been hit by a car; however, in the next breath Mary exclaimed, "The president has been shot!" Everyone was stunned. Helen believed that Mahon was supposed to be riding in the second car in the motorcade and fear began to set in. The women listened to the television in one room and the radio in another for about an hour, but nothing was said about any injuries other than to President Kennedy and Governor Connally. They realized that if there were any other casualties, the news would have reached Helen by that time. Helen also knew that all telephone lines in and out of Dallas would be busy and Mahon would have no way to call her. Later that afternoon, someone from the air force called to say that Mahon was on his way back to Washington in the vice president's plane. Someone also called from Andrews Air Force Base to let her know that the plane had landed safely and he was on his way home in an air force car. Mahon arrived at their apartment at approximately eight o'clock that evening. He was pretty badly shaken by all that had happened that day, and they stayed up until two-thirty watching the news on television. Not being able to sleep well, they were up by six the next morning and started watching television again.

Members of Congress were invited to the White House to pay their respects that Saturday afternoon from two-thirty until five, and on Sunday they received the fallen president's body in the Rotunda of the Capitol when it arrived from the White House. The flag-draped coffin remained closed.

Because of the limited capacity of the church, only the one hundred most senior members of Congress were invited to the funeral. Mahon was included among those members, so Helen planned to remain at home on Monday and watch the services on television. When she learned that buses would take wives and other members from the Capitol to Arlington Cemetery, she decided to go. She and Lera Thomas, wife of Albert Thomas (D-TX), were on the first bus to arrive at the cemetery, so they were able to find a place to stand very close to the walkway where the family and dignitaries would be passing. They waited over an hour for the procession to arrive from the church.

Helen wrote home:

> While we were standing there, Mrs. Maxwell Taylor and General Taylor's aide walked up and Mrs. Taylor recognized me and we spoke. She said to Lera Thomas and me, "Just come and go along with us." So we went right up and were in a position where we could see Jacqueline during the whole ceremony and were very close to all the proceedings. I have never seen anybody who had the courage that Jacqueline Kennedy had. Just before they gave her the flag she walked up and stood by Cardinal Cushing for the last benediction. And then when the flag was presented to her, she broke down and cried for a minute and then she regained her composure and took about four steps out toward where she would walk to her car. Then she turned around and walked back and walked up to General Taylor and put her arm around him and kissed him on the cheek and cried violently for just a minute. Since I was with Mrs. Taylor she said, "That is a kiss my Pappy will never forget." It really was one of the most touching and heartbreaking experiences that any of us have ever had.[114]

In the same family letter that was written on Thanksgiving Day, Helen commented, "Washington has not been the same since and you would be surprised at the people who have said over and over, 'What kind of a place is Texas?' I think more than ever this was said after the killing of Oswald, and the people wonder what kind of state we are. . . . We all say, 'Why did it have to happen in Texas?'"[115] That day the owner of Alban Towers sent the Mahons a Thanksgiving dinner, complete with turkey, dressing, gravy, and cranberries. Mr. Rivitz, who had been very upset about the assassination, was also thankful that Mahon had returned safely. That evening they had another turkey dinner with friends who had rallied around to offer comfort and support.

When President Johnson addressed Congress after Kennedy's assassination, he displayed confidence and knowledge. Since 1931, when he served as a congressional aide, he had been at the center of Washington politics. Unlike

Truman after President Roosevelt's death, Johnson sounded like a president. "It was the peculiar fate of Johnson, master of coalition-building on Capitol Hill, to have to deal with forces that were on their way to fragmenting the United States," wrote historian James Patterson.[116] Mahon and Helen attended and were very impressed. They wrote home, "He was sincere. He was magnificent. I hope the country and the people can accept his challenge of getting rid of some of this hate and some of this horrible way that people are thinking today. It has all been just like a nightmare and it is going to take us a long time to get over such shocking things."[117]

A week after the assassination President Johnson appointed an official committee, chaired by Chief Justice Earl Warren, to conduct a thorough investigation of the tragedy in Dallas. Their report attributed the shooting to a single gunman; however, debate about a conspiracy plot continued for the next half-century.

When the House adjourned on December 23, Mahon had voted to expand the role of the federal government 39 percent of the time, and he supported a smaller federal government on 61 percent of the votes. The *Congressional Quarterly* analyzed the vote of 348 roll call votes. After adjournment Mahon flew to Philadelphia with President Johnson to attend a funeral and then on to Austin. They called on Governor Connally at the Governor's Mansion on Christmas Eve before Mahon left to join his family for Christmas. Mahon described Connally as "pretty tired and worn,"[118] which he attributed to the great emotional shock the governor had recently endured as well as his injury. Helen, knowing that Congress would be a beehive of activity at the end of the session, left the second week in December on the train to Colorado City. That would allow time for a much-needed visit with family, and she would be ready to return when Mahon was. They both needed some time to become reconciled to the fact that a shadow of grief had been cast over the brilliance they saw at the beginning of the Kennedy administration.

Chapter 7

The Limits of Power: 1964–1968

W hen President Johnson took office, he pledged to carry out President Kennedy's commitments, which included a civil rights bill, tax cuts, medical care for the elderly, federal aid to education, improvement of the quality of life in the cities, and a poverty program. Many believed that Cold War tensions had been reduced following the Cuban missile crisis in 1962 and the Nuclear Test Ban Treaty in 1963. Now the political upheaval in Vietnam seemed to be the darkest cloud on the horizon following Ngo Dinh Diem's assassination during a military coup in 1963; however, most Americans believed this problem could be settled before it became an international crisis. The economy was strong, and "it was," as Johnson later described it, "almost as if the world had provided a breathing space within which I could concentrate on domestic affairs."[1] Foreign affairs had been President Kennedy's strength, but President Johnson felt more confident focusing on domestic programs, so he saw this as an opportunity to get his legislative programs through Congress. Most of the president's Great Society programs would be problematic for Mahon because many of his constituents were opposed to social-welfare programs. He also knew that increased spending for domestic programs would compete with defense spending, which he considered vital for the nation's security. The coming years would contain many dilemmas for him.

The year started with a whirlwind of activities for Mahon, including a luncheon at the State Department hosted by Secretary of State Dean Rusk, followed by a luncheon two days later at the White House in honor of Lester Pearson, prime minister of Canada. At the end of January, he was the guest of Ned Brooks, moderator of NBC's *Meet the Press*, at the annual Alfalfa Dinner. This was the first time he had ever attended the event. The Alfalfa Club, founded in 1913 to celebrate the birthday of Confederate Civil War General Robert E. Lee, was, and still is, a social organization that exists primarily to hold a banquet at the end of January. It is named for the alfalfa plant that will supposedly do anything to get a drink. At the dinner Mahon visited with George H. W. Bush and retired general Omar Bradley, who was walking with a cane because of a recent knee operation. Mahon described General Bradley as "one of my great favorites."[2]

Because the previous December had been unusually stressful, the Mahons were late giving the office staff their Christmas gifts. At the end of January, they invited everyone to their apartment for dinner and gave each a set of cotton sheets and pillowcases. Although it was their custom to use cotton gifts whenever possible, in a letter home Mahon wrote, "Frankly, our practice has not made much of a dent in the surplus!"[3] The letter ended, "This is election year and we love everybody!"

After an early morning vote in the House on April 9, Mahon boarded a plane for Louisville, Kentucky, to pick up Sargent Shriver, director of the Peace Corps and special assistant to President Johnson for the War on Poverty. They flew on to Lubbock where Shriver addressed a crowd of thirty-two hundred Texas Tech students and later an audience of eight hundred civic leaders. He cited numerous examples of the effectiveness of the Peace Corps abroad and told his listeners that the War on Poverty would produce similar results at home. He said, "On an outlay of 'less than a billion dollars,' the War on Poverty is expected to reach 600,000 persons in the first year."[4] Help would be provided to individuals to get an education and set up small businesses in hopes of producing contributing members of society among people who would otherwise have ended up on relief rolls. Both students and civic leaders were impressed, crowding around him afterward to express interest in his remarks. Shriver and Mahon left Lubbock the next day.

By the end of April, the Department of Defense appropriation bill (H.R. 10939) was reported out of the Appropriations Committee to the House for consideration. The president's defense budget was approved without major changes. Mahon was floor manager for the $46.7 billion bill, and during his opening remarks he said that the president, as the nation's spokesman in international affairs, must be able to negotiate with other nations from a position of military superiority. The current bill would provide adequate funding to maintain that superiority. The Subcommittee for Defense Appropriations recommended approximately $718 million less than the administration requested and $1.5 billion below the previous year's bill. Funding requests had declined because the build-up of Polaris, Atlas, and Titan missiles was complete, and the Minuteman program was nearing completion. Mahon expressed the committee's confidence that the Department of Defense was doing a good job of management, and as a result, a serious military episode, the Cuban missile crisis, had been turned into an advantage for the United States. Management policies instituted by Secretary McNamara proved to be a major factor in holding down costs. In his annual presentation to the House and Senate Armed Services Committees and Defense Appropriations subcommittees, McNamara testified that the Defense Department's cost-reduction program had resulted in estimated savings in the fiscal year 1965 budget of $2.4 billion. He predicted that by fiscal year 1967 the program would result in recurring annual savings of $4 billion. He said, "A major factor in reducing operating costs was closing down unnecessary military bases and installations."[5] He told the House Defense Appropriations Subcommittee that he had reduced the requested total obligational authority by $10 billion without jeopardizing military readiness.

In his floor remarks Mahon beat back Republican criticism that the administration was not developing new strategic weapons and placed too much reliance on missiles. Unlike the manned bomber, these missiles had never been tested in war. Mahon assured the House that piloted aircraft remained an important part of the strategic defense plans and that the current bill provided for the purchase of two thousand aircraft that would strengthen the existing fleet of six hundred bombers. Also, $52 million had been appropriated for research and development of a follow-on manned bomber to replace the B-52.

During the late 1940s and early 1950s inter-service disputes about ground forces versus manned bombers were widespread. By the 1960s, as technology advanced, the disputes centered on manned bombers versus missiles. Air Force Chief of Staff General Curtis LeMay strongly advocated manned bombers. He argued before the House Subcommittee on Defense Appropriations that American superiority over the Soviets was narrowing because of the heavy reliance on missiles, and this would endanger the defense of the country in the future. Secretary McNamara countered that US military strength was actually increasing, and he favored missiles because they were more cost effective. Moreover, defense experts noted that the Soviets were already spending far more on missiles than bombers. When testifying before

Congress on the fiscal year 1965 defense budget, McNamara argued that a distinction should be made between dependability and reliability. Conceding a greater mechanical reliability to bombers, he stated that "a higher proportion of the Minuteman missile force than that of the B-52 bomber force would reach its targets under war conditions, and concluded that the missile force was thus more dependable than bomber force."[6] Meanwhile, Congress got into the picture when the Armed Services Committees and Appropriations Committees in both chambers allocated unrequested funds for bombers, believing that Secretary McNamara was minimizing the strategic role of piloted aircraft in the nation's strategic forces. In the end the secretary had the last word by refusing to allow the extra funds to be spent.

The struggle between the emphasis on high-technology and conventional weapons had also surfaced in the upgrade of warships in the navy. Early in 1963 the navy and the Atomic Energy Commission requested the installation of a nuclear power plant in the Forrestal-class carrier (CVA-67) that had been authorized in fiscal year 1962. In October 1963 Secretary McNamara announced that the carrier would be built with a conventional, oil-burning power plant. He conceded that while nuclear-powered carriers were superior to conventional carriers, navy studies could not prove that the additional cost of $160 million would provide a commensurate increase in defense strength. This was just another budget skirmish in a long line of confrontations that raged within Congress and between Congress and the Department of Defense over the matter of conventional versus high-technology weaponry.

Voting on the defense appropriations bill was barely over in the House when Clarence Cannon, chairman of the House Committee on Appropriations, died of heart failure in a Washington hospital on May 12. In 1917 Cannon was elected House parliamentarian and held that job until he was elected to represent the Ninth Congressional District of Missouri. Only Representative Carl Vinson (D-GA) outranked Cannon in service. Throughout his career he was considered the top parliamentarian in the House, and he wrote *Cannon's Procedure of the House of Representatives*. Many who had watched the Democratic conventions on TV remembered him as the parliamentarian who stood at Sam Rayburn's side, offering advice on precedents that often got Rayburn out of a tight spot. According to legend Rayburn said privately that he did not know where Cannon got all those precedents, but they sure helped keep the convention under control.

For twenty years Cannon had chaired the House Appropriations Committee. Although he had presided over the spending of more money than any person in the history of the US—more than a trillion dollars—he was proudest of the billions he chopped from budget requests. His determination to save the taxpayers' money was often a hard battle, and he fought it hard. At best he was cantankerous, and he had a low boiling point. Several times he took a poke at another member in the heat of an argument over spending.[7] Now the purse strings that Cannon held so tightly had been passed, through seniority, to his right-hand man, George Mahon. The *Houston Chronicle* called Mahon, known throughout Congress for his quiet, behind-the-scenes approach, "Mr. Anonymous."[8] His integrity and hard work were rewarded with prestige from both the Hill and the Pentagon, making it possible to get bipartisan support for the difficult decisions he made on budget cuts. And he did cut! Like Cannon, his passion was to spend the taxpayers' money wisely. On the morning of May 18, Mahon, as acting chairman, called the House Appropriations Committee together and announced that he had appointed Representatives Harry Sheppard of California, Albert Thomas of Texas, and Ben Jensen of Iowa to prepare and present a suitable resolution on the late chairman Cannon. At that time Representative Thomas and Representative Jensen, on behalf of the whole committee, pledged their cooperation to Mahon and wished him a long and successful term as chairman.[9] Mahon told a reporter for the *Lubbock Avalanche-Journal* that he had lost a good and true friend.[10] He was a member of the delegation appointed by Speaker John McCormack to attend Cannon's funeral in Elsberry, Missouri. President Johnson and former president Truman also attended.

Just as no president ever assumed office more prepared than Lyndon Johnson, no person ever assumed the chair of the House Committee on Appropriations more prepared than George Mahon. He had been appointed to the full committee in 1939 and to the War Department subcommittee in 1940. In 1947, when the military services were united under the Department of Defense, Cannon appointed him chair of the Subcommittee for Defense Appropriations. The only other position that he ever aspired to was chair of the full committee, and now that was his. He decided to continue as chair of the subcommittee because so much of his career was wrapped up with its work, and he understood the defense budget better than most people in Washington. Each president appointed a new secretary of defense, thus Mahon's twenty-three years on the subcommittee provided a depth of knowledge greater than any secretary or most congressmen. Many Washington pundits considered the chair of the House Committee on Appropriations the third most powerful position in the House of Representatives, behind speaker and minority leader. With a Texan in the White House, one at the head of the House Appropriations Committee, another—Wright Patman, chair of the House Banking and Currency Committee—and several others occupying the number-two spot on committees, the Texas drawl was heard often about town. This was an advantage for the new president as he could count on the House of Representatives, as a whole, to support him on legislation.

Early on, Mahon made two important changes. He decided to establish a close working relationship with the ranking minority member on the committee. This meant inviting Frank Bow (R-OH) to attend all subcommittee markup sessions and all conference meetings. Representative Cannon had worked closely with John Tabor (R-NY), but he ostracized Tabor's successor, Ben Jensen, which caused a lot of friction. Mahon's action produced greater harmony and reduced partisanship within the full committee, which allowed more integration of the subcommittees.

Mahon was also determined to integrate new members into the workings of the committee as rapidly as possible. Cannon had remained so aloof from these new members that many believed he didn't even know who they were. Mahon established a policy of conferring with them individually. He also asked them to sit in, as nonvoting members, on hearings of the Subcommittee on Defense Appropriations, and whenever possible he improved their subcommittee assignments. Mahon was proud of the change and remarked that "the younger members are happier than they have been in years."[11] The wisdom of this change of attitude would be borne out in future years.

Mahon vowed to work more closely with party leaders. Cannon's cantankerous personality made collegial relations very difficult, and he often had to send Mahon to mend fences in order to obtain favors from the leadership.[12] During Mahon's chairmanship, interaction with party leaders was greatly increased. His efforts to work harmoniously with others actually created a stronger power base than Cannon had acquired through his dictatorial behavior.

However, the strength of the new chairman was soon tested in a power struggle over the foreign-aid bill. For ten years Otto Passman (D-LA), a well-known opponent of foreign aid, had been chairman of the Subcommittee on Foreign Aid Appropriations, and during that time he made cutting foreign aid his stock in trade. Chairman Cannon supported Passman's "meat-axe" approach to cutting, which created a particularly nettlesome situation for Presidents Eisenhower and Kennedy. Fortunately for President Johnson his annual request of $3.5 billion for foreign aid came before the subcommittee after his colleague from Texas had assumed the chairmanship of the full committee. Johnson was asking for $1 billion less than President Kennedy had requested in 1963, and he asked Mahon to help get a bill passed that would not put the United States at a disadvantage when conducting affairs with other countries. A nation must spend on foreign aid if it intends to be effective overseas. Passman made it clear that he did not believe the president's figure of $3.5 billion was a "bare bones" request and led the charge to cut at least $515 million. Addressing the subcommittee, Mahon asked that the cut be scaled back to $200 million, and for the first time during Passman's chairmanship, his own subcommittee rebelled against him. Passman decided to take the fight to the House floor. In Richard Fenno's history of the appropriations committee, he writes: "In this instance, Chairman Mahon reversed the entire pattern of collaboration which had existed under Cannon. He fought against instead of with his subcommittee chairman; he invited leadership assistance in persuading individual members of his Committee to vote for the higher figure rather than the lower aid figure and the Chairman of the Appropriations Committee and the Democratic party leaders (in Congress and, it must be stressed, in the White House) won a spirited battle in subcommittee, in full Committee, and on the floor."[13]

Newspapers across the country carried the story. Most reporters interpreted the events as a "win" for the president because of the support of his colleague, but it was also a victory for Mahon over a particularly headstrong subcommittee chairman. Because of this incident, other subcommittee members became more cautious about challenging the chairman of the full committee. This also marked the beginning of a more cooperative relationship between the House Appropriations Committee and party leaders.

On June 1 Helen and George were on the campus of his alma mater, Hardin-Simmons University in Abilene, where Mahon presented the commencement address and received an honorary doctor of laws degree. He told the 192 graduates that "future problems would be solved by education, not legislation."[14] Touching on the complexity of the civil rights issue, the war in Vietnam, and the president's social programs, he urged the graduates to "assist with leadership that will provide moderation."[15] After the ceremony they went on to Colorado City for a few days of relaxation with family and friends.

⌐⌐⌐

President Johnson wisely got his tax cut bill of $11.5 billion passed in the early part of the session and signed into law on February 26. It proved to be a stimulant to economic growth and helped put people in a better frame of mind when his civil rights legislation came up for a vote.

Just a few hours after the Civil Rights Act of 1964 was passed by Congress, President Johnson signed the bill in the East Room of the White House. At 6:45 p.m. on July 2, the signing was telecast to the nation, and the president pleaded with Americans to close the springs of racial poison. The East Room was filled with members of Congress, cabinet members, and civil rights leaders on hand to witness the ceremony; however, Mahon was in Texas, having left Washington on July 1 for a family vacation in Colorado City.

The most far-reaching legislation since Reconstruction, the bill guaranteed Negroes the right to vote and access to public accommodations such as hotels and restaurants, authorized the federal government to sue in cases of segregation in public schools or public facilities, allowed federal funds to be cut off for programs where discrimination existed, and prohibited discrimination in labor unions or professional business organizations where membership is required to deal in interstate commerce. It authorized the federal government to end discrimination in a broad range of areas from hiring to public accommodations. Although some sections were considered unconstitutional, on December 14 the Supreme Court upheld the most controversial sections, which dealt with public accommodations. Mahon voted against the bill when it was considered in the House, and there is no evidence that President Johnson expressed his displeasure with Mahon's vote, although he is reputed to have made it known that there would be unpleasant consequences for any Democrat who voted against the bill. Johnson had enough votes to ensure its passage in the House, and he understood that voting in favor of civil rights would cause a problem between Mahon and his constituents. Speaking in the House, Mahon said that he was voting against the civil rights bill because "it gives the Federal Government too much power to meddle in the day-to-day lives of American citizens—all American citizens. It threatens basic American freedoms, and, if the pending bill becomes law, I predict that it will rise to plague many of those who support it."[16] These are the very same words used in answering constituent letters about his position on the legislation. Mahon, and the majority of his constituents, objected most to the idea of integrating public accommodations, arguing that this should be determined by local authority not the federal government; however, time had proven that local governments were not going to deal with this situation. If there were any consequences from President Johnson, there is no evidence of it. This is very likely because the president needed Mahon's help more to get appropriations bills passed than he did to get his civil rights bill through the House. Mahon had also voted against civil rights legislation in 1956, 1957, and 1962.

On July 3 Daphne and her family arrived in Colorado City to join her parents, who had arrived the day before. After celebrating July Fourth, Daphne and Duncan returned to Houston, leaving the children with their grandparents. "I think that we had the best visit with the grandchildren we have ever had. We had two weeks. They were wonderful. They rode Sugarbabe [a favorite horse], went fishing, swimming, shot fire works. Betsy made a dress. George shot the 410 [shotgun] to his heart's content,"[17] Mahon wrote in his Green Journal. George Holt was twelve, Betsy was ten, and Laurie was six. Before returning to Washington Mahon had several repairs made on the house that included a new paint job and a new air conditioner.

In September, the 1965 supplemental appropriations bill included $13 million to implement the civil rights act. When the bill was being debated in the House, Southern members raised objections, to which Mahon responded, "Congress has passed certain legislation relating to civil rights and I believe it is to be the duty of Congress to make it possible to carry out the law. . . . I realize the legislation is controversial, but this was approved by the Committee on Appropriations in a nonpartisan way."[18] No reductions were made.

Initially, Mahon labeled President Johnson's antipoverty program too ambitious, and the publisher of the Lubbock newspaper agreed, praising Mahon as being "an unusually level-headed Congressman who speaks the language of the grass roots."[19] However, because this was his first major program since becoming president, Johnson pressed for the support of Democrats from his home state. In August, thirteen voted in favor, and eight opposed the $947.5 million bill. After voting for the bill Mahon contacted a reporter for the

Avalanche-Journal to say, "I am hopeful that the program will succeed, especially in the area of job training and educational assistance to unemployed youth. . . . I decided to vote to give our President a chance to make a new attack on the problem. The President has personally stated to me that he will proceed with great caution and care in working out the details and management of the program. . . . We in Congress will have control of the appropriations, and we will chop off the funds if the program fails to succeed."[20] He described himself as skeptical but not cynical of the program, and he also made a point of telling the reporter that public assistance was already costing more than $4 billion a year, and if the job training could make taxpayers of these people, it would be a good investment.

This was election year, and as convention time approached, President Johnson seemed certain to be the Democratic nominee. When he ruled out the possibility of choosing anyone from his cabinet as a running mate, Hubert Humphrey became the strongest contender for the vice presidential nomination. He was a liberal, which Johnson thought would help the ticket, and he had proven to be very loyal to Johnson. Doris Kearns, President Johnson's biographer, writes, "Humphrey, with his open, ebullient nature and his unswerving loyalty, had great appeal for Johnson."[21] He served the additional purpose of blocking any further talk of Robert Kennedy as a candidate for the office. When President Johnson arrived at the Atlantic City convention with Humphrey, both were given an enthusiastic welcome. Mahon, however, was not enthusiastic about Humphrey's liberal ideas, and mixed in with the files of newsletters he had sent to the district is a piece of scratch paper on which he had penciled the following:

> I often disagree with the views of Senator Humphrey and he would not have been my choice for Vice President. Indeed, there was no man on the horizon who seemed to be an ideal selection for the job. The President knows him better than I do and he picked him as the man who could be most helpful to him in his burdensome responsibilities. The Senator is an honorable man and a man of exceptional ability. He is capable and highly knowledgeable. The reactions of people to the candidates are not predictable. Only as the people learn more of the issues and candidates will they firmly make up their minds.[22]

The 1964 election produced the biggest Democratic victory since 1936.[23] Mahon had an opponent, but he easily won the election with 78 percent of the votes. Blacks voted in unprecedented numbers for the Democratic ticket and in several states provided a margin of victory for Johnson. A major difference between the two political parties was highlighted during the campaign, when Democrats pledged enforcement of the 1964 Civil Rights Act and Republicans pledged execution of the new law. "The 24th Amendment to the Constitution of the United States, outlawing the use of a poll tax as a prerequisite for voting in federal elections, was ratified by the required three-fourths (38) of the states and became a part of the Constitution Jan. 23, 1964. It barred the use of a poll tax for voting in the 1964 Presidential and Congressional elections, as well as all subsequent elections. The amendment was submitted to the states by Congress Aug. 27, 1962. Efforts to outlaw the poll tax, either by statute or constitutional amendment, had been undertaken in most sessions of Congress since the early 1940s. Five times between 1942 and 1949 bills to ban the poll tax by statute were passed by the House but died in the Senate, three times as a result of Southern filibusters. The last Amendment ratified before 1964 was the 23rd, which took effect in 1961. It gave citizens of the District of Columbia the right to vote in Presidential elections."[24]

During the Thanksgiving holidays in November 1964, the Mahons joined Charles and Emma Beth Thompson from Colorado City, Mr. and Mrs. Bob Whipkey from Big Spring, and Charles and Grace Guy from Lubbock for a day at the Johnson ranch. After winning the election by such a landslide, President and Mrs. Johnson were in great spirits to host company. They took their guests on a hunting trip, showed off their prize cattle, took them on a helicopter ride over the ranch, and treated everyone to a boat ride on the Llano River.[25] Knowing that Guy and Whipkey were newspaper publishers, the president commented, from time to time, on potential solutions to domestic and national problems. Undoubtedly, he was using the opportunity to garner West Texas press support and further influence Mahon, who did not always vote in favor of Johnson's Great Society programs. Johnson succeeded in getting a long, favorable column in the *Lubbock Avalanche-Journal*, and apparently a good time was had by all. Publisher Guy commented that seeing the president so relaxed made him hope that Johnson would return often to the ranch.[26]

When the Mahons returned to Washington after Thanksgiving, the pace picked up immediately. The inauguration of Lyndon B. Johnson was a grand occasion for Texas Democrats, and many of them flocked to the capital city to enjoy the festivities. At the end of December, Mahon sent a newsletter to his constituents with suggestions that would make their visit more pleasant. He recommended bringing warm clothing and extended an invitation to all coming from the district to attend a luncheon that he and Helen were giving in the Capitol on the Tuesday before the inauguration. He also welcomed visitors to drop by his office on Inauguration Day for the usual sandwiches and coffee. For the first time in several years, Mahon and Helen spent Christmas in Washington. "As the new Chairman of the Appropriations Committee I felt I needed to get back and prepare for the new session,"[27] he told his journal. Daphne and her family spent their first Christmas in a new home in Houston.

On Monday night, January 11, 1965, Mahon wrote in his journal:

Yesterday was a snowy Sunday. . . . Around 4 or 5 P.M. I sat in the sun room of the apartment working on the oil painting of a lady's face [the previous December Mahon decided to try his hand at painting and purchased a set of oil paints—his mother had also painted]. President LBJ called and talked with me about 30 minutes or more about his budget problems. He was worried about Otto Passman and the Foreign Aid Subcommittee and said that he just could not get the kind of bill he needed with that type of group. He had not understood that I could enlarge the committee. . . . To make a good showing he wanted to bring in a low budget but he did not want to get hurt by this. . . . I talked at length with the President about the farm situation, the bad effect of the 1¢ per pound cut in the support price for cotton and many other matters. We discussed the V.A. office at Lubbock, the proposed federal building at Lubbock and Big Spring and many other subjects. . . . We talked about keeping the budget at $100 million or less and I was encouraged over his apparent determination to bring in a low budget. . . . He said that he didn't have anybody to talk to like he did when Sam Rayburn was alive and that he liked to talk to me about his problems. At long last the President said good bye.

I went back to painting. Shortly the phone rang and it was Lady Bird asking Helen if we would not come by for "Pot luck" supper and we would look at a movie or just sit by the window and talk and watch the snow fall outside.

The snow was accumulating pretty heavily on the ground. I talked on the phone when Lady Bird called. She said for us to come for dinner at about

7:15. I went back to painting for a short time and then Helen called the guard at the Northwest gate of the White House as to where we should appear. The guard said either the northwest or southwest gate. Helen said we did not have snow tires and that we would probably come in a taxi.

Later Lady Bird called and told Helen that a White House car would pick us up at Alban Towers Hotel at 7:05. We dressed and went down to the porte cachere [sic] about 15 minutes early. The White House car was waiting at the curb. He drove into the hotel drive way, we entered the car, met the driver, and started on our way going through the park. The snow continued.[28]

Shortly after the visit Mahon commented in a family letter that he and Helen were the only guests present that evening and he enjoyed the opportunity to suggest to the president how the country should be run, but he didn't provide any details about his suggestions. In the draft of his letter, he wrote—and later omitted before sending—"It has been my experience that it is pretty hard to tell Presidents very much. Too often they insist on doing most of the talking!"[29] As time went on, it became apparent that lavishing attention on the Mahons was President Johnson's method of trying to bring Mahon around to his way of thinking. According to legend, someone asked Mahon if the president ever tried to arm-twist him or use intimidation on him. Mahon is supposed to have replied that he was always Lyndon's friend, but if he had tried to arm-twist him, Mahon would have become an enemy. In 1979 when interviewed by an oral historian from the LBJ Library, Mahon said he had known Lyndon Johnson for many years and believed Johnson wanted to hear the truth from him. When he disagreed with Johnson, he said so. He said that one of the troubles with being president was getting an honest view of what others in the country think because everyone wanted to be a yes-man. Years later, in an answer to a complaining constituent, Mahon wrote, "Some people think you have to be a yes man when you talk with the President, but I think the President respects me for telling him what I consider to be the truth."[30] While he believed in being honest, Mahon was always respectful of the president and helped in every way possible.

Before the inauguration festivities got under way the Mahons attended the dedication of the statue of Sam Rayburn that had been placed in the entrance to the New House Office Building. Lady Bird Johnson dedicated the statue to "all new members of the 89th Congress and all future Congresses in hopes that—like Sam Rayburn—they will labor under the great white dome of the

Capitol with the same faith in the people and the same nobility of purpose."[31] The statue, sculpted by Felix W. de Weldon, was presented by the Texas State Society. During the ceremonies Helen happened to be standing right next to Rayburn's statue when Randolph Routt, photographer for the *Washington Evening Star*, captured the dedicatory scene that was sent throughout the nation.

Mahon received a new congressional office in the Rayburn Building that was far more spacious than his old one. It had a large work room for employees and office files. He also got a parking space close to an entrance that would make it easier to get in and out. "For most of the past 30 years my office has been in the so called New House Office Building which has been named the Longworth Building. For a couple of terms my office was in the Old House Building now known as the Cannon Building."[32]

Moving into a new office on March 1 was the second move Mahon made that year. During the latter part of January he and Helen went apartment hunting. After discovering that the rent was even higher than they thought, one that was closer to his office caught their eye. The drawback was its location on the eleventh floor. "It is terrific. We liked it very much. Of course I do not like to live up high in the building. . . looking out makes me dizzy,"[33] he wrote to Daphne and her family. Looking out also provided a beautiful view of the city. From the balcony they could see the Iwo Jima statue, the Potomac River, the Washington monument, and the Capitol dome. Despite the height they decided to take the apartment, and Mahon told his Green Journal, "On Feb 23 we moved from Alban Towers Hotel where we had lived for 27 years to Prospect House, 1200 North Ash, Arlington, Virginia. So we have been citizens of the State of Virginia for a few days. The 2 bed room apartment on the 11th floor rents for $325 per month. Add on $30 more for garage space for two cars. This place is by all odds the loveliest place we have ever lived. We were paying $190 per month at Albany Towers but the new place is worth the money."[34]

Another advantage was the two phone lines they had installed in order to have an unlisted number.

On a cold, sunny day the thirty-sixth president of the United States promised to lead the nation toward a Great Society. In an atmosphere of informality symbolizing that he was a man of the people, Lyndon Johnson wore a gray business suit that was not new and a gray felt fedora, instead of the traditional cutaway coat, striped trousers, and silk top hat. He placed his hand on his mother's Bible as he repeated the oath of office. After hosting their usual "office party" for many more constituents than usual, the Mahons attended one of the inaugural balls at the Sheraton Park Hotel. The crowd was so large that the ballroom was uncomfortably hot, so they returned home early to watch the arrival of President and Mrs. Johnson on TV. To Daphne, Mahon described the inauguration as "a great success. Everybody from home seemed to enjoy himself. Mother and I went all out as we always do and as we love to do."[35] However, he told a reporter for the *Lubbock Avalanche-Journal* that the excitement of the inauguration was "hard on the bones."[36]

The following day it was back to work, and Mahon attended a meeting at the White House that included all committee chairmen of the House of Representatives. He was concerned about the president's heavy responsibilities because the situation in Vietnam was growing more critical. The number of United States forces was increasing steadily, and it appeared that the point of no return was drawing closer and closer. The president seemed to be the only chipper one at the meeting—everyone else was worn out. However, exhaustion soon got the upper hand when both the president and Lady Bird entered the hospital to rest and get over their colds.

President Johnson sent his budget message to Congress on January 25, and Mahon received permission to address the House in response. He remarked that "it manifests a determination by the President to deliver what he has promised the country. I personally know that the President and his associates have labored mightily to hold spending at the lowest acceptable levels in many areas of government."[37]

He further praised the president because his $99.7 billion budget was the smallest percentage of GNP in the past fifteen years. In 1965 the budget, including military construction, family housing, and civil defense, but excluding military foreign assistance and space, was 7.1 percent of GNP.[38] He also called attention to the fact that between fiscal year 1954 (just after the Korean War ended) and fiscal year 1961, defense spending increased 1 percent and nondefense spending increased 65 percent; however, the arms buildup between fiscal year 1961 and fiscal year 1965 brought defense spending more in line with nondefense spending. With the completion of the arms buildup, defense spending was expected to taper off, but domestic programs seemed destined to increase, as well as the overall budget.

With the budget officially in hand, the first meeting of the appropriations committee was scheduled for the following day. Nine new Democrats had been assigned to the committee, making a total of thirty-four Democrats and sixteen Republicans. This gave the Democrats a larger-than-usual majority. For the first time since taking over as chairman, Mahon was faced with the task of making subcommittee assignments. Giving the task his usual careful attention, Mahon discovered that figuring out an appropriate assignment for everyone was somewhat difficult. He wrote Daphne, "The problem is trying but rather interesting."[39]

One thing was certain, however. The Foreign Aid Subcommittee would be different. He was determined not to have a repeat performance of the previous year's power struggle with Representative Otto Passman, and he knew this could be avoided by using subcommittee assignments to build in a majority of members who favored foreign aid. First Mahon reduced the size of the subcommittee from eleven to nine members. Two members who supported cuts to foreign-aid appropriations were assigned to other subcommittees, and Representative Gerald Ford (R-MI) resigned from the subcommittee when be became House minority leader. The three newcomers supported foreign aid, as did three returning members. Two additional members were assigned who supported Passman's cuts, and Passman continued as chair. This combination provided a six-to-three majority in favor of foreign aid. Mahon considered this ratio adequate to provide a spirited debate without guaranteeing difficulty for Johnson's foreign policy.

When all assignments were complete, the full committee settled down to business, and Chairman Mahon announced that he hoped to have all appropriation bills through the House by the time the new fiscal year began on July 1. The committee was also briefed, behind closed doors, by Budget Director Kermit Gordon and Secretary of the Treasury Douglas Dillon. They brought the members up to date on the economic and fiscal condition of the nation; then subcommittee members went their separate ways to begin hearings and to scrutinize their portion of the president's budget.

The first appropriation bill to clear the House that year provided funding for the Commodity Credit Corporation, and the president's first legislative test ran into some opposition in the House when it tried to ban all Food for Peace aid to Egypt. The ban was a rider on the bill that would provide supplemental appropriations of $1.6 billion to the Commodity Credit Corporation for continued price supports through June. The CCC sold surplus commodities abroad for foreign currency that was then spent in that country. Nasser had been making public remarks about the United States taking its aid and jumping in the lake. Many congressmen were enraged, and Robert H. Michel (R-IL) attached a rider to the bill, prohibiting the use of the newly appropriated funds to purchase any commodities that would be sold to Egypt. Mahon was floor manager of the bill in the House, and he argued against a negative vote on the grounds that a bill for farm price supports was no place to write foreign policy. The issue at hand was farm price supports, not approval or disapproval of Nasser. He believed the ban against Egypt would only hurt Israel in the long run and also play into the hands of communists, who were always willing to help Egypt in order to make the United States look bad. Additionally, the ban was an affront to the president, who had so recently been elected by a large majority. His efforts were to no avail as seventy-six Democrats joined ranks with the solid block of Republicans to approve the rider.[40] Diligent lobbying in the Senate, by the administration, worked in the president's favor, and the decision to ban food to Egypt remained his to make.

Mahon came under fire in the district for his vote against the rider and the food ban. Sentiment among constituents was overwhelmingly in favor of the ban. They believed that denying food to Egypt would teach Nasser to respect the United States. This was interesting because the food was to be taken from the Commodity Credit Corporation warehouses, where surplus crops from West Texas and the rest of the nation were stored against loans to farmers so they would not have to accept low prices on a glutted market. If surpluses became so large that payments to farmers had to be reduced, it was likely those same West Texas farmers would also learn a lesson—one they didn't like.

Mahon wrote in a family letter:

The President, the Secretary of Agriculture, and others seemed most grateful to me for my successful handling of the Commodity Credit Corporation appropriation bill which contained the riders. You probably read something about the bill in the papers—the first major bill to pass Congress this year. I was the author of the measure in the House. My days are all pretty rugged but many of them are very interesting indeed. To be in the midst of great happenings is quite a privilege, a responsibility and a worry.

Also last week I was invited to the White House with leaders of the House and Senate to discuss the Viet Nam situation. The whole matter is most discouraging and disturbing.

. . . There is a lot of unrest and uncertainty among farmers and I have been requested to come to the Lubbock area and listen to a report from farmers and give a report on the Washington situation.[41]

To show his appreciation for Mahon's efforts, President Johnson invited Helen and George to remain for dinner after a congressional reception at the White House. Vice President and Mrs. Humphrey were among the small group of guests. The president asked Mahon to say the blessing, and being mindful of complaints about long-winded blessings, Mahon limited his words. In a later letter to Daphne and Duncan, he wrote, "The President complained that it was too short!"[42] Johnson also sent an autographed book and an ashtray as a small remembrance for Daphne and Duncan.

On May 4 President Johnson called 150 congressional leaders to the White House to ask for their support of the supplemental defense appropriation request he was sending to Congress. He made it clear that the $700 million request was in no way a routine appropriation, and he would interpret their vote on this request as a vote of confidence concerning the way he was handling the attempt to halt communist aggression. On May 5, Mahon authored the bill that the House Appropriations Committee cleared that morning, and the House waived the three-day waiting period required for most appropriation measures. When introducing the bill in the House, Mahon said:

> I am proud of the fact that when the occasion demands, the House can and does act fast. There is a requirement for action today with respect to the international situation. . . . By the transfer of funds within the frame work of existing law, the President could have met this emergency without the action we will take today. . . . Certainly he could have coped with the situation for a considerable time, but the President asked us to counsel with him and work with him, as members of the team, in dealing with this matter. . . . We have had team work not only with the White House but within the House. The Armed Services Committee waived the requirement for authorization and the Appropriations Committee unanimously approved the request. . . . I do not believe this action to be necessary to show that Congress is behind the President in his determination to follow a firm policy in dealing with Communist aggression. The President and the country already know it. This will simply affirm our position established on August 10, 1964, when Congress passed a resolution placing itself squarely on record in favor of a firm policy in Southeast Asia. By providing these funds and participating in this action we shall set a good example of democracy at work.[43]

The bill passed 408-7, with 18 not voting. President Johnson invited Mahon and Senator Carl Hayden (D-AZ) to the White House for the signing ceremony and gave each of them a pen that had been used to sign the bill. After the ceremony the president told Mahon he had read Mahon's speech on the House floor and was very pleased with it. Before the first session of the Eighty-nineth Congress was over, there would be another supplemental request for $1.7 billion to cover increased activities in Vietnam. The increased cost of escalation was not included in the original budget presented earlier in the year because the amount might have hindered passage of Great Society programs. Covering the expense of a war in Southeast Asia with supplemental appropriations became a pattern that Johnson often followed in an effort to pay for the war because the public was less likely to be aware of these expenditures if they were presented piecemeal. He knew that congressional or public debate on the cost of the conflict would mean the beginning of the end of Great Society programs. He also knew that he could very likely count on Mahon to guide his requests for defense appropriations through the House in such a manner that they could survive in the Conference Committee should the Senate decide to balk at the costs. Mahon was a longtime Cold Warrior who thought survival of the nation was first and liberal domestic programs should come later.

President Johnson made a concerted effort to discuss his proposed legislation with leading congressmen and senators before sending it to the Hill. He often told the story about how chagrined Speaker Rayburn had been when President Roosevelt sent some controversial legislation to the Hill without giving Rayburn any forewarning. During the debate in the House, members complained vociferously about the legislation, and he tried to buy time by telling them everyone would just have to think the matter over. When the day's session ended, Rayburn told Representative Lyndon Johnson that if the president had just let him know this controversial legislation was coming, he could have built a base of support and avoided much of the anger members were feeling. Johnson said he never forgot this incident and always tried to get a buy-in from as many congressional leaders as possible before sending legislation to the Hill.[44] In a 1972 interview Mahon told Joe Frantz, who at that time was conducting interviews for the Johnson Oral History Project, that "Johnson was a professional of the highest quality when it came to dealing with the Hill, with Congress."[45]

The Department of Defense Appropriation Bill for fiscal year 1966, authored by Mahon, was brought to the House floor for debate on June 23, before the end of the fiscal year, as he had planned. The $45 billion bill had been reduced by $60.6 million from the initial budget request. This was $2.5 billion less than appropriated the previous year. For the Defense Department's requests the Subcommittee on Defense Department Appropriations provided funds for the six nuclear-attack submarines initially requested by the Joint Chiefs of Staff, instead of the four requested by Secretary McNamara, and it provided $57 million more than requested to enable the Army National Guard and Reserve programs to be carried on as separate programs for one more year, despite McNamara's request to consolidate them. Also, $20 million more than requested was appropriated to purchase long-lead-time items for a nuclear-powered frigate that was to begin construction the following year. Mahon commented on the House floor that "it seems Congress is again put in a position of leading the way toward encouraging an increase in a nuclear Navy. I also feel there is too much stress by the Secretary of Defense on the initial cost rather than the long-term cost and effectiveness of a weapons system."[46] After four hours of debate, it was approved and sent to the Senate.

Daphne, Duncan, and the grandchildren visited her parents that summer. Everyone enjoyed a short trip to Ocean City, Maryland, over the July Fourth weekend, and when it was time to leave Washington, George Holt, their oldest child, asked to remain with his grandparents for several weeks. He wanted to help with the work in Mahon's congressional office. Of course, the grandparents were happy to have him stay, and Mahon paid him $1.50 a day with board. In a letter home Mahon wrote, "You would think that he is the most important man at the Capitol. We think he can learn a lot, and he can really help show people round, run errands and do things generally."[47] It turned out that there were some pretty exciting things to do besides work in the office. Mahon took his grandson to the Pentagon to see air force officials pin wings on the Gemini astronauts Jim McDivitt and Edward White, who had recently orbited the earth sixty times. They got autographs from the astronauts, their wives, and several congressmen who were on hand for the ceremony. Later they were photographed with the astronauts.[48] Before George Holt returned to Houston, Helen took him to New York to see the World's Fair. She and Mahon had already been there and decided it would be a great experience for their grandson.

Finally it was time to return home, and Mahon wrote in his journal, "Yesterday, Friday the 13th [August] Helen and I drove George Mahon Holt out to Dulles airport to catch the 8:45 a.m. whisper jet flight to Houston. George was obviously a little worried about the first flight alone, and he was concerned about Friday the thirteenth.

"We called him last night and he reported a wonderful flight. . . . George spent more than a month with us. It was a great occasion for us and for George. He matured a great deal. He worked at the office and did innumerable errands for us. . . . I bought George a book, similar book to this [Mahon's Green Journal], encouraged him to write about his adventures in Washington during the summer of 1965."[49]

In addition to the ongoing problem of Vietnam, Americans were worried about the nuclear device being developed by the People's Republic of China. Military experts predicted it would take at least ten years before China became a nuclear threat to the world, but this did not allay the fears of most people. Ten years seemed like a very short time. However, one piece of news sounded good to Americans. Nikita Khrushchev's peaceful removal from power contrasted sharply with the usual violence that accompanies a power transition in totalitarian countries. Despite uncertainty about the direction that the new leaders, Leonid Brezhnev and Alexei Kosygin, would pursue, many saw the transition as a good omen.

Because of his many years in Congress, President Johnson had an unusually keen insight about dealing with the legislative branch, an insight that his predecessor had sometimes lacked. He seemed to know when his role as president should be muted, so as not to offend, and to know when a strong presidential voice and strategy were called for. Thus, by the time the first session of the eighty-ninth Congress adjourned at the end of October, he had been successful in getting a large amount of substantive legislation passed. The president and his White House legislative aides developed a close rapport with Democratic members of Congress by staying in touch with them and offering small favors along the way. Johnson's knowledge of the legislative process, plus a gain of thirty-eight seats in the House from the 1964 election, made 1965 a very productive year for him. Many of the new Democrats were Northern liberals; thus, the old conservative coalition of Southern conservative Democrats and Republicans could not easily form to thwart the president's programs. The new legislation was dominated by domestic programs, many of which Mahon voted against. He voted against medical care for the elderly under Social Security, establishing a cabinet-level Department of Housing and Urban Development, and aid to elementary and secondary education that would provide money for books and library material. He also voted against repealing the right-to-work laws of the Taft-Hartley Act, against liberalization of immigration laws, against Medicare, and against the farm bill. All of the bills were passed by Congress, except repeal of the right-to-work laws of the Taft-Hartley Act, which was defeated in the Senate.[50] In a newsletter he told constituents he had voted against all of the president's welfare legislation. Correspondence from his constituents was heavily in favor of the way he voted; however, one did take him to task. A professor from Texas Tech University wrote, "I do forgive a good man his mistakes—but for those mentioned here I hope you will ask the Lord's forgiveness also—and try in the future to see how badly you betrayed the (for one year of his life) sincere efforts of our President to help those of our people who really need it."[51] A woman from Chicago wrote, "It is indeed good to know that there are men in Congress—and the President's own party—who are not 'afraid' of him and who have the interests of the country ahead of political gain. We have viewed with dismay the dictatorial mandates of Mr. Johnson, and the absolute subservience of the Congress."[52] In July when the Voting Rights Bill was before the House, Mahon wrote to his family, "I would like to vote for it, but the bill goes so far I cannot do so. I find myself voting against the GREAT SOCIETY most of the time. I go along with the party whenever I can, but I cannot always do so. I think our administration is seeking to go too far too fast."[53]

By the end of the session, US involvement in Vietnam had increased enormously. After an attack on an American base in February 1965, Johnson ordered US planes to begin bombing North Vietnam, and by March the Marines were engaged in combat there. American involvement had changed from that of advisor to combatant. At the end of 1963, there were seventeen thousand military advisors in Vietnam: by the end of 1965 "nearly 200,000 U.S. Military personnel were engaged in Vietnam and the buildup was not completed."[54]

In September the Mahons attended a dinner at the Vietnamese embassy, and the next day General Westmoreland, commander of US forces in Vietnam, came by Mahon's office for a visit. "I expressed my unhappiness about our seeming inability to bring the war to a satisfactory conclusion. He remonstrated that the situation was much improved but I pointed out that he had said this years—two years ago and last year and that under the circumstances he might very well say the same thing a year or five years from now. It is a frustrating and disturbing situation," Mahon wrote home.[55] He believed the war should have been waged more aggressively in order to end it. When interviewed in 1980, he recalled, "My personal feeling was that the war should have been won after a decision had been made for the United States to enter the conflict."[56] However, in that same interview he admitted that bombing North Vietnam into oblivion would have brought the Chinese into the conflict, "and besides that, if we had gone in and bombed them back to the Stone Age, where would we have been then? Would we be over there having to police them and establish a government and so forth? Wars don't always settle things as decisively as we would like for them to."[57]

After a beautiful Indian summer day on the golf course, Mahon told his Green Journal, "Today I probably shot my final round of golf for the year. Had a 79 at B.T. [Burning Tree Country Club] playing a twosome with Mel Laird [R-WI]. I learned that if I do not use my arms or hands at all until the back swing is well underway and turn my hips good and try to come into the ball with a close-in right elbow I hit the woods wonderfully. I must try not to kill the ball. This is one of the great golf lessons of 1965 for me and could mean a lot."[58] Early in November he and Helen returned to the district to begin making the rounds to talk with constituents.

On December 4 Mahon addressed the West Texas–New Mexico Civil Defense Council Conference in Big Spring, Texas. He used this opportunity to announce that during the next session of Congress, all requests for new money would be screened very carefully in order to eliminate all unnecessary or marginal spending. He said, "A policy of fiscal caution is important from the standpoint of the war effort and from the standpoint of the threat of inflation."[59] He intended to look at all programs, domestic and defense, to determine where spending could be reduced. He went on to say that he fully supported the president's position in Vietnam and repeatedly mentioned that domestic programs would have to be cut to meet rising defense expenditures. A copy of his speech was sent to the president and to the UPI wire service. It was picked up by several major newspapers.

The Mahon and Holt families spent the Christmas holidays together in Colorado City. It was a poignant time for them because Mitchell County would no longer be in the Nineteenth District, making this very likely the last Christmas they would spend there. Redistricting changes were to become effective the following year. The people renting their house planned to be gone for the holidays and offered them the use of their space, so the family had the whole house to enjoy. Mahon brought in armloads of wood and had a great fire in the fireplace when Daphne arrived with her family. They all enjoyed Christmas Eve dinner with Helen's sister.

Mahon thought the cotton crop on his farm to be the best in his lifetime and was excited about showing it to the Holts. On the way out to the farm he let grandson George drive. He was soon to be fourteen and was so anxious to learn to drive. Mahon picked up some sand and cement in town and early on New Year's Eve day the whole family helped to mix it into a block about two feet square. They added red coloring before Mahon wrote, "Christmas 1965" and "Some write their names in water, some in sand but the Mahons and the Holts write their names in concrete." Then each person scribbled his, or her, name in the concrete. They thought it would be fun to see how long the red block remained in the backyard where they left it.

Before leaving, they gave their 1962 Pontiac station wagon to Daphne and Duncan to use as a second car. Then they boarded the train back to Washington.[60] When they got to Weatherford, Texas, they had a layover. George's sister Cary and her husband picked them up and took them to their house for a steak dinner topped off with pecan pie. "I was reminded of the Prodigal Son and the fatted calf. We had to hurry a bit through the meal in order to catch our train but we made it without mishap."[61] They arrived in Washington on New Year's Day.

On the day that Congress opened in 1966 Helen dropped Mahon off at the church where the president and Congress attended a communion service. Afterward he rode to the Capitol with a congressman from Michigan whose new car was "so comfortable to me with my hat on, and it was so sturdy and attractive and unostentatious I asked what make it was. It was a Chrysler. We ordered one and we should have it within the next two or three weeks. Dark green, and not a station wagon. A few gadgets but not many. We like the simple lines and the absence of showiness. And we didn't like the name <u>Wildcat</u> on the Buick anyway! It's a New Yorker but it's not a big bus like it used to be,"[62] he wrote to Daphne.

"Last Sunday afternoon, January 9, 1966, just after I returned from playing golf the President called and asked us to be at the White House at 7 p.m. for dinner,"[63] Mahon wrote in his Green Journal. Others guests included Texas congressmen Jake Pickle and Jack Brooks and their wives, daughter Luci, Pat Nugent, and Marvin Watson.[64] Mahon wrote that the president was great about giving gifts to people. In fact he gave so many that "giving gifts seems to be a phobia with him."[65] It was almost embarrassing.

> On this particular occasion the President was wearing a red turtle neck sweater. . . . Near the end of the evening I commented favorably on the sweater. He said, "would you like one." I said I certainly would and he went into the next room and soon brought me a couple, one short and one long sleeve. They were light weight and apparently of a synthetic. He had asked me for a color preference and I specified red! Prior to this time on the same evening he had given us men an LBJ Ranch ash tray, a big medallion of his inauguration in 1965 and an exceptionally clever pocket knife. In the course of the conversation during the evening the President talked of his forth coming State of the Union message and asked me what I thought of the Viet Nam section. He spoke of leaks in the State Department but he spoke highly of Secretary Dean Rusk and Gardner, the new Secretary of H.E.W.[66]

Presidents give gifts, but this is usually a routine function handled by the staff. Not so for Lyndon Johnson. In fact, during Johnson's administration the budget for personal gifts was larger than it had ever been before, and he personally took charge of passing them out. He gave what he wanted each person to have, and it didn't matter if the gift was something they wanted or not. During this visit he also gave Mahon an ashtray although he did not smoke. He often gave someone the same gift on numerous occasions.[67] Fortunately, Mahon made no reference to receiving additional red sweaters during his White House visits.

The president's State of the Union address was a very somber one that stressed numerous times the importance of halting communist aggression in Vietnam. The overriding issue of the year became "guns versus butter." Hard choices had to be made between increasing the war efforts and funding the social programs that were part of President Johnson's Great Society. Most members of Congress supported the war effort, but there were differing opinions about how much "butter" the country could afford. The Democrats had suffered above-average losses at the polls in November 1966, thus reducing the number of members who would naturally be inclined to support domestic programs. Adding to the president's woes were conservative Democrats, who often voted with Republicans to defeat social measures, known as the conservative coalition. This group was responsible for outright defeats on civil rights; repeal of Section 14(b) of the Taft-Hartley Act, which authorized state "right to work" laws; and home rule for the District of Columbia. Mahon often voted with the conservative coalition, but his strong support of military appropriations spared him becoming a target of the president's ire. Constituents from the Nineteenth District largely opposed social programs; thus Mahon's votes reflected their wishes.

Mahon decided to begin having a Saturday swim in the pool in the Rayburn Building where the lifeguard was teaching him to exhale under water and to inhale on the surface while gliding along. With snow on the ground, golf was not an option for exercise. His weight was 171 pounds, and he wanted to keep it there. Because of the demands of work, his swimming was erratic, but he started again in June and wrote to Betsy, who was away at summer camp, "I feel very inferior when some of my colleagues go swishing by me when I am swimming with all my might and they pass me up like a rabbit would pass a tortoise."[68] He also wrote that he was sure some of them thought he was an "old odd ball" because he wore a cap to keep his hair dry while swimming, which saved the time it took to dry it again. Then he wrote something revealing, "Of course, I am not embarrassed by this. Embarrass not a word in my vocabulary, as you know, nor in yours, unless I do something that is really stupid or wrong."[69] George Mahon was quite comfortable with his practical, small-town ways, despite the more urbane behavior of many around him, and he encouraged his grandchildren to follow his example.

In February he wrote to Daphne that he had been to the White House "to confer on Vietnam, food for India, the new set-up in HEW, foreign aid legislative changes and once for dinner with Helen. Poor LBJ has an impossible job and so do we all. Did you see the picture in *Time* this week, "Mahon, Mansfield and Fulbright?" I thought it was pretty good until I saw written below the picture, The Peaceniks! Of course, I'm for peace but not in the boat with Mansfield and Fulbright."[70] Both Mansfield and Fulbright spoke out publicly about their opposition to the Vietnam War. Mahon was a Cold Warrior, who supported a strong defense and fighting when the president believed it was necessary. He would never have spoken out publicly against President Johnson on this matter. He continued, "My speech on the budget has been widely quoted. We had the Secretary of the Treasury and the Director of the Bureau of the Budget before our 50-member Appropriations Committee last Monday. We had McNamara two days last week and Admiral Rayburn of CIA two days the previous week. McNamara was supposed to present his new defense budget to us tomorrow."[71]

President Johnson presented a budget of $112.8 billion for fiscal year 1967. This was the first $100-billion-plus budget in the history of the nation. It included $58.3 billion for defense and cited rising expenditures of $5.8 billion for Vietnam. When the president's budget message was presented to Congress, it was Mahon's duty to respond to it. He first noted the small number of members present to hear the message, which indicated "something less than a consuming interest,"[72] despite the importance of the nation's money matters. Mahon went on to declare that the American people want peace in Vietnam and they want domestic expenditures to take a backseat until peace is achieved. He praised the president for showing restraint by limiting the deficit for fiscal year 1967 to $1.8 billion, compared to $6.4 billion in fiscal year 1966. He didn't say so then, but the current deficit was destined to increase as supplemental appropriation bills were passed to fund the war.

Mahon also spoke of the budgetary priorities from his point of view. Defense was first and foremost. It was followed by interest on the national debt and care for veterans through the Veterans Administration. The fourth priority was the agricultural program. He consistently opposed aid for urbanites, whose conditions were often as unfavorable as the rural constituency he represented. By 1970, 26.4 percent of Americans lived in a rural environment, and 73.6 percent were urban. He admonished the House to draw a sharp distinction between needs and wants. He did admit that not all members would have the same definition of needs and wants, but the debate caused by this would be healthy. He closed by saying, "As a great legislative body with independent responsibilities and full and unfettered power over public money, I would hope we would do everything feasible to follow the course of fiscal caution and do nothing to shunt us from it."[73] His policy statement of the previous December, which he made public in Big Spring, Texas, was repeated on the House floor. Money for defense was the top priority, and domestic social programs should be curbed.

On a Sunday evening in late February, Helen and Mahon joined a small group at the White House that included Vice President and Mrs. Humphrey; Senators Symington, Bayh, and Monrony and their wives; and Jake Pickle with his wife. After supper the president invited the men into the Oval Office because he needed someone to talk to. Mahon wrote in his Green Journal, "The President was all steamed up, talking incessantly."[74] He was upset about Senator Robert Kennedy's statements that the Viet Cong were an active force in the South Vietnamese government. "He has a deep distaste for Bobby. He spoke of how he campaigned for Bobby in the New York election, how Bobby had help[ed] mess up the Bay of Pigs situation,"[75] Mahon told his Green Journal. President Johnson located some secret papers in the Oval Office to prove that President Kennedy and his brother had proposed a US takeover, if necessary, in the Dominican Republic, and now Robert Kennedy was not supporting the president on this policy. The president also complained about the Fulbright hearings and "produced FBI reports showing that foreign ambassadors were sending back unfavorable messages as to Fulbright and probably Morse."[76] Senator Fulbright initially supported the war in Vietnam but over time had come to believe it was undermining the credibility of the United States with third-world countries whose support the United States was hoping to gain. When Fulbright turned against the war and decided to have the Senate Foreign Relations Committee conduct televised hearings about the validity of the war, Johnson became quite angry. These hearings fueled the protests that were taking place. He was also angry because Fulbright, a staunch segregationist, voted against all of Johnson's civil-rights bills. Diatribes of this sort were fairly common in private gatherings, especially as the situation in Vietnam worsened. President Johnson often saw conspiracies wherever disagreement existed, and he did not hesitate to vent his anger against the "traitors."[77]

Vice President Humphrey, who had just returned from a trip to Southeast Asia, fell asleep during most of the conversation. Finally, about midnight Mrs. Johnson "came to the door and told the President that the girls wanted to go home."[78] Mahon wrote, "The President has to let off steam at times and has to trust a few people. I am convinced that there is a loneliness about the Presidency. I would not, of course, repeat the things said by the President and I only write this down with the thought that it might interest me in future years."[79]

Mahon also wrote in his Green Journal in early March that he attended a White House reception for members of Congress, and for the first time committee chairmen and ranking minority members were invited to arrive early, park in front, and enter through the front door. In another entry Mahon noted that he had been invited to the White House more in 1966 than any other year, sometimes going as often as twice a week. These visits might be to discuss policies or problems, to attend briefings, to provide a listening post for the president, or to attend a state dinner such as the one honoring the prime minister of India that month. All this served to encourage Mahon to support the president's programs as much as possible. With the exception of defense programs, what was possible was a very small amount indeed. Mahon's lack of support of Johnson's programs was kept pretty low key, except back in the district, where his constituents were in agreement with his votes.

On March 10 President Johnson met with all House committee chairmen from 5:00 to 8:15 p.m. to review their work thus far in the session. Most of the conversation was about Vietnam—past, present, and future aspects. He also expressed satisfaction with the tax bill. Mahon took Wayne Aspinall (D-CO), chairman of the House Interior and Insular Affairs Committee, to the meeting. A bill was before that committee to establish the Guadalupe Mountains National Park, and Mahon asked Johnson how important it was to hold the line on appropriations. Creating a national park, even one in Texas, fell within Mahon's concept of expenditures that could wait until the war was over, and he wanted Aspinall to hear what the president had to say on the matter. Mahon did not record the president's answer in his journal, but on October 16, 1966, President Johnson signed the act establishing the park. However, the park was not actually created until 1972.

In February Mahon wrote to his family:

There has been a lot in the paper about the CIA subsidy for the student organization which has many contacts overseas. As a top man in the House of
Representatives in CIA money matters, I was not taken by surprise by this
revelation. I thought the program was a good one, but I will not undertake to
explain the details in this letter. This was one of the ways of countering communism at youth festivals in various parts of the world. A *Time* magazine
man called me yesterday and asked me if I did not feel the CIA was perfectly
awful and I told him that I didn't. We had the Director of the CIA before the
Appropriations Committee for two days this week. We always have a briefing
on world conditions prior to the time we listen to the military witnesses.
Secretary McNamara and company will appear before us beginning Monday.
The pressures of the session are beginning to mount.[80]

On September 8 Mahon wrote in his journal:

Last night we turned the apartment telephone off as usual. The unlisted line
runs to the kitchen only. It developed that during the night the White House
had tried to locate us. This morning we left the apartment at about 7:20 to go
to National airport to see Secretary Orville Freeman [Secretary of Agricul-
ture] off to Lubbock and Plainview. While waiting for Orville I was paged at
the American Airlines counter. I was asked to be at the White House at 8:45
for breakfast. I said I could make it. We sat at breakfast with the President
for 2 hours. He read the message he had prepared to send to Congress at 3
p.m. recommending the repeal of the 7% Investment Credit. In the message
he discussed revenue and appropriation. He asked for suggestions as to the
message. He accepted several changes including one of mine. It was a small
breakfast. At the President's right was Speaker McCormack, then Mahon,
Postmaster General Larry O'Brien, Joe Califano, Asst. to the President, Wilbur Mills, Chairman of Ways and Means and Acting Majority Leader Hale
Boggs (Carl Albert was in the hospital recovering from a heart attack).[81]

On December 14 the Mahons returned to Washington from Lubbock and
their annual tour of the district. Following a heavy blizzard on Christmas Eve,

they left Washington on Christmas Day to spend ten days in Puerto Rico. It was still snowing when they took off, and they were uneasy about flying in those conditions. However, once in the air their flight of just over three hours was delightful. Mahon did not bring along any work, as he hoped to make this his first real vacation in many years.

Puerto Rico had become increasingly important as a winter resort for vacationers after Castro came to power in Cuba. The temperature ranged from sixty-five to seventy degrees, and the barracks on Ramey Air Force Base, where they stayed for six days, didn't need any heat. In fact, it did not even have glass windows—just metal hurricane shutters. Ramey was a B-52 base, where quarters on the base cost eight dollars per day, plus the cost of meals at the officers' club. This was far more economical than a hotel room in San Juan, which would have cost twenty-one dollars a day for the four days they spent on the island. Although they were able to stay on the base because Mahon was a member of Congress, the seven-hundred-dollar cost of the trip was their own expense. Mahon tried to leave work behind but just couldn't resist meeting with some of the navy and air force people and touring an agricultural experiment station. Possibly these meetings gave his stay on the base more of an appearance of official business. Secretary of the Air Force Harold Brown and Deputy Secretary of Defense Cyrus Vance were also staying on the base, as was Carl Albert, majority leader of the House, who was recuperating from a heart attack. He and Helen declined an invitation to a New Year's Eve party, but Mahon played a lot of golf, with Helen driving the golf cart, and he also read Homer's *Odyssey*. People on the island were US citizens, and many wanted it to become the fifty-first state. However, Mahon did not believe this would happen for a long time.[82]

Soon after they returned to Washington, the Democrats caucused to make committee assignments before the first session of the Ninetieth Congress opened on January 10, and the president delivered his State of the Union address that evening. Money issues were on every congressman's mind; thus the cost of the Vietnam War was the overriding issue of the session. With expenditures reaching as high as $2.5 billion a month, critics of the administration insisted that budgetary priorities be established to avoid slashing domestic programs. The theme of the State of the Union message was the necessity to confront communism in Vietnam. The cost of that action would require a budget, for fiscal year 1967, of $112.8 billion, the first time in the nation's history that a budget request had gone over $100 billion. The president expected the defense budget to grow by $5.8 billion, to approximately $58.3 billion. The president also insisted that Great Society programs must not be abandoned in the effort to meet commitments in Vietnam. Mahon had made public his stand on that matter the previous December in Big Spring, Texas, when he said that all nondefense spending must be closely scrutinized and reduced, even to the point of withholding money that had already been appropriated. If the issue was "guns versus butter," Mahon always supported guns, as did many other conservative members of Congress. However, trying to pay for both a war in Southeast Asia and Great Society programs was costing more than the nation could afford.

> On Thursday at 5 p.m. I went to the White House and sat for 1 hour in the President's office with Speaker McCormack and Leader Albert and talked about the House program, Teacher Corps, and Rent Supplements, foreign aid, model cities, International Education, etc. . . . The Pres. still thinks there will be a threat of inflation late in the year and that the 6% surtax should be passed late in this session.[83]

In May twenty-six farm women from the Nineteenth District came to Washington to plead with Mahon, among other congressmen, to do whatever they could to raise farm income. One of the women told Mahon that her husband's average income was thirty cents per hour.[84] That same month he wrote to his family:

> Yesterday I attended a 5 hour meeting in the conference room of Secretary Rusk with a committee appointed by the President to come up with a recommendation as to how the U.S. should support certain activities overseas which were formerly supported by the CIA. On Thursday and Friday I met with the President's committee on revision of the federal budget. These kinds of things are interesting but very time consuming at a time when we are trying to put the finishing touches on a group of appropriation bills. We plan to finish Defense hearings this week. I have had to miss a lot of things. I think the administration will be shocked at some of the reductions we are propos-

ing. I don't know that we can make them. . . . When Gen. Westmoreland was here I attended the luncheon for him at the White House. Later he came by the office for a visit. Everybody continues to worry about the war and that certainly includes Helen and me.[85]

In July Mahon introduced the Department of Defense $60 billion appropriation bill to the House. He told the House that "a modern war cannot be fought without money, without big money."[86] During the previous four years, 1962–1965, defense appropriations had increased slightly more than $10 billion a year over the amount appropriated during the previous four years. During the last four years the average defense budget was more than $47 billion a year.[87] Despite the size of the bill, supplemental appropriations would be needed before the fiscal year ended, bringing the total outlay to $71.5 billion.

On August 6, 1966, at high noon, the Mahons attended the wedding of Luci Baines Johnson and Patrick Nugent. After the ceremony a splendid reception was held at the White House. As they made their way through the receiving line, Mahon took time to tease the president, "You got strictly second billing today!"[88] For once, Johnson received the comment as praise. After arriving home, Mahon wrote in his journal, "We left at 5 p.m. We started to the wedding at 10 a.m. so we devoted 7 hours of this day to the wedding of the President's daughter. . . . The day was sunny and pleasant. We enjoyed rubbing shoulders with the high and mighty for a day."[89]

George Holt spent a second summer with his grandparents. He worked at the office and played golf with his granddad. "He is a great joy at the apartment and the office."[90] Before he returned to Houston the three of them spent the weekend at Williamsburg. It was a pleasant way to end the summer.

The first session of the Ninetieth Congress was marked by rising federal expenditures, by riots in the nation's urban ghettos, and most of all by frustration over the war in Vietnam. Republicans gained forty-seven seats in the 1966 mid-term election, reducing the Democratic majority to sixty-one. Many of the traditionally Democratic seats were now held by conservative Southerners, which put Great Society programs in danger because of the latter's opposition to domestic programs that they considered too liberal.[91] When the

House Democratic leadership appeared to be losing power, some Democrats called for aging Speaker McCormack's resignation before the next Congress convened in 1968.

In a letter to his sister Mary Agnes, Mahon wrote, "Adam Clayton Powell continues to give Congress a bad name. I believe we are going to be able to do something about him. I shall vote not to seat him. Were it not for the fact that he is a Negro our job would be much simpler."[92]

Two members of Congress—Senator Thomas J. Dodd (D-CT) and Representative-elect Adam C. Powell (D-NY)—received strong reprimands from their respective chambers for alleged misuse of public funds. These two incidents spurred members to demand a new code of congressional ethics; however, interest in the proposal appeared to have died down by the end of the 1967 session. Mahon wrote home, "Last week was rather interesting. Of course, you read all about our bout with Adam Clayton Powell. Adam is always very pleasant on a personal basis. It is too bad that he brought such discredit on Congress and himself. What we did was more than justified in my opinion. . . . We thought the Speaker made a big mistake by opposing action against Mr. Powell."[93] Powell, a former Baptist minister from Harlem, was elected to the House of Representatives in 1944. One of only two black congressmen at the time of his election, Powell became chairman of the Education and Labor Committee in 1961, where he established a record for steering some fifty bills through Congress in a single session. These bills included making lynching a federal crime and mandating desegregation in public schools. In the 1960s Powell was criticized for mismanagement of committee funds, which included travel to his retreat on the Isle of Bimini. By 1967 the allegations of corruption had become so intense that the House Democratic caucus stripped him of his committee chairmanship and refused to seat him until the Judiciary Committee had completed its investigation of his activities. In March the House voted 307–116 to exclude him from membership. Mahon voted against seating him and supported disciplinary action against him. Powell then won a special election to fill his vacated seat, but he did not take the seat. Instead, he took his case to the Supreme Court in 1969, *Powell v. McCormack*. The Supreme Court ruled that Powell was a duly elected member, and the House had acted unconstitutionally when it refused to seat him. The House was required to recognize his right to membership; however, he was stripped of his seniority. In response to a letter from a constituent, Mahon wrote, "I feel that Mr. Powell's actions have been indefensible and he has certainly brought great discredit upon Congress." An editorial in the *Lubbock Avalanche-Journal* agreed with Mahon's assessment of the situation, stating, "Congress' reputation has been hurt, and so has that of every member, including the 160 who voted against the seating. Among the latter is Rep. George H. Mahon of Lubbock."[94]

In January Mahon wrote to his family, "I hardly have any time to read books but I am reading one now that is full of interest for me. Professor Richard Fenno of Rochester University published a book last year entitled 'The Power of the Purse.' He took six years to write it. It is mostly about the House Appropriations Committee. It is chock-full of very interesting things, especially from my view point. I look forward to a very interesting year. My work is a great challenge. The pressures of the job keep me in a state of considerable fatigue but I am at least starting off the year with great zest."[95]

Handling correspondence takes a large amount of every congressional member's time, and those writers not wanting Mahon to do something for them usually had something they wanted to complain about. However, in January 1967, Mahon received a gripe letter that really got his attention. It began:

Dear Congressman,

I am nonplused to learn about the disasterous [*sic*] fact of the horrifying terror that smog is taking over. I am frustrated to learn that nothing has been done about this problem. I am noncommittal of the things that are being done. I think this problem should be analized [*sic*] to find a solution. I know this is time of great dilemma, but I am sure many people feel as I do. It is obvious to see that many people have become ill due to the effects of this condition. . . .

I am sure that the government will act with alacrity although this is indeed a formidable problem. I have a profound respect for your sagacious mind and your integrity. I do not feel that this should be signed with a pseudonym because I am very belligerent. Please do not think this letter is ludicrous because this comes with all sincerety [*sic*]. Thank you for your magnamious [*sic*] help.

Sincerely yours,
Betsy Holt[96]

He quickly answered:

Dear Betsy:

I am glad you did not write me under a pseudonym! You did such a grand job
with your letter it makes me feel proud to observe that it was sent under your
own name. You were very magnanimous in a number of your statements. I
can well understand your concern about the dilemma which is confronting
us. I would like to see our country act with greater alacrity in dealing with
our air and water pollution problems. We must agree that they are quite formidable, however, and that a great deal of sagacity will be required if we are
to find the right road to follow.

I love you.

As ever,
Granddad[97]

On March 10, Mahon attended a meeting in the Cabinet room at the White
House. President Johnson planned to attend a summit meeting in Latin
America in April, and he hoped to get a resolution from Congress pledging
an annual increase of $300 million for five years to the $1.1 billion aid already
pledged annually for the Alliance for Progress. The program was started in
1961 by President Kennedy for the purpose of countering communist influence in Latin America, but it did not prove to be effective. This was George
Holt's birthday, and when Mahon made a note of this in his Green Journal he
reminisced about his meeting with the president, as well as other matters of
the day:

We all told the President we would cooperate and support the Resolution.
I told the President I would support the Resolution but that I thought we
would have great difficulty securing the money. I told him the going would
be tough on the motion to re-commit the appropriation bill.

I accompanied LBJ and Lady Bird from the White House to the Justice
Department for the swearing in of Ramsey Clark as Attorney General of the
United States. The President in the talk said that while walking in the bldg.
Mahon observed that this was the first time there had been a son follow in
the footsteps of his dad and become Attorney General and wouldn't it be
something if the son should later follow his father on the Supreme Court.[98]

On a Saturday morning in late March 1967, Mahon was playing golf at Burning Tree Country Club when the phone rang at home. Helen answered it and learned that someone from the White House was looking for Mahon. She told the caller how to locate him, and after holding the line for a few minutes the president picked up the phone and asked what their plans were for Easter. Helen said they had none, and he said, "Well, can you be at the White House at four o'clock and we will go down to Camp David for the weekend?" He told her to pack casual clothes like one would wear on a farm and only one dress for church on Easter Sunday. She answered that they would be delighted and would be there promptly at four to leave in the helicopter. After hanging up she called Burning Tree to tell Mahon, who finished his game while she packed their clothes. They were the only guests. Most of the others who went along worked for the president. Lynda and Lady Bird also joined the group, along with the Secret Service men and the president's doctor. The sixteen-person helicopter was full when it took off that afternoon. Helen, who was not particularly fond of flying, wrote to Daphne, "It is kind of a thrill when it just raises up and takes off and you fly so low that you can see everything as you go along—all the farm houses and all the roads and things which makes it quite interesting."[99] It took only thirty minutes to travel from the White House lawn to Camp David, and cars were waiting for the party when it arrived. President Johnson took over one of the cars and drove it up to the main house.

Camp David, Maryland, is located about seventy-five miles north of Washington. Established by President Franklin Roosevelt and called Shangri La, the name was changed to Camp David by President Eisenhower. It was just a short distance from Gettysburg, Pennsylvania, where the Eisenhowers retired. The main house, named Aspen, consisted of a large living room, a sitting room, dining room, and three bedrooms, each with its own bath. There were six smaller guest houses. The two-bedroom, two-bath guesthouse that the Mahons occupied was named Witch Hazel. The others had tree names. All the buildings were very rustic but comfortable.

Quickly changing to casual clothes, the Mahons joined the others, and Mahon bowled with the Johnsons before dinner. After dinner Helen enjoyed a bridge game with Lady Bird and Lynda before they all watched a movie. By ten-thirty Mahon decided he had had a full day, so he and Helen retired.

The next morning they all had breakfast together in the main house before leaving, with the president driving, to attend church in the nearby town of Smithburg. The car was "an old beat-up, light-colored Mercury station wagon."[100] It was used in order not to call attention to the president; however, the first family still caused quite a stir in this small town of seven hundred people. Initially the minister was shocked to see the president in his church, but after gaining his composure, he went on to conduct a meaningful Episcopalian service.

Hamburgers were served for lunch, and the remainder of the day was spent walking in the woods, reading, playing bridge, or bowling. Easter dinner, consisting of lamb chops, black-eyed peas, green salad, and desert, was served that evening. After dinner everyone watched *Face the Nation*, featuring Senator Ed Brooke (R-MA). President Johnson was pleased with the way Brooke answered questions about Vietnam and called him after the program to say so. Mahon also talked to Brooke to congratulate him on a good job. Then they watched *Meet the Press*, featuring Sargent Shriver and the Anti-Poverty Program. Shriver was also called so the president and Mahon could express their pleasure with the program. In a letter to Daphne and Duncan, Mahon wrote that the president listened to news reports on the radio and watched them on television as much as possible. Mahon was impressed with the amount of information that Johnson remembered. When the group returned to Washington on Monday, the first family was rested, and the Mahons each had a head full of memories they wanted to share with Daphne and her family.

On April 23 Mahon went to the White House at 5:00 p.m., along with Speaker McCormack and Majority Leader Albert. They were in the Oval Office for an hour and, according to his journal, talked about the "House program, Teacher Corps, Rent Supplements, foreign aid, model cities, Education, etc. . . . The Pres. still thinks there will be a threat of inflation late in the year and that the 6% surtax should be passed late in this session."[101] The surtax bill, intended to help fight inflation by reducing consumer demand, was still pigeonholed in the House Ways and Means Committee at the session's end.[102] Wilbur D. Mills (D-AR), chairman of the Ways and Means Committee, would not send a bill for increased taxes to the House floor for debate unless the appropriations chairman, Mahon, agreed to cut spending by the amount Mills insisted on. The cut Mills demanded went from $2 billion to $4 billion and finally $6 billion. Each time it looked as though an agreement had been reached, Mills would up the ante. Mills was a Southern conservative who was opposed to President Johnson's Great Society programs, and many in the administration believed his real goal was cutting funding for these programs. Mills argued that if the taxpayers were made to pull in their belts, the government should be expected to do the same. This angered Mahon, who strongly believed the Appropriations Committee should determine cuts in expenditures, not the chairman of the Ways and Means Committee.[103] If increased taxes were to be linked to the outlay of money, the Ways and Means Committee should make the necessary amendments to reduce expenditures during the House debate of each appropriation bill and allow the members to vote the reductions up or down. The surtax was President Johnson's program, and Mahon was pulled into it as chairman of the House Appropriations Committee. He sided with the president in wanting the smallest reduction possible. Both believed the current budget was a lean one, and large reductions would be very difficult to make without cutting programs. The power struggle that ensued between Congress and the White House lasted for nearly two years. President Johnson pleaded with Mills to agree to a compromise that would allow the tax bill to come out of committee for debate on the House floor. Ultimately, Mills got the better of this power struggle when the final agreement required a $6 billion cut in expenditures for a 10 percent surtax. The surtax bill did not go into effect until 1969, and President Johnson considered this delay one of his greatest legislative failures. Historian Julian Zelizer writes that this power struggle marked a turning point in American government, a time when conservatives began to push aggressively for smaller government and reduced Great Society programs.[104] The size of the federal government had been growing since New Deal days. It also foreshadowed the national mood of the next decade when many liberal voters became quite vocal about demanding reduced military budgets and increased social welfare programs.

On June 13 George Mahon presented the $70.3 billion defense appropriation bill for fiscal year 1968 to the House. This was the largest single bill ever presented to Congress. Defense spending reached $86.4 billion in 1944; however, money was appropriated in two bills—one for the War Department and one for the Navy Department—and the House Defense Appropriations Subcommittee trimmed $1.2 billion from the amount initially requested. Of the amount appropriated, an estimated $20 billion was required to fund the Vietnam War, and Mahon told members to expect a supplemental bill because "the tempo and cost of the war in Southeast Asia are on an upward trend."[105]

Rather than leaving any extra money in the bill, which would amount to a blank check, the subcommittee wanted the Department of Defense to submit a request for any additional funds that would justify the need and purpose of the money. This would provide tighter congressional control over appropriations, which ultimately totaled more than $84 billion with forthcoming supplements and money for military construction.

The Subcommittee on Defense Appropriations added $404 million above funds requested despite administration opposition to the increase. The subcommittee "did not think we ought to deprive ourselves of B-52 strength or airlift strength" because of the war in Southeast Asia and trouble spots in the Middle East.[106] During the Vietnam War military inventory was not being kept up because every possible penny was being poured into the war. To address these issues the subcommittee added $11.9 million to purchase forty-five planes that were scheduled for elimination, thus maintaining B-52 strength at three squadrons, and added $12.1 million to maintain eight Air Force Reserve units and three National Guard units.[107] Money was also added for additional aeromedical evacuation aircraft and $25 million above the budget for the development of a new long-range bomber, a follow-on for the B-52.

Total reductions made by the subcommittee amounted to $1.6 billion, which included reduced funding of the F-111B program because the crash of a test plane would delay the program. Mahon stressed that none of the reductions were in programs directly related to the war. Although it was possible that some funds in the original request could have been shifted to the war, the subcommittee was clear that it preferred any additional war funds be provided through requests for supplemental appropriations, not through shifting funds from one category to another. The final defense appropriation for $69,936,620,000 cleared Congress on September 13. Before the year was over three supplemental bills brought the total for all activities of the Defense Department to $84 billion.[108] This represented over one-half of all US government budget activities for fiscal year 1968.

After Mahon became chairman of the full appropriations committee, reporters sought him constantly for interviews. He always stressed frugality in spending the taxpayers' money and advocated a pay-as-you-go program. Pay-as-you-go was a euphemism for additional taxes. The national deficit was growing each year; thus, there was no additional money to pay for expenditures at the time they were made. Mahon strongly advocated defense expenditures, which often accounted for one-half of all federal expenditures. As was seen in most years during the administrations of President Kennedy and President Johnson, Mahon's subcommittee often appropriated additional money for defense weapons that the military wanted but that Secretary McNamara did not think were needed. Thus, he would not spend the extra money, much to the chagrin of Congress.

The nation was alarmed by urban riots in 1967, which many people believed indicated a growing militancy of the civil rights movement. Devastating riots in Newark and Detroit caused Congress and the president to demand investigations. Some members of Congress argued that the riots demonstrated the urgent need for more federal aid to overcome the unemployment, substandard housing, and lack of education so characteristic of the ghettos. Others believed that federal assistance should be withheld, thereby punishing the rioters instead of rewarding them. On July 20, a week after the Newark riot, the administration's rat control bill for $40 million came before the House, where some members became quite raucous, calling it a "civil rats bill" that should be voted down "rat now." The bill failed 176-207. However, harsh criticism from liberal members and the press caused opponents to reconsider, and on September 20 a modified bill cleared as an amendment to the Partnership for Health bill.

Mahon received a letter from an irate attorney in Lubbock, who wrote,

How can you explain your FLIP-FLOP on the $40,000,000.00 Rat Control give away bill. On July 20th you took a stand for conservative spending and then immediately you changed on roll call on September 20. . . . I note that you ask for concrete suggestions concerning where reductions in government spending can be made. The chairman of the Appropriations Committee should know better than anyone in congress where these reductions can be made. . . . Foreign aid can be materially reduced and numerous programs of the Health and Welfare department can be diminished considerably. GEORGE, IT TRULY IS LATER THAN YOU THINK.[109]

By return mail Mahon explained his position in a three-page answer. He told his constituent that he had voted against the original bill to establish a division of rodent control under the Housing Department because he believed the Public Health Service should be in charge of that activity. Moreover, the original bill would have applied only to cities that were zoned, and some cities, such as Houston, would not be eligible to participate. He maintained that he clearly understood the seriousness of rodent control and had read literature documenting that "more than 14,000 people, mainly children and babies, were bitten each year."[110] Over the years Congress had authorized programs to help farmers and cattlemen, and he wrote that he believed this program should be authorized, also. When it again came before the House in the Partnership for Health Amendments of 1967, he decided it would serve the public, and he voted for it. He let his constituent know that he had always been attentive to the interests of the agriculture and oil industries. However, he wrote, "I cannot in good conscience and out of my interest in our District's welfare always turn a deaf ear and otherwise be unresponsive to the problems of cities."[111] Although he had misgivings about federal funding of such a program, in order to be successful in meeting the needs of West Texas, he had to have the support of congressmen from urban areas. "As you know, the Members from urban areas far outnumber those of us from non-urban areas."[112] Mahon reminded his constituent that the authorization bill would come before the Appropriations Committee and that "my Committee will carefully screen any request for funds and undertake to deny any appropriation which does not appear to be in the best public interest."[113]

On July 24, 1967, a riot broke out in Detroit, and federal troops were required to quell it. Six days later the mayor of the city, on nationwide television, blamed Congress. Vice President Humphrey publicly agreed that Congress had not done enough to deal with the growing problems of the cities. The mayor said that additional violence might remove the veil from the eyes of congressmen. Mahon was angry and asked for time to speak from the House floor.

> Having failed to provide peaceful leadership in his own city, he seeks to wash his hands by making a whipping boy of the Congress, and I for one propose not to let the matter go unanswered. . . . This Congress, since 1960, has provided $100 million to the city of Detroit in grant reservations for urban renewal. . . . I do not know how much, if any, of it went up in smoke because of the leadership gap. . . . Certainly such irresponsibility deserves a rebuke, which I am undertaking to give today. . . . This arrogant mayor who failed to do his job in the city which elected him . . . wishes to remove what he says

is a veil over the eyes of Members of Congress. . . . Please get the beam out of your own eyes, Mr. Mayor, before trying to get the mote out of the eyes of this body.[114]

He went on to declare that additional spending was not a solution for the problem. However, he made it clear that he did not advocate abandoning any worthwhile programs. He recommended discipline, not dollars. "Discipline, self-respect, and some degree of law and order enforced on the local level by the local people is vital. The more we have appropriated for these programs, the more violence we have had. This refutes the idea that money alone is the answer to this problem,"[115] he told Congress.

The following day, again from the House floor, Les Arends (R-IL) responded that he considered George Mahon one of the finest gentlemen he had ever known. "I think on yesterday he performed a service not only to his country, but especially to our House of Representatives as the body that speaks for the people. I wish to commend the gentleman from Texas for the courage he displayed in standing there in the well of this House on yesterday to make the forthright factual statements he made."[116]

This was not the end of the matter. *Washington Post* columnist Jack Anderson got into the discussion. He wrote that the vice president hit the mark when he blamed Congress for not responding to the crisis growing in cities. "What Humphrey could have said, but discretely did not mention, is that Congress is run by a gaggle of old men from small towns, who have never been much interested in the problems of the cities."[117] Time would prove Mahon's point valid—that it would take more than money to solve the problems of the cities. However, Jack Anderson's point that Congress was ruled by a gaggle of old men who held their position because of seniority, not always because of their ability, was a theme that would surface often throughout the coming decade. Although the House was reluctant to support aid to the ghettos, it did pass an antiriot bill, making it a crime to cross state lines with the intent to incite or engage in a riot, but the bill did not become law because it was not reported out of committee in the Senate and had no support from the administration.

After spending a little more than three weeks in the district, the Mahons returned to Washington just in time for the opening day of Congress on January 15. The trip to Texas had been strenuous. Mahon had been able to cover only about a third of the district, and constituents seemed to have more problems than usual, causing a huge backlog of things to be done for them. While in Texas Helen had the flu and missed visiting with as many people as usual, although she recovered in time to attend a Young Farmers banquet in Levelland the night before they returned. They shook hands with more than eleven hundred people who came from throughout the district. The next day they started the seventeen-hundred-mile trip to Washington. When things settled down after opening day, they flew to Miami, where they rented a car for the seventy-five-mile ride to Palm Beach. They stayed at the Breakers for a week and met some very interesting people. Mahon also enjoyed golfing, and Helen got some much-needed rest. It had been over a year since they had had a real vacation. Mahon wrote to Daphne, "Seeing all the rich, fat cats has brought me reluctantly to a decision. I am going to quit wearing suits over 7 years of age and that have wide bottoms on the trouser legs."[118] He also told Daphne that the average age of the ancient guests at the Breakers was eighty-seven.

While in Florida Mahon called President Johnson to congratulate him on persuading Clark Clifford to become secretary of defense. Earlier, the president had shown him a list of five names he was considering and asked for Mahon's opinion. "I told him that Clifford was the best man for the place in my opinion. I doubt that Clifford would want to serve beyond this year, but he is close enough to the picture to take over immediately. No Secretary of Defense can for long please Congress or the Country. Like Secretary of State and Secretary of Agriculture, it is an impossible job."[119] In November 1967, Secretary McNamara had submitted his resignation to become effective February 29, 1968. During his seven-year tenure, the longest on record, he wrested control of the Pentagon from the military establishment. However, since late 1967 he had become progressively more at odds with President Johnson over Vietnam. He finally came to believe the bombing should be halted and the Vietnamese military should be responsible for more of the fighting. According to Deborah Shapley, McNamara's biographer, President Johnson's appointment of him to be president of the World Bank was a surprise although he had earlier expressed a desire for that position. The stress of the war was taking a heavy toll on his emotions, and the change proved to be a good one. Mahon's comment about the secretary of defense not being able to please Congress or the country was perceptive, especially during a war as frustrating as the conflict in Vietnam. Moreover, McNamara angered many in Congress because he refused to spend appropriated money that was above his budget requests.

Seeing the snow-covered countryside was a pleasant part of the train trip back to Washington, where the Mahons arrived in time to attend a dinner honoring the speaker of the House. Mahon soon got back into the swing of things, although at times it seemed that he had to work all day and half the night. When the defense subcommittee was meeting, he was tied up all day with that business, and then he returned to his Congressional office, where he signed letters, made phone calls, and handled problems that accumulated during his absence.

The Tet offensive, a full-scale assault on South Vietnamese cities, began on January 30, the Vietnamese lunar New Year, a festive national holiday. Earlier, the Vietcong had smuggled arms into South Vietnamese provincial capitals to be used during the surprise attack. A large number of the South Vietnamese military were on leave to celebrate the holiday. The overwhelming effectiveness of the attacks served to show Americans that noncommunist forces really did not control the country south of the Seventeenth Parallel. South Vietnamese and American forces ultimately drove the communist forces back, causing the Vietcong to actually gain little ground and suffer heavy losses. However, the psychological damage was already done. Americans watched the fighting on TV with horror and disillusionment. What they saw had a jarring effect on public opinion and did not confirm General Westmoreland's optimistic version that the United States was winning the war. Criticism of the administration's war policy increased, producing much talk of a credibility gap. People wanted to know why the South Vietnamese were not willing to fight and die to defend their nation if that nation was as viable as the American public had been led to believe it was. General Westmoreland's solution was to escalate the war. However, Defense Secretary Clifford was reluctant to do that and advised sending fewer troops than requested. He believed that South Vietnamese leaders should be emphatically told that they must assume greater responsibility for the war. Later that year General Westmoreland was replaced by General Creighton W. Abrams, and at a farewell press conference on June 10, Westmoreland said that the United States should not expect victory in a "classic sense" because of the administration's refusal to expand the war. The Tet offensive became the chief military development during 1968 and led to increased criticism of the administration's policy in Vietnam.[120]

Early in February 1968, President Johnson held a two-hour breakfast meeting at the White House for congressional leaders to enlist their support for his war policies during the coming weeks. Mahon attended. He had always supported administrative policies to fight communism and backed up his support with adequate defense appropriations. When the press criticized Westmoreland, Mahon told a reporter that Westmoreland had performed well in what was probably the most difficult task ever assigned a US military commander. "Efforts are being made at home and abroad, and this includes the Communist press, to discredit Gen. Westmoreland. In my opinion this is against the best interest of the United States."[121] He believed that those who expected nothing but success against such a determined foe as the North Vietnamese were expecting the impossible.

Those opposed to the war were also working to unseat President Johnson in the 1968 election, causing his political base to diminish even before the Tet offensive. The turning point for Johnson, however, was the New Hampshire primary. He won only 49.5 percent of the votes, and his Democratic opponent, Senator Eugene McCarthy, won 42.4 percent, creating doubts that Johnson could win in November. Then Robert Kennedy decided to enter the race. The president's health had long been a concern for Lady Bird. She knew that Johnson men often died young from heart disease and feared another term would be fatal for her husband. After considering all the forces swirling around him, Lyndon Johnson announced on March 31 that "I shall not seek, nor will I accept the nomination of my party for another term as president." This announcement came at the end of a national address in which he offered to halt the bombing in Vietnam if North Vietnamese officials would come to the conference table for peace talks. He said he believed that in light of the problems in Vietnam, he should not devote a single day of his attention to anything else, including campaigning for another term.

Mahon told a reporter in the Washington bureau of the *Lubbock Avalanche-Journal* that he had been at the White House the evening before Johnson's announcement and had no hint that the president's withdrawal was coming. He said that on a couple of earlier occasions, the president had asked his opinion about running for reelection; however, "I didn't have the faintest idea that he was contemplating not running for another term."[122] Mahon went on to praise the president for adding "stability plus deliberate and thoughtful attention"[123] to the presidency. "He hasn't done things in haste or anger. And no president in our history has worked at the job with more fever and zeal," he said.[124] In 1980 when Mahon was interviewed by the director of the Southwest Collection, he was asked whether he would have encouraged Johnson to run in 1968. Mahon replied, "I don't believe I would have. He had health problems. He was saddled with an almost impossible situation. There didn't seem to be any way at that time to bring to a conclusion, a successful conclusion, the war in Vietnam. I think he made the right decision."[125] He added that he believed Johnson would have been nominated in 1968 and reelected. Charles Guy, editor of the Lubbock paper, who had visited at the president's ranch in November 1964, described Johnson's withdrawal as the biggest shock since President Kennedy's death. He wrote, "We believe he made the supreme personal sacrifice in order to promote peace in Vietnam and the causes of peace everywhere. We think he had his *finest hour* and that his act revealed the pygmy stature of those who ceaselessly have slashed at him from every hidden vantage point."[126]

On a quiet Sunday afternoon Lynda and Chuck Robb came to the Mahons' apartment to play bridge. The Secret Service man who came with Lynda was from Amarillo, Texas, and he sat on the lounge watching the door as the foursome played cards. Later that afternoon Lady Bird called to talk to Helen and decided to join the group when she learned that Lynda and Chuck were there. She also had a Secret Service guard. The next week Helen teased her bridge club, telling them that they, too, must have a Secret Service guard if they wanted to play with her![127]

Although "Congress set limits on expenditures, it found them difficult to apply. Appropriations committees cut back on budget requests but not deeply enough to bring expenditures down to the required level, thus leaving much of the responsibility for politically unpopular cuts to the administration. On October 9, near the end of the session, Mahon estimated that Congress had cut the administration's requests for new spending authority (mostly appropriations) by about twelve billion dollars. He estimated that this would produce a cut in actual expenditures in fiscal year 1969 of $3.5 to $3.7 billion with the balance of the six billion dollars required cut to be made by the Administration."[128] Initially, four major programs were exempt from cuts: defense spending associated with the Vietnam War, interest on the national debt, veterans' benefits, and Social Security payments. Later price support programs of the Commodity Credit Corporation; grants from the Department of Health, Education and Welfare; and education programs administered by the Office of Education were added.[129]

On April 4 the Reverend Dr. Martin Luther King, Jr., was assassinated in Memphis, Tennessee. King was there to lead a demonstration on behalf of striking garbage collectors. Fearing the worst, President Johnson canceled his engagements for that evening and addressed the nation on television. He "condemned King's slaying and implored 'every citizen to reject . . . blind violence,' and to pray for 'peace and understanding.'"[130] He called a meeting of black leaders and the congressional leadership for the next morning at the White House. He asked black leaders to oppose violence and congressional leaders to move civil rights legislation from committees to the floor for debate and a vote. After the meeting they went together to the National Cathedral to attend a memorial service for Dr. King. Despite the president's efforts, rioting broke out in more than one hundred cities across the nation, including Washington, DC. By the evening of Friday, April 5, looting and fires had broken out in the city. The Mahons could see the fires from the balcony of their eleventh-floor apartment in Arlington, Virginia. It was about two miles, as the crow flies, from the Capitol and allowed them a clear view of the government area of the city. Mahon closed his Congressional office about 5:00 p.m. instead of the usual 6:30 p.m., and he and Helen, like many other government employees, tried to get home before the situation worsened. A reporter from the *Lubbock Avalanche-Journal* called that evening to inquire about their safety and learned that they had gotten home easily because they took a different route across a bridge that was used very sparingly. Mahon told the reporter that if they had taken the usual route, they would have been tied up in traffic more than two hours. Mahon had been in a conference that afternoon in the business district of Washington, and when he tried to "return to his office adjacent to the Capitol, in the Sam Rayburn building, he was forced to take a circuitous route because of having to detour around areas where some looting and window smashing was in progress."[131] He did not believe the situation in Washington would get out of control because of the troops and thousands of police officers on duty. The main problem was fighting the fires he believed had been started by rambunctious teenagers.[132]

Many people feared that the morality of the nation in general was breaking down because of the "permissiveness" in American life. Others saw crime and violence as a more complicated issue, resulting from the conditions of mass living that had developed in the nation's major cities. President Johnson was of this school of thought. The latter group condemned crime and violence, while urging programs that would strike at the root of the problem—poverty, ghetto conditions, inadequate police protection, and unsuccessful correctional systems.

Liberals in Congress warned that more aid for the cities was necessary to prevent further riots, and conservatives responded by saying that rioters should not be rewarded, especially in light of the budget cuts voted by Congress. Largely in response to the King murder, on April 10 the House cleared the administration's Civil Rights–Open Housing bill (H.R. 2516), and the next day the president signed it into law (Pub. L. No. 90-284). Mahon voted against this bill. The bill prohibited discrimination in the sale or rental of property. Mahon and many of his constituents believed this was an infringement on personal property rights. As he told the Lubbock Chamber of Commerce when he addressed the group in 1966, "I am not a reactionary. I know that we must continue to strive to improve our country and the lives of the people in every state, but in my opinion, the Federal Government must not be permitted to intrude too far into our lives."[133] At the end of the day, social programs were increased more than they were cut. Meanwhile, rioting and demonstrations spread to college campuses, and students eventually took over Columbia University in the spring of 1968.

Dissatisfaction with the present state of law enforcement was expressed by Congress in several ways—a crime bill that strengthened local law enforcement and attacked the Supreme Court, a refusal to consider the nomination of Fortas to the position of Supreme Court chief justice, antiriot legislation, and provisions to halt federal aid to student rioters. Congress enacted juvenile-delinquency legislation and a bill to control the use of LSD and other stimulant, depressant, and hallucinogenic drugs. Limited gun control legislation was also passed.

Dissatisfaction with law enforcement was a hot topic among Americans. A Gallup poll concerning solutions to the nation's violence revealed that the second most-frequent solution recommended was stricter law enforcement, including more police and less lenient courts. The most frequently voiced solution was stricter gun laws.[134] Mahon wrote in a family letter:

> Helen and I are so angry about the failure in law enforcement that we boil over from time to time. I think the people throughout the nation are angry

and if they are not, they ought to be. Another upsetting thing is the Poor People's March on Washington. The government has provided billions in aid and handouts to the poor and the efforts of the militants to destroy the country is indefensible. We pass by shanty towns on the way from work. The vast amount of the new lumber that is being wasted is a shame. Granted there is some discrimination and inequity but no government in the world has been so liberal as ours—and that is one of the main troubles—and moreover almost anyone who wants a job and is willing to work can get one. I have never seen the people so aroused and I hope they stay aroused until somebody and every law abiding citizen puts his foot down and demands and gets law and order among adults and juveniles. The juveniles are providing the front for much of the damage, but it would be far better to lose a few juveniles than to lose the country—and we are moving toward losing the country. . . . I am trying to do all that I can in long hours in my job and whenever I touch the lives of young people I try to encourage them.[135]

Mahon did not finish his letter until May 27, when the Poor People's Army was already camped near the Lincoln Memorial, just about a mile east of their balcony. He believed most Washingtonians were disgusted with the marchers, and he knew from his mail that the people of West Texas were disgusted and believed the protesters were just troublemakers. He continued in his letter, "I have written every Cabinet head and every agency head of the government and asked them to keep me advised of any federal funds that are expended directly or indirectly in support of the Poor People's Army which has invaded the city, and is undertaking in a measure to take over the reins of government."[136] Black activism aroused negative emotions in many Americans.

King had endorsed the Poor People's March on Washington, and after his death it was led by Ralph Abernathy. The goal was to stimulate federal action to help alleviate black poverty. The disorganized march ended in failure because whites were much less supportive of black problems in the North and there was a pronounced public backlash because of the urban riots. Moreover, King's assassination created a leadership void.[137]

At the beginning of 1968, the outlook for gun control legislation was dim. However, the national mood for gun laws changed after the assassination of Dr. King in April and Robert F. Kennedy (D-NY) in June. Gun control then became a national issue, and two bills were introduced in Congress. The first bill prohibited the interstate sale or shipment of handguns to individuals but did not apply to ammunition, rifles, or shotguns. The National Rifle Association, strongly opposed to any type of gun control, lobbied against the bill. A second bill extended regulation on ammunition, rifles, and shotguns. Both the House and Senate refused to include provisions that would have greatly strengthened gun control enforcement by requiring gun registration and licensing. Supporters of strong gun laws were unsuccessful in their attempts to link gun control legislation to crime control, and both were defeated. Texans in the House voted two to one against the bills, and Mahon was among the opposing group. He received a flood of constituent mail that ran 90 percent against any type of gun control or registration.[138] Unbroken pasture land in Texas provides a natural habitat for game, such as deer, quail, and doves, and many ranchers earn a sizeable portion of their income from hunting leases. More often than not, hunters oppose gun controls. Mahon hunted as a young man and also when he returned to Texas after Congress adjourned each year. Like many other Texans, he owned shotguns and bought one for his grandson, George Holt. He taught his grandson how to shoot and often took him hunting when they were in Mitchell County.

In August Mahon spent ten days in the district while the Republicans held their national convention. After returning to Washington he joined Helen and George Holt for a weekend in Ocean City, Maryland. They had been there only a day and a half when he received a call from the White House, asking that he return in time for a 1:00 p.m. meeting the following day. President Johnson wanted the Congressional leadership to meet with him regarding the war in Vietnam and the Czech invasion. During the night of August 20–21, Soviet tanks invaded Czechoslovakia to crush that country's first freedom movement. "The brutal invasion dashed LBJ's plans for a final summit with Soviet Premier Alexei Kosygin, which he had hoped might pave the way to peace in Vietnam and a new era in Soviet-American relations."[139] Getting an early buy-in from Mahon was Johnson's standard procedure for making it easier to get additional appropriations if needed.

Mahon did not attend the Democratic National Convention, which opened August 26 in Chicago. He had always been lukewarm about Hubert Humphrey, and Eugene McCarthy's liberal views were certainly not compatible with his own. Also, neither he nor Helen had been admirers of Robert Kennedy. The convention was marred by antiwar demonstrations flashed across the nation on television. Taking a hard line against the protestors, Mayor Daley allowed the Chicago police to use whatever force was necessary to subdue them, thus setting off a national debate about police brutality. After watching the events unfold on television, Mahon wrote to his family, "Helen and I were completely out of sympathy with the people who tried to interfere with the convention. We were glad that Mayor Daley did not let things get completely out of hand. He may have made mistakes but I think most Americans were in favor of his efforts to preserve order. . . . I noticed one letter from our district denouncing police brutality in Chicago but I suspect this will be the exception."[140]

Mahon wrote to Daphne that he would be supporting the Democratic ticket, but he expressed his reservations about both the Democratic and Republican candidates. However, he thought the American Independent Party was in the weakest position of all. "Wallace added a new and disturbing dimension to his campaign when he selected LeMay.[141] LeMay is a strong, two-fisted, incorrigible, inflexible, highly-capable military man but he seems out of character on the Wallace ticket and I suspect that he will prove to be more hurtful than helpful to Wallace," he wrote.[142] This is somewhat different from the impression Mahon had of LeMay when he visited the general at Strategic Air Command Headquarters in December 1954. Of course, Mahon could be far more candid in a family letter after LeMay's retirement from the air force than he could be in a formal report to the chair of the Subcommittee on Defense Appropriations, especially since Republicans were in control of the House and Mahon was not chair of the committee at that time. There is no doubt that LeMay's personality and forceful way of working with others would have been undesirable to Mahon.

The office was closed on Labor Day, and Mahon did not go in to catch up on his correspondence. Instead, he played golf at Burning Tree and took a nap that afternoon. That evening he and Helen were dinner guests of Mr. Revitz, the owner of the Alban Towers, where they had lived for so many years. They went to the Rib Room at the Mayflower Hotel, where "the meal was exceptionally good and the conversation most interesting. Mr. Revitz was born in Russia of Jewish parents. His father was killed and Mr. Revitz escaped and came to the U.S. forty-nine years ago. He had not been back to the USSR until about 3 weeks ago. He went over for a ten day visit with his relatives and he gave us a full report."[143] Mr. Revitz brought Mahon a 12-gauge "over and under" shotgun from the USSR. Richard Helms, Mahon's friend who was director of the Central Intelligence Agency, offered to have the gun inspected and the lengthy Russian instructions translated into English. He learned that the Soviets made excellent guns of that type, and the one he had was the very best. The CIA people who test fired it gave Mahon a paper showing the various shot patterns made from different size shots.

On Friday, September 20, the Mahons, Transportation Secretary and Mrs. Boyd, Lady Bird Johnson, and some of the White House staff left Washington at 6:30 p.m. on the president's Jet Star plane. They were headed to the Texas ranch to relax for the weekend and to celebrate Mahon's sixty-eighth birthday. On Saturday they went by helicopter to San Antonio, where they toured the Hemis-Fair and later enjoyed Mexican food at an outdoor restaurant on the river walk. They attended both the Lutheran and Catholic churches in Stonewall on Sunday morning, then spent the afternoon on Lake LBJ on a rather large boat belonging to one of the Johnsons' friends. Helen wrote to Daphne that Lady Bird went below to change into her bathing suit and then jumped over the side into water that was at least forty feet deep and swam for thirty-five minutes without stopping. Her stamina amazed Helen; however, according to entries in her diary, Lady Bird often swam thirty laps in the White House pool. After supper that evening Mahon was honored with a big chocolate birthday cake that Helen described as "the best chocolate cake I think I have ever put in my mouth . . . I told Daddy Sunday afternoon that little did we think when we came to Washington that we would be celebrating his 68th birthday at the home of the President of the United States!"[144] President Johnson made a little speech about his friend George and gave him several little remembrances that he kept in a drawer in his desk. When they got back to Washington a pair of bookends with the president's seal was also delivered to Mahon's office.

Early in October Mahon played golf with a couple of doctors at Woodmont Country Club, a country club for Jewish members. The previous week he had handled a bill for an additional $560 million for public assistance, much of it for Medicare. Mahon told Daphne and Duncan, "I chided the doctors saying, 'If medicare and medicaid does not bankrupt this country eventually, it can't be bankrupted.' They said, 'Yes, we knew that all of the time and that was the reason we opposed medicare and medicaid.' I countered that I had not voted for the legislation. Nevertheless, now that we have medicare and medicaid, I am sure that it will do a tremendous amount of good but it is too bad that there seems to be no adequate way of preventing frequent mismanagement of these programs.'"[145] The doctors were a little late arriving so Mahon visited with other members in the grill. "There was a time when I did not feel comfortable talking to the Jews and Catholics about their religion and their views but this is no longer the case," he wrote.[146]

In October the Mahons attended a dinner following the opening ceremonies of the National Portrait Gallery of the Smithsonian Institution, which was housed in the old Civil Service Building. It was a small gathering, and Mahon had a good chance to visit with Chief Justice and Mrs. Earl Warren. Warren was the chancellor of the Smithsonian Institution, and Mahon was on the board of regents. "The Chief Justice, despite his rulings which in some instances have in my opinion done great injury to the country, is a modest and apparently a very well meaning man. . . . No I did not discuss the Fortas appointment with the Chief Justice," he wrote to Daphne, "nor did I tell him that I was of the opinion that Mr. Fortas should not become Chief Justice. He leans too far to the left. Also, he should not have accepted the $15,000 from American University which was raised by his former law firm of which his wife is still a member."[147] As Mahon was dictating his letter into the Dictaphone, Helen, who was in the kitchen, overheard him and came into the room to say that she sat next to Chief Justice Warren at dinner and discussed the Fortas appointment at length with him and also Warren's desire to retire. She reported that Warren "said that Justice Fortas was a very able man. He apparently offered no criticism of Justice Fortas but said that he, himself, had never accepted an honorarium at any time during his political career."[148] So much for political correctness.

In June 1968, seventy-seven-year-old Chief Justice Earl Warren submitted his resignation to President Johnson because he didn't want to run the risk of Richard Nixon's naming his replacement. After Johnson's withdrawal from the presidential race, there was widespread belief that Nixon would win the election. Warren considered Nixon unethical and he feared that a right-wing appointment would lay the ground for overturning many Great Society programs. The resignation would become effective when a replacement was confirmed. Johnson nominated Associate Justice Abe Fortas, a longtime friend and a liberal, to be the next chief justice of the Supreme Court. He intended to appoint another longtime friend, Texan Homer Thornberry, who had been a circuit judge and was currently on the federal court of appeals, to fill Fortas's seat.[149]

During the chief justice confirmation process Fortas agreed to testify before the Senate Judiciary Committee, although a sitting justice was not required to do so. In fact, the event was historic since it was the first time that a nominee for chief justice had appeared before the Senate. Fortas's cronyism and unethical discussions with President Johnson about cases before the court were made public. However, his acceptance of $15,000 for nine weeks of teaching at American University raised even stronger questions of ethics and propriety. That amount of money was equal to approximately 40 percent of his justice salary.

Despite problems, the committee passed on the Fortas nomination and sent it to the full Senate for confirmation, where a filibuster ensued until Fortas asked President Johnson to withdraw his name from nomination. Ultimately, Nixon did name the next chief justice, Warren Burger.

Mahon had difficulty getting his subcommittees to report their appropriation bills to the full appropriations committee for consideration before being reported to the House. Executive agencies had been operating on emergency funds provided by Congress since July 1, the beginning of fiscal year 1969. The defense subcommittee completed its hearings before the end of fiscal year 1968, but it could not move forward because the House Armed Services Committee was slow in completing its legislative authorizations for the Department of Defense, which had to take place before the appropriations bill could be written. Also, Congress recessed for two months to allow time for the national political conventions, which added to the delay and caused the defense appropriations bill not to make its way to the House until September 11.

When presenting the defense bill to the House, Mahon reminded members that the president's total budget request was for $201 billion, and of that amount approximately $60 billion would have to be used to cover existing obligations, such as interest on the debt, Social Security, and payments from other trust funds. That left approximately $141 billion for expenditures requiring Congressional approval. The bill he was presenting totaled $72.2 billion, more than half of the $141 billion.

He also reminded them that the Revenue and Expenditure Control Act passed the previous June, the first spending cut mandate ever legislated by Congress, required that at least $6 billion must be cut from the new budget in order to get the president's requested 10 percent tax surcharge. The Subcommittee on Defense Appropriations had recommended the president's initial request of $77 billion for defense be reduced to $72.2 billion, thus furnishing $4.8 billion of the required reduction. Combined with reductions in other appropriation bills, the House had cut $11.6 billion from the original presidential budget request. Mahon also told the House that it should expect supplemental requests for money during the year because it was practically impossible to precisely compute war costs very far in advance. As the figures stood at that time, the war in Vietnam was expected to cost at least $28 billion in fiscal year 1969.

He further assured the House that the reductions did not indicate any backing down on America's military strength, nor should anyone believe this was any move toward appeasement just because reductions had been made in non–Southeast Asia budget requests. Overall, the bill supported 3.5 million troops, 960 ships, 35,000 active aircraft, and a high level of research and development. The subcommittee did not believe funds for national security should be determined solely on the need for economy in government.

Most of the reductions came from deferring funds for weapons systems that were not intended to be actual expenditures in fiscal year 1969. During the development of a new weapon, there is a gap of several years between the concept stage and operational application. However, he cautioned members that budget deferments in fiscal year 1969 appropriations would have to be made up in coming years because the failure to sustain weapons development would ultimately threaten national security. An important fact to remember is that because many reductions involved money to be spent in the future on projects, the reductions would actually save only $1.7 billion in 1969 expenditures, not the $4.8 billion that Mahon talked about when he introduced the bill. Addressing the widespread concern about the size of the bill, Mahon said: "I would point out that those who speak of the ending of the conflict in Southeast Asia as the beginning of a time when we can have a mere skeletonized Defense Department are not thinking along realistic lines. Regardless of the ending of the war in Southeast Asia, we will still be confronted with a very ruthless challenge to the security of the United States. The most powerful opponent in the world confronting the United States is not, of course, North Korea or North Vietnam, but the Soviet Union."[150]

Nevertheless, he promised that the subcommittee would always be diligent in its search for and elimination of waste and inefficiency. This prompted Representative Alvin O'Konski (R-WI) to question why the Gateway Ammunition Plant in St. Louis, a business that had not produced a single shell from a $41 million outlay, was being awarded a second contract by the Army for $26.5 million. All of this was happening despite reports that the payroll was rife with Cosa Nostra gangsters. He called attention to an article in the *St. Louis Globe-Democrat* entitled, "Gravy Train—Hoodlums Getting Well-heeled at Shell-less Shell Plant." Mahon responded that the army, a grand jury, and the FBI were all conducting investigations at the time, and he was watching the situation very closely. Mr. O'Konski said he would not pursue it further if Mahon was doing so.[151]

During debate on the defense bill Donald M. Fraser (D-MN) also asked Mahon whether it was true that no outside experts ever testified before the Appropriations Committee, and therefore only the view of the administration and Defense Department was heard. Mahon replied that virtually all testimony did come from government officials. He said the committee did not actively solicit testimony from outside authorities but would welcome it if anyone ever requested to appear. He went on to say that because committee members weighed comments on the subject from the press, constituents, and members of Congress, he believed the input was balanced. Before the debate ended Fraser told the House that he did not believe the US was getting what it really wanted. He stressed the importance of stopping the arms race, curbing the pell-mell expenditure on expensive military hardware, and finding a way to focus on nation-building programs.[152] These challenges foreshadowed the criticisms and dissent of the coming decade.

The bill also contained funds for an anti ballistic missile (ABM) program. Although it would not be completely operational for many months, Mahon said on the floor, "I believe it would weaken us in our position of world leadership vis-à-vis the Soviet Union if we were to slow down at this time the ABM program."[153]

Because the Subcommittee on Defense Appropriations held hearings much earlier in the year, Mahon asked Defense Secretary Clifford and Chairman of the Joint Chiefs of Staff Wheeler to again meet with the committee just before the bill was reported to the House. They agreed that the bill was reasonably adequate and recommended no major changes. Mahon offered this information to many who questioned why defense appropriations were being cut so much when the country was involved in the Vietnam War and the Soviet Union had only recently invaded Czechoslovakia. He agreed with the defense secretary and the chairman of the Joint Chiefs of Staff that the invasion was a matter of grave concern, but, it did not mean that the United States should make any immediate change in its own defense strategy.

Finally, the bill "prohibited the use of funds in the bill to pay the salaries of any Federal employee convicted of inciting, promoting or carrying on a riot or any group activity resulting in damage to property or injury to persons. Prohibited use of funds in the bill for loans or grants to any person convicted of a crime involving force, trespass or seizure of property in an attempt to prevent officials or students at an institution of higher learning from carrying out their normal functions."[154]

On September 12 the House passed the defense appropriations bill for fiscal year 1969 (H.R. 18707). The roll call vote was 333-7. The $72.2 billion bill was basically unchanged from the amount initially recommended by the Subcommittee on Defense Appropriations. It was sent to the Senate, where a filibuster against the Fortas confirmation delayed action.

On October 11, the eve of adjournment, Congress finally completed its work on the defense appropriations bill (H.R. 18707), which amounted to $71.9 billion. This figure was $5.2 billion less than the $77 billion the administration had requested and nearly $400 million below the amount the House had initially passed. Although this was the largest single bill that Congress ever passed, it also represented the deepest cuts ever made in a Department of Defense request for funds.[155] However, of the $5.2 billion reduction, only $1.8 billion of actual spending in 1969 would be reduced, and appropriations committees in both the House and Senate stressed the need to make up the reductions when the fiscal crisis was resolved.

Major appropriations included allotments for the controversial Sentinel ABM system, numerous aircraft development programs, the army's new Cheyenne assault helicopter, ship conversions, and funds for all aspects of the Vietnam War. The bill's $46.3 billion in non-Vietnam funds almost equaled the $46.9 billion appropriated for all defense programs, including Vietnam, in the regular defense money bill for fiscal 1966, passed only three years before, in the 1965 session of Congress.[156]

When combined with appropriations from previous years, the funds available for the Sentinel ABM totaled approximately $1.4 billion, enough for the president to begin installing the new antimissile system. The Sentinel was a missile designed to prevent incoming ballistic missiles from reaching their targets in the United States. It was a missile for missile defense that would be installed across the northern boundary of the United States, as well as in Alaska and Hawaii. Opposition to this system was growing among Americans because of the rising costs of the Vietnam War, which was diverting funds from domestic projects, and the growing opposition to the arms race. Proponents of the system argued that the antiballistic missile system would "strengthen the nation's hand in arms control negotiations, that the system would work effectively and that it would not add fuel to the arms race because it was defensive rather than offensive in nature."[157] Debate about this weapons system would become increasingly heated in the coming decade.

Back in the district the end of 1968 brought happier news for Mahon and his constituents. In November Lubbock got the go-ahead for a $4.5 million federal office building and courthouse. Congress approved the project in 1967, but funds were frozen during the administration's freeze of nonessential building programs.[158] Now they had been released, and the building was named the George Mahon Federal Building.

In mid-December word was received that the Interstate Highway System would be extended from Amarillo to Lubbock. The Department of Transportation had added 1,472.5 miles in twenty-eight states to the forty-one-thousand-mile interstate network. The $43.1 million project would tie Lubbock to I-40, with the federal government covering 90 percent of the cost and Texas taxpayers assuming the remaining 10 percent. For years Lubbock had been one of the three largest cities in the nation not connected to the Interstate Highway System, and this was considered a big disadvantage for industry and for attracting cross-country traffic. Mahon credited President Johnson with making this possible. Also, the fact that the Mahons were friends with Secretary Boyd and his wife, played bridge with them, and lived in the same apartment complex did not hurt either.

According to the *Avalanche-Journal*, the fly in the ointment was the fact that it had not been clearly established that the Interstate would cross the city, rather than end at the northern leg of Loop 289,[159] and prospects for getting the additional mileage appeared dim because all the available miles had been allocated. It was expected that the additional mileage would cost more than $72 million, with no federal help. However, Congress passed a measure allowing those cities planning to install mass transport systems to return mileage allocated to them. Fewer than five hundred miles were returned, and bidding for these miles was very aggressive. It seemed unlikely that Lubbock would be able to get any of them, but chamber of commerce officials placed their hopes on Mahon's continuing interest in the project. Projects of this type generally take as long as ten years to complete, and Mahon and the Lubbock Chamber of Commerce used that time to secure the additional miles.

In 1975, when word was received that an additional five and one-half miles would be allocated to the Nineteenth District, an aide in Mahon's office said he did not know where they came from. William T. Coleman, secretary of transportation during President Ford's administration, tells a different story. The president wanted to limit the reallocation of these returned miles in an effort to cut federal expenses because the deficit was rising so rapidly. However, he had to have the consent of the House and Senate appropriations committees to limit this expenditure from the Highway Trust Fund. An amendment to appropriations would be required, and he knew that would be difficult because the power to allocate interstate highway miles was such a valuable chit. Secretary William T. Coleman was sent to try to work out a deal with Senator Birch Bayh and Representative George Mahon. He talked first with Bayh, who said he was opposed but added as an afterthought that he would vote in favor of the amendment if George Mahon would. Then Coleman scheduled an appointment with Mahon and upon entering the office, before he could say anything, Mahon said, "Mr. Secretary, I have a highway problem in my district. I need eight miles of interstate."[160] Coleman replied that Mahon had the miles, provided all the legal requirements were met. Coleman wrote that when he told Senator Bayh the next day, his response was unprintable, but he honored his word and voted in favor of the president's amendment. Of course, Mahon voted in favor of it, too. Coleman added that a few weeks later President Ford was talking with him; Ford said he was having trouble with Mahon over defense appropriations and asked whether Coleman could find another forty-eight miles of interstate highway for him.[161] It is not clear how the eight miles became five and one-half, but the allocation was ample to cross the city of Lubbock and connect with US 87 South. Mahon's vote could easily be called the "$72 Million Vote."

"Backlash" was the dominant theme of the 1968 presidential election that gave Richard Nixon and Spiro Agnew a slim victory over Hubert Humphrey and Edmund Muskie. The Republican Party garnered 43.7 percent of the total vote, and Democrats got 42.7 percent. Despite the slim difference in popular votes, this was an important election because, as James Patterson writes, "After 1968 the Democratic Party became a less and less purposeful organization when it came to presidential politics."[162] Republicanism was on the rise, and for many Americans this seemed to represent a return to their old familiar ways. Democrats retained control of Congress, which meant that Mahon would continue to chair the House Committee on Appropriations, but the comfort zone that many chairmen thought they had found would prove to be an illusion.

Chapter 8

The Abuse of Power: 1969–1973

The Ninety-first Congress opened with a Republican president and a Democratic Congress. This was the first time since the inauguration of Zachary Taylor in 1848 that a president entering office faced opposition parties in both houses of Congress. President Nixon was also confronted with the problem of an unpopular war that affected every aspect of domestic life. On the campaign trail he repeatedly pledged to end US involvement in the Vietnam War, but he did not specify how or when this would happen. The 1968 Tet offensive stunned Americans into the realization that it was losing the war against a small, war-torn nation, and public frustration began to mount. It didn't make sense that such a small nation could hold out against the world's most powerful military force. What most Americans did not understand was that in reality the North Vietnamese held the advantage. While the United States was fighting a war to contain communism, North Vietnam was fighting for self-determination and national survival. Moreover, it had the ultimate advantage in defending familiar ground—its homeland. The Tet offensive also strengthened the antiwar movement's strident and growing criticism against continuing such a costly venture when domestic programs such as for health, education, and urban problems needed funding. Moderates and liberals demanded a reordering of national priorities that would lead to reduced military expenditures, fewer foreign commitments, and increased spending for domestic programs.

The problems that characterized much of the Nixon administration did not surface until the excitement of the inauguration had subsided. Early in January the Mahons went with Transportation Secretary and Mrs. Boyd to a party given by automobile magnate Henry Ford at the F Street Club.[1] It was the last time that the outgoing secretary was to use his official car and chauffeur.

Many glamorous people were present, including Henry Ford and his young Italian wife, who had a great time mingling with the guests. Ford had chaired President Johnson's National Alliance of Businessmen. Started in 1968, the alliance was made up of several of the nation's leading businessmen, who agreed to train and provide jobs for one hundred thousand of the hard-core unemployed. By January 1969 the goal had been exceeded. Mahon was impressed with the results and described Ford as "rather sensible and down to earth."[2]

Describing the evening to his grandchildren, Mahon wrote, "When we arrived at the Club we had some difficulty getting through the crowds and into the house. We learned that President Johnson had just left following a brief visit. When we left about an hour or more later hundreds of hippies were crowded throughout the block on both sides of the street and in the street. In the old days crowds like this would be dispersed by the police but not now. They were fairly orderly but you could not help thinking someone might fire a gun or toss a bomb. We were glad to leave."[3] The type of crowds that had made Mahon uneasy were also present during the inaugural parade, and in fact interrupted the parade.

This Inauguration Day was different from previous ones, when the Mahons traditionally held an open house in his office and served refreshments to constituents from the district. The office staff had to entertain the visitors this time because he and Helen had an official part in the ceremonies as stand-ins for Preston Smith and his wife, Ima. On that same day in Austin, Smith, a good friend of Mahon's, was being sworn in as governor of Texas. Initially, the Mahons were somewhat reluctant to fill this role, but they had a great time after they got into the swing of things, as Mahon wrote to his grandchildren,

The cars for the Governors proceeded two abreast down Pennsylvania Avenue. Our Dodge convertible had a big Texas sign on each side. The crowds generally were in a jolly mood and seemed to want to have an excuse to cheer and wave. Gram did not complain that I did some clowning. Occasionally, I would rise up part way in my seat, wave my right fist and shout "Yea Texas!" The crowds seemed to love it and they would respond by shouting "Yea Texas!" The Governors themselves were a little more dignified but Texans are supposed to be a bit rowdy! . . . As we were passing the Washington Hotel we received a hearty cheer from some Lubbockites who had a room overlooking the parade route. As we passed the White House and the President's reviewing stand President Nixon waved and gave us a symbolic handshake which we returned, and we exchanged shouts with members of the Cabinet with whom we were acquainted. I told Gram that night as we spoke of how tired we were that maybe we should take some comfort in the fact that we had been the first of the Mahon-Stevenson clan to ride in an Inaugural Parade for a President.[4]

Immediately after completing the sixteen-block ride from the Rayburn Office Building to the White House, they hurried to Andrews Air Force Base, where they hoped to join the farewell festivities for the Johnsons. However, they had departed for Texas just twenty minutes earlier. The next day Mahon sent a letter apologizing for missing the farewell luncheon and departure at Andrews, but being in the inaugural parade had taken longer than expected. He wrote, "Helen and I are very proud of you and Bird for the great job you did throughout your service. . . . We will never forget our experiences here with the Johnsons. May God bless you all."[5] Within days he received a note from Johnson saying there was no need to apologize—he understood the pressures on their time. "Besides, you were always there when it counted—and that's how I'll always remember you."[6]

Earlier that month they had attended a dinner at the home of Marjorie Merriweather Post, the eighty-three-year-old socialite whose father established Post, Texas, a town in the Nineteenth District. The Mahons were invited because George was on the board of regents of the Smithsonian Institution. After dinner, during a conversation with the hostess, she reminisced with Mahon about her visits to Post as a young girl. Later she sent some books from her estate to him.[7] In January Ms. Post announced that she was giving her home, Hillwood, and its many art treasures to the Smithsonian.

Although the Republicans controlled the White House, the Mahons were on the guest list as often as they had been when the Democrats were in office. In fact, just a week after the 1968 election, Nixon telephoned Mahon, who was in Midland, Texas, to address the chamber of commerce. He told Mahon that he had great confidence in him and remembered that they had often voted alike when they served together in the House. He asked for Mahon's support during the coming four years and mentioned that in conversations with President Johnson, he had been told that Mahon could be very helpful to a president. Johnson had spoken highly of him. Mahon replied that Nixon would have his support, that he would do whatever he could to be helpful, and he wished Nixon good luck.[8] Richard Nixon would be the sixth president with whom he had served, and although he belonged to a different political party, Mahon had no difficulty agreeing with many planks in the Republican platform of 1968, especially the promise to reform welfare laws and strengthen national defense.[9] He did not like Hubert Humphrey, but there is no evidence that he voted for Nixon. In fact, Mahon always claimed to have voted for the Democratic nominee in national elections.[10] With the late Sam Rayburn and Lyndon Johnson gone, Mahon became the top Texan in the Ninety-first Congress. Furthermore, because the new president was not of his party, pressure to implement the administration's programs was considerably reduced. However, as a leading member of the loyal opposition, Mahon's support was important to Nixon.

Later Helen wrote in a family letter, "Tuesday night we were invited to the White House for dinner in honor of the prime minister and his wife from Australia. Not since the Eisenhower administration have you worn white tie and tails to an affair at the White House. Kennedy and Johnson both used informal dress for affairs that were given at the White House."[11]

The guests noticed, and commented about the fact, that the dining table was configured in the more formal shape of an *E*, instead of the round tables used during the previous administrations. Mahon and Helen were seated at the very end of the middle part of the *E*, across from the president and the prime minister. They were also across from Secretary of Agriculture and Mrs. Edmund Muskie. Senator Wallace Bennett was Helen's dinner partner. In her letter Helen described the event as "very beautiful with many flowers and a lot of good food."[12]

Helen noticed that Mrs. Nixon ate very little food and wrote that "Pat Nixon is so very thin and I think that it makes her look so much older because her face is sunken in. Someone said that she hardly eats a thing. She is so afraid that she is going to gain a half a pound. I would swear that I could watch her the other night at the dinner and I don't believe she ate three bites of food. She sat and talked and made like she was eating, but the food she took in would certainly not keep a bird alive."[13]

The menu was printed on stiff cardboard paper, and Mahon put his copy in a pocket in his trousers. It was their custom to take a copy of the menu home as a memento of the evening. Later while having coffee, he put his hand into the pocket containing the menu and got a paper cut on the end of the middle finger of his right hand. Someone graciously provided a Kleenex and then a Band-Aid to stop the bleeding. When the guests went into the East Room for the evening's entertainment, Helen showed Secretary of State and Mrs. Rogers the card and joked that Mahon had given blood for the Republicans that night. Someone overheard and remarked that his blood was too thin to do the Republicans any good! Everyone had a good laugh out of this. Helen continued in her letter,

> We have been to Church at the White House twice this year. As I am sure you have read, the President is having church at the White House when he is in Washington. They have about 300 at the time and I told somebody he evidentially [sic] thought the Mahons didn't have much religion since he has had us down there twice for the Sunday services. . . . The services are not [as] long as the usual ones because they don't take up a collection! After the service you go into the dining room and they have orange juice and coffee and different kinds of little cookies and donuts.[14]

In February salaries for members of Congress were raised to $42,500, and each House member was to have an additional office worker. The method of computing pensions for members was changed, and henceforth pension amounts were to be based on the three-highest wage-earning years, instead of the five years previously used.

In order to avoid the politically thorny issue of voting on its own pay rates, Congress, in 1967, established a system whereby new salaries would be recommended by the president. Under the law (Pub. L. No. 90-206), a quadrennial commission would make recommendations to the president, who would review those levels and include his own recommendations in the next budget. The recommendations were to take effect within thirty days unless Congress vetoed them in whole or in part or enacted its own pay bill. An editorial in the *Lubbock Avalanche-Journal* referred to this law as a slick scheme for getting pay raises and encouraged readers to write to their congressmen, insisting that salaries be held at the previous level until the budget was balanced. The editorial also stated that Mahon "holds that the increase is flatly 'indefensible' at a time when top Congressional priority should go to holding the line against inflation."[15] When Mahon initially went to Congress in 1935 his salary was $10,000 per year.

By the first week in February it was back to business with the usual discussions about how to run the country. Starting early in 1969, headlines began reporting heated debates about building an ABM system that would block a nuclear attack from either the People's Republic of China or the Soviet Union. The Nixon administration inherited the Sentinel ABM system, which consisted of radar and missiles placed near metropolitan centers to detect and destroy incoming missiles. Opposition to the Sentinel surfaced during the Johnson administration, when homeowners joined defense critics to argue that nuclear warheads near population centers would make them an enemy target and likely cause the loss of civilian lives. Jack Anderson's column in the *Washington Post* echoed civilian fear when he wrote, "Should a missile site ever blow up, according to Pentagon experts, it would cause total destruction for a radius of at least five miles and would spread radioactive fallout for hundreds of miles."[16] There was also serious doubt that the ABM system could stop all incoming missiles. Moreover, the Sentinel system was not designed to protect military sites capable of mounting a retaliatory strike against an enemy. Anderson wrote critically that the dubious system "was sought by the corporate carnivores who devour defense dollars and by the brass hats who seem willing to lavish staggering amounts on their pet theories and hunches."[17]

Because many of the protesters were articulate, middle-class citizens who had enough political muscle to be felt, the Nixon administration proposed a scaled-down version that became known as the Safeguard ABM. Basically, it was designed to protect the retaliatory, second-strike missile sites, such as Minuteman sites, instead of cities. Defense analysts decided that improving protection of Minuteman missile sites would elevate the US second-strike capacity, thus discouraging a Soviet first-strike. Knowing the United States could retaliate aggressively was considered the best protection against an attack.

In both 1968 and 1969, attempts to block the system were narrowly overcome in Congress. When the defense appropriations bill for fiscal year 1970 reached the House floor, dissent surfaced again over the Safeguard antiballistic missile. However, the administration claimed to need the ABM system as a bargaining chip in the upcoming Strategic Arms Limitation Talks (SALT). The ABM system was soon center stage in the most acrimonious Congressional floor fight of the post–WWII era involving a military weapons system.[18] Members on both sides of the aisle hammered away at waste and mismanagement. However, the small band of antimilitary doves was outvoted by the hawks, who were also strong supporters of the powerful military committees. During heated Congressional debates the press began to reveal speculations about why some congressmen supported high defense expenditures despite the awesome "overkill" capacity of the United States. *Newsweek* blamed the military-industrial complex, which it described as "the nation's largest single activity. It employs one in every ten working Americans, either in service with the military or with its more than 120,000 individual suppliers."[19] Seymour Hersh, former Associated Press correspondent for the Defense Department, blamed the seniority system for the failure of Congress to limit the growth of military power. He cited four elderly chairmen of the military committees, of whom Mahon was one, for chafing at military waste but continuing to approve huge defense bills with only a minimum of debate. "They believe that America's well-being depends upon a preponderance of military might. They feel that a lack of preparedness before World War II and Korea almost brought disaster to the United States," wrote Hersh.[20] And the public blamed politicians from the Kennedy to the Nixon administrations for continuing a war that was paid for in lost lives and higher taxes.

The growing antimilitary sentiment caused defense policies and budgets to be subjected to greater scrutiny than in the past. Huge cost overruns and malfunctioning weapons made the military-industrial complex especially vulnerable to an articulate group in Congress who launched a vigorous debate about these problems in an attempt to reduce defense spending. These antimilitary groups called national attention to waste, inefficiency, and even corruption in the services. "Ill-conceived tactics in Vietnam, battlefield atrocities, problems within the United States, and a changed international environment undermined the position and credibility of the American military."[21] Military brass and contractors were not the only targets of public wrath; the seniority system in Congress also received its share of criticism. Gray-haired "war hawks" were challenged for their mantra of "anything for national security." To younger, more liberal congressmen it seemed that the "old guard" was more worried about protecting its power base than the home front.

Melvin Laird (R-MI) resigned from the House Subcommittee on Defense Appropriations to become secretary of defense. The new secretary had no business or law experience and had never held a full-time job in the private sector. "However, his long career as a legislator had made him sensitive to popular moods, skilled in the art of compromise, and expert in getting along with people with opposing views."[22] At the time of Laird's appointment, military morale was very low because of frustrations with the war, the increasingly negative attitude of Congress and Americans toward the military, and the de- moralizing effect of excluding military input into most decisions made during the tenure of Robert McNamara.

During his previous eight years on the Subcommittee for Defense Appro- priations, Laird had worked closely with McNamara and grew to believe that the Pentagon had become overcentralized under the management and au- thority of the defense secretary. Moreover, decisions were increasingly pred- icated on the "bottom line," with cost analysis often being the sole basis for his decisions. Laird was also concerned that the previous administration had solicited minimal input from experienced military leadership.[23] He moved quickly to institute a policy of "participatory management," which returned more decision-making power to the Chiefs of Staff. The chiefs who were ap- pointed to serve during Laird's tenure brought a much different set of expe- riences from those who served during the previous decade. All of them had combat experience in either Korea or Vietnam and understood the challenges of limited war. Moreover, each had experience in strategic planning and exe- cution and had learned how to facilitate inter-service cooperation, to operate within the parameters of a constitutional government, and to work effective- ly with civilian leadership. These skills were important in Washington and worked well with the skills that Laird had acquired from his years in Congress, where cooperation and compromise were necessary to get the job done. He understood that in the current antimilitary climate, defense budgets would be reduced, and he wanted the chiefs to make the tough decisions about where to cut. A shift toward a more diffuse management style at the Pentagon was a welcome change from McNamara's highly centralized oversight.[24] Some se- nior Pentagon officials who served under both McNamara and Laird believed Laird's management style contained the best of McNamara's revolution while giving the military a more responsible role.[25]

During the late 1960s, peace pressure groups began attacking military programs and expenditures with unusual boldness. By 1969, defense expen- ditures and cost overruns had also become the target of Congressional ques- tions, causing a flurry of investigations as well as criticism from individual members and the press. Military programs were closely scrutinized in an attempt to eliminate waste caused by the poor performance of some weapons systems. A heated debate on the House floor between Mahon and Representative L. Mendel Rivers (D-SC) illustrated the growing attitude of skepticism in some congressmen. Mahon was speaking in favor of an amendment to the $3.8 billion supplemental appropriations bill then being debated. The amendment would have put a $192.9 billion ceiling on all federal spending for fiscal year 1969, including defense expenditures. This was the first time in his career that Mahon had argued for a ceiling on military spending. In a fury Rivers grabbed a microphone and demanded that military expenditures be exempted from spending ceilings. He railed at Congress for being willing to cut military funding but not having the courage to cut funding for some of the crazy programs, which he defined as the Job Corps and OEO and "a lot of those things we are spending money on all over hell's half acre."[26] Outbursts from Rivers were nothing new, and after this one Mahon calmly, but with some irritation, continued his remarks, pointing out that the previous week a nuclear submarine, the USS *Guitarro*, had sunk while under construction at the Mare Island Navy Yard in California. The estimated cost to raise and repair it was projected as high as $22 million. "The military has made so many mistakes it has generated a lack of confidence,"[27] Mahon said. Alluding to a number of other similar fiascos, Mahon could see no reason why the Defense Department deserved the unquestioned confidence of Congress. He also expressed concern that the people responsible for the sinking would probably be transferred rather than being court-martialed. Again, Rivers stormed onto the floor to counter Mahon's strong statements about Pentagon mismanagement. He grabbed a microphone and shouted forth, "You are feeding the Pentagon's enemies and the other body [the Senate] is full of them."[28]

Some members were shocked by the clash of these two titans, who openly displayed their anger on the floor. Such behavior usually took place behind closed doors, and only the most courteous words were spoken in public. In fact, Mahon's very good-mannered behavior contributed to the power base he enjoyed, but now he was angry, partly because he resented being labeled antimilitary when he had always supported a strong national defense while others were shills for social programs. He believed that national security was the nation's number-one priority and without a strong military the social programs would be of no use. However, his antipathy for social programs did not outweigh his concern about poor management in the Pentagon. When it came to fiscal austerity and trimming budgets, he was a realist. He knew that the American public talked a lot about cutting programs, as long as it was done to the other fellow. They did not want any of their favorite projects cut.[29] With the exception of defense and agricultural matters, Mahon was proud of his reputation for being as frugal with government money as his personal money.[30]

After the day's session, both Rivers and Mahon altered their remarks in the *Congressional Record* to reflect a much gentler disagreement. However, newsmen who reported the episode made it part of the public record. A columnist for *US News & World Report* pointed out that the skirmish was representative of the growing debate taking place across the nation about the growth of the military establishment and its exorbitant expenditures. *Washington Post* columnist Drew Pearson saw Rivers's outburst as "one important illustration of why the military continues to ride roughshod over civilian branches of Government . . . The incident is extremely important and gets to the root of why the military get every cent they want while the cities and civilian branches of government are starved."[31]

Rivers was known for bulldozing decisions through his committee without giving other committee members an opportunity to study and debate them. Pearson believed one of the main reasons for such overbearing behavior on his part was the fact that Rivers's district had been showered with military installations, and the employment opportunities from the large inflow of federal money provided him a sure ticket at election time. Ultimately, his reelections gave him the seniority that he needed to chair the powerful House Armed Services Committee and to continue to give the military what it wanted. Despite the gentler remarks in the *Congressional Record*, other representatives knew that Rivers had a long history of blocking appropriate investigations of military waste and negligence. This incident was a harbinger of things to come.

Throughout Capitol Hill there was a growing belief that the defense budget was no longer a sacred cow and it was open season on military expenses, with intense questioning and scrutiny more the norm than the exception. Additionally, public confidence had been shaken by stories of cost overruns stemming from expensive weapons systems that did not work and top-heavy command structures.[32] An interesting sidelight to the story is the tribute that Mahon paid to Rivers in the House after Rivers's death in December 1970. Mahon said, "He was always tolerant in his dealings with his fellow committee chairmen."[33] Mahon, who was so proud of his reputation for honesty, seemed to be taking some liberties with the truth on this occasion. Perhaps silence would have been better.

⤸

At the end of April, Mahon received the George Washington Award of the American Good Government Society. Each year since 1953 the society had presented two awards to public officeholders, many of whom were members of Congress. In 1969 Senator Wallace R. Bennett (R-UT) was also recognized. The two recipients received their awards at a banquet in the Sheridan-Park Hotel. Frank T. Bow (R-OH), the ranking minority member of the House Appropriations Committee, read Mahon's citation, in which he praised the West Texan for his contributions to the nation's fiscal policy and for working hard to provide a strong national defense. In his response Mahon called on the majority of law-abiding Americans to practice a "new militancy." He was not advocating any sort of rebellion. He was encouraging Americans to take steps "to curb the anarchy which is eating ravenously at the very heart of this great country. . . . It is time to see to it that the destructive elements are denied full leeway in their efforts to erode and destroy the very foundation of our institutions."[34] He was advocating more militancy on the part of Americans in practicing old-fashioned virtues in order to counteract those who were advocating changing the mores.

⤸

The demands of work began to weigh more heavily on Mahon as he grew older, and he wrote home, "The pressures of life are so great family letters are almost out of the question. After the tumult of the day and much of the night I don't have that extra ounce of strength."[35] He did, however, find the energy to start a family letter one Sunday morning after finishing the newspaper. He and Helen were waiting for their grandson, George Holt, to awaken before eating breakfast. George had come from Tulsa to spend the summer with them and to work in Mahon's office. Mahon wrote,

> I had to work yesterday. I had been invited to play golf in the afternoon with a foursome which included Clark Clifford, former Secretary of Defense. I don't think Clifford ought to have written the article about pulling out of Viet-Nam. The old Administration should not interfere with the new. Nixon

then, in my opinion, went entirely too far in liquidating his options.

I was on the USS Patricia—formerly the Honey Fitz—with Mel Laird, Secretary of Defense a few nights ago when the President held his press conference. The President "lost his cool" and also made a few slips. The awful responsibility of the Presidency is closing in on him. He has been very nice to me and I continue to help him in any way I can but it is just impossible for anybody to cope adequately with the terrible problems which confront the country.[36]

Clark Clifford served as secretary of defense during the Johnson administration after Robert McNamara's departure. Clifford was an experienced appointee who had previously served as White House counsel under President Truman and was an active member of President Kennedy's Foreign Intelligence Advisory Board. His knowledge of foreign affairs was extensive. Clifford wrote an article for the July 1969 issue of *Foreign Affairs* in which he traced the evolution of his understanding of the conflict in Vietnam. When President Johnson decided to escalate the conflict in 1965, Clifford agreed that it was necessary. However, by 1969 he had changed his mind and delineated three main reasons for the withdrawal of American troops from South Vietnam. First was an ongoing struggle between China and the USSR over which nation would be the leader in influencing and supporting Hanoi, which made future US foreign policy uncertain. Next, rising domestic unrest in the United States was demanding more of the nation's resources, and the war was a distraction to the national will. Finally, the South Vietnamese government was seemingly too weak to survive on its own. He argued that further escalation of US military support would not strengthen the South Vietnamese government but would make it even more dependent on US support. He ended the article: "Unless we have the imagination and the courage to adopt a different course, I am convinced that we will be in no better, and no different, position a year from now than we are today. . . . We should reduce American casualties by reducing American combat forces. . . . Let us start to bring our men home—and let us start *now*."[37] During his press conference President Nixon became quite angry, pointing out that Clifford did not halt the escalation in Vietnam when he was secretary of defense, and in fact, more lives were lost under his tenure that at any other time. The idea of pulling out of Vietnam without victory also angered many Americans who did not understand why the strongest nation in the world could not subdue what President Johnson had referred to as "a little piss ant country" like North Vietnam. Protesters in the street and on campuses were demanding that troops be withdrawn from Vietnam because many of them wanted to avoid being drafted. These protests were a problem for Nixon, and having someone like Clifford publicly advocate immediate withdrawal struck a raw nerve. Mahon was irritated with Clifford's speaking out because he always tried to support the president, regardless of political affiliations, and would have been very reluctant to take a public stand against a president during a time of conflict.

Continuing his letter Mahon wrote,

This morning the Washington Post denounces the House Appropriations Committee for "cutting back funds for the poor" in a bill which we will have before us in the House on Tuesday. The end of the fiscal year is June 30 and since our appropriations bills have not been enacted, I will present to the House this week what is called a "Continuing Resolution" which will provide funds for the government to run until October 31. The House and Senate have both passed a bill setting a limit on spending for next year. I handled it in the House and we are to begin on Tuesday trying to iron out the differences between the House and Senate versions.

The bill to extend the surtax (to raise $9 billion) is to be considered this week. I wish the tax could be avoided but I don't think it can and I shall vote for it.[38]

The letter was put on hold because it was time to get ready for church. That afternoon, while grandson George was playing golf with a friend, Mahon found time to finish.

Now it is Sunday afternoon. . . . I have a lot of studying I must do in preparation for the week. This afternoon the School Board and Superintendent of Schools from Lubbock arrive for a confrontation tomorrow with HEW, but mainly the bills before the House will claim my attention.

I felt a little guilty leaving church this morning with a Hymnal tucked under my coat but I have every intention of returning it next Sunday. (Most embezzlers at banks expect to return the money.) I wanted George to learn to play one of my favorite hymns, "How Great Thou Art." He plays by ear and has mastered it from a George Beverly Shay record we have. We rented a piano for the summer and are having a lot of fun. I'm not sure this can be said for our neighbors!

I must bring this epistle to a close. . . . We do think of you all and we send our love. There may be a generation gap but there is no family gap with us. I was a bit shaken on Father's Day when Daphne gave me a walking cane. I never thought of giving Papa a walking cane until he was past 80! But in mitigation, I should point out that the Holts had just returned from a trip to the Ozarks of Arkansas and had acquired the stick there. It is quite a bludgeon and I would like to think she sent it to me for protection as well as support![39]

Mahon became quite annoyed with syndicated columnist Drew Pearson because of an article that appeared in many newspapers, including several district newspapers, and caused letters from angry constituents to pour into his office. According to Pearson, Mahon was responsible for extending President Johnson's government pay and allowances for staff from six months to eighteen months, which would cost US taxpayers $375,000. He composed a letter that was sent in response to letters he received that June. He pointed out that Pearson's columns often contained incorrect information, and most newspapers in Lubbock and Abilene had dropped his column years ago. The correct facts should read—according to Mahon—that an ex-president's salary stops the day he leaves office; however, all ex-presidents receive generous benefits, including retirement pay for life. In 1964 Congress passed the Presidential Transition Act, "which authorized the appropriation of $900,000, not as salary but as expenses incident to the coming into office of the new President, and the departure from office of the outgoing President, to be divided equally."[40] The author of the bill was Representative Fascell of Florida, and the funds were to be available for six months—or eighteen months if Congress agreed to the extension. In 1968 Congress agreed to extend the time limit to June 30, 1970. Mahon pointed out that there was nothing secret about the law. "I asked the Comptroller General for a ruling, and he wrote me a letter citing the law and pointing out that the expense funds available to President Nixon and President Johnson—and they were equally divided—would remain available until June 30, 1970, as set forth in the law."[41]

"I am receiving a lot of mean letters from throughout the Nation as a result of the Drew Pearson story which I am told also appeared in *Newsweek* last week. Harry Truman and many others have called Pearson a lying blankety-blank and Pearson has never been able to refute the charge. Actually, he has always been nice to me but I have never known firsthand the facts of an incident which he reported when I thought he reported the incident accurately," Mahon wrote home.[42]

In September Mahon joined a couple of army friends at the skeet shooting range at Andrews Air Force Base. He had never taken part in this sport before but enjoyed it. He hit ten targets out of twenty-five. However, others in the group were better shots; one man had missed only four shots out of a hundred. That month he also attended a dinner honoring the golf pros who were departing for the Ryder Cup matches in England. Jack Nicklaus, Lee Trevino, and Sam Snead were in the group. In the Speaker's Dining Room the next day, Mahon, Representative Gerald Ford, and Speaker McCormack made speeches honoring the pros.[43]

"We went to a small seated dinner at the Embassy of South Africa Friday night. Ambassador Taswell invited us because I have sought to be helpful in preventing discriminatory language against South Africa and Rhodesia in the foreign aid appropriation bill. Dean Acheson, former Secretary of State, and Mrs. Acheson were at the dinner. Acheson had been lambasted as being soft on Communism in the State Department during his tenure, but had become more popular with the Republicans because he supported President Nixon's policies in Southeast Asia.

"...Mrs. Acheson discussed with me a letter which she wrote to me several months ago. Her grandfather, born in Ireland, was named George Mahon. We were not able to establish kinship. We have never been able to break the barrier caused by the fact that George Thomas Mahon, my grandfather, who died in 1860, was raised in Tennessee or Virginia as an orphan," he told Daphne and Duncan in a letter.[44] He also wrote,

We had a three day battle in the House this week over the authorization for military program—not the appropriation bill. The appropriation bill should be considered about a month from now. There is an acceleration of unrest over the war in Vietnam. This is by far the most difficult subject with which this Country has to deal and no one seems to know how our course should be charted. A few years ago two or three people in the House were in opposition to our military program and perhaps one or two in the Senate. Now about 90 members of the House and about a third of the Senators are vocal in their opposition to military spending, based generally, I believe, on the unpopularity of the war and the interest of many members for more money for programs relating to the cities and various phases of welfare.[45]

Mahon's analysis was correct, and voices of protest against the war and military spending would only grow louder during the year.

President Nixon had the opportunity to fill four vacancies on the Supreme Court, but he experienced considerable frustration with some of them. His first nominee, Warren Earl Burger of Minnesota, was nominated for chief justice and easily confirmed by a Senate vote of 74-3. Initially, Burger feared that liberal Democrats would oppose his nomination; however, many Democrats, as well as Republicans, were happy about the retirement of liberal Chief Justice Earl Warren and believed that Burger, a moderate, was well qualified for the position.

In 1969 Abe Fortas, President Johnson's controversial nominee for chief justice, resigned his position on the court because of conflict-of-interest charges, and in August Nixon nominated Judge Clement F. Haynsworth, chief judge of the Fourth Circuit Court of Appeals, to fill the vacancy. He was a strict constructionist from South Carolina who opposed integration.[46] This appealed to many conservative Southern Democrats, who were looking about for a new political home after the passage of civil rights legislation in the 1960s.[47] Nixon was currying their favor in hopes of carrying the South in the 1972 election. However, liberal Northern Democrats strongly opposed Haynsworth, some said in retaliation for the Republicans' opposition to the Fortas nomination in 1968. Publicly, Northern Democrats argued that they opposed Haynsworth because he was a "roadblock against organized labor and the civil rights movement."[48] He was also alleged to have ruled in cases where he had a financial interest, although this was never proven. The Senate defeated his nomination by a 55-45 vote. President Nixon was furious. Mahon was in favor of Haynsworth's confirmation and wrote to a constituent, "I do not know Judge Haynsworth but I feel confident from what I have heard about him that he would be a good addition to the Court."[49] In a letter to Daphne and Duncan, Mahon wrote that he believed Haynsworth would be confirmed despite the allegations against him, however Helen thought not. "To my surprise she was right. Some of his dealings were open to question in a minor way but I am sure he must be an honest man. It now seems clear to me that he was unhorsed by the AFL-CIO, the strong civil rights advocates, and the liberal contingent which sees little good in men of conservative views, especially from Strom Thurmond's South Carolina. Late, on the day of the vote I called LBJ on the telephone and had a very interesting conversation upon which I should not comment. I did not call Mrs. Mitchell! But I did read in the paper what she said."[50]

The controversial wife of US attorney general John Mitchell told the *Washington Post* that she was quite upset about the vote in the Senate. "I feel sick for him [Haynsworth] over what he has taken from the country. It's just like the country had slapped him in the face."[51] Martha Mitchell often called reporters to voice her opinion about national affairs. She seemed totally unaware of the adverse reaction to her comments.

Mahon continued in his letter:

Last night at dinner I had a very interesting conservation with the widow of the late General Chennault, of Flying Tiger fame. Martha (Mrs. Mitchell) had called her and discussed the nomination with her. A reporter from Greece told Gram at the dinner that the statement by Mrs. Mitchell about the Moratorium had been published widely in Europe. We have met Mrs. Mitchell but do not have a clear recollection of her. Her husband, the attorney general had seemed like a sourpuss to me but I have decided he is a pretty nice guy. Of course, he should not have made that speech recently blaming all of the ills of our time on LBJ and the Democrats. There is plenty of blame to be sure but the more I see of this Administration the more I am convinced that there is plenty of blame for all to share.[52]

Mahon, like most of his constituents, was a conservative Democrat. He believed civil rights should be handled by the states and was quick to use the urgency of arming against a Soviet threat as a reason for not dealing with civil rights issues. An editorial in the *Lubbock Avalanche-Journal* called Haynsworth's defeat a sorry event. Editor Charles Guy favored the nomination because it held the promise that a philosophical balance might be achieved "to more closely coincide with its constitutional obligation to stick to judicial affairs, leaving executive and legislative action to the proper branches of the Government."[53] Guy went on to say if the same treatment was given to the next nominee "the forces of decency and civility should be rallied in overwhelming strength."[54]

As it turned out, all the forces of decency and civility could not save the president's next nominee. On January 19, 1970, Judge G. Harrold Carswell, of the Fifth Circuit Court of Appeals, was nominated to fill the Fortas vacancy. He was also a strict constructionist and appealed to white Southern conservatives. Bruce Kalk wrote in the *Journal of American Legal History* that "there certainly was no denying that Carswell would be the most conservative Supreme Court nominee in at least the last quarter-century."[55] Opponents charged Carswell with being mediocre because 58 percent of his opinions as a district judge had been reversed and he had a reputation for dismissing a large number of cases in order to keep his workload light. Kalk went on: "Carswell spent little time writing opinions. On average, he turned out less than sixteen pages a year. Typical Carswell work was shallow indeed."[56] As if the charge of incompetence was not enough, Carswell voiced support for segregation when running for a seat in the Georgia legislature, and despite later denials he remained a strong segregationist throughout his life. He was often described as a "man on the make" and certainly not of the caliber of either Louis Brandeis or Felix Frankfurter, men who had previously occupied the position for which he was nominated. According to Kalk, he was possibly one of the worst choices that Nixon could have made,[57] and the Senate rejected the nomination by a vote of 51-45. Not since 1894, during the second Cleveland administration, had a president had two Supreme Court nominees rejected outright by the Senate. Mahon believed the rejection was a mistake; however, he thought the Supreme Court had also been responsible for its poor estimation in the eyes of many Americans. He never missed an opportunity to berate Justice William O. Douglas in letters to constituents, and he believed it was well that Fortas resigned because his conduct was indefensible.[58] In a letter that was modified before mailing, the following paragraph was red-lined:

I am glad to see Justice Warren leaving the Court and I would welcome the departure of certain other Justices who have joined in decisions which I do not feel are in the best public interest. The wisdom of the Court in all too many recent instances has been questionable. Changes in the Court will be forthcoming and I hope and pray that through this vehicle and otherwise, common sense and trust will become the hallmark of the Court.[59]

After all this brouhaha, Nixon nominated Assistant Attorney General William Rehnquist of Arizona and Virginia attorney Lewis Powell as associate justices. Rehnquist was confirmed, 68–26, and Powell, former president of the American Bar Association, was confirmed, 89–1. The only objection this time came from the president's wife, Pat, who was sorely disappointed that her husband did not nominate a woman for one of the positions.[60]

Mahon's support of President Nixon's nominees, along with his record of voting in favor of administration bills 66 percent of the time in 1969 and 1970 did not go unnoticed. In 1972 President Nixon appointed Eldon Mahon, a Fort Worth attorney, to a federal judgeship. George Mahon was Eldon's uncle, and while no one disputed the younger Mahon's qualifications, Republicans complained that appointive plums should go to Republicans during a GOP presidency.[61]

In early December Mahon attended the annual meeting of the Lower Mississippi River Flood Control Association in New Orleans. He was there to generate good will for a project that would transport water from the lower Mississippi to West Texas to be used for crop irrigation. Mahon hoped to allay suspicions that only Texas would benefit. He spent the day talking to leaders of the association, trying to assure them that the project would not be undertaken unless the state of Louisiana, the Mississippi Valley states, and the state of Texas would all benefit.

Mahon had always been interested in the prospect of finding more water for dry West Texas. In the 1950s he introduced legislation requesting "several million dollars to explore the possibility of bringing water from the Missouri River Basin to the high plains."[62] He could not find the necessary support, and the idea died. He also explored the possibility of bringing water in from Canada or the Columbia River, but with no success.[63] In 1966, after he became chairman of the House Appropriations Committee, he was able to secure funding for a study to analyze the possibility of importing water into West Texas and New Mexico from the lower Mississippi. The appropriations committee had the authority to fund preliminary studies by the Bureau of Reclamation without prior authorization of bills that had to clear a legislative committee so he was able to add the sum of $200,000 to the 1966 public works bill to begin the study, and over a seven-year period $6.1 million was appropriated. In 1973 the project was declared not feasible. A joint study by the Army Corps of Engineers, the Bureau of Reclamation, and the Mississippi River Commission indicated that building a trans-Louisiana and trans-Texas canal system would cost at least $20.5 billion. Operation and maintenance of the system was estimated to cost another $1.9 million annually. Water that was delivered to West Texas would cost approximately $125 per acre foot, and at that price the cost would outweigh the benefits by seven to one.[64]

Before going to New Orleans, Mahon had declined an invitation from President Nixon to attend the Texas-Arkansas football game in Fayetteville. However, when he returned late Friday evening he learned that the president had called again, expressing his hope that Mahon would reconsider, which he did. They left in Air Force One just before 10:00 a.m. the next day. Mahon wrote to his brother, "A President has so many burdens and responsibilities, I never find fault with him for making any trip which he thinks is recreation or any other benefit. The presidency is an impossible job and I always felt tolerant toward any president."[65]

Air Force One landed at Fort Smith, Arkansas, and helicopters took the group to the stadium forty miles away in Fayetteville. Mahon was quite surprised when he was greeted by Daphne as he made his way from the helicopter. A friend of Duncan was visiting them in Tulsa, one hundred miles away, and he had game tickets for the three of them. The White House had let her know that her father would also be attending the game with the president. They did not sit near each other, but Mahon had a nice visit with Daphne and Duncan during half-time.

Coach Bud Wilkinson was along for the trip and rode back to Air Force One in the same helicopter as Mahon. Mahon told his brother, "It was fun talking to Bud Wilkinson, the famous coach and commentator, about the game. . . . I do not understand much about football and I found it interesting to listen to Bud tell about the fine points of the contest."[66] Wilkinson, whose fame came from coaching a forty-seven-game winning streak for the University of Oklahoma, was a special consultant to President Nixon in 1969. The group arrived back in Washington about 7:00 p.m., and President Nixon left by helicopter for Camp David, where he spent the weekend preparing for a press conference the following week. Mahon spent the remainder of the weekend finalizing preparations for the fiscal year 1970 defense appropriation bill he was to present to the House the following week.

Debate on the bill opened December 8 in the House, and Mahon told members that the bill provided $69.9 billion in new spending authority, and a supplemental appropriations bill for roughly $2.1 billion would be required to cover a pay raise for military and civilian employees, bringing total defense appropriations to $72 billion. Funds for the raise were not included in the current bill because it would not become effective until the summer of 1970. He pointed out that total defense appropriations were below those of 1969 and would be on a par with appropriations for fiscal year 1967. While defense spending would be approximately 8 percent of gross national product in fiscal year 1970, compared with 9.5 percent in fiscal year 1968, Mahon stressed the importance of slowing the arms race. He pointed out that talks between the US and the USSR had already begun and would hopefully result in a reduction of strategic weapons.

During his presentation Mahon did not miss the opportunity to tell members that while defense spending actually declined from 1968, nondefense spending had increased by $12.4 billion. He also noted that from 1964 to 1970, defense spending increased by $27 billion and nondefense spending increased by over $47 billion. He wanted these facts front and center as a response to the public outcry to reconsider national spending priorities in order to provide a larger share of the national wealth for domestic programs. Mahon always argued that until defense programs were adequate to keep the nation secure it was foolhardy to consider domestic programs.

He went on to say that "we have had excellent cooperation from the Department of Defense. Our former colleague, Secretary Laird, has cooperated with the committee very well indeed."[67] Before President Johnson left office he submitted to Congress an $80 billion defense budget. After taking office President Nixon cut out $2.5 billion. The mood of the Congress had grown for increased social-domestic programs and against heavy defense spending. Knowing Congress would probably gut the budget if given the chance, Secretary Laird directed the Pentagon to make its own cuts before others got a chance. After serving on the House Subcommittee for Defense Appropriations for many years, he was knowledgeable about the defense budget and decided it could stand a $5 billion reduction. After Laird and the chiefs decided on the lowest dollar amount, he sat down separately with the promilitary chairmen of the four defense-related congressional committees and told them the military needed at least $70 billion to survive and also that he was willing to let Congress take credit for the cuts.[68] Laird's biographer, Dale Van Atta, wrote that in August 1969 Mahon became Laird's coconspirator in the House and got legislators to line up behind him. They did not know that Mahon and Laird had already agreed on the final figure for defense appropriations and that the cuts were really due to Laird, not the members in the House, who thought they were actually deciding the final figure. Secretary Laird knew that if the budget-cutting process was left in the hands of the congressional rank-and-file, the whole process could get out of hand, prompting runaway cuts that might have endangered national security. Even under Mahon's cooperation and guidance, congressional colleagues brought tremendous pressure to reduce the budget, and Mahon had difficulty holding the line at $69.9 billion. Nevertheless, Laird had won something important. He won respect for using his political skills to turn what could have been an ugly power struggle into a matter of securing a realistic military budget that both the Pentagon and the public could live with.

During the debate on the bill, there was more opposition than usual. Although Mahon tried to put a positive spin on the cuts, critics complained that the House Appropriations Committee—and Mahon in particular—publicly criticized the Defense Department for slovenly management practices while continuing to fund programs that were wasting taxpayers' money. Critics spoke out against the ABM system for being an expensive program that many, including scientists, believed would not work. They called the cost overruns on the air force's C-5A transport plane a scandal and opposed money that had been added, but not requested by the executive department, for a nuclear attack carrier. They pointed out that the United States already had a twenty-three to zero superiority over the Soviet Union, which did not possess a single carrier. One congressman declared that "while our country's domestic problems have been worsening, 35 defense weapons programs have overrun their original estimated costs by $19.9 billion."[69] This criticism reflected growing public and Congressional opposition to pouring more than half the national budget into defense expenditures. The strong antimilitary attitudes in Congress, largely a product of Johnson's involvement in Vietnam, peaked during the Nixon years.[70]

After the bill cleared the Senate and Conference Committee, Congress on December 18 approved an appropriations bill (H.R. 15090) totaling $69.6 billion, an overall reduction of $10.4 billion from the Johnson request. This was the largest reduction on a defense bill since $6.3 billion had been cut from the fiscal year 1954 bill at the end of the Korean War.

After the fiscal year 1970 defense appropriations bill cleared the House, Mahon was interviewed by George Wilson from the *Washington Post*. He said the military strength of the United States vis-à-vis the Soviet Union had not changed, "but the mood is different."[71] He believed there was a greater feeling that World War III would be averted because the leaders of both nations understood that nuclear war would be fatal for both, thus a "first strike" would be insane. He also believed it was impossible to completely defend the United States from an attack, as the recent penetration of United States airspace by a Cuban MIG had demonstrated. Most people were shocked by the incident, but Mahon insisted that "no one has been able to figure out a complete defense against aircraft, let alone missiles."[72]

Mahon also identified the changing mood as a weariness with war caused by the disappointing experience in Vietnam. He told Wilson, "There is a growing feeling in Congress that we don't have to accept without reservation the allegations made by the Secretary of Defense, the Joint Chiefs of Staff or the State Department."[73] A resurgence of confidence was beginning to surface in Congressional decisions; however, it was obvious that the United States did not know how to deal with national wars of liberation. Because Americans had no stomach for a prolonged limited war, Hanoi had only needed to wait them out.

Overall, Mahon said, the United States was still ahead of the Soviets in nuclear strike forces, "and that is one more reason why the Pentagon is not going to get all the new weaponry it wants from its old friends in Congress."[74] Although the old "war hawk" did not philosophically support social programs, he did understand that the money in the purse whose strings he held was put there by the taxpayers, and he was aware of their changing mood.

In early February Mahon wrote to his family, "This is Sunday night. For a couple of hours I have been studying about a meeting of the Appropriations Committee tomorrow with the Secretary of the Treasury and others in which we are to discuss the fiscal plight of the Country. We are having a lot of business already in my Committee. . . . Last Sunday we went to Church at the White House upon the invitation of the President. Perhaps I wrote you that we had dinner at the White House about three weeks ago. There are many dinners and receptions we nearly have to go to during the first part of the year. We pass up as many as we reasonably can.

"We went to a big party honoring Liz Carpenter who is promoting her book Ruffles and Flourishes. Helen has been reading it today. Of course, old Sam Houston has grabbed the spotlight from Liz, LBJ and about everybody else. I only played dominoes once with Sam. (I think I told you that.) The book is an exaggeration by a very clever writer. The President is not a big 'cusser.' I am so sorry that Sam Houston Johnson wrote that book. I cannot believe that that much swearing took place. The co-author of the book must have manufactured much of the contents in an effort to make it sell. Too bad. I never saw Sam Houston more than a half dozen times. Last year he was my partner in a 4 handed domino game at the White House. We lost but all the across-the-table talk was fun."[75] The language in Sam Houston Johnson's book, *My Brother Lyndon*, is not especially rough, but Mahon's comment in his letter home may indicate that Johnson exercised caution when the Mahons were present. Neither of them would have tolerated the vulgar or coarse language that Johnson is reported to have thought was clever. If he had talked that way around them, it is almost certain they would have found an excuse to decline his invitations—to the White House or anyplace else.

In 1969 the Nixon administration initiated a policy known as Vietnamization, which was intended to gradually shift the responsibility for combat troops from Washington to Saigon. This would allow American troops to be withdrawn according to an orderly timetable. Turning over combat responsibilities to the South Vietnamese was seen as a creditable beginning to meet the president's announced plan of withdrawing 150,000 troops by May 1, 1971. At the end of December, 344,000 troops still remained in South Vietnam, but the termination of US participation in the frustrating war in Southeast Asia had begun.

During March and April 1970, news surfaced of a clandestine war in Laos, and on April 30 President Nixon announced that he had sent US troops into Cambodia to clean out North Vietnamese and Viet Cong sanctuaries along the Ho Chi Minh Trail. He claimed these actions did not constitute a widening of the war; however, both Congress and the public resisted his logic. Antiwar demonstrations sprang up on many campuses, resulting in the death of two students at Jackson State College in Mississippi by police and the fatal shooting of four students by National Guardsmen at Kent State University in Ohio. The decision to extend military action beyond Vietnam brought a sharp response in the Senate. On June 30, in a 55-37 roll call vote, an amendment was passed prohibiting the reentry of US ground forces into Cambodia.[76]

Mahon wrote to constituents that he was skeptical about being able to destroy North Vietnamese sanctuaries in Cambodia. He did, however, believe that in time of war he should support the president as much as possible. He continued, "In my capacity as Chairman of the Committee on Appropriations I have sought to be as helpful as possible in providing strength for our military forces."[77]

And to his family he wrote, "During the past week we had hundreds of college students in Washington. . . . I spent an hour with each of three groups. Most of the students were rather sensible. The most far-out student was one from our district, a student of philosophy who said, if this country did not mend its ways in accordance with his views he would leave it and go to West Germany or Canada. If he were drafted he would go to Cuba. There was at least one student from our district in each group. The favorite group was from Washington and Lee University, Lexington, Virginia. Their views did not seem to be very different from mine. The colleges seem to be disbanding in favor of treks to Washington to straighten out the country! . . . One wonders if our country will survive."[78] Mahon was not the only one who wondered whether the country would survive. Historian Stephen Ambrose was very critical of the rioting in the spring of 1970. He wrote that "some of it was designed to bring down the capitalist system; much of it was random violence and rebelliousness, pure and simple."[79]

President Nixon on June 30 issued a written report about the sixty-day US operation in Cambodia, stating that it had been successfully concluded and no American troops would be returned to that country in the future. He said that the move to clean out communist border sanctuaries would assure the continued withdrawal of American forces from Vietnam.[80] In July Mahon told a reporter for the *Lubbock Avalanche-Journal* that he believed "the Cambodian venture, no doubt, relieved pressure on South Vietnam, protected U.S. servicemen and bought time for the Vietnamese to take over a bigger role in the war as American troops were withdrawn."[81]

Mahon wrote to his family,

This is Saturday night. I quit Lawrence Welk, after a few numbers but I was tremendously impressed with the preceding hour on CBS, LBJ and Cronkite on the program "Tragedy and Transition." I did not think the previous LBJ-Cronkite programs were very good. This one was superb. I hope this one will tend to rescue the series.

It is so difficult after a period of years, even after a period of months and often after a period of days, to reconstruct a happening.

I was, of course, in Dallas on November 23 [should be November 22], 1963 when President Kennedy was shot. I think I was in the fifth car behind the President. I heard the shots, I saw the scurrying about, the forward rush of the cars ahead and the general disorganization.

I thought the Johnson account of the whole event, the transition and the following days and months was outstanding. It was low key, sober, considerate and I think factual. Johnson revealed his true self in this broadcast but not in the others.[82]

During the last week in April, Helen's brother, Malven Stephenson, suffered a heart attack and died in Snyder, Texas. The Mahons immediately booked a flight to Abilene, where they rented a car for the drive to nearby Snyder. Only a month before they had visited with Malven at the funeral of John Mahon, George's brother, and he looked well at the time so his death was a shock. Although he had had heart problems since 1960, his doctor did not believe he was in any immediate danger. After the funeral they drove on to Lubbock to spend the night with Durward, another brother, before returning to Washington. They arrived home on Saturday, May 2, which was primary day in Texas. Mahon did not have an opponent, but both he and Helen were surprised to see Senator Ralph Yarborough trailing in the early evening returns. That evening in a letter to Daphne, he wrote,

Undoubtedly the effective way Bentsen [Lloyd] played up Yarbrough's espousal of McCarthy for President and his support of the moratorium and a few other things which were not favored by rank and file Texans hurt him very much. . . . Secretary Laird is to appear before the Committee tomorrow to discuss Cambodia and defense problems generally. I wish I could be optimistic about the turn of events in Vietnam. Richard Milhous has seemed to cross the Rubicon. I am convinced he is absolutely sincere and I devoutly hope he is right. It seems to me we almost have to support the President in war once a decision is made. I was invited to the White House the night of his speech but I am not sure I am to be there on Tuesday.

. . . We love everybody, some more than others, and we do not hate anyone anywhere. Of course, this should not be interpreted to mean that we admire Justice Douglas![83]

The outcome of the general election on November 3 left Congress under Democratic control.

Near the end of February, Secretary of Defense Melvin Laird told Congress that fiscal year 1971 plans for his department essentially constituted a holding pattern but one that would maintain the nation's military strength. He also revealed that a presidential commission had recommended ending the draft and implementing an all-volunteer army by the time the selective service law expired on June 30, 1971. Opposition to the draft among young people had been growing since the major buildup of forces in Vietnam, and the administration hoped that eliminating the draft would reduce protests against the war.[84]

In September George Holt entered Duke University. In a letter to his grandson, Mahon wrote that University of Texas won a football game with Texas Christian University. "But football is football and your studies and your associations there are the important things."[85]

On December 29 Congress cleared the smallest Defense Department appropriation since fiscal year 1967; Pub. L. No. 91-668 provided $66.6 billion. Debate on the bill in the House was brisk. When Mahon introduced it, he complained about shoddy procurement and management policies. He predicted that if the department's reputation continued to decline in the eyes of Congress and the country, ultimately it would be impossible to get the necessary appropriations to ensure national security. He pointed out that the department poorly managed billions of the taxpayers' money and failed to effectively monitor and oversee the civilian defense contractors.[86] He stressed that the military buy only what was needed and place greater effort into making certain the weapons worked properly before buying them. The whole budget-reduction initiative stemmed from the Congressional hope of encouraging more effective management of funds. Mahon also criticized the Defense Department because it requested money for weapons and other items that it argued were needed, and then during hearings conducted in future years, it was revealed that the money had not been used for the purpose for which it had been appropriated. "For example: over the last nine years, Congress has appropriated over $1,600,000,000 for 71 new ships and ship conversions which have been cancelled by the Navy and most of the funds have been diverted to other shipbuilding programs."[87] He also criticized program changes over past years in the Safeguard ABM, the F-111 aircraft, and the high volume of cost overruns. He went on to say that the subcommittee did not intend to eliminate reprogramming, but the volume of reprogramming was a strong indication that planning had been very poor and not completely thought out.

As a means of tightening Congressional control over appropriations, the subcommittee recommended allowing carryover balances only for a specified number of years, not until the money was expended. Mahon decried the practice of siphoning off remaining and unobligated funds into a discretionary fund that was used at the Defense Department's whim. Mahon called this a "game" that the subcommittee would no longer play. He continued with criticism of the frequent reassignment of military personnel. The subcommittee believed this unnecessary expense also indicated poor planning and made it difficult to fix responsibility when problems arose. Finally, he gave notice that the defense appropriations might have to increase next year if the president's peace attempts failed.

Several members of the House voiced concern that the cuts were too severe and believed that if this practice continued in future years, the US would become a second-rate military power. Another somewhat heated exchange took place between Mahon and L. Mendel Rivers (D-SC), Armed Services Committee chairman. In yielding speaking time to Rivers, Mahon referred to him as a great patriot and a great leader. Rivers thanked him for his kind remarks and promptly tore into Mahon for his remarks about waste and mismanagement in the Department of Defense since Rivers thought this would hurt defense officials. He suggested that Mahon read his remarks and change them for the final version of the *Congressional Record*. This was the second time that Rivers had insisted that Mahon change his actual remarks for the *Record* when the remarks revealed shortcomings in the Pentagon. He didn't get his way this time. Mahon replied, "I do not recall any remarks which are out of character. . . . I am very pro defense and my only interest is to be helpful. I do believe we must face up to our shortcomings if we are to adequately cope with waste and management."[88] As pointed out earlier, the many military installations in Rivers's congressional district were a great economic boon and a sure ticket to his continued reelection. In fact, it was often joked that if he managed to have another installation placed there, the whole district would fall off into the Atlantic Ocean. No wonder that he wanted military spending to continue without much scrutiny.

After clearing the Senate and two conference meetings, the final bill appropriated $66.6 billion for the Department of Defense. A second conference was needed because of House language allowing the funds to be used for the entry of US combat forces into Laos, Thailand, or Cambodia to help with the US withdrawal from Vietnam and the release of US prisoners. House conferees had to agree to drop their proviso permitting US activity in Cambodia.[89] The final bill was $1.9 billion below the administration's initial request.

Toward the end of 1970, the administration served notice that defense spending would rise in fiscal year 1972. Secretary of Defense Melvin R. Laird said: "I see some strong and convincing evidence for possible defense budget increases in order to meet urgent requirements, many of them too long deferred."[90] During the last half of the 1960s, years of intense conflict in Vietnam, money for new weapons took a backseat to money for the war. Under President Johnson money that would have normally been spent on new weapons or repair of weapons on hand was spent on the war. This allowed the defense budget to be lower than it would otherwise have been and helped hide the true cost of the Vietnam War. President Johnson feared that if the true cost was known, some of his Great Society programs would not be funded. Additional concern centered upon the resurgent military strength of the Soviet Union since the Cuban missile crisis. It had reached parity with the United States in long-range missiles. For the first time the Soviet Union could exercise real power far beyond its borders, not just boast about its capabilities.[91]

By the end of the year, Mahon had been pummeled from every side about defense problems. Congressman Rivers was angry about criticisms of management practices in the Pentagon, liberals in Congress were angry about the amount of money spent for defense, journalists were more strident than ever about the dangers of the military-industrial complex, and one woman from Dallas sent Mahon the following note: "For the love of God! Mr. Mahon, quit being a hawk. Cut the military budget ten billion—or more, and lets [sic] get going on the constructive things that must be attended to or we perish. Please show that you are not too old to grasp the terrible situation we are in. You are in a position of responsibility to do something about it."[92] In his answer Mahon thanked her graciously for her letter, explained the reason for high military expenditures, and ended, "We must stay militarily strong and spend whatever is necessary to do. There is no second place in the continuing contest with world communism."[93]

On December 14, 1970, President Nixon nominated former Texas governor John Connally, a Democrat, as treasury secretary to succeed David M. Kennedy. Many people also considered Connally a possible candidate for Nixon's running mate in 1972. Mahon wrote to his family,

The President called me and put John on the line just before the public release. A nice gesture. I talked to the President about a little trip which Helen
and I may make if we are not held here too long. I haven't been to Europe in
12 years and I have prodded myself into thinking that it might be a bit exciting and interesting and informative to take a trip again.

As Chairman of the Appropriations Committee, I approve the spending
of more than two billion dollars each year in Europe and environs. Most of
this goes to support our 300 thousand men in the area and the Mediterranean fleet. Mansfield wants to bring two-thirds of our men home and the
President wants to make no significant change at the moment as we negotiate with the Russians toward a reduction in the arms race.

It might be good for me to get away but don't have much enthusiasm for
it. I tell myself that this is one of the reasons why I should shake myself loose
from my shackles here and seek re-invigoration. Of course, the weather is
bad. We would plan to travel from Naples to Germany and Brussels by train.
I would confer widely with U.S., German and other officials, visit headquarters of the fleet and so forth.

Helen would accompany me with proceeds from the Loraine farm! Her
ticket from here to Rome, first class, on a 747 would be 900 bucks. I would
go government.[94] Maybe the chances are 50-50 that we can get away for the
trip. . . . I have now taken note of all the important things except the following: We think Christmas is wonderful—we love our family—we think of you
often—we pray God's blessings upon you—we remember the ones we have
lost since last Christmas and there is a vacant place in our hearts. But I must
not close with a sad note.

Merry Christmas and Happy New Year.

P.S. One further historic note. Helen and I will have been married 47
years tomorrow—47 wonderful years![95]

At the close of the Ninety-first Congress, House Speaker John W. McCormack (D-MA), seventy-nine years old, retired. He had served nine years as
speaker and forty-two years as a member of the House of Representatives
from Boston. Representative Carl Albert (D-OK) succeeded him as speaker.
It was pointed out that Lyndon Johnson would be the last president born in a
log cabin, and John McCormack would be the last speaker who didn't attend
high school. Both McCormack and Albert had been protégés of Sam Rayburn.[96]

In early January 1971 Mahon and Helen traveled to Europe, where he had extensive discussions with military and civilian leaders concerning the possibility of a significant reduction of US forces in Western Europe. Because of antiwar sentiment and a renewed spirit of isolation, President Nixon had revealed the Nixon Doctrine in 1969, which basically declared that there would be a reduction of US troops on foreign soil. The United States would continue to provide a nuclear shield to protect allies and in the event of aggression would provide military and economic supplies, but henceforth allies had to provide the troops needed for their protection. The goal of the doctrine was to avoid direct US military involvement in remote corners of the globe. The Nixon Doctrine was to take effect at the end of US involvement in Vietnam, and Mahon expected discussions of troop reductions to figure in upcoming hearings on defense appropriations. He believed firsthand information was necessary before his subcommittee made any decisions to reduce funding for troops.

The first leg of the trip took them to Madrid, where the Christmas decorations were still up for the exchanging of gifts on the Twelfth Night of Christmas. That is when the children believed the three Kings came to bring gifts. Helen was impressed that they could walk about the city without having to worry about their safety. The next stop was Rome, where they stayed at the Excelsior Hotel, the same hotel they used during their 1955 trip. The naval commander and his daughter picked them up for a trip to Naples. As they came to the admiral's ship, he and Mahon got out for a tour of the ship and continued the trip to Naples by helicopter. His daughter and Helen stopped along the way to sightsee and shop. The following day they traveled by train to Milan. Helen was most impressed with the trains, but she got a big laugh out of the custom that when the train stopped you had to lower the window and quickly throw your bags out before the train took off again. After spending the night in Milan, they continued on through the Alps to Stuttgart. It was a sunny day, and the scenery was spectacular. The routine was the same in Stuttgart, as in all of the other places they visited. The top military people took Mahon on a tour of the installations, and one of the wives would take Helen sightseeing. That evening they dined in the home of one of the military people. The food they were served was quite good and was typical of the area. They found the houses much colder than in Washington, and Mahon had to wear his "long-handles" to keep warm. Helen, however, did not fare so well in her cocktail dresses and got a bad cold as a result.

Savannah and Julius Walker met them in London as they finished the trip. They all enjoyed a good visit and did some sightseeing. Savannah had worked in Mahon's congressional office before her marriage and again whenever her husband was assigned to Washington. While in London, Mahon and Helen also visited with Ambassador and Mrs. Annenberg. Helen decided their home was the most beautiful of any that she had ever seen. The next day they returned to Washington, and Helen wrote, "I feel that this was the most wonderful thing that ever happened to me even though I dreaded the trip because I do not like to fly but I decided if George wants to take me back I am ready to fly the ocean anytime! I will have to admit that I find it is very nice to be traveling with the Chairman of the Appropriations Committee. I really do not regret what it cost for me to go and I will admit it cost quite a bit but it was worth every penny that we spent."[97] In his usual family letter Mahon wrote that he felt refreshed and better informed for the hearings that were coming up.

Mahon learned from this trip that any force reduction was strongly opposed by all with whom he conferred, especially General Andrew Goodpaster, the supreme allied commander of NATO, who had served in the Eisenhower administration. In fact, the Soviet military buildup in the Mediterranean region was the foremost strategic concern, and a force reduction was the last thing anyone there wanted. At the end of his tour, Mahon reported that,

U.S. military forces in Western Europe, coupled with the forces of our NATO allies, presently appear to be adequate to deter a Soviet invasion of Western Europe. But we will have to modernize our forces and continue to press our allies for greater contributions toward their own security which, of course, is important to our security. I feel that some progress is being made toward convincing our allies that if we are going to continue to keep large U.S. forces in Europe the other NATO partners must make a larger contribution.

I consider world peace as the Number 1 priority. While I found nothing in Europe that would encourage a feeling of complacency, World War III has thus far been averted. I feel that if we continue to maintain our strength and the will to take whatever steps are necessary to maintain peace, the prospects for world stability can be greatly improved.

In Brussels, I met with officials of the European Common Market where the principal subject of discussion related to the possibility of increasing the U.S. export of farm crops to Western Europe. There was no evidence of a change of policy which would permit a greater export of feed grains or other crops to the common market countries. We have a long way to go in seeking to deal successfully with the common market countries.[98]

In the upcoming session of Congress, amendments were twice rejected to reduce the number of US troops stationed in Europe as part of the NATO force.[99] During the previous session Mahon had also opposed the reduction of US forces in Western Europe because he believed that any reduction "would adversely affect the on-going U.S. negotiations with the Soviet Union."[100] However, he did support the president's insistence that Western European nations increase their contributions to their own defense.

When the Democratic caucus met in January 1971 a proposal was put forth to change the traditional system of using seniority to select committee chairmen. Not all committee chairmen agreed with the change, and they were able to make sure that only a modest change was made. Upon demand, ten or more members of the Committee on Committees, which consisted of the Democratic members of the House Ways and Means Committee, would recommend nominees for chairman and membership of House committees. If the nomination was rejected, another would be made. Acceptance by the caucus, not seniority, became the determining factor. No nominations for committee chairman were rejected in 1971. The caucus also agreed that members could chair no more than one committee at a time. These changes would open opportunities for younger members to serve on and chair committees that were previously tied up with older members.[101] In February Mahon wrote to his family, "I am disgusted with the left wing Democrats who are giving the party a bad image. We are to have a meeting on Wednesday at which grievances will be aired. Many of the younger Members want to find a way to remove the old committee chairmen. They like me, I hope and believe, but they are dissatisfied generally and, of course, there is a lot of room for improvement. Their idea of improvement, however, is far different from my own."[102] The House defeated a major challenge to the seniority system by rejecting an amendment that would allow majority committee members to select the chairman from among the three senior majority members of the committee.

In November 1971 a major procedural change in the House was the introduction of the recorded teller vote, which provided a record of how each member voted on amendments before the final passage of major bills. With anonymity no longer guaranteed, members began voting in greater numbers than previously. Statistics for the year reveal that there were 320 recorded votes taken in the House in 1971, an increase of more than 80 percent over the previous year. Of these, 108 were recorded teller votes.

When the House passed the Legislative Reorganization Act on September 17 fewer than half the chairmen of the standing House committees voted in favor. Mahon was among those chairmen who did vote for it.[103]

On March 29, 1971, Lt. William Calley was convicted in a court-martial for killing unarmed civilians in the Vietnamese village of My Lai in 1968. He argued that he was following orders to find and destroy Viet Cong. According to official estimates 347 people, ranging from one to eighty-two years old, were killed. A memorial at the site of the massacre, however, lists 504 deaths. Initially, twenty-five US soldiers were charged with premeditated murder, but only Calley was convicted. As the horrific details of the incident were revealed, people around the world were outraged. In the United States, a wider chasm developed between those who supported the war in Vietnam and those demanding its end. A flood of letters, telegrams, and petitions, some carrying more than one hundred names, swept into Mahon's office. Only a few letters asked Mahon to refuse to be a part of the whitewashing of Calley. At least 99 percent of the writers opposed the war but were angry about the treatment of Calley, who they believed was being used as a scapegoat. The editor of the *Avalanche-Journal* wrote the same. Some asked whether the United States had forgotten about the killing of many civilians when the atom bomb was dropped and why those who bombed whole villages got medals while Calley got a prison sentence. Some stouthearted West Texans even went so far as to write that if Lt. Calley was wrong, then the "long hair demonstrators" must be right!

In a form letter response Mahon wrote that he had been in touch with Defense Secretary Laird, the secretary of the army, and the president to inform them about the huge volume of mail and to summarize the contents. Laird responded that when all of the facts were made public, he believed the American public would be shocked. Mahon hoped all of the facts would not be made public "to avoid further publicity over this explosive matter."[104] He believed the whole matter had been mishandled—that it should have been investigated by the army immediately and appropriate action taken in the field.

He wrote that it was hard to tell back home just what the facts and realities of the war actually were. "Calley should not be made a scapegoat; the right of our men to protect themselves must not be jeopardized, our Government must not discredit our men who hazard their lives in war. If there has been indefensible slaughter—taking into consideration all the facts—then, of course, our country cannot condone it."[105] This viewpoint was very much in keeping with those of his constituents. Along this line there is a note in Mahon's files dated September 29, 1969, concerning a phone call from Secretary of the Army Stanley Resor. It reads, "They are dropping Green Beret trials—<u>Is dismissing all charged</u>. I said case ought to be dropped and should never have been surfaced."[106] Eight Green Berets had been charged with premeditated murder and conspiracy to commit murder of a Vietnamese national who was reported to be a double agent.

By January 1971 the People's Republic of China began reaching out to the world, indicating that its period of self-imposed isolation was nearing an end. Ideological differences with the Soviets that caused armed clashes along their long common border further encouraged Chinese leaders to strengthen their friendships with other nations. In fact, this common fear of the Soviets was an important factor in opening the lines of communications between the United States and the People's Republic of China. In the spring of 1971, Chou En-Lai indicated that he and Chairman Mao would welcome President Nixon for high-level talks in Beijing concerning the withdrawal of US support troops from Taiwan in exchange for urging the North Vietnamese to allow the United States to withdraw its troops and not overthrow the Thieu government before the 1972 election. Chinese officials also insisted that the United States refrain from blocking its entry into the United Nations, as had been the case for the previous two decades. After more than twenty years of hostility, attitudes began to change rather quickly. In June President Nixon announced an end to the twenty-one-year embargo on trade with the People's Republic of China; on July 15 the president announced that he would visit Beijing in February 1972; and on August 2 Secretary of State William Rogers announced that the US would support the seating of the People's Republic of China in the United Nations.

Nixon's announcement about his upcoming visit to the People's Republic of China stunned the world. For two decades Nixon had lambasted Dem-

ocrats for being "soft on communism." However, historian Randall Bennett
Woods writes that it was his strong anticommunist position that allowed Nixon to make these overtures without being accused of being too lenient on
communism.[107]

On the morning of July 19, Mahon attended a four-hour meeting in the
Cabinet Room. Nine House and seven Senate leaders were briefed by President Nixon, National Security Advisor Henry Kissinger, and Secretary of
State Rogers about the trip to China. Mahon's notes provided some insight
into what took place and revealed that the trip was not just for goodwill. The
United States had ample channels of communication with the USSR but very
meager ones with the People's Republic of China. Mahon wrote that Nixon insisted on referring to the nation as the People's Republic of China, its
actual name; however, Mahon and most other Americans continued to re-
fer to it as Communist China or Red China. Those present were told this
was "a promising road but a dangerous road"[108] and were cautioned against
giving the impression that the United States was now anti-Soviet and pro-
Chinese. Nixon asked the group to be very careful when talking to reporters
after the meeting. He intended to reveal very little because Chinese leaders
were concerned about being embarrassed; if congressmen expressed their personal opinions it could jeopardize the meeting in Beijing. To placate allies and
minimize international anxieties Nixon had notified leaders in approximately
twenty other countries about the trip. Most responded favorably, saying it was
long overdue. However, Japanese leaders were uneasy, fearing that the United
States would make a secret agreement with the Chinese; and the Republic
of China (known to many as Nationalist China) was quite concerned about
the trip because of the communist government's determination to replace it
in the United Nations. In a dramatic foreign-policy shift, the group was told
that while the United States might favor the Republic of China's retaining the
seat, the People's Republic of China could no longer be blocked from having
the seat, and that would mean the expulsion of the Republic of China. However, US treaties would continue in force with the Republic of China. Aside
from the dramatic change in store for the Republic of China, Congressional
and Senate leaders were told that the trip "will not be at the expense of our
old friends. Our action is not directed at any other country."[109] Nixon did not
want any of them saying the trip was intended to help with the problems in
Vietnam. Although he hoped it would contribute to peace, he said he wanted
the meeting with Chinese leaders to outlive problems in Vietnam. Many nations responded favorably, but the USSR was noticeably silent.

The next morning a reporter from UPI called Mahon, asking for a statement about the meeting in the Cabinet Room. Mahon said he was not at liberty to comment on the meeting about the president's trip to the People's Republic of China. He went on to say he did not know whether it would bring about an immediate good relationship with China, but it was worth a try.[110]

When the United Nations was formed in 1945, the Republic of China became a charter member and one of the five nations with veto power in the Security Council. Although the communists seized control of the Chinese mainland in 1949 and established the People's Republic of China, the United Nations continued to recognize only the Republic of China, which had fled to the island of Taiwan. However, on October 25, 1971, with the passage of United Nations General Assembly Resolution 2758, the UN recognized the representatives of the People's Republic of China as legitimate delegates and expelled the delegates from the Republic of China. In the events leading up to the UN expulsion of the Republic of China, on October 13 Mahon had been one of 336 members of the House who signed a bipartisan partition opposing the expulsion of the Republic of China from the United Nations. It was presented to President Nixon. However, the administration had already taken the first step in approving the UN admittance of the People's Republic of China when the State Department announced in August that it supported the "two Chinas" policy of the United Nations, which seated the People's Republic of China simultaneously with delegates of the Republic of China.

Although many people believed the time had come to accept reality with regard to the communist control of mainland China, Mahon's mail increased with letters of concern about the future consequences of the United Nations' decision. Most writers wanted the United States to withdraw its membership and financial support. Mahon answered that "I have never been as disappointed with the United Nations as some people have been because I never did expect it to be the instrument through which we would solve all our international problems."[111] He wrote that "when a policy is promulgated, or a program launched, it is not always possible to tell in advance whether it will be successful, especially in the field of foreign affairs. A lot of money has gone down the drain in pursuit of the foreign policies of each of our Presidents since World War II . . . but a third world war has so far been avoided."[112] He did not believe it was in the best interest of the United States to withdraw its membership because that would leave the organization almost totally in the control of the communists. However, he did believe that "we must consider terminating significant financial support."[113] He was in favor of continuing some amount of support for the children's fund. He called the seating of the People's Republic of China and the ouster of the Republic of China outrageous and indefensible. Despite disappointment from the old China bloc,[114] the presidential entourage to the People's Republic of China captured the nation's imagination in addition to prime-time TV coverage and lots of ink in the press.

Not to be outdone by their Chinese rivals, shortly after President Nixon announced his intentions to visit Beijing, Soviet leaders extended an invitation to visit Moscow. That visit was scheduled for May 1972, barely three months after the president's return from Beijing. A diplomatic revolution for the United States seemed to be taking hold. President Nixon was the first US president to visit Moscow. When he returned to Washington on June 1, it was learned that he and the Soviet leaders had signed pacts calling for joint efforts in space missions, technology, the environment, medical research, trade, incidents at sea, and the limitation of strategic arms. The strategic-arms agreement would limit the number of offensive weapons to those already deployed or under construction. It also limited the number of missile-carrying submarines that could be built. The Senate ratified the ABM treaty that limited the number of antiballistic missiles that could be deployed. Trade agreements included $45.6 billion of natural gas, which the United States would purchase from the Soviet Union, and wheat, corn, and feed grain, which the Soviets would purchase from the United States.[115]

Historian John Lewis Gaddis writes, "It is difficult to think of anything the Nixon administration could have done that would have produced a more dramatic shift in world power relationships of greater benefit to the United States at less cost."[116] The People's Republic of China and the USSR were both becoming friendlier to the United States as they became more hostile toward each other. President Nixon and National Security Advisor Henry Kissinger believed this situation created a balance of power that would do more to encourage peace than war possibly could. It also allowed the United States to reduce force requirements because it was now very unlikely that a war would have to be fought in Europe and Asia at the same time. If the Soviets caused problems in Europe, the Chinese would side with the United States, and if the Chinese caused problems in Asia, the Soviets would become an ally. The number of adversaries had been reduced by half, and US commitments to the world could also be reduced, making it easier to implement the Nixon Doctrine announced in Guam in 1969. This doctrine stated that the United States would honor all its treaty commitments and provide a nuclear shield if a nation that was vital to our security was threatened. However, the threatened nation had to provide ground troops for its own defense.[117]

Congress approved $70.5 billion for the Department of Defense for fiscal year 1972, after trimming $3 billion from the president's initial request. This was the second-largest defense appropriations bill in the history of the United States. Antiwar protests in Washington during the spring of 1971 lasted nearly three weeks and focused on Congress. At one point more than 175,000 people surrounded the Capitol. Some of the demonstrators portrayed guerilla battle scenes in the hall of the House and Senate, while others targeted certain members of Congress with sit-ins. Two months later the Senate adopted a bill calling for the withdrawal of US troops from Indochina, which was ultimately signed by the president.[118]

In early December 1971, during a lively debate in the House about a $3.4 billion supplemental bill for health programs, Mahon was strongly questioned about why funds for the Economic Opportunity Act were cut by 5 percent and why funds for Head Start were also being cut. It was customary for the subcommittees of the House Appropriations Committee to recommend some cuts in each bill they considered, and the cuts here were not especially large. However, some members were arguing vigorously for full funding when Representative Findley from Illinois asked Mahon whether it was true that at the current rate of spending the deficit for fiscal year 1972 would be approximately $40 billion. He expressed concern that Congress had lost control over spending and asked Mahon what could be done to bring more discipline into the appropriation process. Mahon replied that it was fundamentally a question of will and predicted that a democracy would fail unless the people had the will and restraint to make it work. He said, "Formerly on the Committee on Appropriations we would take pride in saving the taxpayers' dollars and reducing the budget as much as possible. . . . Now our fight tends to consist in trying to prevent going inordinately above the budget."[119] He went on to say that many of the programs being proposed were attractive, and some members justified the expenditure by saying that the budget was being exceeded by only a few million. He continued, "If we provided full funding for all projects, public spending would go so high that the public debt sooner or later would probably approach a googol. A googol is the figure 1 followed by 100 zeros. Then beyond that you step up to what is called a googolplex. That is, indeed, an astronomical sum. . . . This lack of restraint jeopardizes the dollar. It is perhaps the principal cause of the great economic distress."[120] The press was attracted by the idea of a googol and carried the story far and wide. One reader, the owner of Russell Textile Mills in Alabama, produced a "Googol Rag" to wipe out the debt and sent Mahon a generous supply to pass out.

President Nixon called Mahon on December 31, 1971, to wish him a happy New Year and to tell him that he couldn't have gotten through the past year without Mahon's help. Nixon told him that the bombing of North Vietnam was finished and only one plane was lost the last week in December. . . . They also talked about football, and Nixon said Dallas would win because it had a balanced team that year. He said the Redskins were an ephemeral thing. In his notes Mahon scribbled, "How do you talk to the President?"[121] Mahon asked the president where he was, and Nixon replied that he was in Key Biscayne, Florida. When Nixon asked Mahon where he was, Mahon replied that he was in Washington, sitting around in his double-knit slacks, enjoying life.[122]

On Christmas day President Nixon had ordered the resumption of the bombing of North Vietnam. More than two hundred planes flew in waves of sorties in the largest single raid since President Johnson had halted bombing in November 1968. There were a few demonstrations around the country, but they were not very effective because the movement had lost its momentum. However, antiwar legislators had not lost their momentum, and there were threats to cut off funding.[123] President Nixon understood that he couldn't have gotten through the past year without Mahon's help, and he was certainly going to need that help again next year.

In his second inaugural address President Nixon said, "Let each of us ask not what government can do for me, but what I can do for myself."[124] Nixon's biographer, Richard Reeves, called that statement a good prelude to the $268.7 billion budget that Nixon delivered to Congress on January 27. It countered the trend toward bigger and more socially conscious government that began with Franklin Roosevelt's New Deal in the 1930s and continued through Lyndon Johnson's Great Society. The budget, prepared by Casper Weinberger and Roy Ash of the new OMB, proposed no new programs and eliminated or cut one hundred existing federal programs, including ones benefiting the unemployed, farmers, students, veterans, small businessmen, the mentally ill, and people living in federal housing. Nixon's philosophy was to eliminate specific grants for such programs as vocational education and slum clearance, then give the states block grants, under the name of special revenue sharing, to use at state and local discretion. He made clear his intention of impounding money appropriated by Congress for programs he considered unnecessary. Congressional estimates indicated the president refused to spend at least $12.2 billion already appropriated.[125] It soon became evident that the newly reelected president was ready to challenge congressional authority by refusing to spend appropriated money, by refusing to allow certain members of his administration to appear before congressional committees, and by refusing to halt the bombing in Indochina despite protests from both houses of Congress that it was illegal.

Instead of vetoing bills for programs he found objectionable and risking an override, he let the bills become laws, then refused to spend the money appropriated to bring these programs into existence, thus killing them. Nixon made it plain that he would not raise taxes to pay for social programs, and he considered impoundment a way to reduce them. He justified his actions as representative of his determination to hold down federal spending because Congress would not exercise restraint. The truth of the matter is that the only action the Constitution allows for opposing legislation is the veto. The Constitution gives Congress, not the president, the right to determine levels of spending. Nixon's actions fueled a concern that the president was undermining the power of Congress to legislate and that he was, in fact, legislating through impoundment of funds.

Mahon told a reporter from *US News & World Report*, "The differences between the White House and Congress are very serious, because I do not feel the President has the broad authority which he has exercised to impound funds. I don't think he has the authority under the law just to, willy-nilly, eliminate programs or drastically to reduce them on the ground that he doesn't think they're effective. After all, a law is a law. I think that's going to be a major issue."[126] On March 28 he introduced a bill (H.R. 5193) that would require the president "to inform Congress within 10 days of the impoundment of funds and that Congress have 60 days in which to nullify, in whole or in part, the impoundment actions of the President."[127] Many similar bills were introduced in both the House and Senate that indicated the anger that impoundment caused in Congress. The bill that ultimately became law was introduced in the Senate by Senator Ervin, but it did not pass until 1974 and is known as the Impoundment Control Act of 1974.

The president also asserted that Congress had no legal way to force testimony from members of his administration. This caused a group of senators to begin drawing up rules that could be used to declare uncooperative witnesses to be in contempt of Congress. However, before the end of the year executive privilege was a nonissue, in light of Watergate and other scandals. Ultimately, those in Congress who were attempting to halt the president's usurpation of Congressional powers were victorious in passing the War Powers Resolution, despite a veto. This act set a sixty-day limit on committing US troops to conflict without congressional approval.

On January 22, just two days after President Nixon's second inauguration, Lyndon Johnson died of a heart attack at his Texas ranch. This was also the day that a cease-fire was signed in Vietnam. Johnson's severe heart disease had been further aggravated by smoking and stress. It was reported that Lady Bird feared such as this if he chose to seek a second term, and indeed if he had run successfully his death would have occurred just two days after his second term had ended. His body was taken to Washington for a state funeral. After lying in state in the Capitol, services were conducted on January 25 at National City Christian Church, where he often worshiped. The Mahons had an opportunity to personally express their sorrow to Lady Bird after the ceremony in the Capitol rotunda, but they did not have a chance to speak to her after the burial in the family cemetery in Stonewall, Texas. They made the flight to Texas in Air Force Two, and because a number of others were on the same plane, all the passengers were required to stay together. The plane returned to Washington immediately after the services at the cemetery so they were not able to visit with the family at the ranch house. Within a week in a letter to Lady Bird, Mahon wrote, "Please know of our continued love and sympathy. We want to continue the same warm relationship which has existed through the years. We look forward to coming back to the Ranch one of these days and we want to see you whenever you are in Washington."[128]

In February Mahon wrote to his family, "We have had a busy time of it, many things happening, trip to the LBJ funeral and the Boggs memorial in New Orleans, the Inauguration, mean problems associated with the reconvening of Congress and the organization of the Appropriations Committee, hearing with Secretary of the Treasury about the Budget, and much, much more."[129]

In October 1973 Vice President Spiro Agnew resigned from office. The US attorney's office in Maryland had been investigating him on charges of tax fraud, extortion, and bribery. He was ultimately allowed to plead no contest to charges that he failed to report nearly $30,000 of income received in 1967, if he agreed to resign from office. In doing so, he became the only vice president in history to resign because of criminal charges. President Nixon nominated Representative Gerald Ford (R-MI), the House minority leader, to replace him.

Mahon appeared before the Senate Rules Committee on behalf of the nomination of Gerald Ford for vice president. He noted that this was the first action of its kind under the twenty-fifth amendment to the Constitution. He continued, "It is most fortunate that the President has nominated a man who is so well known and, I should say, so favorably known to the Congress. In May of 1966 I had the honor of presenting the annual George Washington Award to Mr. Ford in behalf of the American Good Government Society. . . . On that occasion I said, 'Great things lie ahead for Jerry Ford in the realm of government.' That prediction is being fulfilled. At the same time I spoke of the reverence which Jerry Ford has for the American constitutional system. I noted his long experience in government which had fitted him for the task of helping strengthen American institutions. His dedicated service since that time has borne out the validity of those remarks."[130] Ford had served on the House Committee for Appropriations since 1951 and on the defense subcommittee since 1953. From the very beginning Mahon was impressed with his calm judgment, and a close friendship soon developed between them. Mahon believed that after working closely with a person for the number of hours required to prepare the appropriations bills, he learned to know that person pretty well. He characterized Ford as sincere, forthright, a hard worker, and one who respects truth and decency. "He represents the best qualities of American manhood and integrity."[131] Mahon went on to say that Ford's service as minority leader, in addition to his service on the Appropriations Committee, had given him a national, rather than a parochial view of government, which would allow him to work productively with any administration that was in power. Mahon believed that knowing where the nation's money was spent provided Ford with an overall knowledge about how the government operated. "Not many people in the House of Representatives know Jerry Ford better than I do. I have had occasion to consult with him on almost a daily basis, first in his membership on the Appropriations Committee and then in his capacity as Minority Leader. I would unhesitatingly place Jerry Ford high on the list of those Members of unassailable character and integrity with whom I have served in my years of Congressional service. He reflects and generates confidence among those with whom he associates. These are qualities devoutly to be sought in a public official."[132] Ford had asked Mahon and five other members of the House to testify on his behalf. Mahon appeared before the Senate committee on October 30, 1973, and a letter from Ford thanking Mahon for testifying is in his files. It is very much the usual formal thank-you letter. However, Ford scrawled across the bottom, "P.S. Your personal comments were great. J."[133] On December 6 Gerald Ford became the fifth vice president who was not elected to the office.

In early November Mahon told his sister in a letter,

> I had a telephone call from a friend at Lubbock in regard to the George and Helen Mahon City and County Library. It is to be dedicated probably in March of next year. He was inquiring as to whether or not it might be suitable for me to place "my papers" in the Library. It seems to be the fashion for Presidents and Members of Congress to place their files and records and papers in libraries. . . . Of course, the Lubbock library was not built for the Mahons, just named for us.
>
> LBJ insisted for a period of years, and he was joined by Lady Bird, that I give my papers to the LBJ Library at Austin. I felt I could hardly do that. Dr. Murray, president of Tech, has asked that I give my papers to Tech. I have an honorary degree from Tech, and Tech is in our home town, and one could make a good case for my giving my papers to Tech, an educational institution. The city library, which is named for us, would be a good candidate, but in a way, it is not the place where students of history a hundred years from now would go for research to the same extent as to a university library.

I have explained to my friends and to archivists that I can see little value in my papers. I do grab a pencil when anyone calls me, and I make notes; but the notes are hardly legible, hardly intelligible, and they wouldn't mean much to anyone but me.

Letters from constituents might, in some cases, be of interest; but it would hardly seem fair for me to release to the public personal-type letters which I receive from constituents. However, it is said that one can specify that his papers shall not be made available for five years, ten years, twenty-five years, or whatever. It is conceivable that a few hundred years from now, barring a nuclear holocaust, some of my papers might be of interest to the historians as to the Watergate era in which we now live![134]

Early on the night of May 11, 1970, Lubbock was hit by a killer tornado that was rated F5 on the Fujita scale, the highest rating on a scale used to measure tornadoes throughout the country. The one-and-a-half-mile-wide storm destroyed fifteen square miles of the city, killed twenty-six people, injured more than five hundred, and left property damage that amounted to over $250 million. Within days Mahon was in Lubbock, along with other government officials, to survey the damage and pledge help in securing federal aid for rebuilding. A citizens advisory commission, made up of business and civic leaders, was quickly formed to begin plans for rebuilding. In less than three months an election was held to approve $13.5 million in redevelopment bonds. This money was to be used to build a civic center complex in memory of those killed, a series of lakes, a new city library, and new parks. Federal money, used for neighborhood redevelopment, was handled by the city's Urban Renewal Agency.

The new $1.2 million library was named for George and Helen Mahon. They were on hand for the dedication in March 1974 and expressed their honor and gratitude at having a library bear their name. When Lubbock Mayor Morris Turner addressed the crowd of more than one thousand, he told them, "We are here to honor two friends who helped us so well."[135] Congratulatory telegrams from President Nixon and Vice President Ford were read. Congratulatory letters also flowed into his Congressional office, and one of these pretty well summarized the feelings of Lubbockites. The writer thought the George and Helen Mahon Library was the greatest library in the world because in honoring two great people who had served others, it would also serve the people of West Texas.[136]

⇝

On December 20 Congress cleared for the president's signature H.R. 11575 (Pub. L. No. 93-238), a bill appropriating $74.2 billion for the Department of Defense in fiscal year 1974. The budget was second only to the fiscal year 1973 total of $74.4 billion as the largest single defense appropriation ever approved by Congress.

Most of the Pentagon's major weapons requests were left intact. The largest reductions were made in funds for the navy's new Trident submarine and the army's new Minuteman ABM system, called Site Defense. Substantial reductions also were made in the military assistance program for South Vietnam and Laos, and Congress took steps toward returning the program to the regular foreign aid program funded through the State Department.

⇝

On December 21, 1973, the Mahons had been married fifty years, and they were honored with a dinner on December 16 at the exclusive 1925 F Street Club in Washington. The private club, formerly a townhouse mansion near the White House, was decorated in gold and had several glowing fireplaces to keep away the cold from the snow-covered city. Hosts for the occasion were Mr. and Mrs. Leslie Carpenter, Texans who worked in Washington. Liz Carpenter had been press secretary for Lady Bird Johnson, and her husband was Washington bureau chief for the *Abilene* (Texas) *Reporter-News*. Vice President and Mrs. Gerald Ford; Speaker and Mrs. Carl Albert; and former vice president and Mrs. Humphrey were among the star-studded politicos who attended the sit-down dinner for forty-eight. Lady Bird Johnson sent a white orchid corsage for Helen along with a card that read, "For Helen, with much love on this big night! Love, Lady Bird."[137] Congratulations and warm wishes for many more years together also came from Mrs. Dwight Eisenhower and Mrs. Harry Truman. President and Mrs. Nixon had earlier expressed their congratulations. The Carpenters presented the honored couple with a golden vermeil bowl from Tiffany's. The bowl contained two inscriptions: "The Golden Formula: A Sense of Purpose and a Touch of Poetry" and a line from Elizabeth Barrett Browning, "Beloved, thou hast brought me many flowers." Many believed these words captured the Mahons' approach to marriage during their fifty years together. Liz Carpenter described Mahon as having "the heart of a poet even though he might have the pen of a miser."[138] When asked to make a few remarks, Mahon began by saying that when he married, "I just threw myself into neutral and went wherever Helen pushed me." He went on to say that he considered every day to be Helen's Day and got the most fun in life from spending time with her. After fifty years of marriage and all the attention then being given to women's lib, he had some definite ideas about the place of a wife. He declared it was not in the professions, not in society, not in the kitchen, nor in the home, but the real place of a wife was in the heart of her husband, where he had enjoyed having Helen for the past fifty years. He closed by saying that they loved each other, their friends, and their country, and they believed better days were ahead.

The Mahons spent the actual day of their anniversary in Dallas with Daphne and her family. They took time away from family activities to drive to the First Methodist Church in Fort Worth, the scene of their wedding. In a note found in Mahon's files, Helen recalled that it was a rainy day that Friday in 1923, and although there were no flowers or music, their love was enough.[139]

Stress became the overriding theme of 1974, beginning in March, when Mahon's brother Durward was killed in a one-car accident. This was the third brother to die, John having died in 1970 and Thomas Marion in 1940.

Then Helen's health became a major concern in the summer of 1974, when she suffered a heart attack on the morning of June 17. She didn't have any pain but was very nauseated. Mahon called the Capitol doctor and made an appointment for her the following morning. After checking her over, the doctor called for an ambulance, which immediately took her to a hospital. Upon arrival her case was turned over to her family doctor, who happened to be a heart specialist. She spent the next six days in intensive care before being put in a private room, where she remained for the next two weeks. When she returned home, Daphne came for a week to care for her mother, and after that Mahon secured the help of a woman who stayed with her five days a week. He was her "nurse" at night and on the weekends. His first task each morning was to check her pulse and weight. During the first week at home she was not allowed to use the stairs, do any housework, or exert herself in any way, but gradually she was able to resume her usual activities.

Helen was getting stronger every day and able to take a three-block walk on late afternoons when the next thunderbolt hit. Mahon had just started to present the $83 billion defense appropriation bill to the House when his office received a call from William Timmons, a close presidential aide. It was 9:00 p.m. before the bill passed, after eight hours of uninterrupted debate. The following morning, when Mahon returned the call, he learned that Timmons was asking key people on the Hill for their opinion about Nixon's problem with the office tapes that had been subpoenaed. Mahon's position was best stated in a family letter, "I explained that, since the President had released three additional tapes and issued a statement directly implicating himself in the cover up; and, since the House Judiciary Committee had recommended impeachment; and, since all of the Members, including 17 Republicans, now advocated if the President did not resign, I thought impeachment by the House by a wide margin was inevitable."[140] Mahon's analysis was in line with the other opinions Timmons had sought.

On June 17, 1972, the Democratic National Committee headquarters in the Watergate office building had been burglarized. What was initially described as "a third-rate burglary" ultimately became a political scandal that involved many in high office, including President Nixon. Two years of investigation uncovered a plethora of illegal activities conducted by administration officials and the president's staff. Through it all Nixon steadfastly claimed to be innocent of any knowledge concerning these activities; however, the tape recording system in his office contained conversations that proved he did know what was going on and that he had obstructed justice by trying to cover up knowledge of the Watergate break-in. Realizing that the conversations on the tapes would incriminate him, making him subject to impeachment, President Nixon attempted to claim executive privilege to avoid turning over the tapes to the Senate Select Committee on Presidential Activities. This committee had been established to investigate the Watergate break-in and other activities surrounding Nixon's reelection. When the Supreme Court ruled that he must release the tapes, it became clear that the damage to his presidency would be devastating.

On Thursday, August 8, Mahon received another call from Timmons, telling him the president would like to see him and a few friends from the Hill at 8:00 p.m. to tell them good-bye before speaking to the nation at 9:00 p.m. About thirty-five people gathered in the Cabinet Room, and when the president entered, they stood, applauding vigorously. Later Mahon wrote home that "it was obvious that the President was under great strain and was struggling with his emotions. . . . He said that his family had been consulted and they all wanted him to fight impeachment and that it was in his nature to do so. When he spoke of the loyalty of his family, he had to stop and struggle with his emotions. He had to pause to gain his composure several times. . . . He ended his discussion by thanking us for being helpful to him through the years, remarking that he hoped we would not feel that he had let us down. He left the room in tears, and there were very few, if any, dry eyes in the room. I had never seen him lose his composure before; but, of course, no public official in the nation had ever been under such stress and strain for so long. . . . He referred to his mistakes but never to any wrongdoing. Nothing like this moment had ever happened before in the history of this country, and it was awesome to have a grandstand seat to witness it."[141]

President Nixon invited those present to watch his television address from the theater room in the White House, but Mahon quickly made the eight-minute trip home to watch the address with Helen. Afterward, there were many calls from reporters, and later he told his family that he was completely satisfied with the article about his reaction that appeared in the *Lubbock Avalanche-Journal*. He told the reporters with whom he talked that he refused to speculate on how he would have voted on impeachment and would not comment on whether or not he thought Nixon should have resigned. "I have studiously sought to keep an open mind with respect to the whole impeachment affair," he told the reporter from Lubbock.[142]

Mahon wrote to his family that he believed there were a lot of political angles to the Watergate affair and that he had always tried to act with complete fairness and objectivity. However, the colleagues he talked with agreed that Nixon's resignation was necessary. He hoped that leaders of all parties would work together to promote a better feeling in the nation and a constructive approach to any new problems.

He and Helen went to bed about eleven o'clock that night. Sometime after one o'clock Helen awakened him to answer the phone in the kitchen. That was their private line; the public line was always turned off when they retired at night. The caller hung up before he could get into the kitchen, but the phone soon rang again. This time the White House operator told him the president was calling. Mahon had always made his private number available to the White House. When Nixon came on the line, Mahon told him that his televised speech had been a masterful job. Then Nixon said he did not want his friends to feel that he had let them down. He went on to reminisce about the three weeks that he and Mahon had spent together in Europe in 1947 as members of the Herter Committee. The president also said that he and Pat loved the Mahons and would always appreciate their friendship. According to notes Mahon made the next day about the conservation, Nixon also said, "We have got to keep this country strong on account of those g.d. Russians. You've got to tell Jerry that."[143] It was 1:20 a.m. when he hung up. In 1980 Mahon recalled that Nixon was very distraught when he called. Although Nixon and Mahon had never discussed personal problems with each other, Mahon assumed he just needed someone to talk to that night.[144]

Richard Nixon left the White House on the morning of August 9, and Chief Justice Warren Burger administered the oath of office to Gerald Ford at twelve o'clock. Mahon was present. On the evening of August 12, President Ford addressed a joint session of Congress, and after the address Mahon went to the appropriation offices, just off the House floor. As he was leaving for the night, he met Ford in the corridor in front of the offices and congratulated him. Ford said they needed to get together for a game of golf, and just a short time later he contacted Mahon.[145] They always enjoyed golfing together, but responsibilities prevented their doing so very often. Earlier that week during a telephone interview, a reporter asked Mahon how many presidents he had served under and was told, "Watch your language, young man, I haven't served under any!" He pointed out that he had served with six presidents and when Gerald Ford became president, he would have served with seven.[146]

Mahon jokingly told his family that he considered canceling his subscription to the *Washington Post* and offering his television for sale. For months the Watergate scandal was all anyone wrote or talked about, and now that it had ended, Mahon assumed they would have nothing at all to report! He also wrote that there seemed to be a new spirit in Washington because when they filled his car with gas the following weekend, the attendant cleaned the windows and that had not happened for months.

A stressful year ended on a positive note. On December 10 a portrait of Mahon was unveiled in the Sam Rayburn Room of the Capitol. The Rayburn Room was chosen because it was Speaker Rayburn who had sponsored his appointment to the House Appropriations Committee in 1939. After the ceremony the portrait was moved to the House Appropriations Committee chambers. Jamie L. Whitten (D-MS), ranking majority member of the House committee, was master of ceremonies. Remarks were made by President Ford, Speaker Carl Albert, and others. Ford opened his remarks with an expression of gratitude for the friendship he had long enjoyed with the Mahons and recalled the golf games that he and Mahon had enjoyed with the comment that Mahon not only had "an interlocking grip on a putter, but he had a hammer-lock grip on unnecessary government spending."[147] After serving for fourteen years on the House Appropriations Committee with Mahon, Ford said he deserved to be called a statesman for consistently rising above party politics to do what was best for his country. He "devoted his total energies, his boundless resources to keep America morally, militarily and fiscally strong."[148] He ended by saying, "Texas, we all know, has been known for its bigness. George Mahon has lived up to its reputation."[149]

Mahon responded by thanking the president for his remarks and assuring him that the burdens of office would be lighter because the Democrats at their mid-term national convention in Kansas City agreed that cooperation was paramount—that the country's welfare must be placed above partisanship.

After the ceremony a luncheon for a select group was held in the Speaker's Dining Room at the Capitol. George Holt, Mahon's grandson, was present for the occasion.

West Texas friends paid for the portrait, which was presented to the government after the dedication. In the Nineteenth District admiration for Mahon was so great that no letters of solicitation were sent to prospective donors for fear of offending someone by failing to contact him.[150] Notice of the project spread by word of mouth, and more money than needed to pay for the portrait, printing expenses, and the luncheon was received. After all expenses were paid, the remaining money was donated to the chambers of commerce in Lubbock, Midland, and Odessa, Texas.

Charles J. Fox of New York City was contracted to produce the portrait for $6,500. He was well-known for his portraits of famous and wealthy Americans, including President John F. Kennedy, Supreme Court Justice Louis D. Brandeis, and Governor John B. Connally, in addition to many legislators and captains of industry. The portraits were painted from a photograph, with a sketch being sent to the subject before the painting was executed. A fly in the ointment surfaced in 1978 when an Internal Revenue investigation revealed that C. J. Fox was really Leo Fox, a great salesman who could not paint. Other artists did his work. From 1972 through 1974, an obscure Manhattan artist named Irving Resnikoff painted portraits for Fox for a fee of $250 to

$300 each and was probably the person who painted Mahon's portrait. Mahon never expressed any dissatisfaction with the portrait, although his files did contain news articles from *Time* and the *Washington Post* about the fraud. Apparently other clients were also satisfied with their portraits because the business was still operative in 2009, and the portraits continued to be painted from a photograph by "who knows who"? In the same vein as the Watergate scandal, Fox's deception was indicative of an attitude that the ends justify the means, an attitude all too prevalent in America during the 1970s.

During the early part of the Ninety-third Congress, the president's use of executive authority threatened the role of the legislative branch. Most legislators understood the difficulty of getting into a power struggle with the newly reelected president; however, problems within the executive branch that led to the resignation of both the president and the vice president created a leadership vacuum that allowed Congress to recapture some of its lost power. This was evidenced in 1973, when Congress overrode Nixon's veto of a bill restricting the president's power to make war, and again in 1974, when it passed a budget reform bill that helped it regain control over federal spending by limiting executive impoundment of funds. Congress also played a role in selecting the new president and vice president. By the time of adjournment in December 1974, the balance of power had shifted away from the "imperial presidency" of the executive branch back to Congress. "The so-called balance of powers in American government is not a static entity; throughout history the balance of that power has shifted among the three branches of government."[151] Beginning with the New Deal and continuing through World War II, power shifted to the executive branch. This shift was evident in the declaration of war without Congressional approval in Korea and Vietnam. The history of presidential deceit that was exposed in the Pentagon Papers caused many in Congress to believe it was time to take back as much power as possible. Finally, the exposure of lies and deceit that led to Richard Nixon's resignation provided the opportunity to do this.[152]

Chapter 9

Transitions: 1974–1978

When Gerald R. Ford assumed the presidency, the vice presidency was vacant for the second time in a year. In December 1974 Congress confirmed President Ford's choice of Nelson A. Rockefeller for vice president, and for the first time in history, Americans had both a president and a vice president who had not been elected.

The new spirit that Mahon thought he noticed in Washington and the new era of integrity that the nation expected in government went up in smoke on September 8, when President Ford granted Richard Nixon a "full, free and absolute pardon." The pardon ended any possibility of an indictment, and Nixon never did admit to any criminal wrongdoing. President Ford granted the pardon in hopes of healing the nation and ending the media frenzy over the former president's involvement with the Watergate scandal. However, rather than healing the nation, the pardon set off a firestorm. The public was further angered when newspapers began printing articles about President Ford's request for funds to ease Nixon's transition to private life. Part of the money he was to receive was provided under the Presidential Transition Act of 1963, the same source of funding that people had complained about so loudly when President Johnson left office. Other funds to cover the expenses of Nixon's office in San Clemente ran into opposition, and Mahon promised that public hearings would intensely scrutinize any requests not covered by law before appropriating any money. Americans were enraged because they believed Nixon should be held accountable under the law just as they were. There was a loud outcry that a deal had been struck that undermined the concept of a single justice for all Americans.

Mahon's office was overwhelmed with letters from angry and confused constituents. Many were furious that there appeared to be a double standard that allowed a politician to walk free, while ordinary citizens were held accountable for their crimes. One woman wrote that "what's fair for Nixon is fair for the dogcatcher. . . . There is a difference between compassion and copout. This is a copout. . . . Nixon has made a fool of the Congress, the people, his family and his lawyers. . . . I can hear his horselaugh all the way from California ringing in my ears. . . . The next thing I know he'll be out campaigning for Ford in '76—or collecting royalties from his new book "Wading Watergate with Pat & Dick."[1] Mahon wrote to constituents that he "was deeply disappointed over President Ford's actions regarding the pardon."[2] He further explained that he was not convinced that the president had the authority under the Constitution to grant a pardon prior to court action and a conviction. However, most legal authorities agreed that, as far as presidential pardons were concerned, Congress did not have the power to nullify the president's actions. Mahon's files contain President Ford's answer to a constituent letter that Mahon forwarded to him. Ford wrote that it was not an easy decision to reach; however, the Constitution granted him the right to pardon Nixon, and he had done so to "heal the wounds of the Nation." He continued, "I felt then, and I feel now, that I made the right decision in an honest, conscientious effort to end the divisions in this country."[3] President Ford had been catapulted into the presidency without time to develop an overall vision concerning what he wanted to accomplish during his presidency, and he had no opportunity to assemble a team that could help implement his vision. In addition to the trauma of Watergate, a plethora of problems existed, such as rising inflation coupled with a recession, unemployment, energy problems, defense costs, and trade deficits. All of this needed attention, but that attention was being diverted to Nixon's problems. In future years it was believed that if President Ford had waited longer, he might have avoided some of the backlash. Because he did not prepare Congress, the public, or the press for what was coming, reaction was swift and ugly. Two decades later, after some of the dust had settled, historian Stephen Ambrose and *Washington Post* reporter Bob Woodward both came to the conclusion that a pardon was inevitable because it would have been nearly impossible to conduct any national business in the chaos that would have accompanied the trial of a former president.[4]

Shortly after he pardoned Richard Nixon, the House of Representatives summoned President Ford to appear before the Judiciary Committee's Criminal Justice Subcommittee, chaired by William L. Hungate (D-MO). "He became the first president to testify before a committee of Congress since Abraham Lincoln."[5] As members of the subcommittee grilled the president, it became evident that political power had shifted from the White House to

Congress. Throughout the hearing President Ford steadfastly maintained that "there was no deal, period, under no circumstances."[6] "No deal" also foreshadowed the future relationship between the president and Congress during his administration. Long-lasting cynicism, not healing, became the legacy of Nixon's pardon.

During the midterm elections in the fall of 1974, the turnout was small—only 36 percent of the eligible voters went to the polls. Democrats gained forty-three seats in the House and three seats in the Senate, giving them a majority in both chambers. A change had taken place in the composition of Congress, and the president would have to govern in this new environment.

The shift of power from the White House to Congress was not the only power shift taking place. During the decade of the 1970s, there were also important power shifts taking place within Congress. In January 1973 the House and Senate began an overall examination of the structure and jurisdiction of the committee system, the first in more than a quarter century. Since the 1960s a surge of Northern Democrats along with the growth of Republicans in the South began to erode the traditional Southern conservative dominance of the Democratic Party. New, younger Democrats who were urban and liberal soon outnumbered the older Southern conservatives, and they believed a larger share of the power and resources should be theirs. Changes that began slowly in the 1960s accelerated during the 1970s and reached a peak in 1974 and 1975. Reforms that challenged the seniority system used to select committee chairs were adopted; sunshine laws that exposed committee meetings to the public were enforced; secret votes on floor amendments were ended; and additional staff was allocated to junior members.[7] Prior to this, almost absolute authority had been vested in the representatives and senators who had served the longest. While not a formal rule, the seniority system was a strongly engrained tradition used to rank committee members according to continuous years of service on the committee. Members who transferred to another committee had to start over again at the bottom of the seniority ladder.

In January 1971, when Democrats were organizing for the Ninety-second Congress, the Committee on Committees, consisting of all the Democrats on the Ways and Means Committee, was admonished that committee members "should *not* consider only seniority when they compiled the list of recommendations for committee chairmen that would be submitted to the entire caucus."[8] Although the caucus had traditionally voted on the whole slate of nominees for committee chairmen, those in charge served notice that if any ten members wanted a separate vote on individual chairmen, that would happen. Only one chairman was voted on individually, and he passed, but in 1973 a new rule was passed requiring a separate vote by secret ballot on each chairman. Never before had committee chairmen had to face such an accounting for how they ran their committees. Only in the rarest of cases had the House blocked a representative from taking a committee chairmanship to which he was entitled by seniority. This was a major break from the past, when freshmen were seen and not heard until they had served several terms. A sizable number of negative votes were cast that year, but no nominee for chairman failed to pass. By 1975 the caucus adopted a rule that nominees from the floor of the caucus would be permitted if any nominee from the Committee on Committees was rejected.

A reorganization of the House committee system in 1974 allowed the caucus of the majority party to organize new Congresses in December of election years, before the next Congress convened the following January. Traditionally this had happened in January, just before the opening of a new Congress. Earlier reforms made Democratic committee chairmen subject to election by the caucus each biennium, and the authority to make Democratic committee assignments was transferred from the House Ways and Means Committee to the Democratic Steering and Policy Committee. Also, for the first time, all thirteen subcommittee chairmen of the House Appropriations Committee were subject to approval by the caucus of the majority party. Proxy votes in committees were banned; all committees were required to have at least four subcommittees; and the speaker gained greater latitude in referring bills to committees.

In December 1974 the newly elected members, who would not be sworn in until January 1975, were permitted to interview committee chairmen, "questioning them mainly on how they planned to run their committees and on what they saw as the prospective input of freshmen."[9] After these interviews the new members voted by secret ballot when the party caucus met in January to elect committee chairs. There were more negative than positive votes for Wright Patman (D-TX), W. R. Poage (D-TX), and F. Edward Hebert (D-LA), and this played a large part in the loss by these men of their chairmanships. Each of the three was accused of arrogant and autocratic behavior that denied fair treatment to other committee members. Although Mahon received some negative votes—193 for and 94 against—his chairmanship survived. Mahon told his family, "That did not seem so bad in light of the atmosphere and in view of the revolution by most of the new Democratic Members."[10] Historian Barbara Hinckley writes that in the case of the three deposed chairmen, there was a Northern liberal challenger around whom the reformers could rally. In Mahon's case Representative Jamie Whitten, an archconservative from Mississippi, was next in line to assume the chairmanship, and there were three more Southern conservatives in line behind him. There was simply no eligible Northern liberal that the reformers could rally around, so nothing would be gained by deposing Mahon.[11] Mahon's congressional aide believed that an important reason he was not deposed was that, when interviewed he spent most of the day showing the freshmen how the Appropriations Committee worked.[12] This very likely did have a bearing on the situation: one of the changes Mahon made in 1964 when he became chairman of the full committee was taking newcomers on the committee under his wing in order to help them find a subcommittee on which they could serve. According to legend he remembered what it was like to be a freshman, and he tried to smoothly integrate newcomers into the Appropriations Committee.

Although by the end of 1975 the seniority system was in shambles as the sole method by which members rose to power, it still functioned as a device for ordering the hierarchy on committees. It was simply no longer the dominant force. "Both chambers had created methods by which committee chairmen had to stand for election by their colleagues in the party caucuses."[13] The reforms produced a Congress that was much different by the end of 1975 than at the beginning of the decade. Not surprisingly, Mahon was skeptical of most of the reforms and wrote home that "we have never had anything like this before during my tenure here."[14]

The *Washington Post* carried an article by Rowland Evans and Robert Novak in which they discussed the concern of several congressmen that a lack of clear guidelines for choosing which chairmen to purge would mean punishment for those chairmen who simply did not please a majority, regardless of whether they were capable of continuing in their position or not. The whole process could degenerate to a biennial bartering orgy for leadership roles, and the chaos created would be worse than the seniority system.[15]

The Defense Department appropriation bill for fiscal year 1975 cleared the Conference Committee on September 23. This was the bill Mahon was working on when White House aide William Timmons called him on August 8 about developments concerning the resignation of President Nixon. The bill that cleared the Senate was for just over $82 billion. The conferees settled on $82.5 billion, $800 million less than the $83.3 billion recommended by the House. This was an increase from the $80 billion—or less—appropriated for the previous seven years. There was a growing concern that the Soviets, despite détente, were continuing their arms buildup, and this was causing Americans to change their minds about reduced defense budgets. However, Mahon did warn the Pentagon that only with great reluctance would Congress entertain a request for supplemental appropriations during that fiscal year. The military brass and the administration were put on notice that they were expected to find a way to live within the appropriation allowed.[16]

When the conference report was debated in the House, members disagreed with the report on several points. Robert N. Giaimo (D-CT) refused to sign it, complaining that he and most other members were not privy to information about the amount and use of CIA money. He argued that it was shameful for the United States to use covert intelligence operations to overthrow governments that were philosophically different from that of the United States. He insisted that it was time to terminate such actions. He was referring to the CIA's actions in Chile to undermine the Allende government, which was overthrown on September 11, 1974. Mahon was reluctant to share much information and responded that "we, of course, do not want to telegraph to the Kremlin the innermost secrets of the U.S. government. . . . The law provides the procedure for keeping this type of information secret."[17] He continued that he and others who approved CIA funds were satisfied that CIA actions were proper and he would feel obligated to tell Congress if that were not so.

Other members complained about providing $205 million for twelve F-111 fighter/bomber planes that the air force had not requested for the past two years. Surely, they argued, this was done to protect employment in aircraft industries in some congressmen's districts. Mahon replied that the nearest aircraft plant was three hundred miles from his district. He said that the F-111 production lines had to be kept open in case the controversial B-1 bomber did not go into production. Several members, including Jim Wright (D-TX), jumped to Mahon's defense, arguing that it was actually more economical to keep the production lines open for the F-111 than to get caught in a position of having to fund the B-1 bomber regardless of the cost. It was pointed out that the air force had not requested F-111s because the air force brass did not want an economical option to the B-1. If the production lines were closed, reopening them again would be very costly, but if Congress kept the lines open by ordering planes, there would be an option to the B-1, which was in serious trouble because of cost overruns. In 1974 it was costing $70 million per plane, with predictions that by the time it went into production, the cost would reach $100 million per plane.

After a vigorous debate on the report, a motion to accept it passed by 293 yeas, 59 nays, and 82 not voting. Although some people were beginning to realize the problem of allowing the Soviet Union to get ahead militarily, one-third of the members present in the House when the final defense appropriation figures were voted on were opposed to the high cost of defense. Clearly, money for defense still had a fight ahead, especially when double-digit inflation was causing reductions in social programs.

From the outbreak of the Korean War until the Tet offensive of 1968, the Department of Defense had a special relationship with Congress. During those years the Pentagon's budget received special treatment compared to requests for nondefense spending. Congressional reductions of requests for defense appropriations averaged less than 2 percent, while requests for non-defense programs averaged more than 9 percent reductions. In fact, it was not unusual for Congress to appropriate more money for defense than the secretary of defense had requested. This was clearly illustrated in 1962, when Representative Carl Vinson insisted that the air force spend more money on the B-70 aircraft than the secretary of defense wanted. However, after the Tet offensive this relationship underwent a dramatic shift because of widespread public disillusionment with the Vietnam War and increasing concern for domestic problems.[18]

By 1974 only about 60 percent of federal spending was subject to annual appropriations. The rest, known as "backdoor spending," consisted of obligations, such as interest on the national debt, that Congress had no choice but to meet through appropriations. It also included mandatory spending, entitlement programs, that had to be funded as a result of legislation. In 1974 Congress passed a budget reform bill that provided more control over back-door spending beginning in 1975. New borrowing authority and contract authority would have to be approved by the Appropriations Committees, and entitlement programs would be subject to tighter review by the Appropriations Committees.[19]

During 1975 the Central Intelligence Agency and the Federal Bureau of Investigation became the target of investigations concerning Watergate-related activities, wiretapping and spying on American citizens such as student protesters, and attempted assassinations of foreign government officials. After an expose by Seymour Hersh in the *New York Times* on December 22, 1974, President Ford appointed a committee to investigate CIA activities within the United States. He appointed Nelson Rockefeller as chair, and the committee became known as the Rockefeller Committee. Additionally, investigative committees were formed in both the House and the Senate. Many people were stirred up and determined to shed light on problems within the agency, many of which CIA Director William Colby declared had already been corrected. Mahon did not agree with the idea of publicly shedding light on CIA activities, as he had pointed out from the House floor in 1963. He did not condone the mistakes that had been made, but he believed that the people who wanted to weaken or destroy the CIA by making information public that should be denied to the country's enemies were "dead wrong."[20] He declared, "The CIA and FBI are indispensible to the welfare and security of the United States. . . . I regret the unfair attacks that have been made, and I shall continue to do what I can to maintain a strong FBI and a strong CIA."[21]

When members finally adjourned for Christmas on December 19, they left behind a year of disagreement over energy, the economy, foreign policy, defense costs, and lack of public confidence in government. President Ford had vetoed seventeen bills during the session, but Congress was able to override only four of those vetoes.

President Ford intended that the $97.5 billion he requested in the fiscal year 1976 defense budget would curtail a decade-long trend of declining US military strength relative to that of the USSR. However, half the 15 percent increase over the previous year was needed to offset the effect of inflation; the other half was needed to begin a program of increasing conventional forces and expanding nuclear capabilities. The fact that the Soviets were thought to be spending more on defense than the United States alarmed Secretary of Defense James Schlesinger. He was determined not only to stop the downward trend in defense spending but to actually increase it for the remainder of the decade.[22] Many congressmen and most Democratic presidential hopefuls disagreed with his position. They argued that military spending was diverting limited federal funds from pressing social needs. Believing the defense budget could be reduced without undue risk, they cited cost overruns on new weapons and wasteful practices among military personnel to prove their point.[23] When the House Subcommittee on Defense Appropriations reduced the budget by $7.5 billion, Secretary Schlesinger called a news conference, where he lashed out at the committee, and at Mahon in particular, calling the reductions "deep, savage and arbitrary cuts."[24] He went on to declare that the cuts were politically motivated, and if allowed to stand, the United States would be weakened militarily. "I question the choice of his words and the tactics employed," Mahon responded. "I doubt that Schlesinger's attack will be helpful to the Pentagon's cause in Congress. The majority of Congress is very defense-minded and certainly cannot be accused of jeopardizing the nation's security."[25] Mahon was convinced that the Department of Defense had put a cushion in the budget it submitted to offset cuts it suspected were coming because the Senate had been asked to restore only $2.6 billion of the $7.5 billion cut in the House. Mahon argued that Schlesinger was determined to keep the overall appropriation high, but the committee had closely scrutinized individual programs instead of the bottom line. He stressed that any of the programs that had been cut were not ready for funding at that time. He called the reductions "paper cuts" that would not hurt the nation's military might and could be restored when programs needed funding. Mahon's formal rebuttal to Schlesinger was that "most Americans would agree that $90.2 billion for the Defense Department—exclusive of military construction and military assistance—is, if managed and spent wisely, adequate at a time when no U.S. military forces are engaged in combat and the nation is faced with a huge deficit and an increase in the national debt of $80 billion."[26] The story got a lot of publicity, and Mahon told a reporter for the *Washington Post*, "I thought Schlesinger made a poor choice of words. But I understood he was trying to get the cuts restored. I did not take it as a personal affront."[27] Nevertheless, the tactics he used did not help him.

President Ford was also annoyed with Schlesinger's tactics. After serving many years on Mahon's committee, he understood how effective it was for Department of Defense witnesses to attempt to sway the committee gently with reason, rather than beating them over the head with insults. However, this was just the latest incident of Schlesinger being overly blunt to the point of arrogance, even with the president and other cabinet members, and it proved to be the last straw. During the days of his vice presidency, Ford had become aware that Schlesinger could not deal effectively with Congress, but he and other cabinet members were kept on after Nixon's resignation in order to portray a sense of continuity. This proved to be an unwise decision when difficulties only grew in volume. In October 1975 President Ford decided to replace several holdover cabinet members with people of his choice, and this latest dustup provided an opportunity to replace Schlesinger. In his memoirs President Ford wrote that when he called those people being replaced into his office to tell them of his decision, the conversations were generally cordial, and some lasted no more than fifteen minutes. However, it was different with the secretary of defense, who argued for over an hour about refusing to resign, forcing the president to fire him.[28]

Mahon typed a memo for his defense appropriations file about the incident in relation to a conversation he had with *Washington Post* reporter Jack Anderson. Anderson asked whether Mahon had suggested, during a golf game with President Ford, that he fire Schlesinger. Mahon replied that he had played golf with the president about that time, but the controversial statement by Schlesinger was not discussed. However, after the game he and the president did have a short conversation, and "the President said that he had felt that we had cut the Defense budget too deeply and I said, 'well, if anyone would read the House report they would find that we had done a very careful and cautious job.'"[29] Mahon also compiled a two-page statement that he included in his answer to letters received from the public. He stated that the defense budget for 1976 had been affirmed by a vote of 353-61 in the House of Representatives. The objective had been to eliminate unnecessary spending without impairing essential defense programs, and the reductions had been made in a nonpartisan atmosphere. Reductions were very specific, with the reasons for each reduction set forth in a 365-page report that accompanied the bill.[30] There is also a memo in Mahon's files about a telephone call from Deputy Secretary of Defense William Clements, who said that "he is glad Schlesinger is out—says it is good for Department, good for President and good for country, because nobody can work with him."[31]

Ford was concerned that the cuts were pretty severe, but he knew the committee had given them careful scrutiny. The final defense appropriation was set in concrete at $90.2 billion.

In September 1975 President Ford angered many farmers when he placed a moratorium on Soviet grain sales. He did this reluctantly because his administration had urged farmers to increase their yield in 1975, but now they were being told that they could not sell their record harvest to the Soviet Union. In his memoirs Ford recalled that he did this because Soviet purchases were very erratic, fluctuating from 1.8 million metric tons one year to 13.7 million tons in another. In contrast, sales to Western European nations were fairly stable, but the fluctuating Soviet sales contributed to unstable prices that were problematic for everyone. Moreover, a longshoremen's strike caused shipments of grain to back up in railroad cars and in elevators when the Soviets insisted their ships be used in order to keep shipping costs low. The AFL-CIO objected, and farm organizations filed suit, hoping to force the loading of grain. The president stepped into the fray by suspending all sales to foreign nations for at least one month.

Representatives of farm organizations in the district immediately contacted Mahon. Despite a busy schedule, he arranged a meeting for these representatives with President Ford and Senator Carl Curtis of Nebraska. Mahon accompanied them to the Oval Office and issued a press release, in which he said, "The suspension of sales is completely contrary to everything the government has been telling the American farmer throughout the past year about all out production and the assurance to free access to foreign markets. . . . I have been urging officials at all levels of government—at the White House, the Department of Agriculture and otherwise—to convince them of the urgency in lifting the moratorium as soon as possible."[32] He always worked to stay abreast of the needs of his constituents—whose livelihood depended on agriculture—not the defense industry.

The problem was soon resolved through a long-term agreement with the Soviets that guaranteed sales of six million metric tons of grain per year for five years, one-third of which was to be transported in US ships. When lifting the embargo President Ford maintained that the American farmer would benefit more from a long-term agreement governing the amount of grain the Soviets would purchase each year than riding the roller coaster of sales and price fluctuations.[33]

A major budget reform bill was passed in 1974, setting a tight timetable for Congress to clear all appropriations bills. Beginning in 1976 the fiscal year was moved to October 1 from July 1 and Congress was to clear all appropria tions bill by seven days after Labor Day.

President Ford's defense budget for fiscal year 1977 received much better treatment than the previous year. His request for $106 billion was 14 percent more than the previous year and became the largest single appropriation in the history of the US government. After conducting hearings, the House subcommittee reduced the initial request by only $800 million. When presenting the bill to the House for debate, Mahon told members that "the Soviet Union is engaging in a terrific buildup of its military strength . . . and if we should stand still we would soon be No. 2 in the arms race."[34] He went on to say that this was the main reason the committee substantially approved the amount the president requested.

He did, however, acknowledge to a *New York Times* reporter that election-year politics played a role in the subcommittee's decision. The Ford administration had actually been warning of a Soviet buildup that justified the request for growth of the military structure, while Ronald Reagan accused President Ford of allowing the nation to become militarily inferior, and the subcommittee hoped to keep the defense budget out of election-year politics.[35] The size of the bill was also a response to the pleas of the Joint Chiefs of Staff and their concern about world conditions. For fiscal year 1977 Congress provided $15.5 billion more for the military than the previous year. This included the supplemental bill for military pay raises passed the following spring.

Although the Soviets had more missiles, the United States had multitargeted missiles (MIRV), giving it an advantage in the number of warheads. Acting somewhat like a shotgun, the MIRV missiles caused much greater damage to a target than a single warhead alone. The United States was also ahead in the number of bombers and carriers, but the Soviets were ahead in tanks and ground troops.

By 1976 George Mahon had not faced a real battle for reelection since 1946. During that time Democrats had controlled Congress for all except the sessions of 1946 and 1952. However, since 1952 the Republican Party had been slowly rebuilding in Texas from its near demise following the Civil War, and by 1976 young Republicans, who had worked hard across the state, believed political victories were possible. Thus forty-six-year-old Jim Reese, former mayor of Odessa, Texas, entered the race and became a strong Republican contender for the Nineteenth Congressional District seat.

Reese declared his candidacy in May with his central theme being that it was time for a change because George Mahon was an old man who had been in office so long that he had become soft on liberalism and was now out of touch with the people in his district. It was time for a younger, more conservative representative, and Jim Reese advertised himself as that person.

In campaign literature Reese charged Mahon personally with all the faults that Reese found in the Democratic-controlled Congress. These included voting for funds to continue negotiations to give away the Panama Canal, voting to abolish the House Internal Security Committee, better known as the House Un-American Activities Committee, voting for a congressional pay raise, voting to increase the federal debt ceiling, and others. He also accused Mahon of being one of those who weakened national defense.

Mahon was concerned about the challenge. He was aware of the growing tide of republicanism in West Texas, and during the past year he had witnessed the problems that younger members of the House could cause for the old-timers. Congress remained in session as usual until well into June, causing Mahon to have to direct his campaign from Washington until he could return home with less than a month remaining before the primary. He kept the staff in his congressional office busy sending out letters and information about legislative activities to supporters throughout the district. He also contacted over forty newspapers in the district whose editors he considered personal friends.

A Lubbock attorney, Harold P. (Bo) Brown, became chairman of the George Mahon for Congress committee. He concentrated on raising money, talking with leading supporters, and carrying out Mahon's instructions from Washington. Brown worked closely with David Langston, another Lubbockite, who was on Mahon's congressional staff in Washington. Mahon also added a political analyst from Lubbock, who checked on public sentiments and reported on how he thought the campaign was going.

Brown believed the biggest challenge was educating young voters about Mahon. Because Mahon seldom had an opponent, his campaigns had been almost nonexistent, and younger people, especially those not involved in agriculture, did not really have a reason to know this man. Older supporters, those of Mahon's generation, were not convinced that this was the case, so one day at lunch in the cafeteria of the Texas Commerce Bank building, Brown and an older supporter canvassed the twenty-two tables, asking people their opinion of George Mahon. Many of the people were young and employed by the bank or one of the offices located in the building. An astonishing number knew little about Mahon. Considering the rising tide of Republicans in the

Nineteenth District, it became obvious that educating the electorate about what George Mahon had done for the district and what he could continue to do, as well as his role in national affairs, was a top priority. His name needed to become a household name, making this situation similar to the one he had faced in his first campaign in 1934. Fliers were sent out, and radio spots were secured. Over forty newspaper editors in the district—staunch supporters—also ran full-page articles about his work. Langston worked with local people to set up rallies where Mahon could speak and have a chance to meet constituents whom he did not already know. As an interesting sidelight, Charles Guy, editor of the *Lubbock Avalanche-Journal*, wrote that, because of Mahon's record and integrity, "the veteran and highly respected Congressman from the 19th District ranks among the giants. . . . Rep. George Mahon has earned not only another term in Congress, but deserves the undying gratitude and thanks of his fellow Americans. He has truly been a faithful public servant."[36] This was the same editor who, in 1934, had cautioned voters against sending a boy to Washington to do a man's job.

Some of Mahon's most loyal supporters had become Republicans, but they crossed lines to campaign for him because they respected and admired him. When these supporters realized the seriousness of the situation, they really pitched in by contacting others in their profession; for example, attorneys wrote to clients and other attorneys in the district, encouraging them to vote for Mahon. Many doctors, bankers, businesspeople, and civic leaders did the same. Mahon proved to be an easy sell because he was really a conservative politician, not the liberal that Reese tried to make him appear to be. Moreover, he was a good speaker, had a great sense of humor, and always looked dignified in his suit, white shirt, and tie. He kept a black book with information about constituents he had met during his forty-two years in office and spent time refreshing his memory before visiting with people in each town to remind himself of their names, their children's names, and small bits of information about their lives. His ability to converse so easily with people made his constituents feel that he was one of them—just as he had done so well during his first campaign in 1934. He genuinely liked people and had a knack for making them feel comfortable when they were around him.

However, none of these qualities spared him the stress of a negative campaign. Jim Reese blasted him at every opportunity, while Mahon spoke only about the issues, never about his opponent. He refused Reese's challenge to a debate because he did not believe it was beneficial to get into an argument about his vote on congressional bills that could easily be skewed one way or another with amendments. He thought his time would be better spent talking with constituents and trying to address their individual concerns. He addressed Reese's criticisms in a flier that was handed out generously. In this way he countered each accusation underlying Reese's conclusion that George Mahon was the biggest spender in US history because of his role in defense appropriations.

On election day Mahon received 87,684 votes, and Reece received 70,593.[37] This was the smallest margin of victory in his entire career, and Mahon understood the growing strength of the Republican Party in West Texas. However, he took all this in stride, just as he did the negative votes he had received when Democrats caucused to choose committee chairmen for another year. He won the election, and he kept his chairmanship, but he clearly understood the changes taking place and how they could affect him.

While Mahon did not receive the overwhelming majority of votes that he was accustomed to in years past, he soon learned that he would be serving with a president whose victory was equally small. Jimmy Carter garnered barely over 50 percent of the votes to Ford's 48 percent. Although America's disillusionment with the Vietnam War and Watergate left scars on President Ford's administration, neither candidate seemed to excite the voters.

As the longest-serving member, Mahon became the dean of the House of Representatives and was designated to act as speaker pro tempore on Inauguration Day. He presided over the House and led its members to the inauguration ceremony where President Carter was sworn in, wearing a business suit. Labeled the People's Inaugural, this inauguration was a dramatic departure from anything seen before, with ordinary people involved in an unprecedented way. Most of the staggering array of festivities and entertainment that took place from January 18 through January 22 were open to the public with no charge. Even free Metro transportation was provided to key inaugural events.

Inaugural festivities were barely over when Mahon began getting pleas for help from constituents. The Occupational Safety and Health Administration (OSHA) was moving forward with cotton-dust standards that could be very expensive for all sectors of the cotton industry. A new standard issued by OSHA in December 1976 would reduce the amount of cotton dust a worker could be exposed to in an eight-hour period from one thousand micrograms to two hundred micrograms. Only cotton harvesting would be exempt. The new standard had to be implemented solely through air-cleaning equipment. Respirators or rotation of workers during a shift was not an option. Cotton dust was alleged to be the cause of byssinosis, commonly known as "brown lung."

Upon investigation Mahon learned that no studies or well-documented evidence existed to establish the amount of respiratory problems generated from cotton dust in cotton gins, compresses, warehouses, or cottonseed-oil mills. He contacted Dr. Eula Bingham, the new assistant secretary of labor for OSHA, to insist that hearings be conducted in the field. He then made arrangements to be in Lubbock for the hearing scheduled to take place there in early May. Mahon told over 1,200 people gathered from Texas, Oklahoma, New Mexico, Arizona, and California that "the imposition of ill-advised cotton dust standards could paralyze the cotton industry from farm to factory and wreak havoc upon the economy of the nation."[38] Appealing to reason he went on to explain that the cost of plant equipment to bring the cotton industry into partial compliance had been estimated at approximately $3.2 billion. This meant that ginning charges would increase approximately 52 percent, causing an increase in the price of domestic cotton for world buyers. As a result, exports would fall at a time when the United States was suffering the worst trade deficit in history. And domestic mills would turn to petroleum to produce synthetic fabrics more cheaply, causing a greater reliance on imported oil, which would make the Unites States more vulnerable to OPEC. He pointed out that this increased demand for imported oil would come at a time when President Carter had proposed a stringent national energy conservation program for the United States. He said, "It is incomprehensible to me that one of the President's agencies would come forward with a proposal to write standards which would mandate such a tremendous increase in energy consumption without the most compelling justification."[39] Because the new standard was widely believed to be unnecessary, it became the target of political debate.

Mahon's speech was followed by that of Texas commissioner of agriculture Reagan Brown, who also opposed the cotton-dust standard because of lack of documentation that it caused respiratory problems. He further stated that before cotton gins were subjected to the new standard, he wanted to see well-substantiated evidence of the harm to workers because the ginning season was generally only six to eight weeks long, and heavy turnover meant that many workers did not work at the gin for the entire season, further reducing the likelihood of their contracting a respiratory disease as a result of the work. Brown lung was not a disease but a condition that progressed slowly over many years from chest tightness and breathing difficulties to obstructive lung disease. However, when workers began to show symptoms and were removed from the dust-laden environment, they lost the symptoms.[40] The two- or three-month duration of the annual cotton ginning and processing cycle automatically removed workers from a dust-laden environment. Nevertheless, OSHA's new cotton-dust standard became effective in June 1978.

Mahon's lack of patience with OSHA dated back to 1973, when he and cotton-industry spokesmen first tried to persuade OSHA officials that cotton gins and cottonseed-oil mills should be excluded from dust standards because there was no evidence of a dangerous work environment. Public Citizen director Sidney Wolfe accused Mahon of using his power to curtail "normal, reasonable, and necessary"[41] inspections of buildings and machinery. Wolfe claimed that this made Mahon responsible for the several deaths and hundreds of injuries in cottonseed-oil mills. He claimed that Mahon had intervened on behalf of oil-mill owners and added that "the Texas congressman should have foreseen that OSHA would over-react to any advance from a man with his strangle-hold on their budget."[42] Mahon called the accusation warped and ridiculous. He claimed that if OSHA officials had neglected to conduct proper inspections, that was their fault, not his. In July 1977 it was revealed that it was actually an OSHA scientist who was responsible for limiting inspections of cottonseed-oil mills. Mahon declared that further studies were needed to determine that a problem existed in cottonseed-oil mills, and he pointed out that conditions in the oil mills were not the same as those in textile mills, for which the dust standard was drawn.[43] Although Mahon refused to argue in the press about accusations leveled against him, he did have a lot to say on the House floor about bureaucratic harassment and bungling. In July 1976 he said that the federal government was increasingly becoming the object of contempt for harassing citizens with the administration of federal laws. Congress purposely wrote legislation in broad terms that must be administered by the executive branch. He believed that "too often one sees examples of foolish and ridiculous rules and regulations which are invented by impractical Government personnel."[44] He cited two examples that had been brought to his attention on a recent visit to the district. The first was a booklet entitled, "Safety with Beef Cattle", that OSHA issued. The booklet contained such statements as "when floors are wet and slippery with manure, you could have a bad fall"; "bare feet or sneakers aren't safe around cattle"; and "be careful that you do not fall into manure pits."[45] Mahon complained that many constituents "do not like to see their tax money used in the publication of such trash."[46] He declared that the time had come to stop tolerating such ineptness, and he presented, for the *Congressional Record*, the names of those associated with the booklet, including those at Purdue University, where it had been prepared. He then called on the secretary of labor to review the performance of these people and determine what corrective action would be best.

Mahon's second complaint was about OSHA's regulations for field sanitary facilities on farms and ranches, which required toilet and hand-washing facilities to be available within a five-minute walk of the workers. He called the regulations ludicrous and said if they were implemented on a large farm or ranch, the result would become "one of the greatest monuments to bureaucratic foolishness and ineptness known to man."[47] When Mahon discussed the matter with the director of OSHA, he was told that the proposed standards were not meant to be a final product but only a way that people could react and make proposals. He responded, "In my opinion, this is an outrageous situation and one that the Department of Labor should not tolerate."[48] He went on to stress that although the bureaucrats did not have to answer to voters, a way must be found to instill in them the knowledge that they are servants of the people. They should not be allowed to harass citizens and make a mockery of programs that were intended to help rather than hinder people. He concluded, "We must stop such actions and we should do it now."[49] He did not say so, but everyone knew that if no corrective action was taken by the secretary of labor, appropriations could be trimmed considerably.

In June 1978 OSHA issued a cotton-dust standard that had been considerably modified from the initial proposal. Warehouses, shippers, and cottonseed-oil mills were required to reduce the exposure of workers to five hundred micrograms per cubic meter of air instead of two hundred micrograms, and cotton gins were not required to meet any dust level. However, gins were required to furnish written schedules to OSHA for keeping the workplace free of dust; to educate employees about the lung problems that can result from cotton dust; to educate them about the importance of using respirators and of medical surveillance; and to place signs warning workers of lung problems from cotton dust. Beginning in 1979, gins were required to provide respirators and medical surveillance at no cost to employees. While the modified level of acceptable dust reduced the expense of compliance equipment, the cost was still prohibitive, and preparations began immediately for court challenges to the new standard. However, in 1981 the Supreme Court upheld OSHA's cotton-dust standard.

Somewhere in the midst of all the stress over the dustup with OSHA, Mahon received the happy news that he was to be the recipient of the James Forrestal Memorial Award. Established in 1954, this award was given annually by the National Defense Industrial Association to the US citizen considered to have most effectively applied Secretary Forrestal's belief that a close working relationship between government and industry is essential to the nation's security. The first recipient had been President Dwight Eisenhower. Mahon told the crowd gathered at the Sheraton-Park Hotel in Washington that "we have come here tonight to further encourage an atmosphere of good will and teamwork among the defense industry. . . . It is necessary for Congress and the military to deal in a manner at arms length with the defense industry, but in an atmosphere of mutual respect and cooperation."[50] He praised the men and women in the defense industry, saying that "without them our defense programs would be in shambles."[51] He ended by saying that there were many challenges and opportunities for members of the military establishment and the National Security Industrial Association to work together.

In his inaugural address President Carter pledged "perseverance and wisdom in our efforts to limit the world's armaments to those necessary for each nation's own domestic safety. And we will move a step toward our ultimate goal—the elimination of all nuclear weapons from this earth."[52] During his presidential campaign Carter had promised savings of $5 billion to $7 billion dollars in defense spending. However, after the election he and Defense Secretary Brown explained that the savings would be gradual and would actually be the difference between the amount that defense spending would have normally risen and reduced defense expenses in the proposed Carter budgets for the next four years. The savings would not represent any cuts in spending. By his second year in the White House, President Carter's budget request for fiscal year 1979 defense spending was $125.57 billion. Although this figure was $8.4 billion less than the Ford administration had predicted for 1979 defense expenditures, Carter's request amounted to a 3.5 percent real increase after inflation was taken into account.

The defense budget for fiscal year 1978, essentially a product of the Ford administration, was submitted to Congress in January 1977. President Carter requested $112.4 billion, which represented a $2.8 billion reduction in President Ford's request. Although Congress reduced the Carter request by $4.1 billion, there were no radical changes in major weapons-production programs.[53] Defense hard-liners decided that it would be impossible to increase weapons authorizations despite concern over the continuing Soviet military buildup because of worries about the size of the rising federal deficit.

However, there were controversies, and the most intense concerned the B-1 bomber. For nearly a decade Congress had debated the necessity and the cost of a follow-on bomber for the B-52. In June 1970 Rockwell International was awarded the contract to build three prototypes at an estimated price of $41 million per plane. Each of the four engines in the new plane was to have a thrust of thirty thousand pounds and could fly at supersonic levels at high altitudes and near the speed of sound at treetop level. Two-thirds the size of the B-52, the B-1 had the maneuverability of a fighter plane. With a maximum range of six thousand miles, it could carry twenty-four short-range attack missiles and was considered one of the air force's greatest aeronautical achievements. It also became one of the costliest weapons ever conceived. By 1975 funding totaled $2.027 billion. Then an additional $661 million was added in 1976, and $1.532 billion was appropriated in 1977.[54] With only four planes ready for testing and money to cover the construction of two more, the price tag of a B-1 had grown to $100 million by 1977. Throughout these years Mahon supported the bomber's production, although the price was growing beyond the American taxpayer's pocketbook. Just the year before he admitted the B-1 was in trouble because of rising costs, and he wanted to keep production lines for the F-111 open in the event that the B-1 was killed.

Additionally, since 1969 a bipartisan group of senators and representatives who were Vietnam veterans, known as Members of Congress for Peace through Law (MCPL), had been highly critical of large military expenditures and the way that military contracts were awarded. They believed that more money should be spent on social programs instead of expensive weapons systems when the nation was not at war. However, they discovered that it was

difficult to stop new weapons systems that were supported by the administration, and both Presidents Nixon and Ford had favored the B-1. As their
number grew and their voices became louder, more attention was focused on
the military and economic flaws of the B-1.[55] Adding momentum to this trend
of criticizing military expenditures was Carter's address at the Democratic
convention in 1976. He cited the B-1 as an example of a proposed weapons
system that should not be funded because it was wasteful of taxpayers' money.[56] Proponents of the B-1 were alarmed, but the Democratic Congress decided to give the new president time to study the situation and reach his own
conclusions about whether or not to continue production of the plane.

On June 30, 1977, during a news conference, President Carter announced
that, after assessing all factors in the production of the B-1, he had directed
that production stop and instead that cruise missiles be deployed using modified B-52s. Cruise missiles were pilotless planes that could carry nuclear or
conventional warheads. Air-launched cruise missiles could carry a nuclear
warhead at least fifteen hundred miles, to within ten yards of a target. This
would allow the triad concept of three delivery systems to continue with
submarine-launched ballistic missiles, intercontinental ballistic missiles, and
cruise missiles launched from B-52s. He announced that he believed these
three systems would provide flexibility and would be sufficient for national
defense. However, he favored continued research on the B-1 so that the United States could still produce the plane if future events warranted it. At the
heart of the congressional debate was a difference of beliefs about what kind
of nuclear threat would most likely deter a Soviet attack. Supporters of the B-1
argued that the Soviets could beat back cruise-missile attacks because these
missiles lacked self-defense electronic gear and flew at subsonic speeds. Only
a manned bomber could outmaneuver a Soviet defensive attack.

Just two days before the president's news conference the House had voted
to appropriate nearly $1.5 billion to procure B-1 bombers in the bill for fiscal
year 1978 defense appropriations. However, when the bill (H.R. 7933) reached
the Senate, that body voted to delete the appropriation for the bomber, partly
based on the president's recent announcement. The House conferees would
not agree with the Senate's version during the conference, and the bill was
returned to the House to address this difference. Ultimately, the full House
voted to delete money for the bomber in order to get the defense appropriation bill passed, but supporters did not intend to let the matter die there.

In October, during consideration of a $6.8 billion supplemental appropriation bill, supporters introduced an amendment to restore the $1.5 billion for the B-1 bomber that had been deleted on September 8 during House consideration of the conference report on Department of Defense Appropriation Act 1978 (H.R. 7933). The two hours allowed for debate of the amendment were completely dominated by proponents of the plane. The amendment had been presented on a Thursday afternoon before a four-day weekend, and the Democratic leadership feared that opponents might slip away before the end of the session. To avoid being defeated, Mahon asked that the House recess without taking a vote. He believed that chances to beat back the amendment would be better when more of the opposing members were present the following week. Proponents for the plane knew that, too, so they moved to close the debate and force a vote on the amendment that afternoon. Mahon reminded the group that neither he nor the speaker had had a chance to speak, and they were allowed ten minutes to do so. Mahon spoke first and reminded the members that his credentials for a strong defense were very good, that, in fact, in twenty-eight years he had guided bills through the House that provided more than $2 trillion for defense—which he believed gave him a pretty good insight into what was needed to keep the nation safe. Based on that, he couldn't understand why this year everyone was acting as though "the bomber was everything that was going to save us from war or win the war if war should come."[57] He went on to stress that if war did come, there would be a massive exchange of intercontinental ballistic missiles and submarine-launched missiles that would destroy the Soviet Union several times over. He continued, "Do we not know that the only purpose of a bomber is to do the cleanup job? And after the atomic exchange, we could probably do the cleanup in an ox cart."[58] He strongly stressed that the United States was not relying on any aircraft as its primary strategic weapon, and a vote to reinstate funds for the B-1 bomber would not accomplish anything because the Senate would not agree to it and the president would veto the bill. He urged members to vote against funds for the bomber because he understood that the only thing the amendment could accomplish was a rebuff to the president and further delay of funds that were sorely needed by other federal agencies. Speaker O'Neill spoke next, beginning, "Now, more than ever, I appreciate how tall the gentleman [Mahon] stands."[59] When the recorded vote was taken, there were 194 ayes and 204 noes, thus the amendment to reinstate funds for the B-1 bomber was defeated. The *New York Times* reported that General Omar Bradley was one of those who watched all of the debate from the gallery, but it did not record his reaction.[60]

Still, the B-1 bomber was not dead. Only money to build copies 7, 8, 9, and 10 had been killed. Copies 1, 2, 3, and 4 were already built, and Congress had appropriated $462 million in 1976 (fiscal year 1977) to build copies 5 and 6. Now B-1 supporters planned to insist that the money be spent in compliance with anti-impoundment legislation passed in 1974, while President Nixon was in office. In July 1977 President Carter had requested rescission of the unspent money, and on September 28 the House Appropriations Committee voted 34-21 against the president's request. However, the Senate had voted in favor and added the rescission request to the fiscal year 1978 supplemental appropriations bill (H.R. 9375) that had already had a rough time in the House. When the bill that now included the rescission request was returned to the House, it was rejected 166-191 on December 6. This meant final action on the fiscal year 1978 supplemental would be delayed until after the first of the following year. Just to be certain everyone understood its position, on February 1, 1978, the Senate reaffirmed its decision to cancel the $462 million by a 57-38 vote. The supplemental bill was now in the hands of the House, thus delaying needed funds for federal agencies until an agreement could be reached. On February 28 on the House floor, Mahon made a motion that "the House recede from its disagreement to Senate amendment numbered 43 and concur therein."[61] He offered the same reasoning as previously—that the Senate continued to oppose spending any money for further production of the plane and the president would veto any bill containing money for production. Some supporters realized the battle was lost, and others continued to grouse, but the final vote was 234 for the motion and 182 against.[62]

President Carter wrote to Mahon, saying, "Our victory on the B-1 bomber last week was due largely to your guidance and leadership. I am gratified to have worked with you on this and many other issues. I value your judgment and counsel."[63] Concerned constituents also began calling and sending mail. Mahon tried to reassure them: "The B-1 has been a controversial plane for a number of years. I had always supported it until it became apparent that the B-1 for the present is dead."[64] But the B-1 was not really dead. It had only been knocked out during the Carter administration. During the Reagan administration it was revived, and in 1986 it began flying as the follow-on bomber to the B-52.

On the morning of July 7, 1977, Mahon's office released news that caused all heads in Washington to turn his way. "At the end of my present term, I will have served 44 years in Congress and a total of 52 years in public office. I promised myself long ago that I would not seek to serve in Congress after reaching age 80, a milestone I would pass prior to the conclusion of another two-year term."[65] Only six other members in the entire history of the United States had served longer in the House of Representatives.

With Mahon's departure Congress would lose one of its strongest voices for fiscal conservatism. Mahon said, "Having an opportunity to participate in some of the most momentous decisions of our time has been a great privilege. I have dealt with the high and mighty in government, but perhaps my greatest satisfaction has been helping the people of the 19th District who have called upon me. Throughout my service I have been sustained by the feeling that I had the trust and support of the folks at home."[66] Normally congressmen announce their political intentions sometime in December prior to election year. However, Mahon believed that because he would not be a candidate he should give voters ample time to consider a successor.

Several days later George Will wrote in the *Washington Post* that being eighty years old was a poor reason for the House to lose the services of a man whose abilities remained formidable.[67] He went on, "Mahon is an American type—an alloy of piety, industriousness, reticence and abstemiousness—that once was as common, and soon may be as scarce as, the homing pigeon."[68] Mahon was six-feet-two, erect and lean, and Will described him as looking as "though he was whittled from a fence post by the West Texas wind."[69] He went on to say that government was better than it would have been if Mahon had not served and that he was still as good a person as when he came.

In a family letter of the same date as George Will's column, Mahon wrote, "Some of our media friends have really put us (Mahon and Helen) on a pedestal."[70] He then told his family the story of a minister at a funeral going on about how angelic the deceased was; the wife said to her son, "Willie, go up there and open that casket and see if it is really your Pappy!" He urged reporters not to praise him so much that they knocked him off his pedestal.

Reporters were not the only ones dismayed with his announcement. Former president Nixon penned a letter in his own hand, "I read of your decision with mixed emotions. You personally have served your country far beyond the call of duty. But never has the nation needed a man of your statesmanship more. . . . I have always rated you at the top of my list of men who had rare intelligence, great wisdom and a unique devotion to duty. I shall always be grateful for your wise counsel and friendship during the years I was in the White House."[71] Senator John C. Stennis (D-MS) also wrote in his own hand, "If one word only could be used to sum up your public career, I would use the word 'usefulness.' This usefulness has been bottomed on the essential qualities that go to make character, and reinforced by a strong will to work. To me, this spells out and adds up to one of the greatest careers in Congressional history. I know too that your wife had a big part in all of this so to each of you—thanks and God bless each of you."[72] And from President Carter: "It is with regret that I learned of your decision to retire after 44 years of service in the House of Representatives. I share your pride and that of your family in the record of your accomplishments as a Member of Congress and as Chairman of the Appropriations Committee. The dedication and the expertise which you have brought to your work have earned you the respect and admiration of your colleagues and the Nation."[73]

Although Mahon revealed nothing about his plans for the future in the press release, he did announce that he had many interests and would continue to lead an active and vigorous life. This inspired the dean of the School of Business at the University of Southern California to write, suggesting to Mahon that he consider joining the university as "a part time professor, a full time professor, or an administrator in residence for any period of time that your schedule will permit. This could be a joint appointment with our Graduate School of Business Administration and our Graduate School of Public Administration in Los Angeles; or, if you choose you could remain in Washington, our Public Administration has a program there in which they would be most pleased for you to participate."[74] The dean wrote that he knew no one who more justly deserved retirement than Mahon, "however, it is a shame for a person of your experience and capability not to continue to contribute to our country."[75]

In September 1977 two treaties governing the future operation and defense of the Panama Canal were signed by President Carter and General Omar Torrijos. These treaties replaced the seventy-four-year-old Hay-Bunau-Varilla Treaty signed in 1903, which granted the United States, in perpetuity, the right to build and operate a canal across Panamanian territory, with all the rights as if it were sovereign. Panama was paid $10 million and $250,000 annually, beginning in 1913. The annual annuity was raised until it ultimately became $1,930,000 in 1955. Information in Mahon's files that had been received from the White House indicates that the initial cost was $387 million, and by 1977 $690 million had been paid to the US Treasury from canal revenues.[76] "Aside from presidential election campaigns and the anti-Vietnam war effort, there have been few political battles in recent years to match the national emotion roused by the treaties."[77] When the treaty received Senate approval, letters began to pour into Mahon's congressional office. Constituents were just as emotional as the rest of the nation. One woman wrote, "I'm concerned with the trend our country is taking toward the evil, communism and socialism. I beg you to do all you can as our Representative to stop the evil. Please keep our canal in Panama. Please stop giving away our money to those evil causes. We can't afford to support everyone in the world, especially the servants of the devil. I'm counting on you to get us back to God's way in this country. We have to follow God, or we will end in destruction. Please show us that you will follow God. Everyone I know feels the same."[78] Mahon answered that he was opposed to any giveaway of the Panama Canal and was disappointed that the Senate had ratified the treaties that would return the Canal Zone to Panama. Another constituent wrote that he was concerned not only about the return of the canal, but also about a United Nations resolution he believed President Carter had signed, giving the United Nations the right to confiscate the private property of American citizens. He added the following postscript, "I did not ask 'left-wing' Lloyd for his help on this matter. I now know where he stands on matters concerning the safety of this country."[79] Senator Lloyd Bentsen (D-TX) had voted in favor of ratifying the Panama Canal treaties.

President Carter requested $125.5 billion for the Department of Defense for fiscal year 1979. This was an increase of $10.3 billion over the $115.2 billion provided for fiscal year 1978. The budget request did not represent an across-the-board increase; rather it represented an increase that would allow the army to modernize conventional forces to improve US capabilities within the NATO alliance.

In an effort to wrap up all business before the second session of the Ninety-fifth Congress ended, it was necessary to have a Saturday session in the House. Mahon was busy trying to get a vote on the last of the appropriations bills. At the end of debate on a bill for continuing appropriations for fiscal year 1979, he took a moment to acknowledge that "this appropriation measure is the last piece of legislation which I will have the honor of handling in the House of Representatives. . . . I just wish to say that the Speaker, the majority leader, the minority leader and other officials of the House have been wonderful in helping us to handle the often complex and demanding work-load of the Committee on Appropriations."[80] After all debate had ended, ac-colades were expressed for those members who were leaving Congress. Eligio "Kika" de la Garza (D-TX) paid tribute to Mahon, saying, "What can you say about a man who was first elected to this august body back in 1934? Where do you begin? . . . Knowing how much George Mahon hates unnecessary ex-penditure, I must resist the temptation to try to catalog his many, many fine deeds for Texas and the Nation."[81] He went on to say that Mahon had set his imprint on just about every important bill passed by the House since becom-ing chair of the Appropriations Committee in 1964, and because of that, "this country has directed its resources in the direction of efficiency, imagination, and commonsense."[82] De la Garza speculated that the nation would one day commemorate George Mahon Day. He ended, "So sit back in your rocking chair, Mr. Chairman—enjoy and savor your rest. You have certainly earned it and the entire country is richer for the great work you have done."[83] Thus ended George Mahon's service in the US House of Representatives.

On October 24 Mahon was honored by the army with the Distinguished Civilian Service Award, the army's highest award for a civilian. The ceremony took place at Fort Myer, Virginia, where General Bernard Rogers, army chief of staff, told the crowd that Mahon was being honored for long and distin-guished service to national defense. He said that despite working with im-personal numbers and dollars, Mahon "never lost sight of how those figures impact on the persons that are the reason and the end of all our endeavors. The citizens and the service members of the United States."[84] He called Ma-hon "a gentleman of honor and integrity, a statesman of vision and wisdom, a patriotic and dedicated American."[85] He ended by thanking Mahon for what he had contributed to the nation and the dignified manner in which he made that contribution. The ceremony included a seventeen-gun salute, four ruffles and flourishes, and a special musical tribute that included "The Yellow Rose of Texas," "The Eyes of Texas," and "The Caissons Go Rolling Along." The Third Infantry Division passed in review wearing Revolutionary War uniforms. Re-porters noted that Mahon appeared to be quite moved by the ceremony. Put-ting his prepared speech in his coat pocket, he spoke informally, recalling the day he had asked Speaker Rayburn about accepting a seat on the House Committee on Appropriations. He remembered that Rayburn told him to take it fast because the war clouds were gathering in Europe and that committee would become very important—and so it did. He praised the many people with whom he had worked on the committee and ended by expressing his gratitude for the whole experience of being involved in national defense. All the members of the Subcommittee on Defense Appropriations and all those on the full House Committee on Appropriations were present. A reception followed in the army chief of staff's quarters. Later Mahon wrote to his family: "The Army award and the 17-gun salute on October 20th was, I must admit, a most thrilling occasion."[86] George Mahon had seen his childhood dream come true. He had become somebody, and his public service was recognized at the highest level. He could truly be proud of his accomplishment.

In the same letter Mahon wrote that he expected his office schedule for the remainder of the year to be quite hectic as he vacated "two offices and four storerooms chock full of papers, files and books."[87] He wrote that if he didn't get the work done while he still had his loyal and efficient staff, he would be facing a hopeless situation. He went on, "The Speaker has written all retiring Members to try to vacate their offices by December 15. We just won't be able to do that. Our term expires January 2nd."[88]

Sometime during the next two weeks he and Helen planned to leave for the district, where he had committed to attend chamber of commerce dinners and events honoring them, but after that they would be very busy packing material that would be shipped to the Southwest Collection at Texas Tech University in Lubbock for permanent storage and future use by scholars.

Kent Hance, a Texas state senator, won the November election to become the representative from the Nineteenth Congressional District. At every opportunity Hance reminded voters that he was a native-born West Texan, unlike his opponent George W. Bush, who grew up mostly in the northeast and only moved back to Midland, Texas, as an adult. Although Bush tried to convince voters that his conservative ideology was more closely aligned to theirs, they elected a Democrat to replace Mahon. Mahon let it be known that he supported Hance but otherwise stayed out of the race. This proved to be the only race that Bush ever lost.

Many boxes of papers and other memorabilia documenting Mahon's congressional career began arriving on the Texas Tech University campus in late October. The last large shipment of material arrived in January 1979 just as the snow was melting from a recent storm. Three men supervised the unloading, and the remaining staff crowded in the windows to watch. They managed to get the forklift stuck in the mud, which brought gales of laughter and tapping on the window, but soon the pallets of boxes were on their way inside with papers that would ultimately be transferred to acid-free boxes with aids developed to help researchers find their way through the 624 boxes in this collection. I was one of those at the window. It all seemed exciting at the time, but I had no idea just how important that day would be in my life.

A fter vacating his congressional office, Mahon began to use an office in L'Enfant Plaza that had been provided by Litton Industries, a defense company. Secretarial help was also provided. At that time Bates "Tex" Thornton was president of Litton Industries, and his friendship with Mahon dated back to 1934. They became friends when both rode the same train to Washington, DC. At that time Thornton was looking for a job, which was hard to find during the Depression, and after getting settled in Washington, Mahon recommended him to someone in the Department of Agriculture, who hired him. Thornton never forgot this favor and provided an office for Mahon to use during his retirement. In Mahon's file concerning Litton Industries is a note saying, "Great thing about Bates—he is a friend always— once your friend, always your friend—not fair weather friend."[1] Indeed, he was a great friend and admirer of Mahon. In 1980 he donated two hundred thousand dollars to Texas Tech University to establish the George H. Mahon Professorship in Law.

Initially, retirement was not easy for Mahon. For many years he had worked very hard, even taking work home to finish on evenings and weekends. He wanted to stay busy, and from his new office he continued to work on Smithsonian committees. He was serving on the audit and review committee and the personnel committee, and he had been appointed a Smithsonian regent emeritus. He also served on a committee to fight inflation chaired by Arthur Burns.

On February 6, 1979, the House Committee on Appropriations voted unanimously to name Room H-140 in the Capitol the George H. Mahon Room. The full Committee on Appropriations had met regularly in this room with Mahon presiding since 1964, and it was also the meeting room for the Subcommittee on Defense Appropriations, over which Mahon had presided since 1949. The committee believed it was unlikely that Mahon's long record would be broken in the foreseeable future; they wanted the room where he did so much of his work to be named in his honor.[2] Speaker O'Neill concurred.

In March 1984 George and Helen Mahon moved back to Colorado City to the house on Chestnut Street that they had purchased in 1936. It had been rented out during the fifty years they were in Washington. Health issues, Parkinson's disease, and knee problems slowed Mahon down, so it was time to come home. The Washington pace had become too much, and now he just wanted to be among the people he had known most of his life, to check on the cotton crops from time to time, and to savor the memories he had acquired over the last half century. He told a reporter, "I've had my day in the sun. I'm trying to leave present-day politics to present-day politicians."[3] He also tried to avoid publicity and interviews.

In mid-November 1985 a wave of sadness washed over the Nineteenth Congressional District. On November 19 George Mahon died in Shannon West Texas Memorial Hospital in San Angelo, Texas. He was eighty-five when he died of complications from knee surgery. As word spread over the district, many stories were told about how Mahon had helped his constituents and the district. Former Texas governor Preston Smith told a reporter for the *Lubbock Avalanche-Journal*, "George Mahon is regarded now and, factually so, as an institution more so than a man because of the outstanding services he rendered this community, this state and this nation."[4] Phone calls and sympathy cards came from around the world. Former president Gerald Ford called Helen from London to express his sympathy. One especially touching note came from the staff and students of George Mahon Elementary School in Lubbock. It ended, "This school will serve as a living memorial to a great man and a true friend."[5]

Funeral services were held in the First United Methodist Church in Lubbock. Nearly fifteen hundred people from all walks of life, including a delegation from Washington, DC, gathered to pay tribute to Mahon. Representative Larry Combest, a Republican and the current congressman from the Nineteenth District, was among the group. House Minority Leader Jim Wright delivered the eulogy. Wright told those gathered, "He was a gentle man. The word honorable was not just a title for George Mahon. It was a way of life."[6] Graveside services were held later that afternoon in Loraine, Texas.

Helen was devastated from grief. She could not understand why she was not taken along with her husband. For sixty-two years they had been a team, and now she was left alone. She told people that the Lord must have something for her to do and that was why she was left behind. Daphne, Duncan, and the grandchildren spent more time than usual with her, hoping to ease some of her grief. Soon after the funeral, granddaughter Laurie wrote that she would be in Colorado City for Helen's birthday on December 15 and to decorate the Christmas tree. This was to be a special tree just for Gram and Laurie. As time went on Helen seemed to rally a bit, but on December 10, 1987, she died, just five days short of her eighty-seventh birthday. Her grandson, George Mahon Holt, told the mourners gathered in the First Methodist Church of Colorado City that his grandmother's failing health and grief were just too much for her to overcome. Helen Stevenson Mahon was buried next to her husband in the cemetery at Loraine, and the team that had been her source of strength for so many years was united once again.

Notes

Preface

1. *Lubbock* (Texas) *Avalanche-Journal*, November 1, 1964.
2. George H. Mahon Papers (hereafter cited as GHM), 1887–1986, Southwest Collection, Texas Tech University, Lubbock, Texas, Box 22, folder 23.
3. *Houston Chronicle*, May 17, 1964.

Chapter 1

1. GHM, Box 29, folder 4, letter to Judge W. R. Ely, dated January 3, 1935.
2. Ibid., letter from Judge W. R. Ely, dated January 10, 1935.
3. "New Speaker's Family, Secretary Are Thrilled," *Washington Post*, January 4, 1935.
4. Ibid.
5. Robert V. Remini, *The House: The History of the House of Representatives* (New York: HarperCollins, 2006), 258. Democrats and Republicans each have a party whip, whose position ranks in importance just below the majority and minority leaders. The Democratic whip position was established in 1899. Whips are elected by each party and are responsible for mobilizing votes to support the program of the party leaders. They poll members to learn how they intend to vote on specific bills, and then they make certain that members are present for close votes. Each party whip has a number of assistants who help with oversight of voting on specific bills.
6. E. P. Pendleton Herring, "First Session of the Seventy-fourth Congress, January 3, 1935, to August 26, 1935," *American Political Science Review* 29, no. 16 (Dec. 1935): 985.
7. "Byrns, Bankhead Named, Congress to Meet at Noon," *Washington Post*, January 3, 1935.
8. The "hopper" is the mahogany box on the House rostrum where members place the bills they are introducing.
9. James T. Patterson, *Congressional Conservatism and the New Deal: The Growth of the Conservative Coalition in Congress, 1933–1939* (Lexington: University of Kentucky Press, 1967), 3, 4.

10. A county in Louisiana is called a parish.

11. A fourth-class post office was one with fewer than thirty-six employees.

12. US Census Bureau: State and County Quick Facts, rev. March 11, 2013. According to the 2010 census, Claiborne Parish, Louisiana, had a population of 17,195 in 2010.

13. GHM, Box 2, folder 15, typescript entitled "The Name and Family of Mahon."

14. GHM, Box 2, folder 19, "Notes about George Mahon."

15. Mary Agnes (b. 1893), Cary (b. 1895), Bryan (b. 1896), Thomas Marion (b. 1898), George Herman (b. 1900), Elmer Overton (b. 1902), Cecil (b. 1905), and Durward Dale (b. 1908).

16. GHM, Box 2, folder 15, Note in "Genealogy" file that after Mahon went to Congress, he corresponded with John Nelson, who was then an old man but remembered his father.

17. GHM, Box 2, folder 19, "Notes about George Mahon."

18. GHM, Box 2, folder 16, unpublished manuscript entitled "My Father," c. 1955; and GHM, Box 2, Folder 9, letter to Mrs. S. E. Meadows, dated July 26, 1955.

19. GHM, Box 2, folder 16, "My Father," c. 1955.

20. Ibid. and GHM, Box 2, folder 9, letter to Mrs. S. E. Meadows, dated July 26, 1955.

21. GHM, Box 2, folder 16, "My Father," c. 1955.

22. Ibid.

23. Ibid.

24. Ibid.

25. Ibid.

26. Ibid.

27. Ibid.

28. GHM, Box 588, copy of letter from J. K. Mahon to Herman (George), dated July 30, 1924, inserted in Brown Journal.

29. GHM, Box 2, folder 19, letter from George Mahon to J. K. Mahon, dated October 11, 1939.

30. GHM, Box 3, folder 22, George Mahon to William Pearce and David Murrah, Washington, DC, September 25, 1980, interview transcript, p. 5 (hereafter cited as Mahon to Pearce and Murrah).

31. *Texas Almanac and State Industrial Guide, 1904* (Galveston, TX: A. H. Belo, 1904), unnumbered front pages; 329–30; 1910 issue, 10, 306, 321. This last issue carried over fifty pages of similar ads.

32. Initially the town was named Colorado, Texas. It was pronounced with a long "a." In 1939 local businessmen voted to change the name to Colorado City because much of their mail was going to the state of Colorado, and it was sometimes lost or several days late arriving at its true destination.

33. *Lore and Legend: A Compilation of Documents Depicting the History of Colorado City and Mitchell County* (Colorado City, TX: Colorado City Record, 1976), 35–36.

34. *Texas Almanac*, 329.

35. *New Handbook of Texas* (Austin: Texas State Historical Association, 1996), 4: 781–82.

36. *Lore and Legend*, 74, 86.

37. GHM, Box 4, folder 2, photocopied material, "Our School," by Mildred Johnson Smith, 1, 84; *Lore and Legend*, 110.

38. GHM, Box 2, folder 16, "My Father," c. 1955.

39. *New Handbook of Texas*, 781–82.

40. Ibid., 290.

41. *Lore and Legend*, 281.

42. GHM, Box 3, folder 22, Mahon to Pearce and Murrah, 5.

43. Ibid.

44. GHM, Box 4, folder 41, Notebook, unnumbered pages.

45. GHM, Box 3, folder 22, Mahon to Pearce and Murrah, 8.

46. Ibid., 8–9.

47. Ibid.

48. Ibid., 9, 10.

49. GHM, Box 2, folder 19, "Notes about George Mahon."

50. Ibid.

51. GHM, Box 561, Scrapbook, 1953.

52. GHM, Box 2, folder 19, "Notes about George Mahon."

53. Ibid., undated letter to Mary Agnes from Nashville, Fall 1918.

54. GHM, Box 588, folder entitled "Literary Productions," letter to "Dear Homefolks," dated November 22, 1918.

55. Ibid., letter to "Dear Mary Agnes," dated November 8, 1918.

56. GHM, Box 2, folder 19, letter to Mary Agnes, dated "Sunday Eve," March 1919.

57. GHM, Box 5, folder 13, letter to "Dear Children," dated October 21, 1969.

58. Rupert Norval Richardson. *Famous Are Thy Halls: Hardin-Simmons University as I Have Known It* (Abilene, TX: Abilene Printing and Stationery), 1964, 18–20, 23.

59. GHM, Box 2, folder 19, letter to "Dear Mary Agnes," dated Fall 1919.

60. *The Bronco: A Pictorial Yearbook* (Abilene, TX: Simmons College, 1920), 12:68, 140.

61. GHM, Box 3, folder 22, Mahon to Pearce and Murrah, 13.

62. GHM, Box 588, folder 4, Brown Journal, 53.

63. Ibid.

64. "Batching" was a term used to describe young men who were living alone.

65. GHM, Box 2, folder 19, letter to Mary Agnes, dated 1919.

66. GHM, Box 588, folder 4, Brown Journal, 59.

67. *Bronco*, 179.

68. GHM, Box 2, folder 19, "Notes about George Mahon."

69. "Students Pull Faculty Stunt in Unique Chapel Program April First," *Simmons Brand* (Abilene, TX: Simmons College, April 9, 1921).

70. Richardson, *Famous Are Thy Halls*, 102.

71. Ibid., 102, 116.

72. GHM, Box 7, folder 3, letter to "Dear Mama and all," dated "Sunday Evening, 1921."

73. GHM, Box 588, folder 4, Brown Journal, copy of Uniform Transfer Blank for Texas Colleges inserted between 113 and 114.

74. *The Cactus*, University of Texas Yearbook, 1923, 135; *Texas Law Review*, as copied from *The Cactus*, 1924, 130.

75. Helen Stevenson Mahon was born in Floresville, Texas, on December 15, 1900.

76. Helen Mahon to David Murrah and Dale Cluff, December 18, 1985, Oral History Files.

77. GHM, Box 2, folder 6. The hotel cost $3 and the train $2.70.

78. GHM, Box 3, folder 22, Mahon to Pearce and Murrah, 12–13; Helen Mahon to David Murrah and Dale Cluff, December 18, 1985, Oral History Files.

79. GHM, Box 588, folder entitled "Speeches, 1946–1979."

80. GHM, Box 588, folder 4, Brown Journal, 245; copy of University of Minnesota transcript, August 1, 1925.

81. GHM, Box 3, folder 22, Mahon to Pearce and Murrah, 11.

82. The judge was probably referring to Mahon as a "young Lochinvar" because he was helping the defendant escape the full brunt of the law.

83. GHM, Box 2, folder 19, "Notes about George Mahon."

84. GHM, Box 3, folder 22, Mahon to Pearce and Murrah, 17; GHM, Box 2, folder 19, "Notes about George Mahon."

85. GHM, Box 3, folder 22, Mahon to Pearce and Murrah, 17.

86. "Mahon Announces He Will Run for Seat in Congress," *Sweetwater* (Texas) *Daily Reporter*, May 19, 1933.

87. *Texas Almanac*, 1931, 296–97; and *Texas Almanac*, 1936, 324.

88. A bonus granted to veterans of World War I in 1924 by the World War Adjusted Compensation Act; however, bonus certificates were not redeemable until 1945.

89. "George Mahon Club for Congress Was Launched at Rally Monday Night," *Colorado* (Texas) *Record*, January 19, 1934.

90. "Temporary Organization Young Democrats' Club Perfected at Colorado," *Colorado* (Texas) *Record*, December 8, 1933.

91. Certificates from the state promising to pay at a later date.

92. "Mullican-for-Congress Club Is Organized by Friends," *Lubbock* (Texas) *Evening Journal*, August 2, 1934.

93. "Judge Mullican Says Lubbock County Not Taking Interest in Congress Race," *Lubbock* (Texas) *Evening Journal*, June 10, 1934.

94. GHM, Box 7, folder 3, letter from Durward Mahon, dated August 12, 1933.

95. "Europe's Peace Is America's Problem," *Sweetwater* (Texas) *Reporter*, June 2, 1933.

96. GHM, Box 374, folder 34.

97. "Candidates Brought Views to Large Local Crowd," *Plainview* (Texas) *Evening Herald*, July 5, 1934.

98. Lawrence L. Graves, ed., *A History of Lubbock* (Lubbock: West Texas Museum Association, 1962), 109, 257. "Trades days" were usually held the first Monday of each month and often coincided with cattle sales days.

99. "George Mahon Leaves for West Texas Tour," *Colorado* (Texas) *Record*, July 13, 1934.

100. "The Choice Is Yours," *Lubbock* (Texas) *Avalanche-Journal*, August 12, 1934.

101. Paying a poll tax was a requirement for registering and voting in some states. Along with other measures, such as a literacy test, it was widely used in Southern states to bar blacks and poor whites from the polls. After the Fifteenth Amendment extended the right to vote to all races, a poll tax was devised as a way to circumvent the amendment. Payment of a poll tax, as a precondition for voting, was outlawed by the ratification of the Twenty-fourth Amendment to the Constitution in 1964.

102. Freda McVay, *The Paradoxical Plainsman: A Biography of the (More or Less) Honorable Charles A. Guy* (Lubbock: Texas Tech University Press, 1983), 27.

103. "George Mahon, Ending Brilliant Record as District Attorney in This Judicial District, Realizes Boyhood Ambition in Going to Congress," *Sweetwater* (Texas) *Reporter*, September 9, 1934.

104. "George Mahon Develops Strong Lead over Judge Mullican for Congress," *Colorado* (Texas) *Record*, August 31, 1934.

105. GHM, Box 400, folders 32 and 33.

106. "Big Majority Piled Up for Colorado Man," *Lubbock Avalanche-Journal*, August 26, 1934.

107. Ibid.

Chapter 2

1. Kenneth R. Mladenka and Kim Quaile Hill, *Texas Government: Politics and Economics*, 2nd ed. (Pacific Grove, CA: Brooks/Cole, 1989), 88.

2. Ibid.

3. A game played with dominoes.

4. GHM, Box 2, folder 9, typescript of undated manuscript entitled "Early Days as a Member of Congress."

5. GHM, Box 92, folder 20, letter from Marvin Jones to George Mahon, August 29, 1934.

6. Ibid., letter from Marvin Jones to George Mahon, September 21, 1934; and letter dated September 24, 1934. Letter from George Mahon to Marvin Jones, December 3, 1934.

7. Ibid., letter from Sam Rayburn to George Mahon, September 29, 1934.

8. Ibid., letter from Joseph W. Byrns to George Mahon, August 4, 1934.

9. GHM, Box 92, folder 20. Letter from Marvin Jones, dated November 12, 1934.

10. Ibid.; and GHM, Box 32, folder 13, letter from George Mahon to Sam Rayburn, November 20, 1934.

11. Ibid., letter from Sam Rayburn to George Mahon, November 24, 1934.

12. Ibid., letter from Hatton Sumners to George Mahon, dated September 4, 1934.

13. Ibid., letter from Thomas L. Blanton to George Mahon, dated September 26, 1934.

14. Ibid., letter from Thomas L. Blanton to George Mahon, August 31, 1934.

15. Ibid., letter from Sam Rayburn, dated August 27, 1934; letter from John O'Connor, dated September 16, 1934; letter from A. J. Sabbath, dated November 12, 1934; letter from Jim Farley, dated November 14, 1934.

16. GHM, Box 2, folder 9, undated manuscript entitled "Early Days as a Member of Congress."

17. GHM, Box 588, Green Journal, 20, 35.

18. Ibid., 20.

19. Ibid., 19.

20. Ibid.

21. Ibid., 21.

22. GHM, Box 3, folder 22, Mahon to Pearce and Murrah, 20.

23. Franklyn Waltman, Jr., "Roosevelt Goes before Congress with Plan to Employ 3,500,000," *Washington Post*, January 5, 1935.

24. *Congressional Record*, 74th Congress, 1st Session, 116–18.

25. "5 Billions—Relief Bill, Boodle Bill?" *Washington Post*, February 17, 1935.

26. GHM, Box 588, Green Journal, 27–28.

27. Conrad Black, *Franklin Delano Roosevelt: Champion of Freedom* (New York: Public Affairs, 2003), 349.

28. "Federal Grants Are Approved," *Lubbock* (Texas) *Morning Avalanche*, September 17, 1938.

29. GHM, Box 29, folder 27, Elizabeth West to George Mahon, November 14, 1934; and Mahon to West, January 10, 1935.

30. GHM, Box 579, Scrapbook, 1935.

31. GHM, Box 2, folder 9, typescript of undated manuscript entitled "Early Days as a Member of Congress."

32. Alan Brinkley, *Voices of Protest: Huey Long, Father Coughlin, and the Great Depression* (New York: Knopf, 1982), 3.

33. Joseph M. Siracusa and David G. Coleman, *Depression to Cold War: A History of America from Herbert Hoover to Ronald Reagan* (Westport, CT: Praeger, 2002), 30.

34. Alan Brinkley, *Voices of Protest*, 7.

35. Kingfish was a character in the popular and deeply racial *Amos 'n Andy* radio program.

36. Alan Brinkley, *Voices of Protest*, ix.

37. Arthur Meier Schlesinger, Jr., ed., *The Age of Roosevelt: The Politics of Upheaval.*,3 vols. (Boston: Houghton Mifflin), 35.

38. GHM, Box 588, Green Journal, 29.

39. GHM, Box 365, folder entitled "Legislation: Old Age Pension, 1934-1935, General."

40. GHM, Box 365, folder 3, name withheld to protect the privacy of the writer.

41. David M. Kennedy, *Freedom from Fear: The American People in Depression and War, 1929–1945* (New York: Oxford University Press, 1999), 262.

42. Ibid., 262; and Frances Perkins, *The Roosevelt I Knew* (New York: Viking Press, 1946), 286.

43. Perkins, *Roosevelt I Knew*, 279.

44. Nicholas A. Masters, "Committee Assignments in the House of Representatives," *American Political Science Review* 55, no. 2 (1961): 346.

45. US National Archives and Records Administration, Records of the Committee on Insular Affairs (1899–1946), 13.96, http://www.archives.gov/legislative/guide/house/chapter-13-insular-affairs.html.

46. GHM, Box 588, Green Journal, 23–24.

47. GHM, Box 2, folder 19, typescript of letter to "Dear Papa and Aunt Laura," dated March 10, 1935.

48. Ibid.

49. Ibid.

50. GHM, Box 92, folder 36, George Mahon to Jesse W. Davis, dated October 3, 1936.

51. *Congressional Record*, 74th Congress, 1st Session, 3554–55.

52. GHM, Box 248, folder 24, copy of letter to President Franklin D. Roosevelt, dated August 16, 1935.

53. GHM, Box 29, folder 19, letter from Clark Mullican, dated June 22, 1935.

54. Dr. Elwood Mead, an internationally known irrigation engineer, was in Washington, DC, serving as commissioner of reclamation when Mahon contacted him.

55. GHM, Box 579, 1935 Scrapbook, news article from *Sudan* (Texas) *News*, April 25, 1935.

56. "Mahon Loses in His Effort to Get West Texas Survey," *Lubbock* (Texas) *Morning Avalanche*, February 1, 1936.

57. *The Cross Section* 17, no. 8 (August 1971): 1–2 (publication of the High Plains Underground Water Conservation District No. 1, published in Lubbock, Texas).

58. Ibid.

59. GHM, Box 598, folder 34, letter to Judge O. E. Stevenson, dated July 25, 1935.

60. Schlesinger, *Age of Roosevelt: The Politics of Upheaval*, 306.

61. Patterson, *Congressional Conservatism*, 51.

62. Ibid., 41.

63. GHM, Box 29, folder 19, letter from Durward D. Mahon, dated July 15, 1935.

64. GHM, Box 588, Green Journal, 36.

65. Ibid., 37.

66. "Mahon Back from Capital Sees Brighter Days for US," *Sweetwater* (Texas) *Reporter*, September 8, 1935.

67. Ibid.

68. The bill for early payment of the veterans' bonus.

69. "Mahon Back from Capital Sees Brighter Days for US," *Sweetwater* (Texas) *Reporter*, September 8, 1935.

70. GHM, Box 29, folder 4, letter from W. R. Ely, August 26, 1935.

71. "Mahon Back from Capital Sees Brighter Days for US," *Sweetwater* (Texas) *Reporter*, September 8, 1935.

72. GHM, Box 588, Green Journal, 64–65.

73. Ibid., 124–25.

74. Ibid., 127.

75. Ibid., 70.

76. Ibid., 108.

77. Ibid., 73.

78. Ibid., 85.

79. Ibid., 86.

80. Ibid., 95.

81. Ibid., 97.

82. Ibid., 104.

83. Ibid.

84. Ibid., 115.

85. Ibid., 129–30.

86. Ibid., p. 133.

87. "Garner to Visit Japan in Fall; Formal Welcome Is Planned," *Washington Post*, August 20, 1935.

88. GHM, Box 588, Green Journal, 134.

89. The Agricultural Adjustment Act (AAA) and the Bankhead Bill were federal efforts to restrict cotton acreage and provide payments to producers for acres not planted in cotton.

90. GHM, Box 588, Green Journal, 140–46.

91. Ibid., 149.

92. Ibid., 150–51.

93. "Mahon, Back from Capital Sees Brighter Days for US," *Sweetwater* (Texas) *Reporter*, September 8, 1935.

94. David Kennedy, *Freedom from Fear*, 278–79.

95. *Congressional Record*, 74th Congress, 2nd Session, 6–7.

96. Ibid., 7; David Kennedy, *Freedom from Fear*, 278–79.

97. "Klansmen Attend Funeral of Fellow Member," *Washington Post*, January 5, 1936.

98. "Fight for Agriculture Only Begun—Mahon's Challenge," *Colorado* (Texas) *Record*, January 17, 1936.

99. "Mitchell Citizens Paid over One Million in AAA Cash," *Colorado* (Texas) *Record,* January 10, 1936.

100. GHM, Box 257, folder 14, letter from Walter Young, Levelland, Texas, dated February 14, 1936.

101. Ibid., letter to Walter Young, Levelland, Texas, dated February 17, 1936.

102. Dr. George Gallup, "Poll Finds All Sections Except South Opposed," *Washington Post*, January 5, 1936.

103. Franklyn Waltman, Jr., "President Declares US Must Pay Debt to Farmers," *Washington Post*, January 8, 1936.

104. Janet Neugebauer, ed., *Plains Farmer: The Diary of William G. DeLoach, 1914–1964* (College Station: Texas A&M University Press, 1991), 170–71.

105. Irvin M. May, Jr., *Marvin Jones: The Public Life of an Agrarian Advocate* (College Station: Texas A&M University Press, 1980), 144.

106. *Congressional Record*, 74th Congress, 2nd Session, 3611–12.

107. "Texas Cowboy Congressman Easily Lassoes Democrats," *Danville* (Virginia) *Register*, March 3, 1936.

108. "Hear President Praised as 'Greatest Home-Saver,'" *Mansfield* (Virginia) *News*, April 18, 1936.

109. Thomas P. Wolf, William D. Pederson, and Byron W. Daynes, *Franklin D. Roosevelt and Congress: The New Deal and Its Aftermath* (Armonk, NY: M. E. Sharpe, 2001), 80; *Congressional Record*, 74th Congress, 1st Session, 3989–94.

110. *Congressional Record*, 74th Congress, 1st Session, 7993–96.

111. Editorial, "Cash for the Veterans," *Lubbock* (Texas) *Evening Journal*, June 18, 1936.

112. Ibid., "Wife Takes Vet's Bonus; Charged," June 27, 1936.

113. "Rep. Bankhead Follows Byrns in Speakership," *Washington Post*, June 5, 1936.

114. GHM, Box 29, folder 18, letter from James Little to George Mahon, dated June 3, 1936.

115. *Lubbock* (Texas) *Morning Avalanche*, July 23, 1936.

116. Editorial, "The Plainsman Says," *Lubbock* (Texas) *Evening Journal*, May 19, 1936.

117. Editorial, "The Plainsman Says," *Lubbock* (Texas) *Evening Journal*, May 19, 1936., Editorial, "Mahon Moves Up," *Lubbock* (Texas) *Evening Journal*, October 18, 1936.

118. "George Mahon, Ending First Congress Term, Sees Victory for Party after Much Work," *Abilene* (Texas*) Reporter News*, July 8, 1936.

119. "Crowds Enthusiastic in Honoring Garner," *Dallas Morning News*, August 6, 1936.

120. GHM, Box 92, folder 19, letter to Sam Rayburn, dated September 24, 1936.

121. Ibid., letter to George Mahon from Sam Rayburn, November 24, 1936.

122. "Mahon and Neutrality," *Lubbock* (Texas) *Morning Avalanche*, December 30, 1936.

123. "Rayburn Wins in Fight for House Leadership; Congress Opens Today," *Washington Post*, January 5, 1937.

124. Ibid.

125. *Congressional Record*, 75th Congress, 1st Session, 12.

126. Hope Ridings Miller, "Senator Caraway Interested in Old-Age Pensions and Farm Question," *Washington Post*, January 5, 1937.

127. *Congressional Record*, 75th Congress, 1st Session, 83.

128. Ibid., 84.

129. Ibid., 85.

130. Ibid., 86.

131. "President Views New Amendment as Unnecessary," *Washington Post*, January 7, 1937.

132. David Kennedy, *Freedom from Fear*, 328.

133. Ibid., 325.

134. D. B. Hardeman and Donald C. Bacon, *Rayburn: A Biography* (Austin: Texas Monthly Press, 1987), 221.

135. Page Smith, *Redeeming the Time: A People's History of the 1920s and the New Deal* (New York: McGraw-Hill, 1987), 684.

136. O. R. Altman, "First Session of the Seventy-fifth Congress, January 5, 1937–August 21, 1937," *American Political Science Review* 31, no. 6 (1937): 1071.

137. GHM, Box 28, folder 64, letter to Fred C. Haile, dated March 13, 1937.

138. "Mr. Mahon Is Doing His Job," *Lubbock* (Texas) *Avalanche-Journal*, September 12, 1937.

139. GHM, Box 28, folder 77, letter to Jack Wester, dated March 11, 1937.

140. Ibid.

141. Ibid.

142. Ibid.

143. *Congressional Record*, 75th Congress, 1st Session, 5767.

144. Jewel Barrett, "Congressman George Mahon's Belief in President Roosevelt Unshaken; Says Demo Split Not Serious," *Abilene* (Texas) *Reporter News*, September 5, 1937.

145. Ibid.

146. "Public Interest in Governmental Affairs Will Curb Threat of Dictator, Mahon Asserts," *Big Spring* (Texas) *Herald*, September 21, 1937.

147. "Congressman Mahon Believes He Knows What Type of Cotton Program West Texas Farmers Want," *Abilene* (Texas) *Reporter News*, November 7, 1937.

148. David Kennedy, *Freedom from Fear*, 340; Frank Friedel, *Franklin D. Roosevelt: A Rendezvous with Destiny* (Boston: Little, Brown, 1990), 185.

149. David Kennedy, *Freedom from Fear*, 340.

150. GHM, Box 257, folder 11, letter to L. D. Saint, dated January 17, 1938.

151. Irvin May, *Marvin Jones*, 127.

152. Murray R. Benedict, *Can We Solve the Farm Problem?* (New York: Twentieth Century Fund, 1955), 254.

153. GHM, Box 2, folder 9, undated manuscript entitled "Early Days as a Member of Congress."

154. Ibid.

155. "George Mahon and Family Drive in from Washington," *Colorado* (Texas) *Record*, July 1, 1938.

156. "Congressman Marvin Jones Pays a Visit to Lubbock," *Lubbock* (Texas) *Morning Avalanche*, September 11, 1938.

157. "Work of Congressman Mahon Receives Praise from Speaker Bankhead," *Colorado* (Texas) *Record*, July 8, 1938.

158. Masters, "Committee Assignments," 346.

159. GHM, Box 92, folder 21, letter from Sam Rayburn, dated August 31, 1938.

160. Ibid., letter to Ewing Thomason, dated August 23, 1938.

161. GHM, Box 3, folder 22, Mahon to Pearce and Murrah, 29.

162. Patterson, *Congressional Conservatism*, 281.

163. Ibid., 284.

164. Ibid., 290.

Chapter 3

1. GHM, Box 575, Scrapbook, 1939.

2. Richard F. Fenno, Jr., *The Power of the Purse: Appropriations Politics in Congress* (Boston: Little, Brown, 1966), 6.

3. Ibid., 8.

4. Riders are amendments that are not germane to the subject matter of the bill they are attached to. They are often proposals that would not likely become law by themselves. However, when attached to urgent bills, such as funding necessary to run the government, the amendment has a better possibility of becoming law.

5. Fenno, *Power of the Purse*, 1.

6. Legislative committees, in both chambers, approve the bill required to establish a program and often decide the maximum amount to be spent annually on the program. After being approved in both chambers, the bill is sent to the president for signing before being sent to the House Committee on Appropriations to begin the funding process.

7. *Congressional Record*, 89th Congress, 1st Session, 3959–63.

8. Ibid., statement by the chairman in the House, March 2, 1965.

9. Fenno, *Power of the Purse*, 7.

10. Treasury and Post Office Appropriations; Legislative Establishment Appropriations; Interior Department Appropriations; Agriculture Department Appropriations; War Department Appropriations; District of Columbia Appropriations; Labor Department and Federal Security Agency Appropriations; State, Justice, and Commerce Department Appropriations; Deficiency Appropriations; House Subcommittee Acting under H. Res. 130 Appropriations (this subcommittee investigated activities of the WPA). In future years the number of subcommittees was increased to twelve.

11. A safe district was one in which the representative felt secure about the likelihood of being returned to Congress in future elections. This often happened in one-party states.

12. Fenno, *Power of the Purse*, 51–78.

13. Ibid., 93.

14. Ibid., 11.

15. *Congressional Record*, 76th Congress, 1st Session, 121.

16. Only standing committees would be considered important because others did not meet regularly or handle major legislation.

17. Bernard Weisberger, *The District of Columbia: The Seat of Government* (New York: Time-Life Books, 1968), 43; David Brinkley, *Washington Goes to War* (New York: Alfred A. Knopf, 1988), 75.

18. GHM, Box 593, folder 9, letter to Durward Mahon, dated May 31, 1944.

19. James D. Secrest, "Mahon to Get D.C. Finance Post, Is Report," *Washington Post*, July 21, 1939.

20. David Brinkley, *Washington Goes to War*, 11.

21. *Congressional Record*, 77th Congress, 1st Session, 3918–21.

22. "Our New Chief of Purse," *Washington Post*, January 16, 1941.

23. David Brinkley, *Washington Goes to War*, 107.

24. Ibid., 16.

25. Bernard Baruch, a financier, accepted administrative positions for one dollar a year instead of a regular salary. It was necessary to find executives from the corporate world who would do this because there was no large cadre of civil-service personnel to undertake many of the jobs that needed filling.

26. GHM, Box 212, folder 23, news article from *New York Journal American*, December 21, 1942; letter from Mahon to Honorable Leon Henderson, dated January 4, 1943.

27. Ibid., unsigned memorandum.

28. "George Mahon Believes America Can Stay out of European War," *Lubbock* (Texas) *Avalanche-Journal*, September 3, 1939; *Congressional Record*, 74th Congress, 2nd Session, 2253; *Congressional Record*, 75th Congress, 1st Session, 2410; *Congressional Record*, 76th Congress, 2nd Session, 8511–14.

29. *Congressional Record*, 76th Congress, 3rd Session, 8.

30. Black, *Roosevelt*, 482.

31. James MacGregor Burns, *Roosevelt: The Lion and the Fox* (New York: Harcourt, Brace, 1956), 383.

32. David M. Kennedy, *Freedom from Fear*, 400.

33. GHM, Box 303, folder 27, letter from B. F. Robbins, dated October 26, 1939.

34. Ibid., letter to B. F. Robbins, dated October 30, 1939.

35. Ibid., letter from Jesse M. Osborn, dated September 16, 1939.

36. Ibid., letter to Jesse M. Osborn, dated September 25, 1939.

37. Mark Sullivan, Editorial, *Washington Post*, July 2, 1939.

38. GHM, Box 3, folder 22, Mahon to Pearce and Murrah, 29.

39. Ibid.

40. Ibid., 30.

41. James L. McConaughy, Jr., "Congressmen and the Pentagon," *Fortune* (April 1958), 167.

42. Fenno, *Power of the Purse*, 141.

43. Ibid., 142.

44. "5,500-Plane Bill Sent to White House," *Washington Post*, July 1, 1939.

45. David Kennedy, *Freedom from Fear*, 429.

46. *Congressional Record*, 76th Congress, 3rd Session, 8516–17.

47. Ibid.

48. GHM, Box 306, folder 26, letter to J. A. Freeland, dated May 4, 1942.

49. GHM, Box 593, folder 1.

50. The gears on a windmill had to be greased periodically, and someone had to climb the tower to perform this job, which could be difficult for anyone afraid of heights.

51. Bolling Field became Bolling Air Force Base in 1948.
52. GHM, Box 588, Green Journal, 162.
53. GHM, Box 3, folder 22, Mahon to Pearce and Murrah, 30.
54. GHM, Box 80, folder 11.
55. GHM, Box 593, folder 1, unsigned letter from Lloyd Croslin to Mahon, dated August 9, 1940.
56. GHM, Box 588, Green Journal, 182.
57. GHM, Box 134, folder 29.
58. *United States News* 11, no. 15 (October 10, 1941): 26.
59. *Congressional Record*, 77th Congress, 1st Session, 2994.
60. GHM, Box 303, folder 25, letter from Mrs. C. A. McDonald, dated May 15, 1941.
61. Ibid., letter to Judge Louis B. Reed, dated April 29, 1941.
62. David Kennedy, *Freedom from Fear*, 639.
63. GHM, Box 593, folder 9, letter to "Dear Owen," dated February 1, 1944.
64. GHM, Box 5, folder 13, letter to "Dear Folks at Home," dated May 2, 1943.
65. *Congressional Record*, 77th Congress, 1st Session, 9519–20.
66. GHM, Box 589, folder entitled "Correspondence, 1935–1980," letter to "Dear Dad," dated December 15, 1941.
67. Ibid.
68. Ibid. Mahon misspelled "genius" in his letter.
69. "War Draft Passes Both Houses; Ages Set at 20-44," *Washington Post*, December 20, 1941.
70. GHM, Box 589, folder entitled "Correspondence 1935–1980," letter to "Dear Dad," dated December 15, 1941.
71. John K. Mahon would have lived when Washington, DC, was a war capital during the Civil War, the Spanish-American War, World War I, and World War II.
72. GHM, Box 589, folder entitled "Correspondence 1935–1980," letter to "Dear Dad," dated December 15, 1941.
73. "Production for Victory: What It Means to Industry," *United States News* 11, no. 25 (December 19, 1941): 35.
74. Ibid.
75. GHM, Box 5, folder 13, letter to "Bro. Tompkins and Miss Ewella" (the Charles Thompsons in Colorado City), dated December 22, 1941.
76. Ibid.
77. Editorial, "New Year," *Washington Post*, January 1, 1942.
78. Ibid.
79. *Congressional Record*, 77th Congress, 2nd Session, 32–35.
80. Ibid.
81. Ibid.

82. Barnet Nover, "Victory and Beyond," *Washington Post*, January 7, 1942.

83. GHM, Box 589, folder entitled "Correspondence 1935–1980," letter to "Dear Dad," dated January 25, 1942.

84. *Congressional Record*, 77th Congress, 2nd Session, 602–3.

85. "Daylight Saving," *Washington Post*, January 11, 1942.

86. "History of Lubbock Army Air Field, Lubbock, Texas, to 1 March 1944," unpublished manuscript located in Reference File, Southwest Collection, Texas Tech University, Lubbock, Texas, 9.

87. Pilots who are trained to fly with the aid of instruments when the weather conditions make visual flight impossible.

88. Walter Wilcox, *The Farmer in World War II* (Ames: Iowa State College Press, 1947), 257.

89. *Congressional Record*, 78th Congress, 1st Session, 9760.

90. The increases seem miniscule in 2014; however, it was a noticeable price increase by 1940s standards.

91. *Congressional Record*, 78th Congress, 1st Session, 9760.

92. Ibid., 750.

93. "The Gallup Poll," *Washington Post*, December 4, 1943.

94. Allan M. Winkler, *Home Front USA: America during World War II* (Arlington Heights, IL: H. Davidson, 1986), 32.

95. GHM, Box 598, folder 33, letter to "Dear Folks at Home," dated May 27, 1943.

96. Ibid., letter to "Dear Dad and all others to whom this letter may come," dated February 7, 1943.

97. Ibid.

98. *Congressional Record*, 78th Congress, 1st Session, 1108–9.

99. Spencer Moosa, "Congress Cheers Mme. Chiang as Foe Drives to Crush China," *Washington Post*, February 19, 1943.

100. David Kennedy, *Freedom from Fear*, 624.

101. GHM, Box 5, folder 13, letter to "Dear Folks at Home," dated May 2, 1943.

102. Editorial, "Telling Congress," *Washington Post*, May 25, 1943.

103. GHM, Box 5, folder 13, letter to "Dear Folks at Home," dated May 2, 1943.

104. GHM, Box 287, folder 29.

105. *Congressional Record*, 78th Congress, 2nd Session, 1959.

106. GHM, Box 5, folder 14, letter to J. K. Mahon, dated March 2, 1944.

107. Winkler, *Home Front USA*, 104.

108. GHM, Box 5, folder 14, letter from Charles L. South, dated February 2, 1944.

109. Hardeman and Bacon, *Rayburn*, 301–2.

110. *Congressional Record*, 79th Congress, 1st Session, 91–96.

111. Ibid., 96.

112. David McCullough, *Truman* (New York: Simon and Schuster, 1992), 332.

113. David Kennedy, *Freedom from Fear*, 799–806.

114. GHM, Box 5, folder 13, letter to Daphne Mahon, dated April 18, 1945.

115. GHM, Box 3, folder 22, Mahon to Pearce and Murrah, 120–22.

116. Truman was in Lubbock to campaign for President Roosevelt in 1944.

117. GHM, Box 5, folder 14, letter to "Dick, Tom, and Harry," dated May 5, 1945.

118. Ibid., letter to J. K. Mahon, dated June 16, 1945.

119. GHM, Box 3, folder 22, Mahon to Pearce and Murrah, 56–57.

120. Henry Wallace had also served as secretary of agriculture and vice president before becoming secretary of commerce.

121. GHM, Box 5, folder 14, letter to "Dick, Tom, and Harry," dated May 5, 1945.

122. Vincent C. Jones, *Manhattan: The Army and the Atomic Bomb* (Washington, DC: Center of Military History, United States Army, 1985), 11–12.

123. Ibid., 19.

124. Ibid., 33.

125. Roland Young, *Congressional Politics in the Second World War* (New York: Columbia University Press, 1956), 235.

126. Leslie R. Groves, *Now It Can Be Told: The Story of the Manhattan Project* (New York: Harper & Row, 1962), 361.

127. Ibid., 361–63.

128. In September 1941 Edward T. Taylor (D-CO) died, and Clarence Cannon (D-MO) became chairman of the House Committee on Appropriations.

129. Groves, *Now It Can Be Told*, 364.

130. Ibid., 365.

131. Ibid., 360.

132. GHM, Box 3, folder 34, "A Fantastic Interlude."

133. GHM, Box 3, folder 33, "Notes Made by George Mahon during the 1970 Period in Regard to the Development of the Atomic Bomb."

134. Groves, *Now It Can Be Told*, 413.

135. R. C. Hankins, "Cong. George Mahon in on 'Atomic" Secret," *Lubbock* (Texas) *Avalanche-Journal*, August 7, 1945.

136. GHM, Box 3, folder 22, Mahon to Pearce and Murrah, transcript of interview, 41.

137. Ibid.

138. GHM, Box 3, folder 33, "Notes Made by George Mahon during the 1970 Period in Regard to the Development of the Atomic Bomb."

139. GHM, Box 80, folder 2, "Preliminary Report of the War Department Sub-Committee on Appropriations, House of Representatives, on an Overseas Inspection Made during the Period August 16–September 23, 1945."

140. GHM, Box 5, folder 31, unpublished manuscript entitled "Around the World in Thirty-nine Days."

141. Ibid.

142. GHM, Box 5, folder 30, "Diary of Round-the-World Trip of Congressional Sub-Committee on Military Appropriations, 16 August–23 September 1945 incl."

143. GHM, Box 5, folder 31, unpublished manuscript entitled "Around the World in Thirty-nine Days."

144. GHM, Box 5, folder 30, "Diary of Round-the-World Trip of Congressional Sub-Committee on Military Appropriations, 16 August–23 September 1945 incl.," written by Robert E. Lambert, committee clerk.

145. Ibid.

146. Ibid.

147. GHM, Box 588, Green Journal, 104.

148. GHM, Box 5, folder 30, "Diary of Round-the-World Trip of Congressional Sub-Committee on Military Appropriations, 16 August–23 September 1945 incl.," written by Robert E. Lambert, committee clerk.

149. GHM, Box 5, folder 31, manuscript titled "Around the World in Thirty-nine Days," 2.

150. "The Hump" was the name Allied pilots gave to the eastern end of the Himalayan Mountains during World War II. Flying over the Hump was risky because of bad weather and turbulence; however, it was the only way to bring supplies into China from Assam, India, after the Japanese captured the Burma Road.

151. GHM, Box 5, folder 31, unpublished manuscript entitled "Around the World in Thirty-nine Days."

152. Ibid.

153. Ibid.

154. Ibid.

155. Ibid.

156. Ibid.

157. Ibid.

158. Ibid.

159. Ibid.

160. Ibid.

161. Ibid.

162. Ibid.

163. Ibid.

164. Ibid.

165. Ibid.

166. Ibid.

167. Ibid.

168. Ibid.

169. Ibid.

170. Ibid.

171. GHM, Box 5, folder 30, "Diary of Round-the-World Trip of Congressional Sub-Committee on Military Appropriations, 16 August–23 September 1945 incl.," written by Robert E. Lambert, committee clerk.

172. Ibid.

173. Ibid.

174. Ibid.

175. GHM, Box 5, folder 13, letter to "Dear Homefolks," dated September 23, 1945.

176. Ibid.

177. GHM, Box 80, folder 8, Memorandum of Conclusions Submitted to the President.

178. Ibid.

179. Ibid.

180. Ibid.

181. GHM, Box 80, folder 8.

182. Edward T. Folliard, "Christmas Tree Glows for First Time since Dark Days of Tobruk," *Washington Post*, December 25, 1945; William Seale, *The President's House: A History*, vol. 2 (Washington, DC: National Geographic Society, White House Historical Association, 1986), 975.

183. Editorial, "Christmas," *Washington Post*, December 25, 1945.

Chapter 4

1. William H. Chafe, *The Unfinished Journey: America since World War II* (New York: Oxford University Press, 1986), 31–35.

2. James T. Patterson, *Grand Expectations: The United States from 1945–1974* (New York: Oxford University Press, 1996), 113; John Lewis Gaddis, *The United States and the Origins of the Cold War, 1941–1947* (New York: Columbia University Press, 2000), 283–84, 299–301, McCullough, *Truman*, 486; Chafe, *Unfinished Journey*, 62.

3. Patterson, *Grand Expectations*, 113.

4. John Lewis Gaddis, *George F. Kennan: An American Life* (New York: Penguin Press, 2011), 215–22, Stephen E. Ambrose and Douglas G. Brinkley, *Rise to Globalism: American Foreign Policy since 1938*, 9th rev. ed. (New York: Penguin Books, 2011), 95.

5. Gaddis, *Origins of the Cold War*, 302–4; Katherine A. S. Sibley, *The Cold War* (Westport, CT: Greenwood Press, 1998), 132; Randall Bennett Woods, *Quest for Identity: America since 1945* (New York: Cambridge University Press, 2005), 43–44; and Patterson, *Grand Expectations*, 114–15.

6. Patterson, *Grand Expectations*, 115; Sibley, *Cold War*, 136–39.

7. Ambrose and Brinkley, *Rise to Globalism*, 71.

8. GHM, Box 133, folder 13, letter to Mrs. L. S. Hay, dated January 19, 1946.

9. "Mahon Says Shipping Supplies Factor in Getting Troops Home," *Lubbock* (Texas) *Avalanche-Journal*, September 30, 1945.

10. McCullough, *Truman*, 741.

11. Warner R. Schilling, Paul Y. Hammond, and Glen H. Snyder, *Strategy, Politics and Defense Budgets* (New York: Columbia University Press, 1962), 30.

12. Ibid., 17; Edward A. Kolodziej, *The Uncommon Defense and Congress, 1945–1963* (Columbus: Ohio State University Press, 1966), 453; Samuel P. Huntington, *The Common Defense: Strategic Programs in National Politics* (New York: Columbia University Press, 1961), 47.

13. Elias Huzar, *The Purse and the Sword: Control of the Army by Congress through Military Appropriations, 1933–1950* (Ithaca, NY: Cornell University Press, 1950), 403.

14. Kolodziej, *Uncommon Defense*, 439.

15. Ernest R. May, "Cold War and Defense," in *The Cold War and Defense*, ed. Keith Neilson and Ronald G. Haycock (New York: Praeger, 1990), 38–39.

16. An administrative unit composed of two or more squadrons. Generally, a group is a subdivision of a force assigned for a specific purpose.

17. Aaron Wildavsky, *The Politics of the Budgetary Process*, 2nd ed. (Boston: Little, Brown, 1974), 52.

18. A bill must be passed in identical form by both the House of Representatives and the Senate before it can be sent to the president for his signature, or veto, as the case may be. Frequently, the two chambers pass different versions of the same bill, and a conference committee is then established to work out the differences. Although conference committee members are formally appointed by the speaker of the House and the president of the Senate, actually the chair and ranking minority member of the committee that originally handled the bill choose who will serve on the committee. Both Republicans and Democrats are represented on the committee and are chosen based on seniority and knowledge of the bill. After discussion, conferees from each chamber vote separately on the differing issues, and a majority from each group must agree before a compromise bill can be returned to each chamber for its approval. When the identical bill passes both chambers, the conference committee ceases to exist.

19. GHM, Box 593, folder entitled "Campaign, 1946," letter from Robert H. Bean, dated May 7, 1946.

20. Ibid, folder entitled "Campaign, 1946," "The George Mahon Journal."

21. Ibid.

22. GHM, Box 593, folder entitled "Campaign, 1946," letter to John Baze of the *Colorado* (Colorado City, Texas) *Record*, dated June 21, 1946.

23. Ibid.

24. "Twelve Candidates Endorsed by Lubbock's Negro Voters," *Lubbock* (Texas) *Morning Avalanche*, July 27, 1946.

25. "Mahon to Return to Capital for Duties," *Lubbock* (Texas) *Morning Avalanche*, July 24, 1946.

26. GHM, Box 5, folder 14, letter to Eldon Mahon, dated January 2, 1947.

27. Kolodziej, *Uncommon Defense*, 60–70.

28. Eric F. Goldman, *The Crucial Decade—and After: America, 1945–1960* (New York: Knopf, 1966), 57; Chafe, *Unfinished Journey*, 66.

29. Ambrose and Brinkley. *Rise to Globalism: American Foreign Policy since 1938*, 9th rev. ed., 76.

30. *Congressional Record*, 80th Congress, 1st Session, 1981.

31. Ambrose and Brinkley, *Rise to Globalism*, 82.

32. GHM, Box 319, folder 21, letter to Hon. George H. Mahon, dated March 15, 1947.

33. Ibid., letter to Mr. Marshall NcNeil, dated April 23, 1947.

34. The atomic bomb would be a big stick.

35. GHM, Box 319, folder 21, letter to G. E. Long, dated March 25, 1947.

36. Ibid., letter from Georgia W. Dingus (Mrs. William Dingus), dated February 25, 1947.

37. Ibid., letter to Mrs. William Dingus, dated March 28, 1947.

38. John Lewis Gaddis, *The Cold War: A New History* (New York: Penguin Press, 2005), 95.

39. Ibid., 32.

40. A select committee is one that is created for a specific purpose and disbanded when the goal is met. In this case the select committee was to study the situation in Europe and report recommendations for aid that became known as the Marshall Plan.

41. Arthur Krock, "House Playing Big Role in US Foreign Policy," *New York Times*, August 3, 1947.

42. Ibid.

43. GHM, Box 599, folder 52; the newsletter, entitled "Sidelights from Washington," was to be released August 7, 1947.

44. Editorial, "Mahon in Group: It's Something New," *Lubbock* (Texas) *Morning Avalanche*, August 17, 1947.

45. Ibid.

46. GHM, Box 79, folder 8, handwritten notes from folder entitled "Office Trips, 1947," 1. Underlining is Mahon's.

47. Ibid.

48. GHM, Box 79, folder 16, "A Report from Europe."

49. Ibid.

50. *Preliminary Report Eight of the House Select Committee on Foreign Aid Pursuant to H. Res. 296 A Resolution Creating a Special Committee on Foreign Aid*, "Proposed Principles and Organization for Any Program of Foreign Aid, November 22, 1947" (Washington: Government Printing Office, 1947), 1.

51. GHM, Box 79, folder 8, handwritten notes from folder entitled "Office Trips, Italy," September 9, 1947, 6. Underlining is Mahon's.

52. GHM, Box 79, folder 8, "Statement by the Chairman of the Italy-Trieste-Greece Subcommittee to the General Committee."

53. Ibid.

54. Ibid, Trieste handwritten notes in folder entitled "Office Trips, 1947," 1.

55. GHM, Box 79, folder 9. Taken from notes scribbled on a copy of "Monitoring Report" published by News and Monitoring Division HQ AIS, Trieste.

56. GHM, Box 79, folder 8, "Statement by the Chairman of the Italy-Trieste-Greece Subcommittee to the General Committee."

57. The Import-Export Bank is the official export credit agency that assists in financing US goods that are exported to international markets.

58. Patterson, *Grand Expectations*, 131.

59. *Congressional Record*, 80th Congress, 1st Session, 11474–76.

60. Ibid., 11475–76.

61. Ibid., 11476.

62. Nicolaus Mills, *Winning the Peace: The Marshall Plan and America's Coming of Age as a Superpower* (Hoboken, NJ: John Wiley and Sons, 2008), 168.

63. Patterson, *Grand Expectations*, 132–33.

64. McCullough, *Truman*, 583.

65. GHM, Box 5, folder 13, letter to Mrs. S. E. Meadows, dated May 3, 1948.

66. Ibid., letter to Mr. and Mrs. J. B. Mahon, dated June 30, 1948.

67. Ibid.

68. Ibid.

69. Each bill assigned to a committee receives careful scrutiny, which involves holding hearings to gather information, carefully deliberating each part, and rewriting any parts as needed.

70. GHM, Box 5, folder 13, letter to Mrs. S. E. Meadows, dated May 3, 1948.

71. Patterson, *Grand Expectations*, 156.

72. McCullough, *Truman*, 710.

73. *Current Developments in United States Foreign Policy* 2, no. 4 (November 1948): 3.

74. Fair Employment Practices Committee.

75. "Mahon Deserves Unopposed Campaign," *Big Spring* (Texas) *Herald*, April 4, 1948.

76. Schilling, Hammond, and Snyder, *Strategy, Politics,* 11; Patterson, *Grand Expectations,* 133.

77. Ralph Preston to Lawrence Graves, September 24, 1992, Oral History Files.

78. *Congressional Record*, 79th Congress, 2nd Session, 6862–63.

79. *Congressional Record*, 81st Congress, 1st Session, 4432.

80. GHM, Box 286, folder 21, letter from William C. O'Mara, dated April 14, 1949.

81. An air force group is an organizational unit made up of two or more squadrons and usually commanded by a colonel. Two or more groups can make a wing, the highest level of command on an air force base. There is no set number of personnel in any of these organizational units.

82. On March 1, 1949, James Forrestal resigned as secretary of defense, and Louis Johnson replaced him. During his tenure as secretary of defense, Johnson built a strong political base from his philosophy of economizing defense expenditures. Foreign economic aid (Marshall Plan) and military aid (NATO) competed with national defense expenditures for resources.

83. *Congressional Record*, 81st Congress, 1st Session, 4427.

84. Ibid., 4428.

85. Ibid.

86. Schilling, Hammond, and Snyder, *Strategy, Politics*, 57; Huzar, *Purse and Sword*, 401–4.

87. Schilling, Hammond, and Snyder, *Strategy, Politics*, 28–94.

88. *Congressional Record*, 81st Congress, 1st Session, 4428.

89. Ibid., 4430.

90. Kolodziej, *Uncommon Defense*, 81.

91. Harold B. Hinton, "White House Gets Defense Fund Bill," *Washington Post*, October 19, 1949.

92. Walter C. Hornaday, "70 Air Groups OK'd by House," *Dallas Morning News*, April 16, 1948.

93. *Congressional Record*, 81st Congress, 1st Session, 14922.

94. Ibid., 4428.

95. GHM, Box 286, folder 3, report labeled "Department of Defense Utilization of New Obligational Authority for the Military Functions of the Department of Defense."

96. GHM, Box 589, folder entitled "Correspondence 1935–1980," letter to Mrs. O. E. Stevenson, dated March 21, 1949.

97. McCullough, *Truman*, 749.

98. Ambrose and Brinkley, *Rise to Globalism*, 106.

99. National Security Council, hereafter referred to as NSC.

100. Huntington, *Common Defense*, 51.

101. Ambrose and Brinkley, *Rise to Globalism*, 111.

102. Ibid.

103. Huntington, *Common Defense*, 50.

104. Ibid., 51.

105. Bill Clark, "Lubbock Air Force Base to Be Reopened in Near Future," *Lubbock* (Texas) *Evening Journal*, April 22, 1949.

106. GHM, Box 589, folder labeled Correspondence 1935–1954, letter to "Dear Daph & Dunc," dated Sunday, December 11, 1949.

107. Huntington, *Common Defense*, 28.

108. Siracusa and Coleman, *Depression to Cold War*, 131.

109. John Lewis Gaddis, *We Now Know: Rethinking Cold War History* (New York: Oxford University Press, 1997), 70–75; and Gaddis, *Cold War*, 40–42.

110. Gaddis, *Cold War*, 42–43.

111. McCullough, *Truman*, 790.

112. GHM, Box 386, folder 359-2, letter from Mrs. Grace Martin, dated July 10, 1950.

113. *Congressional Record*, 81st Congress, 2nd Session, 16040–41.

114. Ibid.

115. Kolodziej, *Uncommon Defense*, 132.

116. "Rep. Mahon Would Welcome MacArthur Return to States," *Lubbock* (Texas) *Morning Avalanche*, April 12, 1951.

117. GHM, Box 134, folder 19, copy of Mahon's statement to the press concerning MacArthur's release.

118. Editorial, "It Could Be Costly," *Lubbock* (Texas) *Morning Avalanche*, April 12, 1951; "Rep. Mahon Would Welcome MacArthur Return to States," *Lubbock* (Texas) *Morning Avalanche*, April 12, 1951.

119. GHM, Box 134, folder 20, letters from and to Dr. Glen Simmons, dated April 18, 1951, and April 21, 1951, respectively.

120. Ibid., folder 20, letters from and to E. J. Brandt, dated April 1951 and April 21 1951, respectively.

121. GHM, Box 134, folder 19, copy of form letter sent to constituents.

122. McCullough, *Truman*, 855.

123. E. Merl Young, formerly an examiner for the Reconstruction Finance Committee, gave his wife a pastel mink coat costing over $9,500. Mrs. Young was a White House stenographer, and the coat she received was paid for by an attorney whose firm had a long track record of successfully getting RFC loans. She was (finally) fired because there appeared to be a problem associated with her husband's influence peddling.

124. GHM, Box 598, folder 32, letter to "Dear Folks at Home," dated April 28, 1951.

125. Kolodziej, *Uncommon Defense*, 140.

126. Ibid., 146.

127. *Congressional Record*, 82nd Congress, 2nd Session, 3620.

128. GHM, Box 589, folder labeled "Correspondence, 1950–1955," letter to "Dear Folks at home," dated April 10, 1952.

129. Ibid.

130. Ibid.

131. GHM, Box 598, folder 32, letter to "Dear Loved Ones," dated January 27, 1952.

132. GHM, Box 5, folder 19.

133. Ibid.

134. GHM, Box 598, folder 32, letter to "Dear Dad," dated July 24, 1952.

135. Former Illinois governor Adlai E. Stevenson, the Democratic presidential nominee in 1952.

136. GHM, Box 598, folder 32, letter to "Dear Dad," dated July 24, 1952.

137. Ibid.

138. Kenneth May, "Mahon Says US Power Growing," *Lubbock* (Texas) *Morning Avalanche*, September 2, 1952.

139. Ibid.

140. Ibid.

141. "Texas '$100 Million Heat Wave' Cracked," *Lubbock* (Texas) *Morning Avalanche*, September 3, 1952.

142. "Mahon Backs Demo Choices," *Lubbock* (Texas) *Evening Journal*, September 4, 1952.

143. Stephen E. Ambrose, *Eisenhower: The President* (New York: Simon and Schuster, 1984), 15.

144. GHM, Box 437, folder 29, memo given to news reporters on December 24, 1952.

145. Ibid.

146. Ibid.

147. Ibid.

148. GHM Papers, Box 588, Green Journal, 187.

149. Ibid., 184–85.

150. Ambrose and Brinkley, *Rise to Globalism*, 126.

Chapter 5

1. Ambrose and Brinkley, *Rise to Globalism*, 128.

2. Patterson, *Grand Expectations*, 250–51.

3. Ambrose, *Eisenhower*, 42.

4. *Congressional Record*, 83rd Congress, 1st Session, 451–52.

5. Robert J. Donovan, *Eisenhower: The Inside Story* (New York: Harper and Brothers, 1956), 22.

6. Checkers was the small dog that Vice President Nixon refused to return although it was one of the gifts he had taken while a senator. During the campaign he had to defend on national television contributions he had received, and he said that the dog would never be returned because the children were so fond of it.

7. GHM, Box 598, folder 32, letter to Mary Agnes and Earnest, dated January 28, 1953.

8. Liberty Hill was a small town north of Austin, Texas, where Mahon taught school in 1924. He had to drop out of the University of Texas Law School to earn enough money to continue his education the following year.

9. GHM, Box 598, folder 32, letter to Mary Agnes and Earnest, dated January 28, 1953.

10. Ambrose, *Eisenhower,* 42–43.

11. GHM, Box 598, folder 32, letter to Mary Agnes and Earnest, dated January 28, 1953.

12. Ibid.

13. Ibid.

14. GHM, Box 589, folder entitled "Correspondence, 1948–1959."

15. Lawrence J. Korb served as assistant secretary of defense from 1981 through 1985. In that position he administered approximately 70 percent of the annual defense budget.

16. Lawrence J. Korb, "The Budget Process in the Department of Defense, 1947–77: The Strengths and Weaknesses of the Three Systems," *Public Administration Review* 37, no. 4 (1977): 334.

17. William Reitzel, Morton A. Kaplan, and Constance G. Coblenz, *United States Foreign Policy, 1945–1955* (Washington, DC: Brookings Institution, 1956), 347.

18. Kolodziej, *Uncommon Defense,* 167–68.

19. Huntington, *Common Defense,* 65–66.

20. Kolodziej, *Uncommon Defense,* 169–71.

21. Iwan W. Morgan, "Eisenhower and the Balanced Budget," in *Reexamining the Eisenhower Presidency,* ed. Shirley Anne Warshaw (Westport, CT: Greenwood Press, 1993), 121.

22. Ambrose, *Eisenhower,* 50.

23. Glen H. Snyder, "The 'New Look' of 1953," in *Strategy, Politics, and Defense Budgets,* ed. Warner R. Schilling (New York: Columbia University Press, 1962), 425.

24. McCullough, *Truman,* 935.

25. Ambrose, *Eisenhower,* 52.

26. Gaddis, *Cold War,* 59.

27. Drew Pearson, "Congressmen Meet Genial Host," *Washington Post,* February 21, 1953; Sarah McClendon, "Eisenhower 'Impresses' Group of Texas Solons Invited to White House Luncheons, *Lubbock* (Texas) *Morning Avalanche,* February 22, 1953.

28. GHM, Box 437, folder 29, press release, dated February 26, 1953.

29. Ibid.

30. GHM, Box 589, folder entitled "Correspondence, 1948–1959."

31. GHM, Box 28, folder 13, letter to "Dear Homefolks," dated February 15, 1953.

32. Gilbert C. Fite, *American Farmers: The New Minority* (Bloomington: Indiana University Press, 1981), 102.

33. Parity is a federal monetary supplement to farmers of certain crops designed to make the exchange rate between farm and nonfarm products fair to farmers. For example, if parity is set at 90 percent for cotton, farmers who agree to limit production will receive a government check for the difference between the current market price of their cotton and a price that would be equal to 90 percent of the cost of nonfarm products. The dollar amount of the supplement is figured using a formula devised by the Department of Agriculture. The percentage amount of parity is set by Congress and the president in each year's farm bill.

34. Fite, *American Farmers*, 102–3.

35. "152 Texas Counties Will Receive Help," *Lubbock* (Texas) *Morning Avalanche*, June 30, 1953.

36. T. W. Bridges, "Benson Speech Ends Congress," *Lubbock* (Texas) *Morning Avalanche,* June 28, 1953.

37. Ibid.

38. Ibid.

39. GHM, Box 28, folder 13, letter to "Dear Ernest," dated July 5, 1953; *Congressional Record*, 83rd Congress, 1st Session, 7803–55.

40. Elizabeth Carpenter, "Mahon's Rise—From $2.35 to $5 Billion," *Houston Post*, June 14, 1953.

41. Kolodziej, *Uncommon Defense*, 508–13.

42. *Congressional Record*, 83rd Congress, 1st Session, 7808.

43. *Congressional Record*, 83rd Congress, 1st Session, 7817.

44. Kolodziej, *Uncommon Defense*, 175.

45. GHM, Box 437, folder 29, Press Release, dated February 19, 1953.

46. Ibid.

47. C. W. Ratliff, "Mahon Lauds 'New Spirit' in Capital," *Lubbock* (Texas) *Morning Avalanche*, August 30, 1953.

48. Ibid.

49. "The Plainsman," *Lubbock* (Texas) *Evening Journal*, November 6, 1953.

50. Editorial, *Lubbock* (Texas) *Morning Avalanche*, October 29, 1953.

51. *Congressional Record*, 83rd Congress, 2nd Session, 78–82.

52. Kolodziej, *Uncommon Defense*, 199–200.

53. Ibid., 194.

54. James Forrestal, the first secretary of defense, died from falling out a hospital window. It is not known whether this was an accident or suicide.

55. GHM Box 589, folder entitled "Correspondence 1950–1955," letter to "Dear Folks," dated February 8, 1954.

56. Kenneth May, "Mahon Favors Gallery Curbs," *Lubbock* (Texas) *Morning Avalanche*, March 2, 1954.

57. *Congressional* Record, 83rd Congress, 2nd Session, 5672.

58. GHM, Box 589, folder labeled "Correspondence 1950–1955," letter to "Dear Daph and Dunc," dated April 30, 1954. Mahon often abbreviated Daphne's and Duncan's name in letters written to them.

59. GHM, Box 433, folder 14, typescript of the remarks originally made by Mahon but not printed in the record.

60. Editorial, "Unstoppable Attack," *Lubbock* (Texas) *Morning Avalanche*, May 1, 1954.

61. Ibid.

62. Ambrose, *Eisenhower*, 184.

63. Sam Fogg, "Air Force 'Unstoppable' If War Erupts, Mahon Says," *Lubbock* (Texas) *Morning Avalanche*, April 29, 1954; *Congressional Record*, 83rd Congress, 2nd Session, 5771.

64. Kenneth May, "Medal of Honor for a Hero," and Jerry Hall, "Troop Use in Indochina Hit," *Lubbock* (Texas) *Morning Avalanche*, May 15, 1954.

65. GHM, Box 589, folder labeled "Correspondence 1950–1955," letter to "Dear Addresses," dated "Easter Sunday, 1954."

66. GHM, Box 5, folder 13, letter to "My Dearest," dated May 24, 1954.

67. GHM, Box 589, folder labeled "Correspondence 1950–1955," letter to "Dear Daphne," dated May 6, 1954.

68. Box 598, folder 17, manuscript entitled "Biographical Notes."

69. Helen Mahon to David Murrah and Dale Cluff, December 18, 1985, Oral History Files.

70. Robert David Johnson, *Congress and the Cold War* (New York: Cambridge University Press, 2006), 75.

71. GHM, Box 589, folder labeled "Correspondence 1950–1955," letter to "M. A. and E.," dated August 1, 1954.

72. Mahon was teasing his son-in-law, Duncan, about being able to pass the Texas Bar exam on his first try despite being a South Carolina native and perhaps not as familiar with Texas ways as native Texans.

73. GHM, Box 589, folder entitled "Correspondence 1950–1955," letter to "Dear Duncan," dated August 7, 1954.

74. Ibid., letter to "M. A. and E.," dated August 1, 1954.

75. Major Floynee M. Houle, "Angel Tells Own Story of Dien Bien Phu," *Washington Post*, July 29, 1954.

76. "Dr. Rhee's Preventive War," *Washington Post*, July 30, 1954.

77. At the Geneva Conference, Korea was divided at the 38th Parallel, with the hope that future elections would unite the country. After the war, control of the territory remained the same; thus, the loss of lives accomplished nothing.

78. Tanner Laine, "Mahon Sees 'Bright Spots' in Gloomy International Situation," *Lubbock* (Texas) *Morning Avalanche*, September 5, 1954.

79. Ibid.

80. GHM, Box 589, folder labeled "Correspondence 1950–1955," letter to "Dear Helen," dated December 2, 1954.

81. GHM, Box 284, folder 4, report submitted to Richard Wigglesworth, chairman of the House Subcommittee on Appropriations for Armed Forces, dated January 3, 1955.

82. Ibid.

83. Ibid.

84. GHM, Box 589, folder labeled "Correspondence 1950–1955," letter to "Dear Helen," dated December 2, 1954.

85. Until he entered college George was called Herman by family and friends.

86. GHM, Box 589, folder labeled "Correspondence 1950–1955," letter to "Dear Helen," dated December 9, 1954.

87. GHM, Box 28, folder 9, letter from Mahon to Mr. and Mrs. Lloyd Croslin, dated March 15, 1955.

88. Between sessions of Congress, the Mahons returned to the district and rented an apartment in Lubbock until they returned to Washington.

89. GHM, Box 589, folder labeled "Correspondence 1950–1955," letter to "Dearest Children," undated.

90. GHM, Box 28, folder 9, letter to Honorable Alvah Allen, dated April 4, 1955.

91. Ibid., letter to Mr. and Mrs. J. K. Mahon, dated July 2, 1955.

92. Postum was a caffeine-free, roasted grain sold by Kraft Foods and used as a substitute for coffee.

93. GHM, Box 28, folder 9, letter to "Dear Homefolks," dated February 27, 1955.

94. Ibid.

95. "Ike's Military Cutback Okayed by Unanimous Vote of House," *Lubbock* (Texas) *Morning Avalanche*, May 13, 1955.

96. "Taxpayer Is 'Losing Shirt' in Defense Buying, Mahon Claims," *Lubbock* (Texas) *Morning Avalanche,* May 12, 1955; and Frank Eleazer, "Defense Buying Probe Ordered," *Washington Post*, May 12, 1955.

97. "Ike's Military Cutback Okayed by Unanimous Vote of House," *Lubbock* (Texas) *Morning Avalanche,* May 13, 1955.

98. Ibid.; "Mahon Protests: 'Ride' for Taxpayer," May 16, 1955.

99. Darrell Garwood, "Mahon Urges Speedup in Plane Output," *Lubbock* (Texas) *Morning Avalanche,* July 5, 1955.

100. Ibid.

101. Ibid.

102. Stephen M. Meyer, "Verification and Risk in Arms Control," *International Security* 8, no. 4 (1984): 116.

103. GHM, Box 5, folder 13, letter to "Dear Homefolks," dated August 23, 1955.

104. Ibid.

105. Ibid., letter to "Daph and Dunc," dated August 5, 1955.

106. GHM, Box 3, folder 18, press release, dated August 4, 1955.

107. GHM, Box 5, folder 13, letter to "Dear Homefolks," dated August 15, 1955.

108. Ibid.

109. Editorial, "Congress Goes Abroad," *Ralls* (Texas) *Banner*, September 2, 1955.

110. GHM, Box 598, folder 32, letter to "Dear Folks," dated September 8, 1955.

111. US Congress, House of Representatives, House Report No. 2104, 18–19; Huntington, *Common Defense*, 87.

112. US Congress, House of Representatives, House Report No. 2104, 18–19.

113. Kolodziej, *Uncommon Defense*, 226.

114. Ibid., 230–31.

115. A Cold War term to describe the diplomatic tactic of threatening to use nuclear force to get concessions from the Soviets.

116. Kolodziej, *Uncommon Defense*, 228.

117. *Congressional Record*, 84th Congress, 2nd Session, 7802.

118. Kenneth May, "Mahon Warns of Red Gains," *Lubbock* (Texas) *Morning Avalanche*, September 5, 1956.

119. Ibid.

120. Ibid.

121. Ken Kennamer, "Mahon Blames GOP for Defense Cuts, Defends H-Test Ban Plan," *Lubbock* (Texas) *Morning Avalanche*, October 30, 1956.

122. Ibid.

123. Ibid.

124. Ibid.

125. Ibid.

126. Korb, "Budget Process," 335.

127. Kolodziej, *Uncommon Defense*, 245.

128. GHM, Box 446, folder 420-15, Notes on Defense Bill Speech, 1957.

129. Kolodziej, *Uncommon Defense*, 252.

130. "Mahon Urges Ike to 'Knock Heads' for Military Unity," *Lubbock* (Texas) *Evening Journal*, August 5, 1957.

131. GHM, Box 446, folder 420-15, Notes on Defense Bill Speech, 1957.

132. "Mahon Urges Ike to 'Knock Heads' for Military Unity," *Lubbock* (Texas) *Evening Journal*, August 5, 1957.

133. Samuel P. Huntington, "Interservice Competition and the Political Roles of the Armed Services," *American Political Science Review* 55, no. 1 (1961): 42.

134. Anne Markusen and Joel Yudken, *Dismantling the Cold War Economy* (New York: BasicBooks, 1993), 18.

135. GHM, Box 589, folder labeled "1948–1959," letter to "Dear Folks," dated June 30, 1957.

136. Dorance Guy, "Mahon Is Disturbed by Slashes in Defense Spending," *Lubbock* (Texas) *Morning Avalanche*, September 12, 1957.

137. Ibid.

138. Ibid.

139. Patterson, *Grand Expectations*, 418.

140. Editorial, *Washington Post*, October 7, 1957; Neil Sheehan, *A Fiery Peace in a Cold War: Bernard Schriever and the Ultimate Weapon* (New York: Random House, 2009), 362–64.

141. Ambrose and Brinkley, *Rise to Globalism*, 159.

142. Ambrose, *Eisenhower*, 427.

143. Ibid., 433–34.

144. "They Carry Weight: Mahon's Suggestions," *Lubbock* (Texas) *Morning Avalanche*, November 21, 1957.

145. *Congressional Record*, 85th Congress, 2nd Session, 204.

146. Elizabeth Carpenter, "Mahon Has Ideas on Pentagon Problems," *Houston Post*, September 2, 1958.

147. GHM, Box 589, folder labeled "Correspondence, 1948–1959," letter to "Homefolks and Mary Agnes," dated February 16, 1958.

148. *Congressional Record*, 85th Congress, 2nd Session, 10016, 10020–21.

149. Ibid.; Kolodziej, *Uncommon Defense*, 281–83.

150. GHM, Box 5, folder 13, letter to Mary Agnes, dated April 16, 1958.

151. Ibid.

152. GHM, Box 589, folder labeled "Correspondence, 1948–1959," letter to "Dear Helen," dated May 5, 1958.

153. "The Plainsman," *Lubbock* (Texas) *Evening Journal*, August 25, 1961.

154. Woods, *Quest for Identity*, 112.

155. Ambrose, *Eisenhower*, 463.

156. GHM, Box 599, folder 49, notes by George Mahon regarding trip to Middle East.

157. Ibid., letter to Honorable Clarence Cannon, dated November 25, 1958.

158. Ibid., notes by George Mahon regarding trip to Middle East.

159. Ibid.

160. Ibid.

161. *Congressional Quarterly Almanac*, 86th Congress, 1st Session, 15:24.

162. Ibid., 25.

163. *Congressional* Record, 86th Congress, 1st Session, 9698. According to a comment in the *Congressional Record* by Representative Flood, he and Mahon agreed on defense appropriations only about half the time. Representative Flood was

strongly in favor of increasing conventional ground forces, and Mahon was just as strongly in favor of strategic air-atomic forces. Flood characterized Mahon as being a hard worker with the patience of Job—because he had to put up with Flood!

164. Errett Scrivner (R-KS) and Richard B. Wigglesworth (R-MA).

165. GHM, Box 589, folder labeled "Correspondence, 1948–1959," letter to "Dear Savannah and Julius," dated February 8, 1959. Savannah Walker, from Taho-ka, Texas, had worked in Mahon's congressional office prior to marrying Julius Walker.

166. Ibid.

167. Atlas was the United States' first successful nuclear-armed intercontinental ballistic missile. Built by the Convair Division of General Dynamics, this liquid-fueled missile was first tested in 1959. When Soviet progress with ICBMs was discovered, the Atlas program assumed national importance.

168. The Titan was a big brother of the Atlas, both of which were phased out in favor of the Minuteman missile.

169. Manufactured by the Boeing Corporation, the Minuteman was a land-based ICBM. It was a solid-fueled missile that could be stored for a long period of time and launched with the turn of a key, making it faster to launch than liquid-fueled missiles.

170. Bomarc was a surface-to-air missile manufactured by the Boeing Corporation and the Michigan Aerospace Research Center; hence the name ("BO" for Boeing and "MARC" for Michigan Aerospace Research Center). Becoming fully operational in 1959, it was a joint United States–Canada project used to defend the east and west seacoasts. The Bomarc was a long-range antiaircraft missile capable of carrying either a nuclear or conventional warhead. These missiles were intended to create a perimeter of defense that would prevent enemy bombers from reaching industrial regions.

171. The Nike-Hercules missile was a solid-fueled surface-to-air missile that could be equipped with either a nuclear or conventional warhead. It was designed to destroy enemy bombers or missiles at high or medium altitudes and could also be used for surface-to surface defense. It was used by NATO as well as the United States and remained in service in Europe until the army replaced it with PATRIOT missiles in the 1980s.

172. Nike-Zeus was designed to intercept ballistic missiles at a very high altitude. Initially the missile had to be restrained to stay within the two-hundred-mile range for army missiles; however, after Sputnik that restriction was lifted.

173. Clark A. Murdock, *Defense Policy Formation: A Comparative Analysis of the McNamara Era* (Albany: State University of New York Press, 1974), 43.

174. *Congressional Quarterly Almanac*, 86th Congress, 1st Session, 75.

175. Ibid., 76.

176. Ibid., 76, 325.

177. GHM, Box 589, folder labeled "Correspondence, 1948–1959," letter to "Dear Homefolks," dated August 8, 1959.

178. GHM, Box 5, folder 13, letter to "Dear Ones," dated June 27, 1959.

179. The Dixon-Yates controversy involved a conflict of interest in a contract awarded to two public utilities to supply energy for the Atomic Energy Commission. Strauss was alleged to have been involved in the affair.

180. *Congressional Quarterly Almanac*, 86th Congress, 1st Session, 83.

181. GHM, Box 589, folder labeled "Correspondence, 1948–1959," letter to "Dear Homefolks," dated September 7, 1959.

182. GHM, Box 598, folder 32, letter to "Dear Helen," dated September 10, 1959.

183. *Congressional Quarterly Almanac*, 86th Congress, 1st Session, 144–45.

184. Ambrose, *Eisenhower*, 497.

185. *Congressional Quarterly Almanac*, 86th Congress, 1st Session, 80, 291–94.

186. Emil Carmichael, "Helen Mahon Is Busy from Dawn to Dusk," *Lubbock* (Texas) *Evening Journal*, October 19, 1959.

187. "Backdoor spending" is spending that is authorized to meet federal obligations without going through the normal appropriations process. Examples are interest on the national debt, entitlements, or money to cover guaranteed student loans when they are defaulted. The money is borrowed from the treasury.

188. Editorial, "Hits Pork Barrel," *Lubbock* (Texas) *Morning Avalanche*, November 1, 1959.

189. Ambrose, *Eisenhower*, 568.

190. Ibid., 573.

191. Ibid., 580.

192. GHM, Box 589, folder labeled "Correspondence 1960–1965," letter to "Dear Homefolks," dated May 30, 1960.

193. GHM, Box 313, folder 12, letter to Mr. L. D. Casey, dated June 28, 1960.

194. Ibid., office memo to staff.

195. GHM, Box 313, folder 12, letter to Mrs. Helen Woods, dated June 8, 1960.

196. GHM, Box 589, folder labeled "Correspondence 1960–1965," letter to "Dear Daphne and Duncan," dated March 17, 1960.

197. *Congressional Quarterly Almanac*, 86th Congress, 2nd Session, 16:65.

198. Ibid., 104–5, 128, 140.

199. Ibid., 65.

200. Kolodziej, *Uncommon Defense*, 301–6.

201. Ibid.

202. GHM, Box 588, Green Journal, 208.

203. GHM, Box 589, folder labeled "Correspondence 1960–65," letter to "Dear Duncan and Daphne," dated June 22, 1960.

204. *Congressional Record*, 86th Congress, 2nd Session, 19524–29.

205. Ibid.

206. Ibid.

207. Ambrose, *Eisenhower*, 594.

208. Charles H. Donnelly, "United States Defense Policies in 1961," in *American Defense Policy in Perspective*, ed. Raymond G. O'Connor (New York: John Wiley and Sons, 1965), 347.

209. *Congressional Quarterly Almanac*, 86th Congress, 2nd Session, 16:93.

210. Ambrose and Brinkley, *Rise to Globalism*, 167.

211. *Congressional Quarterly Almanac*, 86th Congress, 2nd Session, 16:65.

212. GHM, Box 589, folder labeled "Correspondence 1960–1965," letter to "Dear Babe," dated "9-13-60."

213. Patterson, *Grand Expectations*, 439.

214. President Eisenhower's grandson.

215. GHM, Box 589, folder labeled "Correspondence 1960–1965," letter to "Dear Homefolks," dated August 23, 1960.

216. Ibid., letter to "Dear Daph and Dunc," dated "Friday Morn 11-4-60."

217. Ibid., letter to "Dear Home Folks."

218. Ibid.

219. Ibid.

220. Ibid.

Chapter 6

1. Alfred Steinberg, *Sam Rayburn: A Biography* (New York: Hawthorn Books, 1975), 335; David Halberstam, *The Best and the Brightest* (New York: Random House, 1972), 41.

2. *Congressional Quarterly Almanac*, 87th Congress, 1st Session, 17:25.

3. GHM, Box 589, folder labeled "Correspondence 1960–65," letter to "Dear Folks," dated January 9, 1961.

4. Ibid., letter dated January 15, 1961, no salutation.

5. Richard Nixon.

6. GHM, Box 589, folder labeled "Correspondence, 1960–65," letter to "Dear Folks," dated January 9, 1961.

7. Ibid., letter dated January 15, 1961, no salutation.

8. President Kennedy encouraged his new cabinet and others to wear top hats for the inauguration because the hat industry in Massachusetts complained that going bareheaded, as he did during the campaign, hurt the industry. He did this to placate his constituents, but obviously Mahon, who was known for his Stetson, felt no obligation to do likewise.

9. GHM, Box 589, folder labeled "Correspondence, 1960–65," letter to "Dear Home folks," dated January 28, 1961.

10. Ibid.

11. *Congressional* Record, 87th Congress, 1st Session, 1012; Richard Reeves, *President Kennedy: Profile of Power* (New York: Simon and Schuster, 1993), 36.

12. Deborah Shapley, *Promise and Power: The Life and Times of Robert McNamara* (Boston: Little, Brown, 1993), 97.

13. Ibid., p. 102.

14. GHM, Box 589, folder labeled "Correspondence 1960–65," letter to "Dear Folks," dated January 9, 1961.

15. Ibid.

16. Ibid.

17. Ibid., letter to "Dear Daph and Dunc," dated April 8, 1961.

18. "Federal Aid to Education Opposed Here," *Lubbock* (Texas) *Avalanche-Journal*, June 8, 1961; GHM, Box 313, folder 5, letter to Honorable George Mahon, dated June 6, 1961.

19. Ibid.

20. Reeves, *President Kennedy*, 58.

21. Shapley, *Promise and Power*, 91.

22. Charles J. Hitch, *Decision Making for Defense* (Berkeley: University of California Press, 1965), 39.

23. Robert S. McNamara, "Decision Making in the Defense Department," in *American Defense Policy in Perspective: From Colonial Times to the Present*, ed. Raymond G. O'Connor (New York: John Wiley and Sons, 1965), 345.

24. GHM, Box 589, folder labeled "Correspondence, 1960–65," letter to "Dear Daph and Dunc," dated April 8, 1961.

25. Carol Foley, "Budger-Cutter Mahon Wields Sharp Ax with a Clean Whack," *Houston Chronicle*, May 17, 1964.

26. Kolodziej, *Uncommon Defense*, 328.

27. Ibid.

28. Reeves, *President Kennedy*, 245; *Congressional Record*, 87th Congress, 1st Session, 11439–40.

29. John Lewis Gaddis, *Strategies of Containment* (rev., exp. ed.) (New York: Oxford University Press, 2005), 202.

30. Frank Eleazer, "McNamara Would Halt Extra Bomber Outlay," *Lubbock* (Texas) *Avalanche-Journal*, June 24, 1961.

31. GHM, Box 279, folder 14, letter from Robert S. McNamara, dated August 26, 1961.

32. Mark J. White, ed., *Kennedy: The New Frontier Revisited* (New York: New York University Press, 1998), 10–11.

33. Shapley, *Promise and Power*, 99.

34. Kolodziej, *Uncommon Defense*, 369.

35. Robert Johnson, *Congress and Cold War*, 74–75.

36. George Fielding Eliot, "The High Cost of Hardware," *National Guardsman* 18 (April 1964): 2–6, 40.

37. Ambrose, *Eisenhower*, 612.

38. William D. Hartung, "Eisenhower's Warning the Military-Industrial Complex Forty Years Later," *World Policy Journal* 18, no. 1 (Spring 2011): 39.

39. GHM, Box 279, folder 14, letter to Honorable Frank Pace, Jr., chairman of the board of General Dynamics Corporation, dated April 21, 1961.

40. Ibid., letter from Robert S. McNamara, dated June 5, 1961.

41. Shapley, *Promise and Power*, 105–7.

42. GHM, Box 279, folder 14.

43. Charles H. Donnelly, "United States Defense Policies in 1961," House Document Number 502, 87th Congress, 2nd Session (Washington, DC: US Government Printing Office, 1962), 2–5.

44. *Congressional Quarterly Almanac*, 87th Congress, 1st Session, 18:147.

45. Frank Eleazer, "McNamara Would Halt Extra Bomber Outlay," *Lubbock* (Texas) *Avalanche-Journal*, June 24, 1961; Shapley, *Power and Promise*, 105–7.

46. GHM, Box 589, folder labeled "Correspondence, 1960–65," letter to "Dear Homefolks," dated August 18, 1961.

47. Kenneth May, "US Stronger Militarily Than Russia, Mahon Claims," *Lubbock* (Texas) *Avalanche-Journal*, October 24, 1961.

48. GHM, Box 589, folder labeled "Correspondence, 1960–65," letter to "Dear Daph and Dunc," dated September 18, 1961.

49. *Congressional Quarterly Almanac*, 87th Congress, 1st Session, 17:25.

50. Hardshell Baptists are a very conservative branch of the Baptist denomination. Each congregation is autonomous, resisting any type of centralization. They also resist the formation of missions, Sunday school, etc., and believe in predestination.

51. GHM, Box 589, folder labeled "Correspondence, 1960–65," letter to "Dear Children," dated November 19, 1961.

52. Ibid.

53. Ibid., letter to "Dear Daph and Dunc," dated September 9, 1961.

54. Ibid., letter to "Dear Children," dated September 29, 1961.

55. Ibid., letter to "Dear Daph and Dunc," dated September 25, 1961.

56. Kenneth May, "US Stronger Militarily Than Russia, Mahon Claims," *Lubbock* (Texas) *Avalanche-Journal*, October 24, 1961.

57. Ibid.

58. Ibid.

59. Ibid.

60. Ibid.

61. In July 1961 a two-year extension of the Bracero Farm Labor Law cleared Congress. This was the extension of an agreement between Mexico and the United States that allowed Mexican nationals to do manual labor in the United States on a temporary basis.

62. Jerry Hall, "Slaton Granted Delay in Integrating Pool," *Lubbock* (Texas) *Avalanche-Journal*, December 24, 1961.

63. Letters to the Editor, *Lubbock* (Texas) *Avalanche-Journal*, December 17, 1961.

64. Letters to the Editor, *Lubbock* (Texas) *Avalanche-Journal*, December 24, 1961.

65. GHM, Box 589, folder labeled "Correspondence, 1960–65," letter to "Dear Folks," dated January 1, 1962.

66. GHM, Box 588, Green Journal, 189.

67. GHM, Box 589, labeled "Correspondence, 1960–65," letter to "Dear Folks," dated January 1, 1962.

68. "McCormack Seen as Successor: Texas' Rep. Mahon in Darkhorse Role," *Lubbock* (Texas) *Avalanche-Journal*, October 6, 1961.

69. GHM, Box 27, folder 45, "Memo in Regard to a Telephone Call, Dec. 2, 1961, from Congressman Clarence Cannon."

70. GHM, Box 588, Green Journal, 189.

71. Ibid., 190.

72. Mahon's abbreviation for "John."

73. GHM, Box 589, folder labeled "Correspondence, 1960–65," letter to "Dear Children," dated March 4, 1962.

74. Woods, *Quest for Identity*, 168.

75. GHM, Box 589, folder labeled "Correspondence, 1960–65," letter to "Dear Relatives," dated May 19, 1962.

76. Ibid., letter to "Dear Homefolks," dated July 2, 1962.

77. Ibid., letter to "Dear Homefolks," dated July 29, 1962.

78. Ibid.

79. The John Birch Society, a right-wing political advocacy group that supported limited government and was anticommunist, believed it could find a sympathetic ear in Mahon.

80. GHM, Box 588, Green Journal, 192.

81. Paul Duke, "Vinson Drops Plan to 'Direct' Pentagon to Spend Extra $320 Million on B-70 Plane," *Wall Street Journal*, March 21, 1962.

82. Ibid.

83. Ibid.

84. *Congressional Record*, 87th Congress, 2nd Session, 4693.

85. Ned Curran, "Vinson-Mahon Tussle Key to Tiff over R-7 Plane," *Abilene Reporter-News*, March 25, 1962.

86. *Congressional Quarterly Almanac*, 87th Congress, 2nd Session, 147.

87. Ibid.

88. *Congressional Record*, 87th Congress, 2nd Session, 6831–32.

89. GHM, Box 450, folder 21.

90. Ibid.

91. Ibid.

92. GHM, Box 78, folder 23, Mahon's copy of navy orders for the trip.

93. GHM, Box 78, folder 23; Box 589, folder labeled "Correspondence, 1960–65," letter to "Dear Children," dated December 4, 1962.

94. GHM, Box 589, folder labeled "Correspondence, 1960–65," letter to "Dear Homefolks," dated "11-27-62."

95. Ibid., letter to "Dear Helen," dated November 30, 1962.

96. GHM, Box 78, folder 23, letter to Robert Michaels, fellow member of the House Appropriations Committee, dated February 22, 1964.

97. Ibid., Memo regarding the Caribbean Trip, December 10, 1962.

98. "Reduced Military Budget Mahon Goal, But Much of Spending for Armed Forces Justified, Texan Feels," *Lubbock* (Texas) *Avalanche-Journal*, January 20, 1963.

99. *Congressional Quarterly Almanac*, 88th Congress, 1st Session, 420.

100. *Congressional Record*, 88th Congress, 1st Session, 3736–37.

101. Ibid.

102. Ibid.

103. GHM, Box 32, folder 18, "Four Get Political Science Awards," *ROLL CALL: The Newspaper of Capitol Hill*, September 11, 1963.

104. GHM, Box 23, folder 18, letter from Kenneth McFarland, dated September 9, 1963.

105. Ibid., letter from Ray Joe Riley, dated September 7, 1963.

106. Ibid., letter from Ann England, dated September 11, 1963.

107. Editorial, "In This Area: Wide Approval a Certainty," *Lubbock* (Texas) *Avalanche-Journal*, September 7, 1963.

108. GHM, Box 3, folder 12, Notes written by George Mahon while returning from Dallas, Texas, in Air Force Two, following the assassination of President Kennedy.

109. Ibid.

110. Ibid. (no spelling corrections were made in the typed transcript).

111. Ibid.

112. GHM, Box 614, folder 12; these notes were added on February 7, 1980, when Mahon was preparing his papers for deposit in the Southwest Collection.

113. Patrick Cox, *Ralph W. Yarborough: The People's Senator* (Austin: University of Texas Press, 2001), 189.

114. GHM, Box 5, folder 13, letter from Helen Mahon to "Dear Folks," dated November 28, 1963.

115. Ibid.

116. Patterson, *Grand Expectations*, 525; Robert Divine, *Exploring the Johnson Years* (Austin: University of Texas Press, 1981), 16.

117. GHM, Box 5, folder 13, letter from Helen Mahon to "Dear Folks," dated November 28, 1963.

118. GHM, Box 589, folder entitled "Correspondence, 1960–65."

Chapter 7

1. Doris Kearns, *Lyndon Johnson and the American Dream* (New York: Harper and Row, 1976), 179.

2. GHM, Box 589, folder entitled "Correspondence, 1960–65," letter to "Dear Homefolks," dated January 25, 1964.

3. Ibid.

4. Kenneth May, "Peace Corps Gets Shriver's Praise," *Lubbock* (Texas) *Avalanche-Journal*, April 9, 1964.

5. *Congressional Quarterly Almanac*, 88th Congress, 2nd Session, 20:156.

6. Ibid., 445.

7. William S. White, "George Mahon—A Statesman with a Big Job to Do," *Houston Chronicle*, May 21, 1964.

8. "New House Money Man: Mahon Discloses Views on Spending," Houston Post, May 21, 1964.

9. Journal, Committee on Appropriations, 88th Congress, 2nd Session, 67.

10. Les Carpenter, "Mahon Succeeds to Vital House Post," *Lubbock* (Texas) *Avalanche-Journal*, May 13, 1964.

11. Fenno, *Power of the Purse*, 260.

12. Ibid., 430–31.

13. Ibid.

14. "Mahon Says Extremists Not for Public Interest," *San Angelo* (Texas) *Standard-Times*, June 2, 1964.

15. Ibid.

16. *Congressional Record,* 88th Congress, 2nd Session, 2566–67.

17. GHM, Box 588, Green Journal, 210.

18. *Congressional Quarterly Almanac*, 88th Congress, 2nd Session, 178; *Congressional Record*, 88th Congress, 2nd Session, 22425.

19. "Mahon's View: 'Poverty War' Creates Doubt," *Lubbock* (Texas) *Avalanche-Journal*, July 7, 1964.

20. Leslie Carpenter, "Salons Keep Funds Rein," *Lubbock* (Texas) *Avalanche-Journal*, August 9, 1964.

21. Kearns, *Lyndon Johnson*, 202.

22. GHM, Box 437, folder 411–14.

23. *Congressional Quarterly Almanac*, 88th Congress, 2nd Session, 65.

24. Ibid., 381.

25. Daily Diary of President Lyndon B. Johnson, November 28, 1964, Lyndon Baines Johnson Library, Austin, Texas, 2, 4, 8.

26. Editorial, *Lubbock* (Texas) *Avalanche-Journal*, December 1, 1964.

27. GHM, Box 588, Green Journal, 193.

28. Ibid., 194–97.

29. GHM, Box 5, folder 13, letter to "Dear Homefolks," dated January 14, 1965.

30. GHM, Box 3, folder 24, George Mahon to Anthony Champagne, October 1979; Box 387, folder 25, letter to Mrs. L. E. Davis, dated February 17, 1967.

31. "Johnson Watches as Wife Dedicates Rayburn Statue," *Evening Star* (Washington, DC), January 6, 1965.

32. GHM, Box 588, Green Journal, 198.

33. GHM, Box 5, folder 13, letter to "Dear Children," dated January 24, 1965.

34. GHM, Box 588, Green Journal, 197.

35. GHM, Box 5, folder 13, letter to "Dear Children," dated January 24, 1965.

36. Ned Curran, "Morning after Inaugural Finds Rep. Mahon Working," *Lubbock* (Texas) *Avalanche-Journal*, January 22, 1965.

37. *Congressional* Record, 89th Congress, 1st Session, 1100.

38. *Congressional Quarterly Almanac*, 89th Congress, 1st Session, 21:174.

39. GHM, Box 5, folder 13, letter to "Dear Children," dated January 24, 1965.

40. Richard L. Lyons, "House Votes Curbs on Aid to Nasser," *Washington Post*, January 27, 1965.

41. GHM, Box 589, folder entitled "Correspondence, 1965–69," letter to "Dear Children," dated February 15, 1965.

42. Ibid.

43. *Congressional Record*, 89th Congress, 1st Session, 9518–19.

44. Lyndon Baines Johnson, *The Vantage Point: Perspectives of the Presidency, 1963–1969* (New York: Holt, Rinehart and Winston, 1971), 447–48.

45. GHM, Box 3, folder 24.

46. *Congressional* Record, 89th Congress, 1st Session, 14477.

47. GHM, Box 589, folder entitled "Correspondence, 1965–69," letter to "Dear Home Folks," dated July 9, 1965.

48. GHM, Box 588, Green Journal, 211–12.

49. Ibid., 199.

50. GHM, Box 437, folder 411–10, Newsletter, November 1965.

51. Ibid., letter to Honorable George Mahon, dated October 17, 1965.

52. GHM, Box 549, folder 96, letter to Honorable George Mahon, dated September 7, 1965.

53. GHM, Box 589, folder labeled "Correspondence, 1965–69," letter to "Dear Home Folks," dated July 9, 1965.

54. US Congress, House of Representatives, "United States Defense Policies in 1965," House Document No. 344, 89th Congress, 2nd Session, 1–3.

55. GHM, Box 589, folder entitled "Correspondence, 1965–69," letter to "Dear Children," September 13, 1965; and GHM, Box 276, folder 6, Memorandum for the file, Subject: Visit of General Westmoreland.

56. GHM, Box 3, folder 22, Mahon to Murrah and Pearce, 1980, transcript of interview, 70.

57. Ibid., 71.

58. GHM, Box 588, Green Journal, 219.

59. Jerry Adams, "No Choice. Mahon Says Civil Defense May Bow to War Effort Spending," *Big Spring* (Texas) *Daily Herald*, December 5, 1965.

60. GHM, Box 588, Green Journal, 201.

61. GHM, Box 5, folder 13, letter to "Dear Homefolks," dated January 3, 1966.

62. GHM, Box 5, folder 13, letter to "Dear Daphne," dated February 6, 1966.

63. GHM, Box 588, Green Journal, 201–2.

64. Marvin Watson, a fellow Texan, was a longtime advisor to Lyndon Johnson. He began working for Johnson in 1948 during his Senate campaign, and in 1965 he was known as Johnson's "informal" White House chief of staff.

65. GHM, Box 588, Green Journal, 201–2.

66. Ibid.

67. Kearns, *Lyndon Johnson*, 9–11.

68. GHM, Box 5, folder 13, letter to Miss Betsy H. Holt, dated June 4, 1966.

69. Ibid.

70. GHM, Box 5, folder 13, letter to "Dear Daphne," dated February 6, 1966.

71. Ibid.

72. *Congressional Record*, 89th Congress, 2nd Session, 917.

73. Ibid., 924.

74. GHM, Box 588, Green Journal, 212.

75. Ibid., 213.

76. Ibid.; Robert Dallek, *Flawed Giant: Lyndon Johnson and His Times, 1961–1973* (New York: Oxford University Press, 1998), 288–89. Johnson considered Fulbright and Morse to be tormenters because they openly disagreed with his stand on Vietnam. In this particular instance, Dallek writes that FBI information linking Fulbright to communism in the Dominican Republic was not correct.

77. Kearns, *Lyndon Johnson*, 317.

78. GHM, Box 588, Green Journal, 213.

79. Ibid., 213–14.

80. GHM, Box 589, folder entitled "Correspondence, 1965–69," letter to "Dear Homefolks," February 18, 1967.

81. GHM, Box 588, Green Journal, 9. When Mahon got to the end of the pages in his Green Journal he went back to the first pages and added entries wherever there was empty space. He dated these new entries which correspond to what was happening in his life at the time of the date recorded.

82. GHM, Box 5, folder 13, letter to "Dear Mary Agnes," dated December 31, 1966.

83. GHM, Box 588, Green Journal, 14.

84. GHM, Box 589, folder entitled "Correspondence, 1965–69," letter to "Dear Homefolks," dated May 7, 1967.

85. Ibid.

86. *Congressional Record*, 89th Congress, 2nd Session, 16186.

87. Ibid., 16187.

88. Mary McGrory, "The President Played His Role Well," *Washington Star*, August 7, 1966.

89. GHM, Box 588, Green Journal, 8.

90. Ibid.

91. The conservative coalition, the voting alliance of Republicans and Southern Democrats against Northern Democrats, had been successful in defeating social welfare legislation since the days of the New Deal. An influx of liberal Democrats in 1965 (the 89th Congress) weakened the coalition, but it found new strength with the forty-seven seats the Republicans picked up in 1966. According to *Congressional Quarterly*, it won more victories in 1967 than in any year since 1957. During the 90th Congress (1967–1968) Mahon voted with the conservative coalition 54 percent of the time and against it 44 percent of the time. In the 89th Congress he voted with the coalition 63 percent of the time and against it 38 percent of the time.

92. GHM, Box 5, folder 13, letter to "Dear Mary Agnes," dated December 31, 1966.

93. GHM, Box 589, folder entitled "Correspondence, 1965–69," letter to "Dear Homefolks," dated January 15, 1967.

94. Editorial, "Congress Hurt by Powell Seating," *Lubbock* (Texas) *Avalanche-Journal*, January 6, 1969.

95. GHM, Box 589, folder entitled "Correspondence, 1965–69," letter to "Dear Homefolks," dated January 15, 1967.

96. GHM, Box 5, folder 13, letter to "Chairman of the Appropriations Committee," dated January 26, 1967. Betsy Holt was Daphne's second child.

97. GHM, Box 5, folder 13, letter to Miss Betsy Holt, dated February 8, 1965.

98. GHM, Box 588, Green Journal, 12–13.

99. GHM, Box 5, folder 13, letter to "Dear Children," dated March 28, 1967.

100. Ibid., letter to "Dear Children," dated April 2, 1967.

101. GHM, Box 588, Green Journal, 14.

102. A surtax is a tax on a tax. If the amount of the tax is $1,000 and the surtax is 6 percent, then the total tax is $1,060.

103. Letter to the President from Barefoot Sanders, dated April 22, 1968, White House Central Files, Name File "M," Box 36, Lyndon Baines Johnson Library, Austin, Texas; letter from Charles J. Zwick, Bureau of the Budget, dated April

24, 1968, White House Central Files, Name file "M," Box 36, Lyndon Baines Johnson Library, Austin, Texas.

104. Julian E. Zelizer, *Taxing America: Wilbur D. Mills, Congress, and the State, 1945–1975* (New York: Cambridge University Press, 1998), 257–77; Lyndon Baines Johnson, *Vantage Point*, 445–60; Joseph A. Califano, Jr., *The Triumph and Tragedy of Lyndon Johnson: The White House Years* (New York: Simon and Schuster, 1991), 284–88.

105. *Congressional Record*, 90th Congress, 1st Session, 15540.

106. Ibid., 15541.

107. Ibid., 15540–41.

108. *Congressional Quarterly Almanac*, 90th Congress, 1st Session, 23.

109. GHM, Box 387, folder 27, letter from Elmer East, dated October 5, 1967.

110. Ibid., letter to Elmer East, dated October 12, 1967.

111. Ibid.

112. Ibid.

113. Ibid.

114. *Congressional Record*, 90th Congress, 1st Session, 20596–97.

115. Ibid.

116. Ibid., 20757-58.

117. Jack Anderson, "Rural-Ruled Hill Slights City Needs," *Washington Post*, August 25, 1967.

118. GHM, Box 589, folder entitled "Correspondence, 1965–69," letter to "Dear Children," dated January 24, 1968.

119. Ibid.

120. *Congressional Quarterly Almanac*, 90th Congress, 2nd Session, 24:125–26.

121. "Mahon Assails Critics of Westmoreland," *Lubbock* (Texas) *Avalanche-Journal*, February 13, 1968.

122. "Mahon Says President's Disclosure 'Bombshell,'" *Lubbock* (Texas) *Avalanche-Journal*, April 1, 1968.

123. Ibid.

124. Ibid.

125. GHM, Box 3, folder 22, Mahon to Pearce and Murrah, 90.

126. Editorial, "Only Time Will Tell Full Story," *Lubbock* (Texas) *Avalanche-Journal*, April 2, 1968.

127. GHM Papers, Box 589, folder entitled "Correspondence, 1965–69," letter to "Dear Homefolks," February 21, 1968.

128. *Congressional Quarterly Almanac*, 90th Congress, 2nd Session, 1968, 70.

129. Ibid., 70–71.

130. Califano, *Triumph and Tragedy*, 273.

131. "Mahons Watch on Balcony as Fires Rage in Capital," *Lubbock* (Texas) *Avalanche-Journal*, April 6, 1968.

132. Ibid.

133. GHM, Box 372, folder 65.

134. George H. Gallup, *The Gallup Poll: Public Opinion 1935–1971* (New York: Random House, 1972), 2130.

135. GHM, Box 589, folder entitled "Correspondence, 1965–69," letter to "Dear Homefolks," dated May 18, 1968.

136. Ibid., letter to "Dear Homefolks," dated May 27, 1968.

137. Patterson, *Grand Expectations*, 688–89.

138. "Texans Veto Gun Curbs," *Lubbock* (Texas) *Avalanche-Journal*, July 20, 1968.

139. Califano, *Triumph and Tragedy*, 319.

140. GHM, Box 5, folder 13, letter to "Dear Homefolks," dated "Labor Day 1968."

141. Retired Air Force General Curtis LeMay was chosen to be the vice presidential candidate on the American Independent Party ticket.

142. GHM, Box 5, folder 13, letter to "Dear Children," dated October 6, 1968.

143. Ibid., letter to "Dear Homefolks," dated "Labor Day 1968."

144. Ibid., letter to "Dear Children," dated September 24, 1968.

145. Ibid., letter to "Dear Children," dated October 6, 1968.

146. Ibid.

147. Ibid.

148. GHM, Box 5, folder 13, letter to "Dear Children," dated October 6, 1968.

149. Dallek, *Flawed Giant*, 557.

150. *Congressional Record*, 90th Congress, 2nd Session, 26462.

151. Ibid., 26477–78, 26481.

152. Ibid., 26562, 26567–68.

153. Ibid., 26458.

154. *Congressional Quarterly Almanac*, 90th Congress, 2nd Session, 583.

155. Ibid., 80.

156. Ibid., 577, 578.

157. Ibid., 578.

158. Dave Knapp, "Funds Freed for Project," *Lubbock* (Texas) *Avalanche-Journal*, November 20, 1968.

159. Kenneth May, "Route Slated via Amarillo," *Lubbock* (Texas) *Avalanche-Journal*, November 20, 1968.

160. William T. Coleman, Jr., with Donald T. Bliss, *Counsel for the Situation: Shaping the Law to Realize America's Promise* (Washington, DC: Brookings Institute, 2010), 232.

161. Ibid.

162. Patterson, *Grand Expectations*, 706.

Chapter 8

1. A private club that had once been a private mansion located near the White House.
2. GHM, Box 5, folder 13, letter to "Dear George, Betsy and Laurie," dated January 22, 1969.
3. Ibid.
4. Ibid.
5. GHM, Box 1, folder 3, letter to "Dear Mr. President," dated January 21, 1969.
6. Ibid., letter to "Dear George," dated January 30, 1969.
7. GHM, Box 5, folder 13, letter to "George, Betsy and Laurie," January 22, 1969.
8. GHM, Box 205, folder 19.
9. Woods, *Quest for Identity*, 321.
10. "Letters to the Editor," *Lubbock* (Texas) *Avalanche-Journal*, February 26, 1969.
11. GHM, Box 5, folder 13, letter to "Dear Everybody," May 8, 1969.
12. Ibid.
13. Ibid.
14. Ibid.
15. Editorial, *Lubbock* (Texas) *Avalanche-Journal*, January 29, 1969.
16. Jack Anderson, "ABM Sites Could Imperil Cities," *Washington Post,* February 11, 1969.
17. Ibid.
18. Julius Duscha, "The Pentagon under Fire," *Progressive* 33, no. 9 (1969): 32.
19. *Newsweek* (June 9, 1969), 74–80.
20. Seymour M. Hersh, "The Military Committees," *Washington Monthly* 1, no. 3 (April 1, 1969).
21. Lawrence J. Korb, *The Fall and Rise of the Pentagon: American Defense Policies in the 1970s* (Westport, CT: Greenwood Press, 1979), 83.
22. Ibid.
23. Ibid., 87.
24. Andrew Hamilton, "Defense: Laird Decentralization Alters Civilian, Military Roles," *Science*, New Series 167, no. 3920 (Feb. 13, 1970): 965.
25. Ibid., 965–67.
26. *Congressional Record*, 91st Congress, 1st Session, 13128.
27. Ibid.; *Newsweek* (June 2, 1969): 29–30.
28. *Newsweek* (June 2, 1969): 30.
29. Duscha, "George Mahon: Tall Tightfisted Texan," *Washingtonian Magazine* 4, no. 12 (September 1969): 23.
30. Ibid., 22.
31. Drew Pearson, "Rivers Hampering Probes of Military," *Washington Post*, May 28, 1969.

32. Robert S. Benson, "The Military on Capitol Hill: Prospects in the Quest for Funds," *Annals of the American Academy of Political and Social Science* 406 (March 1973): 49.

33. *Congressional Record*, 91st Congress, 2nd Session, 43744.

34. GHM, Box 372, folder 55, speech delivered by Mahon when accepting his award.

35. GHM, Box 589, folder entitled "Correspondence, 1965–69," letter to "Dear Home Folks," June 22, 1969.

36. Ibid.

37. Clark M. Clifford, "A Viet Nam Reappraisal: The Personal History of One Man's View and How It Evolved," *Foreign Affairs* 47, no. 4 (July 1969): 622.

38. GHM, Box 589, folder entitled "Correspondence 1965–69," letter to "Dear Home Folks," June 22, 1969.

39. Ibid.

40. Ibid., form letter, dated June 21, 1969.

41. Ibid.

42. Ibid., letter to "Dear Home Folks," June 22, 1969.

43. GHM, Green Journal, Box 588, 15.

44. GHM, Box 589, folder entitled "Correspondence, 1965–69," letter to "Dear Children," dated October 6, 1969.

45. Ibid.

46. A strict constructionist is one who interprets the Constitution using a literal and narrow definition of the language. No allowance is made for differences between conditions that existed when the Constitution was written and modern conditions. In contrast, a broad constructionist considers the intent of the framers of the Constitution.

47. William E. Leuchtenburg, *A Troubled Feast: American Society since 1945* (Boston: Little, Brown, 1973), 249–51.

48. Bruce H. Kalk, "The Carswell Affair: The Politics of a Supreme Court Nomination in the Nixon Administration," *American Journal of Legal History* 42, no. 3 (July 1998): 265–66.

49. GHM, Box 236, folder 23, letter to James M. Hamilton, November 12, 1969.

50. GHM, Box 589, folder entitled "Correspondence, 1965–69," letter to "Dear Children," November 23, 1969.

51. Dorothy McCardle, "Attorney General's Wife 'Sick' over Haynsworth Rejection," *Washington Post*, November 22, 1969.

52. GHM, Box 589, folder entitled "Correspondence, 1965–69," letter to "Dear Children," November 23, 1969.

53. Editorial, "Haynsworth Defeat Sorry Event," *Lubbock* (Texas) *Avalanche-Journal*, November 22, 1969.

54. Ibid.

55. Kalk, "The Carswell Affair: The Politics of a Supreme Court Nomination in the Nixon Administration," *American Journal of Legal History* 42, no. 3 (July 1998): 268.

56. Ibid., 276.

57. Ibid., 278.

58. GHM, Box 236, folder 23.

59. Ibid., letter written to O. B. Ratliff, May 19, 1969, but revised before mailing.

60. Stephen Ambrose, *Nixon: The Triumph of a Politician, 1962–1972* (New York: Simon and Schuster, 1989), 2:469.

61. GHM, Box 598, folder 30.

62. GHM, Box 614, folder 416-40.

63. Ibid., letter to Brian Shirley, dated November 18, 1974.

64. GHM, Box 614, folder 416-40; and Art Wiese, "West Texas Diversion Plan 'Infeasible,' Study Concludes," *Houston Post*, August 5, 1973.

65. GHM, Box 589, folder entitled "Correspondence, 1965–69," letter to John B. Mahon, December 7, 1969.

66. Ibid.

67. *Congressional Record*, 91st Congress, 1st Session, 37662.

68. Dale Van Atta, *With Honor: Melvin Laird in War, Peace, and Politics* (Madison: University of Wisconsin Press, 2008), 309.

69. *Congressional Record*, 91st Congress, 1st Session, 37687–88.

70. Gaddis, *Strategies of Containment*, 319.

71. George C. Wilson, "Public's New Tune Spurs Mahon to Cut Arms Funds by $5 Billion," *Washington Post*, December 22, 1969.

72. Ibid.

73. Ibid.

74. Ibid.

75. GHM, Box 589, folder entitled "Correspondence, 1965–69," letter to "Dear Children," November 23, 1969.

76. *Congressional Quarterly Almanac*, 91st Congress, 2nd Session, 26:99.

77. GHM, Box 589, folder entitled "Correspondence, 1970–74."

78. Ibid.

79. Ambrose, *Nixon*, 333.

80. *Congressional Quarterly Almanac*, 91st Congress, 2nd Session, 947.

81. Kenneth May, "Mahon Warns Congress on Spending, Deficits," *Lubbock* (Texas) *Avalanche-Journal*, July 24, 1970.

82. GHM, Box 5, folder 13, letter to "Dear Children," May 2, 1970.

83. Ibid.

84. *Congressional Quarterly Almanac*, 91st Congress, 2nd Session, 381.

85. GHM, Box 5, folder 13, letter to "Dear George," November 15, 1970.

86. *Congressional Record*, 91st Congress, 2nd Session, 35744.

87. Ibid., 35776.

88. Ibid., 35779.

89. *Congressional Quarterly Almanac*, 91st Congress, 2nd Session, 414.

90. Ibid., 101.

91. Gaddis, *Strategies of Containment*, 284.

92. GHM, Box 5, folder 13, note from Mrs. Cordye Hall, dated January 24, 1970.

93. GHM, Box 5, folder 13, letter from Mahon to Mrs. Cordye Hall, dated February 6, 1970.

94. There is a memo in Mahon's files that on February 4, 1971, Lt. Colonel Art Wells picked up a check payable to the Treasurer of the United States for $1,612.16 to cover Helen's expenses for the trip. Mahon's official expenses were $1,311.28.

95. GHM, Box 5, folder 13, letter to "Dear Homefolks," dated December 20, 1970.

96. *Congressional Quarterly Almanac*, 91st Congress, 2nd Session, 116.

97. GHM, Box 5, folder 13, letter to "Dear Children," dated January 25, 1971.

98. GHM, Box 78, folder 18; Box 589, folder entitled "Correspondence, 1970–74."

99. *Congressional Quarterly Almanac*, 92nd Congress, 1st Session, 28.

100. GHM, Box 78, folder 18.

101. *Congressional Quarterly Almanac*, 92nd Congress, 1st Session, 17.

102. GHM, Box 589, folder entitled "Correspondence, 1970–74," letter to "Dear Homefolks," dated February 15, 1970.

103. *Congressional Quarterly Almanac*, 91st Congress, 2nd Session, 119.

104. GHM, Box 385, folder 7.

105. Ibid.

106. GHM, Box 131, folder 12.

107. Woods, *Quest for Identity*, 305.

108. GHM, Box 383, folder 10.

109. Ibid.

110. Ibid.

111. GHM, Box 185, folder 3.

112. Ibid.

113. Ibid.

114. The old China bloc, sometimes called the China lobby, is a term from the 1940s used to describe Americans who tried to influence politicians and public opinion in favor of the Nationalist Chinese government and against the communist government of the People's Republic of China.

115. *Congressional Quarterly Almanac*, 92nd Congress, 2nd Session, 111.

116. Gaddis, *Strategies of Containment*, 295.

117. Ibid., 296.

118. *Congressional Quarterly Almanac*, 92nd Congress, 1st Session, 39–40.

119. *Congressional Record*, 91st Congress, 1st Session, 45885.

120. Ibid.; Felix R. McKnight, "Of Googols and Googolplexes," *Dallas Times Herald*, December 19, 1971.

121. GHM, Box 205, folder 19.

122. Ibid.

123. Richard Reeves, *President Nixon: Alone in the White House* (New York: Simon and Schuster, 2001), 413–14.

124. Ibid., 566–67.

125. Ibid.

126. *U.S. News & World Report* 74, no. 7 (February 12, 1973): 37.

127. GHM, Box 348, folder 12, "Statement before the House Committee on Rules in Regard to H.R. 5193."

128. GHM, Box 27, folder 11.

129. GHM, Box 589, folder entitled "Correspondence, 1970–74," letter to "Dear Homefolks," February 10, 1973.

130. Ibid., "Statement of Hon. George Mahon before the Senate Rules Committee on the Nomination of Gerald R. Ford to the Office of Vice President of the United States," dated November 5, 1973.

131. Ibid.

132. Ibid.

133. GHM, Box 27, folder 11.

134. GHM, Box 589, folder entitled "Correspondence, 1970–74," letter to Mrs. W. E. Meadows, November 3, 1973.

135. Worth Wren, "'Marvelous Tribute' Paid Mahons," *Lubbock* (Texas) *Avalanche-Journal*, March 17, 1974.

136. GHM, Box 22, folder 30, letter from Claude Cravens.

137. "Mahons to Observe Anniversary," *Abilene* (Texas) *Reporter-News*, December 16, 1973.

138. Betty Beale, "Liz to the Rescue on White House P-R," *Washington Star*, December 19, 1973.

139. GHM, Box 3, folder 27.

140. GHM, Box 5, folder 13, letter to "Dear Home Folks."

141. Ibid.

142. GHM, Box 542, folder 7; "Neutrality Affirmed by Mahon," *Lubbock* (Texas) *Avalanche-Journal*, August 6, 1974.

143. GHM, Box 205, folder 10.

144. GHM, Box 3, folder 22, Mahon to Pearce and Murrah, transcript of interview, 101.

145. Ibid., 103.

146. GHM, Box 5, folder 13.

147. GHM, Box 1, folder 10.

148. Ibid.
149. Ibid.
150. GHM, Box 29, folder 35.
151. John Robert Greene, *The Presidency of Gerald R. Ford* (Lawrence: University Press of Kansas, 1995), 53.
152. Ibid., 53–54.

Chapter 9

1. GHM, Box 384, folder 16.
2. Ibid.
3. Ibid.
4. Bernard J. Firestone and Alexej Ugrinsky, eds., *Gerald R. Ford and the Politics of Post-Watergate America*, 1:22, 74.
5. Greene, *Gerald R. Ford*, 57.
6. Ibid.
7. Eric Schickler, Eric McGhee, and John Sides, "Remaking the House and Senate: Personal Power, Ideology, and the 1970s Reforms," *Legislative Studies Quarterly* 28, no. 3 (August 2003): 297.
8. Sarah Brandes Crook and John R. Hibbing, "Congressional Reform and Party Discipline: The Effects of Changes in the Seniority System on Party Loyalty in the US House of Representatives," *British Journal of Political Science* 15, no. 2 (April 1985): 208.
9. Barbara Hinckley, "Seniority 1975: Old Theories Confront New Facts," *British Journal of Political Science* 6, no. 4 (October 1976): 389.
10. GHM, Box 5, folder 13, letter to "Dear Homefolks," dated January 25, 1975.
11. Hinckley, "Seniority 1975," 395.
12. Ralph Preston to Lawrence Graves, September 24, 1992, Oral History Files.
13. *Congressional Quarterly Almanac*, 94th Congress, 1st Session, 695.
14. GHM, Box 5, folder 13, letter to "Dear Homefolks," dated January 25, 1975.
15. Rowland Evans and Robert Novak, "Something Worse Than Seniority?" *Washington Post*, January 25, 1975.
16. *Congressional Record*, 93rd Congress, 2nd Session, 26967.
17. Ibid., 32031.
18. Korb, *Fall and Rise*, 50–51.
19. *Congressional Quarterly Almanac*, 93rd Congress, 2nd Session, 40.
20. GHM, Box 273, folder 7, letter to Richard W. Everett, dated November 20, 1975.
21. Ibid.
22. Korb, *Fall and Rise*, 104.
23. Barry M. Blechman and Edward R. Fried, "Controlling the Defense Budget," *Foreign Affairs* 54, no. 2 (January 1976): 234.
24. George C. Wilson, "Pentagon Tactics Resented on Hill," *Washington Post*, Oc-

tober 26, 1975.

25. Ibid.

26. Ibid.

27. Mary Russell, "Retribution Not Mahon's Style," *Washington Post*, November 10, 1975.

28. Gerald R. Ford, *A Time to Heal: The Autobiography of Gerald R. Ford* (New York: Harper and Row, 1979), 320–24, 329–30.

29. GHM, Box 273, folder 3.

30. Ibid.

31. Ibid.

32. GHM, Box 205, folder 2.

33. Ford, *Time to Heal*, 313.

34. *Congressional Record*, 94th Congress, 2nd Session, 18946.

35. John W. Finney, "Arms Budget Cut in House Is the Smallest in a Decade," *New York Times*, May 14, 1976.

36. Editorial, "Mahon—True Public Servant," *Lubbock* (Texas) *Avalanche-Journal*, September 26, 1976.

37. GHM, Box 400, folder 20.

38. Keth Henley, "Mahon Rips into OSHA, Dust Limits," *Lubbock* (Texas) *Avalanche-Journal*, May 10, 1977.

39. Ibid.

40. W. Kip Viscusi, "Cotton Dust Regulation: An OSHA Success Story?" *Journal of Political Analysis and Management* 4, no. 3 (1985): 326.

41. Pat Patrick, "Mahon Lashes Nader Gin Safety Views," *Lubbock* (Texas) *Avalanche-Journal*, June 14, 1977.

42. Ibid.

43. *The Cotton Gin and Oil Mill Press* 78, no. 15 (July 16, 1977): 17.

44. *Congressional Record*, 94th Congress, 2nd Session, 24805.

45. Ibid.

46. Ibid.

47. Ibid.

48. Ibid.

49. Ibid.

50. GHM, Box 22, folder 23.

51. Ibid.

52. *Congressional* Record, 95th Congress, 1st Session, 1862–63.

53. Congressional Quarterly, *U.S. Defense Policy: Weapons, Strategy and Commitments* (Washington, DC: Congressional Quarterly, 1978), 46-A.

54. Ibid., 14.

55. Ibid.

56. Ibid.

57. *Congressional Record*, 95th Congress, 1st Session, 34715.

58. Ibid., 34716.

59. Ibid.

60. Martin Tolchin, "President Is Upheld as the House Rejects Funds for B-1 Bomber," *New York Times*, October 21, 1977.

61. *Congressional Record*, 95th Congress, 2nd Session, 4061.

62. Ibid., 4074.

63. GHM, Box 271, folder 4, letter from Jimmy Carter, dated February 28, 1978.

64. Ibid., letter to "Honorable Roy Bass, Mayor," dated February 28, 1978.

65. GHM, Box 3, folder 2, press release, dated July 7, 1977.

66. Ibid.

67. George F. Will, "An Unretiring Chairman Has Decided to Retire," *Washington Post*, July 24, 1977.

68. Ibid.

69. Ibid.

70. GHM, Box 5, folder 13, letter to "Dear Family," dated July 24, 1977.

71. GHM, Box 1, folder 3, letter from Dick Nixon, dated July 7, 1977.

72. Ibid., letter from Senator John C. Stennis, dated July 7, 1977.

73. GHM, Box 26, folder 25, letter from Jimmy Carter, dated July 21, 1977.

74. GHM, Box 589, folder labeled "Correspondence, 1975–1980," letter from Jack D. Steele, dated October 3, 1977.

75. Ibid.

76. GHM, Box 316, folder 16.

77. Congressional Quarterly, *U.S. Defense Policy*, 108.

78. GHM, Box 316, folder 15, letter from Mrs. R. B. Hunnicut, dated March 7, 1978.

79. GHM, Box 316, folder 14, letter from Kenneth B. Paynter, dated April 26, 1978.

80. *Congressional Record*, 95th Congress, 2nd Session, 38616.

81. Ibid., 38766.

82. Ibid.

83. Ibid.

84. GHM, Box 26, folder 8, letter to "Dear Homefolks," October 29, 1978.

85. Ibid.

86. Ibid.

87. Ibid.

88. Ibid.

Epilogue

1. GHM, Box 591, folder entitled "Litton Industries."

2. GHM, Box 1, folder 3, letter from Jamie Whitten to Honorable Thomas P. O'Neill,

dated February 14, 1979.

3. Cindy Rugeley, "By George, Mahon Has Come Home," *Fort Worth Star Telegram*, March 18, 1984.

4. "Congress Veteran George Mahon Dead at 85," *Lubbock* (Texas) *Avalanche-Journal*, November 20, 1985.

5. GHM, Box 7, folder 4.

6. "Friends Honor George Mahon," *Lubbock* (Texas) *Avalanche-Journal*, November 23, 1985.

Manuscript Collections

George H. Mahon Papers, 1887–1986, Southwest Collection, Texas Tech University, Lubbock, Texas

Lyndon Baines Johnson Library, Austin, Texas
Daily Diary
White House Central Files
Name file "M"

Government Documents

Congressional Record, 1935 through 1979.

Donnelly, Charles H. "United States Defense Policies in 1961." House Document Number 502, 87th Congress, 2nd Session. Washington, DC: Government Printing Office, 1962.

US Congress, Department of Defense Appropriation Bill, House Report 1561, 86th Congress, 2nd Session, 1961.

US Congress. Final Report on Foreign Aid of the House Select Committee on Foreign Aid, House Report No. 1845, 80th Congress, 2nd Session, 1948.

US Congress. House Report, 86th Congress, 1st Session, vol. 3, 1959.

US Congress, House of Representatives. Appropriation Bill, 1061, House Report No. 1561, 86th Congress, 2nd Session, 1960.

US Congress, House of Representatives, Committee on Armed Services. Authorizing Appropriations for Aircraft, Missiles, and Naval Vessels, House Report No. 1406, 87th Congress, 2nd Session, 1962.

US Congress, House of Representatives, Committee on Appropriations, Department of Defense Appropriation Bill, House Report 95-451, 95th Congress, 1st Session, 1978.

US Congress, House of Representatives, Committee on Appropriations, Department of Defense Appropriation Bill, House Report 93-1255, 93rd Congress, 2nd Session, 1975.

US Congress, House of Representatives, Committee on Appropriations, Department of Defense Appropriation Bill, House Report No. 1607, 87th Congress, 2nd Session, 1963.

US Congress, House of Representatives, Committee on Appropriations. Department of Defense Appropriation Bill, 1957, House Report No. 2104, 84th Congress, 2nd Session, 1956.

US Congress, House of Representatives, Committee on Appropriations. Journal, 88th Congress, 2nd Session.

US Congress, House of Representatives. National Military Establishment Appropriation Bill, 1950, House Report 417, 81st Congress, 1st Session.

US Congress, House of Representatives. United States Defense Policies in 1965, House Document No. 344, 89th Congress, 2nd Session.

US Congress. Preliminary Report 8 of the House Select Committee on Foreign Aid Pursuant to H. Res. 296, A Resolution Creating a Special Committee on Foreign Aid, "Proposed Principles and Organization for Any Program of Foreign Aid, November 22, 1947. "Washington, DC: Government Printing Office, 1947.

US National Archives and Records Administration, Records of the Committee on Insular Affairs (1899–1946), 13.96, http://www.archives.gov/legislative/guide/house/chapter-13-insular-affairs.html.

Books

Acheson, Dean. *Present at the Creation: My Years in the State Department.* New York: Norton, 1969.

Alexander, Thomas E. *The One and Only Rattlesnake Bomber Base: Pyote Army Airfield in World War II.* Abilene, TX: State House Press, 2005.

Alsop, Stewart. *The Center: People and Power in Political Washington.* New York: Harper and Row, 1968.

Ambrose, Stephen E. *Eisenhower: The President.* New York: Simon and Schuster, 1984.

———. *Nixon: The Triumph of a Politician, 1962–1972.* Vol. 2. New York: Simon and Schuster, 1989.

Ambrose, Stephen E., and Douglas G. Brinkley. *Rise to Globalism: American Foreign Policy since 1938.* 9th rev. ed. New York: Penguin Books, 2011.

Art, Robert J., Vincent Davis, and Samuel P. Huntington, eds. *Reorganizing America's Defense: Leadership in War and Peace.* Elmsford, NY: Pergamon Press, 1985.

Axelrod, Alan. *Bradley.* New York: Palgrave Macmillan, 2008.

Bacevich, Andrew J., ed. *The Long War: A New History of U.S. National Security Policy since World War II.* New York: Columbia University Press, 2007.

Ball, Desmond. *Politics and Force Levels: The Strategic Missile Program of the Kennedy Administration.* Berkeley: University of California Press, 1980.

Beard, Charles Austin. *American Foreign Policy in the Making, 1932–1940.* New Haven: Yale University Press, 1946.

Benedict, Murray R. *Can We Solve the Farm Problem?* New York: Twentieth Century Fund, 1955.

Black, Conrad. *Franklin Delano Roosevelt: Champion of Freedom.* New York: Public Affairs, 2003.

———. *Richard M. Nixon: A Life in Full.* New York: Public Affairs, 2007.

Bolling, Richard. *House Out of Order.* New York: Dutton, 1965.

Bowie, Robert, and Richard H. Immerman. *Waging Peace: How Eisenhower Shaped an Enduring Cold War Strategy.* New York: Oxford University Press, 1998.

Bradley, Mark Philip, and Marilyn B. Young, eds. *Making Sense of the Vietnam Wars: Local, National and Transnational Perspectives.* New York: Oxford University Press, 2008.

Bradley, Richard. *American Political Mythology from Kennedy to Nixon.* New York: Peter Lang, 2000.

Brands, H. W. *Cold Warriors: Eisenhower's Generation and American Foreign Policy.* New York: Columbia University Press, 1968.

———. *The Devil We Knew: Americans and the Cold War.* New York: Oxford University Press, 1993.

Brinkley, Alan. *Voices of Protest: Huey Long, Father Coughlin, and the Great Depression.* New York: Knopf, 1982.

Brinkley, David. *Washington Goes to War.* New York: Alfred A. Knopf, 1988.

Brinkley, Douglas. *Gerald R. Ford.* New York: Times Books, 2007.

Brown, D. Clayton. *Globalization and America since 1945.* Wilmington, DE: Scholarly Resources, 2003.

Bundy, McGeorge. *Danger and Survival: Choices about the Bomb in the First Fifty Years.* New York: Random House, 1988.

———, ed. *The Pattern of Responsibility (from the Record of Secretary of State Dean Acheson).* Boston: Houghton Mifflin, 1952.

Burns, James MacGregor. *Roosevelt: The Lion and the Fox.* New York: Harcourt, Brace, 1956.

Burns, James MacGregor, and Susan Dunn. *The Three Roosevelts: Patrician Leaders Who Transformed America.* New York: Atlantic Monthly Press, 2001.

Califano, Joseph A., Jr., *The Triumph and Tragedy of Lyndon Johnson: The White House Years.* New York: Simon and Schuster, 1991.

Caro, Robert A. *The Path to Power.* New York: Knopf, 1982.

Castillo, Jasen, Julia Lowell, Ashley J. Tellis, Jorge Munoz, and Benjamin Zycher. *Military Expenditures and Economic Growth.* Santa Monica, CA: Rand, 2001.

Chafe, William H. *The Unfinished Journey: America since World War II.* New York: Oxford University Press, 1986.

Chernus, Ira. *Eisenhower's Atoms for Peace.* College Station: Texas A&M University Press, 2002.

Cimbala, Stephen J. *US Military Strategy and the Cold War Endgame*. Portland, OR: F. Cass, 1995.

Clark, Asa A., Peter W. Chiarelli, Jeffery S. McKitrick, and James W. Reed, eds. *The Defense Reform Debate: Issues and Analysis*. Baltimore, MD: Johns Hopkins University Press, 1984.

Cline, Omer W. "History of Mitchell County to 1900." Master's thesis, East Texas State Teachers College, 1948.

Clotfelter, James. *The Military in American Politics*. New York: Harper and Row, 1973.

Coleman, William T., Jr., with Donald T. Bliss. *Counsel for the Situation: Shaping the Law to Realize America's Promise*. Washington, DC: Brookings Institute, 2010.

Congressional Quarterly, Inc. *U.S. Defense Policy: Weapons, Strategy, and Commitments*. Washington, DC: Congressional Quarterly, 1978.

Congressional Quarterly Almanac, 1945–1978. Washington, DC: Congressional Quarterly Service.

Converse, Elliott V. *Rearming for the Cold War*. Washington, DC: Historical Office of the Secretary of Defense, 2012.

Cox, Patrick. *Ralph W. Yarborough: The People's Senator*. Austin: University of Texas Press, 2001.

Current Developments in United States Foreign Policy. Vol. 2, no. 4 (November 1948).

Dallek, Robert. *Flawed Giant: Lyndon Johnson and His Times, 1961–1973*. New York: Oxford University Press, 1998.

———. *Harry S. Truman*. New York: Tome Books, 2008.

———. *Lone Star Rising: Lyndon Johnson and His Times, 1908–1960*. New York: Oxford University Press, 1991.

———. *Nixon and Kissinger: Partners in Power*. New York: HarperCollins, 2007.

Dickson, Paul, and Thomas B. Allen. *The Bonus Army: An American Epic*. New York: Walker, 2004.

Divine, Robert A. *Eisenhower and the Cold War*. New York: Oxford University Press, 1961.

———. *Exploring the Johnson Years*. Austin: University of Texas Press, 1981.

Donnelly, Charles H. "United States Defense Policies in 1961." In *American Defense Policy in Perspective: From Colonial Times to the Present*, edited by Raymond G. O'Connor, 346–52. New York: John Wiley and Sons, 1965.

Donovan, Robert J. *Eisenhower: The Inside Story*. New York: Harper and Brothers, 1956.

———. *Tumultuous Years: The Presidency of Harry S. Truman, 1949–1953*. New York: W. W. Norton, 1996.

Dudley, William, ed. *The Great Depression: Opposing Viewpoints*. San Diego, CA: Greenhaven Press, 1994.

Dulles, Allen Welsh. *The Craft of Intelligence.* New York: Harper and Row, 1963.

Dumbrell, John. *The Carter Presidency: A Re-evaluation.* Manchester, UK: Manchester University Press, 1995.

Duscha, Julius. *Arms, Money, and Politics.* New York: Washburn, 1965.

Eisenhower, Dwight D. *Mandate for Change, 1953–1956: The White House Years.* New York: Doubleday, 1963.

Eliot, Thomas H. *Recollections of the New Deal: When the People Mattered.* Boston: Northeastern University Press, 1992.

Ellis, Joseph J. *American Creation: Triumphs and Tragedies at the Founding of the Republic.* New York: Alfred A. Knopf, 2007.

Endicott, John E., and Roy W. Stafford, Jr., eds. *American Defense Policy.* Baltimore, MD: Johns Hopkins University Press, 1977.

Evans, Wanda Webb. *One Honest Man: George Mahon.* Canyon, TX: Staked Plains Press, 1978.

Fenno, Richard F., Jr. *Congressmen in Committees.* Boston: Little, Brown, 1973.

———. *The Power of the Purse: Appropriations Politics in Congress.* Boston: Little, Brown, 1966.

Fehrenbach, T. R. *Seven Keys to Texas.* Bridgewater, NJ: Replica Books, 1999.

Fein, Melvyn L. *Race and Morality: How Good Intentions Undermine Social Justice and Perpetuate Inequality.* New York: Kluwer Academic/Plenum Publishers, 2001.

Feld, Werner J. *Congress and National Defense: The Politics of the Unthinkable.* New York: Praeger, 1985.

Ferrell, Robert. *Harry S. Truman: A Life.* Columbia: University of Missouri Press, 1996.

Fink, Gary M., and David Graham Hugh, eds. *The Carter Presidency: Policy Choices in the Post–New Deal Era.* Lawrence: University of Kansas Press, 1998.

Firestone, Bernard J., and Alexej Ugrinsky, eds. *Gerald R. Ford and the Politics of Post-Watergate America,* 2 vols. Westport, CT: Greenwood Press, 1993.

Fite, Gilbert. *American Farmers: The New Minority.* Bloomington: Indiana University Press, 1981.

Fitzgerald, A. Ernest. *The High Priests of Waste.* New York: Norton, 1972.

Fontaine, William Thomas. *Reflections on Segregation, Desegregation, Power, and Morals.* Springfield, IL: Thomas, 1967.

Ford, Gerald R. *A Time to Heal: The Autobiography of Gerald R. Ford.* New York: Harper and Row, 1979.

Frantzich, Stephen E. *Write Your Congressman: Constituent Communications and Representation.* New York: Praeger Publishers, 1986.

Friedel, Frank. *Franklin D. Roosevelt: A Rendezvous with Destiny.* Boston: Little, Brown, 1990.

Froman, Lewis A., Jr. *Congressmen and Their Constituencies.* Chicago: Rand Mc-

Nally, 1963.

Fulbright, J. William. *The Pentagon Propaganda Machine*. New York: Liveright, 1970.

Gaddis, John Lewis. *The Cold War: A New History*. New York: Penguin Press, 2005.

———. *George F. Kennan: An American Life*. New York: Penguin Press, 2011.

———. *Strategies of Containment*. Rev., exp. ed. New York: Oxford University Press, 2005.

———. *The United States and the End of the Cold War*. New York: Oxford University Press, 1992.

———. *The United States and the Origins of the Cold War, 1941–1947*. New York: Columbia University Press, 2000.

———. *We Now Know: Rethinking Cold War History*. New York: Oxford University Press, 1997.

Galloway, George B. *History of the House of Representatives*. New York: Crowell, 1976.

Gallup, George H. *The Gallup Poll: Public Opinion, 1935–1971*. New York: Random House, 1972.

Gansler, Jacques S. *Affording Defense*. Cambridge, MA: MIT Press, 1989.

Garson, Robert A., and Stuart S. Kidd, eds. *The Roosevelt Years: New Perspectives on American History, 1933–1945*. Edinburgh: Edinburgh University Press, 1999.

Gellerman, William. *Martin Dies*. New York: John Day, 1944.

Goldman, Eric F. *The Crucial Decade—and After: America, 1945–1960*. New York: Knopf, 1966.

Goodwin, Doris Kearns. *No Ordinary Time: Franklin and Eleanor Roosevelt: The Home Front in World War II*. New York: Simon and Schuster, 1994.

Gottlieb, Sanford. *Defense Addiction: Can America Kick the Habit?* Boulder, CO: Westview Press, 1997.

Gould, Lewis L. *The Modern American Presidency*. Lawrence: University of Kansas Press, 2003.

Graham, Otis L. *Perspectives on Twentieth-Century America*. New York: Dodd, Mead, 1973.

Graves, Lawrence L., ed., *A History of Lubbock*. Lubbock: West Texas Museum Association, 1962.

Green, Constance M. *Washington: Capital City, 1879–1950*. Princeton, NJ: Princeton University Press, 1963.

Green, George Norris. *The Establishment in Texas Politics: The Primitive Years, 1938–1957*. Westport, CT: Greenwood Press, 1979.

Greene, John Robert. *The Presidency of Gerald R. Ford*. Lawrence: University Press of Kansas, 1995.

Greenstone, J. David. *Labor in American Politics*. Chicago: University of Chicago Press, 1977.

Groves, Leslie R. *Now It Can Be Told: The Story of the Manhattan Project*. New York: Harper and Row, 1962.

Guhin, Michael A. *John Foster Dulles*. New York: Columbia University Press, 1972.

Halberstam, David. *The Best and the Brightest*. New York: Random House, 1972.

———. *The Fifties*. New York: Villard Books, 1993.

Halperin, Morton H. *The Political Economy of the Military-Industrial Complex*. Berkeley: University of California, 1973.

Hardeman, D. B., and Donald C. Bacon. *Rayburn: A Biography*. Austin: Texas Monthly Press, 1987.

Heale, M. J. *Franklin D. Roosevelt: The New Deal and the War*. New York: Routledge, 1999.

———. *The Sixties in America: History, Politics and Protest*. Chicago: Fitzroy Dearborn, 2001.

Hendrickson, Kenneth E., Jr., and Michael L. Collins, eds. *Profiles in Power: Twentieth-Century Texans in Washington*. Arlington Heights, IL: Harlan Davidson, 1993.

Herken, Gregg. *The Winning Weapon: The Atomic Bomb in the Cold War, 1945–1950*. New York: Alfred A. Knopf, 1980.

Higgs, Robert, ed. *Arms, Politics, and the Economy: Historical and Contemporary Perspectives*. New York: Holmes and Meier, 1990.

———. *Depression, War, and Cold War: Studies in Political Economy*. New York: Oxford University Press, 2006.

Hill, Kim Quaile, and Kenneth R. Mladenka. *Texas Politics and Government*. Boston: Allyn and Bacon, 1997.

Hinckley, Barbara. *The Seniority System in Congress*. Bloomington: Indiana University Press, 1971.

Hitch, Charles J. *Decision Making for Defense*. Berkeley: University of California Press, 1965.

Hitch, Charles J., and Roland N. McKean. *The Economics of Defense in the Nuclear Age*. Cambridge, MA: Harvard University Press, 1960.

Huitt, Ralph K. *Working within the System*. Berkeley, CA: IGS Press, 1990.

Hult, Karen Marie. *Empowering the White House: Governance under Nixon, Ford, and Carter*. Lawrence: University of Kansas Press, 2004.

Huntington, Samuel P. *The Common Defense: Strategic Programs in National Politics*. New York: Columbia University Press, 1961.

———. *The Soldier and the State: The Theory of Politics of Civil-Military Relations*. Cambridge, MA: The Belknap Press of Harvard University Press, 1957.

Huzar, Elias. *The Purse and the Sword: Control of the Army by Congress through Military Appropriations, 1933–1950*. Ithaca, NY: Cornell University Press, 1950.

Ismay, Lord. *NATO, the First Five Years, 1949–1954*. Netherlands: Bosch-Utrecht, 1954.

Janeway, Michael. *The Fall of the House of Roosevelt: Brokers of Ideas and Power from FDR to LBJ*. New York: Columbia University Press, 2004.

Jeffers, H. Paul. *Marshall: Lessons in Leadership*. New York: Palgrave Macmillan, 2010.

Jeffries, John W. *Wartime America: The World War II Home Front*. Chicago: I. R. Dee, 1996.

Jenkins, Roy. *Franklin Delano Roosevelt*. Completed with the assistance of Richard E. Neustadt. 1st ed. New York: Henry Holt, 2003.

Jennings, Peter, and Todd Brewster. *The Century*. New York: Doubleday, 1998.

Johnson, Haynes B. *In the Absence of Power: Governing America*. New York: Viking Press, 1980.

Johnson, Lady Bird. *A White House Diary*. New York: Holt, Rinehart and Winston, 1970.

Johnson, Lyndon Baines. *The Vantage Point: Perspectives of the Presidency, 1963–1969*. New York: Holt, Rinehart and Winston, 1971.

Johnson, Robert David. *Congress and the Cold War*. New York: Cambridge University Press, 2006.

Johnson, Sam Houston. *My Brother Lyndon*. New York: Cowles Book Company, 1969.

Jones, Vincent C. *Manhattan: The Army and the Atomic Bomb*. Washington, DC: Center of Military History, United States Army, 1985.

Kanter, Arnold. *Defense Politics: A Budgetary Perspective*. Chicago: University of Chicago Press, 1979.

Kaplan, Lawrence S. *The Long Entanglement: NATO's First Fifty Years*. Westport, CT: Praeger, 1999.

Kaufman, Burton Ira. *The Presidency of James Earl Carter, Jr.* Lawrence: University of Kansas Press, 1993.

Kaufman, Richard M. *The War Profiteers*. Indianapolis, IN: Bobbs-Merrill, 1970.

Kearns, Doris. *Lyndon Johnson and the American Dream*. New York: Harper and Row, 1976.

Kennedy, David M. *Freedom from Fear: The American People in Depression and War, 1929–1945*. New York: Oxford University Press, 1999.

Kennedy, Gavin. *Defense Economics*. New York: St. Martin's Press, 1983.

Kennedy, Robert, and John M. Weinstein. *The Defense of the West: Strategic and European Security Issues Reappraised*. Boulder, CO: Westview Press, 1984.

Kinch, Sam, and Stuart Long. *Allan Shivers: The Pied Piper of Texas Politics*. Austin, TX: Shoal Creek, 1973.

Kinnard, Douglas. *The Secretary of Defense*. Lexington: University Press of Kentucky, 1980.

Kolodziej, Edward A. *The Uncommon Defense and Congress, 1945–1963*. Columbus: Ohio State University Press, 1966.

Korb, Lawrence J. *The Fall and Rise of the Pentagon: American Defense Policies in the 1970s.* Westport, CT: Greenwood Press, 1979.

Lapp, Ralph Eugene. *Arms beyond Doubt: The Tyranny of Weapons Technology.* New York: Cowles, 1970.

———. *The Weapons Culture.* New York: W. W. Norton, 1968.

Lebow, Richard Ned, and Janice Gross Stein. *We All Lost the Cold War.* Princeton, NJ: Princeton University Press, 1994.

Leebaert, Derek. *The Fifty-Year Wound: How America's Cold War Victory Shapes Our World.* Boston: Little, Brown, 2002.

Leffler, Melvyn P. *A Preponderance of Power: National Security, the Truman Administration, and the Cold War.* Stanford, CA: Stanford University Press, 1991.

Leuchtenburg, William E. *In the Shadow of FDR: From Harry Truman to George W. Bush.* Ithaca, NY: Cornell University Press, 2001.

———. *The Supreme Court Reborn: The Constitutional Revolution in the Age of Roosevelt.* New York: Oxford University Press, 1995.

———. *A Troubled Feast: American Society since 1945.* Boston: Little, Brown, 1973.

Lightbody, Bradley. *The Cold War.* New York: Routledge, 1999.

Lippman, Walter. *The Cold War: A Study in U.S. Foreign Policy.* New York: Harper and Row, 1947.

Lore and Legend: A Compilation of Documents Depicting the History of Colorado City and Mitchell County. Colorado City, TX: Colorado City Record, 1976.

MacCorkle, Stuart A., and Dick Smith. *Texas Government*, 6th ed. New York: McGraw-Hill, 1968.

MacNeil, Neil. *Forge of Democracy: The House of Representatives.* New York: D. McKay, 1963.

Major Problems of United States Foreign Policy, 1951–1952. Washington, DC: Brookings Institution, 1952.

Markusen, Anne, and Joel Yudken. *Dismantling the Cold War Economy.* New York: BasicBooks, 1993.

Martin, George W. *Madam Secretary, Frances Perkins.* Boston: Houghton Mifflin, 1976.

Martin, Joe. *My First Fifty Years in Politics.* New York: McGraw Hill, 1960.

Mason, John W. *The Cold War, 1945–1991.* New York: Routledge, 1996.

May, Ernest R. "Cold War and Defense." In *The Cold War and Defense*, edited by Keith Neilson and Ronald G. Haycock, 7–73. New York: Praeger, 1990.

May, Irvin M., Jr. *Marvin Jones: The Public Life of an Agrarian Advocate.* College Station: Texas A&M University Press, 1980.

Mayhew, David R. *Divided We Govern: Party Control, Lawmaking, and Investigations, 1946–1990.* New Haven, CT: Yale University Press, 1991.

McCullough, David. *Truman.* New York: Simon and Schuster, 1992.

McKay, Seth Shepard. *Texas and the Fair Deal, 1945–1952*. San Antonio, TX: Naylor, 1954.

——. *Texas Politics, 1906–1944*. Lubbock: Texas Tech University Press, 1952.

McMaster, H. R. *Dereliction of Duty: Lyndon Johnson, Robert McNamara, the Joint Chiefs of Staff, and the Lies That Led to Vietnam*. New York: HarperCollins, 1997.

McNamara, Robert S. "Decision Making in the Department of Defense." In *American Defense Policy in Perspective: From Colonial Times to the Present*, edited by Raymond G. O'Connor, 357–64. New York: John Wiley and Sons, 1965.

McVay, Freda. *The Paradoxical Plainsman: A Biography of the (More or Less) Honorable Charles A. Guy*. Lubbock: Texas Tech University Press, 1983.

Millis, Walter, ed. *The Forrestal Diaries*. New York: Viking Press, 1951.

Mills, Nicolaus. *Winning the Peace: The Marshall Plan and America's Coming of Age as a Superpower*. Hoboken, NJ: John Wiley and Sons, 2008.

Mladenka, Kenneth R., and Kim Quaile Hill. *Texas Government: Politics and Economics*. 2nd ed. Pacific Grove, CA: Brooks/Cole, 1989.

Morgan, Iwan W. "Eisenhower and the Balanced Budget." In *Reexamining the Eisenhower Presidency*, edited by Shirley Ann Warshaw, 121–32. Westport, CT: Greenwood Press, 1993.

——. *Nixon*. New York: Oxford University Press, 2002.

Morgenthau, Hans J. *Politics of the Twentieth Century*. Chicago: University of Chicago Press, 1962.

Morrow, William L. *Congressional Committees*. New York: Charles Scribner's Sons, 1969.

Murdock, Clark A. *Defense Policy Formation: A Comparative Analysis of the McNamara Era*. Albany: State University of New York Press, 1974.

Nader, Ralph. *Ralph Nader Congress Project: The Revenue Committees*. New York: Grossman, 1975.

Neilson, Keith, and Ronald G. Haycock. *The Cold War and Defense*. New York: Praeger, 1990.

Neugebauer, Janet, ed. *Plains Farmer: The Diary of William G. DeLoach, 1914–1964*. College Station: Texas A&M University Press, 1991.

New Handbook of Texas. Austin: Texas State Historical Association, 1996.

O'Brien, Kenneth Paul, and Lynn Hudson Parsons. *The Home-Front War: World War II and American Society*. New Haven, CT: Yale University Press, 1995.

Olien, Roger M. *From Token to Triumph: The Texas Republicans since 1920*. Dallas, TX: Southern Methodist University Press, 1982.

Olson, James C. *Stuart Symington: A Life*. Columbus: University of Missouri Press, 2003.

O'Neill, Tip, with William Novak. *Man of the House: The Life and Political Memoirs of Speaker Tip O'Neill*. New York: Random House, 1987.

Orfield, Gary. *Congressional Power: Congress and Social Change*. New York: Harcourt Brace Jovanovich, 1975.

Parmet, Herbert S. *Eisenhower and the American Crusades*. New York: Macmillan, 1972.

Patterson, James T. *America's Struggle against Poverty, 1900–1980*. Cambridge, MA: Harvard University Press, 1981.

———. *Congressional Conservatism and the New Deal: The Growth of the Conservative Coalition in Congress, 1933–1939*. Lexington: University of Kentucky Press, 1967.

———. *Grand Expectations: The United States from 1945–1974*. New York: Oxford University Press, 1996.

———. *Restless Giant: The United States from Watergate to Bush v. Gore*. New York: Oxford University Press, 2005.

Paulson, May Nelson, and Carl McQueary. *Miriam: The Southern Belle Who Became the First Woman Governor of Texas*. Austin, TX: Eakin Press, 1995.

Payne, James E., and Anandi P. Sahu, eds. *Defense Spending and Economic Growth*. Boulder, CO: Westview Press, 1993.

Peabody, Robert L., and Nelson W. Polsby, eds. *New Perspectives on the House of Representatives*. Chicago: Rand McNally, 1963.

Perkins, Frances. *The Roosevelt I Knew*. New York: Viking Press, 1946.

Peters, Charles. *Lyndon B. Johnson*. New York: Times Books, 2010.

Pogue, Forrest C. *George C. Marshall*. New York: Viking Press, 1963.

Polenberg, Richard, ed. *America at War: The Home Front, 1941–1945*. Englewood Cliffs, NJ: Prentice-Hall, 1968.

———. *The Era of Franklin D. Roosevelt, 1933–1945: A Brief History with Documents*. Boston: Bedford/St. Martin's, 2000.

———. *War and Society: The United States, 1941–1945*. Philadelphia: Lippincott, 1972.

Polsby, Nelson W., ed. *Congressional Behavior*. Berkeley: University of California Press, 1971.

Pursell, Carroll W. *The Military-Industrial Complex*. New York: Harper and Row, 1972.

Rae, Nicol C. *Southern Democrats*. New York: Oxford University Press, 1994.

Ralph Nader Congress Project. *The Revenue Committees: A Study of the House Ways and Means and Senate Finance Committees and House and Senate Appropriations Committees*. New York: Grossman Publishers, 1975.

Ray, Joseph M., ed. *Marvin Jones Memoirs, 1917–1973: Fifty-Six Years of Continuing Service in All Three Branches of the Federal Government*. El Paso: Western Press, University of Texas at El Paso, 1973.

Reeves, Richard. *President Kennedy: Profile of Power*. New York: Simon and Schuster, 1993.

——. *President Nixon: Alone in the White House*. New York: Simon and Schuster, 2001.

Reichley, James. *Conservatives in an Age of Change: Nixon and Ford Administrations*. Washington, DC: Brookings Institution, 1981.

Reitzel, William, Morton A. Kaplan, and Constance G. Coblenz. *United States Foreign Policy, 1945–1955*. Washington, DC: Brookings Institution, 1956.

Remini, Robert V. *The House: The History of the House of Representatives*. New York: HarperCollins, 2006.

Richardson, Rupert Norval. *Famous Are Thy Halls: Hardin-Simmons University as I Have Known It*. Abilene, TX: Abilene Printing and Stationery, 1964.

Roherty, James M. *Decisions of Robert S. McNamara: A Study of the Role of the Secretary of Defense*. Coral Gables, FL: University of Miami Press, 1970.

Roman, Peter J. *Eisenhower and the Missile Gap*. Ithaca, NY: Cornell University Press, 1995.

Safire, William. *Before the Fall: An Inside View of the Pre-Watergate White House*. Garden City, NY: Doubleday, 1975.

Sanders, Jerry W. *The Committee on the Present Danger of the Politics of Containment*. Boston: South End Press, 1983.

Sarkesian, Sam C., ed. *Defense Policy and the Presidency: Carter's First Years*. Boulder, CO: Westview Press, 1979.

Schaffer, Ronald. *Wings of Judgment: American Bombing in World War II*. New York: Oxford University Press, 1985.

Schilling, Warner R., Paul Y. Hammond, and Glen H. Snyder. *Strategy, Politics and Defense Budgets*. New York: Columbia University Press, 1962.

Schlesinger, Arthur Meier, Jr. *A Thousand Days: John F. Kennedy in the White House*. Boston: Houghton Mifflin, 1965.

——, ed. *The Age of Roosevelt: The Politics of Upheaval*. 3 vols. Boston: Houghton Mifflin, 1960.

Schlesinger, Arthur Meier, Jr., and Morton White, eds. *Paths of American Thought*. Boston: Houghton Mifflin, 1963.

Seale, William. *The President's House: A History*. Vol. 2. Washington, DC: National Geographic Society, White House Historical Association, 1986.

Shapley, Deborah. *Promise and Power: The Life and Times of Robert McNamara*. Boston: Little, Brown, 1993.

Sheehan, Michael. *The Arms Race*. New York: St. Martin's Press, 1983.

Sheehan, Neil. *A Fiery Peace in a Cold War: Bernard Schriever and the Ultimate Weapon*. New York: Random House, 2009.

Sherry, Michael S. *In the Shadow of the War: The United States since the 1930s*. New Haven, CT: Yale University Press, 1995.

Sibley, Katherine A. S. *The Cold War*. Westport, CT: Greenwood Press, 1998.

Siracusa, Joseph M., and David G. Coleman. *Depression to Cold War: A History of America from Herbert Hoover to Ronald Reagan.* Westport, CT: Praeger, 2002.

Sitkoff, Harvard, ed. *Perspectives on Modern America: Making Sense of the Twentieth Century.* New York: Oxford University Press, 2001.

Small, Melvin. *Johnson, Nixon, and the Doves.* New Brunswick, NJ: Rutgers University Press, 1988.

Smiley, Gene. *Rethinking the Great Depression.* Chicago: Ivan R. Dee, 2002.

Smith, Howard K. *Washington, D.C.: The Story of Our Nation's Capital.* New York: Random House, 1967.

Smith, Page. *Redeeming the Time: A People's History of the 1920s and the New Deal.* New York: McGraw-Hill, 1987.

Snead, David L. *The Gaither Committee, Eisenhower, and the Cold War.* Columbus: Ohio State University Press, 1999.

Snyder, Glenn H. *Deterrence and Defense: Toward a Theory of National Security.* Princeton, NJ: Princeton University Press, 1961.

———. "The 'New Look' of 1953." In *Strategy, Politics, and Defense Budgets,* edited by Warner R. Schilling, 383–524. New York: Columbia University Press, 1962.

Spinney, Franklin. *Defense Facts of Life: The Plans/Reality Mismatch.* Boulder, CO: Westview Press, 1985.

Stein, Harold, ed. *American Civil-Military Decisions: A Book of Case Studies.* A Twentieth-Century Fund Study. Tuscaloosa: University of Alabama Press, 1963.

Steinberg, Alfred. *Sam Rayburn: A Biography.* New York: Hawthorn Books, 1975.

Stone, I. F. *The Haunted Fifties.* New York: Random House, 1963.

Taylor, Maxwell D. *The Uncertain Trumpet.* New York: Harper and Brothers, 1959.

Texas Almanac and State Industrial Guide, 1904. Galveston, TX: A. H. Belo, 1904.

Tillman, Barry. *LeMay.* New York: Palgrave Macmillan, 2007.

Towle, Michael J. *Out of Touch: The Presidency and Public Opinion.* College Station: Texas A&M University Press, 2004.

Turner, John. *The Arms Race.* Cambridge: Cambridge University Press, 1983.

Van Atta, Dale. *With Honor: Melvin Laird in War, Peace, and Politics.* Madison: University of Wisconsin Press, 2008.

Vogler, David J. *The Politics of Congress.* Boston: Allyn and Bacon, 1974.

Wall, Wendy L. *Inventing the "American Way": The Politics of Consensus from the New Deal to the Civil Rights Movement.* New York: Oxford University Press, 2008.

Warshaw, Shirley Anne, ed. *Reexamining the Eisenhower Presidency.* Westport, CT: Greenwood Press, 1993.

Weeks, O. Douglas. *Texas Presidential Politics in 1952.* Austin: Institute of Public Affairs, University of Texas, 1953.

Weisberger, Bernard A. *The District of Columbia: The Seat of Government.* New York: Time-Life Books, 1968.

Whisenhunt, Donald W. *The Depression in Texas: The Hoover Years*. New York: Garland Publishing, 1983.

White, Donald Wallace. *The American Century: The Rise and Decline of the United States as a World Power*. New Haven, CT: Yale University Press, 1996.

White, Mark J., ed. *Kennedy: The New Frontier Revisited*. New York: New York University Press, 1998.

Wilbanks, James H., ed. *Generals of the Army: Marshall, MacArthur, Eisenhower, Arnold, Bradley*. Lexington: University Press of Kentucky, 2013.

Wilcox, Walter. *The Farmer in World War II*. Ames: Iowa State College Press, 1947.

Wildavsky, Aaron. *The Politics of the Budgetary Process*. 2nd ed. Boston: Little, Brown, 1974.

Williams, Vernon J. *The Social Sciences and Theories of Race*. Urbana: University of Illinois Press, 2006.

Winant, Howard. *Racial Conditions: Politics, Theory, Comparisons*. Minneapolis: University of Minnesota Press, 1994.

Winkler, Allan M. *Home Front USA: America during World War II*. Arlington Heights, IL: H. Davidson, 1986.

Wolf, Thomas P., William D. Pederson, and Byron W. Daynes, eds. *Franklin D. Roosevelt and Congress: The New Deal and Its Aftermath*. Armonk, NY: M. E. Sharpe, 2001.

Woods, Randall Bennett. *Quest for Identity: America since 1945*. New York: Cambridge University Press, 2005.

Wright, Jim. *Balance of Power: Presidents and Congress from the Era of McCarthy to the Age of Gingrich*. Atlanta: Turner Publishing, 1996.

Young, Nancy Beck. *Wright Patman: Populism, Liberalism, and the American Dream*. Dallas, TX: Southern Methodist University Press, 2000.

Young, Roland. *The American Congress*. New York: Harper, 1958.

Zelizer, Julian E. *Congressional Politics in the Second World War*. New York: Columbia University Press, 1956.

———. *Taxing America: Wilbur D. Mills, Congress, and the State, 1945–1975*. New York: Cambridge University Press, 1998.

Articles

Altman, O. R. "The First Session of the Seventy-fifth Congress, January 5, 1937–August 31, 1937." *American Political Science Review* 31, no. 6 (1937): 1071–93.

Aspin, Les. "Games the Pentagon Plays." *Foreign Policy*, no. 11 (1973): 80–92.

———. "Why Doesn't Congress Do Something?" *Foreign Policy*, no. 15 (1974).

Benson, Robert S. "The Military on Capitol Hill: Prospects in the Quest for Funds." *Annals of the American Academy of Political and Social Science* 406 (1973): 48–58.

Blechman, Barry M., and Edward R. Fried. "Controlling the Defense Budget." *Foreign Affairs* 54, no. 2 (1976): 233–49.

Brands, H. W. "The Age of Vulnerability: Eisenhower and the National Insecurity State." *American Historical Review* 94, no. 4 (1989): 963–89.

Cameron, Juan. "Those Frayed Congressional Purse Strings." *Fortune* (February 1973): 98–110.

Carter, Donald Alan. "Eisenhower versus the Generals." *Journal of Military History* 71, no. 4 (2007): 1169–99.

Carter, Luther J. "The McNamara Legacy: A Revealing History—Death of the B-70." *Science,* New Series 159, no. 3817 (1968): 859–63.

Clifford, Clark M. "A Viet Nam Reappraisal: The Personal History of One Man's View and How It Evolved." *Foreign Affairs* 47, no. 4 (1969): 601–22.

Crook, Sarah Brandes, and John R. Hibbing. "Congressional Reform and Party Discipline: The Effects of Changes in the Seniority System on Party Loyalty in the US House of Representatives." *British Journal of Political Science* 15, no. 2 (1985): 207–26.

Cuddy, Edward. "Vietnam: Mr. Johnson's War—Or Mr. Eisenhower's?" *Review of Politics* 65, no. 4 (2003): 351–74.

Dick, James C. "The Strategic Arms Race, 1957–61: Who Opened the Missile Gap?" *Journal of Politics* 34, no. 4 (1972): 1062–1110.

Duscha, Julius. "George Mahon: Tall Tightfisted Texan." *Washingtonian* 4, no. 12 (1969): 22–23.

———. "The Pentagon under Fire." *Progressive* 33, no. 9 (1969): 32–37.

Eliot, George Fielding. "The High Cost of Hardware." *National Guardsman* 18 (April 1964): 2–6, 40.

Ericson, J. "The Military-Industrial Complex." *Science Studies* 1, no. 2 (1971): 225–33.

Ferrell, Robert H. "Truman's Place in History." *Reviews in American History* 18, no. 1 (1990): 1–9.

Finley, James T. "The 1974 Congressional Initiative in Budget Making." *Public Administration Review* 35, no. 3 (1975): 270–78.

Fisher, Louis. "The Politics of Impounded Funds." *Administrative Science Quarterly* 15, no. 3 (1970): 361–71.

———. "Reprogramming of Funds by the Defense Department." *Journal of Politics* 36, no. 1 (1974): 77–102.

Fleming, D. F. "The Costs and Consequences of the Cold War." *Annals of the American Academy of Political and Social Science* 366, American Civilization: Its Influence on Our Foreign Policy (July 1966): 127–38.

Gist, John R. "The Impact of Annual Authorizations on Military Appropriations in the U.S. Congress." *Legislative Studies Quarterly* 6, no. 3 (1981): 439–54.

Gordon, Bernard. "The Military Budget: Congressional Phase." *Journal of Politics* 23, no. 4 (1961): 689–710.

Gray, Colin S., and Jeffery G. Barlow. "Inexcusable Restraint: The Decline of American Military Power in the 1970s." *International Security* 10, no. 2 (1985): 27–69.

Greenstein, Fred I., and Richard H. Immerman. "What Did Eisenhower Tell Kennedy about Indochina? The Politics of Misperception." *Journal of American History* 79, no. 2 (1992): 568–87.

Griffith, Robert. "Old Progressives and the Cold War." *Journal of American History* 66, no. 2 (1979): 334–47.

Hamburg, Roger. "Massive Retaliation Revisited." *Military Affairs* 38, no. 1 (1974): 17–23.

Hamilton, Andrew. "Defense: Laird Decentralization Alters Civilian, Military Roles." *Science,* New Series 167, no. 3920 (1970): 965–67.

———. "Defense: Laird Warns of 'Soviet Technological Threat.'" *Science,* New Series 167, no. 3923 (1970): 1360.

Hammond, Paul Y. "Effects of Structure on Policy." *Public Administration Review* 18, no. 3 (1958): 175–79.

Harris, Joseph P. "The Social Security Program of the United States." *American Political Science Review* 30, no. 3 (1936): 455–93.

Healy, Paul F. "Nobody Loves Clarence." *Saturday Evening Post* 222, no. 39 (1950): 38–137.

Henry, John B., II. "February, 1968." *Foreign Policy,* no. 4 (1971): 3–33.

Herring, E. Pendleton. "First Session of the Seventy-fourth Congress, January 3, 1935, to August 26, 1935." *American Political Science Review* 29, no. 6 (1935): 985–1005.

Hersh, Seymour M. "The Military Committees." *Washington Monthly* 1, no. 3 (1969): 84–92.

Hinkley, Barbara. "Seniority in the Committee Leadership Selection of Congress." *Midwest Journal of Political Science* 13, no. 4 (1969): 613–30.

———. "Seniority 1975: Old Theories Confront New Facts." *British Journal of Political Science* 6, no. 4 (1976): 383–99.

Huntington, Samuel P. "Interservice Competition and the Political Roles of the Armed Services." *American Political Science Review* 55, no. 1 (1961): 40–52.

Huzar, Elias. "Reorganization for National Security." *Journal of Politics* 12, no. 1 (1950): 128–52.

Hyman, Herbert H., and Paul B. Sheatsley. "The Political Appeal of President Eisenhower." *Public Opinion Quarterly* 17, no. 4 (1953–1954): 443–60.

Jefferies, John W. "The 'Quest for National Purpose' of 1960." *American Quarterly* 3, no. 4 (1978): 451–70.

Kalk, Bruce H. "The Carswell Affair: The Politics of a Supreme Court Nomination in the Nixon Administration." *American Journal of Legal History* 42, no. 3 (1998): 261–87.

Kim, Sun Kil. "The Politics of a Congressional Budgetary Process: 'Backdoor Spending.'" *Western Historical Quarterly* 21, no. 4 (1968): 606–23.

Kinnard, Douglas. "President Eisenhower and the Defense Budget." *Journal of Politics* 39, no. 3 (1977): 596–623.

Koistinen, Paul A. C. "The 'Industrial-Military Complex' in Historical Perspective: The InterWar Years," *Journal of American History* 56, no. 4 (1970): 819–39.

Komer, Robert W. "What 'Decade of Neglect'?" *International Security* 10, no. 2 (1985): 70–83.

Korb, Lawrence J. "The Budget Process in the Department of Defense, 1947–1977: The Strengths and Weaknesses of the Three Systems." *Public Administration Review* 37, no. 4 (1977): 334–46.

Krock, Arthur. "House Playing Big Role in U.S. Foreign Policy." *New York Times*, August 3, 1947.

Kurth, James R. "Why We Buy the Weapons We Do." *Foreign Policy*, no. 11 (1973): 33–56.

Laird, Melvin. "A Strong Start in a Difficult Decade: Defense Policy in the Nixon-Ford Years." *International Security* 10, no. 2 (1985): 5–26.

Laurance, Edward J. "The Changing Role of Congress in Defense Policy-Making." *Journal of Conflict Resolution* 20, no. 2 (1976): 213–53.

Leffler, Melvyn P. "The Cold War: What Do 'We Now Know'?" *American Historical Review* 104, no. 2 (1999): 501–24.

Licklider, Roy E. "The Missile Gap Controversy." *Political Science Quarterly* 85, no. 4 (1970): 600–615.

Longley, Charles H. "McNamara and Military Behavior." *American Journal of Political Science* 18, no. 1 (1974): 1–21.

Masters, Nicholas A. "Committee Assignments in the House of Representatives." *American Political Science Review* 55, no. 2 (1961): 345–57.

McConaughy, James L. "Congressmen and the Pentagon." *Fortune* (April 1958): 156–68.

McFarland, Stephen L. "The Air Force in the Cold War, 1945–60." *Airpower Journal* (Fall 1966): 4–15.

McNaugher, Thomas L. "Weapons Procurement: The Futility of Reform." *International Security* 12, no. 2 (1987): 63–104.

Meyer, Stephen M. "Verification and Risk in Arms Control." *International Security* 8, no. 4 (1984): 111–26.

Molander, Earl A. "Historical Antecedents of Military-Industrial Criticism." *Military Affairs* (April 1976): 59–63.

Preble, Christopher A. "Who Ever Believed in the Missile Gap?" *Presidential Studies Quarterly* 33, no. 4 (2003): 801–26.

"Price-Priority System Fails—Stronger Controls Coming." *United States News* 11, no. 15 (October 10, 1941): 11.

"Production for Victory: What It Means to Industry." *United States News* 11, no. 25 (December 19, 1941): 34–35.

Quester, George H. "Was Eisenhower a Genius?" *International Security* 4, no. 2 (1979): 159–79.

Ravenal, Earl C. "The Political-Military Gap." *Foreign Policy*, no. 3 (1971): 22–40.

Rayner, F. A. "Water Import Studies." *Cross Section* 17, no. 8 (1971): 1–2.

Rieselbach, Leroy N. "In the Wake of Watergate: Congressional Reform?" *Review of Politics* 36, no. 3 (1974): 371–93.

Roszak, Theodore. "A Just War Analysis of Two Types of Deterrence." *Ethics* 73, no. 2 (1963): 100–109.

Schickler, Eric, Eric McGhee, and John Sides. "Remaking the House and Senate: Personal Power, Ideology and the 1970s Reforms." *Legislative Studies Quarterly* 28 (2003): 297–331.

Silver, Howard J. "Presidential Power and the Post-Watergate Presidency." *Presidential Studies Quarterly* 8, no. 2 (1978): 199–214.

"Talks with OSHA Assistant Secretary Fail to Satisfy California Delegation. "*The Cotton Gin and Oil Mill Press* 78, no. 15 (1977): 16–17.

Viscusi, W. Kip. "Cotton Dust Regulation: An OSHA Success Story?" *Journal of Political Analysis and Management* 4, no. 3 (1985): 326.

Waldman, Sidney. "Majority Leadership in the House of Representatives." *Political Science Quarterly* 95, no. 3 (1980): 373–93.

Weidenbaum, Murray L. "The Federal Budget for 1975." *Financial Analysts Journal* 30, no. 4 (1974): 20–24, 61–63.

York, Herbert F. "ABM, MIRV, and the Arms Race." *Science*, New Series 169, no. 3942 (1970): 257–60.

Newspapers

Abilene *Reporter News*
Big Spring (Texas) *Daily Herald*
Colorado (Texas) *Reporter*
Dallas *Morning News*
Dallas *Times Herald*
The Evening Star (Washington, DC)
Houston *Chronicle*
Houston *Post*
Lubbock (Texas) *Morning Avalanche*
New York Times
Ralls (Texas) *Banner*

ROLL CALL: The Newspaper of Capitol Hill
San Angelo (Texas) *Standard-Times*
Sudan (Texas) *Beacon*
Sweetwater (Texas) *Reporter*
Wall Street Journal
The Washington Post

Oral Histories (located in the Oral History Files, Southwest Collection, Texas Tech University, Lubbock, Texas)
Carl Albert to Lawrence Graves, July 28, 1992.
Donald Anderson to Lawrence Graves, September 24, 1992.
Harold "Bo" Brown to Lawrence Graves, July 1, 1999.
Liz Carpenter to Lawrence Graves, March 4, 1993.
Gerald Ford to Lawrence Graves, May 10, 1994.
H. C. Griffith to Lawrence Graves, February 3, 1994.
Jerry Hall to Lawrence Graves, December 14, 1992.
Joe Kilgore to Lawrence Graves, February 27, 1996.
David Langston to Lawrence Graves, June 28, 1999.
Eldon Mahon to Lawrence Graves, March 7, 1991.
Helen Mahon to Dale Cluff and David Murrah, December 18, 1985.
Keith Mainland to Lawrence Graves, September 23, 1992.
Laura McElroy to Lawrence Graves, March 2, 1994.
William Natcher to Lawrence Graves, November 20, 1991.
J. J. Pickle to Lawrence Graves, December 4, 1992.
Ralph Preston to Lawrence Graves, September 24, 1992.
Tom Purdom to Lawrence Graves, November 5, 1996.
Melba Rickman to Lawrence Graves, October 31, 1994.
Dorothy Rylander to Lawrence Graves, January 1988.
Preston Smith to Lawrence Graves, August 6, 1991.
Savannah Walker to Lawrence Graves, May 19, 1991.
Jim Wright to Lawrence Graves, September 9, 1999.
Admiral Elmo Zumwalt to Lawrence Graves, April 16, 1999.

Index

Page numbers in *italics* represent photographs.

Abernathy, Ralph, 383
Abrams, Creighton W., 378
Acheson, Dean, 198, 204, 409
Adams, John, 89
African Americans: activism of late 1960s, backlash against, 383; and election of 1964, 344; migration to Washington, DC, 104–5
African American voting rights: Democratic Party power struggle and, 110–11; and membership restrictions of Texas Democratic Party, 44, 171; obstacles to, in South, 485n101
Agnew, Spiro, 394, 437
Agricultural Adjustment Act of 1933 (AAA): administration efforts to replace, 76–78, 79; Mahon's support for, 68, 74, 77–78; public opinion on, 78–79; Supreme Court strikedown of, 76
Agricultural Adjustment Act of 1938, 93–94
Agricultural Appropriations Subcommittee, Mahon's interest in, 112
agricultural policy: of Eisenhower administration, 222–24, 237–38, 255; Mahon on, 36, 169–70, 237–38, 255; Mahon's interest in, xix, xx, 91, 92, 93, 95, 102, 222–24, 229–30, 345, 350, 426–27, 457

Agriculture Committee, Mahon's interest in, 60–61
Aid to Dependent Children, introduction of, 59, 60
air force: and B-1 bomber debate, 452–53, 466–69, *plate w*; and bomber funding as issue, 303–5, 317–20, 321, 325, 336–37; creation of, 187; as deterrent, 163, 173, 193, 197, 199–200, 230, 233, 244; size of, as budget issue in 1950s, 190–94, 225–27, 244, 246, 252, 254–55, 273
Alaska, Mahon's inspection trip to, 114–15
Albert, Carl, 319, 364, 365, 371, 424, 440, 445
Alfalfa Dinner, 334–35
Allen, George, 274
Alliance for Progress, 369
ambition of Mahon, 15–16, 20, 29, 474; appointment to War Department Subcommittee and, 111; college and, xxi, 26; early days in Congress and, 53; hopes for Appropriations Committee chair, xx, 187, 210, 338
Ambrose, Stephen, 195, 220, 260–61, 419, 448
American Cotton Congress, 222–24, *plate f*
American Liberty League, 57
Anderson, Clinton P., 326
Anderson, Jack, 376, 400, 456
Andrews, George, 244

Appropriations Committee, House: Cold War importance of, xxi; criteria for choosing members of, 101; cuts from Johnson budgets, 380–81; frugality vs. Senate committee, 167; functions of, 99–101; growth of federal budget and, 102; history of, 99–100; leather chairs purchased for, 227; Mahon's assignment to, xvi; Mahon's changes to, 339; Mahon's early committee assignments, 102; and Mahon's expertise, 338; and Mahon's frugality, 356; Mahon's length of time on, xix; Mahon's lobbying for appointment to, 96–97; Mahon's subcommittee appointments in, 349; media criticisms of, 407; and outside experts, 390; power of, 339; subcommittees of, 100–101, 492n10; subcommittees served on by Mahon, 170; as tightly-knit group, 101–2; turf battles with Ways and Means Committee, 372. See also *specific subcommittees*

Appropriations Committee chair: Mahon as, 300, 338, 373, 450–51; Mahon's appointment as, xvii, 97, 98–99; as Mahon's goal, xx, 187, 210, 338

Arends, Les, 235, 376

Armed Services Committee, House, 318–20

arms control, U-2 incident and, 277–78

arms race: air power and, 245–46, 252; criticisms of, 390; Eisenhower on, 260–61; ICBMs and, 252, 260, 261; Kennedy escalation of, 299; Mahon on, 254–55, 259–60, 310, 415; missiles and, 320; renewed concerns of 1970s, 452; Sputnik and, 260. See also missile gap

Ash, Roy, 435

Ashurst, Henry F., 88

Aspinall, Wayne, 362

atomic bomb(s): bombing of Japan, 143–44; Mahon on, 144, 160, 169; Nazi efforts to develop, 136, 142; Soviet acquisition of, 194–95, 197. See also Manhattan Project

awards and honors for Mahon, 326–27, 340–41, 405, 465, 473–74, 477–78, *plate ae*

B-1 bomber, *plate w*; debate on funding of, 452–53, 466–69

balance of power in US government: Nixon pardon and, 448–49; shifting of over time, 446

Bankhead, William B.: and AAA, 76–77; death of, 116; as House Speaker, 82, 87; on Mahon, 95; as majority leader, 7, 75–76; and Supreme Court reform efforts, 88

Bankhead Bill, 74

Barkley, Alben W., 88, 133, 186

Baruch, Bernard, 105, 493n25

Bates, Bill, *plate s*

Battley, Joseph F., 145

Bayh, Birch, 361, 393

Bay of Pigs, 305–6, 323

Benedict, Murray, 93

Bennett, Wallace, 398, 405

Benson, Ezra Taft, 222–24, 255, *plate f*

Bentley, Alvin M., 232

Bentsen, Lloyd, 420, 472

Berlin crisis, 306–7, 310

Berlin Wall, 306, 322

Bingham, Eula, 462

Black, Conrad, 55

Blanton, Tom, 49–50, 87

blind persons, Social Security program for, 59, 60

Boggs, Hale, 363, 437

Bohlen, Charles E., 180

Boland, Pat, 7

Bow, Frank, 339, 405, *plate s*

Boyd, Alan, 386, 392, 395, *plate t*

Bradley, Omar, 191, 204, 208, 221, 335, 468–69

Brezhnev, Leonid, 354

Brinkley, Alan, 57

Brinkley, David, 104, 195, 260

Brooke, Ed., 371
Brooks, Jack, 228, 358
Brooks, Overton, 271
Brown, Barbara Narcissa Thomason
   (grandmother), 9
Brown, Harold, 364, *plate ae*
Brown, Harold P. (Bo), 459–60
Brown, Thomas Marion (grandfather), 9
Brown v. Board of Education (1954),
   Southern Manifesto on, 260
budget. *See* federal budget
Budget and Accounting Act of 1021, 99
Burger, Warren, 388, 410, 444
Burke, Arleigh, 273
Bush, George H. W., 335, *plate t, plate ad*
Bush, Prescott, *plate j*
Bush, Vannevar, 139
Byrns, Joseph W.: death of, 49, 82;
   election as House speaker, 5–6, 6–7,
   48–49; on Japan and potential for war,
   73; and trip to Philippines, 69, 72

Cabot, John, 247
Calley, William, 428–29
Calver, George, 82
campaigning by Mahon: in election
   of 1934, 36–42, 42–44; in election
   of 1936, 80, 83–84, 85; in election
   of 1938, 94–95; in election of 1944,
   133–34; in election of 1946, 167–71;
   in election of 1948, 186, 187–88; in
   election of 1952, 211; in election of
   1956, 254–55; in election of 1960,
   287, 288; in election of 1976, 459–60;
   individual contact as key to, 38, 41;
   newspaper editors and, 38, 40–41,
   43, 83–84; and populist image, 43,
   45; public speaking skills and, 41–42;
   as speaker's bureau speaker, 80, 84;
   strength of voice and, 10, 37; and
   supporters, "little black book" list of,
   43–44, 460; techniques for, 43–44
campaigns of 1930s, standards of civility
   in, 41, 42, 65

Camp David: Mahons at, 370–71; Nixon
   at, 414
Cannon, Clarence, *plate d*; as Appropriations chair, 187, 216, 240, 248, 268,
   269, 279, 300, 339–40; and atomic
   bomb, 140; career of, 337–38; death
   of, 337; on defense budget, 264; Mahon as protégée of, 187, 189, 210, 240,
   314; on New Look policy, 244–45
Cannon, Joseph G., 270
career of Mahon: early jobs, 17–19,
   28–29; early plans for, 26. *See also*
   House of Representatives, Mahon in;
   law career of Mahon
Carpenter, Leslie, 440
Carpenter, Liz, 417, 440, 441
Carswell, G. Harrold, 411–12
Carter, James E. "Jimmy," *plate ac, plate
   ae*; and B-1 bomber debate, 466–67,
   469; budget deficits under, 466; defense budgets under, 465–66, 472; and
   election of 1976, 461; inauguration of,
   461, 465; on Mahon, 471; and Panama
   Canal, 471–72
Case, Francis, 126, 145, 154, *plate b*
CCC (Civilian Conservation Corp),
   creation of, 55
Census Committee, Mahon's service on,
   61, 95
Central Intelligence Agency (CIA): appropriations for, 279; and Bay of Pigs,
   306; criticisms of in 1970s, 452, 454;
   Mahon on, 363, 454; Mahon's briefings by, 314; Mahon's investigation of,
   268–69; Mahon's relationship with,
   386; U-2 flights, 262–63, 277–79, 314
character of Mahon: ability to work
   with others, xxi, xxi–xxii, 189, 339;
   constituents' faith in, 36, 46; father's
   influence on, xxi, 11; friendliness and
   concern for others, xv, xx, 22, 26, 40,
   56; frugality, xxi, 17, 20, 46, 227, 338,
   356, 373, 404; as gentleman, xv, xxi,
   403; incapacity for embarrassment,

359; as level-headed and fair-minded, 36; resistance to pressure politics, xx; sense of humor, 20; on smoking and drinking, 10; as statesman, xxii. *See also* ambition of Mahon

Chiang Kai-shek, xvi, 148, 149, 194

Chiang Kai-shek, Madam, 129–30, *plate o*

childhood of Mahon, 8; ambition and, 15–16, 20; education, 9, 14, 16, 17; father's personality and, 9–11; interest in history, 16; move to Texas, 13–14; poverty of, xv, 14–15, 17; and rural West Texas life, 14–15

China: fall to Communists, 194, 197; Mahon on future of, 150; Mahon's visits to, 71, 147–50, *plate c*; US aid to, 149. *See also* People's Republic of China

Chou En-Lai, 148, 429

Churchill, Winston, 131–32, 134, 159, 163

CIA. *See* Central Intelligence Agency (CIA)

civil defense, Kennedy administration and, 299

civil rights: conservative southern Democrats and, 89, 186, 208, 260, 275, 281, 330, 342, 344, 359, 410, 411, 485n101; and election of 1960, 288; Johnson and, 334, 341–42, 381; Mahon and, 187, 208, 260, 281, 330, 340–41, 341–42, 382, 411; and swimming pool integration in Mahon's district, 311–13. *See also* African American voting rights

Civil Rights Act of 1960, 281

Civil Rights Act of 1964, 341–42, 344

civil rights movement, alleged ties to communism, 307

Civil Rights–Open Housing Bill of 1968, 382

Civil Service Committee, Mahon's service on, 61–62, 95

Clark, Ramsey, 369

Clay, Lucius D., 157, 170

Clements, William, 456, *plate aa*

Clifford, Clark, 377, 390–91, 405–7, *plate s*

Clifton, Ted, 329

climate, and culture, Mahon on, 73

club and organization memberships of Mahon, 32, 33, 47

Colby, William, 454

Cold War: and arms race, 215; division of globe in, 195; Eisenhower on, 262; and importance of defense spending, xxi; length of, 161; Mahon and, 163–64, 310, 352, 416–17; Marshall Plan and, 177–78; NSC-68 and, 195–96, 198, 219; origins of, 161–63; public opposition to, 162, 164, 174–75, 196; and Soviet buildup in Mediterranean, 426; US aid to Greece and Turkey, 173–78; US postwar demobilization and, 163–64. *See also* arms race; containment policy, US

Cole, David, 57

Coleman, William T., 393

college: Mahon's ambition and, xxi, 26; Mahon's debate training in, 22, 23–24, 27. *See also* Simmons College; University of Texas, Austin

Colley, Harold, 312

Collins, Ross, 102–3

Colorado City, Texas: history of, 12, 13; Mahons' campaign for Congress and, 35, 36, 37, 47; Mahon's move of district office from, 106; Mahons' residence in, 30–31, 32, 33; Mahon's return to after retirement, 478; return visits to, 68, 75, 85, 94, 96, 239, 324, 333, 341, 342, 357

Commodity Credit Corporation, 126, 349–50

Communism: government fearmongering about, 113, 174–75, 185; Mahon on, 113, 175, 176

Communist bloc: Mahon on advances

by, 237; proxy war strategy of, 234, 250–51, 297

Congress: committee system, reforms of, 449–51; ethics of, 367–68; and funding of World War II, 122–23; and Great Depression, 7–8; growth of Vietnam War opposition in, 409, 433, 434, 436, 466–67; Nixon's challenge to power of, 435–36, 446; patronage power of members, 47–48, 64, 84; recorded teller votes, introduction of, 427–28; salaries in, 53, 399; seniority system, criticisms of, 376, 401; seniority system reforms, 427, 449–51; Southern conservative control of in 1930s, 5. *See also* House of Representatives

congressional committees: assignment process for, 61, 96, 112; committees served on by Mahon, xix, 170; Mahon's early committee assignments, xvi, 60–63; Mahon's early frustration with, 94; reorganization of (1946), 172

Congressional District Nineteen: anti-union sentiment in, 168; creation of, 32–33, 34; economic benefits delivered by Mahon to, 84, 115–16, 123–24, 136, 169–70, 193, 196, 240–41, 317, 392–93; and election of 1960, 287; Mahon's frequent touring of, xx, 51, 68, 92, 169, 171, 211, 253, 275–76, 317, 356, 363, 376–77, 384; as predominantly agricultural, 95; redistricting and, 357; Republican criticisms of Mahon in, 312–13; Republican rise in, 458–61; swimming pool integration issue in, 311–13; voter demographics in, 46. *See also* constituents

Congressional District Nineteen election of 1934: candidates for, 34; challenges of campaigning for, 34, 35, 38; Democratic primary election, 42; Democratic runoff election, 42, 44; Mahon's

campaign for, 36–42, 42–44; Mahon's decision to run for, 33, 34–35; Mahon's platform in run for, 35–36, 39; Mahon's victory in, xv–xvi, 46

Connally, John: and Kennedy assassination, 329, 330, 331, 333; Mahons' friendship with, 333; rift in Texas politics and, 330; as Treasury Secretary, 423–24

Connally, Tom: Mahon's first meeting with, 51; Mahon's legislative efforts and, 65; as navy secretary, 292; and trip to Philippines, 69, 70, 74

conservatives, opposition to New Deal, 57

conservative southern Democrats, 521n91; and civil rights, 89, 186, 208, 260, 275, 281, 330, 342, 344, 359, 410, 411, 485n101; Eisenhower and, 221, 275, 281; influence in Congress, 5, 7, 133, 281, 359; influence in Congress, waning of, 288, 354–55, 410, 449, 451–52; Johnson and, 330, 359, 366–67, 371–72; Kennedy and, 288–89, 330–31; Mahon as, 5, 97, 275, 281, 295, 330; in Mahon's constituency, 179, 208, 223, 330; Nixon Supreme Court nominees and, 410, 411, 412; Roosevelt's court packing scheme and, 89; Roosevelt's efforts to purge, 89, 97, 110; Truman and, 186, 208

constituents: on civil unrest of 1960s, 383; complaints by, 105, 365, 368, 374–75; conservatism of, 330, 334, 359; on defense industry strikes, 116–17; at Eisenhower inauguration, 217; faith in Mahons' character, 36, 46; on food aid to Egypt, 350; on gun control, 384; increased correspondence from in 1960s, 307; on Korean War, 199, 203–4; Mahon's attention to agriculture and, 95; Mahon's desire to listen to, 229; Mahon's explanations of policies to, 83; Mahon's "little black book" of, 43–44, 460; Mahon's policy of welcoming in Washington, 56–57, 217, 345; Mahon's sense of responsibility toward, xvii, 218; on Marshall Plan, 179; on Panama Canal, 472; on pardon of Nixon, 447–48; popularity of New Deal programs in, 55; pride in Mahon, xx, 85, 95, 179–80, 196, 327, 445; support for House Un-American Activities Committee, 113, 204; support for Mahon, 127, 187; on Truman Doctrine, 175–77; on Vietnam War, 428, 429; views on neutrality issue, 108–10; views on Supreme Court reform efforts, 89–90

containment policy, US: air power as focus of, 163, 173; Eisenhower's replacement with deterrence policy, 219, 220; Mahon on, 173; Marshall Plan and, 184; and nuclear arms as deterrent, 163, 167, 174, 197, 199–200; as US policy, 185. *See also* Truman Doctrine

cotton: Great Depression and, 39, 53; Japan as consumer of, 69, 71; and Mahon family farm, 18; OSHA dust standards and, 461–63, 464–65; postwar prices for, 33; production controls on, 229–30; US policy, Mahon on, 74; West Texas and, 12–13, 14, 33, 71, 74, 170, 222–24, 229–30, 335

Couderat, Frederic R., Jr., 234

Coughlin, Charles E., 57, 75

Crittenberger, Willis D., *plate d*

Crosby, Sam, *plate e*

Crosby, Scott, 268, 270

Croslin, Lloyd: death of, 283; and Mahon first campaign, 36, 37–38; as Mahon's secretary, 50, 70, 85, 94, 115; as Mahon supporter, 187; as Texas attorney, 240–41

Cuba: Bay of Pigs invasion, 305–6, 323; Latin American views on, 323; missile crisis, 321–23, 325, 336; US policy in, 322, 324–25, 326

Cullen, Hugh Roy, 187

Cummings, Homer S., 59, 76, 88–89

Curtis, Carl, 457, *plate z*

Curtis, Thomas B., 326

Czechoslovakia, Soviet invasion of, 384

Daniel, Price, 222, 229, 253, *plate f*

Davis, Chester C., 76–77, 131

Davis, Glen, 213, *plate e*

Davis, Roy, *plate z*

daylight-saving time, introduction of, 123

death and funeral of Mahon, 478

Defense Appropriations Subcommittee, *plate i*; air force subcommittee, *plate e*; and bomber purchases, as issue, 319–20; challenges of work in, xxi; Cold War importance of, xxi; control of military public works, 248; Eisenhower defense cuts and, 218; election of 1952 and, 216; growth of defense budget and, xxi, 215; and impact of Mahon, xix; investigation of defense contractor profits, 245; line item adjustments to budget, 244, 273–74, 301, 302, 373–74; Mahon as chairman of, xvi–xvii, 216, 238, 240, 254, 256, 270, 271, 338; Mahon on work in, 271; Mahon's expertise and, 266, 286, 301, 302; McNamara reforms and, 300; as nonpartisan, xxii; reluctance to question Eisenhower budgets, 251, 256; and response to missile gap, 265. *See also* War Department subcommittee

defense industry strikes, Mahon's opposition to, 116–19

defense policy: of Eisenhower, criticism of, 264, 272–73, 279, 280, 282, 293; under Kennedy, 297; Mahon on, 233; McNamara and, 297; under Nixon, 400; NSC-68 and, 195–96, 198, 219. *See also* New Look policy; Truman Doctrine

Defense Reorganization Act of 1958, 293, 301, 303

defense spending: B-1 bomber debate, 452–53, 466–69, *plate w*; on bombers, as issue, 303–5, 317–20, 321, 325, 336–37; budget process and, 187–88, 189–90, 192; under Carter, 465–66, 472; Cold War and, 195–96; congressional efforts to control details of, 244, 262, 272, 273–74, 282, 283–84, 299–300, 302, 303, 305, 318–20, 337, 353, 373, 415–16, 422; Congress's deferral to president on, 166, 197; consolidation of military administration and, 187; cutbacks in 1953 budget, 205–7; under Eisenhower, 218–20, 225–27, 230–31, 232–33, 244–45, 250–52, 255, 256–57, 264–66, 270–71, 272–74, 282, 283–85, 318; Eisenhower on appropriate levels of, 219; under Ford, 451–53, 454–56, 458; increased congressional opposition to, 402–4, 416, 417, 452–53, 455, 466–67; increased opposition to in 1960s, 401, 402–4, 416; as issue in 1960 election, 284–85; under Johnson, 335–37, 351–52, 353, 365–66, 372–73, 389–90, 415, 423; under Kennedy, 293–94, 297–98, 299, 310, 320–21, 325–26; Korean War and, 200, 202, 205; Mahon on appropriate levels of, 191–92, 194, 197, 205, 206, 210–11, 213, 228, 254–55, 259–60, 265, 310, 311, 389–90, 403–4, 423, 455, 468; Mahon on waste in, 211, 213; Mahon's line item changes in, 244, 273–74, 301, 302; Mahon's resistance to Eisenhower cuts in, 225–27; McNamara reforms and, 296–97, 300–301; under Nixon, 414–16, 421–24, 433, 440; nuclear arms race and, 161; postwar cuts in, 164–65, 166, 173; postwar lack of coordination in, 165–66, 188–89; process before Defense Reorganization Act, 301–3;

rapid technological advances and, 166; resistance to in 1960s, 400–401; size of air force as issue in, 190–94, 225–27, 244, 246, 252, 254–55, 273; Sputnik's impact on, 264–66, 270–71; technological advances and, 303; Truman and, 189, 190–91, 193–94, 197, 205–6; waste and inefficiency in, 256, 272–73, 282–83, 285, 301–2, 401, 403, 404, 421–22

Democratic National Convention of 1936, 82–83, 110

Democratic National Convention of 1948, 186, 187

Democratic National Convention of 1952, 209, 210

Democratic National Convention of 1956, 253

Democratic National Convention of 1960, 280, 283

Democratic National Convention of 1964, 343

Democratic National Convention of 1968, 384–85

Democratic National Conventions, Cannon as parliamentarian at, 337

Democratic Party: decline of after 1968, 394; fragmentation of in response to Roosevelt's court reform efforts, 89, 91, 93; liberal-conservative split in, 97, 281, 327, 330–31; Mahon on his disagreements with, 211–12; Mahon's rise in, 80, 95; rise of liberal wing, 5, 210, 372, 395, 401, 449, 450–51; Roosevelt-Garner power struggle in, 110–11. *See also* conservative southern Democrats

Department of Defense, consolidation of military under, 187, 258

Detroit riots of 1967, 375–76

Dien Bien Phu, battle of, 234, 236–37

Dies, Martin, 53, 113

Dillon, Douglas, 349

District of Columbia Appropriations subcommittee, Mahon as chair of, 102–5, 132

Dodge, Joseph M., 221

domestic spending: increased pressure for in 1960s-70s, 407, 415, 453, 455; Mahon on, 227, 334, 357, 360–61, 415

Donovan, Robert J., 217

Douglas, William O., 162, 412, 420

draft, debate on ending, 421

Duggan, Arthur, 34, 40, 42

Dulles, Allen, 221, 269, 279, 294, 326

Dulles, John Foster, 220, 251

"Early Days in Congress" (Mahon), 47

Eaton, Charles A., 178

education, federal funding for, 294–95

Edwards, Jack, *plate ae*

Egypt, foreign aid to, 349–50

Eisenhower, Dwight D., *plate c, plate j;* agricultural policy of, 222–24; and arms race, 260–61; and Bay of Pigs plan, 306; and Camp David, 370; Congress and, 227–28, 286; courting of Southern Democrats, 221; defense budgets of, 218–20, 225–27, 230–31, 232–33, 244–45, 250–52, 255, 256–57, 264–66, 270–71, 272–74, 282, 283–85, 318; and defense policy, criticism of, 264, 272–73, 279, 280, 282, 293; deficit under, 234–35; and election of 1952, 209–10, 212; and Formosa (Taiwan), 240, 244; frustrations of final year as president, 286; as general, 191, 193, 194; and golf, 235, 259, 274, 287–88; inauguration of, 216–18; on Indochina War, 234; and interservice rivalry, efforts to reduce, 263; on Kennedy defense spending, 321; Mahon on, 221, 222, 254–55, 279; Mahon's meetings with, 221–22; Mahon's relationship with, 209, 274, 279; Mahon's votes for and against, 229; on military-industri-

al complex, 303; as native Texan, 221; and NSC-68, 219; at Rayburn funeral, 308; retirement of, 370; on Soviet threat, 262–63; State of the Union addresses, 230, 259, 262–63, 264; and tax cuts, 231, 243–44; and Texas tidelands issue, 212, 229; and Truman, 212, 308; and U-2 incident, 277–79. *See also* New Look policy

election of 1934: advice from fellow Democrats following, 47–48, 49–50; Democratic gains in, 4–5; issues in, 39–40; Mahon's victory in, xv–xvi, 46. *See also* Congressional District Nineteen election of 1934

election of 1936: counting of electoral votes in, 87; and Democratic control of House, 86; Mahon's campaign for reelection, 83–84; Mahon's campaigning for Democrats in, 80, 85; reelection of FDR in, 86

election of 1938: Mahon's campaigning in, 94–95; Republican gains in House, 97; Roosevelt's efforts to defeat conservative Democrats in, 97

election of 1940: incumbents' limited campaign time in, 110; reelection of Roosevelt in, 116; war as issue in, 110

election of 1944: Mahon's victory in, 133–34; Roosevelt's victory in, 134

election of 1946: Mahon's campaign for, 167–71; and Republican control of Congress, 171, 172

election of 1948: Democrats' recapture of Congress in, 186–87, 189; Dixiecrat challenge to Truman, 186; Mahon's campaign in, 186, 187–88

election of 1952, 209–10; and defense cuts, 207; Eisenhower platform in, 216; Eisenhower victory in, 212; Mahon's victory in, 211; Republican capture of Congress in, 216; Truman and, 207 election of 1954, 238

election of 1956: Eisenhower victory in, 256; Mahon's campaigning in, 254–55; Mahon's victory in, 253

election of 1960: and civil rights issue, 288; Mahon's campaigning in, 287, 288; Mahon's victory in, 288; missile gap as issue in, 285

election of 1964, 343–44, 354–55

election of 1966, 366, 521n91

election of 1968: Johnson's withdrawal from, 379–80; Nixon's victory in, 393–94

election of 1970, 420

election of 1972, 410

election of 1974, 449

election of 1976: Carter victory in, 461; challenge to Mahon in, 458–61

Elections committee, Mahon's service on, 95

Ely, Walter R.: advice to Mahon on congressional travel, 69; Mahon's gratitude to, xv, xxii; support for Mahon's education, xv, 3–4, 23, 28; support for Mahon's political career, 31, 34–35; at Texas congressional delegation meeting, 63

Emergency Relief Appropriations Act of 1935, 55

Engel, Albert J., *plate d*, *plate b*; as chairman of War Appropriations subcommittee, 172; efforts to trim military spending by, 173; and Manhattan Project, 138–39, 140, 143; and postwar inspection tour, 145, 146, 148, 152

Engel v. Vitale (962), 315–16

entitlement programs, efforts to control spending on, 453

Ervin, Sam, 436

Estes, Billy Sol, 315–16, 317

Europe: Mahon on views on Americans in, 248–49, 269; Mahon's inspection tours in, 179–83, 213–14, 248,

269–70; Mahons' vacations in, 248, 424–26; reduction of US forces in, as issue, 424–27

Evans, Rowland, 451

executive branch: growth in power, 446; Roosevelt's efforts to reorganize, 87, 92, 93

Export-Import Bank, 183

family of Mahon: ancestry, 8–9; move to Texas, 11–13

Farley, Jim, 50

Farm Bureau, Mahon address to, *plate p*

FBI: criticisms of in 1970s, 454; Mahon on, 454

Federal Aid to Education Bill (1961), 294–95

federal budget: growth of, 102, 391; under Johnson, 348–49, 360–61, 380–81, 388–92. *See also* defense spending

federal budget, balancing of: Eisenhower and, 216, 218–20, 223, 225–27, 261, 270, 285; as issue, 75, 80; Mahon on, 310, 311, 325, 373–74; public's calls for, 399; Truman and, 164, 165, 173

federal budget deficits: under Carter, 466; under Eisenhower, 234–35; under Johnson, 360; Mahon on, 373–74, 433–44

federal bureaucratic, Mahon on harassment and bungling by, 463–64

federal government growth, 372; conservative push for limiting, 372; Mahon's voting record and, 333

federal judiciary, Roosevelt's efforts to reform, 88–90

Fenno, Richard, 99, 101–2, 112, 340

Ferguson, Miriam, 46

films of Mahan, Mahons' review of, 291

Flood, Daniel, 244, 271, 510–11n163

Ford, Gerald R., *plate x*, *plate k*, *plate y*, *plate z*; appointment as vice president, 437–38; assumption of presidency, 444; as congressman, 349, 409, 437–

38; cost cutting by, 393; and death of Mahon, 478; defense spending under, 451–53, 454–56, 458; and election of 1976, 461; Mahon's relationship with, 440, 444, 445, 456; Mahon's work with, 271; moratorium on Soviet grain sales, 457; Nixon cabinet members replaced by, 456; pardon of Nixon, 447–49; vice presidential pick by, 447; weakness as president, 448–49

Ford, Henry, 395–96

foreign aid, battle over funding for, 339–40, 345, 349

foreign policy, US, Mahon on, 324–25

Formosa. *See* Republic of China

Forrestal, James V., 187, 191, 199, 502n82, 506n54, plate *d*

Fortas, Abe, 382, 387–88, 391, 410, 412

Fox, Charles J., 445–46

France: and Indochina War, 234; Mahon's postwar visits to, 157, 213

Frantz, Joe, 352

Fraser, Donald M., 390

Freeman, Orville, 315, 363

Fulbright, J. William, 360, 361, 520n76, *plate t*

Gaither, H. Roland, 261

Gaither Report, 261–62

Galard-Terraube, Genevieve de, 236–37

Garner, John Nance: as congressman, 40; and election of 1936, 87; and Garner Day in Texas, 84–85; power struggle with Roosevelt, 110–11; and Supreme Court reform efforts, 88–89; as Texas, 5; and trip to Philippines, 69, 72, 73–74; as vice president, 86; welcoming of Mahon to Congress, 51

Garner Day celebration (1936), 84–85

Gates, Thomas S., Jr., 282

Gentry, Brady, 228

"The George Mahon Journal," 169–71

Germany, Mahon's postwar visit to, 156–57, 181, *plate c*

Gerry, Peter G., 62

Giaimo, Robert N., 452

Gibson, Ernest V., 62

Gilpatric, Roswell L., 310–11

Glass, Henry, 301

Glenn, John, 315

golf, Mahon and, 32, 235–36, 259, 274, 287–88, 308–9, 313, 325, 356, 358, 364, 366, 370, 377, 385, 386, 405, 409, 444, 456, *plate j*

Goodpaster, Andrew, 426

Goodwin, Robert, *plate m*, *plate k*

Googol Rags, 434, *plate v*

Gordon, Kermit, 349

Government Corporations subcommittee, Mahon as chair of, 170

Great Britain, Mahon's postwar visits to, 180–81, 213

Great Depression: Congress and, 7–8; cotton prices and, 39, 53; and patronage power of members of Congress, 47; and Social Security, need for, 59; West Texas and, 38–39, 45, 68

Great Society programs: congressional opposition to, 366–67, 371–72; Mahon on, 334, 355, 359, 362, 365; and Vietnam War, funding conflict between, 352, 359, 362, 364–65, 423; War on Poverty, 335, 342–43

Greece, US Cold War aid to, 173–78, 182

Greenland, Mahon's visit to, 208–9, 210

Groves, Leslie R., 137, 138, 140, 141, 143, 169

gun control legislation, of late 1960s, 383–84

Guy, Charles, 43, 83–84, 105–6, 268, 326, 344, 380, 411, 460

Guy, Grace, 43

Haile, Fred, 34, 38, 42, 89

Hailey, Bob, 324

Halberstam, David, 290

Hall, Jerry, *plate n*

Halleck, Charles A., 232, 270

Halsey, Marcus "Hop," 168–71

Harris, C. L., 133

Hawaii, Mahons' visits to, 74, 145

Hayden, Carl, 352, *plate s*

Haynsworth, Clement F., 410–11

health of Mahon: back problems, 317; cause of death, 478; diverticulitis, 283, 314; in retirement, 478; swimming and, 359

Hebert, F. Edward, 450

Helms, Richard, 385–86, *plate s*

Henderson, Leon, 105

Hendricks, Joseph E., 145, *plate b*

Herrington, E. P., 7

Hersh, Seymour, 454

Herter, Christian A., 178, 279

Herter Committee: creation of, 178–79; fact-finding tour of Europe, 179–83; and Mahon's relationship with Nixon, 209–10, 443–44; report by, 182–83

Hofstetter, C. F., 138

Holiday, William, *plate j*

Holt, Betsy Helen (granddaughter), 230, 239, 268, 276–77, 342, 359, 368–69

Holt, Duncan (son-in-law), 185, 208, 214, 236, 256, 276, 414

Holt, George Mahon (grandson): and 1964 World's Fair, 353–54; birth of, 208; at Duke University, 421; and family Christmas, 214; Mahon's portrait unveiling and, 445; at Mother's funeral, 479; visits with grandparents, 239, 342, 354, 357, 366, 384, 405, 407; work in Mahon's office, 353, 354, 366, 405

Holt, Laurel Ann (granddaughter), 267, 342, 479

Hoover, Herbert, 39, 127, 155

Hopkins, Harry, 59

House of Representatives: importance of knowing rules of, 50; Puerto Rican nationalists' attack on, 232; in World War II, 121

House of Representatives, Mahon in:

ambition to rise in, xx, 53, 187, 210, 338; attendance and voting record, 228, 281; development of contacts, 69; disillusionment after first session in, 67–68; early advice from colleagues, 52; events witnessed by during, xix–xx; first bill introduced by, 63–64; first day in, 4–7; first session in (1935), 54–68; first speech in the House, 63; frustration with congressional inaction, 93, 94; frustration with lack of advancement, 94; interesting people met in, 128–29, 194; lack of interest in Senate seat, 253; learning of rules, 94; office in, 347; and power networking, 235–36; preparation for departure for, 46–47, 51; rise in, 189, 190, 215, 216, 240, 286, 338, 398; shunning of public credit, xxii, 194, 327, 478; and Speaker position, opening for, 314; stress of, 264, 267, 405; and time-saving devices, 289; and typical day's activities, 186; work load of, 309

House Un-American Activities Committee, Mahon's support for, 113, 204, 459

House Ways and Means Committee: and committee assignments, 61, 96, 98; Mahon's lobbying for appointment to, 96

Hughes, Charles Evans, 90, 227

Hughes, Sarah, 330

Humphrey, Hubert, *plate p*; and election of 1968, 384–85, 393–94; Mahon on, 343, 384–85, 398; on neglect of urban areas, 375, 376; as Treasury Secretary, 256; as vice president, 351, 361, 362, 440; as vice presidential candidate, 343

Hungate, William L., 448

Huntington, Samuel, 197, 258

Hurley, Patrick J., 147–48, 149

ICBMs. *See* intercontinental ballistic missiles

Ickes, Harold, 65

Impoundment Control Act of 1974, 436, 446

Independent Offices subcommittee, Mahon's work on, 170

India, Mahon's visit to, 151–52

Indochina War: efforts to bar US involvement in, 234; and Medal of Freedom for Galard-Terraube, 236–37; and New Look policy, 244; and Soviet proxy war strategy, 234

influenza epidemic (1918), 18

Insular Affairs Committee, Mahon's service on, 62–63, 69, 91, 95

intercontinental ballistic missiles (ICBMs): antimissile defense against, 272, 282, 284–85; and arms race, 252, 260, 261, 262, 296; US bases for, 309; US development of, 284, 511n167–72

Interdisciplinary Union meeting (1955), 246–48

International Bank for Reconstruction and Development, 183

International Monetary Fund (IMF), 183

Interstate Highway System, Mahon's influence and, 392–93

Iran, Mahon's visit to, 152–55

Iron Curtain speech of Churchill, 163

isolationism, postwar: Cold War and, 174–75; impossibility of, 162, 164, 184; Mahon on, 184; Marshall Plan and, 179; public's preference for, 162, 164

isolationism, prewar, 106–10

Japan: atomic bombing of, 143–44; as cotton consumer, 69, 71; declaration of war on, 119–20; invasion of China by, 129; Mahon on laborers in, 71, 73; Mahons' visit to, 69, 71; and prospect for war in 1935, 73; surrender of, 144

Jenkins, Thomas A., 181, 182

Jensen, Ben, 338, 339

John Birch Society, 307, 317, 516n79

Johnson, J. A. "Swede," 34, 38

Johnson, Lady Bird: concerns about husband's health, 379, 436; Daphne Mahon's meeting of, 288; dedication of Rayburn statue by, 346–47; Johnson's funeral and, 436; and Kennedy assassination, 328; Mahons' relationship with, 345–46, 369, 370, 380, 386, 440; and stress of office, 348

Johnson, Louis, 191, 193, 197, 502n82

Johnson, Luci Baines, wedding of, 366

Johnson, Luther, 53

Johnson, Lynda Bird, 370, 380

Johnson, Lyndon B., plate f, plate p, plate r, plate s; and Alliance for Progress, 369; angry rants by, 361–62; and Billy Sol Estes, 315; and Bobby Kennedy, 361; and bomber construction as issue, 336–37; budgets under, 348–49, 360–61, 380–81, 388–92; and civil rights, 260, 334, 341–42, 381; Congress and, 339, 353, 354, 359, 378, 384; death and funeral of, 436–37; defense budgets under, 335–37, 351–52, 353, 365–66, 372–73, 389–90, 415, 423; departure from Washington, 397; and domestic spending, 348; and election of 1960, 280, 283, 288; and election of 1964, 343–44; and election of 1968, 379–80; focus on domestic issues, 334; foreign aid under, 339–40, 345, 349; gift-giving by, 358, 386; health problems of, 379, 380; inauguration of, 345, 347–48; on Indochina War, 234; on Kennedy administration intellectuals, 290; and Kennedy agenda, 334; and Kennedy assassination, 327–28, 329–30, 332–33, 420; and King assassination, 381; liberal agenda of, 281; on Mahon, 397; Mahon on, 271, 352, 360, 362, 411; Mahon's relationship with, xvii, 333, 344–46, 351, 352, 358,

362, 363, 369–71, 377, 379, 386, 411, 418, 424; Mahon's support for, 340, 349, 351–52; as moderate Democrat, 330; as senator, 222, 229, 264, 275, 280; and Soviet relations, 384; State of the Union addresses, 359, 364–65; and Supreme Court, 387–88; tax policy under, 341, 365, 371–72, 389; and urban problems, 382; and Vietnam War, 351–52; and White House dinners, 398. *See also* Great Society programs

Johnson, Sam Houston, 417–18

Joint Chiefs of Staff: and defense budgets, 270–71, 282, 300–301, 402; Eisenhower and, 220, 263; Mahon on, 263–64

Jones, Marvin: and AAA, 76–77, 79; advice for newly-elected Mahon, 47–48; as Agriculture Committee chair, 61, 79, 85; as Eighteenth District representative, 34; and House Speaker election (1934), 48–49; legislation by, 64; on Mahon, 95; as Mahon mentor, 48, 50, 52, 94

Jones, Vincent, 137

journals kept by Mahon: after high school and in college (Brown Journal), 24; in Washington years (Green Journal), 51–52, 58, 62, 70–71, 72, 75, 283, 313, 314, 342, 347, 358, 361, 362, 369

Kalk, Bruce, 412

Kearns, Doris, 343

Kennan, George, 162–63, 177

Kennedy, David M., 4–5, 88, 108–9, 112, 118

Kennedy, Jacqueline, 330, 332

Kennedy, John F., *plate l*; and arms race, 299; assassination of, 327–33, 420; and Bay of Pigs, 305–6, 323; and Berlin crisis, 306–7; and bomber construction as issue, 303–5, 317–20; and civil defense, 299; Congress and, 290, 317–20; and Cuban missile crisis, 321–23, 325; defense policy

under, 297; defense spending under, 293–94, 297–98, 299, 310, 320–21, 325–26; education policy of, 294–95; and election of 1960, 280, 283, 287, 288; funeral of, 331–32; inauguration of, 291–93, 513n8; intellectuals in administration of, 290; liberal agenda of, 281; Mahon's acquaintance with, 290–91; Mahon's friends in administration of, 293–94; Mahon's meetings with, 306–7; Mahon's voting record, 315; on missile gap, 295–96; and New Frontier, 290; thanks to Mahon, 298–99; and White House dinners, 398; youth and vigor of administration, 290, 292, 293, 294

Kennedy, Robert F., 290, 343, 361, 379, 383, 385

Kessler, J. K., *plate ae*

Keyes, Roger, 225

Khrushchev, Nikita: and arms race, 261; and Berlin Wall, 306; and Cuban missile crisis, 322, 323; peaceful handover of power by, 354; and U-2 incident, 277–78, 279

Kim Il-Sung, 198, 201

King, Martin Luther, Jr., 381, 382, 383

Kishi, Nobusuke, *plate j*

Kissinger, Henry, 429, 432

Knapp, Bradford, 56

knowledge, Mahon's hunger for, 16, 24

Kolodziej, Edward A., 231, 257, 297

Korb, Lawrence, 218

Korea, postwar division of, 198

Korean War, 198–205; armistice agreement, 220–21, 228; and commodity prices, 223, 224; and defense spending, 200, 202, 205; and defense strategy, 321; Mahon on, 202–4, 228; and nuclear weapons, 199–200, 201, 221; origins of, 198; public opinion on, 201, 202–4; rapid US/UN response in, 198–99; shifting fronts in, 200–201;

and Soviet threat, revised perception of, 200; US military's poor preparation for, 199

Kosygin, Alexei, 354, 384

Krock, Arthur, 178, 179

Labor Department: Mahon on, 118, 464; and swimming pool integration issue in Texas, 311–12

Laird, Melvin, *plate v*; in Congress, 402; and My Lai massacre, 428; Nixon's response to Clifford and, 405–6; relationship with Mahon, 356; as Secretary of Defense, 401–2, 415–16, 420, 421, 423, 428

Lambert, Robert E., 145, *plate d*, *plate b*

Langston, David, 459–60

Lanham, Fritz, 52

law career of Mahon: choice of, 27; as county attorney, 30, 172–73; as district attorney, 30–31, 33, 35, 46; law degree, 29, 30; opportunities provided by, xxi; private practice, 30, 33; as valuable experience, 31–32

law enforcement, late-1960s calls for stiffening of, 382–83

Legislative Reorganization Act of 1946, 172

Legislative Reorganization Act of 1970, 428

LeMay, Curtis, 238–39, 318, 319, 336, *plate g*

Lemnitzer, Lyman, 300–301, 309

Lewis, Elmer A., 56

Lewis, John L., 118, 119

Long, Huey, 55, 57, 59

Lubbock, Texas: deadly tornado in (1970), 439; George and Helen Mahon Library in, 438–40; Mahon's move of district office to, 106; wartime air base construction in, 123–24

MacArthur, Douglas, *plate n*; and budget cuts, 207; and Korean War, 200–205;

Mahon on, 120; Mahon's support of, 208

Magnuson, Don, 253

Mahon, Bryan (nephew), 185

Mahon, Daphne (daughter): birth of, 30; cane given to father by, 408; child of, 208; and declaration of war on Japan, 119–20; and election of 1960, 288; and Mahons' 50th anniversary, 441; marriage of, 185; married life of, 214; mother's heart attack and, 441; parents' visits with after marriage, 208, 235, 239, 243, 250, 267, 342, 353, 357, 414, 441, 479; as student, 121–22

Mahon, Durward (brother), 38, 67, 196–97, 441

Mahon, Eldon (nephew), 172–73, 413

Mahon, George Thomas (grandfather), 8–9

Mahon, Helen Stevenson (wife), *plate g, plate t, plate y*; background of, 27; birthday celebration during Philippines trip, 74–75; christening of USS *Skipjack*, 267–68; and Churchill's address to Congress, 131–32; club and organization memberships of, 33; and Congressional opening days, 250; death of, 479; death of brothers, 256, 420; death of Mahon and, 478–79; and election of 1934, 35; entertaining of visiting constituents by, 56–57; health of, 314; heart attack of, 441–42; high school romance with, 16, 20, 27, 28; and Kennedy assassination, 331–32, 333; and Kennedy Inauguration, 292; and Mahon's first day in Congress, 5, 6; and Nixon inauguration, 396–97; and Rayburn statue dedication, 346–47; renewal of relationship with, 27; and Roosevelt State of the Union address (1935), 54; teaching career of, 27–28, 28–29; as teammate in Mahon's career, xviii, xx, 57, 217, 276, 294, 377; travel with Mahon, 144–59,

247, 249; and Washington social life, 53; wedding and honeymoon, 28. *See also* married life of Mahons

Mahon, John (brother), 420, 441

Mahon, John Kirkpatrick "J. K." (father): air conditioner purchased for, 242; death of, 11, 266–67; and family move to Texas, 11–14; family of, 8, 9; frugality of, 10, 17; life of, 9; Mahon on, 9–11; and Mahon's wool suit, 6; marriages of, 9, 266; visits to, 256

Mahon, Lola Willis Brown (mother): character of, 11; death of, 11, 266; family of, 9; marriage of, 9

Mahon, Marion (brother), 18

Mahon, Mary Agnes (sister), 19, 20

Mahon, Pollyann Kirkpatrick (grandmother), 8, 9

Mahon, Thomas Marion (brother), 441

Mahon name, pronunciation of, 22

Malenkov, Georgy M., 220

Manhattan Project, 136–44; Allied knowledge of, 142–43; Appropriations Committee briefing on, 140–43; Appropriations Committee inquiries about, 137–40; briefing of congressional leadership on, 139; establishment of, 136–37; Mahon's knowledge of, xvi; Mahon's tour of Knoxville facility, 140–43; naming of, 137. *See also* atomic bomb

Mansfield, Mike, 317, 360, 424

Mao Tze-Tung, 148, 150, 429

married life of Mahons: apartment renovations, 241–42, 272; Christmas, 1935, 75; Christmas, 1952, 214; Christmas, 1954, 239; Christmas, 1955, 250; Christmas, 1959, 276–77; Christmas, 1960, 289; Christmas, 1961, 313; Christmas, 1964, 335, 345; Christmas, 1965, 357; Christmas, 1966, 364; early years, 28–29; grandchildren and, 208, 230, 239, 267, 276–77, 289, 313, 342,

353–54, 357, 366, 368–69, 405; leisure activities enjoyed in, xx, 32, 47, 119, 208, 235, 236, 242–43, 309–10, 345, 346, 368, 409; Mahon's busy schedule and, 186; Mahon's domestic confusion during Helen's absences, 235, 275; move to new apartment, 347; new car purchases, 258–59, 357–58; social life in, 53, 56, 62–63, 128, 129–30, 290–91, 292, 317, 344, 345–46, 348, 351, 360, 361, 370–71, 380, 385–86, 387, 395–96, 397, 398–99, 409; souvenirs collected for family, 148, 235, 351, 352, 353, 398; vacations, 186, 248, 309, 353, 364, 377–78, 424–26; visits with daughter and family, 208, 235, 239, 243, 250, 267, 342, 353, 357, 414, 441, 479; wartime gardening, 127–28; wartime social life, 128, 129–30; wedding anniversary celebrations, 121, 440–41

Marshall, George C., 139, 143, 158, 177, 184, *plate b*

Marshall Plan: amount of aid delivered through, 184; goals of, 177–78; Herter Committee and, 178–83; Mahon on, 180, 183–84, 213–14; passage of, 183–84; propaganda benefits of, 181; and Truman Doctrine, 184

Martin, Joseph W., 139, 178, 201, 232

Mauzey, A. R., 34

Maverick, Maury, 210

May, Irwin M., 79

May, Kenneth, 310

McAdoo, William Gibbs, 62

McCarthy, Eugene, 379, 384–85

McClellan, John, *plate t*

McCone, John, 314

McCormack, John W.: election as Speaker, 313–14; as Majority Leader, 307; and Manhattan Project, 139; retirement of, 424; as Speaker, 315, 319, 338, 363, 365, 367, 371, 409

McCullough, David, 134, 186, 204

McElroy, Neil, 265, 272
McFarlane, W. D., 97
McGroarty, John S., 58
McNamara, Robert S., *plate o, plate s*; and bomber construction, as issue, 304–5, 318–20, 321, 325, 336–37; and civil defense program, 299; defense department reforms by, 293, 402; defense policy under, 297; Mahon on, 290, 297, 298; on missile gap, 295–96; and missiles, emphasis on, 304, 305, 336–37; reform of defense budgeting process, 296–97, 300–301, 320–21, 336; resignation as Secretary of Defense, 377; and waste reduction, 298, 336, 353, 374; as World Bank president, 377
McNeil, William, 225
McNeill, Marshall, 175
McVey, Freda, 43
Meadows, Ernest (brother-in-law), 136
media: criticism of Appropriations committee, 407; criticism of Mahon, 408; Mahon on, 80, 222; Mahon's use of, 106
medicare and medicaid, Mahon on, 387
Mediterranean region, Mahon's postwar trips to, 155–56, 181–82
Members of Congress for Peace Through Law (MCPL), 466–67
Mexico, Mahon's travel to, 70, 323–24
Michel, Robert H., 350
Middle East: CIA in, 268, 269; Mahon's visit to, 155–56, 268–69
military: build-up prior to World War II, 106–7, 108, 112–13; consolidation under Department of Defense, 187, 258; and Korean War readiness, 199; McNamara reforms of, 293; and modern warfare, standing army required for, 164, 166–67, 173, 195–96; opposition to Eisenhower budgets, 257, 264, 270, 273; postwar demobilization, 163–64; wartime build-up, 121, 122, 123. *See*

also defense spending; Korean War; Vietnam War; World War II
military, and inter-service rivalry: decrease of in 1960s, 402; effects of, 257–58, 272–73, 285–86; Eisenhower's efforts to reduce, 263; Mahon on, 263–64; McNamara's reduction of, 297, 300
Military Establishment Subcommittee of Appropriations Committee: budget process in, 189–90; creation of, 189; criticisms of, 191–92; Korean War and, 200; Mahon as chair of, 189, 190, 196
military-industrial complex: economic leverage of, 303–4, 304–5; Eisenhower on, 303; increasing criticisms of, 401, 423; as necessity for modern weapons production, 285
Miller, L. W., 145
Mills, Wilbur, 317, 363, 371–72
minimum wage debates, 280–81, 288
Minshall, William E., 323, *plate v*
missile gap: congressional action on, 262, 272, 282, 284–85; and defense budget, 272–74; Eisenhower on, 261–62, 262–63, 280, 295; Gaither Report on, 261–62; as issue in 1960 election, 285; Kennedy on, 295–96; Mahon on, 259–60, 265, 277, 296; McNamara on, 295–96; public concerns about, 259, 277
missiles: guided, development of, 227, 233, 250; McNamara's emphasis on, 304, 305, 336–37
missiles, anti-ballistic (ABMs): arms agreement on, 432; debate on, 392, 400–401, 416; funding of, 390, 392
missiles, intercontinental ballistic (ICBMs): antimissile defense against, 272, 282, 284–85; and arms race, 252, 260, 261, 262, 296; US bases for, 309; US development of, 284, 511n167–72
Mitchell, Martha, 411

Mitchell, William L., 145
Mitchell County, Texas: history of, 12–13; isolation of, 15; Mahon family move to, 13–14
Moody, Dan, 31
Moore, Frank, *plate ae*
Moore, Fred, *plate m*
morality of US, concerns about decline of, 381–82
Morgan, Iwan, 220
Morgenthau, Henry, Jr., 59
Mueller, Frederick H., 275
Mueller, George E., *plate u*
Mullican, Clark: and election of 1934, 33–34, 38, 40, 42, 43, 44–45, 83–84; work with Mahon on West Texas issues, 64–65
Murphy, Frank, 62, 72
Muskie, Edmund, 394, 398

Nasser, Gamal Abdel, 268–69, 349–50
National Alliance of Businessmen, 396
national debt: Eisenhower and, 234–35; Mahon on, 276, 433–34
national defense, strong, Mahon's support for, xxi, 126, 183–84, 266
National Defense Act of 1920, 107
National Portrait Gallery opening, 387
National Security Act of 1947, 187
National Security Council: creation of, 187; and Gaither Report, 261
NATO, Mahon on, 426, 427
Nelson, Donald M., 105
neutrality, in World War II: cash-and-carry plan and, 107–10; Mahon's support for, 86, 106, 108–10, 137; Neutrality Acts, 76, 107; US isolationism and, 106–10
New Deal programs, 55; Mahon's support for, 80; opposition to, 57, 97, 110; special congressional session of 1937 and, 92–93; Supreme Court strikedown of, 76, 88

New Look policy, 219–20, 230–32; criticisms of, 233–34, 244–45, 250–51, 264–66
Ngo Dinh Diem, 334
Nixon, Pat, 398, 412, 444
Nixon, Richard M., *plate x*, *plate t*; and anti-war activism, 405–7; and Cambodian incursions, 418, 419, 422–23; challenge to congressional power, 435–36; character of, 446; and China, opening of, 429–33; and Congress, 395; in Congress, xvi, 178, 181, 209–10, 443–44; defense budgets under, 414–16, 421–24, 433, 440; defense policy of, 400; dog (Checkers), 217, 504n6; and election of 1952, 209, 212, 291; and election of 1960, 288; and election of 1968, 387–88, 393–94; and election of 1972, 410; Ford's pardon of, 447–49; and Herter Committee, 178, 181, 209–10, 443–44; impounding of allocated funds by, 435–36, 446; inaugurations of, 396–97, 434; leisure activities, 414; on Mahon, 470–71; Mahon on, 411; Mahon's relationship with, xvii, 209–10, 397–98, 413–14, 417, 434, 440, 442–43, 443–44; Mahon's support for, 397–98, 407, 412, 418–19, 420, 434; Nixon Doctrine, 425, 432–33; resignation of, xvii, 442–44; and social welfare programs, 434–35; and Soviet Union, improved relations with, 432; and stress of presidency, 405–6; Supreme Court appointments, 387–88, 410–13; and US forces in Europe, 424; Vietnamization strategy of, 418; and Vietnam War, pledge to end, 418; and White House church services, 399, 417; White House dinners with, 398–99
Norrell, William F., 145, 154, *plate b*
Norstad, Lauris, *plate k*
Norton, Mary T., 87

Novak, Robert, 451

NSC-68, 195–96, 198, 219

nuclear arms race: and defense spending, 161; and US containment policy, 163, 167

Nuclear Test Ban Treaty of 1963, 334

nuclear weapons: bomber bases for, 208–9; China and, 354; Kennedy's views on, 297; Korean War and, 199–200, 201, 221; Mahon on, 233, 310–11; and militarization of space, 260; and New Look deterrence policy and, 219, 220, 221, 230, 234, 244; Rhee's interest in using, 237; US containment policy and, 163, 167, 174, 197, 199–200

Nugent, Pat, 358

Nye, Gerald P., 107

O'Brien, Larry, 317, 328, 329, 330

Occupational Safety and Health Administration (OSHA), Mahon's battle against, 461–65

O'Connor, John J., 50, 86

O'Konski, Alvin, 390

O'Neill, Tip, 468, 478, *plate ac*

OSHA. *See* Occupational Safety and Health Administration

Ostertag, Harold C., 253

Pace, Frank, Jr., 197, 267, 303–4

Paine, Thomas O., *plate u*

Panama, Mahon's visits to, 324, *plate d*, *plate m*

Panama Canal, 459, 471–72

Passman, Otto, 339–40, 345, *plate o*

Patman, Wright, 81, 96, 126, 308, 339, 450

Patman Bill, 81

patronage power of members of Congress, 47–48, 84; federal judicial appointments and, 64

patronage power of president, and Washington DC administration, 102

Patterson, James, 8, 139, 186, 287, 333, 394

Patterson, Robert, 138, 143, 169

Patton, Nat, 98

Pearson, Drew, 408

Pearson, Lester, 334

Pentagon Papers, 446

People's Republic of China: delay in international recognition of, 198, 247, 429–32; establishment of, 194, 197; and Korean War, 198, 201; Nixon's opening of, 429–33; and nuclear weapons, 354

Perkins, Frances, 59, 118

Pfluger, Bill, *plate k*

Pharr, Homer L., 34, 42

Philippine Islands: Mahon's views on independence for, 72, 73, 90–91; trip to (1935), 62, 69–75; trip to (1945), 147, *plate b*

Pickle, Jack, 358, 361, *plate t*

Plumley, Charles A., 190, *plate d*

Poage, W. R., 96, 222, 308, 312, 450, *plate f*

poll taxes, 43, 80, 187, 344, 495n100

Poor People's March on Washington, 383

pork projects, Mahon's avoidance of, xvii

Porter, Ray E., *plate d*

portrait of Mahon for Appropriations Committee chambers, 444–46, *plate y*

Post, Marjorie M., 397

postmasters, political role of, 47–48, 84, 133

postwar inspection tour of US bases overseas, 144–59; in Azores, 157–58; in China, 147–50, *plate c*; committee's report on, 158–59; and election of 1946, 170; in France, 157; in Germany, 156–57, *plate c*; in India, 151–52; in Iran, 152–55; meetings with soldiers in, 146, 148–49, 151–52, 157–58, *plate c*; members of group for, 145; in Middle East and Mediterranean, 155–56;

on Pacific islands, 146–47, *plate b*;
    purpose of, 144–45, 145–46
Powell, Adam Clayton, 367–68
Powell, Lewis, 412
Powell v. McCormack (1969), 367
Powers, Francis Gary, 277
prayer in public schools, 315–16
Presidential Transition Act of 1964, 408,
    447
presidents: Mahon on burdens of, 414;
    Mahon's acquaintance with, 136. See
    also *specific presidents*
Preston, Ralph, 189
Price, Bob, *plate t*
protesters, at Nixon inauguration, 396
public speaking skills of Mahon: college
    and university debate training and, 22,
    23–24, 27; high school debate training
    and, 17; law career and, 32; Mahon's
    campaigns and, 41–42
public-utility holding companies, efforts
    to regulate, 66–67
Puerto Rico, Mahons' vacation in, 364
PWA (Public Works Administration),
    creation of, 55

Quarles, Donald, 252
Quezon, Manuel, 72–73

race, Mahon on, 73
Radford, Arthur, 235
railroad companies, and settlement of
    West Texas, 12
Rainey, Henry, 6, 48
Rayburn, Sam, *plate f*; birthday dinner
    (1961), 290–91; "Board of Educa-
    tion" hideout of, 135; and civil rights
    issue, 260; death and burial of, 307–8;
    on defense budget, 193, 264; and
    Democratic Convention of 1936, 82;
    and Democratic conventions, 337;
    and election for Speaker of the House
    (1934), 48–49; and election of 1948,

186; as House Speaker, 116, 270, 308;
    influence of, 49, 424; Johnson and,
    345, 352; on Kennedy administration
    intellectuals, 290; letter of support to
    newly-elected Mahon, 50; as Mahon
    mentor, xvi, 94, 111, 135, 444, 474;
    and Mahon's committee assignments,
    61, 98; and Mahon's speaker's bureau
    duties, 84; Mahon's support for,
    85–86, 116; as majority leader, 85–86,
    96; and Manhattan Project, 139; and
    public-utility holding company regu-
    lation, 66–67; and Southern conserva-
    tive control of Congress, 5; statue to,
    346–47; and Supreme Court reform,
    90; wartime social life of, 128
REA (Rural Electrification Administra-
    tion), creation of, 55
Reagan, Ronald W., and B-1 bomber, 469
Reduction of Nonessential Federal
    Expenditures Committee, Mahon on,
    270
Reed, Louis B., 118
Reese, Jim, 458–61, 460–61
Reese Air Force Base, 196
Reeves, Richard, 434
Rehnquist, William, 412
religious faith of Mahon, 25, 32, 33, 47,
    115, 185, 209, 266–67, 287, 291, 317
Republicans: and AAA, 78; criticisms of
    Roosevelt, 75; gains in Texas, 127, 212,
    308; rise in Mahon's district, 312–13,
    458–61
Republic of China (Formosa; Taiwan):
    US defense of, 240, 244; US recog-
    nition of Communist China and,
    430–32
Resor, Stanley, 429
Retirement Act of 1937, 89
retirement of Mahon: announcement
    of, 470; last day in Congress, 472–73;
    return to Texas, 478; USC offer of
    position after, 471; vacating of office,

474; Washington office space used in, 477

Revenue Act of 1942, 130

Revenue and Expenditure Control Act of 1968, 389

Rhee, Syngman, 198, 236, 237

Richards, George J., 144, 145, 152, *plate b*

Rickenbacker, Eddie, 128

Rickover, Hyman, *plate k*

Ridgway, Matthew, 213, 250

Riley, John, 213

riots: of 1967, 374–76; of 1968, 381, 382; of 1970s, 419; theories on response to, 374, 382

Rivers, L. Mendel, 173, 403, 404, 422, 423, *plate s*

Robb, Chuck, 380

Roberts, Ray, 329

Robinson, Joseph T., 87

Rockefeller, Nelson, 447, 454, *plate ab*

Rogers, Bernard, 473

Rogers, Edith Nourse, 237

Rogers, Walter, 328

Rogers, William, 198, 429

Roosevelt, Eleanor, 5

Roosevelt, Franklin D.: and Camp David, 370; conservative opposition to, 57, 97, 110, 133; declining support for in Texas, 126–27; and defense industry strikes, 116, 118, 119; efforts to purge conservative Democrats, 89, 97, 110; and election of 1936, 86; and election of 1938, 97; and election of 1940, 116; and election of 1944, 134; and Emergency Relief Appropriations Act, 55; and executive branch reorganization, 87, 92, 93; fireside chats of, 4–5; on humanitarian era, 76, 80; illness and death of, 134–35; judicial reform efforts, 88–90; Mahon's support for, 65–66, 68, 91, 92, 98, 110–11; and Manhattan Project, 136–37, 140; and national Christmas tree, 159; and radio, 75; and Social Security, 59–60;

State of the Union address (1935), 54–55; State of the Union address (1936), 75–76; State of the Union address (1937), 87–88; State of the Union address (1940), 106; State of the Union address (1942), 122; and veterans' bonuses, 39, 68, 81

Roosevelt, and World War II: decision to enter, 106, 108; declaration of war, 119–20; preference for aerial warfare, 112; war powers of, 121; wartime taxes, 132–33

Roosevelt Supreme Court reform efforts, 88–90; impact on Democratic unity, 89, 91, 93; Mahon's views on, 89–90; and rise of conservative opposition, 93

Rusk, Dean, 334, 358, 365, *plate s*

Russell, James, 268

Russell, Richard, 263

Sabath, A. J., 7, 50

Sachs, Albert, 137

Saltonstall, Leverett, 326

Sandefer, Thomas Jefferson, 3, 16–17, 21, 31

Sanders, Morgan, 95–96

Schlesinger, James, 454–56

Schneider, George J., 6

Schriever, Bernard, *plate j*

Scott, Hugh, 257

Scrivner, Errett, 226, 233, 235, 253, *plate e*

Secretary of Defense: and budget process, 286; creation of position, 187; difficulty of job, 377; shortage of expertise in, 286–87, 293, 301, 338

secrets, national, Mahon on, 279, 325–26, 452

Select Committee on Foreign Aid, 178. *See also* Herter Committee

Shah of Iran, xvi, 154–55

Shao Litze, 148

Shapley, Deborah, 293, 296, 377

Sheppard, Harry R., 189, 338, *plate d*
Sheppard, Morris, 51, 52, 65
Shivers, Allan, 210
Shriver, Garner E., *plate o*
Shriver, Sargent, xv, 335, 371
Sikes, Robert L., 233, 234, *plate v, plate d*
Simmons College: Ely's support for Mahon at, xv, 3–4, 23; father's support for Mahon at, 19, 22, 23; history of, 21; Mahon at, 20–27; Mahon's choice of, 19; Mahon's part-time jobs at, 22, 23; Mahon's student government experience at, 22, 25; social life at, 25
Siracusa, Joseph, 57
Smith, Margaret Chase, *plate s*
Smith, Preston, 478
Smith, Wilmer, *plate z*
Smithsonian Institution, 387, 397, 477
Snell, Bertrand H., 6, 75
Snyder, J. Buell, 114–15, 140, 144, 145, 146, 148, 154, 155, *plate b*
Social Security: Mahon's support for, 58, 68, 83; passage of, 58–59, 60; plans in competition with, 57–58, 59; programs included under, 59, 60; public relations campaign for, 59–60
Soil Conservation and Domestic Allotment Act (1936), 79, 93
South, Charles L., 133–34
Southern Manifesto, 260
Soviet Union: aggressive response to US weakness, 226; air power, US concerns about, 245–46, 252; Eisenhower on threat from, 262–63; invasion of Czechoslovakia, 384; Mahon on threat from, 253–54, 264, 310, 320, 389–90; Mahon's mistrust of, 247–48; Marshall Plan and, 178; Middle East influence, fear of, 269; Nixon's visit to, 432; and nuclear weapons acquisition, 194–95, 197, 227, 230–31; and peaceful transition to Brezhnev, 354; postwar aggressiveness of, 161, 162, 164; postwar goals of, 161; proxy war strategy of, 234, 250–51, 297. *See also* arms race; Cold War; Sputnik
space program, US, 315, 353
Speck, E. B., 83
Sputnik: launch of, 260; US response to, 260–61, 262, 264–66, 270–71, 295
Stalin, Joseph: and Cold War, 161–62; death of, 220–21, 226; and Korean War, 198–99, 220–21; postwar goals of, 161; and World War II, 134
States' Rights Democratic Party (Dixiecrats), and election of 1948, 186
Stennis, John C., 471, *plate s*
Stevenson, Adlai, 209, 211, 212, 254, 255
Stevenson, O. E. (father-in-law), 27
Stimson, Henry, 139, 140–41, 169
Stone, Harlan, 135
Strategic Air Command, 238–39, 304, 309
Strategic Arms Limitation Talks (SALT), 400
Strauss, Lewis L., 274–75
Summers Bill, 89–90
Sumners, Hatton, 49, 61, 64, 88
Supreme Court: history of, 89; Mahon on, 412; and Nixon tapes, 442; on OSHA cotton dust standards, 465; *Powell v. McCormack* (1969), 367; and prayer in schools, 315–16; rejection of New Deal programs, 68, 76, 88
Supreme Court reform efforts by Roosevelt, 88–90; impact on Democratic unity, 89, 91, 93; Mahon's views on, 89–90; and rise of conservative opposition, 93
Symington, Stuart, 226, 246, 252, 271, 283, 361

Taber, John, 113, 140, 193, 216, 227, 339
Taiwan. *See* Republic of China
taxes: Eisenhower and, 231, 243–44; Mahon on, 130–31, 133; wartime in-

creases in, 130, 132–33; withholding, introduction of, 130

Taylor, Edward T., 6, 7, 102, 111, 112

Taylor, Maxwell, 273, 282, 332, *plate o, plate s*

Teague, Olin Earl, 329, 330

Telles, Raymond, 324

Texas: Democratic dominance in, 34, 46; Democratic factions in, 330–31; and election of 1960, 288; high number of tenant farmers in, 93; Republican gains in, 127, 212, 308; tidelands ownership as issue, 211–12, 229. *See also* West Texas

Texas congressional delegation: biweekly meetings of, 63; House delegation, Mahon as chair of, 171–72

Texas Democratic Party, race restrictions on membership, in 1930s, 44

Texas Negro Voters League, 171

Texas Technological College: designation as federal documents depository, 56; Mahon's honorary degree from, 315; Mahon's support for, 56

Texas Tech University, *plate l, plate m*; George H. Mahon chair at, 477; Mahon's donation of papers to, 438–39, 474–75. *See also* Texas Technological College

Thomas, Albert, 308, 328, 332, 338

Thomas, Clyde, 31

Thomason, Abbie, 51, 70

Thomason, Ewing, 34, 51, 70, 94, 96, 111, 115

Thomason, R. E., 53

Thompson, Charles: as county judge, 30, 33; and Democratic Convention of 1936, 82; and election of 1934, 36, 37, 38; Mahon's friendship with, 121–22, 344; as Mahon's law partner, 30, 33; wife's death, 243

Thompson, Joe H., 34, 38

Thornton, Bates "Tex," 477

Thurmond, J. Strom, 186, 410

Tibbott, Harve, 145, *plate d, plate b*

Timmons, William, 442, 451–52

Tower, John, 312

Townsend, Francis E., 57–58, 59, 82

Townsend Plan, 57–58, 82–83

travel by Mahon as Congressman: to Alaska (1940), 114–15; to Central and South America, 323–25; to China, 71, 147–50, *plate c*; criticisms of, 249–50; to Europe, 179–83, 213–14, 248, 269–70; first air flight experience, 114; to France, 157, 213; funding of, 249; to Germany, 156–57, 181, *plate c*; to Great Britain, 180–81, 213; to Greenland, 208–9, 210; to Hawaii, 74, 145; to India, 151–52; inspection tours of US bases, 238–39, 253, 261–62, 283, 309, *plate g*; to Interdisciplinary Union meeting in Helsinki, 246–47; to Iran, 152–55; justifications of to constituents, xvii, 69–70, 114–15, 179; knowledge gained in, xvi, 69, 70, 113, 120; to Manhattan Project facility, 140–43; to Mediterranean region, 155–56, 181–82; to Middle East, 268–69; to Philippines, 62, 69–75, 120, 147, *plate b*; tours of defense contractors, 253, 262. *See also* postwar inspection tour of US bases overseas

Truman, Harry S., *plate n*; assumption of presidency, 135; budget balancing by, 164, 165, 173; and Cannon funeral, 338; and Cold War, 161, 163; corruption allegations against, 216; and defense budget, 189, 190–91, 193–94, 197, 205–6; Eisenhower and, 212, 308; and election of 1948, 186; and election of 1952, 207; expansion of US global role under, 214–15; and Korean War, 198, 199, 201–2; Mahon on, 204–5, 207–8; Mahon's acquaintance with, 135–36; and Manhattan Project, 140; and Marshall Plan, 184; and national Christmas tree, 159–60; and NSC-68,

195–96; postwar policies of, 159; on press, 408; at Rayburn funeral, 308; as senator, 165; and Texas tidelands issue, 212; and unions, 168; wedding of Daphne Mahon and, 185

Truman Doctrine, 174, 177; Mahon on, 175, 176–77; Mahon's constituents on, 175–77; Marshall Plan and, 184. *See also* containment policy, US

Turkey, US Cold War aid to, 173–78

Turki, Prince of Saudi Arabia, *plate aa*

Turner, Morris, 439

24th Amendment, 344

U-2 flights over Soviet Union, 262–63, 314; Mahon on, 278–79; public disclosure of, 277–79

Udall, Morris, 317

unemployment insurance, introduction of, 59

unions: and defense industry strikes, 116–19; Mexican laborers and, 311–12; Soviet grain sales and, 457; and wartime production, 124; West Texas backlash against, 168

United Nations: and Korean War, 198–99; Mahon on, 431–32; and recognition of Communist China, 198, 429–32

University of Minnesota, Mahon at, 29

University of Texas, Austin: Mahon at, 26–27, 28; Mahon's graduation from, 29

urban problems: blaming of Congress for, 375–76; Johnson's efforts to address, 382

Van Atta, Dale, 415

Vance, Cyrus, 364

Vandenberg, Arthur, 174, 191

Vandenberg, Hoyt S., 226

Vandergrift, A. A., 128–29

veterans' bonuses, 81; FDR's opposition to, 39, 68, 81; as issue in Congress,

54, 76; as issue in election of 1934, 39; payment of in bonds, 81

victory gardens, 127–28

Vienna Summit (1961), 322

Vietnam, partitioning of, 234

Vietnam War: bombing of North Vietnam, 355, 356, 434, 435; Cambodian incursions, 418, 419, 422–23; cost of, 364–65, 372, 391, 423; escalation of, 348, 355; Fulbright hearings on, 361; and Great Society, funding conflict between, 352, 359, 362, 364–65, 423; growth of opposition to, 378, 395, 401, 406–7, 409, 416, 417, 418, 421, 433, 434, 436; and increased resistance to defense spending, 453; Johnson's supplemental appropriations to fund, 351–52, 360, 372, 373, 389; Mahon on, 350, 356, 418–19, 420; Mahon's support for, xvii, 35, 351–52, 356, 360, 379; My Lai massacre, 428–29; Nixon's pledge to end, 395; Nixon's Vietnamization strategy, 418; North Vietnam's advantages in, 395, 417; Tet Offensive, 378

Vinson, Carl, 263, 271, 308, 318–20, 321, 337, 453

von Braun, Wernher, *plate u*

Voting Rights Act of 1965, 355

Walker, Julius and Savannah, 426

Walker, Walton, 200

Wallace, Henry, 59, 76–77, 136, 149

War Department subcommittee (later, Defense Appropriations Subcommittee): briefing on Manhattan Project, 140–43; Cold War and, 161; inquiries about secret Manhattan Project spending, 137–40; Mahon as chair of, 170; Mahon's appointment to, 111–12; Mahon's work for, 114–15, 124, 129, 132; and prewar build-up, 112–13; and Republican victory of 1946, 172

War Powers Resolution, 436, 446

Warren, Earl, 307, 333, 387–88, 410, 412

Warren Commission, 333

Washington, DC: federal administration of, 102–5; Mahons' arrival in, 51; Mahons' early sightseeing in, 53–54; Mahon's first days in, 51–54; riots of 1968, 381; wartime in, 120; World War II growth of, 103

Washington, George, 6

Watergate scandal, 442

Watson, Marvin, 358

Wedemeyer, Albert, 147–48, 149, 191

Weinberger, Casper, 435

West, Elizabeth Howard, 56

West, Milton, 96, 98, 99, 172

Westmoreland, William, 355–56, 366, 378, 379, *plate r*

West Texas: and cotton, 12–13, 14, 33, 71, 74, 170, 222–24, 229–30, 335; drought of 1920s, 23; drought of 1930s, 38–39, 45, 68, 79–80, 94; drought of 1950s, 211, 222–24, 229; and Great Depression, 38–39, 45, 68; groundwater issues in, 240–41; growth of, and addition of congressional districts, 32–33; Mahon's efforts to create new federal judicial district for, 63–64; Mahon's opposition to media portrayal of drought in, 80; settlement of, 12, 14, 33; water and, 413; WPA survey of groundwater resources, Mahon's initiation of, 65–66. *See also* Congressional District Nineteen

Wheeler, Earle, 296, 390–91

Whipkey, Bob, 344

White, Taylor, 34, 38

Whitten, George, 94, 128, 148–49

Whitten, Jamie, 444, 451, *plate e*

Wickard, Claude R., 105, 169–70

Wilkinson, Bud, 414

Will, George, 470

Wilson, Charles E., 219, 225, 226, 231–32, 245, 251, 254, 255, 266, *plate h*

Wilson, George, 416

Wilson, Woodrow, 107

Wolfe, Sidney, 463

women, in Seventy-fifth Congress, 87

Wood, Robert J., 145

Woods, Randall Bennett, 429

Woodward, Bob, 448

Works Project Administration (WPA), creation of, 55

World's Fair (1958), 268

World's Fair (1964), 353–54

World War II: Allied progress of 1945, 134; Churchill-Roosevelt consultations on, 131; consumer subsidies, Mahon on, 125–26; declaration of war on Japan, 119–20; draft and, 120; food rationing in, 105; funding for, 122–23, 124, 130–31, 132–33; and growth of Washington, DC, 103; industrial production in, 120–21, 122, 123; and inflation, 124, 130; Mahon's support for, 119, 120; and need for sacrifice, Mahon on, 125–26; postwar demobilization, 163–64; profiteering, Mahon on, 123; rationing and price controls, 120–21, 124–25; US isolationism and, 106–10; and US postwar global leadership, 161; and victory gardens, 127–28; voters' concerns about preparations for, 40; Yalta Conference, 134. *See also* Manhattan Project; neutrality, in World War II; postwar inspection tour of US bases overseas

WPA (Works Project Administration), creation of, 55

Wright, Fielding L., 186

Wright, Jim, 304, 452, 478, *plate t*

Yarborough, Ralph, 304–5, 329, 330, 331, 420

Zelizer, Julian, 372